EMERGING COMPANIES GUIDE: A RESOURCE FOR PROFESSIONALS AND ENTREPRENEURS

SECOND EDITION

EDITORS
ROBERT L. BROWN
ALAN S. GUTTERMAN

D1223759

AMERICAN BAR ASSOCIATION
Business Law Section

Cover design by ABA Publishing.

Page layout by Quadrum Solutions.

Printed in the United States of America.

15 14 13 12 11   5 4 3 2 1

Library of Congress Cataloging-in-Publication Data

Emerging companies guide : a resource for professionals and entrepreneurs / editors: Robert L. Brown, Alan S. Gutterman. — 2nd ed.
    p. cm.
  Includes bibliographical references and index.
  ISBN 978-1-61632-831-3 (alk. paper)
  1. New business enterprises—Law and legislation—United States. 2. Entrepreneurship—United States. I. Brown, Robert, 1949— II. Gutterman, Alan S., 1955—
  KF1355.E46 2011
  346.73'065—dc22
                     2011001427

Discounts are available for books ordered in bulk. Special consideration is given to state bars, CLE programs, and other bar-related organizations. Inquire at Book Publishing, ABA Publishing, American Bar Association, 321 N. Clark Street, Chicago, Illinois 60654-7598.

www.ababooks.org

Summary of Chapters

Contents

Preface

In the late 1990s, high-tech and start-up companies were the rage of the stock market, investors and the media. Following the stock collapse, or dot.bomb, a sense of reality returned and people began to study emerging companies from a more balanced view. A similar trend followed the global financial crisis that started in 2008. Many people who lost their jobs started their own companies.

On the other hand, over the past several decades, most of the jobs in the United States have been created by emerging companies. In fact, most of the economic growth in the United States is due to the expansion of emerging companies. At the same time, larger companies, including those on the Fortune 500, have seen their total employment shrink. The years following the recent global financial crisis have underscored this trend.

This book attempts to bring together current thoughts on how to establish, organize, develop and eventually sell an emerging company. Over 15 chapters, we have tried to address basic organizational issues, tax and non-tax planning issues, and employment issues, as well as how to grow the business through distribution, licensing and sales. We have also included chapters on protecting your intellectual property rights and how to handle media and public relations. Unfortunately, only about one third of all emerging companies make it to a second generation, with only about 25 percent making it to a third generation. Frequently, this failure is because of an inability to address important estate-planning issues. This book is unique in that it includes a detailed discussion of these types of issues.

The editors have brought together leading experts from around the country to address, in the chapters that follow, each of these critical matters:

- Deciding to Start a New Business
- Preparing the Business Plan
- Non-Tax Aspects of Forming and Organizing a New Entity
- Tax Aspects of Forming and Organizing a New Entity
- Tax Reporting and Compliance
- Accounting and Financial Reporting Issues
- Technology and Intellectual Property Rights
- Financing the Business
- Product Development and Distribution
- Human Resources
- The Internet and Online Business Activities
- Public Relations
- Growing the Business
- Purchasing and Selling Businesses
- Estate Planning

Guided by our own experiences of attempting to locate this type of a reference book and not being able to do so, we endeavored to put together in one handy resource, all of the issues relating to emerging companies that we address on a day-to-day basis. We hope you find this book helpful.

We also have made a great effort to keep it user friendly and hope that you will find it to be so. To facilitate your usage, we have included a CD-ROM that contains the agreements referenced in the book as exhibits. You can use any of the forms to prepare and customize your own documents as needed for your clients.

We wish you the best of luck, success and good fortune in using this book. We hope that the information provided here will be a one-stop reference for those who are interested in forming a new company as well as for those who are advising them.

Robert L. Brown
Greenebaum Doll & McDonald PLLC
Louisville, KY

Alan S. Gutterman
Gutterman Law & Business
Piedmont, CA

CHAPTER 1

Starting a New Business

Robert L. Brown

Greenebaum, Doll & McDonald, PLLC
Louisville, KY

Alan S. Gutterman

Gutterman Law & Business
Piedmont, CA

Contents

Starting a New Business[1]

1.01   Preliminary Considerations

In deciding to start a business the entrepreneur should consider whether it is financially, professionally and personally worthwhile to do so. The entrepreneur may find that the reality of starting and running a business differs from what has been expected. Entrepreneurs need to seriously consider whether they are ready to assume the risks of forming a business entity before taking this step. Perhaps they will be afforded protections by forming a business entity such as a corporation or a limited liability company, but they will also be assuming more responsibility.

Many entrepreneurs want to start a new business because they want the independence of being their own bosses. To an extent, when the entrepreneur forms his or her own business entity, the entrepreneur will be his or her own boss. However, there will always be someone to answer to. The entrepreneurs of a new business entity will soon realize a new set of dynamics that will make their work a challenge. This challenge could be different than the challenges faced by a typical employee. An entrepreneur with a new business entity will have to answer to investors who will want to know how the business plans to perform. Once the business begins operations, the investors will want to see results and to see how their investment is growing and succeeding. Throughout the life span of a typical new business entity, the entrepreneurs and then the management of the business entity will continue to respond to requests and inquiries of the investors while also anticipating their needs and concerns. Management must inform its investors on a regular basis as to the status, progress and concerns of the business entity, while at the same time protecting the business entity to the extent possible. The entrepreneurs need

---

1.   Anna Capelle and Eunice J. Paik were the authors of this chapter in the first edition of the *Guide*.

to determine early on in the life span of the new business entity whether or not they will be able to respond to the sometimes constant demands and pressures of investors.

The entrepreneur with a new business will also have to respond to, inform and meet with its board of directors or similar authority on a regular basis. This authority should provide periodic guidance to the management of the newly formed business entity. However, often the members of this authority are also investors, so these investors are in turn looking out after their investments. The balancing act comes from dealing with members of the authority, providing them with information and building a consensus. This is a difficult skill for most to achieve because there are inevitably varying personality types that must be attended to and appeased. Sometimes the members of the authority can seem more like bosses than advisors.

Another drawback to starting a new business and becoming one's own boss is that the entrepreneur is now in the position of the boss, a place that may have been despised at one point. As the founder or management of a new business entity, that person will now be responsible for hiring and firing employees and dealing with personnel issues on a daily basis. Being the boss and dealing with employment or management issues is often a large part of starting a new business. Entrepreneurs would be well advised to consider whether or not this is a role that they want to assume.

In summary, an entrepreneur may want to be the chief executive officer of his very own new business entity, but he or she still has to perform and answer to someone, whether that is to an investor, board member or employee. Before taking on the role, the would-be entrepreneur should carefully consider whether he or she is prepared to assume the responsibilities of such role.

A.   Joint Ventures

If the entrepreneur is not sure about forming a business entity or assuming additional responsibilities by him or herself, one alternative is to form a joint venture. There are no statutory requirements to forming a joint venture. Joint ventures are typically strategic alliances or business projects undertaken cooperatively by two or more parties where each contributes different skills and resources and then share in the results of the project. Joint ventures usually include active participation by all joint venturers, with each of them bringing something unique or particular to the venture, which in turn complements the other venturers.

Joint ventures are very flexible and can be structured in many different ways. They can be created as a contractual arrangement or can appear as complicated partnerships. Joint ventures are not as rigid as some corporate structures and may allow the participants greater creativity in structuring their project. It is a flexible enough business vehicle to later develop into a more formal business entity as well. Joint ventures can be seen by entrepreneurs as a good opportunity to partner or experience with others a business project with a common goal without all of the formalities of a corporate structure. It allows the participants to determine if the product, service or idea has the potential of succeeding in the marketplace. Finally, because of the potentially fluid structure of the joint venture, others may be willing to participate as one of the many joint venturers without feeling like they are taking on a large risk by investing in a newly formed business entity or getting deeply involved in a new industry.

B.   Sole Proprietor

Instead of starting a new business and forming an entity, the entrepreneur may want to consider starting small by doing business simply as a sole proprietor. The sole proprietorship is the basic noncorporate form that an individual may use for operating a business. A business owner who engages in business personally is a sole proprietorship. The sole proprietorship is simple to start or terminate, but poses difficulties in planning the transfer of the business and estate planning for the entrepreneur. The entrepreneur has limited income tax savings opportunities and is not personally protected from the liabilities of the business.

The sole proprietorship is not a separate legal entity from its owner, the entrepreneur. No organizational documents or other formalities are required to begin the operation as a sole proprietorship. The sole proprietor can hire employees or contract with third parties to perform services for the business, but remains the sole owner of the business. As the sole owner, the proprietor has the right to all of the profits of the business and can make all of the management decisions of the business. The income, loss and other tax items of the business are represented on the owner's individual income tax return. The sale of a sole proprietorship is typically the selling of assets used by the owner in conducting the business. This may cause the seller to recognize gain on the sale of the net assets, depending on the tax basis of the assets.

The proprietor is also personally liable for all obligations of the business. Thus, if the business incurs losses, the owner will be personally liable and will put his or her entire personal assets at risk. To cover this risk the proprietor may obtain liability insurance to protect personal assets.

The sole proprietorship as a business organization requires no formalities and few fees, and there are less regulatory and reporting requirements than for other forms of business. The sole proprietorship is a good form of business for an individual starting a new business that is relatively small and simple. In particular, the form can be appropriate for businesses that can obtain insurance to protect against liability such as architecture, legal services or accounting services. A sole proprietorship may be the right choice if the tax benefits associated with a corporation are outweighed by the complexity of the form. A sole proprietorship may also be a good alternative to consider for an entrepreneur that wants to see if the idea for the business makes sense and can be put to practice, while at the same time being independent.

C.   Employment

Remaining or becoming an employee may be an alternative to starting a business and forming a business entity. The key to being or remaining an employee is finding the right employer and the right position. The entrepreneur should consider whether being an employee could afford protections from liability as well as security, depending on the type and nature of employment. Starting a new business entity could result in liability or monetary loss if the business fails and is often very risky. It may be possible for the entrepreneur to find the right employer and the right position to allow the entrepreneur, as an employee, to explore whether the business or idea could develop, while at the same time protecting the entrepreneur from liability and providing security and benefits. Depending on the employer and the position, the entrepreneur could use the employment opportunity as a test ground for the business itself. Further, working as an employee with a company in the industry in which the entrepreneur hopes to start a business could provide the entrepreneur with additional experience, knowledge and contacts that the entrepreneur would not have otherwise been able to obtain—elements that may prove valuable when applied in starting and growing a new business at a later time.

1.02   Hiring Professionals

Once an entrepreneur has decided to start a business, he or she will need professionals to assist them in forming and operating the business. Depending on the type of business, different types of professionals may be necessary to form the entity. Generally, when starting a business, the entrepreneur will need to contact an attorney and an accountant to assist with the many determinations and alternatives that need to be considered before actually forming the business entity. Without this type of advice and guidance, an entrepreneur could end up with an unsuccessful or poorly organized business, or worse, he or she could incur liabilities and debts. Therefore, it is critical that the entrepreneur contact and engage professionals who can add insight and value to the decision to start a business and protect the entrepreneur during the formation and operation of the business.

A.   Attorney

The attorney's function is essential in deciding to start and form a new business entity. The attorney will assist in determining which entity is the most suitable for the new business, as well as forming the new business entity once the choice is made. Once the business entity is formed, the attorney will continue to advise and guide the new business with its growth and strategies.

More specifically, in deciding on the choice of business entity, an attorney's services to the entrepreneur as a client include the following:

- Identifying client objectives and concerns
- Analyzing client's objectives and information obtained in light of applicable legal considerations (corporate, securities and tax laws)
- Advising client on alternative entities available
- Implementing plan for the selected business entity

1. Selection Factors

In choosing an attorney, the entrepreneur will have to determine if a particular attorney is well suited to represent the entrepreneur in starting the business, forming it and supporting the business through its cycles. The entrepreneur should review and consider the entire package of services and relationships presented by the individual attorney, his or her team and the attorney's law firm as a whole. The entrepreneur should consider the following characteristics of the attorney, among others, when determining whether the attorney is competent and compatible:

- Diligence
- Skill
- Expertise in representing emerging companies
- Relationships in the entrepreneur area of business
- Reach of firm

To further expand on these characteristics, a good business attorney must be very diligent and detail-oriented in representing the entrepreneur or any client. Diligence can appear in many forms in the legal context, such as an attorney's attention to detail and carefulness. The details involved in deciding to start a new business and forming the business, such as the entity's principal place of business, are some of the most crucial in the life of the business entity. An attorney representing an entrepreneur needs to be careful in analyzing applicable law in light of the entrepreneur's particular factual situation to determine the choice of entity and to form the entity. The characteristic of diligence encompasses not only attention to detail and carefulness, but also a zeal for and attention to the entrepreneur. This characteristic could mean not giving up on a transaction for a client that the attorney deems unimportant or of little significance, but instead diligently representing the client to achieve the best possible outcome for the client, as well as effectively communicating with the client to apprise it of the terms and issues of a particular transaction.

The characteristic of skill can also take many forms and is equally important. Skill of course includes legal skills and aptitudes, which are very important in representing businesses as the law affecting entities is always adapting and new trends are developing. A good business attorney needs to have experienced legal skills within reach to adequately represent the entrepreneur in business dealings. These skills can be acquired through legal practice or education, but in either case they must be present. Another skill that is not so tangible, but equally important for a business lawyer, is negotiating skill, used to reach agreements with other attorneys and financial professionals, including venture capitalists and other sources of financing. This type of skill is most often obtained through experience in the practice of law affecting businesses and familiarity with these types of transactions. Finally, the attorney must have personal skills to interact with the entrepreneur. An entrepreneur, like any other client, needs and expects attention to legal matters, which includes promptly returning telephone calls and advising on deadlines. More generally, the attorney should have the skill to be able to interact freely and candidly with the entrepreneur. This leads to a more open professional relationship and better service to the entrepreneur client.

Expertise is another characteristic that has many significant aspects. Again, the attorney must have the requisite legal expertise in corporate, securities and tax law in order to effectively represent and advise the entrepreneur. If the attorney does not have the particular legal expertise in a specialty area, the attorney should be able to refer the matter or issue to an attorney who has the expertise, either in the same firm or externally. Attorneys should speak candidly to their clients regarding their expertise and memorialize the limits of the advice that will be provided in the engagement agreement. This avoids misunderstandings later between attorney and client and helps to frame the matters that the client can reasonably depend on the attorney to handle. If the attorney does refer a particular issue to another attorney in the same firm or outside, this does not mean the attorney should consider that the client is completely passed on. The initial attorney should work with the second attorney to provide comprehensive guidance to the client. This also ensures that the initial attorney will be apprised of the particular matter and will continue to have a relationship with the client.

One of the most important characteristics of a good business attorney often is measured by the number and types of contacts or relationships the attorney has with the business community. An entrepreneur usually comes to an attorney first when deciding to start a business and may not have engaged an attorney previously or had much contact with attorneys or others in a particular industry. The entrepreneur often looks to the attorney to assist in finding other professionals that may be of assistance to the entrepreneur and the new business entity, such as specialized attorneys, accountants, financial professionals, venture capitalists, human resource managers and bankers. Therefore, it is important for a business attorney to cultivate these types of relationships and recommend them to clients as appropriate. These contacts also provide the attorney with valuable resources that the attorney may draw on at a personal level as well.

2. *Ethical Issues*

The representation of an entrepreneur deciding to start a business may create several ethical issues as the attorney provides services to the business. These issues should be carefully considered and documented. Actual and potential conflicts can involve many players, including entrepreneurs forming an entity, the entity, the founders, and/or the entity and its parent or subsidiary, and can vary depending on the jurisdictions where the attorney practices law.

The attorney frequently should assess whether actual or potential conflicts are present during the varying stages of deciding to start a business, forming a business and continuing the representation of the business, because the response to the inquiry may change during each stage. Frequently, in the initial stages of deciding to start a business and forming a business, the attorney is interacting with one or more entrepreneurs or founders. In this stage, the business entity that the attorney represents is not yet formed. The attorney should, therefore, be concerned with joint representation and the representation of more than one client in a matter in which the clients' interests actually or potentially conflict. Once the entity is formed, the attorney should request clear guidance from the entrepreneurs and the entity to determine who is the client. Will the client now be the newly formed entity or will it continue to be the entrepreneurs or only one of them? The formation of the entity may necessitate new disclosures and written consents by the entrepreneurs regarding representation. Determining the client for representation purposes also arises if the newly formed entity has affiliated business entities that are being represented by the same attorney. This often arises in the context of a parent-subsidiary relationship. During each stage of the new business entity, the determination of the client representation should be considered, addressed and documented as necessary.

To elaborate, conflicts of interests between an attorney and a current or former client may arise in a variety of circumstances surrounding the formation of a new business entity. Conflicts have occurred in the following circumstances:

- An attorney is requested to provide legal services to all parties involved in a transaction.
- An attorney represents only one party in a particular transaction while simultaneously representing another client with adverse interests in an unrelated matter.
- An attorney has successive representations of conflicting interests (i.e., the attorney may represent only one party, but may have formerly represented another party whose interest conflicts with the current client).
- An attorney has an interest in the subject matter of the representation or a present or past legal, business, financial, professional or personal relationship with another party in the same transaction.

Attorneys are not prohibited from representing a client in any of the above situations. However, at a minimum, the attorney must provide the affected clients with written disclosure of the potential conflicts of interest, and where the conflict arises out of concurrent or successive representation of conflicting interests, representations may ethically proceed only with the affected clients' informed written consent.[2]

Absent each client's informed written consent as discussed above, an attorney cannot accept or continue representation of more than one client in a matter in which the clients' interests actually or potentially conflict, or simultaneously represent two clients in separate matters where their interests conflict.

Simultaneously representing clients with actually or potentially conflicting interests in the same matter occurs each time an attorney is asked to represent two or more persons starting a new business. Business attorneys will be faced with these circumstances on a regular basis. It is not uncommon for each client to have different goals and concerns for the new business, which may or could conflict with the other client's goals or concerns. In the event this occurs, the attorney may continue representation, but it must be clear that the attorney's duty is to provide undivided loyalty to the entity or business that is being formed, not to the individuals. The individual clients should be instructed to seek independent counsel. The attorney may also represent the clients jointly as long as their fully informed written consent is obtained. It is best to state the representation and actual or potential conflict in writing and also to include, in the event of conflict between the clients, that the attorney will only represent the entity.

An attorney may not simultaneously represent two or more clients on separate matters where the clients' interests conflict unless each client gives his or her informed written consent.[3] Again, the main concern in this scenario is the attorney's duty of loyalty. Generally, matters arising under this type of scenario are subject to a per se disqualification absent the clients' consent.

3. Engagement Agreements

Following the determination of the client to be represented by the attorney with any conflicts disclosed and/or waived in writing as appropriate, it will be necessary for the attorney and the client to enter into a written engagement agreement for the payment of fees by the client in exchange for legal services from the attorney.[4] The three typical fee arrangements include flat fee, hourly rate and retainer fee arrangements. The flat fee arrangement is advisable when the services are routine and easily quantifiable. Otherwise, an hourly rate

---

2. Cal. Rules of Prof. Cond. 3-310(B) through (E); Nev. Rules of Prof. Cond. 1.7; N.Y. Rules of Prof. Cond. 1.7 and 1-8.
3. Cal. Rules of Prof. Cond. 3-310(C)(3); *see also supra* note 1.
4. Cal. Bus. & Prof. Code § 6148; Nev. Rules of Prof. Cond. 1.5; N.Y. Rules of Prof. Cond. 1.5.

arrangement with or without a retainer fee is usually the preferred arrangement. The attorney will need to determine the type of services that will be provided in deciding to start a business, forming the business entity and continuing the representation of the business entity, and if possible, to include the types of services in the engagement agreement. One fee arrangement may make more sense at one stage of the representation but less sense later as the business entity grows. Therefore, the engagement agreement should be periodically reviewed during the representation of the business entity in light of ethical issues discussed above and to evaluate the fee arrangements.

B.   Accountant

To assist in the business and tax decisions of starting a business, an attorney will most likely want to recommend an accountant. The attorney should consider the type of accountant he or she recommends. For instance, in California there are two types of accountants, Certified Public Accountants ("CPA") and public accountants. Both perform the same services. The distinction between the two lies in the method of licensing. CPAs are persons who have passed the certified public accountant examination in California.[5] Public accountants in California, for example, are persons who registered with the applicable state board of accountancy as such before 1956 and were not required to take this examination.[6]

Accountants typically provide the following professional services to their clients:

- Perform audit, examination, verification, investigation, certification, presentation or review of financial transactions and accounting records
- Prepare or certify reports on audit or examination of books and records of account, balance sheets and other financial, accounting and related schedules, exhibits, statements or reports that are to be used for publication, for the purpose of obtaining credit, for filing with a court of law or with any governmental agency or for any other purpose
- Render professional services in any or all matters relating to accounting procedure and with respect to the recording, presentation or certification of financial information or data
- Keep books, make trial balances, prepare statements, make audits or prepare reports, all as a part of bookkeeping operations
- Prepare or sign, as the tax preparer, tax returns
- Prepare personal financial or investment plans or provide products or services of others in implementation of personal financial or investment plans

---

5.   Cal. Bus. & Prof. Code § 5033; *see also* Nev. Rev. Stat. 628.190.
6.   Cal. Bus. & Prof. Code § 5034.

- Provide management consulting services

Accountants can be particularly helpful to clients and their attorneys in determining the structure of the business entities to be formed from an accounting or tax perspective, examining the tax implications of debt or equity issuances to investors or employees, and formulating employment packages for key employees of the newly formed entity. The business entity will seek assistance from its accountant almost as frequently as it will seek guidance from its attorneys. Therefore, it is important for the client to retain an accountant that will continue to grow with the entity and anticipate its tax and accounting needs.

While the services of accountants may seem expensive for a client starting a business, the attorney should impress on the client that the tax or accounting implications of starting a new business are of immediate importance and require the attention and consideration of the client for the entity to be properly formed and operational. The relationship with an accountant also adds future value to the newly formed entity and may reduce the time and cost of hiring an accountant at a later date. Many accounting firms have experience with growing entities and can help management decide what types of financial records the entity should prepare and what types of regular reports management should receive to help it manage its business and attract investment. They can also help companies prepare projections and draft business plans.

Overall, working with an accountant from an early stage can help an entity improve its reporting, enhance management's ability to run the business and therefore attract capital. A relationship with a good accounting firm can also provide a reference for potential investment sources at a later date.

After deciding on an accountant or accounting firm, the client will need to document the relationship with the accountant or firm. As is the case with clients and attorneys, a confidential relationship exists between an accountant and its client or former client. This relationship prevents the accountant from disclosing any information obtained from a client, unless the client consents or disclosure is required by law.

1.03   Initial Client Interview

It is extremely important for the attorney and the entrepreneur to hold an initial client meeting, preferably in person, when deciding to start a business. At the initial client meeting the entrepreneur can describe the ideas, goals and prospects for the new business entity. For the attorney, the initial client meeting is critical in order to begin assessing the background, ideas, goals and prospects of the entrepreneur and forming an overall corporate plan for the entrepreneur, including choice of entity, financing sources, operating issues and exit strategies. Although there will be many meetings between the entrepreneur and the attorney, the initial client meeting serves as a time to outline the business goals and objectives of the entrepreneur and to begin the process of building the necessary legal foundation for achieving them.

In preparation for the meeting, the attorney should consider the prior experience of the entrepreneur, including prior employment and business experience. Also the attorney should consider the industry focus of the business and review the relevant and current business and legal information relating to that industry. This initial preparation will permit the attorney to better know and understand the entrepreneur and the industry in which the entrepreneur and the new business will become involved.

The attorney may wish to prepare a checklist of items to discuss at the initial meeting. The preparation and use of a checklist will assist the attorney in framing the discussion and ensuring that all pertinent issues are discussed. Many attorneys have standard checklists that they use for initial client meetings where an entrepreneur is deciding to start a business. These checklists can be tailored to a particular client or industry focus. After several initial client meetings, it may not be necessary to use a checklist during the actual meeting; however, it is often useful to consider the issues raised in a checklist prior to beginning an initial client meeting. The attorney should update the checklist based on the current state of the law or business atmosphere. Attached as **Exhibit 1A** is a form of checklist that may be useful for an initial client meeting.

During the actual initial client meeting, it is important for the attorney to listen to the entrepreneur. This may seem simple and obvious but is often overlooked. The attorney should allow the entrepreneur to describe his or her personal background and employment experience as well as the entrepreneur's ideas, plans, goals and objectives for the new business entity. The more the entrepreneur is able to discuss these items with the attorney, the more likely the attorney will be able to obtain a complete understanding of the entrepreneur and the proposed business, as well as gauge the sophistication and knowledge of the entrepreneur.

Once the entrepreneur has expressed his or her ideas, plans, goals and objectives as well as any relevant background information, it is appropriate for the attorney to provide initial advice and insights into the proposed business and to assess the overall corporate structure for the proposed business. It is not necessary to give the entrepreneur all the legal answers at the initial meeting, but the attorney should raise possible alternatives for the structure of the business and issues that should be of particular concern based on the entrepreneur, the proposed business and the industry. The finer legal points can be addressed at a later time or subsequent meeting.

One of the important issues to consider during the initial client meeting, and throughout the business formation process, is whether the entrepreneur should launch the proposed business alone or with others. Many advantages and disadvantages exist as to each. When entering into a business alone, the sole entrepreneur is able establish goals and direction for the entity without the influence or distraction of others. If the entrepreneur is clearly focused and can execute the goals and direction, then it may be appropriate for the entrepreneur to act alone. Also, if the entrepreneur has specialized skill or knowledge in the field or industry where the new business entity will be operating, then the entrepreneur may not require guidance and support of additional entrepreneurs.

Forming and operating a successful business entity involves difficult and often complex tasks. It is rare that a sole entrepreneur would have the requisite skills and knowledge to form and operate a successful business alone. For the business to succeed, the entrepreneur will require assistance from other entrepreneurs who have skill sets that are different and compatible. The entrepreneur will need to determine when to invite other entrepreneurs to the business entity as founders of the entity, who the new entrepreneurs will be, and how to document the relationship. The entrepreneurs can be invited to join the business entity as founders prior to or at its formation. If the original entrepreneur chooses, additional entrepreneurs may be sought out on an as-needed basis either as employees or perhaps as consultants or advisors. The business collaboration can take many forms. Whatever the form, when deciding to go into business with another person, the individuals involved should consider the following:

- What is their current relationship, and how long have they known each other? That is, are they friends, classmates or relatives?
- How do they currently interact with each other? Are they communicative, responsive and supportive of one another?
- What will be the outcome of their relationship if the business succeeds or fails?

These factors need to be carefully evaluated by the entrepreneurs as they decide to start a business together. It is better to consider the above issues prior to the formation of the business at a time when it is still possible for the individuals to walk away from the business on good terms.

Before ending the initial client meeting, it is a good idea for the attorney and entrepreneur to schedule a follow up meeting and to discuss the items that need to be analyzed or resolved and presented at the next meeting. Both the attorney and the entrepreneur should conclude the initial client meeting with a task list to be completed prior to the next meeting. This will help the entrepreneur feel like actions are being taken to form the business entity and will focus both parties on the key legal issues that need to be addressed. Attached as **Exhibit 1B** is an example questionnaire that may be used at the end of the first meeting to help the client focus on the information required to incorporate the new business entity.

1.04   Planning for Control and Management

A.   Control Structure

Part of deciding to start a business is determining how the financial and control elements of the business will be structured. Time spent on considering the structural issues is well spent as it forces clients and their attorneys to consider their overall goals for the business and it reveals how much the entrepreneur is willing to concede to investors and employees.

1.   *Allocation of Financial Interests*

The allocation issue first arises with the initial investment of the founders in the business. Typically, the founders will either purchase equity in the business for nominal amounts of cash or will contribute assets or services to the business in exchange for equity in the business. Following the initial investments of the founders, a determination needs to be made as to how additional financial interests will be allocated in the business. Before determining the actual allocation, the type of financial interest should be considered. Will financial interests allocated take the form of debt or equity? Simply stated, debt involves a loan of money to the business that must be repaid by the business at some point in time. Debt may also be converted into equity pursuant to a predetermined event. Equity involves an ownership interest in the business that is evidenced by an issuance of shares in the business, which may vary in its rights and preferences depending on the formation and investment documents of the entity.

It may be advantageous for a business to allocate financial interests as debt for several reasons. For example, if a business established as a corporation allocates interests as debt, the business can likely avoid a valuation of the business. This can be very important for a business in its initial stages. Also, debt instruments can be drafted to include automatic or discretionary conversions of debt into equity based on certain events, such as subsequent financing of a certain amount or the achievement of certain business milestones. Despite the advantages of the allocation of financial interests as debt, debt typically must be repaid and includes interest that can be expensive for a newly formed business.

Instead of debt, a new business may consider issuing financial interests as equity. Equity allows newly formed businesses to raise much needed capital, but at the same time offers attractive ownership interests in the business. One disadvantage of issuing equity is that all other owners are diluted by each subsequent issuance of equity. This may be of specific concern for the founders who are unwilling to give up control. Therefore, it is important to discuss with the entrepreneur how much control he or she is willing to relinquish. The answer will assist in structuring the allocation of financial interests and the ability of the entity to attract equity financing.

Ultimately the final structure is a business decision to be made by the client. Some of the factors the client may want to consider in determining the structure include the flexibility of the structure, the delegation of control of the entity, and the financial impact of the structure. The structure can be quite complicated or quite simple depending on the objectives and goals of the client. Most often debt and equity is combined in some form to allocate financial interests of a newly formed business.

2.   *Allocation of Control*

Similar to financial interests, control of the business entity may be structured in many different ways. Again, the client will need to examine the objectives of the business to determine which structure works best and will enable the business to grow, meet its needs and allow flexibility.

Since the corporation is the most common form of business entity, the corporation's structure must be considered in allocating control. In a corporation, the board of directors makes the decisions regarding the management of the corporation, but it serves at the discretion of the shareholders.

Another level of control structure exists among the shareholders of the corporation. Depending on the jurisdiction of the formation of the corporation or where it principally does business,[7] the minority shareholders of the corporation may be afforded certain protections. In California, these protections include the right to cumulatively vote for directors of the corporation. The right of the shareholders to cumulate their votes, if the right is exercised, enables minority shareholders to elect directors where they would not be able to do so if the votes were not cumulated.[8] Also depending on the type of corporation, majority shareholders often have a fiduciary duty to treat minority shareholders fairly in approving transactions.

These basic control measures may be supplemented through several mechanisms. First, the shareholders of a corporation may agree among themselves to enter into shareholder agreements such as voting agreements, voting trusts, or similar arrangements[9] where the shareholders agree to vote their shares in a certain manner.[10] These agreements are enforceable as contractual relationships among the shareholders. The basic control measures may also be modified or elaborated on in the articles or certificate of incorporation. This

---

7.   *See* Cal. Corp. Code § 2115.

8.   *See* Cal. Corp. Code § 708; N.Y. Bus. Corp. Law § 618; Del. General Corp. Law § 214.

9.   *See* Cal. Corp. Code § 706; N.Y. Bus. Corp. Law § 621 N.Y.; Del. General Corp. Law § 212.

10.   Shareholders of unlisted California corporations or foreign corporations subject to California corporate law may not agree to extinguish their right to cumulatively vote. *See* Cal. Corp. Code § 708, § 2115 and § 301.5.

can be achieved by the creation of different classes of voting shares as well as distinct rights and preferences for different classes and series of shares. The drafting of the articles or certificate can become quite complex by including control provisions among the different classes or series of shares. For example, the rights and preferences of the shareholders may include requirements for greater levels of approvals for certain events or changes in the corporation. Other control provisions in the articles or certificate may provide that certain classes or series may vote for and elect particular members of the board of directors. The variations of control provisions in the articles or certificate may be drafted to create a very flexible or rigid control structure, and the possibilities are unlimited.

3. Typical Structure

A typical structure for a corporation issuing debt and equity may include the following:

- Founders: equity comprising issuances of common stock in exchange for nominal cash or contributed assets
- Employees: equity issued pursuant to an equity incentive plan and consisting of options to purchase common stock or issuances of restricted common stock
- Investors: equity consisting of issuances of preferred stock in exchange for cash
- Investors: debt leading up to equity investments consisting of issuances of promissory notes convertible to equity

Again the structure can take many forms and variations that are dependent on the objectives of the client and the corporation's need for financing. We describe the choice between debt and equity, as well as the different forms of equity, in Chapter 7 (Financing a Business).

4. Retaining Control

In addition to the alternatives in allocating control of a corporation during the initial issuance of debt or equity, control of the corporation may also be allocated by imposing conditions on how a shareholder or noteholder disposes of the interest acquired.

In the case of debt, the corporation could simply provide in the promissory note that the note is nontransferable in order to control the interest. In the case of equity, the corporation may impose in a contractual arrangement, such as an investors' rights agreement, that the shareholders cannot transfer their equity or can only in limited circumstances. Such an agreement may also provide that prior to transferring any equity to a third party, the shareholder must first offer to the corporation and/or the other shareholders the opportunity to purchase such shares (i.e., right of first refusal). These types of provisions allow the corporation and/or the current holders of shares to control the structure of the corporation and, as necessary, to maintain their percentage ownership interest in the corporation.

Similarly with the corporation's equity incentive plan, the corporation may institute a repurchase program that allows the corporation to repurchase exercised options or restricted stock in the event the employee leaves the corporation. This type of program allows the corporation to control the ownership of the pool of shares in the stock option plan as well as replenish the option pool with the repurchased shares.

Again there are many alternatives for the corporation and its shareholders to retain control of the structure of corporation, but these alternatives must be adequately evaluated and implemented prior to the issuance of the debt or equity.

B.   Management

One of the greatest challenges faced by newly formed business entities is building a management team. A key component of a successful business is a strong and competent management team. Without a good management team, the product, service or idea will not develop, get funded or attract talented employees. From inception, potential investors will review the management team, its style, competence, depth and leadership in deciding whether or not to invest in the business. Many investors will not consider a business for potential investment if the management team does not possess the capability of leading the business to success. Potential investors may even request changes to the management team prior to or as a condition to investing in the business. Sophisticated investors also know that businesses with strong and capable management teams tend to attract and retain productive and loyal employees. Many employees will follow their managers to new businesses based on their trust in the managers' abilities.

Once the entrepreneurs understand the importance of a strong management team, then they must start building it. Not all entrepreneurs make good managers. For entrepreneurs to transition from the role of entrepreneur to manager, they must be willing to give up some control in the business and begin to concentrate on discrete aspects of the business. This may be very difficult for an entrepreneur to do depending on his or her experience and personality. In order for an entrepreneur to transition to a role of a manager, the individual must have the requisite experience and competence to act as a manager. After the entrepreneurs have filled management positions or decided to step aside, other management positions will need to be filled. Professional recruiting firms can be used to locate competent and appropriate management candidates, but often the entrepreneurs will be able to network among themselves or with contacts to obtain potential candidates for management positions.

Part of the process of building a management team is determining the qualities and skill sets that each member of the management team must possess. This takes careful planning on the part of the entrepreneurs who may seek guidance from third parties or from the board of directors or similar authority. It is important for the entrepreneurs to have an overall picture of the management structure and the necessary qualities and skills that make up each management position before going out in the market to find candidates.

As the management team is assembled, it is critical that managers work well together as a team. In addition to having compatible personalities and working styles, managers will have to learn to rely on each other and know each other's strengths and weaknesses. Once assembled the management team will collectively be responsible for many tasks, including developing relationships with third parties, such as investors, financial institutions, vendors and strategic partners, to name a few. The management team will become the voice of the business when it seeks financing. The management team will need to sell the business, the product or service and the team itself to potential investors and strategic partners. If the management team is not collectively integrated with all of these aspects of the business, then it will have a difficult time raising necessary capital to sustain the business. Internally, the management team will need to interact well with the board of directors or similar authority, as well as lead and inspire employees. Overall management needs to work and act as a team to build a successful business.

1.05   Arrangements Prior to Forming Entity

A.   Formation Expenses

The costs and expenses associated with starting a business and actual formation of the entity could be substantial for the participants and the newly formed entity. These costs and expenses usually include professional service fees such as attorneys' and accountants' fees, filing fees with the Secretary of State and Department of Corporations or similar governmental entities, minimum annual state taxes, and perfecting ownership in intellectual property, such as patents, copyrights, know how, domain names and/or trademarks. Typically, these costs and expenses are advanced by the entrepreneurs prior to formation, however they are usually repaid to the entrepreneurs by the business entity, or else the items obtained from the initial costs and expenses are contributed to the business entity in exchange for an ownership interest. The percentage of ownership and the value contributed can be determined by the entrepreneur or management team with the assistance of the board of directors or similar authority of the business entity. The individual client should carefully consider any tax implications of receiving stock or other securities either as repayment of the costs and fees advanced or from contributing tangible or intangible assets generated from the costs and fees advanced.

In any event, the repayment or the contribution of the formation expenses and costs should be well documented by the directors or similar authority of the business entity. This documentation can take the form of a resolution at the organizational meeting of the business entity.

B. Pre-formation Subscription Agreements

The participants or organizers of the business entity, usually a corporation, may, before forming the entity, enter into agreements among themselves or with third parties to subscribe for an ownership interest in the proposed entity. These types of agreements were used often in the past to provide the organizers with funds during the time that the entity was being formed. Now with the ease and speed of forming an entity, it is not usually necessary for the organizers to subscribe for equity using this agreement.

The pre-formation subscription agreement may be used when the organizers feel that another organizer or a third party, such as a potential investor, appears likely or willing to withdraw from the business entity or the investment prior to the completion of the formation. In such a case, the organizers may want to enter into a subscription agreement to ensure that all parties, organizers or investors are committed to the business entity. The subscription should encompass the organizers' or investors' obligation to purchase an ownership percentage in the business entity when and if certain events occur, such as the formation of the entity.

The client needs to be aware that these agreements are generally enforceable by the organizers or the business entity itself under the theory that the entity is a third party beneficiary to the agreement.[11] Like other issuances of securities interests, the pre-formation subscription agreements are subject to corporate securities laws and must either be qualified or exempted.[12] The pre-formation subscription agreement is subject to certain requirements in order to be exempt from qualification under state and federal law.

C. Pre-formation Transactions by Promoters

Often organizers of a proposed business need or wish to enter into a contract or commitment for property or services that will be required by the business entity before it has been formed. The attorney needs to carefully advise the organizer regarding the limitations and problems associated with entering

---

11.   *Cf.* Moser v. Western Harness Racing, 89 Cal. App. 2d 1, 12 (1948); Positype Corp. of America v. Flowers, 36 F.2d 617 (1930); Reid v. Detroit Ideal Paint Co., 132 Mich. 528 (1903).

12.   Cal. Corp. Code § 25110; Nev. Rev. Stat. 90.470.

into pre-formation transactions. First, the business entity may be liable for the goods and services ordered by the promoters on behalf of the entity if the entity ratifies such contracts or commitments. This ratification may either be express or implied. An express ratification occurs when the board of directors or similar authority adopts a resolution accepting the contracts or commitments, while an implied ratification may occur when the entity accepts the benefits of the contracts or commitments by using the property or services obtained with knowledge of the terms of the contract.[13]

Regardless of whether or not the business entity is formed or the business entity ratifies the pre-formation contracts and commitments, the promoters may remain personally liable on such contracts except to the extent the promoters have disclosed that they are negotiating the contract or commitment on behalf of a business entity not yet formed and the other party agrees to look solely to that business entity after its formation, in which case they will not be liable even if the business entity is never formed.

It is a good practice to have the business entity indemnify its promoters against any liability incurred under the pre-formation commitments made on its behalf, even where it appears that the promoters did not incur any liability. This allows the promoters to feel more secure when working with the formed business entity and demonstrates the business entity's commitment to its promoters.

1.06   Intellectual Property and Business Names

A.   Business or Trade Name

Before a business entity may be formed with a state agency, the entrepreneurs must typically choose the name of the business that will be included in the formation documents and filed with the appropriate Secretary of State, or in other words, they must select a trade name.

The Secretary of State will not accept for filing formation documents in which the business entity's name is the same as or deceptively resembles the name of any other corporation already on file. It is worth the time and the minimal expense to check the name availability with the Secretary of State prior to filing formation documents. The attorney or client may also check the Secretary of State's website to obtain a general idea of whether or not a particular business entity name is available, but it is best to formally request

---

13.   Smith v. Glo-Fire Co., 94 Cal. App. 2d 154, 160 (1949); Stringer v. Electronics Supply Corp., 23 Del. Ch. 79 (1938).

such information from the Secretary of State's office.[14] The process of obtaining a business entity name is most efficient if the client provides the attorney with several potential business entity names to check for availability.

Once the business name, or trade name, has been determined to be available through the Secretary of State's Office, the attorney may be able to reserve the name with the Secretary of State's Office for a period of time. Once the business entity name has been reserved and the formation documents are ready for filing, the name reservation confirmation should be mailed with the filing of the formation documents to ensure that the Secretary of State's Office does not deny the filing on the grounds that the name is already taken or reserved.

The entrepreneurs should be instructed that although the business entity has a particular name filed or reserved with the Secretary of State's Office, that does not ensure that the business entity has intellectual property rights, such as trademark rights, to the name under state or federal law. See the discussion below regarding trademarks and domain names.

B.   Fictitious Business Name

In addition to a business name, the entity may consider obtaining a fictitious business name. A fictitious business name is different from a trade name or trademark. State and local laws typically govern a fictitious business name or "DBA." Typically, the Secretary of State does not handle the filing or administration of fictitious business names. City or county clerks or recorders where the principal place of business is located must be contacted regarding filing or registering fictitious business names. Usually, the procedure for obtaining a fictitious business name is simple and merely administrative.

C.   Identifying and Protecting Names and Marks

In choosing the name of the business entity, it is important not only to file with the Secretary of State, but also to recognize that its use is a fundamental operation in the life of the business entity. Prior to choosing a business entity name, a thorough search of the uses of the potential name should be done for availability reasons, which will avoid problems and costs in the future, as well as ensure the strength of the name chosen. Each potential business entity name should be reviewed as either a trade name, trademark or domain name.

A *trade name* as discussed above is a name used by the business to identify itself, but not necessarily any products or services the business offers. The

---

14.   *See* www.sos.ca.gov/business/be/name-availability.htm; delecorp.delaware.gov/tin/EntitySearch.jsp; nvsos.gov/index.aspx?page=139 and www.dos.state.ny.us/corps/bus_entity_search.html. The procedures for checking availability and reserving business entity names can also be found at these websites.

trade name is usually the name specified in the formation documents filed with the Secretary of State. However, just because a business entity name is accepted in a filing with the Secretary of State, this does not mean that the name is protected from use by others or that it is not being currently used by others in different states. It only means the Secretary of State approved the name in the filing as not being deceptively similar to another business name in this particular state.

Most business entities will be more protective of the name of their products and services. In this aspect, the business name will be functioning as a *trademark*. The business name of the entity, as a trademark, should be chosen not just based on availability, but also on the strength of the trademark. There are two components to the strength of the trademark. First, the trademark should be used to distinguish the business entity's products or services from those of their competitors. This ability to distinguish should be perceived from the perspective of the average consumer of the product. Second, the trademark should be strong enough to prevent others from using the trademark or something similar to it, in a way that would be confusingly similar to consumers as to the origin of the products or services.

An experienced trademark counsel can assist a business entity in choosing an appropriate trademark. Trademark counsel can perform initial searches of potential trademarks to eliminate any exact or closely similar marks. Once the client has narrowed on a potential trademark, trademark counsel can assist the client in focusing the trademark search on a particular geographical area or industry. In choosing a trademark for a business entity, it is important to consider where the business entity anticipates selling and/or marketing its products or services. A client will need to begin to protect the trademark in jurisdictions where it anticipates doing business in the future.

Once the trademark is chosen and the jurisdictions are considered, the business entity should file a federal trademark application in the United States (based on actual or intent to use the mark in interstate commerce) as well as accompanying applications in other jurisdictions. A qualified trademark attorney can assist the company in determining other foreign jurisdictions in which to file for trademark protection, as well as coordinate with foreign counsel as to the filing of such applications.

In addition to protecting the trademark of the business entity, a business entity will typically obtain a *domain name* to present its products or services on the Internet. Most business entities want their domain names to be identical to their trademarks and trade name. Although a business may have a particular trademark, it may be difficult to obtain the exact domain name as an owner's trademark rights and domain name rights may be in conflict. The law and regulations are quickly attempting to sort out the discrepancies in the rights, but the conflicts are far from resolved, although an owner of a trademark may have an advantage in obtaining the corresponding domain name.

An experienced trademark counsel can also assist the business entity in navigating through the Internet and obtaining the appropriate domain name for the entity. The initial searching for a trademark should normally include a domain name search as well. Once the domain name is determined to be available and chosen, the registration of the domain name is a surprisingly simple task.

Many companies select a company name only after checking name availability with all four sources—state name as a business, fictitious business name, trademark and domain name. Once the business entity has reviewed its trade name, fictitious business name, trademark and domain choices and has selected them, then the business entity can proceed with the other steps that are necessary in forming a business entity.

D.   Identifying, Protecting and Owning Intellectual Property

Today, the intellectual property of a new business entity is of key importance to sources of financing, founders of the entity, employees and the continuation of the entity. The first step in protecting a business entity's intellectual property is identifying what the intellectual property is. The entrepreneurs of the newly formed business entity need to be aware of the types of intellectual property and know generally how intellectual rights may be protected once they are created. Some of the types of intellectual property include patents, trademarks, copyrights, domain names, trade names, trade secrets, know how, confidential information and other similar concepts. Depending on the type of business entity and the industry in which it operates, certain intellectual property rights may be more critical than others. Also, certain intellectual property rights are more difficult and expensive to perfect and protect, making it not cost effective to protect them. The client should make the decision of whether or not to proceed with protecting intellectual property. The business entity should engage experienced intellectual property counsel to assist in deciphering the types of intellectual property that the entity may create, and to protect such rights by perfecting the ownership of such rights with the appropriate state, federal or international authorities.

The fact that a business entity has proprietary, enforceable intellectual property rights is extremely important and valuable to a new business entity. The existence of intellectual property ownership is particularly important to investors in the entity and other sources of financing for the entity. The intellectual property is important to them as it prevents competitors or potential competitors from doing what the new business entity is doing, making the new business entity itself valuable. Also the protected intellectual property rights are considered intangible assets of the new business entity that may be sold, assigned, transferred or collateralized by the entity. Enforceable intellectual property rights are also valuable to the entity and to investors in that the rights may be licensed to third parties in exchange for payments or royalties. The licenses may be exclusive or nonexclusive depending on the type of intellectual property right and/or the geographical limits of the license. The license arrangements may be very valuable to a new business entity in that it potentially can license certain or the same rights to more than one party creating revenue for the entity almost at inception. Without enforceable intellectual property rights, it is difficult for a new business entity to demonstrate its value.

One of the more difficult aspects of protecting intellectual property rights is knowing what to protect and when. Depending on the type of intellectual property right and how it is created will determine how a business entity needs to take steps to protect the rights. Therefore, a new business entity must be advised or trained to recognize what an intellectual property right is. This involves knowing the basic types of intellectual property rights, how they are created and how ownership of the rights is perfected. An experienced intellectual property attorney can instruct the new business entity as to what each type of intellectual property is and how to identify it. The attorney can also assist the entity in creating and implementing an internal process for the business entity where inventions and intellectual property rights are tracked from creation and employees are rewarded for following the process.

Once the business entity's management is able to identify and track an intellectual property right that is created within the business entity, the business entity must then take appropriate steps to protect such rights. Typically, many of the intellectual property rights of a business entity are created by the founders, employees or contractors of the business entity. In other words, in the course of their providing services to the business entity, such services resulted in the creation of intellectual property rights. The key issue for the new business entity is making certain that such rights are properly owned by the entity and are documented accordingly. Intellectual property rights owned by a founder, employee or contractor who happens to work at the entity and that have not been transferred to the business entity do not add value to the entity, and in fact, may decrease the entity's value based on fear that the particular employee may take the intellectual property rights to another entity on termination or that the particular employee or contractor may seek to prevent the new business entity from using the intellectual property rights or rights incidental to such property rights on termination.

To adequately protect intellectual property rights once they are identified and created, the business entity must ensure that such rights are held by it and not by the individuals who are providing services to the entity. To accomplish this, the business entity must first make certain that the intellectual property rights of the founders created prior to the formation of the entity are transferred and assigned to the entity and that the founders relinquished their rights to such property. Often the intellectual property rights of the founders are transferred to the business entity in exchange for an ownership interest in the entity. This can be beneficial to the entity in that it receives the valuable asset of the intellectual property and the founder receives equity in the business entity. Often this exchange can be structured in a way that the exchange is tax free to the founder.[15]

Similarly, all intellectual property rights created by employees of the business should be owned by the business entity. A presumption exists that intellectual property developed by an employee during the course of the employment is owned by the business entity as the employer.[16] However, it is recommended to have all employees execute a Proprietary Information and Assignment Agreement at the time of hiring to avoid confusion and problems later. For example in California, a business entity may not require the employee to transfer or assign inventions that are created outside of the scope of employment without the use of materials owned by the business entity.[17] A sample form of acknowledgment is included as **Exhibit 10C**. In addition to confirming the ownership of the intellectual property, employees of the business entity are typically required to agree that they will not disclose or use any proprietary or confidential information outside of the scope of their employment.

In addition to employees, new business entities often engage contractors or consultants to perform services for the entity. As discussed in Chapter 8 (Technology and Intellectual Property Rights), the relationships with these contractors should be clearly defined in writing and include the assignment of any inventions and intellectual property rights created by them while performing services for the business entity or while using the business entity's materials. Likewise and probably more importantly than employees, contractors should be required to execute an appropriate nondisclosure or confidentiality agreement with the business entity to ensure the protection of the business entity's intellectual property and confidential information disclosed during the performance of the services.[18]

Lastly, in order for the new business entity to protect its confidential information, it should routinely enter into nondisclosure or confidentiality agreements with third parties such as potential investors, strategic partners, vendors or others that may have access to the business entity's confidential information. Sample nondisclosure agreements are included as **Exhibit 14A** and **Exhibit 14B** and are discussed in more detail in Chapter 14 (Purchasing and Selling a Business).

---

15. I.R.C. § 351.
16. Nev. Rev. Stat. 600.500.
17. Cal. Lab. Code § 2870.
18. *See also* Cal. Lab. Code § 3351 and Nev. Rev. Stat. 608.010 (defining employee).

1.07   Choosing the Business Entity's Jurisdiction

Two important considerations in forming a business are the choice of business entity and the state in which the entity will be formed. Chapter 3 (Non-Tax Aspects of Forming and Organizing a New Business) provides an in-depth discussion of the various types of entities that are available to an entrepreneur. In general, a business can be organized as a sole proprietorship, a partnership, a limited partnership, a limited liability company or a corporation.

Sole proprietorships and partnerships are deemed to be formed when individuals (in the case of the sole proprietorship) or two or more persons (in the case of the partnership) engage in business. As a general rule, the state in which the sole proprietor or the partners are domiciled will be the state in which the sole proprietorship or partnership is formed.

However, if a limited partnership, limited liability company or corporation is the choice of business entity, the entrepreneur may select the jurisdiction in which to form the entity. Limited partnerships, limited liability companies and corporations are creatures of state law. A corporation may be formed in any one of the 50 states of the United States and the District of Columbia. Most state laws provide for the formation of limited partnerships and limited liability companies, and the entrepreneur will have a number of jurisdictions to choose from.

The business entity will be governed by the laws of the jurisdiction in which it is formed. The entity may also be subject to the laws of other jurisdictions, such as states in which it does business.[19] The entity's jurisdiction of formation may have a significant impact on the cost and complexity associated with forming and maintaining the entity. There are a number of factors to consider when choosing the state in which to form the business entity. The entrepreneur should seek the advice of an attorney when deciding where to form the business entity. An attorney can advise the entrepreneur of the legal considerations of forming an entity in a particular jurisdiction.

A.   General Considerations in Choosing the State of Formation for the Business Entity

Many people assume that Delaware is the most favorable state in which to form a business entity, whether the business entity be a corporation, limited liability company or limited partnership. Delaware has long been regarded as a state whose laws provide flexibility and protection to corporations. These

---

19.   *See* Cal. Corp. Code § 2115.

principles also apply to Delaware limited liability companies and limited partnerships. In many cases, Delaware will be the appropriate choice of jurisdiction for an entity. However, many states have liberalized their laws to become more similar to those of Delaware in order attract businesses. Thus, the tax and corporate law advantages of forming an entity in Delaware (which are discussed in greater detail below) are less significant than they once were. Nevada, in particular, is a state that has revised its corporate laws to compete with Delaware as the situs of choice for corporations and limited liability companies. Another choice that is often appropriate for smaller or closely held businesses is formation in the state where the business is operated.

1. *Formation of Business Entity in the State Where Operation Is Located*

Forming the entity in the state in which the entity operates is often the appropriate choice for small businesses. If the entrepreneur plans to operate his or her business in a particular state and chooses to form a corporation, limited liability company or limited partnership in another state, the business entity that is formed will likely be required to qualify to do business in the state in which it operates. For example, if an entrepreneur forms a Delaware corporation for a business operated in California, the Delaware corporation would have to register with the State of California. This is commonly referred to as qualification by a foreign entity, which is foreign in that it was formed in a foreign jurisdiction. An entity that does business outside of its state of formation will most likely be required to file annual reports and pay taxes in the state of formation and the state or states in which it does business. The additional paperwork and cost involved with forming an entity outside the state where the business operates are factors an entrepreneur should consider.

2. *Model and Uniform Laws Adopted by States*

As discussed above, many states have amended their laws so that they are more consistent with Delaware's laws. Many states have adopted all or portions of the Model Business Corporation Act and the Revised Model Business Corporation Act. The Acts are intended to balance the interests of the corporation's shareholders, its management and the public. States have also adopted the Uniform Limited Partnership Act, and the Uniform Limited Liability Company Act. Some states, however, have not adopted these acts, and as a result, their laws differ markedly from the general trend. For example, New York has adopted only limited sections of the Model Business Corporation Act or the Revised Model Business Corporation Act. Although cost and ease of maintenance may dictate forming the entity in the state in which it operates, the advantages offered by states whose laws provide additional protections and flexibility may weigh in favor of choosing a jurisdiction outside of the state of operations.

3.   Tax and Corporate Law Considerations

As indicated above, the laws governing corporations, limited liability companies and limited partnership differ from state to state. Some of the differences that influence the choice of formation are the degree to which management of the entity is personally liable to the owners of the entity and third parties, the rights of owners of the entity, taxes, takeover defenses, protection of owners of the entity, flexibility in taking actions and clarity of the law governing the entity. For instance, some states allow single member limited liability companies and others require that a limited liability company have at least two members. In general, states with more flexible corporate laws allow shareholders representing a majority of the outstanding voting shares to take actions by written consent without a meeting.

B.   Advantages and Disadvantages of Some Popular Jurisdictions

Delaware continues to be a favorite choice of jurisdiction for corporations, limited liability companies and limited partnerships. Nevada has grown increasingly popular in recent years as a place in which to form business entities. California and New York, as large states with important economies, are often chosen as the place of formation for companies. The main advantages of each jurisdiction are discussed below.

1.   Delaware

Delaware is well known as a state that is friendly to corporate entities. Over half the companies on the New York Stock Exchange are incorporated in Delaware, and Delaware is the place of incorporation for more than one half of the Fortune 500 companies. Delaware was one of the first states to offer great flexibility to corporations, making them easy and inexpensive to form and maintain. Delaware's laws protect the interests of stockholders, directors, officers and the corporation itself. There are a number of advantages to forming a business in Delaware.

Delaware's laws primarily protect stockholders, and as a result, many large companies whose securities are traded on national exchanges are drawn to Delaware. Delaware also protects the management of the corporate entity by allowing for limitation on personal liability and indemnification by the corporation. Delaware law also allows management to put protections in place to resist corporate takeovers.

Delaware's laws are sophisticated and well established. Through approximately a century of being the domicile of choice for corporations, Delaware has built up a body of precedent for a multitude of corporate scenarios. Delaware is singular in the fact that it has a designated five-judge tribunal, the Court of Chancery, whose sole responsibility is to adjudicate corporate matters. Delaware's legislature also is active in addressing corporate issues as they arise and amending the laws to keep up with the changing corporate landscape. For example, Delaware has amended its laws to specifically allow boards of directors of corporations to hold meetings electronically. A Delaware business entity will have many sources of guidance when faced with a question of whether it can take a particular action. Delaware's moderate tax policies make it attractive to businesses. Delaware offers two methods of franchise tax calculation so that businesses can choose the method that is most cost-effective for them. The minimum franchise tax levied by Delaware is $75.00 for corporations using the "Authorized Shares" method and $350.00 for corporations using the "Assumed Par Value Capital Method." The corporate laws allow stockholders and management to conduct business with minimum formalities and procedural expense. The procedures for action are clearly defined. The Division of Corporations, which handles corporate filings, allows for expedited filing (i.e., one hour filing for an added fee) and preclearance, so businesses can quickly effect changes such as amendments to the charter to designate stock for financings and mergers. As an additional example of Delaware's flexibility, filings can be made by fax.

2. Nevada

Nevada's laws governing corporate entities are in many respects as liberal or more liberal than those of Delaware. In some ways, Nevada seems to have taken its laws one step further than Delaware. While Delaware's laws cater to large corporations, especially those whose stock is publicly traded, Nevada's laws are geared towards smaller, private companies.

Nevada is an attractive choice to the management of entities because it provides them with protection arguably stronger than the protection provided under Delaware law. While Delaware requires that directors and officers act in the best interest of the corporation or in a manner not opposed to the best interest of the corporation, Nevada does not allow the courts to compare a director or officer's behavior with an objective standard. This makes it more difficult for directors and officers to be found personally liable. The shareholders of smaller, privately held companies are often the officers and directors of the companies as well. As a result, the shareholders do not need as much protection under the laws, and are more concerned with protection as officers and directors against third parties.

There are also tax advantages that are available to Nevada corporations and limited liability companies. Nevada does not levy a franchise tax, nor does it tax corporations for Nevada-based income.

3. *California*

California has not traditionally been a business-friendly state, due to the fact that many of its laws are designed to protect minority shareholders. California is unique among the 50 states in that it applies certain California corporate laws to foreign corporations who are deemed to be quasi-California corporations.[20] Thus, even if the entrepreneur forms a corporation in a jurisdiction with more flexible laws, the business may still be subject to the more stringent laws of California.

There is a large number of California corporations, limited liability companies and limited partnerships. For companies that primarily do business in California, it is often the most practical choice of jurisdiction. California has a large population and is home to a number of important industries. If the entrepreneur plans to have significant business operations in California, he or she should consider whether it is worthwhile to form the business outside of California.

A business entity formed in California will be subject to California law. A California business corporation or limited liability company is subject to the state's franchise tax. The tax rate is relatively high, and is applied to net income allocated to California. The minimum annual franchise tax for corporations and limited liability companies is $800, and must be paid regardless of whether the entity has earned any income from California sources. The minimum franchise tax must be paid by both California entities and entities qualified to do business in California. Shareholders of a California corporation or a corporation headquartered in California have powerful rights to inspect and copy corporate records.[21]

Due to Section 2115 of the California Corporations Code, foreign corporations operating in California cannot avoid the California laws by incorporating outside of California. If a corporation incorporated in a foreign jurisdiction meets certain requirements, it will be required to comply with certain California General Corporation Law provisions relating to corporate governance. The determination is based on the combination of several factors, which include the amount of the outstanding securities held by Californians and the amount of income from sources in California.

In general though, the California laws are modern and updated regularly. The General Corporation Law allows boards of directors to act by written consent, telephonic or electronic video screen meetings and delegation of powers to committees of the board. The California Secretary of State's office allows for expedited filing of documents, but requires that any document to

---

20.   *See* Cal. Corp. Code § 2115. *See* VantagePoint Venture Partners 1996 v. Examen, Inc., 871 A.2d 1108 (Del.Supr., May 05, 2005) regarding Delaware Supreme Court's opinion on the non-applicability of Cal. Corp. Code § 2115 to a Delaware Corporation.

21.   *See* Cal. Corp. Code §§ 1600 *et seq.*

be filed on a four-hour expedited basis be first precleared with the office. California does not allow filings to be made by fax.

California does have a number of laws that protect shareholders and create obstacles for management. For example, loans to officers and directors usually require shareholder approval,[22] a purchaser usually cannot issue a promissory note to purchase stock from a corporation,[23] the shareholders of a corporation cannot be deprived of their right to cumulatively vote (unless the corporation is publicly held),[24] and staggered boards are prohibited.[25] The shareholders' right to cumulatively vote and the disallowance of staggered boards (where directors serve terms of longer than one year) also apply to "quasi-California" corporations under Section 2115 of the General Corporations Law.

4. New York

An entrepreneur who plans to do business in New York can choose to form a New York business entity or form an entity in another jurisdiction and qualify that entity to do business in New York. Many businesses choose to form in New York. Like California, New York is both heavily populated and a center of commerce. New York, like California, has modern and regularly updated laws. Like California, the New York Department of State, Division of Corporations reviews documents before filing them, so that it is less likely that a defective document is filed.

New York law provides more flexibility than California law in some respects, leaving it up to the corporation's certificate of incorporation and/ or bylaws to dictate whether the shareholders have the right to cumulatively vote[26] and whether classification of directors is allowed.[27]

New York, however, does require that the 10 largest shareholders of a closely held domestic corporation have unlimited personal liability for unpaid wages and fringe benefits of the corporation's wage earners.[28] A foreign corporation would not be subject to this provision.

Doing business in New York, regardless of whether the business entity is formed in New York or not, may subject the business to the significant taxes levied on the state and local level in New York. In addition to a state-level franchise tax imposed on business corporations, there is also a $300 annual "maintenance fee" (which will be available as a credit against any franchise tax due in New York), and local taxes on the city level.[29] Foreign entities that do a certain level of business in New York will also be subject to franchise

---

22.   *See* Cal. Corp. Code § 315.
23.   *See* Cal. Corp. Code § 409(a)(1).
24.   *See* Cal. Corp. Code § 708.
25.   *See* Cal. Corp. Code § 301(a).
26.   *See* N.Y. Bus. Corp. Law § 618.
27.   *See* N.Y. Bus. Corp. Law § 704.
28.   *See* N.Y. Bus. Corp. Law § 630.
29.   *See* N.Y. Tax Law § 209-A.

taxes and will be required to pay the annual maintenance fee and a license fee, which is payable only once unless the corporation's capital share structure changes or the amount of the corporation's capital stock employed in New York State increases from the time the last license fee return was filed.[30]

---

30. *See* http://www.tax.state.ny.us/pdf/publications/multi/pub20_1007.pdf

Preparing a Business Plan

AiMinh T. Nguyen

Associate General Counsel, ASI Computer Technologies, Inc.
Fremont, California

Alan S. Gutterman

Gutterman Law & Business
Piedmont, CA

Contents

Preparing a Business Plan[1]

2.01 Preliminary Considerations

The business plan is the entrepreneur's "resume" for interviewing with potential investors and for prospecting for investment capital. In addition, the business plan should be viewed and valued as an important tool for planning and managing the business. Most entrepreneurs begin drafting a business plan by providing general information about the company, its business model, plans, capital needs, strategy, and the like. Such a business plan may need to be modified substantially, however, in order to be of utility to the entrepreneur in providing the specific information requirements that may be mandated by law. An experienced business counselor should be able to assist the entrepreneur in developing the initial business plan and then adapting the document to suit the requirements of investors and regulators. The business plan is a living and evolving document that should be revisited regularly to ensure that all information is current and that the contents reflect the latest activities and strategies of the business.

A business plan that conforms to the information requirements of the Securities Act of 1933 as amended and its rules ("1933 Act") is a more versatile tool since the business plan can be used both for obtaining investment capital (in a manner that comports with legal requirements) as well as for managing and developing the entrepreneur's business.[2] (Although this chapter

---

1. Damon Lim was the author of this chapter in the first edition of the *Guide*.

2. An entrepreneur generally drafts a business plan in order to obtain equity capital. Section 5 of the 1933 Act makes the issuance of securities without an effective registration statement unlawful. In addition, state laws may govern the issuance of securities in that state or to a resident of that state. Generally, such laws require that every security must be registered or qualified prior to issuance unless an applicable exemption from the registration or qualification requirements can be met. A failure to comply with the

will discuss securities issues in the context of information contained in a business plan and provided to investors, Chapter 7 (Financing a Business) covers securities issues in more detail.)

A portion of the business plan will provide information regarding the specific investment structure and financial documentation for the proposed investment necessary to comply with legal requirements,[3] and the strategic and financial section of the business plan can serve as a guide to manage the operation of the planned business once the investment funds have been obtained. More generally, a business plan describes the business opportunity that the entrepreneur intends to exploit. It also describes the market that the proposed business serves, the existing and potential competitors to such proposed business, the management team's experience and capabilities in exploiting such opportunities, as well as the amount of funds needed to execute the business plan and sustain the company's competitive advantage in the marketplace once the business begins shipping its product or service.

2.02   Purposes of a Business Plan

A.   Introduction

When drafting a business plan, the entrepreneur should be cognizant that the business plan can serve multiple functions. Initially, the business plan is a key that opens the door to investment. However, once the door to investment has been opened, the well-written business plan should also provide prospective investors with certain information to meet legal requirements, as well as information regarding the business's capital structure.

An entrepreneur must also realize that because the investment door shuts very quickly, the entrepreneur must use the little time allotted by prospective investors efficiently and effectively. In those short moments that an entrepreneur has to present his business plan, the entrepreneur must articulate the current business environment, how the entrepreneur's business concept addresses a need or solves a problem in the existing environment, and the potential rewards to the person who implements the underlying plan. The entrepreneur must also be able to grasp and then sustain the investor's interest so that the prospective investor will want to learn more about the business. In this

---

registration requirement or a failure to obtain an exemption from such requirements will create potential liabilities to the issuing company, its officers and directors from governmental enforcement through criminal, civil and administrative proceedings, or from private law suits seeking refunds of their purchase price.

3.   The information requirements of the 1933 Act are meant to provide investors with "full disclosure" of all "material facts," that the typical investor would find important in making an investment decision to purchase the securities of the issuing company. Raising capital effectively and legally from investors, especially investors who are not "accredited investors," as defined in Rule 501(a) of the 1933 Act requires very specific documentation that normally surpasses the information contained in a business plan.

sense, the business plan, or more properly, the executive summary of the business plan, is the teaser that gets the investor to look more closely at the plan itself.

Professional investors spend a good portion of their time overseeing and managing their investments in addition to reviewing countless new business plans every day. Thus, the professional investor has precious little time to carefully review the myriad of business plans that they receive daily. Given the brevity of time that the professional investor can spend on any individual business plan, the entrepreneur's goal is to get his business plan culled from all of the other business plans that the professional investor receives so that his business plan will actually be reviewed in detail.

Because the pitch of the business plan generally precedes the formal presentation of the actual plan, the entrepreneur should be prepared to give his pitch in either a chance meeting or after a formal introduction. As a rule of thumb, in order to get his plan reviewed, the entrepreneur should be able to pitch the business plan in a matter of three minutes. In those three minutes, a prospective investor should be able to decide whether or not the business plan deserves further scrutiny. Thereafter, the entrepreneur can forward the actual business plan to the prospective investor if after such preliminary introduction/meeting, the prospective investor is interested in the underlying business.

B.   Management Tool

The business plan also serves as a management tool. Once the entrepreneur has been successful in obtaining an investment in his business, the business plan morphs from a tool of introduction to an operational and budgetary document that can be used internally and externally for the management of the business enterprise, as well as identifying the specific milestones that management should attempt to achieve during the relevant funding period to keep management focused on the execution of the business plan.

The pro forma financial portion of the business plan and its underlying assumptions form the foundation of the business plan as a management tool. A detailed business plan will contain a time line, specific financial variables, identifiable milestones, and key assumptions about the underlying business and market. The business plan will permit both the entrepreneur and investor to gauge the success of the entrepreneur in executing the business plan and in assessing the actual market size and its potential, and to judge the accuracy of the various forecasts and assumptions that underlie the financial projections in the business plan.

Generally, the pro forma is made for a period of one to three years. It begins with basic assumptions, where the entrepreneur sets forth the framework in the form of a timeline for executing the plan for capitalizing the perceived market opportunity. The initial pro forma begins with greater specificity, that is, monthly detail of significant milestones for a period of 12 to 18 months.

Later periods are presented on a quarterly or annual basis. In creating the forecasts and financials, the entrepreneur must associate significant milestones (e.g., product development, production, or marketing) with the inputs that will enable the milestones to be achieved, and the related costs for each such input. Such pro forma financial statements should include inputs for the following:

- Sales by unit or total dollar volume and product mix
- Gross margin in total and by product
- Accounts receivable collection period
- Inventory turnover
- Useful lives of the company's assets and related depreciation schedules
- Capital expenditures
- Interest income on temporary investments of excess funds
- Effective income tax rate

Once the pro forma financial statements have been developed for periods of one to three years, the entrepreneur has a preliminary financial package that he can show to the prospective investor. Such pro forma will include a balance sheet, income statement and a statement of cash flows.

The preparation of the pro forma financial statement requires some expertise in finance and accounting. Expert advice and assistance should be obtained in preparing the financial statements and the underlying assumptions so that the entrepreneur does not lose credibility from the presentation of an inaccurate or incomplete pro forma.

C. Capital Request

The business plan, or more correctly, the creation of the business plan, assists the entrepreneur in developing his request for capital. Once the pro forma financial statements are complete, in particular the statement of cash flow, the entrepreneur will have a better idea of how much investment capital he or she should be seeking. Specifically, by taking a cumulative total of the total cash flow for each period in the statement of cash flow, the entrepreneur has an indication of how much capital will be required to get the business to a particular milestone, for a time period, or to a break-even position. This cumulative total forms an approximation of the amount of capital that the entrepreneur should be seeking from prospective investors. However, the cumulative total is only an approximate of the amount of capital that the entrepreneur should seek because the actual request should allow for some flexibility in the event that the detail of the company's capital costs, operating expenditures and projected revenue assumptions vary from the initial projections. By asking for more than the cumulative total, the capital request will cover the capital requirements for the relevant period, plus an additional amount for unforeseen expenditures or shortfalls.

D. Strategic Plan

The business plan also forms the foundation for the development of a company's strategic plan.

Although companies may be initially successful in developing their products or technology, the development of such products or technology is not a guarantee of long-term success. The key to the success of a business is developing a product or technology into a sustainable business. Thus, the entrepreneur, in addition to thinking about the product or technology being developed, must also create a business that can bring in follow-on revenues based on several products or a family of products as opposed to a single product or technology, or he must develop plans for the acquisition of his business (i.e., create an exit strategy for his potential investors).

When developing the outline for the creation of a business from a product idea or technology, the entrepreneur should strive to develop a strategy that sets forth an initial blue print for developing related or similar products that may utilize the proposed product or technology to create a sustainable and growing business. The failure to do so would suggest to the prospective investor that the entrepreneur has a one product idea that may be prone to "shooting star" syndrome (that is, the proposed business is likely to get off to a flying start, but fade out soon thereafter unless it is acquired).

E. Private Placement Memorandum

A well-drafted business plan that contains sufficient detailed information can be used to comply with the information requirements of both federal and state securities laws as well as provide the entrepreneur and his company with further protection against suits for fraud. By creating a business plan and the offering documentation at the same time, the entrepreneur facilitates the development of a congruent and accurate package for prospective investors in a cost effective and time efficient manner.

The most common offering document is a private placement memorandum ("PPM"), which is more fully discussed in Chapter 7 (Financing a Business). The PPM includes the company's business plan, a description of the company's management, and proposed offering terms. Generally, in drafting a business plan and PPM, the desire is to raise needed capital to finance the enterprise. There is a significant body of state and federal law that governs PPM contents and the manner of identifying potential investors and soliciting their investments. We will cover these issues in Chapter 7. As noted in that chapter, to the extent that the entrepreneur is unable to raise monies from accredited investors,[4] state law and federal law may require that the company make additional disclosures to its prospective investors.[5]

Because the securities disclosure requirements for nonaccredited investors are quite onerous and extremely costly to provide, during the initial capital raising stage, most entrepreneurs accept investments only from *accredited* investors. In so doing, the entrepreneur can avoid the tremendous costs of preparing adequate disclosures to meet the requirements under the 1933 Act. Generally, if an issuing company utilizes a Regulation D exemption to sell to accredited investors, the entrepreneur may provide the accredited investors only with such information as the prospective investor requires.[6] Access to the issuer's facilities, financial information and records, and access to management to ask questions relating to the investors' investment have been found to satisfy the information requirements of Regulation D.[7] Because all securities transactions, even exempt transactions, are subject to the antifraud provisions of both federal and state securities laws, the entrepreneur should provide sufficient information that is neither false nor misleading (i.e., statements that might contain a material omission that would make the statement made false or misleading) in order to avoid potential liability under the relevant securities law's antifraud provisions. Therefore, even if no specific disclosure requirements are mandated by law, the entrepreneur should take care to provide sufficient information to prospective investors who are accredited so that the prospective investor can make an informed decision.

---

4.   An "accredited investor" is generally regarded as an investor who is sophisticated and has the financial wherewithal to make an investment in a risky security. The 1933 Act defines the following general categories of persons as being accredited: (a) banks, insurance companies, registered investment and development companies; (b) employee benefit plans and plans that have total assets in excess of $5 million; (c) charitable organizations, corporations, trusts not formed to acquire the securities offered, and whose purchases are directed by a sophisticated person, or partnerships with assets exceeding $5 million; (d) any director, executive officer, or general partner of the issuing company; (e) a business in which all the equity owners are accredited investors; (f) natural persons with a net worth of at least $1 million or with incomes exceeding $200,000 in each of the two most recent years or have joint income with a spouse exceeding $300,000 and a reasonable expectation of the same income level in the current year.

5.   The entrepreneur/issuer's disclosure requirements to accredited investors are substantially less, and in some cases, mere access to its facilities, records, financial information and other material may be deemed sufficient. See for example, Barrett v. Triangle Mining Corp., Fed Sec. L. Rep. P. 95,438 (1976). In *Barrett*, the investors' access to the issuing company's books, the opportunity to investigate the company's operations and access to other information was considered to meet the type of information that a registration would disclose.

6.   See for example, Livens v. William D. Witter, Inc., 374 F. Supp. 1104 (1975). In *Livens*, the court upheld the offering as being exempt from registration under the 1933 Act and stated that the exemption depends on the practical needs of the investors and not any particular fact or circumstance. Thus, the offering in *Livens* was exempt from the registration requirements even though no financial information or other information normally provided in a registration was made available to the investors. "The determinative question," the court stated, was "how much reliance would the offerees probably have placed upon the particular missing information, had it been discoverable and disclosed to them, in deciding whether to invest." Livens at 1111–12.

7.   *Barrett*, Fed. Sec. L. Rep. P. 95,438 (1976).

If the company plans to utilize Regulation D, and to sell its securities to *nonaccredited* investors, the level of detail and information required under the rules of Regulation D are greatly increased. Under Rules 505 and 506, the entrepreneur must (a) give the nonaccredited investors disclosure documents that contain the same information in Part II of Form 1-A (see **Exhibit 2A**) or Part I of a registration statement (see **Exhibit 2B**);[8] (b) provide the nonaccredited investors with the same information provided to the accredited investors; and (c) be available to answer questions from prospective purchasers.[9]

Alternatively, the initial capital raising efforts may be made via a private placement of equity securities among family and friends. To the extent that the family members and friends are not accredited investors, state law generally provides an exemption from the registration and qualification requirements of the securities for sales to a limited number of persons if such purchasers each represent that they are purchasing the securities for their own account and the offer and sale is not accomplished by the publication of any advertisement.[10] As noted in Chapter 7 (Financing a Business), these same purchasers may be exempted from federal registration requirements under Section 4(2) of the 1933 Act.[11] However, whether or not a company chooses to rely on Section 4(2) would depend on the facts and circumstances involving the issuance of the shares. In some cases, sales to a limited number of people have been deemed to be public offerings, and therefore, the issuer will need to examine (a) the relationship between the investor and the company and between its officer and directors and the information available to the investors and (b) whether those investors intended to acquire the securities with an intent towards distribution.[12]

2.03   Elements of Business Plan

While it has been said that the length of a business plan is inversely proportional to the entrepreneur's ability to raise money, the overall trend is toward shorter business plans to accommodate the investors' limited time to review such plans. Nonetheless, the amount of information that should be provided to a prospective investor depends on whether the investor is a sophisticated or an

---

8.   Rule 502 under Regulation D provides that if the company is able to use Regulation A (an exemption from registration for securities offerings of up to $5 million), the information to be provided to any investor is the same kind of information as is required in Part II of Form 1-A. Otherwise, it must provide the same kind of information that is required in Part I of a registration statement filed under the 1933 Act.

9.   See Rule 502(b) of the 1933 Act.

10.   See for example Section 25102(f) of the California Corporate Securities Law of 1968.

11.   Certain transactions by an issuer that do not involve a public offering are exempted from the registration requirements of the Securities and Exchange Commission. However, in order to fall within the protection provided by statute, rather than relying on Section 4(2) of the 1933 Act, most issuers would try to fit under the safe harbor provided under Regulation D.

12.   SEC v. Ralston Purina Co., 346 U.S. 119 (1953).

accredited investor,[13] or whether such investor is a nonaccredited investor. For nonaccredited investors, the information requirements are mandated by law. If the entrepreneur/issuing company did not prepare documents that provide the level of detailed information required under Part II of Form 1-A or Part I of a registration statement, the issuing company should consider providing such detailed information for its nonaccredited investors.

The information required under Part II of Form 1-A, includes information in the following general categories:

- Company
- Risk factors
- Business and properties
- Offering price factors
- Use of proceeds
- Capitalization
- Description of securities
- Plan of distribution
- Dividends, distributions and redemptions
- Officers and key personnel of the company
- Directors of the company
- Principal stockholders
- Management relationships, transactions and remuneration
- Litigation
- Federal tax aspects
- Miscellaneous factors
- Financial statements
- Management discussion and analysis of certain relevant factors

The information required by Part I of a registration statement includes information in the following general categories:

- Summary information
- Risk factors
- Ratio of earnings to fixed charges
- Use of proceeds
- Determination of offering price
- Dilution
- Selling security holders
- Plan of distribution
- Description of securities to be registered
- Interests of named experts and counsel
- Information with respect to the issuer, including

---

13.   The amount of information sought by a sophisticated or accredited investor varies by the investor. Some investors want short, five-page summaries, while others seek full-blown business plans. In each case, the elements of the business plan are the same.

- Description of business
- Description of property
- Legal proceedings
- Market price of and dividends on the registrant's common equity and related stockholder matters
- Financial statements, as well as additional financial information
- Management's discussion and analysis of financial condition and results of operations
- Changes in and disagreements with accountants on accounting and financial disclosure
- Quantitative and qualitative disclosures about market risk
- Directors and executive officers
- Executive compensation
- Security ownership of certain beneficial owners and management
- Certain relationships and related transactions
- Corporate governance

- Material changes
- Disclosure of indemnification provisions
- Expenses of issuance and distribution
- Undertakings

To the extent that an issuing company has the detailed information of Part II of Form 1-A or Part I of a registration statement available, the issuing company should provide this information to both its nonaccredited as well as its accredited investors (even though such detailed information is not required in the case of accredited investors) in order to comply with the antifraud provisions of both state and federal laws.

Generally, the information in the business plan, when coupled with the information contained in the term sheet (see for example, the form attached as **Exhibit 2C**) should provide an accredited investor with sufficient disclosure of company's business, risk factors, proposed capitalization, and use of proceeds. To the extent that an accredited investor finds such information to be insufficient, the accredited investor will have the opportunity to seek more information and to ask questions of management.

For the balance of this chapter, we will assume that the entrepreneur is an initial stage company seeking investment capital only from accredited investors under Regulation D. This assumption is generally typical of companies seeking venture capital because the typical entrepreneur does not wish to expend a large portion of any investment capital raised paying for the drafting of legal documents that meet the detailed requirements of the 1933 Act; however, the fact that an offering is limited to accredited investors does not excuse the entrepreneur from making full and fair disclosure of all material information relating to the proposed business and terms of the offering.

This chapter divides the business plan into 13 principal sections. However, because there are no formal legal requirements regarding disclosures for accredited investors, the sections may be combined or in some cases omitted, so long as the business plan and term sheet provide the prospective investor with sufficient information to make the investment decision.

A.   Executive Summary

The executive summary is possibly the single most important section of the business plan because it is the section that most readers will either scan or read. Therefore, in order to get maximum impact, it is critical that this section be brief, precise and clear. In short, the executive summary must provide sufficient information to prospective investors that is both interesting and informative so that the reader will (a) find answers to key questions and (b) be sufficiently engrossed to want to read and learn about the opportunity further.

The entrepreneur must keep in mind that venture capitalists and other sophisticated investors receive numerous requests for funding but only desire to fund a few select projects. Therefore, knowing that the investor generally has a short attention span and that the actual business plan contains detailed information relating to markets, opportunities, finances, risk and the like, the successful entrepreneur will distill such detailed information for the prospective investor, thereby providing the prospective investor with a summary that highlights the business and market opportunity in a compelling manner.

As a rule of thumb, the executive summary should be no more than one and a half pages or about three paragraphs in length. The first paragraph should generally cover the scope of the opportunity. The second paragraph should generally cover the proposed business, and to a certain extent, the management team's capabilities. The final paragraph should be a brief statement about the financing required. To the extent that actual figures (size of market, size of opportunity, and summary financial information) are available, such figures should be used in the executive summary. For the typical investor, the figures are like pictures, and are an excellent substitute for more lengthy prose. If the executive summary is drafted correctly, the prospective investor will be able to understand the opportunity in a few minutes time, and will be able to decide if further reading and a more thorough investigation is warranted.

B.   Table of Contents

The table of contents facilitates the reading of the business plan. The table of contents should be prepared in a way that facilitates its use as a tool for quickly finding information that may be critical to the reader's assessment of the underlying business. To this end, not only should the table of contents provide quick thumbnails of the pertinent sections of the business plan, it also should provide information as to what page each section can be found. If the business plan is to be tabbed, the table of contents should reference the relevant tab. By making the table of contents informative and useful, the entrepreneur maximizes the time that the investor has allocated to reading the business plan.

Because in general, there are many ideas chasing a limited pool of capital, maximizing the exposure that the business plan gets is important.

C.   Business Description

A business plan should provide information on the market, as well as information on how the idea, concept or strategy behind the business being proposed can be converted from its conceptual stage into a commercial product or business. In its simplest form, the business description begins with a general overview of the current marketplace and its existing parameters. From this general overview, the entrepreneur has created a stage from which he can provide a comparative reference on how the entrepreneur's business will be an improvement over the existing market. The entrepreneur achieves this by providing in slightly greater detail, *what* the proposed business is and how it fits into and is superior to the existing market. For example if the current marketplace is using a particular "generation" of an evolving technology, the entrepreneur might explain that current technology limits the types of goods and services the market currently provides. However, by using the entrepreneur's technology, which is based on a next generation technology, not only will new products and services become available, but current existing levels of services might be improved as well.

While it may seem self-evident that in formulating the business description, sufficient thought should be spent on creating a business that has a comparative advantage over other businesses in the existing marketplace, what is less self-evident is that the process should also include introspection about the marketplace and creating a business that is broad enough in scope to stimulate further thinking about potential business opportunities and synergies that the proposed business might have with the other portfolio companies of the potential investor. In short, the business description should be made in a manner so as not to be defined so narrowly as to constrain the possible boundaries of the potential market, partners, synergies or market size. However on the other extreme, the entrepreneur should be aware that in creating the business description, care should also be taken so that the description of the business is not so overly broad as to necessarily envelope additional competitive areas or touch upon issues that would obfuscate or distract the reader. As an example, a company that is interested in making integrated circuits for the telecommunications market should not define its product so broadly as to encompass all integrated circuits, nor should it include a discussion of every integrated circuit producer as its potential competitor.

Finally, the business description section should include a summary description on *how* the company's products or services are to be produced or rendered and how and when the company intends to carry out its activities.

If the entrepreneur has special capabilities, strategies or access to special facilities to produce or provide the products, goods or services, such access should be adequately described so as to be construed as a unique advantage. If the company plans to offer new products, this business description section should also provide detailed information on the present stage of products in development, including whether or not working prototypes are in existence; or alternatively, provide a description of the current stage of development of the products as well as information about what additional requirements are necessary to complete the products. If the company is or is expected to be dependent on one or a limited number of suppliers for essential raw materials, energy or other items, the company may want to describe this situation as part of its business description. Alternatively, if such situations suggest a risk factor, this information could be included in a section on risk. See Section 2.03.I below.

In addition to the overview of the market and the products to be offered by the new company, the business description section should include a quick summary of the following information as well:

- A brief description of the management team and why the team is especially well poised to exploit the idea or market
- A brief description of marketing strategy
- A summary of key financial data relevant to the proposed business, including amount requested

The business description should include a quick reference to the key players who are going to enable the company to develop the proposed products or deliver the proposed services. This reference can be especially helpful in creating credibility for the enterprise in that the more successful or talented the management team, the more willing the investor may be in investing capital in an enterprise run by the members of the management team. As more fully described in Section 2.03.H, investors are not betting on products, so much as they are betting on the management team to get the products to market.

This business description may include a short description of the marketing strategies that the company will be employing, to the extent that such plans have been developed. The strategies should describe the manner in which the management team believes it can use targeted efforts to penetrate or develop a new market. To the extent that the company may already have customers, it would be beneficial to either name such customers (if the customers are willing), or to generally describe the customers.

Finally, the business description may include a short description of relevant financial information and capital needs. Of course, this information should also be found in more detail in the financials section. See Section 2.03.L.

D. Identification of Opportunity/Target Market

One of principal reasons most entrepreneurs engage in a new business is to capitalize on a perceived opportunity in the marketplace. While the entrepreneur may understand the opportunity due to an understanding of the market deficiency or inefficiencies in the existing market, or from his work within a new technology or an application of a different technology to the current product mix, or from his acute perceptiveness about the nuances of a particular product, not all opportunities are as universally apparent to potential investors. Therefore, in order to present the opportunity in a manner that is sufficiently compelling to warrant a further look, and then ultimately an investment, the entrepreneur must be able to describe the opportunity clearly and precisely so that the potential investor is also able to identify and understand the potential opportunity and its financial merits.

In this part of the business plan, the entrepreneur needs to spell out in copious detail the current market, the market players, and the problems inherent in the status quo. The analysis would identify competitive products, the competitors and each such product and competitors' relative strengths and weaknesses. The entrepreneur's analysis should then be followed by a detailed presentation of the company and its solution to the current market inefficiency. This presentation will further explain how and why the entrepreneur is better equipped to exploit the current market environment than the current competitors in the marketplace, and how the entrepreneur's products are not only superior to existing products, but how the entrepreneur intends to defend his product and position from future attack. In this section, it would not be inappropriate for the entrepreneur to extol upon the virtues of its management team and products. Explanations of past experience in expanding the market and protecting market share would also be appropriate.

In short, the presentation of the market opportunity should support the entrepreneur's contention that he can take the initial idea or concept from the idea stage to commercial viability in the identified niche. Thereafter, the section should set forth the manner in which the entrepreneur would protect its target niche from larger companies and other start-ups who may attempt to exploit the same or similar niche. This may include the development of related products, a family of products, or a series of follow-on products that would create a sustainable business not subject to the risks of one idea.

To the extent that the market opportunity section is sufficiently developed, the section may form the basis of the company's strategic plan. In any case, this section should be updated as the opportunity and markets develop.

E. Offering

In deciding whether to make an investment in a new enterprise, prospective investors review information that is external to the company as well as information that is company specific. The investor reviews the current financial landscape for private equity investment as well as the latest trends in equity investments. Armed with this information, and the information provided by the company, the investor will be in a position not only to judge the possible financial returns that would accrue to any investment from the successful execution of the business plan, but also to assess the ability or power that he might be able to exert over the company in the event that the company's business does not go as planned.

The company-specific information that all investors require begins with information about the securities that the company is proposing to offer. As an example, the company can consider offering common stock, convertible debt, warrants, preferred stock convertible into common stock or any combination of the forgoing or other securities. Depending upon the type of securities being offered, additional pertinent information, which often is contained in a term sheet (see, for example, **Exhibit 2C**), will include the following information: dividend rights; terms of conversion; sinking fund provisions in the event that the stock is redeemable; redemption provisions; voting rights, including any protective provisions; liquidation rights; and preemption rights. The capitalization information should include a brief description of any potential dilution from the existence of stock option or stock plans, as well as from the existence of warrants or other rights to purchase shares.

The detailed information of the security being offered and the information on the existing capitalization of the company provide the investor with a snapshot of the capital structure of the company pre- and post-investment. If the capital structure is not to the investor's liking, the investor may seek additional protections in the form of future participation rights, board observer rights, rights of first refusal, codevelopment rights or priority licensing rights.

The description of the existing and proposed capitalization structure is generally followed by a written description, in summary fashion, of the following factors, which may be relevant to the price as well as the terms of investment sought by the investor:

- Net, after-tax earnings for the last fiscal year
- Net, after-tax earnings per share for the last fiscal year (calculated on a weighted average of shares outstanding for the fiscal year)
- Offering price as a multiple of earnings or sales
- Book value and book value per share
- Pre- and post-capitalization of the company on a fully diluted basis
- Minimum and maximum number of securities to be issued/money to be raised
- Information regarding material amounts of funds from sources other than the offering, if any, that are to be used in conjunction with the proceeds from the offering

Finally, the offering section may include information regarding the proposed use of the funds raised. This information, if included in this section (or in the financial section—see Section 2.03.L), would include information on whether any material part of the proceeds from the offering will be used to discharge indebtedness or to acquire assets.

F.   Customers

The section regarding customers is a very important section, because customers are the source of revenue and success to the enterprise. To the extent that the entrepreneur's existing business has customers or persons performing beta testing of the products to be marketed, these facts should be disclosed because such information will assist potential investors in gauging the size of the potential market as well as the level of interest in the products. Alternatively, to the extent that key management personnel have contacts in the desired industry, this information should also be disclosed, along with any interest in the entrepreneur's products being offered (as may be evidenced by the list of prospective customers).

To the extent that an entrepreneur either does not have customers for its products, or the company's management team has not been fully assembled so that it can state that it has contacts to key customers, the entrepreneur is still well served by being able to identify potential customers. This process is relatively straightforward, and a list of customers as well as information about potential customers can be quickly obtained by a search through standard industrial codes for businesses operating in the relevant section, as well as through research on publicly filed documents of publicly traded companies doing business in such sections.

G.   Assessment of Competition

This section is closely related to, and sometimes included in the section regarding identification of opportunity/target market. This section, however, more particularly identifies the competitors or potential competitors in the entrepreneur's market.

In preparing this section, the entrepreneur must be able to describe the industry in which the company is selling or expects to sell its products or services and, where applicable, any recognized trends within that industry. To the extent possible, and if applicable, information should be provided describing that part of the industry and the geographic area in which the proposed business competes or will compete, as well as any assessment of the company's competitor's position in terms of pricing, service or other basis. Finally, information should be provided with respect to the relative size and financial and market strengths of the company's competitors in the area of competition.

Great care should be spent in preparing this section so that the information provided is both current and accurate. The entrepreneur's analysis, as provided in this section, immediately shows prospective investors whether the entrepreneur truly understands its product, market, and the niche he or she intends to exploit. Failure to identify an existing competitor or competitors in the market alerts the potential investor that the entrepreneur has not adequately assessed the market or that the entrepreneur is not in tune with fast developing market or the key players in such market. Such failures are warning signs that the entrepreneur is not adequately prepared and may not adequately understand the competitive pressures or obstacles that must be overcome to be successful. Such lack of diligence is a sign of other impending problems with the entrepreneur's assessment of the business.

When developing this section of the business plan, the entrepreneur needs to be able to identify his present and potential competitors' major weaknesses and strengths, and identify how the proposed business will capitalize on such weaknesses and overcome such strengths. In so doing, the entrepreneur can differentiate the company and products, as well as position the proposed business and its products in such a way as to avoid detection or direct competition from larger rivals. If feasible, the entrepreneur should attempt to position the company's products, features and services so that they will be perceived as being superior to those offered by other competitors or potential competitors.

It is not enough to identify existing companies which are current competitors or might become competitors. The entrepreneur should also research and be aware of any potential business that is in the formation process and will be competing in the same market. This can be crucial information especially when the entrepreneur's products or services involve a new technology or a need that is apparent. Executing the business plan and the different milestones would be incredibly more challenging with the pressure of a new company following a similar path to the entrepreneur's company.

When preparing this section, special care should be made to verify that all information and assumptions are reasonable. As part of the due diligence process, professional investors will take great pains to verify the underlying assumptions and to determine if the entrepreneur has made any gaping oversights or oversimplifications. If the assumptions are inaccurate or unreasonable, the entrepreneur and his business plan will lose credibility.

H. Management

Many companies with great potential have fallen by the wayside because they were not well managed or had management infighting, and as a result, were unable to properly exploit their competitive advantages. Similarly, companies with technically inferior products have been successful because they managed their business well and were able to place their products and market them effectively. The moral of the two diverging stories is that a key to the success or failure of a business rests with the experience, talent, integrity and ability of the management team.

Because of the importance of the management team to the overall success of an enterprise, a professional investor is very concerned with the persons who comprise the management team. The business plan should identify how the company will be organized, the key positions that will need to be filled, including the duties and responsibilities of each position, as well as the persons the entrepreneur has selected to fill such key positions. Businesses that have positions filled by experienced personnel with a demonstrated ability to work with each other are more attractive than businesses staffed with persons who have not worked together. This is because, in small business, the interpersonal style or interactions of the officers and employees are key to developing the company's culture and values.

To the extent that an investor knows that the founders can work together, there is less risk of internal management conflict. With less potential for conflict, the company will operate more smoothly and will be less prone to experiencing product slip and management infighting. Therefore, in drafting this section of the business plan, the entrepreneur should provide information indicating whether any of the officers have ever managed any other company in the start-up or development stage and describe the circumstances; whether any of the officers ever worked for or managed a company (including a separate subsidiary or division of a larger enterprise) in the same business as the company; and whether such officers worked for or managed a company in the same industry as the company. In the latter case, if so, the entrepreneur should disclose whether adequate precautions (including obtaining releases or consents from prior employers) have been taken to preclude claims by prior employers for conversion or theft of trade secrets, know-how or other proprietary information.

On the other hand, teams filled with inexperienced managers or persons who have not demonstrated an ability to work with other key players present increased risks to a prospective investor's investment. Inexperience means less knowledge and contacts, which can result in missed opportunities and deadlines. The lack of demonstrated teamwork presents increased risk of personnel conflict.

The section on management should be supplemented by a fairly comprehensive description of each of the key management employees, including a resume of such person's relevant experience. The resume is usually contained in the appendix to the business plan. Such resumes should demonstrate that the key managers have adequate experience and are qualified to fill such positions.

Generally, in the start-up phase of a new business, the company will have an incomplete management team. Therefore, the business plan should include a plan for filling out the management team with key personnel[14] with the necessary skills and qualifications to make the business a success. To the

---

14.   The term "key personnel" means persons such as vice presidents, production managers, sales managers, or research scientists and similar persons who make or are expected to make significant contributions to the business of the company, whether as employees, independent contractors, consultants or otherwise.

extent that any person filling a position does not have the requisite experience, provision should be made in the management section for the person to be replaced when a suitable candidate for the position is found.

Finally, to give investors an idea of the stake that the key personnel and officers of the company have in the enterprise, information should be provided with respect to each officer and key personnel's stake in the company, including all stock, options and warrants held by each such person.

I. Risk

The business plan should identify the risks related to the technology or market to be exploited. Disclosure of risk factors relating to a proposed investment is required in any Regulation D offering in excess of $1 million, and is prudent in all cases. From a legal perspective, an issuer that makes a comprehensive disclosure of potential risks to investors is less likely to have securities fraud or rescission liability.

Generally, this section should identify unique and specific risks to the business. While legal requirements seek detailed disclosure of risk factors relating to cash flow and liquidity problems, inexperience of management, dependence of the issuer on an unproven product, absence of an existing market for the product, and the like, such disclosures, while pertinent, are not needed in such mind-numbing detail for accredited investors. Therefore, rather than reciting the litany of possible risks that may face the new business, the entrepreneur is best served by presenting the key risks to his business as he sees it. Thus, information that would dissuade the management team from continuing its efforts at developing a product or finding a market for its products would be most useful and germane to the investor. Management should describe the most substantial risks in order of importance.

J. Strategy

Developing a strategy includes a thorough analysis of the industry in which the company competes and the identification of its sources of competitive advantage over existing and potential competitors. In addition, the strategy should cover probable competitive responses from competitors, as well as how the company intends to build on its perceived competitive advantage and sustain such advantage. The entrepreneur must also incorporate seasonal fluctuations and effects in the strategy. For example, a lower demand for the products or services at a certain time of the year will significantly affect the company's operations and income. Therefore, the entrepreneur should have a plan for additional products or services that will complement the company's portfolio and growth throughout the year. This section often is included with the identification of opportunity/target market or assessment of competition sections. In some cases, if the company has a plan for follow-on products, or a family of products, this section can be separated into a separate section on corporate strategy and maintaining the company's differential and competitive advantage.

Generally, after the company has developed a commercial product from the initial concept or product idea, it must focus on protecting its niche from competitors as well as developing follow-on products and technology to form a defensible and sustainable business. Developing a sustainable business from a product or technology usually comes from modifying existing products or technology to create continued growth in a market niche or cultivating a new market with follow-on products.

The development of follow-on products, however, goes beyond developing a product that is faster or cheaper than one's competitors. Instead, it hinges on developing a family of products or technology than can be defensible. To the extent that a company bets its future success on being faster, smaller or cheaper, it is entering a highly competitive arena where others can learn from the first to market, and improve on the initial product. However, by developing a family of products, the company's products envelop a larger market universe that becomes more defensible. Although one product might be replaced by a superior competitive product, the company has additional products from which to draw needed revenue and financial resources to develop and improve on existing products as well as new products.

Thus, the development of a competitive strategy or strategic plan revolves on how a company takes its product, and builds a business to support its market share and to build on such market share.

K.   Operations

The business plan should include a description of the various pertinent functional areas of the proposed business that are essential to the success of the business. In many cases, for the beginning enterprise, this section would be similar to, or be contained in the description of Management in that this section might include a description of key personnel or operational groups including engineering, sales and marketing, administration, manufacturing and sales support.

To the extent the proposed business actually has operations, the entrepreneur should spend time developing this area to show its capabilities, both in terms of meeting current needs, and its ability to flex to meet future growth, better known as "scaling." In addition, to the extent that special processes or procedures are in place, the entrepreneur may want to showcase the sophistication of the group, and the difficulty that potential competitors might have in trying to replicate the capabilities of the proposed company. Such capabilities might include logistical advantages to sourcing or markets, as well as specialized contacts to obtain competitive advantages in cost (e.g., software house in India or manufacturing in China).

L.   Financial

Another section of the business plan that is thoroughly reviewed is the financial section. As discussed in more detail in Chapter 7 (Financing a Business), because the preparation of this section forms the basis for the entrepreneur's capital request, great care should be exercised in developing it. The underpinnings of the financial section contain in numerical form, all of the underlying assumptions of the proposed business including products, costs, general and administration costs, operating costs and capital costs.

Developing the financial section begins with a basic timeline, beginning with where the company is now, until such time that the company anticipates achieving a certain milestone breakeven, or a certain level of profitability. Once the timeline is formulated, the details and related expenses and revenue associated with the timeline must be filled in. Thus, the entrepreneur must, for instance, project salaries, benefit costs and employee taxes to coincide with hiring dates corresponding to the milestones identified in the timeline, as well as extrapolate engineering costs, capital costs, legal, travel and other related costs associated with product development, product marketing and fund raising activities.

A common tendency of entrepreneurs is to either overestimate the amount of revenues or the time when first revenues or product milestones (e.g., prototypes) are reached, and to underestimate costs related to product development and marketing. Similarly, entrepreneurs also overestimate products and delivery capabilities and underestimate equipment needs. Therefore, the preliminary budget tends to underestimate a company's capital needs.

Marketing is a critical part of the new business that is often underestimated or underfunded. It is the bridge between the entrepreneur's products or services and the source of income, the customers. Regardless of how great the products or services are, they will not sell if the customers do not know about them. Because marketing occurs at a later stage in the timeline, the entrepreneur must ensure that funds are not prematurely depleted and that the estimation of marketing costs is accurate and sufficient.

Therefore, when developing the financials (which include a financial statement, balance sheet and statement of cash flows) the entrepreneur must incorporate slippage, cost overruns and delays. By including such factors in the creation of pro forma financial statements for obtaining the company's capital requirements, the entrepreneur will have sufficient resources to get the company to the intended endpoint/milestone if there is an actual slippage or cost overrun or some other unanticipated event. The failure to ask for sufficient capital will force the investor to seek additional capital when the entrepreneur is running out of money and is at its lowest level of negotiating strength.

Once the pro forma financial statements have been prepared, the entrepreneur needs to include in such statements a discussion of management's assessment of the causes of such results, including a description of any trends in the company's industry, and any changes now occurring in the underlying economics of the industry or the company's business that, in the opinion of management, would have a significant impact (either favorable or adverse) on the company's pro forma results. Such discussion should also take into account an analysis of margins and foreign sales as a percent of total sales. The overall conditions in the economy, as well as the specific markets in which the company will be operating, should also be incorporated into the discussion.

M. Appendix

The appendix is where supporting material for the entrepreneur's assumptions are normally kept. The entrepreneur wants to limit the amount of material that he presents prospective investors in the business plan to those key facts and information that are germane for the investment decision. All other information that is not germane, but rather is supporting or helpful, is best left to the appendix section. For example, background articles, market research and collateral material relating to the product, technology or market are placed in the appendix. In addition, if the entrepreneur desires to place a curriculum vitae or more complete resumes than those presented in the management section, they would be placed in this section. In short, the appendix is where interesting reading, which is in a non-summary form, is placed to the extent that the investor may want more detailed background information than is provided in the business plan.

2.04   Presentation of Business Plan

Once the business plan has been drafted, the next step is the presentation of the business plan. Just as the presentation of a resume, by itself, does not generally lead to a job offer, similarly, the presentation of a well-written business plan, by itself, will not lead to funding. The entrepreneur's ability to obtain investment funding depends on how the entrepreneur manages the process of capital formation, of which the business plan only provides a written document supporting capital investment. In addition to the business plan, the entrepreneur must know when, how and to whom to present the business plan, either orally, or in written form. Timing is critical.

Before presenting the business plan, the entrepreneur must know the details of the business plan so that he or she can recite and discuss pertinent aspects of the plan from memory and without resorting to the plan itself. Only after carefully reviewing and understanding the business plan can the entrepreneur be ready, in an instant, to give a short explanation of the proposed business and business opportunity should the opportunity present itself.

However, even before the entrepreneur can present the business plan, the entrepreneur needs an introduction to potential investors. Formal and informal introductions succeed more often than cold calling. Therefore, people who know the potential investor, either personally or professionally, are in the best position to make an introduction of both the entrepreneur and his idea. Therefore, the entrepreneur should engage the assistance of the entrepreneur's attorney, accountant or financial advisor to obtain an introduction to potential investors who have expressed an interest in the entrepreneur's particular field, or who are amenable to making an investment in the proposed business.

Once the entrepreneur has gained an audience with the potential investor or investors, the entrepreneur must be able to articulate the contents of the executive summary of the business plan. Thereafter, the entrepreneur should be able to successfully answer any follow-on questions in a manner that will generate further follow-on questions regarding the underlying technology, differential advantages and management team. If the investor is not interested in the market or business that the entrepreneur is engaged in, no further time need be spent on explaining the business plan and no written business plan need be sent to the prospective investor. If, however, the investor is interested in the business, the entrepreneur can go into more detail about the business, the market and the product. If the entrepreneur is successful in catching the target audience's attention, he or she will have more time to provide support for the business opportunity. The support for the business opportunity is the business plan.

It is at this stage, and in successive meetings with the prospective investors, that the entrepreneur should know about the investor's experience and knowledge of the entrepreneur's target market and business. This knowledge is important. The entrepreneur's goal should not be just to obtain an investment, but to obtain an investment from those investors who can assist the entrepreneur in getting the product to market, and to identify potential resources, vendors and key personnel to help the company. In addition, at some point, the investor may be able to assist the entrepreneur in seeking customers as well as potential acquirors of the entrepreneurs' business. What the entrepreneur seeks to avoid is spending valuable time educating an investor about his target market and business. In many cases, unbeknownst to the entrepreneur, the investor may have a competing investment in the targeted market, and his knowledge of the entrepreneur's business plan may be used to help a competing business.

Once the entrepreneur has found an investor interested in his business or technology, the entrepreneur can send a copy of his business plan to the investor. To the extent possible, the entrepreneur would want to control the dissemination of the business plan. Therefore, prior to delivering a copy of the plan, the entrepreneur should seek to have the investor sign a nondisclosure agreement whereby the investor agrees not to disclose the business plan or confidential information of the company to others.[15] To further protect the company and track the dissemination of the business plan, each plan should be individually numbered, so the entrepreneur can identify the source of any copies that may be disseminated in violation of the nondisclosure agreement.

Finally, the entrepreneur must realize that the business plan should evolve over time. It should be a living and breathing document, with a life of its own. The business plan will be and should be modified and refined as the entrepreneur works with potential investors, vendors and customers. The business plan should also be further modified as the company develops, as it faces new or increasing competition, and as it discovers new opportunities and product extensions.

---

15. This may be difficult because some venture capitalists do not sign nondisclosure agreements.

Non-Tax Aspects of Forming and Organizing a New Business

Robert L. Brown

Greenebaum Doll & McDonald
Louisville, KY

Alan S. Gutterman

Gutterman Law & Business
Piedmont, CA

Contents

Non-Tax Aspects of Forming and Organizing a New Business

3.01   Preliminary Considerations

This chapter discusses the basic elements of formation and organization of a new corporation, which is the primary form of business entity used by emerging growth companies. It is assumed that the reader has reviewed the first two chapters of this book, which address pre-formation activities and preparation of a preliminary business plan. If desired, the parties can usually incorporate a business on a tax-free basis; however, tax aspects of formation and organization are discussed in the following chapter.

The information included in this chapter is intended to provide readers with a brief overview of the common issues that arise at the time a corporation is formed. There are numerous treatises dealing with various aspects of this process and readers should refer to them for further detail and elaboration.

3.02   Selecting the Form of Business Entity

One of the most significant decisions a business will make is choosing the form of entity it will use. The choice of entity is governed by many considerations, including tax, non-tax, application of relevant state and federal laws, and the objectives and desires of the participants in the business. The form the business takes determines who is responsible for the business's obligations, what property may be contributed to the business, whether the business will continue after the founding individuals leave, how interests are transferred, the taxation of the business, the financial risk of the business and the complexity of the legal affairs of the business.

In this section, the various forms of entity a business may choose from will be described, and a general overview of the non-tax and tax considerations for choosing a particular entity will be discussed. The section will then examine more closely the principal non-tax factors in choosing an entity, including management and control of the business, limited liability, transferability of the business's ownership interests, the ability to raise capital for the business, the necessity for complying with securities laws, administrative costs, continuity of the business and anonymity of the owners of the business. The checklist included as **Exhibit 1A** can be used to assist in determining the appropriate form of entity.

State law governs many of the non-tax considerations in choosing a form of entity, and thus the business owner or legal counsel will need to examine the applicable laws of the state in which the entity is to be formed. Since this section provides a general overview of the business law aspects of selecting a form of entity, it references the Uniform Partnership Act ("UPA") and the Revised Uniform Limited Partnership Act ("RULPA").

A. Choices in Forms of Entity for Emerging Companies

While it is possible to launch an emerging company as a sole proprietorship, it is more likely that the entity will need to accommodate at least two, if not more, owners from the very first day that it is established. Accordingly, this discussion does not include sole proprietorships, nor does it include limited liability partnerships, a common organizational form for professional businesses. While the corporate form remains the most popular choice for prospective emerging companies, limited liability companies and two partnership forms may also be used at the outset depending on the circumstances.

1. General Partnership

The partnership is the basic noncorporate form for two or more owners to operate a business. According to Section 6(1) of the Uniform Partnership Act, which has been adopted in some form in all states except Louisiana, a partnership is "two or more persons associating themselves to carry on business as co-owners for profit." There is no requirement that the partnership have a written partnership agreement. The persons may be individuals, corporations, estates, trusts, limited liability companies or other partnerships.

Traditionally, a partnership is not a separate legal entity from its owners, and the partners are personally liable for the partnership's liabilities. The drawback of partnerships is the unlimited liability of each partner, including liability for acts of other partners acting as agents of the partnership under the principals of agency law. This is the case even if the acts are not authorized by the partnership. The partnership will hold the property of the business, not the partners. Although partnerships generally dissolve when one of the partners leaves the partnership or when a new partner joins the partnership, some states now allow for the continuation of the partnership even after a change in membership.

Persons simply coming together and doing business together can form a partnership without a written agreement. However, a written agreement can provide protection by providing for the division of profits and losses of the business, the ability of a partner to engage in outside activities and the effect on the partnership when a partner withdraws from the partnership. Management of the partnership can be difficult if the partnership has many partners. The partnership agreement is the basic governing document of the partnership, which is essentially a private contract. Since the partnership is primarily governed by the partnership agreement, it is subject to minimal restrictions imposed by law. The partnership is generally less expensive and easier to organize and operate than a corporation.

A general partnership is typically not subject to state and federal income taxes, however it is required to file information returns with the Internal Revenue Service ("IRS"). The partnership's income, deductions and other tax items are calculated at the partnership level and passed through to the partners' tax returns. The primary tax benefits of the partnership form is that partners may deduct the partnership losses on their own income tax returns and the partnership avoids the potential double taxation that can result in a corporation.

Generally partnerships as documented in partnership agreements do not allow for free transferability of partnership interests. This is because partners do not want unknown persons to join the partnership, since the partners remain personally liable for the partnership's liabilities. There may also be negative tax consequences to the incoming partner or the continuing partners as a result of a transfer.

The partnership is an appropriate choice of entity for a business that does not have great exposure to personal liability, or if such liability can be insured against. The partnership can be a good form of business for professionals because they can obtain liability protection through insurance without great difficulty. However, if liability is a significant concern, then a limited liability company may be more advantageous. If the business involves a large number of owners, a partnership is not recommended because of the difficulty in administration and the risk of personal liability to the partners.

2. Limited Partnership

A limited partnership is a partnership with one or more limited partners and one or more general partners. Limited partners are limited in their personal liability for the business's obligations and in their ability to participate in the management of the business. A limited partner is generally an investor whose liability for the partnership's obligations is limited to the limited partner's contributions, recourse debt and/or obligation to make future contributions. To maintain the protections of limited liability, a limited partner is prohibited from participating in the management of the business. General partners have unlimited personal liability for business obligations but have control over the business. A limited partnership must have at least one general partner.

Typically, a limited partnership is formed by filing a certificate with the appropriate state agency. If the applicable statutes recognizing limited partnerships are not complied with, the entity may be treated as a general partnership, which exposes all partners to personal liability.

Limited partnership interests may be considered securities, requiring their issue and sale to be in compliance with state and federal securities laws. In most cases, a general partner's interest will not be considered a security.

A limited partnership is typically not subject to state and federal income taxes, and can avoid the potential double taxation that can result in a corporation. In general, a general partner will have the same tax benefits as a partner of a general partnership, and will be able to deduct the limited partnership's losses on the partner's own tax returns. The limited partners are generally not allowed to use the limited partnership's tax credits and tax losses on their personal income tax returns.

Since the limited partnership offers limited partners limited liability and its income will not be subject to double taxation, the form can be used to attract income-seeking investors who do not intend to participate in the management of the business.

3. Corporation

There are two types of corporations under the federal tax laws. The C corporation is governed by Subchapter C of the Internal Revenue Code of 1986, as amended ("Code"). The S corporation is governed by Subchapter S of the Code, and a corporation must elect S status to be recognized as an S corporation. An S corporation, or "small business" corporation, is restricted as to the number and type of stockholders it may have, but its primary advantage is the flow-through tax treatment that allows S corporations to avoid the double taxation of the C corporation. An S corporation is also limited as to the type of securities it can issue.

a. C Corporation

A corporation is a creature of state law and is a separate legal entity from its owners for both tax and liability purposes. The owners of a corporation are its stockholders and the interests of a corporation are generally represented by stock. The stockholders will generally be personally liable for the corporation's liabilities only to the extent of their respective investments.

To be recognized as a legal entity, a corporation must generally (a) file a written corporate charter or articles of incorporation with the state in which it is incorporating, (b) adopt written bylaws, (c) elect a board of directors and (d) hold an organizational meeting.

A corporation can issue various types of stock that can provide for varying types of control over the corporation and varying risk and return on a stockholder's investment. C corporations provide the most flexibility in allowing for varying control and types of stockholders' equity in corporations. The shares of a corporation are generally freely transferable and the transfers are relatively uncomplicated for tax purposes. The stockholders and the corporation may provide for transfer restrictions in a stockholders' agreement.

Corporations are usually centrally managed. The board of directors of the corporation possesses the power to manage the corporation, but typically the board will establish the fundamental corporate policies and delegate the day-to-day management of the business to the officers. The board of directors appoints the officers, and the board is elected by the stockholders of the corporation. The stockholders do not participate actively in the management as a general rule, but their approval may be required for certain organic corporate acts, such as a merger or liquidation.

If the stockholders approve a liquidation, the corporation must then file articles of dissolution with the state and notify its creditors. The creditors will be paid first out of the corporation's available assets and then any remaining assets will be distributed among the stockholders. The corporation can sell its assets and distribute the cash, distribute the assets directly or combine the methods. In any case, the receipt of cash or assets will result in a taxable event for the stockholders.

The corporation, rather than the stockholders, recognizes the income, deductions, losses and credits of the business. Distributions to stockholders are taxed as dividends. Thus, the corporation's income is potentially subject to double taxation when it issues distributions to its stockholders as dividends or upon liquidation. The corporation will be taxed on any gain of a distribution or upon the sale of the corporation's assets and the stockholders will then be taxed on any gain from receiving property or cash in exchange for their stock.

The limitation on personal liability for the owners of a corporation makes the form useful if business will be conducted in multiple jurisdictions or if more than one type of business will be conducted. The corporation may also be considered if the ownership interests will be transferred frequently and if the business is expected to continue beyond the initial principals. Stock options and shares are good tools for providing incentives to employees of a business. A corporation also enables the business to raise large amounts of capital through the sale of interests, and is the most desirable form if a business anticipates "going public." However, the formalities, administration and legal requirements to be followed, in addition to the potential double taxation, may outweigh the benefits of incorporation.

b.   S Corporation

If a corporation makes an S election with the IRS it can become a pass-through entity for federal tax purposes and avoid the double taxation that can occur as a C corporation.

S corporations differ from C corporations only with respect to tax treatment. To be eligible for an S election, a corporation must have 100 or fewer stockholders. The type of stockholder an S corporation can have is limited to individuals and certain qualifying trusts, estates and tax-exempt organizations. The corporation may not have nonresident aliens as stockholders. Additionally, the S corporation may have only one type of stock, but the stock may have different voting rights.

A corporation may want to make an S election if it anticipates losses during the early years of operation that the owners can use on their personal income tax returns.

4.   *Limited Liability Company*

If neither the form of partnership nor a corporation seems to meet an entrepreneur's needs, a limited liability company may be a good compromising choice of entity. A limited liability company ("LLC") is a hybrid entity that combines the qualities of a partnership with a corporation. LLCs are, like corporations, creatures of state law. An LLC may be comprised of one or more persons, depending on the state. Members of an LLC may be individuals, partnerships, limited partnerships, trusts, estates, associations, corporations, other limited liability companies or other entities. LLCs typically combine the corporate characteristic of limited liability with the general flexibility and pass through tax treatment of a partnership. LLCs can elect to be taxed on the federal level as a corporation or a partnership, and in general opt for partnership tax treatment.

An LLC is formed by filing articles of organization with the state. The owners of the LLC are members, and the business of the LLC may be run by its members, or by some other person who need not be a member of the LLC. Some states require that LLCs have more than one member, but most states allow single-member LLCs. If an LLC has at least two members it can elect to be treated as either a partnership or corporation under the federal tax laws. A single-member LLC will be taxed as either a corporation or an entity disregarded from its owner. Thus, to avail itself of partnership tax treatment an LLC must have at least two members.

LLCs offer great flexibility in the business's management. Most states have adopted laws that allow the members of LLCs the ability to determine the organization's management structure, such as how management will be organized, rights of members, allocations and distributions of profits and losses and transferability of membership interests.

The management structure and other rights and obligations of the LLC members are set forth in an operating agreement, which typically contains the same provisions found in partnership and shareholders agreements. The operating agreement is the basic governing document of the LLC. The agreement is a contract among the members of the LLC that provides for the operation and organization of the LLC. The agreement usually contains the details on how distributions, profits and losses will be divided among the members and capital account allocations for tax gain and loss. To ensure that an LLC does not inadvertently lose partnership tax status, the operating agreement and the state law may provide default provisions on this matter.

Membership interests in an LLC may be classified as securities and as such will be subject to federal and state securities laws. A membership will likely not be considered a security if all of the members of the LLC actively participate in the management of the LLC. Some states require that the members approve a transfer of an interest to a nonmember, and if such a transfer is not approved that the nonmember who has been assigned the LLC interest can only receive the share of profits from the interest but cannot participate in the LLC management. The members may provide for any restrictions on transfer in the operating agreement.

Some states prohibit LLCs from engaging in certain business purposes, for example, the practice of a profession.

The LLC is not subject to tax at the entity level; however, because the LLC is a relatively new form of entity, there is a lack of case law and precedent surrounding it. The LLC may be less desirable because of less certainty of the legal and tax ramifications of LLC transactions. Also, the interests may not be freely transferable.

B. Principal Non-Tax Considerations in Selecting the Form of Business Entity

1. Management and Control of the Business

Business entities may be governed in different ways. The entrepreneur needs to consider as part of choosing an entity what type of entity will provide the most flexibility and ease of operation. The level of formality that must be observed within the entity in order to maintain the entity is an important factor. Corporations tend to have the most stringent requirements for corporate governance. Meetings, minutes, resolutions and notices are required on a regular basis for the entity to maintain its status as a corporation. For some entrepreneurs, the day-to-day governance requirements of a corporation are too intensive. Other entities such as limited liability companies and partnerships offer much greater flexibility as far as corporate governance. Generally, LLCs and partnerships are not statutorily required to hold formal meetings, nor are they required to document actions with minutes, resolutions and notices.

For many entrepreneurs, the relative administrative ease of a limited liability company or partnership is very attractive.

a. Corporation

Management and ownership are usually separated in a corporation. Stockholders of a corporation (the owners) elect a board of directors, and the board in turn appoints the officers of the corporation. The business and affairs of the corporation are managed by or under the direction of the board. The board may delegate its power to committees of the board and to others, but the directors have the ultimate power to determine how the corporation is run. Typically the board will delegate the day-to-day management of the corporation's affairs to the officers, but retain the power to decide corporate policy and authorize corporate actions outside the ordinary course of business, such as raising capital, borrowing money, and acquiring or disposing of substantial assets. Stockholders, except in the case of a statutory close corporation as provided for in certain states, do not possess the power to manage the corporation's day-to-day affairs by virtue of holding a corporation's shares.

A correlation between ownership and management of a corporation can be established by creating voting and nonvoting classes of stock, voting trusts, committees of the board, management agreements and stockholders agreements and by requiring more than a majority vote for certain actions in the certificate of incorporation.

If a corporation has a large number of stockholders who are passive investors, the management of the corporation is likely to be centralized. If there are only a few stockholders who are also the directors and officers of the corporation, the corporation will be managed more like a partnership.

b. General Partnership

In general, all partners in a general partnership have the equal right to manage the partnership. The partners may agree by contract to a different management structure. The partners may decide that a partner's control over management depends on the partner's partnership interest, or to elect a management committee or managing partner to be responsible for the day-to-day business decisions of the partnership. The partners may also limit the ability of certain partners to take certain actions. The partnership laws of most states provide that the acts of any one partner may bind the partnership as an entity, so the partners could agree that the acts of a particular partner do not have authority to bind the partnership. However, the partnership may still be bound by the acts of such a partner if the third party was not aware that the partner did not have authority to bind the partnership.

c. Limited Partnership

Limited partnerships are managed by one or more general partners. Limited partners cannot participate in the management of the limited partnership, and if they do, they may lose the protection of limited liability.

A limited partnership typically has a more centralized management and control than general partnerships or corporations. The partnership agreement can provide that the limited partners have no power to remove the general partner. Unlike officers or directors of a corporation, who are subject to appointment by the directors and election by the stockholders, respectively, the general partner can be more independent and autonomous. In a general partnership, the partners are required to work with the other partners, but a general partner or partners will make all of the limited partnership's business decisions.

d. Limited Liability Company

In general, LLCs can be member managed or manager managed and provide great management flexibility. The management of an LLC can be similar to a corporation, or more similar to a partnership, depending on the contractual arrangement among the members. The governing provisions of an LLC are usually set forth in a written operating agreement.

If the LLC is member managed, the members will manage the business and affairs of the LLC. Like a partnership, each member will have the power to bind the LLC.

If the LLC is managed by managers, members do not participate in the management of the LLC and do not have the authority to bind the LLC. The acts of the managers in carrying out the business and affairs of the LLC are binding on the LLC. If allowed by the LLC laws of the state in which the LLC is formed, the operating agreement may provide that members do not have the ability to remove managers.

The charter documents of the LLC can limit a manager or member's authority to bind the LLC. The members or managers of the LLC can appoint officers, whose roles are prescribed by the members or managers. The operating agreement can specify the voting powers of the members and managers. Members may be entitled to a vote in accordance with their percentage membership interest in the LLC, and may have the right to vote on certain matters, even if the LLC is managed by managers.

If the LLC is managed by its members, the management can be similar to a partnership in which all owners have power to manage the entity. An LLC can emulate the centralized management style of a corporation with managers who act as a board of directors and appointed officers. The LLC may also be set up in the mode of a limited partnership, with a manager who makes all the management decisions and who cannot be removed by the members.

2. *Liability of Owners for Business Obligations*

A significant factor for most entrepreneurs who are deciding to start a business is personal exposure to the liabilities of the business. Will the liability flow to the individual owners of interests or to the board of directors and officers or similar authority of the entity? Or will the assets of the entity itself be the sole recourse for liability? A similar concern of the owners of interests and the entity's management is how the obligations or liabilities of the entity will be handled within the entity itself.

The significance of liability is a factor that is easily understood from the perspective of the entrepreneur who is a founder of the entity. Typically, founders will want to make sure that they cannot be liable to a creditor or a shareholder (or similar ownership interest) for any acts or omissions committed in the course of doing business. Similarly, investors assess the level of protection against liability when deciding whether or not to make an investment in the business. They want to know that as an owner of an interest in the entity, they are also protected from creditors or other interest holders. Basically, all owners of interest and participants in the business are concerned with the level of protection against liability for the entity and how such protection may apply to them individually.

With these concerns in mind, the most protective types of business entities are either a limited liability company or a corporation. Both of these entities generally restrict the liabilities and obligations of the entity to the actual entity and do not flow to the members or shareholders as long as the entities are properly formed and maintained. The entity that offers the least protection to the owners of interests in the entity is the general partnership. All partners in a general partnership are generally liable for the obligations of the partnership.

Although corporations are generally recognized as providing the greatest protection against liability for business debts and obligations, it does not protect against all potential sources of personal liability. On the other hand, owners of an unincorporated business may be able to adequately protect themselves against personal liability by obtaining liability insurance.

a. Corporation

The officers, directors and stockholders of a corporation are generally not liable for the debts and other obligations of the corporation. The liability of the owners of the corporation is limited to the extent of the stockholders' investments. The corporation is a separate legal entity and is liable for its own debts and obligations. Even if the corporation declares bankruptcy, the stockholders' personal assets will be protected from judgment and their personal credit ratings are generally not impaired. Individuals may be personally liable if they have personally guaranteed corporate debts or to the extent stockholders have received improper distributions. If the corporation does not observe corporate formalities, a court may treat the stockholders as if the corporation does not exist and "pierce the corporate veil" to impose personal liability on the stockholders of a corporation. A director, officer or stockholder who breaches a duty to other stockholders or the corporation may also be found personally liable.

A business may consider insurance to guard against liability incurred from doing business. However, some businesses involve substantial risk of tort liability or other catastrophe that may expose the owner of the business to personal liability. For these businesses, incorporation is a way of minimizing the risk of personal exposure to liability that arises from doing business. For owners to avail themselves of the protection of limited liability granted by incorporation, corporate formalities should be observed.

b. General Partnership

Partners of a general partnership are jointly and severally liable for the debts and obligations of the partnership, and each partner's personal liability is unlimited. Generally each partner is jointly and severally liable for the actions taken by the partner's copartners that are taken in furtherance of the partnership's business. Liability may be imposed if the partnership authorized the act either impliedly or apparently. Partners can be liable for torts, contracts and criminal acts of their copartners that are deemed to be in furtherance of the partnership's business. In this respect a partnership poses a greater risk of personal liability for the owners than a sole proprietorship—liability for the actions of one (self) versus many (partners).

The partners may provide for indemnification in the partnership agreement to address the risk of personal liability. Usually, a partner that is admitted into the partnership is not liable for the debts of the partnership prior to joining the partnership. A judgment against the partnership is not a judgment against a partner, unless the judgment is also against the partner. Thus, a judgment that is not against a partner cannot be satisfied from the partner's assets.

If limited liability is an important consideration to the owners of the business, then the partnership is probably not the appropriate form for the business. A partner is exposed to personal liability at all times, even if the partner has not acted individually. The personal liability of partners can be mitigated by obtaining insurance, limiting the grants of agency, monitoring the acts of the partners, and providing for indemnification for certain acts. Generally, the more partners there are in a partnership the greater the potential liability that can be caused by the acts of others. If the partnership can be organized as a limited liability partnership under the laws of the state in which it is being organized, a partner's liability for the acts of others can be limited.

c. Limited Partnership

The general partner of a limited partnership has the same liability for the limited partnership's debts and obligations as a partner of a general partnership. Limited partners are usually not liable for the debts of the limited partnership. Like stockholders of a corporation, the liability of limited partners is typically limited to the amount of the limited partners' contributions to the limited partnership and any distributions received from the partnership at the time when the partnership's assets were not adequate to satisfy the partnership's liabilities.

Section 303 of RULPA provides that a limited partner is not personally liable for a limited partnership's obligations unless the limited partner is also a general partner, or, in addition to the exercise of rights and powers as a limited partner, the limited partner takes part in the control of the business. In general, a limited partner will be found to have participated in the management of the business if the partner was really acting as a general partner in a matter and if unknowing third parties were misled by the behavior. Granting the limited partners broad voting rights so they can participate in decisions affecting the limited partnership may be deemed to be active participation in the business. Limited partners may be liable for debts of the limited partnership if they have guaranteed a partnership debt as partners.

d. Limited Liability Company

In general, the members of an LLC are not personally liable for the debts and obligations of the LLC. However, the same exceptions that apply to the limited liability of stockholders of a corporation apply to the members of an LLC. A member may be liable if the member agrees to be liable or personally guarantees a debt of the LLC, if the member commits a tortious act against a third party, if the LLC is an alter ego of the member, or if the member has received distributions from the LLC unlawfully. The determination of whether the corporate veil should be pierced is analogous to the analysis for a corporation. The court will look to the LLC's adherence to corporate formalities, such as holding meetings of managers and members, as required by the operating agreement of the LLC. Unlike a limited partner, a member of an LLC can participate in the management of the business without losing the protection of limited liability.

3. *Transferability of Interests and Liquidity for Business Owners*

The ability to transfer interests of a business entity is not generally a significant factor in determining the appropriate choice of entity for a business. For most forms of business entity that are closely held, there is no real market for the ownership interests in the business, even if the interests were transferable. The only truly transferable interests that may be freely traded are shares of registered stock of a publicly traded corporation. A business with fewer owners will consider this factor less important, while a business with more owners will be more interested in the ability to transfer interests of a business.

a. Corporation

A corporation's shares of stock are the most transferable interests among the various types of business entities. Each owner's interest in the corporation is represented by corporate stock. The transfer of stock of a corporation is limited by any applicable state and federal securities laws, but in general there are no other statutory limitations on the transfer of stock. Absent a separate arrangement, shares of a corporation may be transferred without obtaining the consent of the other stockholders. The stockholders may separately contract to restrict the transfer of shares, or the corporation's charter may require stockholder approval prior to a stock transfer. The transfer of stock does not alter the status of the entity.

b. General Partnership

A partner's ability to transfer a partnership interest is generally limited, and unless otherwise provided for in the partnership agreement, will require the unanimous consent of the partners (see Section 27 of the UPA). However, the partnership agreement may contain provisions restricting the transfer of partnership interests, since partners will not want unknown parties to become partners. Some states provide that the recipient of a transferred partnership interest receives only the economic rights that accompany the interest, but will not possess the right to vote as a member of the partnership or participate in the management of the partnership's business, or the right to inspect the partnership's books and records. The transferee would have the right to share in distributions, as well as profit and loss allocations of the partnership.

The transfer of a partnership interest can also have adverse tax consequences for the remaining partners or the incoming partner. The partnership may be required to "step up" the basis of the partnership's assets, and this will involve an administrative burden. Thus, a partnership may not be the appropriate form of entity for the business if many transfers of interests are anticipated.

c. Limited Partnership

As in the case of a partner in a general partnership, a limited partner may transfer his or her economic interest in the limited partnership, but generally cannot automatically transfer the right to vote. The limited partnership agreement may allow for the admission of the transferee as a substitute limited partner if the other partners consent.

A general partner may transfer only the economic interest of his or her limited partnership interest, subject to any transfer restrictions in the limited partnership agreement. The limited partners may be required to approve the addition or substitution of a new general partner.

d. Limited Liability Company

In general, a member can only transfer the economic interest of his or her LLC interest, unless the LLC operating agreement provides for the admission of the transferee who received the economic interest as a new or substitute member. Thus, as is the case with partnerships, a transferee of an LLC interest will only be entitled to receive distributions and profit and loss allocations, but will not automatically receive the transferor's voting and management rights.

4. *Ability to Raise Capital*

As most business entities will need to obtain financing from outside sources in order to sustain or grow the business, entrepreneurs need to consider the types of legal entities that would most easily permit investments by third parties. Generally, the C corporation is the best vehicle if the business anticipates a need for future financing. The C corporation has been the preferred entity for investment by venture funds due to the fact that the funds are not usually permitted to invest in flow-through entities that are engaged in trade or business. Based on this fact, an entrepreneur may also consider a limited liability company that may be taxed as a corporation, since presumably a venture fund would be able to invest in that type of entity. However, over time, venture funds and other investors have grown accustomed to investing in C corporations and tend to be most familiar with C corporations.

a. Corporation

A corporation is capitalized through debt and equity. The debt may include loans from stockholders and third parties, and may be secured, unsecured, convertible or nonconvertible. Equity capital is raised from the sale of the corporation's stock. Investors in a corporation may contribute a combination of equity and debt, in the form of convertible or hybrid securities, including promissory notes, common or preferred shares, warrants, stock options and preemptive rights.

The corporation is a preferable vehicle for raising capital for several reasons. First, the form of entity is generally well understood by investors, and the consequences of investing in a corporation are generally better understood than the consequences of investing in a partnership or LLC. Second, a corporation's limited liability is attractive to investors. Investors may prefer investing in a corporation because its shares, especially if the corporation goes public and its shares are traded on an established securities market, are transferable. Investors who want to be active in the management of a corporation can do so without personal liability in a corporation.

b.   General Partnership

A general partnership is also capitalized through debt and equity. The debt may come from loans from partners or third parties, and may be secured or unsecured. The equity generally comes from the capital contributions of the partners. The ability of a partnership to obtain a loan usually depends on the creditworthiness of the individual partners and the value of the partnership assets that can be pledged as collateral for the loan.

Investors do not find general partnerships attractive vehicles for passive investment since there is a risk of personal liability for the partnership debts and because the partnership interests are not freely transferable.

c.   Limited Partnership

A limited partnership is capitalized from the same sources as a general partnership, but the limited partners typically contribute capital in addition to the general partner.

Certain passive investors will find limited partnership interests attractive because the investment affords them limited personal liability for the debts and obligations of the limited partnership. Also, the pass-through tax treatment of the limited partnership can be advantageous to investors. Limited partnerships may be used in connection with real estate ventures and tax-advantaged investments. As a result of the limited partnership interests' attributes, they can be a significant source of equity capital for limited partnerships. Investors interested in participating in the business, such as venture capitalists, however, would not tend to invest in limited partnerships, since participation in management may cause a limited partner to become a general partner, and thus expose the investor to unlimited liability.

d.   Limited Liability Company

An LLC is capitalized through debt and equity. The LLC may borrow from its members or third-party lenders, and the loans may be secured or unsecured. The LLC may raise capital through capital contributions from its members.

LLCs tend to be an attractive investment vehicle for venture capitalists for a variety of reasons. First, the LLC's structure and organization are extremely flexible. Due to the limited liability protection that LLCs offer, venture capitalists can participate in the management of the business without fear of liability. The pass-through tax benefits of investment in an LLC are also attractive to venture capitalists and passive investors as well. The investor can make special allocations and deduct losses.

5.   *Administrative Requirements and Costs*

Generally, corporations require more administrative costs. A corporation usually requires filing documents with the state and IRS, and the entity will file tax returns. The requirements can make the financial affairs of the business owner or owners more complicated, but the complexities may be worthwhile. A more administratively complex form of business may provide the owners with greater protection from personal liability and tax savings. If the business's governing rules are clearly documented in writing, the business may avoid litigation when disputes arise.

a.   Corporation

The corporation laws of a state generally require that a number of formalities be observed, but in the end the form may be simpler and less expensive to form because the perimeters are set by statute. Since the statutory provisions of state corporate law prescribe the general structure and operating of the corporation, the need for a detailed agreement governing these matters is reduced. Formal documents must be generated and filed on a regular basis. If the parties forming the corporation want to provide for transfer restrictions on the issued stock of the corporation, or the voting of the outstanding shares, or provide for different classes of stock, then a separate agreement or particularized charter documents will be drafted.

The initial administrative requirements for a corporation include articles of incorporation that must be filed with the state in which the corporation is being formed. An incorporator signs the articles, and is not required to be an officer, director or stockholder of the corporation. Once formed, the corporation's directors and stockholders will adopt bylaws that govern the corporation's internal affairs.

In a corporation, the ownership interests of the entity and control over the management of the business are separated. The stockholders elect the board to manage the entity, and do not directly control the operation of the business themselves. The board of directors conducts the business affairs of the corporation. State law may dictate the number of directors and restrictions on whom may be a director. The directors are typically elected each year by the stockholders of the corporation. Since the corporation's business is conducted by the board, it must meet at least annually and should document actions taken at such a meeting in writing. Shares of the corporation's stock should be issued to the stockholders. The initial actions taken by the incorporator, directors and stockholders should be memorialized in organizational minutes.

Stockholders' meetings will also be required from time to time, and the actions taken will also need to be memorialized in writing. Stockholders generally have the right to approve any amendment of the articles of incorporation, or a corporate merger, sale or share exchange.

The corporation is a legal entity separate from its owners and is subject to federal income taxation. The corporation must file an annual income tax return with the IRS. An S corporation will file a federal income tax return, but since taxation occurs at the owner level rather than the entity level, the S corporation will not be subject to federal income taxation.

The corporation requires more administrative paperwork on a regular basis than other forms of entity, but the form offers its owners limited liability and the ability to raise capital from the public. The paper trail can also be helpful in resolving disputes that arise. Additional administrative complexity can arise from the choice by the stockholders to create diverse types of equity holdings, incentive compensation plans and buyout agreements, which are permitted in the corporate form.

b.   General Partnership

A general partnership is easier to form than a limited partnership, a corporation or LLC because there is no requirement that a document be filed with the state. The partners should enter into an agreement, preferably written, describing the terms and conditions of their business association, since the statutory provisions for partnerships are not comprehensive. The complexity and cost of the agreement will be dictated by the structure of the partnership and the nature of its business. The more parties involved and the alliance of their interests will determine how much time will be spent drafting and negotiating the agreement. Attorneys' fees then can vary significantly.

A partnership is required by Section 19 of the Uniform Partnership Act to keep books reflecting partnership receipts and disbursements, and each partner is entitled to access to the books. Each partner is also required to render an account of partnership affairs to any partner. Thus, partners, like stockholders in a corporation, are granted certain rights to ensure that the business is run in a fair and equitable manner.

The partnership must file annual information returns with the IRS, though it is not generally taxable.

c.   Limited Partnership

A limited partnership is formed by filing with the state of formation a prescribed form executed by all the general partners. The state will usually allow the certificate to be amended and will require amendment on the admission or withdrawal of a partner.

The partners, both general and limited, can enter into a limited partnership agreement either before or after the certificate is filed. A written agreement is preferred, and the agreement should address all material issues among the partners. The complexity and cost of the agreement will depend upon the structure and business of the partnership. The Revised Uniform Limited Partnership Act provides that limited partners are entitled to certain information from the partnership, and thus the general partner will be required to maintain books and records for the limited partnership.

The limited partnership has the same federal tax filing obligations as a general partnership.

d.   Limited Liability Company

The state LLC statute will dictate the procedure to be followed for forming an LLC. An LLC is formed by filing articles of organization with the state. The LLC's articles of organization are similar to a corporation's articles of incorporation. The articles can be signed by an organizer who is not required to be a manager or member of the LLC, and should be accompanied by a filing fee.

The members of the LLC should enter into an operating agreement either before or after the certificate is filed with the state. The operating agreement should be in writing, and like a partnership agreement, the cost and complexity of the agreement will relate to the business and structure of the LLC. The operating agreement should address how the day-to-day operations of the LLC will be run and a statement of the LLC's purpose.

Like a partnership, the LLC files an annual information return with the IRS.

6.   *Continuity of Business*

A client deciding what form of entity to choose for a business should consider the effect of the loss of one of the principals of a business. A principal of a business may cease being part of the business as a result of death, withdrawal, expulsion, disability or bankruptcy. If a particular individual is critical to the business, it may be impossible for the business to continue in that individual's absence. On the other hand, a particular participant may not be necessary for the enterprise, and it may be very desirable to continue the business even when that participant leaves.

In planning what form a business should take, the advisor should consider that some types of entities dissolve upon the loss of one of the principals, and whether the longevity of a business should be connected to a particular individual.

Although the client may decide to initially form as one type of entity, the entity is not prevented from changing or converting to another form of entity at some time in the future. The change can often be done easily depending on the timing and nature of the change. However, the client should be aware that such a reorganization may be a taxable event and as a result should be carefully considered. A change of entity may be necessary for tax reasons or ownership of assets and financings. The entrepreneur should carefully review the alternatives and chose the type of entity that overall suits the objectives of the business.

a. Corporation

A corporation has an independent existence and the withdrawal, death or other loss of a director, officer or stockholder will not cause the corporation to terminate. Unless its certificate of incorporation states otherwise, the corporation will continue to exist indefinitely. The existence of a corporation can be terminated by the act of its stockholders or by judicial decree.

The legal entity of the corporation will continue regardless of the departure of any particular individual, but the business may be highly dependent on a particular person. Though the entity exists, the business of the corporation may be affected.

A stockholder wishing to leave a corporation may not be able to find a market for the shares held by the stockholder, and may not be able to liquidate his or her interest in the corporation. A stockholder may prefer that a corporation liquidate and dissolve when the stockholder wants to leave the corporation so that he or she can liquidate their interest in the corporation.

b. General Partnership

Pursuant to Section 31 of the UPA, a partnership technically dissolves on the occurrence of certain events, including the death or withdrawal of a partner. The remaining partners can continue the business, but the partnership is technically a new one (see Section 41 of the UPA.) The partnership is dissolved by the vote of the partners required by statute or as provided in the partnership agreement.

c. Limited Partnership

The limited partnership is essentially identical to the general partnership in legal form, and will "dissolve" on the death or withdrawal of a general partner. However, the limited partnership agreement may provide that the remaining general partners can elect to continue the enterprise, or the other partners may vote to continue the partnership's business and elect a successor general partner.

The death or incompetence of a limited partner or the transfer of a limited partnership interest will not cause the dissolution of a limited partnership. If the limited partner is an entity such as a corporation, LLC or trust, the dissolution or termination of the entity will not cause the limited partnership to dissolve.

A limited partner typically cannot withdraw from the limited partnership unless the limited partnership agreement specified the time or events for the withdrawal.

d.   Limited Liability Company

An LLC will be dissolved at the date set forth in the articles of organization or operating agreement, if a date or event of dissolution has been established. Most state statutes that govern LLCs provide that the members of the LLC can vote to continue the LLC after a dissolution event has occurred.

The members of the LLC may choose to dissolve the LLC. The LLC statute or LLC's articles of organization or operating agreement may set forth the required approval of the members necessary to dissolve the LLC.

7. Tax Considerations

Tax considerations play a significant role in respect to the choice of business entity. Often the owners of interests in the entity want to know if they will be subject to tax. Additionally, the owners of interests are typically concerned with tax imposed on the entity itself. Taxes imposed on the entity and its owners decrease their profits. Generally, the preferred tax structure for a business entity is to have one level of taxation. Partnerships, limited liability companies and Subchapter S corporations have "flow through" taxation that permits one level of taxation on the partners, members or shareholders, as the case may be, but does not tax the entity itself.

However, most corporations cannot qualify for the Subchapter S election as either they do not meet the requirements or the corporation is seeking financing from investors that are not permitted to invest in Subchapter S corporations. Therefore, C corporations are often formed when financing is a concern, but are taxed at the entity level as well as the shareholder level. For more information on taxes and business entities, please see Chapter 4 (Tax Aspects of Forming and Organizing a New Business).

A chart summarizing the features of partnerships, LLCs, and S and C corporations from the standpoint of California law appears in **Exhibit 3A**.

3.03   Formation and Organization

Once the decision has been made to incorporate an existing or proposed business, a number of steps must be completed. The principals will need to gather a good deal of information and will need to make some fundamental decisions regarding the legal organization of the corporation, including the relative voting rights among shareholders, selection of directors and officers, and the form and scope of any restrictions on transfers of shares. Expert advice from counsel and outside accountants will also be required to ensure that all of the formalities associated with formation of the corporation are completed, business licenses and permits are obtained, and capital contributions are made in a way that suits the tax requirements of the principals.

A.   Preliminary Considerations

As discussed in previous chapters, the process of launching a new business begins well before the corporation is formed. The principals and their advisors should carefully collect all the information regarding the proposed business, prepare a business plan, and review the various forms of business entity and select the appropriate one for the specific situation. In addition, the principals should treat the formation process seriously, just as they might treat the development of a new product. This means setting a target date for completion of the formation process, making sure to anticipate delays in obtaining information, signatures and approvals. If it appears that a significant period of time may elapse before the corporation can be formed, the parties may want to memorialize their understanding regarding the ownership and operation of the business in some form of preincorporation agreement.

B.   State of Incorporation

While selection of the corporation as the form of entity for the new business is certainly a key decision, further consideration must be given to the state in which the new corporation is to be formed and organized. While the laws of each state with respect to operation of corporations are similar in many respects, owing to the guidance of model corporation laws followed by drafters in the various states, there are some important differences. As such, the principals and their legal advisor should check the law of the state where the company will be headquartered against the statutes of neighboring states and major incorporating states (e.g., California, Delaware, Nevada).

Please see Chapter 1 (Starting a New Business) for a more complete discussion of this issue.

C.   Articles of Incorporation and Organization

It is well known that the articles of incorporation are the principal record of the rights, preferences, and privileges of the shareholders. The form and content of the articles of incorporation, sometimes referred to as the certificate of incorporation, will be dictated by the law of the state of incorporation; however, the following issues will usually be addressed:

- Name
- Duration of corporate existence
- Corporate purposes and powers
- Number of authorized shares, including common and preferred shares
- Par value, if any, of the authorized shares
- Specific rights, preferences and privileges of each class or series of shares, including dividend rights, liquidation preferences, preemptive rights (if any) and voting rights
- Election of directors
- Shareholders' meetings and actions
- Indemnification rights and limitations on liability

An example of a Delaware certificate of incorporation appears as **Exhibit 3B**.

It is likely that the articles of incorporation will be substantially amended at the time the corporation receives its initial round of outside financing. At that time, the investors will generally insist on preferred stock with various preferences and special voting rights.

LLCs are organized by the filing of articles of organization, which if the LLC will operate in a corporate form will contain many of the above provisions. Otherwise, the articles will only list the organizer and contain a mailing or location address.

This process is described in greater detail in Chapter 7 (Financing a Business).

D. Bylaws

The bylaws of the corporation are the rules and procedures that govern the conduct of its affairs and the rights and powers of its directors, officers and stockholders. Provisions that merit attention include the following:

Annual Meeting of Shareholders: The date for the annual meeting of shareholders should be fixed long enough after the end of the fiscal year so the corporation will have sufficient time to prepare any year-end financial information for distribution to stockholders. A shareholder vote by means of proxy or conference telephone or other communications equipment constitutes presence at a meeting, provided such participation is permitted in the bylaws. The bylaws should also cover notice, quorum and voting requirements.

Special Meetings of Shareholders: Special shareholders' meetings may be called by the board of directors, certain officers of the corporation, or a specified percentage-in-interest of the shareholders. The bylaws should include the procedure for calling such a meeting, as well as any notice requirements. Voting and quorum requirements for special meetings are usually identical to annual shareholders' meetings.

Meetings and Actions of Directors: Generally, most boards prefer notice requirements for meetings that provide the maximum flexibility permitted by state law. This may be accomplished by allowing meetings to be called on relatively short notice and by permitting notices to be given by telex, copier or even telephone. Like shareholder meetings, director meetings may be held by proxy or telephone conference or other communications equipment as provided in the bylaws.

Officers: The bylaws generally describe the principal duties and responsibilities of the principal officers of the corporation. Often, standard form bylaws will designate the president as both the chief executive officer ("CEO") and chief operating officer ("COO"). The offices of CEO and COO are generally not statutory designations and care should be taken to make sure that the bylaws accurately specify the different functions of the president and the chairman of the board of directors, especially if it is expected that they will be different individuals.

Indemnification: Most state corporate statutes enable corporations to indemnify their officers, directors and other persons against certain liabilities arising out of the performance of their duties. Bylaws are generally drafted to allow for the broadest indemnification permitted by the applicable state statute. However, directors may desire as a matter of corporate policy to limit the indemnification provisions, particularly if such provisions provide for mandatory, rather than permissive indemnification. For example, directors may desire to extend mandatory indemnification to officers, directors and plan fiduciaries, but only permissive indemnification to other employees and agents of the corporation.

Other issues that are generally covered in the bylaws include the following:

- Location of office
- Share certificates, transfer agent, and stock register
- Authority to execute contracts and checks
- Corporate seal
- Amendments

An example of Delaware bylaws appears in **Exhibit 3C**.

E.   Filing of Articles of Incorporation

As discussed above, corporations and LLCs are creatures of statute and do not come into existence until the articles of incorporation or organization have been properly filed with the secretary of state in the state of establishment. Counsel should be sure that all requirements are satisfied, including the payment of any fees or franchise taxes. A copy of the filed articles, certified by the office of the secretary of state, should be placed in the corporation's minute book.

F.   First Meeting of Directors

In some states, the first meeting of directors follows a meeting of the incorporators, the subscribers or the first stockholders, to elect directors. In other states, the first directors are named in the articles, and no elections are needed unless the first directors were accommodation directors or "dummies," who must resign or be replaced.

Consider including some or all of the following in the agenda for the first meeting:

- Selection of chairman and secretary
- Filing of notice of meeting or waiver of notice in minutes
- Receipt of report of filing of articles of incorporation and placement into the record of the meeting
- Adoption of bylaws
- Opening of stock subscription books
- Receipt of report of subscriptions to capital stock and placement into the record of the meeting
- Authorization of issuance of stock and fixing the terms and conditions for the issuance of preferred stock
- Election and swearing in of officers
- Adoption of corporate seal
- Authorization of form of stock certificate and establishment of corporate record books
- Designation of principal office
- Appointment of resident agent
- Authorization of filing and recording of required reports
- Authorization of officers to open bank account and pay organization expenses

G.   Miscellaneous

Aside from the issues and events described above, the formation and organization process may also include one or more of the following tasks and activities:

- Filing of designation of service of process
- Acquisition of corporate outfit (e.g., seal, stock register, and minute book)
- Payment of expenses of organization
- Acquisition of necessary insurance of corporate property and employees

- Evaluation of employee benefit plans (accident and health, medical reimbursement, and wage continuation)
- Formalization of agreements covering transactions between corporation and insiders (e.g., lease arrangements or employment agreements)
- Establishment of a legal compliance program, particularly for the protection of the corporation's intellectual property rights
- Documentation of any transfer of physical or intangible assets to the corporation
- Acquisition of all required business licenses and permits
- Creation of calendar of important dates, including filings of tax returns, board of directors and shareholders' meetings

3.04   Owners' Agreement

Regardless of the entity chosen, there will usually be an agreement among the owners reflecting their rights and obligations. In the limited and general partnership, it is a partnership agreement. In an LLC, it is an operating agreement. In an S or C corporation, it is a shareholders' agreement. In any case, the process of preparing an effective owners agreement begins with the collection of information about the entity and the owners who are to be a party to the agreement. The scope of information depends on the primary purpose of the agreement. For example, a comprehensive form of agreement may cover future share issuances, management, employment of the owners, and buy-sell arrangements. In any case, the preparer should also review the charter documents of the entity (i.e., articles and bylaws) and any separate form of employment or buy-sell agreement to make sure that there are no inconsistent or conflicting terms that might lead to disputes at a later date. Since the primary form of doing business for emerging companies is the S or C corporation, in this section we focus on shareholder agreements for corporations. However, examples of the most frequent agreements, limited partnership agreements and manager-managed LLC operating agreements, are attached as **Exhibit 3D** and **Exhibit 3E**, respectively.

A.   Background

Careful drafting of a shareholders agreement, such as **Exhibit 3F**, begins with proper identification of the names and addresses of each of the shareholders that are to be a party to the agreement. While there is a tendency not to include holders of small amounts of shares as parties to the agreement, it is important not to omit groups of shareholders that collectively could impact the balance of power otherwise created by the agreement. In most cases, holders of at least 1% of the outstanding shares of the corporation will be required to join the agreement.

Counsel should also review the proposed scope of the agreement with the shareholders. While it is possible to limit the agreement to voting on specified issues, such as election of directors or major capital expenditures, an extensive agreement may touch on future issuances of securities, the terms of any employment relationship between the corporation and any of its shareholders, and buy-sell procedures.

Ironically, another preliminary issue is the term of the agreement itself. Counsel and the parties must carefully consider the projected growth of the corporation and events that might render the covenants and promises included in the original agreement moot or inappropriate. In many cases, the parties decide to have the agreement remain in effect for a fixed term unless sooner terminated by a vote of all or a specified percentage-in-interest of the parties. The agreement may also terminate automatically on the occurrence of certain events, such as the closing of a private placement financing of a specified size (e.g., $10 million) or the initial public offering of the common stock of the corporation.

Finally, while counsel should make an effort to cover all of the material issues that might arise in connection with the subject matter of the agreement, provision for amendment or modification of the contract should be included. It should come as no surprise that a key issue is the level of consent that would be required to amend or modify the agreement. Requiring consent of all shareholders may lead to deadlock. The better provision is to provide that an amendment or modification can be effected by the consent of a specified percentage-in-interest of the shareholders, with the percentage set high enough to include most of the major shareholders of the corporation. Protection for the minority shareholders can be included through a provision that restricts any amendment or modification that adversely impacts less than all of the shareholders without the consent of each of the shareholders so affected.

B.   Future Issuances of Securities

Shareholders' agreements generally address the procedures and restrictions relating to future issuances of securities by the corporation. The key issue, of course, is how an issuance of additional securities will impact the balance of voting power that exists among the shareholders at the time that the agreement is originally executed. Shareholders may have legitimate concerns that one or more of the other shareholders may cause additional shares to be issued to themselves, thereby diluting the interest of shareholders not allowed to participate in the issuance.

While concerns regarding dilution of voting power through the issuance of new securities can be addressed, at least in part, by customized consent requirements on various issues, another common method of protection is to include preemptive rights. While preemptive rights can be drafted in a number of ways, the fundamental principle is that each of the shareholders must be offered the opportunity to maintain his or her pro-rata ownership of shares in future financings. Exceptions might be allowed for shares issued pursuant to employee stock option or bonus plans approved by the board and for securities issued to outside investors. Venture capitalists will typically eliminate any preemptive rights previously granted to the founders; however, they will also demand that such rights be granted to them with respect to future financings.

C.   Directors and Officers

Various issues relating to the directors and officers of the corporation will normally be addressed in the shareholders' agreement, as well as in the charter documents of the corporation. For example, the number of directors, and their terms of office, must be specified in the bylaws (and sometimes in the articles of incorporation) and will be reinforced by provisions in the shareholders' agreement relating to voting or election of directors. The bylaws and shareholders' agreement may also include provisions regarding special voting requirements on certain matters to be considered by the board. Finally, while the board has the discretion to appoint the corporate officers identified in the bylaws, shareholders' agreements for smaller corporations may also include covenants regarding designation of certain shareholders to fill specified offices. These provisions will be eliminated as the company grows and outside investors become involved with the business and serve on the board.

Venture capitalists generally insist on some form of formal voting agreement among the key investors, the founders and other major shareholders of the company. These voting provisions may be included as part of a single shareholders' agreement or the parties may opt for a separate voting agreement, such as **Exhibit 3G**. Best practice, although not always followed, is to incorporate the voting arrangements into the charter documents of the corporation. While this does increase the cost and time required for amendments to the procedures, it provides a greater level of protection to all parties.

When venture capitalists or other outside investors provide funding for the company, one of the key issues is the composition of the board of directors. While there is obviously a wide range of possible solutions, it is common to find that, assuming a five-person board, outside investors will be permitted to designate two directors and the founders will be permitted to designate either two or three directors. If less than all of the directors are to be named by either the investors or the founders, the vacancies will generally be filled by independent directors that must be mutually agreed upon by the other directors. In cases where it is contemplated that a new chief executive officer will be brought in to replace one of the founders in that position, one of the seats on the board may be reserved for the CEO once he or she has been approved by the other directors. Default provisions are sometimes included for those situations where the parties cannot agree on the independent director (e.g., the seat will be filled by the representatives of the investors with the founders having the right to nominate other appropriate candidates in the future if they desire).

The shareholders' agreement should include procedures for designation of the nominees from the investor and founder groups. For example, nominees of the investor group may be designated by specified investors or may be selected by a majority vote of members of the investor group. Similarly, one or more employee founders may be specifically designated as board members or the designees may be selected by a majority vote of members of the founding group. In some cases, the "founder group" will be expanded to include other employee shareholders, thereby giving significant officers and employees who came on board after formation an opportunity to participate in the designation process.

Care must be taken to try and accommodate changed circumstances among the members of a particular group with designation rights. For example, if a specific investor has the right to designate a nominee, such rights may terminate if the investor's shareholdings drop below a certain amount (e.g., 50% of original holdings), and other procedures should be included for designating that nominee. As for any founders and/or employee shareholders who may be designated as board members, continued service should not extend beyond termination of employment or reduction of shareholdings below a specified minimum amount.

A number of investors insist on "vote switch" provisions that would allow them to designate additional directors on the occurrence of certain events. Obviously, this procedure will only be used in situations where the investors do not otherwise have control of the board. Possible events that might trigger a change in composition of the board include the following:

- Failure of the corporation to make a required redemption or pay a required dividend
- Commencement of insolvency or bankruptcy proceedings with respect to the corporation
- Default by the corporation under any covenants contained in the charter documents
- Failure of the corporation to meet specific financial tests

Other procedural issues include describing the composition of the board following a vote switch (e.g., investor group becomes entitled to elect a majority of the board of directors) and whether or not the vote switch provisions will terminate once the event causing the switch has been cured. If cure provisions are included, some effort should be made to describe the duties of the designees of the investor group, such as using their best efforts to attempt to cure the problem.

Once the composition of the board has been settled, consideration should be given to the procedures for conducting the activities of the board, including special voting requirements on certain fundamental matters. For example, the consent of more than a simply majority of the directors may be required for the appointment of certain officers, capital expenditures in excess of a certain amount, approval (and amendment) of the corporation's business plan, and a sale or merger of the company. Some or all of these actions may also require shareholder consent.

Other issues relating to day-to-day activities of the corporation that might be covered in the agreement include distributions of corporate funds, selection of accountants and auditors, and preparation and distribution of periodic financial reports. Indemnification of directors and officers, to the extent permitted under applicable statutes, should also be addressed in the agreement as well as in the charter documents of the corporation.

D. Shareholders

The most commonly regulated issues with respect to shareholders are matters subject to shareholder consent and the number or percentage of shareholders who must consent to a particular action for it to be effective. Among the most common issues that might require some form of shareholder consent are the following:

- Issuances of additional shares, other than an agreed number of shares that might be issued under employee stock option or other incentive plans approved by the board
- Sales of significant assets of the corporation
- Execution of contracts that impose material financial obligations on the corporation
- Significant increases in salaries
- Mergers and consolidations
- Material changes in the business of the corporation

In general, corporations with backing from venture capitalists will have shareholder voting requirements that provide the investor group with class or series voting rights on various issues. In other words, the corporation will not be permitted to take certain actions without the consent of a specified percentage-in-interest of the shares of a single class or series, with the percentage being determined by the composition of the investor group. For example, if the corporation raises $4 million from four large investors through the sale of Series A Preferred shares, and each of the investors provides $1 million in funding, it is likely that major actions will require the consent of at least three of the four investors. So, the voting percentage will be set at 75%-in-interest of the Series A Preferred shares. Note that an increase of 1% to 76% would require the approval of all four of the investors and could lead to deadlock.

E.   Terms of Employment and Buy-Sell Procedures

In some cases, the shareholders' agreement will address the terms of employment of any employee-shareholders, as well as buy-sell procedures that include restrictions on transfers and mandatory or optional transfer at the time that an employee-shareholder ceases to be active on a daily basis with the corporation. The provisions may be included in the agreement or in separate contracts.

Employment agreements can be quite comprehensive and cover a wide range of issues. In any event, it is important for the employee-shareholders and investors to reach agreement on the following areas:

- Duties of each employee-shareholder and the amount of time that each shareholder will spend on the activities of the corporate business
- The amount of compensation to be paid to each employee-shareholder (including benefits)
- The circumstances under which employment of a shareholder may be terminated

Employee-shareholders will also be required to enter into agreements regarding protection of confidential information and restrictions on competitive activities during employment. In some states, post-termination restrictions on competition may be allowed under applicable state laws.

Buy-sell provisions, including restrictions on share transfers, can take a number of different forms. In general, any attempted transfer of shares by employee-shareholders will be subject to a right of first offer or refusal in favor of the corporation and/or the other shareholders. Transfers should be broadly defined to include all possible voluntary and involuntary means of transfer including gift, pledge, operation of law (e.g., divorce), and intestate succession.

In addition to voluntary transfers, the parties must consider the need to include procedures that will cover other significant events. Among the issues to be addressed are the following:

- Should the agreement provide for optional mandatory purchase of shares upon disability of a shareholder? If so, how should disability be defined?
- Should the agreement provide for purchase of shares following termination of employment of a shareholder? If so, what events should constitute termination of employment? Generally, mandatory purchase may be appropriate if a shareholder is terminated "without cause" or retires in accordance with the corporation's retirement policies. An option, without an obligation, to repurchase should be created in favor of the corporation and/or other shareholders if termination is "for cause" or the shareholder retires prior to the agreed retirement age.
- Should the agreement provide for mandatory purchase of shares of a deceased shareholder? Generally, the corporation should obtain life

insurance to cover the costs of its obligations to purchase the shares of a deceased shareholder. The ability to purchase such shares is important in recruiting a replacement.

- Should the agreement provide for optional/mandatory purchase of shares that become subject to transfer to a third party in an involuntary transfer (e.g., a transfer pursuant to a judicial order or enforcement of pledge)?

Once the repurchase events are identified, the parties must agree on how the purchase price for the shares will be determined. For example, the parties may agree that the value of the shares will be the sum of the book value of the shares as reflected in the financial statements of the corporation plus an amount equal to the value of the goodwill associated with the shares. The price may vary depending on the event that triggers the buy-sell provision, such as when shares subject to involuntary transfers are purchased at the lower of the price determined pursuant to the above formula or the price actually paid by the third party for the shares.

Finally, provisions should be included for payment of the purchase price for shares bought and sold under the buy-sell agreement. For example, a portion of the price may be paid immediately in cash and the balance may be paid out in installment payments under a promissory note.

3.05   Responsibilities of a Corporate Director

In recent years, one of the biggest legal issues concerning business entities is the responsibilities and liabilities of corporate directors. In light of the failure of Enron and other major businesses, and complaints about the role of their boards, and the adoption of the Sarbanes-Oxley Act of 2002, the issue is likely to continue. In this section, we turn to the issues and uncertainties in this area.

A.   Oversight Responsibilities

The board of directors has the power and authority to oversee the management of the corporation's business and affairs. Directors, other than directors who are also officers and employees of the corporation, are generally not involved in the day-to-day management of the corporation. Instead, directors should focus on the following:

- Operating, financial and other corporate plans, strategies and objectives
- Evaluating the performance of the corporation and its senior management and taking appropriate action, including removal, when warranted
- Fixing and regularly evaluating the compensation of senior executives

- Requiring, approving and implementing senior executive succession plans
- Adopting policies of corporate conduct, including compliance with applicable laws and regulations and maintenance of accounting, financial and other controls
- Reviewing the process of providing appropriate financial and operational information to decision makers (including board members)
- Evaluating the overall effectiveness of the board

In discharging his or her duties, a director is obligated to promote the best interests of the corporation and its shareholders. In order to fulfill these obligations, directors must ensure that the corporation fulfills its disclosure obligations to shareholders and the investment community and establishes legal compliance programs and internal controls. In addition, the board must protect the assets of the corporation and review and approve all material contracts relating to the business and affairs of the corporation.

B. Fiduciary Duties

Corporate directors owe a duty of care that requires that they discharge their duties (a) in good faith, (b) with the care that an ordinary prudent person in a like position would exercise under similar circumstances, and (c) in a manner that he or she reasonably believes to be in the best interests of the corporation. In order to satisfy the standard of care, directors must exercise independent judgment for the overall benefit of the corporation. Directors must also be diligent and invest significant amounts of time and energy in monitoring management's conduct of the business in compliance with the corporation's operating procedures, including regular attendance at board and committee meetings.

In order for directors to fulfill their responsibilities, management must keep the board sufficiently informed about the affairs of the company. While directors must make an effort to gather the information necessary for them to make informed decisions regarding the corporation, they do have a right to rely on others, including the following:

- The corporation's officers or employees whom the director reasonably believes to be reliable and competent in the matters presented
- Legal counsel, public accountants, or other persons as to matters that the director reasonably believes to be within their professional or expert competence
- Duly authorized committees of the board on which the director does not serve, unless in any such case the director has knowledge that would make such reliance unwarranted

The duty of care is qualified by the business judgment rule, which protects a disinterested director from personal liability to the corporation and its shareholders, even though a corporate decision the director approved is unsuccessful or unwise. Upon review of a director's conduct, a court will not substitute its judgment (particularly in hindsight) for that of the director, provided the director (a) acted in good faith, (b) is reasonably informed, and (c) rationally believes the action taken was in the best interests of the corporation.

In addition to the duty of care, directors must abide by a duty of loyalty that requires that they act in the interests of the corporation. For example, if the corporation is a party to a transaction in which a director has a financial or personal interest, the transaction must be approved by the other "disinterested" board members. Also, directors may not usurp corporate opportunities for their own interest and advantage. In determining whether an opportunity must first be offered to the corporation, the following factors must be considered:

- Circumstances in which the director became aware of the opportunity
- The significance of the opportunity to the corporation and the degree of interest to the corporation in the opportunity
- Whether the opportunity relates to the corporation's existing or contemplated business
- Whether there is a reasonable basis for the corporation to expect that the director should make the opportunity available to the corporation

In general, the duty of loyalty requires that a director not use his or her position to enjoy a personal benefit, gain or other advantage at the expense of the corporation. However, conflicts of interests (including interested director transactions and corporate opportunities) are not inherently improper and should not be regarded as an adverse reflection on the board or the interested director. It is the manner in which an interested director and the board deal with the conflict situation that determines the propriety of the transaction and the director's conduct.

Finally, directors should always deal in confidence with respect to all matters involving the corporation until such time as there has been general disclosure.

C. Board Composition and Compensation

Effective boards exercise independent judgment and are perceived by shareholders to exercise independent judgment. Board environments likely to nurture independence and the appearance of independence have independent members on the board of directors. A director will be viewed as independent only if he or she is a nonmanagement director free of any material business or professional relationship with the corporation or its management.

One possible model for effective board composition is as follows:

- An independent director serves as chair of the board
- If the CEO serves as chair, the independent directors designate one of the independent members to act as lead director
- Members of board oversight committees, a majority of whom should be independent, choose their own committee chairs, rather than having the chairs designated by the CEO
- Independent directors meet periodically as a body to review the performance of management and of the members of the board
- Independent directors are available to meet with substantial shareholders, particularly when those shareholders are not satisfied with responses they have received from management

Directors should be fairly compensated and have the responsibility to determine their own compensation. Necessary data to reach a fair conclusion includes comparisons, together with analysis of special factors that relate to the particular corporation. Directors' compensation may take a number of different forms, including annual retainers and attendance fees for board and committee meetings, deferred compensation plans, retirement programs, matching educational or a charitable contribution, and accident or other insurance. Stock options and restricted stock grants to directors strengthen directors' interests in the overall success of the corporation.

D. Effect of Sarbanes-Oxley Act

As a result of a number of well-publicized financial frauds involving Enron, Global Crossing, WorldCom and others, Congress passed the Sarbanes-Oxley Act in 2002. The Securities and Exchange Commission ("SEC") followed with a number of new rules, as did the major stock markets, including the New York Stock Exchange and NASDAQ Stock Market. The new law and rules apply to the following:

- Reporting companies, that is companies that have registered equity or debt securities with the SEC under the Securities Exchange Act of 1934
- Companies that have equity securities listed on an exchange or on NASDAQ

As such, most will not be applicable to emerging companies such as those covered by this book, although Chapter 6 contains an overview of the law. Nevertheless, founders of new companies should understand that while these rules may not be legally applicable, they may establish "best practices" that investors and lenders will insist upon.

3.06   Facilities

A.   Preliminary Considerations

In the earliest stages of business development, almost all companies, regardless of their projected growth, elect to use leased or rented premises as opposed to actually purchasing a building to house their facilities. Leasing is a good way to preserve scarce capital, and with a properly negotiated lease agreement, it allows the founders to retain the flexibility to move to a new location if the requirements of the business should change in the future.

Regardless of whether the facilities are to be leased or purchased, careful consideration must be given to identifying the best location for the business. While real estate agents can provide some input on this issue, their opinion is no substitute for a complete analysis by management of the impact that location will have on access to customers, suppliers, other potential business partners, and human resources.

The first issue to address is whether or not location is really important for the success of the business. In some cases, proximity to the customer base is almost irrelevant if the company generally distributes its products or services primarily through the Internet or other distribution channels such as field sales offices and representatives. In that case, management can focus on other factors, such as lowering rental costs or choosing a site that is convenient for those working in the headquarters office.

On the other hand, if it is anticipated that customers and other potential business partners will need to visit the company's facilities on a regular basis, several other questions need to be asked and answered. For example, consideration must be given to how customers and business partners will get to the company's facilities. Proximity to roadways or some other form of reliable transportation infrastructure is a key issue. For that matter, if the company is engaged in manufacturing activities, care should be taken to ensure that the company can easily transfer finished products to couriers and delivery companies.

Companies involved in product development activities often prefer to locate near universities or research parks. This is a logical step in situations where the founders previously worked at a university and the company is based on technology that may have been originally developed in the academic environment. By locating close to the origin of the technology, the company can take advantage of the founder's continuing contacts and the usual eagerness of the university to continue to provide research assistance on a contract basis. This type of site selection can also improve the recruitment efforts of the company, as it is likely that a larger base of qualified technical candidates will migrate to a technology center.

Research parks, as well as business incubators, provide opportunities for small companies to set up shop alongside businesses with similar interests and compatible skills, thereby increasing the likelihood of formation of strategic business relationships. However, it is important for management to carefully analyze the composition of the tenant population of the research park or incubator before signing on. In many cases, companies find that the real opportunities for functional business partnerships, as opposed to consultants and professional advisors, are limited and that location in proximity to certain large firms may preclude relationships with other partners.

B. Real Estate Lease Agreements

A commercial real estate lease, such as the basic office lease appearing as **Exhibit 3H**, is often one of the first large contracts that will be taken on by an emerging company. In many cases, the projected payments of rent and other assessments under the lease can be staggering, although the company certainly assumes that there will be offsetting revenues during the lease term to cover all of the costs of the operation of the business, including facilities expenses. Many lease agreements come as a standard form promulgated by local real organizations. The landlord almost always is the party responsible for preparing the initial draft and processing any agreed changes, which are often in the form of a lengthy addendum to the standard form. The amount of time and effort that the company spends on negotiating the lease terms is proportional to the length of the projected lease term and the costs associated with moving the facilities if other opportunities arise or the relationship with the landlord is problematic. In any case, it is important for management to have advice of counsel on the proposed lease, even if no changes are negotiated, so that everyone understands the risks of the arrangement and the need to carefully administer the lease once it is signed.

1. Term

Management must carefully consider the length of the lease, often referred to as the "lease term," and the company's ability to renew the lease for subsequent terms if it elects to do so and is not otherwise in default with respect to its obligations under the lease agreement. The optimal lease term depends on the projected expansion of the firm in the foreseeable future and the impact that growth may have on the space requirements for the business. Also, consideration should be given to possible need for different types of space as the company grows. For example, while the company may be engaged in product development activities for the first 18–24 months, manufacturing space may be needed once the company's products have been tested and are ready for introduction on a large scale into the marketplace.

2.   Rent and Other Assessments

Obviously the consideration to be paid by the lessee to the landlord over the term of the lease is a major factor in negotiating and accepting a lease agreement. Consideration will include not only the periodic rental payments, generally assessed on a monthly basis, but also additional amounts for insurance, property taxes and a pro-rata share of maintenance and improvement expenditures by the landlord.

Rent will be determined by market conditions and may vary depending on the length of the proposed lease. The lessee should carefully explore whether or not the landlord will be allowed to increase the rent over the lease term, perhaps to take into account changes in the consumer price index in the area where the facility is located. The big issue with respect to other assessments is defining which items will be charged through to the lessee and any other tenants in the facility. If possible, the lessee should obtain some sort of projected budget from the landlord, as well as a limitation on the total amount that can be charged without the additional consent of the lessee. Finally, the timing of assessments should be discussed so that the lessee can make appropriate cash management plans.

3.   Security Deposit

As with rent, the amount of the security deposit will vary depending on market conditions. The security deposit is an "up front" payment of funds to establish a reserve that the landlord can use to pay for expenses associated with the lessee's breach of its obligations under the lease. The laws and regulations regarding use and return of security deposits are complex and applicable local laws should be reviewed. In any event, from a business perspective, the lessee will obviously want to minimize the amount of cash that will need to be invested in the security deposit. Prospective lessees with a strong balance sheet and good credit history may be able to negotiate a small security deposit, often in the form of a letter of credit in favor of the landlord. Other lessees, particularly those that have not completed their initial round of funding, may find that the required security deposit is relatively large and must be paid in cash at the time the lease is signed.

4.   Space and Improvements

It would seem obvious that the parties must agree on the space that will actually be subject to the lease agreement; however, disputes often arise as to use of common areas, such as hallways, restrooms and elevators. All of this needs to be made clear from the beginning of the relationship, particularly since access to these areas can be important for increasing the comfort of customers and employees.

Improvements and modifications to the space should also be resolved well in advance. In down markets, landlords are often willing to pay for certain changes in the space as a way to entice lessees that might have a number of different options. This is particularly true if the lessee is willing to sign a long-term lease. In any event, the lease should specify who will own any improvements or modifications at the end of the lease term. Also, the parties should clarify the timing, extent and cost of improvements required in order to comply with regulatory requirements, such as the Americans with Disabilities Act.

5.   Other Terms and Conditions

Other issues that will be commonly be addressed in the lease agreement include the following:

- Responsibility for maintenance and repair of the leased premises, particularly heating and air conditioning systems that are not easily accessed by the lessee and may even be in parts of the facility not covered by the lease
- Right of both parties to assign the lease and the right of the lessee to sublease all or a portion of the leased premises
- Notice and other procedural requirements for early termination of the lease and the penalties associated with early termination
- Dispute resolution procedures, including mediation or arbitration

3.07   Personal Property

Businesses generally require substantial amounts of personal property, including equipment and furnishings, to conduct operations. The exact requirements for the company will vary depending on the line of business. In some cases, for example, a company may require bulky and expensive manufacturing equipment. Companies involved in the life sciences area will need to make large investments in laboratory equipment. All businesses will need computers and other information technology hardware for internal and external communications.

Suffice to say that a major issue for any new company is deciding whether to purchase capital equipment and other personal property required for the business or to lease the property until a better decision can be made on actually buying the items. Clearly, the decision will depend on all of the investment projects available to the business at that point in time, since the purchase of personal property is a decision that will diminish the capital immediately available for other uses, such as human resources or technology. Management will also need to consider the possibility that purchased equipment may become obsolete in the near future or otherwise lose its value as technology changes and/or the needs of the company change faster than planned.

It is important to remember that the buy-or-lease decision will usually be impacted by the company's ability to obtain some form of equipment financing from a commercial lender or other institutional lender specializing in funding for such items. Equipment financing, which will include a security interest in the purchased equipment, turns the purchase decision into an installment payment arrangement similar to a lease. Small companies may discover, however, that equipment financing will only be available if supported by personal guarantees offered by the founders of the business.

If the decision is made to lease items of personal property, management and company counsel will need to consider some of the following issues.

Property: Is the personal property subject to the lease fully and adequately described? What procedures, if any, should be included for adding new items in the future? In many cases, the company will forge a long-term relationship with a lessor that allows for lease of new items on an "as needed" basis on the same terms and conditions originally included in the lease. This type of relationship can be particularly useful if the requirements of the lessee change and it is able to return all or a portion of the originally leased equipment prior to the end of the lease term in exchange for updated items.

Payment and Deposit: What are the lease payments and when will they be due? In some cases, lease payments may be based on actual usage of the property. Some lessors will require a security deposit prior to delivery of the property. Payments for use of the property may be supplemented by additional assessments for taxes and similar charges relating to the property.

Term: What is to be the term of the lease? In many cases, the lease extends for a fixed term; however, the parties may include provisions relating to automatic renewal or an option in favor of the lessee to renew the lease at a specified rental. As is the case with purchased equipment, the lessee must consider the possibility that the leased property will become obsolete or that the need of the lessee will change prior to the end of the lease term. Lessors may be willing to agree to exchanges during the lease term without penalty or for a nominal assessment.

Repair: What provisions should be included regarding maintenance and repair of the leased property? The lessee will often be obligated to maintain and repair the property at its own cost over the lease term, although the lessor may offer a separate service contract at additional cost. Alternatively, rental payments may include service and repairs. If the lessor will be providing maintenance services, the contract should carefully describe the scope of the work, the hours during which the services will be provided, and the charges for any additional services.

Loss and Damage: What will be the obligations of the parties with respect to loss of, or damage to, the leased property? In generally, the risk of loss and damage to the property will be borne by the lessee. The contract will often include covenants by the lessee that it will obtain adequate insurance coverage for the leased property and that it will compensate the lessor for any loss or damage to the leased property, including replacement of the property. In addition, lessees are often placed under various restrictions relating to use and location of the property and required to allow the lessor to enter the lessee's premise to inspect the property.

Representations: What representations and warranties will be provided by the lessor with respect to the leased property? In general, the lessor will explicitly disclaim any express and implied warranties regarding the leased property, and will seek to limit any liability for damages or losses suffered by the lessee from the use of the property. In some cases, the lessor will grant a limited warranty to the lessee to maintain the property in good working order. Problems that fall outside of the warranty will be covered by a separate maintenance agreement.

Default: What events will constitute a default under the terms of the agreement? Generally, early termination of the lease by the lessor will be permitted on (a) the lessee's failure to pay lease payments on a timely basis, (b) the lessee's continuing noncompliance with any material term or condition in the lease following notice and opportunity to cure, and (c) the occurrence of certain events that evidence financial difficulties for the lessee (e.g., bankruptcy filing or seizure of assets for the benefit of creditors). The lessor's remedies should be specified, and may include the right to repossess the property, release it to a third party and charge the lessee for the cost of repossessing and leasing the property.

Other issues that should be covered in the lease agreement include procedures for assignment of the lease obligations, return of the leased property at the end of the term, and dispute resolution.

3.08   OSHA

The Occupational Safety and Health Act ("OSHA") contains detailed rules on the types of information that must be kept and the reports that must be filed by employers. Recently, OSHA adopted new rules. Employers should review the details of the new rules; however, the following list summarizes some of the major differences between the old and new rules. Employers should consult the exact language of the new regulation to answer specific questions.

A. Scope

OSHA contains detailed rules on which industries are covered by its rules. The list of service and retail industries that are partially exempt from the rule has been updated. In addition, there is a partial exemption for employers who had 10 or fewer workers at all times in the previous calendar year.

B. Forms

Employers must use OSHA Form 300, 301 and 300A to report injuries or illnesses at the workplace. The forms have been simplified and made more "user-friendly." In addition, flexibility has been added so employers can keep the information on computers at a central location or in alternative forms, as long as the information is compatible and the data can be produced when needed.

C. Work-Related

The reports required to be made to OSHA cover work-related incidents. Events at the workplace are presumed to be work-related. Employees traveling on company business or working out of their home are also covered.

D. Recording Criteria

Employers are required to record work-related injuries or illnesses if they result in one of the following:

- Death
- Days away from work
- Restricted work or transfer to another job
- Medical treatment beyond first aid
- Loss of consciousness
- Diagnosis of a significant injury or illness by a physician or other licensed health care professional

Different criteria for recording work-related injuries and work-related illnesses have been eliminated under current rules; one set of criteria is now used for both.

There are definitions for medical treatment and first aid. First aid is defined by treatments on a finite list. Any treatment not on this list is medical treatment.

In some cases, businesses must record "light duty" or restricted work cases. Employers are required to record cases as restricted work cases when injured or ill employees only work partial days or are restricted from performing their "routine job functions" (defined as work activities the employee regularly performs at least once weekly).

Musculoskeletal disorders ("MSDs") are treated like all other injuries or illnesses; they must be recorded if they result in days away, restricted work, transfer to another job or medical treatment beyond first aid.

E.   Day Counts

Employers are required to record days away, days of restricted work or transfer to another job. The term "lost workdays" is no longer used. Employers are not required to count days away or days of restriction beyond 180 days. In making the calculations, the day on which the injury or illness occurs is not counted.

F.   Employee Involvement

Employers must establish a procedure for employees to report injuries and illnesses and tell their employees how to report. Employees must be given access to OSHA 301 forms to review records of their own injuries and illnesses. In addition, employee representatives are allowed to access those parts of OSHA 301 forms relevant to workplace safety and health.

G.   Protecting Privacy

OSHA is very concerned about employee privacy. Employers are, therefore, required to protect employee privacy by withholding individual names on Form 300 for certain types of sensitive injuries and illnesses (e.g., sexual assaults, HIV infections, mental illnesses). Employers are allowed to withhold descriptive information about sensitive injuries in cases where not doing so would disclose the employee's identity. In addition, employers are required to remove employees' names before providing injury and illness data to persons who do not have access rights under OSHA rules.

H.   Reports

Within four hours, employers must provide records to any OSHA compliance officer who requests them. Employers must also report all fatal heart attacks to employees occurring in the work environment.

3.09   Record Retention Policy

In order to make tax, OSHA and other government reports, a company must maintain records sufficient for it to make the reports. For instance, taxpayers, including businesses, are required to maintain records supporting their tax filings for six years. This includes information on income, as well as expenses. If the IRS challenges information in a tax filing within such six-year period, however, the obligation to maintain such records continues until the challenge is resolved. In addition, as noted above, many agencies and laws mandate what records must be maintained.

On the other hand, a company does not want to keep unnecessary documentation that takes up expensive space. With a fixed disposal schedule that is beyond the time periods mandated by law, the company can comfortably destroy unneeded documents without being accused of destroying records for improper purposes.

Included as **Exhibit 3I** is a records retention policy for a company. Each emerging company should adopt it (or one like it).

Tax Aspects of Forming and Organizing a New Business

David T. Collins

Bellarmine University
Louisville, KY

CHAPTER **4**

Contents

Tax Aspects of Forming and Organizing a New Business[1]

4.01 Preliminary Considerations

The previous chapters have described some of the many issues surrounding the choice of business entity. This Chapter continues that discussion with information about the tax consequences associated with different business entities. Those tax consequences often will prove decisive when selecting an appropriate entity form through which to conduct a business. Familiarity with this material can help the reader avoid substantial tax liabilities later, which also may include significant legal and/or accounting fees to correct or mitigate mistakes (mistakes that are frequently avoidable).

A. Tax Planning Goals in Business Formation

A common tax-planning goal of many new business owners is to minimize taxation of business profits. Of almost equal concern, particularly during the start-up phase, is the ability to use business losses to offset other income—especially the owner's personal income from other sources. Most tax planning related to business entity choice focuses on one or both of those issues.

Other issues of importance (although not always seen as such by new business owners) relate to the efficient transfer of assets into and out of the business entity and the taxation of future increases in equity value. It is desirable to defer tax on assets contributed to business enterprises,

---

1. Patricia Selvy and Benjamin J. Evans were the authors of this chapter in the first edition of the *Guide*.

particularly for assets that have appreciated in value. Since entrepreneurs eventually will want to recover their investment, it is desirable to consider the tax consequences of future increases in equity value. Thus, adequate tax planning also will consider factors such as flexibility in transferring assets and ownership interests.

B. Federal Income Tax Treatment of Businesses

During the planning stage, entrepreneurs should consult with knowledgeable tax practitioners to determine the type of business entity that best meets their tax goals. Each of the different business entities require a particular tax treatment; though there are a few cases when the entrepreneur can elect a desired tax treatment. Broadly speaking, federal income tax law taxes business entities under one of the following four categories:

- Disregarded entities
- Partnerships
- C corporations
- S corporations

As the name suggests, for disregarded entities, the tax law disregards the separate existence of the business entity and treats all of the income as the owner's personal income and permits the owner to deduct the business's expenses. Sole proprietorships are disregarded entities, even if the owner properly segregates business and personal accounts in separate accounting records. Also, single-member limited liability companies can elect disregarded entity treatment.

Under partnership taxation, governed by Subchapter K of the Internal Revenue Code ("Code"), the business entity's income and deductions flow through to the partners, keeping their character (ordinary, capital, etc.). The law imposes no entity-level taxes on partnerships. The partners pay tax on their distributive share of the partnership's income, regardless of whether the partnership distributes money or property to the partners.

The income of C corporations, governed by Subchapter C of the Code, is taxed at the entity level. C corporation earnings and profits also face income taxation when distributed to the business owners—the shareholders. Thus, at present, the law provides for the "double taxation" of C corporation income in many instances.[2] Generally, entrepreneurs try to avoid the double taxation that takes place when the law imposes both an entity-level and an owner-level tax. It is important to note that the law taxes all publicly traded entities as C corporations.

---

2. Currently, qualified dividends are subject to a maximum 15% tax rate through the end of 2010, when that provision is scheduled to end. If it does, all dividends will be subject to ordinary tax rates starting in 2011.

Corporations that meet certain requirements can elect treatment as S corporations (under Subchapter S of the Code). The tax law, with a few exceptions, does not impose an entity-level tax on S corporations. Similar to partnerships, the income and deductions of S corporations flow through to the shareholders. The use of S corporations, however, affords no flexibility in allocating gains and losses among shareholders. Partners have more freedom to allocate gains and losses than S corporation shareholders. Furthermore, the strict requirements of "small business corporations," with the possibility of an inadvertent termination of the S corporation election, can make this form less desirable for some business enterprises.

C. Scope of Discussion

In the remainder of this chapter, we will discuss the following topics:

- Individual, corporate and capital gains tax rates and the alternative minimum tax
- Concepts of basis, realization and recognition of gain
- Mechanics of tax treatment election under the "Check-the-Box" regulations
- Taxation of contributions to, operations of and distributions from, C corporations, S corporations and partnerships

Rather than reviewing each entity type in turn, the discussion will adopt a "follow-the-money" approach, examining differences in tax treatment as assets move into business entities, generate profits and move back out.

The tax treatment of specialized business entities (real estate investment trusts, regulated investment companies, real estate mortgage investment conduits, foreign sales corporations, domestic international sales corporations, etc.) falls outside the scope of this discussion. This chapter also will not consider the special rules applying to banks and insurance companies or the tax issues posed by an affiliated group of corporations filing consolidated returns. This chapter will focus on active business enterprises; the situation of passive investment for profit will receive less discussion. Citations to Code sections refer to the Internal Revenue Code of 1986, as amended, unless otherwise indicated.

The reader is reminded that this chapter offers a rudimentary understanding of federal income tax laws relating to business formation and entity selection. It seeks to facilitate conversation with seasoned tax professionals, not to replace them. As thousands of pages have been penned on this topic, the present discussion suffices only as a first step—the rest of the journey requires a tax professional.

4.02   Tax Rates

Section 1 of the Code imposes progressive rates on the taxable income of individuals. For 2010 the Code imposes six marginal tax rate brackets—10%, 15%, 25%, 28%, 33% and 35%. Those tax rates were set by the Jobs and Growth Tax Relief Reconciliation Act of 2003, which is set to expire at the end of 2010. If Congress allows that to happen, starting in 2011, there will be five tax brackets: 15%, 28%, 31%, 36% and 39.6%—in other words, taxes will effectively increase at all income levels. The income brackets that the tax rates are applied to differ for individuals, heads of households, married filing joint, and married filing separate. Those brackets are adjusted annually for inflation but are not otherwise affected by the possible sunset provisions of the 2003 Act.

With the Revenue Reconciliation Act of 1990, Congress reintroduced a differential between the individual tax rates for ordinary income and for capital gains. This tax rate differential provides astute planners with opportunities to minimize tax liability by structuring transactions to recognize capital gains rather than ordinary income. As a result of the 2003 tax law changes, the Code currently taxes most gains from capital assets held for more than 12 months at 0% or 15%, though there are rates of 25% and 28% for specific capital assets (real estate, collectibles, and small business stock). If the provisions of the 2003 Act are allowed to expire at the end of 2010, the base capital gains rates will rise to 10% or 20%. However, the differential in rates will still result in a preference for capital gains rather than ordinary income.

Section 11 of the Code establishes the progressive rate structure for the entity-level corporate income tax. The 2010 corporate tax rates are shown in the following table.

Taxable Income Over	Not Over	Tax Rate
0	50,000	15%
50,000	75,000	25%
75,000	100,000	34%
100,000	335,000	39%
335,000	10,000,000	34%
10,000,000	15,000,000	35%
15,000,000	18,333,333	38%
18,333,333	…………..	35%

The 39% and 38% brackets eliminate the overall progressivity of corporate taxes at higher income levels. Thus, for taxable income above $18,333,333 the effective corporate tax rate on ALL income is 35%.

Prior to 1986, individual marginal tax rates significantly exceeded the corporate rates. This created an incentive for business owners to shield income in C corporations. The Tax Reform Act of 1986 eliminated this vast rate disparity and, because of the double taxation issue, precipitated a flight from the C corporation as a preferred entity status for many business enterprises. Because it was no longer necessary to leave the income in the business, flow-through entities (partnerships and S corporations) became the entity form of choice. Although the top individual rate is scheduled to rise from 35% to 39.6%, the difference may not be large enough to restore C corporations to positions of prominence. Thus, while differences in tax rates may play a role in the entity form decision, a wider array of tax consequences determines the final outcome of that decision.

Finally, a note about the alternative minimum tax ("AMT"): In response to cases where taxpayers could avoid income taxation by availing themselves of the Code's many tax planning opportunities, Congress decided to impose some minimum level of taxation on income. The Code includes within taxable income certain "tax preference items" that are subject to the AMT; Code sections 55 through 59 contain highly technical provisions affecting both individuals and corporations. For individuals, the AMT is essentially 28% of AMT income above a specified exemption amount. However, since the exempted AMT income is not indexed for inflation, it "captures" more and more middle-income taxpayers—not the group of high-income taxpayers originally contemplated when the AMT was created. This often is cited as a reason to repeal the AMT. On the other hand, it can be shown that the Federal government would lose less revenue if it repealed the regular income tax and kept the AMT. Still, entrepreneurs with a penchant for fancy compensation packages, particularly those that include incentive stock options, may want to beware of the AMT.

4.03   Key Concepts

There are two aspects of taxation that often hold a primary place in tax planning: the character of the income earned and the time period when the tax must be paid. Minding the character of income affords taxpayers one way of minimizing tax liability. Because the Code taxes long-term capital gains for individuals at lower rates than ordinary income, taxpayers desire to structure transactions to recognize capital gains. Taxpayers also can seek to lighten their tax burden through the timing of income and deductions—deferring income or accelerating deductions. As an example of the latter, section 168 of the Code permits taxpayers to use the double declining balance method of depreciation instead of the straight-line method of standard accounting practice. This provision accelerates the taxpayer's ability to deduct the cost of assets.

Other provisions of the Code (e.g., Section 1031) allow the taxpayer to defer until later years the recognition of realized gains during the taxable year.

As the above indicates, taxpayers prefer to pay income tax later, rather than sooner. This does not suggest that taxpayers should pay their taxes after the due date. The Internal Revenue Service ("IRS") vigorously will collect interest and harsh penalties from those who do not pay their taxes when due.[3] Rather, taxpayers should prefer to *owe* the tax in later years.

This tax-planning maxim reposes on the concept of the time value of money. A dollar today is worth more than a dollar tomorrow. If a taxpayer invests one dollar today, for five years with an 8% annual return, the taxpayer will end up with $1.47. From 1926 to 1995, stocks in Standard & Poor's 500 gained an average annual return of 10.5%. (They have not done quite so well in the past years.) Deferring $1.00 in tax for 10 years gives the taxpayer the opportunity perhaps to turn that dollar into $2.60. Inflation too will take its toll on the purchasing power of the dollar that is eventually paid. Therefore, taxpayers will want to avail themselves of the Code's many deferral and nonrecognition provisions.

Those provisions most often involve the tax treatment of transactions involving property. Section 61 of the Code includes within its broad definition of gross income, "Gains derived from dealings in property." Section 1001(a) of the Code explains how to calculate gains from the sale or other disposition of property. The taxpayer must subtract, from the total amount "realized" on the transaction, the taxpayer's adjusted basis in the property to calculate the amount of the gain. Section 1001(c) of the Code requires the recognition of all gains determined under section 1001(a) of the Code unless otherwise provided by some other Code section. The amount realized equals the sum of any money received, the fair market value of any property received and the amount of liabilities discharged in connection with the sale or other disposition of property. Section 1012 of the Code defines "basis" as the cost of property. The Code provides for many adjustments to basis—such as the adjustment for depreciation. A taxpayer must include all recognized gains when computing taxable income.

For example, a taxpayer sells 100 shares of stock for $100,000, the amount realized. He originally purchased the shares for $25,000, the adjusted basis. Under section 1001(a) of the Code, the taxpayer has realized a $75,000 gain from the disposition of the stock, which the taxpayer will recognize under section 1001(c) of the Code.

A basic understanding of the concepts of realization, basis, and recognition is helpful when grappling with the income-deferring and nonrecognition provisions in corporate and partnership taxation.

---

3. Under no circumstances should a business fail to remit employment taxes withheld from employee compensation. Section 6672 of the Code holds those individuals responsible personally liable for any willful failure to remit taxes held in trust for the Government.

Just as the character of income is important (ordinary or capital), it also is important to distinguish types of expenses. Capital expenses refer to expenditures for assets that will last for more than a year. Buildings, equipment and even organizational costs are examples of capital expenses. These expenses can be allocated (depreciated) over the life of the asset.[4] All other expenses are ordinary and can be recorded in the year of expenditure. Since ordinary expenses give taxpayers an immediate deduction against income, they are preferred.

4.04   Electing Tax Treatment

On December 17, 1996, the Treasury Department released the final Check-the-Box regulations, effective January 1, 1997, replacing the old *Kintner* regulations and radically reconfiguring the tax consequences of entity selection. Under the prior *Kintner* regulations, the IRS determined the tax treatment of an entity with reference to six corporate characteristics:

- Presence of associates
- Objective to carry on a business and divide its profits
- Limitation of owners' liability to the extent of their investment
- Free transferability of interests
- Continuity of life of the business enterprise
- Centralized management

Given that both partnerships and corporations have associates who do business together for profit, the analysis turned on the presence of the final four factors. The presence of any two such factors would suffice to require corporate tax treatment. Under the *Kintner* regulations, members of limited liability companies often entered operating agreements limiting the transfer of company interest and inhibiting company longevity to qualify for partnership tax treatment. The mandatory corporate tax treatment of limited liability companies would have severely affected their viability as a business form.

The adoption of the Check-the-Box regulations changed the landscape, giving entrepreneurs more flexibility in selecting the tax treatment of their chosen entities. Treasury Regulation ("Treas. Reg.") § 301.7701-2(a) states that the law will classify any business entity as either a corporation or a partnership. Treas. Reg. § 301.7701-2(b) defines "corporation" for federal tax purposes to include the following:

- Federal, state or Indian tribe corporations
- Associations (other business entities electing corporate tax treatment)

---

4.   Section 179 of the Code allows businesses to immediately expense up to $250,000 of expenditures for capital assets (in 2010).

- Joint-stock companies
- Insurance companies
- FDIC, state-chartered banks
- Business entities wholly owned by a state or local subdivision
- Certain specified foreign entities (usually foreign entities equivalent to U.S. corporations)

Federal law will tax these entities as corporations. They cannot elect tax treatment as partnerships, although such a corporation could make an S corporation election if it meets the statutory requirements.

In addition, there are a number of specialized rules and options available for certain entities:

- Treas. Reg. § 301.7701-2(c)(1) provides for partnership tax treatment for any business entity with multiple members that Treas. Reg. § 301.7701-2(b) does not define as a corporation
- Treas. Reg. § 301.7701-2(c)(2) states that the law will disregard single-owner, noncorporate entities (other than banks) as separate from their owners
- Treas. Reg. § 301.7701-3(a) allows business entities to elect corporate treatment as associations
- Treas. Reg. § 301.7701-3(b) establishes the default rule that the law will treat as partnerships business entities eligible to elect corporate taxation as associations, but that do not so elect

Although the Code taxes all legally incorporated entities as corporations (either C or S), other multiple-member entities can choose between partnership and corporate tax treatment. Noncorporate, single-member entities (other than banks) can choose between disregarded entity treatment or corporate tax treatment. Multiple-owner entities that do not elect to be treated as corporations will receive the default partnership tax treatment. Eligible entities that do not want the default tax treatment should timely file the appropriate election on Form 8832 with the IRS. Form 8832 features a number of boxes and instructs the electing taxpayer to check the appropriate box—thus the name, "Check-the-Box" regulations.

An eligible corporation or association that qualifies as a "small business corporation" can elect treatment as an S corporation. Section 1361(b)(1) of the Code defines a "small business corporation" as any eligible corporation that has none of the following characteristics:

- More than 75 shareholders
- A shareholder other than an individual (with several exceptions discussed below)
- A nonresident alien as a shareholder
- More than one class of stock

The Code allows the following nonindividual shareholders of S corporations:

- Estates
- Bankruptcy estates
- Trusts listed in section 1361(c)(2) of the Code
- Certain exempt organizations
- Qualified Subchapter S trusts

For purposes of the 75-shareholder limitation, the Code treats husband and wife as one shareholder. For the class of stock restriction, mere differences in shareholder voting rights will not create different classes of stock.

Small business corporations make the S corporation election by filing Form 2553 with the IRS. All shareholders must consent to the S corporation election on the Form 2553. Small business corporations wanting to make an S corporation election for their current tax year must make the election before the 16th day of the third month of the current taxable year. The law treats elections made after the first two months of a taxable year as effective for the following year. A new corporation has two months to make the election from the date the corporation first has shareholders, acquires assets or begins doing business, whichever occurs first.[5] Incorporators should take care to timely make the S corporation election. Section 1362(b)(5) of the Code does give the IRS some discretion to accept untimely S corporation elections when the IRS determines the taxpayer had reasonable cause for the delay. But most entrepreneurs will prefer not to rely on the mercy of the IRS.

The S corporation election remains effective until its termination by one of the following three events:

- Shareholders holding more than half of the corporation's shares agree to its revocation
- The corporation loses its status as a small business corporation (e.g., because of a divorce, the corporation finds itself with 76 shareholders)
- The corporation has accumulated earnings and profits at the close of three consecutive taxable years and has gross receipts for each of these three taxable years more than 25% of which constitute passive investment income.[6] Passive investment income includes gross receipts from interest, royalties, dividends, rents and annuities and gains from the sale of stock or securities.

Electing shareholders should take care to prevent an inadvertent termination of the S corporation election, which could saddle the entity with the double taxation of C corporations or trap income-offsetting losses within the entity potentially for five taxable years. Shareholders contemplating an S corporation

---

5. Treas. Reg. 1.1362-6(a)(2).
6. Section 1362(d) of the Code.

election often will include covenants within their shareholders' agreement to prevent the election's termination.

S corporations generally do not pay an entity-level income tax. Instead, income and deductions flow through to shareholders. However, when a C corporation with built-in gains makes an S corporation election, it must pay a tax on the built-in gains if it sells the appreciated assets within 10 years of the election. The law also collapses the last-in first-out ("LIFO") inventory layers of the converting corporation, with a tax on the LIFO recapture.

4.05   Contributions to Capital

When property is transferred to a business in exchange for an ownership interest, a realization event occurs and a gain is realized to the extent the value of the ownership interest received exceeds the adjusted basis in the contributed property. Also a contribution could cause the realization of a loss if the adjusted basis in the contributing property exceeds the value of the ownership interest received. Under section 1001(c) of the Code, a taxpayer will recognize a gain when realized unless a nonrecognition provision applies. Ordinarily new business owners will not want their capital contributions to constitute taxable events. Accordingly, they must ensure that they comply strictly with the Code's appropriate nonrecognition provisions.

Most of the Code's nonrecognition provisions have requirements to which a transaction must conform to qualify for nonrecognition treatment—see, for example, section 1031 (like-kind exchanges), section 1034 (involuntary conversions) and section 1041 (transfers of property between divorcing spouses). The provisions deferring the recognition of gain realized from the contribution of property in exchange for an ownership interest likewise have certain requirements. New business owners should plan to structure these transactions carefully to avoid inadvertently precipitating a taxable event.

A.   C Corporations

Section 351 of the Code governs contributions to the capital of a C corporation and requires the following for the nonrecognition of gains realized from the contribution of property in exchange for stock in a C corporation:

- One or more persons ("transferors")
- Must transfer property
- In exchange for stock
- The transferors immediately after the exchange must own shares representing at least 80% of the stock entitled to vote and at least 80% of all other classes of stock

The transferors must comply with *each* of these requirements or they will recognize any realized gains from the capital contribution or stock receipt. Section 351 of the Code applies to contributions both to start-up C corporations and to existing C corporations. Under section 1032 of the Code, corporations do not recognize gains when transferring their own stock for property.

The requirement that the transferors contribute property merits further elaboration. Property here includes real and personal property, tangible and intangible property—for example, land, buildings, equipment, patents, copyrights, customer lists and secret processes. *Neither past services nor the promise to perform future services constitutes property under section 351 of the Code.* Section 83 of the Code treats stock received in consideration for services rendered, whether past or promised in the future, as compensation income which the taxpayer must include in the taxable year in which the taxpayer's rights in the stock are no longer subject to a substantial risk of forfeiture.

An example illustrates the hazards involved. Taxpayer A and Taxpayer B decide to incorporate a business. A contributes to the corporation real and personal property, with a fair market value of $750,000 in which A has an adjusted basis of $200,000, in exchange for 75 shares. In exchange for B's agreement to contribute B's managerial genius to the business enterprise, the corporation issues B 25 shares. What happens? B must include $250,000 in compensation income from the transaction. Because the property transferor controls less than 80% of the voting shares immediately after the transfer, A must recognize the $550,000 realized gain on the contribution. A and B now face stiff tax liabilities.

When section 351 of the Code applies, the corporation takes a basis in the contributed property equal to the property's basis in the transferor's hands, and the transferor takes a basis in the stock equal to the transferor's basis in the contributed property. Thus, section 351 of the Code can defer the realized gain on appreciated property contributed to a corporation. If the contribution fails to qualify for nonrecognition treatment, then the transferor recognizes the gain realized on the transfer, and the corporation takes a basis in the contributed property equal to the value of the stock exchanged.

On occasion, a transferor may receive property from the corporation in addition to stock in exchange for contributing property. Alternatively, the corporation may assume a transferor's liability in addition to issuing stock in exchange for the transferor's capital contribution. The Code has special rules applicable in each case. Practitioners refer to property received along with stock in exchange for a capital contribution as "boot." If section 351 of the Code otherwise applies to a transaction, but for the fact the transferor receives boot in addition to stock, the transferor will recognize gain (if any), but not in excess of (i) the amount of money received as boot and (ii) the fair market value of other property distributed as boot. Section 351(b)(2) of the Code prevents a transferor from recognizing loss when the transferor receives stock and boot with a value under the transferor's adjusted basis in the contributed property. When a transferor receives boot in addition to stock, the transferor must reduce his or her basis in the stock received by the value of the boot. In addition, the transferor must increase his or her basis in the stock received by the amount of gain recognized. The corporation increases its basis in the property received by the amount of the gain recognized by the transferor.

Proprietors incorporating their business will want the new corporation to assume the liabilities of the preexisting business. Treating the assumption of liabilities like the receipt of boot would require the new shareholder to recognize income. To facilitate the incorporation of ongoing businesses, Congress decided to treat the assumption of liabilities differently. Under section 357(a) of the Code, a transfer otherwise qualifying for nonrecognition under section 351 of the Code will remain tax-free to the transferor, even when the corporation assumes the transferor's liabilities or takes property subject to a liability, unless the liabilities exceed the transferor's basis in the contributed property or the transferor lacked a *bona fide* business purpose for transferring the liability and thereby only sought to escape federal income tax liability. Where the assumed liability exceeds the transferor's adjusted basis in the contributed property, the transferor recognizes a gain to the extent the liability exceeds the basis.[7]

Corporation owners starting or growing their businesses may find tax advantages in lending their corporations money rather than from making additional capital contributions. First, a corporation generally may deduct interest payments but cannot deduct dividends. Accordingly, structuring the transaction as one involving debt rather than equity helps to mitigate the double taxation of corporate income. Secondly, if the business goes poorly, the lender potentially could claim a bad debt deduction if the corporation cannot repay the loan.

Section 385 and case law prevents business owners from becoming too aggressive in their attempts to increase the assets of their corporations through "loans" that more closely resemble capital contributions than debt. Because a particular investment of money in a corporation can reflect characteristics of both debt and equity, courts have employed a multifactored analysis when classifying a particular arrangement as either debt or equity. Courts generally consider the following factors when examining a particular "loan," "note" or "bond":

- Names given the certificates evidencing the indebtedness
- Presence or absence of a fixed maturity date
- Source of the payments on the obligation
- Right to enforce payment of principal and interest
- Participation in management flowing as a result of the loan

---

7. Section 357(c) of the Code.

- Subordination
- Intent of the parties
- "Thin" or inadequate capitalization
- Identity of interest between the creditor and the stockholder
- Payment of interest only out of dividend money
- Ability to obtain loans other than from lending institutions
- Extent to which the funds were used to acquire capital assets
- Failure of the corporation to repay on the due date

Courts examine the facts of the arrangement—both its form and its substance—in light of these factors to see whether the arrangement is more like debt or like equity. For example, if the corporation purposefully and systematically subordinates its payments to the putative lender in favor of all other creditors of the corporation, this fact suggests that the transfer is more like a capital contribution than a loan.

A related issue is original issue discount ("OID"). If the corporation issues a long-term debt instrument for a price less than its face value, the difference is OID. In general, holders of these instruments must include OID in gross income over the term of the issue, regardless of accounting method. This rule applies even though OID will not be paid until maturity. Issuers of publicly offered OID instruments must report OID to the IRS for inclusion in Publication 1212. Under section 6049, brokers and other middlemen must file annual information returns (Form 1099-OID) with the IRS and forward a copy to the instrument holder of record. Any OID included in taxable income in any tax year should be added to the taxpayer's basis for purposes of determining gain or loss on any future disposition.

B. S Corporations

Section 1371 of the Code provides that, except as otherwise provided in Subchapter S, Code provisions applicable to C corporations will apply as well to S corporations. Accordingly, the nonrecognition rules of section 351 of the Code apply regardless of whether the transferee operates as a C corporation or an S corporation.

C. Partnership Contributions

Similar rules apply to capital contributions to partnerships. Section 721(a) of the Code provides that a transferor need not recognize gain realized on the transfer of property to a partnership in exchange for a partnership interest. Section 721(a) of the Code only imposes the exchange requirement, unlike section 351(a) of the Code that further requires transferors to control 80% of the corporation's voting shares and each other class of stock immediately after the transfer. The partner has a basis in his or her partnership interest equal to his or her adjusted basis in the contributed property, plus any amount recognized as a result of the contribution. The partnership has a basis in the property equal to the property's adjusted basis in the hands of the contributing partner, plus any amount recognized as a result of the contribution. If a partner contributes money to the partnership, the partner's basis in the partnership interest equals the value of money contributed. However, if a partnership is an investment company (within the meaning of section 351(e) of the Code), then section 721 of the Code does not afford nonrecognition treatment to realized gains from contributed property.

Again, the reader should observe that section 721 of the Code offers nonrecognition treatment to realized gains from property contributed to a partnership, not *services*. The law treats the receipt of a partnership interest in consideration for services rendered, whether past or future services, as compensation income in the year the individual receives the partnership interest. Different rules apply, however, when a person receives only a profits interest in consideration for services rendered. For example, if Taxpayer A contributes $100,000 to the partnership and Taxpayer B contributes her managerial genius, if Taxpayers A and B agree to split gains and losses evenly, and if Taxpayer A will get his entire investment back at liquidation before they split the remaining assets, then Taxpayer B will recognize no income upon the receipt of the profits interest because B has no interest in the original capital upon liquidation. Taxpayer B will recognize income, however, when the partnership actually allocates profits to her. In Rev. Rul. 93-27, 1993-2 C.B. 343, the IRS has ruled that the receipt of only a profits interest in a partnership does not constitute a taxable event unless (i) the profits interest represents a substantially certain and predictable income stream, (ii) the individual disposes of the profits interest within two years of receipt or (iii) the individual receives a limited partnership interest in a publicly traded partnership.

Several other Code provisions affect capital contributions by partners. The first provision governs the treatment of contributed property that had appreciated in the hands of the partner prior to its contribution. Section 704(c) (1)(A) of the Code provides that partners must share the income, gain, loss or deduction with respect to property contributed by a partner so as to take account of the variation between the basis of the property to the partnership and its fair market value at the time of contribution. For example, Taxpayer A has an office building, with an adjusted basis of $100,000 and a fair market value of $200,000. A contributes the building to partnership ABC. Ten years later, the partnership sells the building for $350,000. Ignoring depreciation, the transaction would have the following results: (i) the partnership must allocate to A the first $100,000 of the gain on the sale of the building and (ii) the partnership can allocate the remaining $150,000 as it sees fit, provided such allocation has substantial economic effect (see discussion of substantial economic effect below). The reader should note with respect to depreciation, that section 704(c)(1)(a) of the Code normally has the effect of shifting a disproportionate amount of subsequent depreciation deductions away from the contributing partner. To prevent partnerships from escaping the effects of section 704(c)(1)(A) of the Code by distributing the property to a partner other than the contributing partner, Congress enacted section 704(c)(1)(B) of the Code. This section provides that the contributing partner must recognize as much gain upon the distribution of contributed property as under the provisions of section 704(c)(1)(A) of the Code, unless the property distribution occurs more than seven years after its contribution.

Furthermore, section 737 of the Code provides that any partner who (i) transfers appreciated property to a partnership and (ii) receives other property from the partnership within five years of the contribution must recognize the pre-contribution gain in the contributed property to the extent that the distribution exceeded the partner's basis in the partnership interest.

Finally, section 724 of the Code limits a partner's ability to re-characterize property by contributing the property to a partnership. If a partner contributes an unrealized receivable to a partnership, section 724 of the Code characterizes any gain or loss recognized by the partnership on the disposition of the unrealized receivable as ordinary gain or loss—even if the partnership holds the property as a capital asset. The same holds true for inventory, provided that the partnership disposes of the inventory within five years of the contribution. No analogous rules apply to contributions to corporations.

4.06   Operations

New business owners should plan to minimize the tax consequences of contributing capital when forming their entities. But the planning cannot end with the contribution phase. As the new business reaps profits (or generates losses), important tax consequences will result from the initial selection of an entity through which to conduct the business. Furthermore, as discussed in Chapter 5 (Tax Reporting and Compliance) the selection of a particular type of entity can impose certain tax accounting methods on a business. The nature of the business itself may require a particular method of accounting. Tax accounting principles govern the timing of income and deductions. While tax accounting methods will not affect a taxpayer's lifetime gross income, these methods can accelerate the taxpayer's inclusion of income or can defer inclusion until later years. Given the time value of money, taxpayers generally will want to accelerate deductions and defer income. Tax accounting rules limit the taxpayer's ability to control the timing of income and deductions. Still, taxpayers working within these rules can achieve tax benefits through careful planning. Taxpayers also will want to remain mindful in early years of how they treat items of income and expense during their formative years, because the taxpayer must obtain prior permission to change a method of accounting from the IRS once the taxpayer has established a method of tax accounting for a particular item.

A.   Gains, Losses, and Their Allocation

1.   C Corporations

When a C corporation generates taxable income in a tax year, it must pay the corporate income tax on this income at the rates set forth in section 11 of the Code. The shareholders do not pay income tax upon corporate earnings and profits until the corporation distributes the earnings and profits to them by means of a dividend.

When a C corporation's deductions for a given year exceed its gross income, the corporation has generated a net operating loss. The corporation can utilize losses from lean years to offset income in fat years. Section 172 of the Code allows corporations to carry losses back for two years and carry losses forward for 20 years. However, shareholders cannot utilize corporate losses to offset their individual income. The losses remain trapped within the corporation and do not flow through to the shareholders. Accordingly, if a C corporation never earns a profit, the losses never will generate a taxable benefit. This potential for not deriving the benefits from losses constitutes an important downside to utilizing C corporations.

2.   S Corporations

An S corporation passes through to the shareholders any income, gain, loss, deduction or credit generated by the corporation. The S corporation generally does not pay an entity-level corporate tax. The S corporation passes these items through to the shareholders in direct proportion to their stockholdings. The shareholders must report the income with the same character as the income had in the hands of the S corporation. The shareholders' basis in their stock will increase by the amount of the income passed through to them. It is important to note that shareholders of an S corporation must pay income tax on the taxable income allocable to their shares, *regardless of whether the corporation distributes funds to the taxpayers with which to pay the tax*. In other words, if an S corporation recognizes substantial income during a taxable year but decides to reinvest all of the profits, the shareholders still must pay the income tax on the portion of the gains allocable to their shares. Their basis in their stock, however, increases by the amount of the taxable gain.

Net operating losses flow through to the shareholders as well. Under section 1366(d) of the Code, however, shareholders can only deduct their losses to the extent that the net operating loss allocable to their shares does not exceed their adjusted basis in their shares plus the shareholders' basis in loans to the corporation. The pass-through of losses to S corporation shareholders reduces their basis in their stock and then their basis in loans to the corporation by the amount of the loss.

The Code imposes two additional limits on an S corporation shareholder's ability to deduct losses. First, under section 465 of the Code, shareholders can deduct such losses only up to the amount the shareholder is "at risk" in the investment. The following factors determine the shareholder's risk:

- Amount the shareholder has invested in the corporation
- Debts for which the shareholder faces personal liability relating to the activity or for which the shareholder has pledged property
- Shareholder's share of the corporation's qualified nonrecourse financing

Second, shareholders of S corporations looking to deduct losses also must comply with the passive loss rules of section 469 of the Code. A purely passive investor ordinarily can only deduct these passive losses to the extent of passive gains. If the shareholder fails to participate materially in the activity, the shareholder is a passive investor. "Material" participation requires that the taxpayers participate in the business regularly, continuously and substantially.

3. Partnerships

As with S corporations, partnership income, gains, expenses, deductions and credits flow through to the partners. The partners increase their basis in the partnership by the amount of income that flows through. Unlike S corporations, however, which must rigidly allocate income and deductions to shareholders according to their number of shares, partnerships have considerably more flexibility in allocating such items among partners under section 704(a) of the Code. Generally, the law will respect the allocation of income, gains, deductions, expenses or credits in the partnership agreement so long as the allocation has "substantial economic effect." If the allocation lacks substantial economic effect, then the law determines a partner's distributive share of partnership items in accordance with the partner's interest in the partnership (taking into account all the facts and circumstances). While the "substantial economic effect" regulations can prove somewhat onerous, they do afford something of a safe harbor when partners desire to make a special allocation.

First an allocation must have economic effect. For allocations under a partnership agreement to have economic effect, the partnership agreement must provide for the following:

- Partners must maintain capital accounts in accordance with the regulations under section 704 of the Code
- Partnership must make liquidating distributions in accordance with capital accounts
- Partners must be obligated to make up capital account deficits or have a qualified income offset in the partnership agreement[8]

---

8.   Treas. Reg. § 1.704-1(b)(2)(ii).

Furthermore, the effect must be "substantial," that is, the allocation must affect the dollars received by the partners independent of the tax consequences.[9]

As with a shareholder of an S corporation, a partner only can deduct losses allocated to the partner to the extent such losses do not exceed the partner's basis in the partnership interest, to the extent the partner is at risk in the venture, and to the extent allowed by the passive loss rules of section 469 of the Code. Generally, a limited partner cannot materially participate in the business for tax purposes. (Besides, such participation could endanger the limited partner's limited liability for other purposes.) However, a regulation does afford three narrow exceptions where a limited partner (i) has more than 500 hours of participation, (ii) materially participates in five of the last 10 years or (iii) has materially participated in any three prior years in a personal service activity.[10] In addition, in the case of certain real estate professionals, the limited partner rule is inapplicable.

B.   Research and Development

A popular strategy for start-up companies has been the research and development partnership ("R&D partnership"). It uses capital contributed by outside investors to finance research work of a firm ("start-up"), usually one with a promising base technology. Under this arrangement the following would occur:

- Start-up contributes the base technology to the R&D partnership
- Investors contribute capital as limited partners
- Start-up performs research work for the benefit of the R&D partnership that approximates in value the amount contributed by the limited partners
- Investors receive a return on their investment from royalties on the sale of products using the technology developed in the research program

The start-up generally has a right to "buy out" the interests of the investors at a formula price.

R&D partnerships provide start-ups with an opportunity to finance development work without using their own funds. The risks that the development work will be unsuccessful are shifted to the investors.

Originally, investors sought the tax benefits of being able to deduct the expense of the research work against ordinary income from all other sources. In addition, investors often were able to achieve substantial income from the royalties generated by product sales. In some cases, investors received a warrant to purchase shares of the start-up's stock, which also enhanced their

---

9.   Treas. Reg. § 1.704-1(b)(iii).
10.   Treas. Reg. § 1.469-5T(a).

total return. However, the "passive income" rules have substantially eroded the benefits of the R&D partnership from a tax perspective, and many investors have concerns about the illiquidity of their partnership interests.

In response to some of these drawbacks associated with R&D partnerships, some start-ups attempt to secure financing for development work by contributing the base technology to a new wholly owned subsidiary. Capital is raised by a public offering of "units" that consist of callable shares of common stock of the new subsidiary and warrants to purchase shares of common stock of the start-up. The start-up performs the development work on behalf of the subsidiary. The shares of the subsidiary's common stock, hopefully, appreciate in value upon the successful completion of the development work. The "call" feature allows the start-up to repurchase the technology from the subsidiary at a fixed price. Investors would still be able to share in the success of the technology, however, through the warrant component of the investment.

C. Tax Accounting for Start-Ups

Section 446 of the Code provides that taxpayers shall compute their taxable income under the accounting method by which the taxpayer regularly computes income in keeping the taxpayer's books, provided that the taxpayer regularly uses the method and that the method clearly reflects income. Otherwise, the IRS will select the accounting method it thinks most clearly reflects the taxpayer's income. The law requires two things of an accounting method: (i) consistency and (ii) a clear reflection of income. Section 446(d) of the Code provides that taxpayers conducting more than one trade or business can use different methods of accounting for each trade or business. Ordinarily, once a taxpayer has elected or established through consistent practice a particular method of accounting, the taxpayer must obtain the prior consent of the IRS before computing taxable income under the new method. Accordingly, taxpayers should plan carefully to adopt sound tax accounting practices early, rather than seeking permission later. The concept of "accounting method" includes not just the taxpayer's overall accounting scheme but also the treatment of particular accounting items.

Section 446(c) of the Code includes among permissible accounting methods the cash receipts and disbursements method and the accrual method. When computing taxable income under the cash method, a taxpayer includes all items that constitute gross income in the taxable year actually or constructively received and deducts all expenditures in the year actually made. Accrual method taxpayers include income in the year when all the events have occurred that fix the right to receive the income and the amount of income can be determined with reasonable accuracy. Under the accrual method, a taxpayer can take a liability into account in the tax year in which the following occurs:

- All the events have occurred that fix the fact of the liability
- The amount of the liability can be determined with reasonable accuracy

- Economic performance has occurred with respect to the liability[11]

Because the use of the cash method usually results in the deferral of income, most taxpaying businesses would prefer to compute their taxable income under the cash method. A number of limitations exist, however, on the use of the cash method. Indeed, current law disfavors the use of the cash method, requiring many businesses to compute taxable income using the accrual method.

Section 448 of the Code imposes limitations on the use of the cash method that could affect entity selection deliberations. With a few exceptions, C corporations, partnerships with C corporations as partners and tax shelters cannot use the cash method to compute taxable income. Two pertinent exceptions to this general rule exist. First, personal service corporations can use the cash method. Second, a C corporation or partnership can still use the cash method provided its average annual gross receipts for the three-taxable-year period ending with the prior taxable year does not exceed $5 million. Section 461(i)(3) of the Code defines tax shelter to include (i) an entity that has offered interests in the entity for sale in an offering requiring federal or state registration, (ii) syndicates and (iii) other tax shelters. Any publicly traded entity must use the accrual method. Section 1256(e)(3)(13) of the Code defines "syndicate" to include any entity (other than a C corporation) in which 35% of the entity's losses are allocable to limited partners or limited entrepreneurs. This provision could prevent many limited partnerships from using the cash method. In the early 1990s, some tax practitioners expressed concern that the law would deem limited liability companies as syndicates, and therefore as tax shelters unable to use the cash method because of the limited liability of members. The IRS determined in a series of rulings that limited liability companies could utilize the cash method provided that a sufficient number of members in the company actively participated in the management of the business. Business enterprises otherwise eligible for the cash method will want to consider these limitations on cash method use when choosing an entity form.

One other important limitation, which pertains to the nature of the business enterprise, applies to the use of the cash method. Treas. Reg. § 1.471-1 requires taxpayers to use inventories whenever taxpayers produce income from the manufacture, purchase or sale of merchandise. As of 2002 a taxpayer whose average annual gross receipts do not exceed $1,000,000 and certain taxpayers whose average annual gross receipts do not exceed $10,000,000 are generally not required to use inventories or the accrual method of accounting. However, as stated in Treas. Reg. § 1.446-1(c)(2)(i) taxpayers required to use inventories must compute taxable income using the accrual method. Partnerships, limited

---

11. Treas. Reg. § 1.446-1(c).

liability companies or personal service corporations that sell personal services generally can use the cash method.

The law affords some flexibility to taxpayers required to keep inventories. Taxpayers can elect various inventory flow assumptions (e.g., first-in, first-out, "FIFO"; or last-in, first-out, "LIFO") and various ways of valuing the closing inventory. Generally, in times of increasing costs, the LIFO method will result in lower closing inventory. The lower the closing inventory, the higher the cost of goods sold. A higher cost of goods sold means lower gross income. Generally, under section 472 of the Code, taxpayers who use the LIFO method for tax reporting purposes, however, must use the LIFO method for all purposes. Entrepreneurs required to utilize inventories will want to retain competent professionals to assist them in keeping inventories and to prevent costly mistakes.

Some erroneous accounting methods, including inventory methods, can have a cumulative effect. While a three-year statute of limitations applies to most tax assessments, the IRS can utilize a special adjustment under section 481 of the Code when it compels a taxpayer to change from an erroneous method of tax accounting. While an accounting error only affects the timing of income, not a taxpayer's lifetime income, most taxpayers would prefer not to pay tax on income from a section 481 adjustment resulting from several dozen years of cumulative accounting errors. Entrepreneurs should seek professional help, especially in the inventory context, both to avail themselves of planning opportunities and to avoid problems in audits down the road.

Finally, entity selection can affect a business's ability to choose its taxable year. Most taxpayers report on the calendar year. Individuals report on the calendar year. Sole proprietorships and disregarded entities effectively report according to the same taxable year as their owners. Those owned and operated by individuals will report on the calendar year. Partnerships report according to the taxable year of those partners having an aggregate interest in partnership profits and capital of more than 50%, and, if none, to the taxable year of all principal partners, or, if none, to the calendar year by default. C corporations, however, can adopt a fiscal year different from the calendar year. Personal service corporations can adopt a fiscal year, provided they can demonstrate, to the satisfaction of the IRS, the existence of a business purpose. Similar rules apply to S corporations.

4.07   Distributions and Liquidations

Thus far, this chapter has examined the tax consequences of money flowing into a business and of the generation of taxable business income. This final section will consider the tax consequences as money and property flow out of a business into the hands of its owners.

A. Corporations

C Corporations make two kinds of distributions to shareholders. First, a C corporation can make a distribution to a shareholder without receiving anything in return. Second, a C corporation can make a distribution in exchange for its own stock.

When a C corporation makes a distribution of money or property to shareholders in their capacity as owners without receiving any of its stock in return, the tax consequences to the shareholders depend upon whether the distribution constitutes a return *on* the shareholders' investment. To determine the tax consequences of such a distribution, the law utilizes the corporate account earnings and profits ("E&P"). Generally speaking, E&P is a corporation's "economic" income. It includes taxable income, plus excluded receipts (e.g., interest on tax-exempt bonds), minus nondeductible expenditures (e.g., federal income tax). Section 316(a) of the Code defines a dividend as any distribution of property (or money) from a C corporation's accumulated E&P or from its E&P for the taxable year calculated as of the end of the year. Shareholders must include dividends as ordinary income, yet once again these distributions will receive preferential tax rate treatment at the long-term capital gains rates of 5% or 15%. To the extent the distribution exceeds the corporation's E&P, the law treats the distribution as a return *of* the shareholder's investment. If such a distribution exceeds the shareholder's basis in the stock, the shareholder must recognize a gain on the distribution. A distribution that is not taxable to a C corporation shareholder reduces the shareholder's basis in the stock by the value of the distribution. On the corporation's side, when a C corporation distributes property, the corporation must recognize any gain if the fair market value of the distributed property exceeds the corporation's basis in the property. The corporation adds any recognized gains from the distribution to its E&P, but must subtract the fair market value of the distributed property from the E&P.

Section 317 of the Code defines "redemption" as a corporation distributing property in exchange for its own stock. The law will not always treat a stock redemption as a return *of* the shareholder's investment, qualifying for capital gains treatment on any gains. Such a redemption will qualify for capital gains treatment under section 302(b) of the Code as a "payment in exchange for stock" only if the redemption meets any of the following four criteria:

- Redemption is not essentially equivalent to a dividend
- Shareholder, after the redemption, owns less than 50% of the corporation's common stock and owns, after the redemption, less than 80% of the voting power that the shareholder previously held
- Redemption completely terminates the shareholder's interest in the corporation
- Redemption partially liquidates a noncorporate shareholder's interest.

Each of these criteria has further guidelines. Furthermore, attribution rules apply to the stock ownership requirements. For example, the law treats a husband as owning his wife's stock, a parent as owning her daughter's stock, and so on. If the law treats the redemption as a dividend, the distributing corporation must subtract the value of the distributed property from its E&P. If the law treats the redemption as the corporation's purchase of its stock, the corporation must reduce its E&P by the ratable share of E&P attributable to the redeemed stock.

At this point in the discussion one idea might occur to a law student or reader. If a corporation wanted to help shareholders avoid the double taxation of corporate income, could the corporation simply not pay dividends and retain its E&P and invest it in the stock market, therefore helping the shareholder avoid all taxation on the corporate income (even though the rates have been reduced on dividend income to equal those on long-term capital gains)? No doubt this possibility occurred to Congress, as evidenced by the two corporate penalty taxes it has enacted—the accumulated earnings tax and the personal holding company tax. Section 531 of the Code imposes a tax on corporations formed or availed of for the purpose of avoiding the income tax with respect to its shareholders by permitting E&P to accumulate, instead of distributing the E&P. Beginning in 2003 the Code imposes an additional 15% tax on the accumulated earnings of the corporation in addition to their regular tax liability. The corporation is allowed a $250,000 accumulated earnings credit or $150,000 credit for personal service corporations. Accordingly, C corporations cannot allow E&P to accumulate beyond the reasonable needs of the business. So, while state corporate law may limit the power of a corporation to pay dividends on the one hand, the accumulated earnings tax effectively requires corporations to declare dividends (or expand) on the other.

The accumulated earnings tax does not apply to personal holdings companies. Section 541 of the Code also taxes at the highest marginal rate for individuals the undistributed income of personal holdings companies. This tax generally applies to closely held corporations in which no more than five individuals own more than 50% of the stock and which earn too great a proportion of their income from dividends, interest, royalties, rents, and the like, without distributing sufficient dividends.

Several other means exist to avoid the potential double taxation of C corporation income. First, entrepreneurs and professionals forming closely held corporations can pass some of the corporation's gross income to the shareholders by compensating the shareholders for services rendered to the corporation. For example, if a shareholder serves as the corporation's president, the corporation can compensate the president for her services. The corporation can claim a deduction for the compensation paid, under section 162 of the Code. The shareholder includes the amount in ordinary income. The corporation must pay its share of FICA taxes and pay the unemployment insurance on the compensation. The employee must pay its share of the Social Security and Medicare taxes on the compensation. Even with the employment taxes, the shareholder ends up with a larger share of the income than if the corporation paid the entity-level tax and then distributed a dividend from its E&P. Such compensation must be reasonable. The IRS, otherwise, will deny the corporation the deduction. A host of cases exists addressing this question of what constitutes "reasonable" compensation. Although limits of reasonableness exist, compensation affords one method of mitigating the total tax liability on corporate income.

One other way to mitigate the tax liability of a corporation concerns the corporation's capital structure. While the Code allows no deduction for dividends paid, section 163 of the Code does permit a deduction for interest paid or accrued on indebtedness. This eliminates the portion of the entity-level tax on the interest paid. Generally, the Code affords more favorable tax consequences to debt than to equity. A corporation that can claim a dividends-received deduction (discussed below), however, would prefer the dividend. Corporations have experimented with a host of types of securities in an effort to obtain the favorable tax treatment accorded to debt. As noted above, there is a jungle of cases in which courts juggle myriad factors determining whether or not indebtedness really exists. An owner bears more economic risk than a lender. The intention of the parties matters in this determination. Courts also look at the formal rights and remedies on the face of the securities or instruments themselves. The thin or inadequate capitalization of a corporation can push a court to deem putative debt as really equity. Courts examine the economic reality of the corporation's capital structure. Limitations exist on the ability of corporations to utilize debt to mitigate tax liability, but planning opportunities remain.

To prevent triple taxation of corporate income when a corporation holds stock in another corporation, Congress enacted section 243 of the Code, which allows corporations a dividends-received deduction. Generally, section 243 of the Code allows corporations to deduct an amount equal to 70% of the dividends received from domestic corporations. If the corporation owns 20% or more of the voting stock of the issuing corporation, then the dividends-received deduction increases to 80%. If the dividend recipient operates as a small business investment company under the 1958 Small Business Investment Act, the deduction increases to 100%. Section 243(b)(1) of the Code makes a 100% dividends-received deduction available for corporations receiving dividends from members of the same affiliated group of corporations.

Finally, if a corporation liquidates, section 336(a) of the Code provides that the corporation generally will recognize gain (or loss) as if the corporation had sold all of its assets to its shareholders at fair market value. Thus, the corporation pays an entity-level tax at liquidation. Section 336(d) of the Code imposes limits on a corporation's ability to recognize losses at liquidation when the corporation does not distribute the property to the shareholders pro rata or when the corporation received the property under section 351 within five years of the liquidating distribution. Congress imposed the entity-level tax on liquidating distributions in 1986, repudiating prior corporate tax law established in *General Utilities & Operating Co. v. Helvering*[12] and thereafter codified in the Code.

Normally, the sale of stock constitutes the sale of a capital asset. While beneficial tax rates apply to capital gains, the law limits the ability of individual taxpayers to claim capital losses. Generally speaking, an individual taxpayer only may claim capital losses to the extent of capital gains plus the lower of either (i) $3,000 or (ii) the excess of capital losses over capital gains. Even with the capital loss carryforward/carryback rules of section 1212 of the Code, an individual trying to sell his stock in his business for a loss may have trouble gaining an income tax benefit from the full amount of the loss—particularly if the individual has no capital gains to offset. A $3,000-per-year capital loss deduction may not afford the individual much income tax relief.

One exception to this rule exists for the sale of "section 1244 stock" for a loss. Section 1244 of the Code allows an individual to treat his loss on the sale of section 1244 stock as an ordinary loss—that is, not subject to the $3,000 capital loss limitation in section 1211 of the Code. Section 1244 of the Code limits to $50,000 ($100,000 for a married couple filing a joint return) the amount of loss such an individual can treat as an ordinary loss. "Section 1244 stock" means stock issued by a domestic corporation for money or other property in a "small business corporation" which during the period of its five most recent taxable years derived more than 50% of its aggregate gross receipts from sources other than royalties, rents, dividends, interests, annuities and sales or exchanges of stocks or securities. A corporation is a "small business corporation" if the aggregate amount of money and other property received by the corporation for stock, as a contribution to capital and as paid-in surplus does not exceed $1,000,000.

B.   S Corporations

Income of an S corporation passes through to its shareholders, who must pay tax on the income. Accordingly, S corporations themselves do not generate E&P. Because the shareholders already have paid the tax on the income, when an S corporation distributes some (not all) of its property to its shareholders in their capacity as shareholders, the law treats the distribution as a return *of* the shareholder's investment, not a return *on* the investment. Generally, shareholders decrease their basis in their stock by the value of the distributed property and only recognize a gain to the extent the property's value exceeds their basis in their stock. S corporations, however, must be careful when appreciated property is distributed to shareholders. Section 1363(d) requires

---

12.   296 U.S. 200 (1935).

S corporations to recognize a gain upon the distribution of appreciated property equal to the amount of the property's value exceeding its basis. This gain will flow through to the shareholders.

S corporations can have accumulated E&P, either because of merging with a C corporation with E&P or because of making an S corporation election after having operated profitability as a C corporation. The law treats distributions from E&P as dividends—currently taxed at capital gains rates of 5% or 15%. To determine the tax treatment of S corporation distributions when the S corporation has accumulated E&P, section 1368 of the Code requires S corporations to maintain a special "accumulated adjustments account" ("AAA"). AAA measures the amount of earnings accumulated by an S corporation for which the shareholders already have paid the tax. The law permits an S corporation to distribute first from its AAA. When such distributions reduce the AAA to zero, then the corporation begins to distribute from its accumulated E&P. Shareholders reduce their basis in their stock by the value of the property distributed from AAA and recognize a capital gain to the extent the value of the property exceeds their basis in the stock. Shareholders must include distributions from E&P as ordinary income (taxed as capital gains rates) and do not adjust their stock basis under section 1368 of the Code.

When an S corporation distributes property to shareholders, the S corporation recognizes a gain to the extent the property's fair market value exceeds the corporation's basis in the property. This gain flows through to the shareholders.

S corporations have the opposite problem from C corporations with respect to compensation for shareholder employees. The shareholder must pay ordinary income taxes on the S corporation's income, regardless of whether such income flows through or is paid as compensation. However, the shareholder only pays self-employment taxes—Social Security and Medicare—on the compensation. In Rev. Rul. 74-44, 1974-1 C.B. 287, the IRS has ruled that an S corporation cannot pay a shareholder/employee an unreasonably low salary to avoid self-employment taxes.

When an S corporation liquidates, the same rules apply as when a C corporation liquidates. Doing business as an S corporation affords investors the opportunity to use a tax-free reorganization as an exit strategy, if the reorganization qualifies under sections 354 and 368 of the Code.

C. Partnerships

Because the partners pay tax on the partnership income that flows through to them, the law generally treats distributions to a partner as a return *of* the partner's investment, to the extent the distribution does not exceed the partner's basis in the partnership interest—i.e., the partner's "outside basis." The tax treatment depends upon whether the partnership makes a current distribution to a continuing partner or makes a distribution in liquidation of the partner's interest. When a partnership makes a current distribution of money, the partner will recognize a capital gain only to the extent that the money distributed exceeds the partner's outside basis immediately before the distribution. When a partnership repays a debt, the law treats each partner as having received a distribution of money equal to the partner's share of the liability.

Section 731 of the Code does not treat the current distribution of property to a partner as a taxable event. Upon receipt of the property distribution, the partner must reduce the partner's outside basis in the partnership by the partnership's basis in the distributed property. The recipient partner takes a transferred basis in the distributed property—i.e., the partnership's basis in the property. If the partnership's basis in the distributed property exceeds the partner's outside basis, then the distribution wipes out the partner's outside basis in the partnership, and the partner takes a basis in the partnership equal to the partner's outside basis in the partnership prior to the distribution. The character of the distributed property also transfers to the receiving partner. For example, when a partnership distributes an unrealized receivable to a partner, the partner must recognize ordinary gain when subsequently selling or collecting the distributed property. Likewise, a partner must recognize ordinary income when selling distributed inventory, if the partner makes the sale within five years of the distribution, even if the partner holds the inventory as a capital asset.

Partnerships generally do not recognize gain or loss upon the distribution of property to partners. Thus, the law treats partnership property distributions differently than S corporation property distributions, which can trigger tax to the corporation. When a partnership distributes property to a partner and the partner recognizes gain or loss, or a partner sells the partner's partnership interest to a new partner, the partnership may elect under section 754 of the Code to adjust the partnership's basis in its property ("inside basis") as set forth in sections 743 and 734 of the Code. The partnership increases its "inside basis" by the amount of gain recognized by the distributee (or departing) partner. When a partner sells her partnership interest, with a 754 election in effect, the law reserves the benefit of the stepped-up inside basis for the new partner. When a partner recognizes a gain upon a distribution, with a 754 election in effect, all the partners share the inside basis adjustment.

A self-employed individual must pay the self-employment tax on the individual's net earnings from self-employment. A general partner pays self-employment tax on the partner's entire distributive share. A limited partner's distributive share does not constitute net earnings from self-employment. A member's distributive share of a limited liability company's income may or may not constitute net earnings from self-employment. In a manager-managed limited liability company, the law might subject some or all of a managing member's distributive share to the self-employment tax. In a member-managed limited liability company, all income allocated to the members might fall liable to the self-employment tax. In 1997, the IRS proposed regulations to clarify the self-employment tax issues faced by limited partners and members of limited liability companies, but the IRS to date has not adopted final regulations.[13]

4.08   Conclusion

Although Congress is considering its elimination, as of now, double taxation constitutes the principal disadvantage of using C corporations. Although dividends are currently taxed at lower rates than ordinary income, there are still additional taxes levied on previously taxed corporate earnings distributed to shareholders. This single fact continues to support the use of pass-through entities (partnerships and S-corporations) for new businesses. In addition, while the current top tax rate for both individuals and corporations is 35%, individual tax rates start at 10% while corporate rates start at 15%. At lower levels of business income (common for start-up periods), this adds to the advantage enjoyed by pass-through entities.

However, if double taxation/tax rate issues are not of primary concern, C corporations afford business owners more flexibility in devising compensation and fringe benefit packages for shareholder employees. This can produce a number of additional tax planning opportunities for business owners.

When choosing between partnership or S corporation status, most business owners will prefer partnership treatment for the following reasons:

(i)   Partnerships can make special allocations of income and deductions.

(ii)   Generally, the distribution of property to a partner does not trigger a taxable event (unless the partner contributed appreciated property to the partnership).

(iii)   Partners can include their share of partnership debt in their basis in the partnership interest.

The use of S corporations requires the rigid allocation of income and deduction among shareholders. Also, property distributions will trigger a taxable event that flows through to the shareholders. S corporations must take care not to inadvertently terminate the S corporation election. The use of S corporations does provide two tax planning benefits. First, an S corporation shareholder need not treat all S corporation income as self-employment income subject to the self-employment tax. Second, investors forming businesses as S corporations can use tax-free reorganizations under sections 354 and 368 of the Code as an exit strategy.

---

13.   Prop. Treas. Reg. § 1.402(a)-2(b).

Tax Reporting and Compliance

David T. Collins

Bellarmine University
Louisville, KY

Contents

Tax Reporting and Compliance

5.01   Preliminary Considerations

Nearly everyone is aware of the pervasiveness of taxes imposed on a wide array of business and personal activities. Certainly the large number of different taxes stems from the multiple jurisdictions (federal, state and local) that must use taxation as their primary source of revenue. However, it also stems from the multiple ways in which taxes may be imposed, and the knowledgeable business manager understands not only the impact of multiple tax jurisdictions but of multiple tax bases. The goal of effective tax planning is not simply to minimize any one particular tax, but to minimize the total cost of all taxes to the company.

Adam Smith, in *The Wealth of Nations*, was one of the first economists to suggest standards for taxation. One of his standards was that taxes should be equitable or fair. There is much disagreement on how "fair" a particular tax may be; however, there is much agreement that for fairness to exist, taxes should be related to some measurable event. That is, the amount of tax to be paid should be related to a defined tax base and not simply a random amount imposed by the tax authorities. This results in taxes generally being linked to either transactions or activities.

Transaction-based taxes occur only when a particular event takes place. Sales, use and excise taxes are examples of transaction-based taxes that are imposed by a variety of federal, state and local tax jurisdictions. The value-added tax ("VAT") is another type of transaction-based tax that is imposed by a number of foreign (non-U.S.) tax jurisdictions and can be very important to businesses engaging in transactions within those foreign jurisdictions.[1] In theory, transaction-based taxes can be avoided simply by not engaging in the taxed transaction. In practice, while avoiding the tax may be possible in selected cases (e.g., taxes on cigarettes), it may not be possible in more general cases (e.g., sales taxes on office supplies). Thus, transaction-based tax planning coincides with good business planning—to acquire items subject to taxation at the lowest price possible.[2] This not only minimizes the tax cost, but also minimizes the overall expense to the company. While transaction-based tax planning is not unimportant, it is limited when compared to the planning possibilities for activity-based taxes.

Activity-based taxes are imposed on the ongoing activities of an individual or a business. For these taxes, taxpayers must maintain records of the activity, summarize the results at periodic intervals and pay the appropriate tax. Income and ad valorem property taxes are examples of activity-based taxes, and each type may have multiple opportunities to reduce taxes through effective planning. For many firms, ad valorem taxes (on both real and personal property) can be minimized by decisions on where to locate the property and on insuring that the taxing authorities have appropriately determined the property's tax valuation. In some cases, these taxes also can be ameliorated by agreements between the firm and the tax jurisdiction to reduce or eliminate the taxes as an enticement for the firm to locate (or remain) in a particular area. Such opportunities should not be overlooked. However, once siting decisions have been made, as with transaction-based taxes, the tax planning considerations are limited when compared to income-based taxes. Given this fact, the remainder of the discussion will focus on income-based taxes and the tax planning opportunities available to minimize them.

A. Tax Planning

The objective of management decision-making is to maximize shareholder value, which is usually defined as maximizing the value of the firm and usually operationalized as maximizing firm profits. Since taxes reduce firm profits, maximizing profitability is, at least partly, effected by minimizing taxes. Tax planning, then, is focused on tax minimization, with a particular emphasis on minimizing income-based taxes.

One approach to minimizing taxes is to alter the characteristics of an activity or transaction to achieve a particular tax objective. For example, with ad valorem property taxes, it may be preferable to lease the property

---

1.   Value-added taxes can be a very powerful revenue source. Michigan is the only U.S.-based tax jurisdiction that uses this type of tax. The Michigan Single Business Tax, enacted in 1976 to replace the state's corporate income tax, is a modified VAT system.

2.   This may not be true for value-added taxes. That is, it may not be in the firm's best interest to "minimize" its value added in order to minimize the tax. However, the cost of the tax must be considered when assessing how much of a product's total value added can be captured by the firm.

rather than own it. With a properly structured lease, it may be possible to control the "tax cost" to the firm regardless of subsequent changes in property valuations or tax rates. For employment taxes, using independent contractors rather than employees may reduce total payroll taxes to the firm. Still, one should not disregard the joint effects of multiple tax rates across multiple tax bases. Forgoing one tax at a lower tax rate that results in paying a different tax at a higher tax rate is not good tax planning—particularly if the first tax offsets the second. For example, if reducing (deductible) property or payroll taxes results in higher income taxes, the total tax cost to the firm could be higher.

It also can be important to carefully consider both the tax and non-tax outcomes of the transaction. Changing some characteristics of a transaction to achieve a particular tax objective should be weighed against the desired non-tax objectives of the activity. For example, in the employee vs. independent contractor case, the firm's ability to directly control the work of the employee may provide benefits that exceed the additional payroll taxes incurred. The problem here is that many non-tax factors may not be monetary, or even quantifiable, and so difficult to evaluate against the very real monetary tax cost. The measurement difficulty should not prevent managers from considering the impact of the non-tax factors in their tax planning decisions.

B.   Tax Entity

Chapter 4 (Tax Aspects of Forming and Organizing a New Entity) discusses the overall tax implications and consequences of different business entities: corporations, partnerships, limited liability companies and others. Each has its own unique tax considerations that were discussed in that chapter and will not be repeated here. However, it is often useful to consider the tax consequences of groups of related entities. For example, what is the overall tax picture presented by two partnerships that jointly own a corporate entity? How does the corporate entity relate to the partnerships? How does each partnership relate to its own group of partners (investors)? Are there any tax benefits that can be achieved in such an arrangement?

One approach to tax planning is to recognize that total income tax incurred can be reduced by shifting income from an entity with a high tax rate to an entity with a low tax rate. Similar effects can be achieved by shifting deductions from the low tax rate entity to the high tax rate entity. The first case can occur when an individual stockholder is hired by the corporate entity. The stockholder is paid a salary (commensurate with employment services provided to the corporation) that is taxed at a presumably lower individual tax rate and that also escapes the double taxation issue associated with dividend distributions. The second case underlies the common advice to adopt S-Corporation status during start up years when the business produces losses. The losses are shifted from the corporate entity (with a current low tax rate because it has no taxable income) to the individual investors (who presumably are facing higher individual tax rates).

Other income- or deduction-shifting possibilities exist. Consider the case of the two partnerships that jointly own a corporate entity described above. With proper planning, each source of income or deduction can be assigned to one of the three entities so as to minimize the overall tax cost to the individual partners in the partnerships. Similar effects can be accomplished in a completely corporate (i.e., parent and subsidiary) group or in a noncorporate (only partnerships) structure.

While the tax benefits of income or deduction shifting are real, they must be structured with care. Tax shifting usually involves related parties in a way that the parties, in the aggregate, are financially better off by the tax savings generated. Congress has long recognized that such activities reduce tax revenues and has often closed such avenues for tax planning. Indeed, the IRS has been vigilant in policing related party transactions that produce beneficial tax shifts. If the transaction serves no genuine business purpose (other that tax avoidance) the IRS may disallow the transaction.

C. Tax Time Period

Each taxpayer (whether individual or business) must determine taxable income on an annual period called a tax year. The calendar year is the most common tax year; however, some taxpayers are allowed to select a fiscal year for their tax year. Chapter 4 (Tax Aspects of Forming and Organizing a New Business) notes the following:

- Individuals report on the calendar year
- Sole proprietorships and disregarded entities effectively report according to the same taxable year as their owners
- Partnerships report according to the taxable year of principal partners
- Personal service corporations can adopt a fiscal year if they demonstrate the existence of a business purpose
- Similar rules apply to S corporations
- C corporations can adopt a fiscal year different from the calendar year

Each taxpayer adopts a tax year when the first tax return is filed. This first tax year rule must be made by the original due date (not including any extensions) of your first tax return. As noted in Chapter 4, once a tax year has been adopted, it is necessary to obtain IRS approval to change to a different tax year.

Substantially all individuals and most businesses use the calendar tax year (the 12 consecutive months from January 1 to December 31). Any taxpayer can adopt a calendar tax year. If any of the following apply, the taxpayer must adopt a calendar tax year:

- Taxpayer does not keep adequate records
- There is no natural annual accounting period other than the calendar year
- Current tax year does not qualify as a fiscal year

Since most individuals do not keep adequate records and/or do not have a natural annual accounting period other than the calendar year, they are required to adopt the calendar tax year. However, many businesses may be able to meet those rules and adopt a fiscal tax year. A fiscal tax year is any 12 consecutive months ending on the last day of any month except December. With proper record keeping it also is possible to select a 52/53-week tax year that ends on the same day of the week (although not necessarily on the last day of the month).

The benefit of a fiscal tax year is that it allows a business to include all of its normal business cycle within a particular tax year. For example, a lawn mower manufacturer may find a June 1 to May 31 fiscal year advantageous since it includes all of the production, shipping and sales efforts for its product within one annual cycle. If the firm had stayed with a calendar year, the bulk of production activities would be placed in one tax year and the shipping and selling efforts in another tax year.

Although the requirement for estimated tax payments mitigates the effect, there also can be tax deferral possibilities in the selection of an appropriate fiscal year. For example, the final corporate estimated tax payment is due on the 15th day of the last month of the corporate year. For calendar-year firms, this is December 15th. If a retail firm makes most of its sales in November and December, but collects most of its open accounts receivable on those sales in January and February, a calendar year would require the firm to make its final estimated tax payment, based on those sales, in December—before it has received payment from its customers. However, a fiscal year ending on March 31 would defer that final estimated tax payment until March 15th—well after all collections on customer accounts. Such an approach can significantly benefit the firm's cash flow position.

D. Tax Accounting Method

An accounting method is a set of rules used to determine when and how income and expenses are reported. The accounting method includes not only the overall method of accounting, but also the accounting treatment used for any material items. For tax purposes, an accounting method is chosen when the first tax return is filed. Once established, IRS approval is required to change from one method of accounting to another method of accounting.

No single accounting method is required of all taxpayers. Each must use the method that clearly shows income and expenses and allows a correct tax return to be filed. In addition to the permanent books of account, appropriate records are necessary to support all entries on the tax return. The same accounting method must be used consistently from year to year. If the accounting method used does not clearly reflect income, the IRS can determine income under the accounting method that, in its opinion, does clearly reflect income.

The tax code (Internal Revenue Code or Code) recognizes two primary methods of accounting (cash and accrual) and two secondary methods of accounting (special and hybrid). Each taxpayer adopts one of the primary methods, as possibly modified by one of the secondary methods. The special method of accounting is used for certain items of income or expense, primarily related to farming, installment sales and depreciation. The hybrid method of accounting is usually the cash method modified by some accrual method requirements. For example, individuals may use the accrual method for business income and expenses and the cash method for personal income and expenses. For businesses that sell products (where inventory is necessary to account for income), the accrual method must be used for sales and purchases but the cash method can be used for all other items of income and expense.

The cash method treats as income all taxable items actually or constructively received and as expenses all deductible items actually or constructively paid. The cash method generally is allowed only for individuals and certain small businesses (those with annual gross receipts less than $5 million). When it is allowed, the cash method can provide useful tax planning opportunities. Income will be taxed only in the year it is received. Thus, the tax due on that income can be deferred to later years simply by delaying the receipt (within certain guidelines) of the related income to those later years. Expenses (again within certain guidelines) become deductible in the year paid. Thus, the tax benefit of future expenses can be accelerated simply by paying the expense within the current tax year.

Under the accrual method, income is taxable in the year earned—whether or not it has been actually or constructively received—and expenses are deductible in the year incurred—whether or not it has been actually or constructively paid. This provides fewer opportunities to shift the tax effect of income or expenses between different tax years. The accrual method generally is required of all business entities with gross receipts that exceed $5 million annually. Also, as noted above, the accrual method is required for all sales and purchases for those entities in which accounting for inventory is necessary. In addition, while advance payments for product sales generally can be deferred to the year of the sale, advance payments for services often must be included in income in the year received rather than in the year when the services are actually performed.

In addition to the above issues of entity, tax year and accounting method, a new business must learn and understand a variety of federal, state and local tax issues, including the following:

- Applying for appropriate employer identification numbers
- Variety of income, employment (or self-employment) and excise taxes that will affect business operations, and how to deposit (pay) those taxes
- Types of information returns that tax authorities may require to be filed

- Types of penalties that might be applied to late or underpaid tax obligations
- Special tax rules for certain types of business expenses, including start-up costs, depreciation of tangible property and car and truck expenses
- Recordkeeping requirements, including the kinds of records to keep and how long to keep records

A useful source of information about these and other start-up questions can be found in IRS Publication 583: *Starting a Business and Keeping Records.*

5.02   Withholding and Estimated Tax Payments

Taxes are either withheld as income is earned, or estimated and paid. In this section, we consider both alternatives.

A.   Withholding

Most income and employment related taxes, whether federal or state, are pay-as-you-go taxes. That is, the tax is paid as the income is earned. A number of income sources (wages, bonuses, commissions, pensions, gambling winnings, etc.) are subject to withholding. In these cases a third party (often the employer) deducts (withholds) an amount from the income earned and remits it to the proper tax authority to be applied against the taxpayer's tax liability for that year. If this is the taxpayer's primary (or only) source of taxable income, then additional (estimated) tax payments are unnecessary.

If the business is an employer, it is responsible for certain employer taxes. In some cases, it will have to pay the tax directly. In other cases, employees pay the tax, but the business is responsible for withholding the tax payment from their wages and making periodic deposits of these funds into an authorized bank.

States generally have their own withholding requirements with respect to amounts to be credited toward the employee's state income tax liability. In addition, states may require that amounts be withheld and paid toward various other types of taxes, including unemployment and disability insurance taxes. In addition, some cities have payroll taxes that are imposed on employers doing business in the city.

The employer's responsibility to pay employment taxes, to withhold taxes imposed on its employees, to file tax returns and to make periodic tax deposits are substantial and the penalties for noncompliance can be severe. For example, partners and officers with responsibility for tax withholdings can be held personally liable for 100% of the unpaid withholding taxes.

1. Wage Withholding

Businesses must withhold federal income tax from the taxable wages paid to their employees (section 3402 of the Code). As part of their obligations, businesses must obtain from each employee a properly executed Employee Withholding Allowance Certificate (IRS Form W4) under section 3402(f)(2) of the Code. Before January 31, following the close of each calendar year, section 6051(a) of the Code requires businesses to provide each employee with an annual Wage and Tax Statement (IRS Form W2).

2. Social Security Taxes ("FICA")

Social Security taxes are imposed on both employers and employees under sections 3101 and 3111 of the Code). The business must withhold FICA taxes from each employee's wages according to section 3102 of the Code and pay a tax equal to the amount paid by each employee under section 3111 of the Code.

3. Federal Unemployment Tax ("FUTA")

Although a few exceptions exist, nearly all employers are subject to the federal unemployment tax, as required by sections 3301 et seq. of the Code. This tax is imposed on the employer, not on the employee.

4. Federal Self-Employment Taxes

Proprietors are subject to self-employment tax, which is similar to the regular Social Security (FICA and Medicare) employment tax imposed on employees. This tax on self-employment income includes an old age, survivors and disability insurance tax, as well as a hospital insurance tax, as reflected in sections 1401(a) and (b) of the Code.

Self-employment income is the individual's net earnings from self-employment. Under sections 1402(a) and (b) of the Code, it is calculated as the individual's gross income from any trade or business less deductions allowed under the income tax law attributable to that trade or business.

The portion of self-employment tax attributable to the FICA portion does not apply to income in excess of a specified maximum amount, which changes on an annual basis, as reflected in section 3121(a)(1) of the Code. The maximum amount subject to tax for any individual is reduced by the amount of any wages earned by the individual while employed by another employer under section 1401(b) of the Code.

5. *Return and Deposit of Taxes*

With some exceptions, employers subject to either income tax withholding or Social Security taxes must file a quarterly return on federal Form 941.[3] They must also deposit the income tax withheld and the FICA taxes with an authorized commercial bank depositary or a Federal Reserve Bank or branch.[4]

B. **Estimated Tax Payments**

Making estimated tax payments is the method used to pay tax on those sources of income not subject to withholding. For corporations, this includes all taxable income of the corporation. For individuals, this includes self-employment business income, interest, dividends, alimony, rent and gains from the sale of assets. Estimated tax payments for individuals also may be necessary if the amount of tax being withheld from salary, pension or other income is not sufficient to meet the total tax liability of the individual.

Paying the proper amount of estimated taxes by the due date of each payment period is important as significant penalties can result even if there is a refund due on the tax return. For each tax year, federal estimated tax payments are required if total tax liability is expected to be $500 or more. For individuals, federal estimated tax payments are required if both of the following apply:

- Total estimated tax liability for the year less any withholdings and credits is $1,000 or more
- Total withholdings and credits will be less than the smaller of:

  - 90% of the total tax liability for the year or
  - 100% of the total tax liability for the previous year

In other words, estimated tax payments for individuals will **NOT** be required if:

- Total amount owed will be less than $1,000
- Current withholdings and credits equal last year's tax liability
- Current withholdings and credits will be at least 90% of this year's tax liability

States (or cities) often adopt the federal requirements for making estimated tax payments. However, given the large number of different states and cities and given the large number of possible regulations concerning estimated tax

---

3. Reg. section 31.6011(a)-1.
4. Reg. section 31.6302-1.

payments, care should be taken to know and understand the specific regulations for the location(s) in which the business firm operates.

Estimated tax payments are normally made four times per year. For corporations, each payment should be made by the 15th day of the 4th, 6th, 9th and 12th months of the tax year. When a corporation adopts the calendar year as its tax year, the due dates are April 15, June 15, September 15 and December 15. For individuals, their estimated payment due dates are April 15, June 15, September 15 and January 15 (if the tax return is filed by January 31, the January 15th payment can be made with the tax return). If a payment due date falls on a Saturday, Sunday or legal holiday, the payment is due on the next regular business day.

Corporations use one of two methods to calculate each required estimated tax payment. Under method one, each required payment is 25% of the income tax that the corporation expects to report on its tax return for the current year. Under method two, each required payment is 25% of the income tax shown on the corporation's tax return for the previous year, but only if the following is true:

- Corporation filed a tax return for the previous year
- Tax return was for a full 12 months and
- Tax return reported a positive tax liability (not zero)

Other restrictions may apply if the corporation has at least $1 million of modified taxable income in any of the last three tax years. Additional computation methods may be available if the corporation's income is expected to vary during the year because of, for example, seasonality. IRS Form 1120-W is a worksheet that corporations can use to calculate their required estimated tax payments. Corporations make their estimated tax payments through the Electronic Federal Tax Payment System or by mailing their payment together with IRS Form 8109. Also see IRS Publication 542 for more information about federal estimated taxes for corporations.

Individuals also use one of two methods to calculate each required estimated tax payment. Method one is based on 100% (in some cases 110%) of the prior year's tax liability. Under this method, each payment would be 25% of the prior year's liability less any withholding applied to that payment. Method two is the annualized income installment method, which is essentially a determination of the expected tax liability for the current year less any withholding to be applied. Each payment is then 25% of that amount. However, unlike corporations, any individuals that reported zero tax liability for the prior year are not required to make estimated tax payments during the current year. IRS Form 1040-ES includes a worksheet to aid individuals in calculating their required estimated tax payments. Individuals make their estimated tax payments through one of the following methods:

- Crediting an overpayment (refund) from a prior year to the current year's estimated taxes

- Mailing the payment with IRS Form 1040-ES tax payment voucher
- Paying electronically using the Electronic Federal Tax Payment System
- Direct debit, for those who file their tax returns electronically
- Credit card using the IRS pay-by-phone system

Also see IRS Publication 17 for more information about federal estimated tax payments for individuals.

5.03   Federal, State and Local Tax Returns

The multiplicity of tax jurisdictions in the United States gives rise to an almost incomprehensible multiplicity of tax returns. Those many jurisdictions— federal, state and local—tax individuals and businesses on a variety of income-producing activities, each with its own type of tax return.[5] The large number of different state and local tax jurisdictions, and the large number of different kinds of taxes they impose, make it nearly impossible to provide examples of each type of tax return a business may be required to file. However, it is possible to provide a broad description of the kinds of taxes that business may be subject to and, for income tax in particular, the effects of operating in more than one state or locality.

A.   State and Local Taxes

States and localities generate most of their tax revenues from income, sales and use and/or property taxes. States also may impose a variety of other taxes, including employment taxes, excise taxes (alcohol, tobacco, etc.) and estate or inheritance taxes. Each kind of tax requires its own tax return to be filed with the state or local jurisdiction, and it is necessary for the business manager to know which taxes the firm is subject to and on which forms those taxes are reported and paid.

B.   State and Local Property Taxes

Notification to the taxing authorities of property subject to taxation usually is accomplished by recording the title for the property with the appropriate clerk (i.e., county clerk). The tax authority (i.e., county) values the property rolls, sets the appropriate tax rate and mails the tax bills to the listed property owner(s). Thus, the tax return is prepared by the tax authority and presented to the property owner, usually annually. Beyond paying the tax due, the property

---

5. A useful source of information on the filing deadlines for a large number of federal tax returns is IRS Publication 509: *Tax Calendars*.

owner's involvement with property taxes often is limited to insuring that the tax valuation is appropriate relative to the property's actual value.

C. State and Local Sales Taxes

Sales taxes are most often "pass along" taxes; that is, they are collected by businesses from their customers and remitted to the state or local sales tax authority. Sales tax authorities are most concerned that the correct amount of sales tax has been collected on each taxable transaction and that the total amount of tax required to be paid has been remitted. Sales taxes usually must be remitted at least quarterly, however, firms that collect large amounts of sales taxes often are required to remit their payments weekly or even daily. Most sales tax returns are required to be filed quarterly. Most of those returns are not complex; essentially requiring the firm to list both sales and taxes collected by month. However, the complexity of recording and reporting the appropriate information can be quite large for firms that operate in multiple sales tax jurisdictions, each with a different variety of taxable and nontaxable items subject to the sales tax.

D. State and Local Income Taxes

The bad news is that no two state or localities are exactly the same in the way that income taxes are determined; the good news is that most of them are based on the federal income tax. A large number of states and localities start with federal taxable income and adjust (add or subtract) that number to arrive at taxable income for the state or locality. This makes the state or local income tax return less complex and costly to prepare, at least in theory. For businesses that operate in more than one state or locality, the biggest income tax issue often is how to apportion federal taxable income among the various states and/or localities.

A state's taxing authority applies to all individuals who reside in the state and all corporations formed under the laws of the state. Also, this jurisdiction extends to nonresident individuals and corporations conducting a business activity within the state. Firms engaged in interstate commerce may be subject to the taxing authority of any number of states and/or localities in which they have a business nexus. It is the degree of nexus that controls the imposition of taxes.

Article 1 of the U.S. Constitution grants the federal government the power to "regulate commerce with foreign Nations, and among the several states, and with the Indian Tribes." This Commerce Clause empowers the federal government to establish rules for state taxation. For a state tax to be constitutional, it must not discriminate against interstate commerce. Also, state taxes can be levied only on business enterprises having nexus with the state.

Nexus means a degree of contact between a business and a state necessary to establish jurisdiction by the state.

At its most basic, nexus requires an actual physical presence (plant, office, etc.) by a business in a state. Thus, firms do not establish nexus simply by selling tangible goods to customers residing in a state. However, this concept of nexus does not apply to activities other than the sale of tangible goods. Thus, firms that provide services or sell intangible property have an economic nexus and are subject to tax jurisdiction by the state. Several states have expanded economic nexus to include the sale of tangible goods, and, to date, Congress and the courts have remained silent on that issue.

The nexus issue is particularly uncertain for Internet firms. Traditional nexus concepts make little sense when applied to business activities in cyberspace. On October 1, 1998, the Internet Tax Freedom Act went into effect.[6] The act includes a ban on new state and local taxes imposed on Internet access and a congressional declaration that the Internet should be free of all international tariffs, trade barriers and other restrictions.

Once the nexus issue is determined, the next issue is to apportion the firm's income among the various state tax authorities. The federal courts have established the principle that states may tax only the income attributable to a firm's in-state business activity. In 1957, a National Conference of Uniform State Laws drafted the Uniform Division of Income for Tax Purposes Act ("UDITPA") and most states today use an apportionment formula conforming to or modeled after the UDITPA. The UDITPA formula, based on three equally weighted factors of sales, payroll and property, is below:

State Percentage = (Sales Factor + Payroll Factor + Property Factor) / 3

Each of the factors is itself a percentage:

Sales Factor = Gross receipts from in-state customers / Total gross receipts

Payroll Factor = Compensation to in-state employees / Total compensation

Property Factor = Cost of tangible property in state / Total tangible property

In theory, 100% of the firm's income is subject to state taxation and no amount of income is either taxed twice or escapes taxation altogether. Practically, this ideal is never achieved. States use variations on the UDITPA formula, which inevitably results in some overlap or omission.

---

6.   The IFTA was renewed in 2001, 2004, and 2007. In 2009, as in 2007, bills were introduced (H.R. 1560 and S. 43) to make the provisions permanent. Those bills have not yet been reported out of committee. Thus, the future status of IFTA is uncertain at this time.

E.   Federal Income Taxes

A large percentage of federal tax revenues comes from individual and corporate income taxes. All corporate entities must file a federal income tax return, whether or not they had taxable income. All individuals who earn self-employment income of $400 or more must file a federal income tax return. All other individuals must file a federal income tax return if their gross income exceeds a specific amount. This amount ranges from $3,650 for married taxpayers filing separate returns to $20,900 for married taxpayers filing joint returns where both spouses are 65 or older.

F.   Corporations

A corporation generally files IRS Form 1120 to report its income, gains, losses, deductions and credits and to figure its income tax liability. A corporation may file IRS Form 1120-A if its gross receipts, total income and total assets are each under $500,000 and it meets certain other requirements. A corporation must file its tax return by the 15th day of the 3rd month after the end of its tax year. If the due date falls on a Saturday, Sunday or legal holiday, the due date is extended to the next business day. Also, corporations can request an automatic six-month extension of time to file their federal income tax return.[7] The extension is automatic if the proper form is completed correctly, it is filed by the original due date of the corporate tax return and any tax due on the original return is paid.

The extension of time to file the corporate tax return does not extend the time to pay any tax that might be due. Failure to pay any tax due (either through previous estimated tax payments or with the extension request) may subject the corporation to penalties for late payment of tax. Those penalties can reach a maximum of 25% of the unpaid tax.[8] As with federal income taxes, states impose similar rules for the payment of taxes due in their jurisdictions. Thus, it is important to properly estimate and pay any taxes due by the due date of the original return.

Federal taxable income for corporations is essentially its gross receipts less its deductible expenses. However, there are special rules, and/or limitations imposed, for various types of income or deduction, including below-market loans (usually low-interest loans from the corporation to employees or officers), capital losses, charitable contributions, corporate tax preferences, dividends received, business start-up costs, certain transactions with related parties (employees or officers), net operating losses and passive investment

---

7.   This is not necessarily an automatic extension of time to file the corporation's state or local income tax return. While a number of jurisdictions accept the federal form, some do not; so care should be taken in this area.

8.   The federal penalty for late filing also can reach a maximum of 25% of the tax due; so it is most advantageous to file for an extension in a timely manner.

activities. As noted in Chapter 4 (Tax Aspects of Forming and Organizing a New Business), federal tax rates for corporations range from 15% for taxable income below $50,000 to 35% for taxable income that exceeds $18,333,333—with two special tax brackets, 39% for taxable income between $100,000 and $335,000 and 38% for taxable income between $15,000,000 and $18,333,333. Those unusual tax brackets, coupled with the provisions of the corporate alternative minimum tax, add complexity for corporate tax planning.

A corporation's tax liability can be reduced by a number of special tax credits. These include, credit for federal taxes on fuels used for nontaxable purposes, nonconventional source fuel credits, qualified electric vehicle credits, foreign tax credits and credit for prior year minimum taxes. While those credits are very specialized, there are a number of general business credits available to corporations. These credits include alcohol used as fuel credit, contributions to selected community development corporations credit, disabled access credit, employer Social Security and Medicare taxes paid on certain employee tips credit, empowerment zone employment credit, enhanced oil recovery credit, Indian employment credit, investment credit, low-income housing credit, orphan drug credit, renewable electricity production credit, research credit, welfare-to-work credit and work opportunity credit. Certainly not all of those credits would be available to the same corporation in the same tax year. However, the workings of the tax law do provide special treatment to some types of income and allow special deductions or credits for some types of expenses. However, to make certain that corporations are not too aggressive in avoiding taxes, the alternative minimum tax as discussed in Chapter 4 (Tax Aspects of Forming and Organizing a New Business) will apply.

G. Individuals

Individuals generally file IRS Form 1040, plus supporting schedules, to report income, gains, losses, deductions and credits, and to determine federal income tax liability. Certain taxpayers (single or married filing jointly), and primarily those with only wage and salary income below $50,000, may file IRS Form 1040-A or 1040-EZ. Individuals must file their tax returns by April 15th of each year. If the due date falls on a Saturday, Sunday or legal holiday, the due date is extended to the next business day. Individuals can file IRS Form 4868 to request an automatic four-month extension of time to file their federal income tax return.[9] The extension is automatic if the form is completed correctly, it is filed by the original due date of the corporate tax return and any tax due on the original return is paid.

---

9.   As with corporations, this is not necessarily an automatic extension of time to file the individual's state or local income tax return. While a number of jurisdictions accept the federal form, some do not; so care should be taken in this area. Also as with corporations, there is no extension of time for payment and similar penalties apply to any late payment of tax due or late filing of tax returns.

Federal taxable income for individuals is more complex than it is for corporations. Gross receipts include wages and salaries, interest and dividends, rents and royalties, business income,[10] pensions (and possibly Social Security benefits) and other miscellaneous sources of income (prizes, awards, etc.). Also, while individual deductions include all necessary and reasonable business expenses (used to offset business income), other individual deductions include amounts paid into individual retirement accounts, moving expenses, alimony, personal exemptions for the taxpayer and any dependents and a choice between a standard deduction (based on filing status—i.e., single, married filing joint, etc.) or itemized deductions (such as medical costs, other kinds of taxes paid, mortgage interest paid, charitable contributions, or non-reimbursed employee expenses).

Federal tax rates for individuals depend on filing status with married taxpayers filing separate returns, in general, paying the highest rates on income and married taxpayers filing joint returns, in general, paying the lowest rates on income. As noted in Chapter 4 (Tax Aspects of Forming and Organizing a New Business), all individual tax rate schedules apply the highest rate (35%) to income above $372,950 ($186,475 for married filing separate). Also, all of the schedules have tax rates at 10%, 15%, 25%, 28%, 33% and 35%. The biggest impact is the size of the first (10%) tax bracket. It is $8,350 for single, $16,700 for married filing joint, $8,350 for married filing separate and $11,950 for head of household. Similar differences exist for the other tax rate brackets.

Once an individual's federal income tax liability has been determined, a number of tax credits may be available. These credits include child and dependent care credit, credit for the elderly or the disabled, child tax credit, education credits and earned income credits. Other, more specialized, credits can include rate reduction credit, adoption credit, foreign tax credit, mortgage interest credit, credit for prior year minimum tax, credit for electric vehicles, credit for excess Social Security tax withheld and credit for tax on undistributed capital gains. As with corporations, individuals that use the benefits of the tax laws to significantly reduce their tax liability face an alternative minimum tax liability. Thus, individuals may owe the alternative minimum tax even when thorough planning for income, deductions and credits has reduced their regular tax liability.

---

10.   Individuals engaged in self-employed business activities must report their business income and all necessary and reasonable expenses related to that income on Schedule C. In addition, for any self-employment income in excess of $400, the taxpayer must calculate the amount of Social Security taxes due on Schedule SE.

CHAPTER 6

Accounting and Financial Reporting Issues

David T. Collins

Bellarmine University
Louisville, KY

Contents

Accounting and Financial Reporting Issues

6.01   Preliminary Considerations

What if there were no accounting rules? What if each company decided for itself how to measure its business activities and what information to disclose about its financial position and results of operations? If that were true, then investors, creditors and other users of financial statements could neither depend on the information about a company nor compare it to any other company. There is an old joke in accounting about not following proper accounting rules.

> The CEO of a large business was interviewing accountants for the CFO position. As each interview ended he asked the candidate one final question: "What is 2 plus 2?" The first candidate answered 4 and was told, "Don't call us, we'll call you." The second candidate said, "Well, it is most often 2, but sometimes it is 3 and sometimes it is 5." He was put on the short list and told to wait by the phone. The third candidate, nodding knowingly, replied, "What do you want the answer to be?" He was hired on the spot.

Consistent rules, consistently applied, are critical to the proper flow of information about business activities because they produce a common business vocabulary, promote uniform accounting methods and encourage full disclosure in financial reports. In the United States, the rules that govern business accounting practices are called *generally accepted accounting principles* ("GAAP").[1] These are the authoritative standards that describe the basic methods for measuring and reporting business activities.

This is one role of the public accounting profession, to define the standards by which companies measure and report their business activities. In the United States, the legal authority to set accounting standards for publicly traded companies is given by Congress to the Securities Exchange Commission ("SEC"). However, since SEC regulations only apply to publicly traded companies, it is necessary to have a source of GAAP that applies to all companies. Members of the U.S. accounting profession have given professional authority to define accounting standards to the Financial Accounting Standards Board ("FASB"). Both SEC regulations and FASB standards make up the body of GAAP in the United States.[2]

When analyzing the financial condition of U.S. businesses, it is assumed that GAAP was followed when the financial statements were prepared. Further, since it also is assumed that GAAP is applied consistently[3] across businesses, it is assumed that the financial results of one business are comparable to those of another. That is, 2 plus 2 is 4 for us and for them and for everyone else—2 plus 2 is *always* 4.

Yet it does not always work that way, especially for complex transactions. Even when businesses try to follow the rules honestly, GAAP does not always produce a clear-cut result. Therefore, GAAP should be thought of as accounting guidelines, rather than rules, because they allow flexibility that requires judgment. Deciding how to measure and report many complex business transactions requires careful interpretation of the rules—interpretations that can create honest differences of opinion on what the rules mean or how they should be implemented.[4]

Some businesses take advantage of GAAP and use *creative accounting* to make themselves look better financially. In fact, the need to interpret the rules often allows those businesses to meet the letter of GAAP even while they violate its spirit. The external audit by independent certified public accountants ("CPAs") exists to prevent, or at least reduce, the worse abuses of creative accounting.[5]

An audit by an independent CPA provides additional assurance (but not a guarantee) that the financial statements not only follow GAAP but that they

---

1. The SEC is developing a plan to transition from U.S. GAAP to International Financial Reporting Standards (IFRS). Current expectations are that IFRS will be required for U.S. corporations in 2015.

2. When IFRS is adopted for use in the United States, the current roles of the SEC and FASB likely will continue, with one or both of those organizations serving as significant members of the International Accounting Standards Board (which sets IFRS).

3. One aspect of this is consistency from year to year. If the SEC mandates IFRS for 2015, corporations will need to retroactively apply those standards to 2013 and 2014.

4. IFRS is less rule-based than GAAP; it is more principles- or judgment-based. Some argue that this will make the application of accounting standards more complex and more confusing.

5. While this is one of the expectations for independent audits, as recent events have shown (Enron, WorldCom, etc.), neither CPA firms nor the audit processes are infallible when it comes to preventing all abuses caused by creative (or even fraudulent) accounting practices.

fairly present the financial condition of the business. Thus, users of audited financial statements should be able to assume that not only did the company follow GAAP but also that it exercised reasonable judgment and good faith in applying GAAP to its own business activities.

Auditing is another role of the public accounting profession. It exists to meet a societal need. The auditor has a legal and professional responsibility to the public, not to the company that is paying for the audit. An audit is an examination of a company's financial statements and records that is sufficient to provide an opinion on whether or not the financial statements are materially correct in all respects to GAAP, including the proper and reasonable application of judgment in those areas where judgment is required.

Audits are conducted only by CPAs, who are licensed by state governments to provide necessary and appropriate accounting services to the public in support of societal goals and objectives. CPAs are required to conduct themselves ethically and responsibly in accordance with a Code of Professional Conduct. CPAs should carry out their responsibilities in the public interest with integrity, objectivity and independence and should use due care when performing their services.

In addition, the Sarbanes-Oxley Act requires that the CEO and the CFO of each issuer shall prepare a statement to accompany every audit report to certify the "appropriateness of the financial statements and disclosures contained in the periodic report, and that those financial statements and disclosures fairly present, in all material respects, the operational and financial condition of the issuer."[6]

Further, the Sarbanes-Oxley Act established a Public Company Accounting Oversight Board ("PCAOB") to oversee the audit of public companies that are subject to the securities laws of the United States.[7] The SEC shall have "oversight and enforcement authority" over the PCAOB. The SEC can, by rule or order, give the PCAOB additional responsibilities. The PCAOB, subject to action by the Securities and Exchange Commission, is charged with the following:

- Registering public accounting firms that prepare audit reports for issuers of financial statements of publicly held companies
- Establishing "auditing, quality control, ethics, independence, and other standards relating to the preparation of audit reports for issuer"
- Conducting inspections of registered accounting firms

The Sarbanes-Oxley Act defined the following services as outside the scope of practice of auditors (i.e., prohibited transactions). The PCAOB may,

---

6.   The question of how Sarbanes-Oxley will be affected by the IFRS framework has not been answered.

7.   As of the second edition of this book, there has been recent legal action regarding the constitutionality of the PCAOB that has not yet been resolved. Many argue that this action will not eliminate the PCAOB but only change how its members are chosen and appointed.

on a case-by-case basis, exempt from these prohibitions any person, issuers, public accounting firm or transaction, subject to review by the SEC.

- Bookkeeping or other services related to accounting records or financial statements of the audit client
- Financial information systems design and implementation
- Appraisal or valuation services, fairness opinions or contributions-in-kind reports
- Actuarial services
- Internal audit outsourcing services
- Management functions or human resources
- Broker or dealer, investment adviser or investment banking services
- Legal services and expert services unrelated to the audit
- Any other service that the Board determines, by regulation, to be impermissible

Prospectively, the Sarbanes-Oxley Act, as implemented through the SEC and the PCAOB, will change both the way GAAP is implemented and the way audits are conducted for all U.S. corporations.

6.02   Accountant's Role in Assisting Emerging Companies

A company exists to increase the wealth of its owners. General management focuses on decisions concerning what products to produce and the methods to produce and distribute those products. Financial management focuses on decisions concerning how financial resources (debt or equity) are acquired and used to meet the production and distribution needs of the company.

Finance has traditionally been thought of as the area of financial management that focuses on the acquisition and disposition of cash. Recently, finance has expanded significantly from being concerned only with borrowing funds and investing excess cash resources. The finance function today involves analyzing the financial information produced by the company to improve decisions that will impact the wealth of the owners.

Accounting provides the financial information used in financial management, and it is generally divided into financial accounting and managerial accounting. Financial accounting records the financial history of the company and, from time to time, reports that history to interested parties outside the company (external users such as creditors and investors). Financial accounting must measure and report on the company's business activities in accordance with generally accepted accounting principles. Also, for many companies, the reports produced by the financial accounting system must be audited by independent certified public accountants.

Managerial accounting provides information useful for making decisions about the future of the company. Where financial accounting looks to the past—at what happened—managerial accounting looks to the future—at what might happen. Also, while financial accounting must follow GAAP—a formal, externally defined structure—managerial accounting is free to provide any information in any format to support virtually any decision—an informal, internally defined structure.

Financial and managerial accounting work together to support financial management. Managerial accounting provides information to support future-oriented decisions—how to achieve company goals and objectives. Financial accounting provides information to support past-oriented feedback—how well were the goals and objectives achieved? Neither part of the accounting process, by itself, is sufficient to meet managerial decision-making needs.

While financial management is concerned with maximizing owner wealth (often defined as the market price of company stock), it is often operationalized as maximizing company profits. That goal, in turn, is often influenced by or dependent on other goals—maximizing revenues through sales or sales growth or minimizing expenses. To reach its maximization goals the company needs to produce a return on its activities greater than its costs and it needs to continue in business. From the point of view of company management, this creates two overriding goals: profitability and viability.

When maximizing profits, there is always a tradeoff with risk. The greater the risk of an action, the greater the expected outcome needs to be to undertake the action. Given two equally risky business activities, the company would always choose the one with the greater expected return. That does not mean that all would choose the same level of risk. Some companies will be more willing than others to accept a high risk in order to achieve a high potential profit.

More often than not the decision is not about the level of risk itself. Risk-averse companies may not be willing to engage in high-risk activities regardless of the size of the expected return. Once the risk tolerance of the company is determined, the key decision is whether the expected return is large enough to justify the perceived level of risk undertaken. This is where accounting plays an important role; not in determining risk, but in measuring expected return.

GAAP defines how profit is measured and reported, which is an important element in the risk vs. return relationship. If the rules are too conservative, or applied too conservatively, the expected return will not appear large enough for the level of risk undertaken. If the rules are too liberal, or applied too liberally, the expected return will appear too large relative to the level of risk undertaken. Both extremes produce less-than-optimal results and prevent the firm from maximizing profits. The role of accounting is to apply the GAAP rules with good faith and reasonable judgment to avoid either of those two extremes. The role of managerial accounting is to apply those rules to proposed actions so that managers can decide what actions to take next. The role of financial accounting is to apply the rules to prior actions so that managers can evaluate the effectiveness of past decisions.

In addition to maximizing profits, companies must ensure financial viability. Companies have no desire to go bankrupt. Even risk-seeking managers probably will not engage in activities that will lead to the demise of the company.[8] Financial viability often is measured in terms of liquidity and solvency. Liquidity is a measure of the company resources that are or will be available to meet company obligations coming due in the near term (usually one year or less). That is, can the company pay its current bills as they become due? Solvency is essentially the same concept applied to the long term (more than one year). That is, is the cash generation potential for the next three, five or ten years sufficient to meet major cash needs (company obligations) over those periods of time?

While the goal is to maintain financial viability, the strategy is not to maximize liquidity and solvency. Companies maximize liquidity by holding liquid resources (cash and cash equivalents). However, doing so reduces the resources employed in longer-term, higher-yielding investments and, so, does not maximize profitability. Companies can maximize solvency by reducing long-term cash needs (usually by reducing long-term debt). Again, doing so reduces the resources available for longer-term, higher-yielding investments and, so, does not maximize profitability.

The role of accounting is to provide information on the sources and uses of company resources and how those resources are changing over time. Financial management uses that information to evaluate the level of liquidity and solvency in the company. The goal is to maintain viability while maximizing profits. The role of managerial accounting is to provide information on the expected impact of future actions on viability. The role of financial accounting is to provide information on how well viability is being maintained.

The tradeoff between viability and profitability is essentially equivalent to the tradeoff between risk and reward. Companies that maximize viability (they create a low risk of bankruptcy) cannot maximize profitability (they earn a low reward). Alternatively, companies that maximize profitability (they want a high reward) cannot maximize viability (they must accept some possible risk of bankruptcy). It is usually obvious that viability does not guarantee profitability, and without profitability the company eventually will be bankrupt. Unfortunately, the opposite also is true; profitability does not guarantee viability. Highly profitable companies can and do go bankrupt.

The negative results happen because profitability and cash flow are not the same things. Profitability is determined by the difference between revenues and expenses during a particular period of time, whereas cash flow is determined by when the revenues are collected and the expenses are paid. If expenses must be paid before the revenues are collected the company

---

8. Again, recent events (particularly the collapse of Enron) show that this is not always the case.

may be profitable but it also may face a liquidity crisis. This crisis can be magnified by rapid growth that is not properly planned for and can lead to bankruptcy of the company. Consider the hypothetical result for High Growth Company shown in Figure 6A below. Without proper planning to support its sales growth, although the company is enjoying high profitability, it could be bankrupt rather quickly.

FIGURE 6A HIGH GROWTH COMPANY—PROFITABILITY VS. VIABILITY			
	January	**February**	**March**
Sales Revenues ($10 per unit sold)	100,000	150,000	200,000
Cost of Sold Inventory ($8 per unit sold)	(80,000)	(120,000)	(160,000)
Profitability	20,000	30,000	40,000
Beginning Cash Balance	180,000	60,000	0
Cash Received from Sales (from previous month)	0	100,000	150,000
Cash Paid Out for Purchases (for current month)	(120,000)	(160,000)	(200,000)
Ending Cash Balance	60,000	0	(50,000)
Number of Units Sold This Month	10,000	15,000	20,000
Number of Units Purchased This Month	15,000	20,000	25,000

Will growing companies always go bankrupt? Obviously not. Yet, liquidity and solvency are crucial to a company's viability and must be planned for to support growth. The key is to focus on both short-term and long-term needs for cash. Even for profitable companies, there is a constant demand for the cash flow projections provided by accounting. They can be every bit as, or more important than, measures of profitability.

6.03   Accounting Elections

When starting a new business the number and type of choices, elections, judgments, estimates and the like can seem overwhelming. A great many of these concern legal and tax issues discussed elsewhere in this book. However, there are a number of accounting issues where the choices made can affect how managers, employees, customers, creditors and investors view a company. Many of these issues concern how an accounting standard is implemented and, so, how that standard impacts the measurement and reporting of process.

This is part of the judgment process in accounting that can make GAAP less than clear-cut.[9]

Within financial accounting, there are a number of very basic issues for which managers may not be aware that an alternative even exists. For these issues the standard (default) approach is so common that, absent compelling reasons to the contrary, it is automatically implemented by accountants. Thus, only those familiar with the workings of GAAP would know that an alternative approach could have been considered, under the right circumstances.

A good example is in the area of revenue recognition, where two issues could be considered. The first concerns the choice between accrual accounting and cash accounting, as briefly described in Chapter 5 (Tax Reporting and Compliance). The standard approach is to recognize revenues in the time period when earned (accrual accounting) rather than in the time period when received (cash accounting). The use of accrual accounting is so basic to GAAP that only in the smallest businesses (essentially those that only maintain a checkbook) do accountants even raise the issue of accrual vs. cash accounting.

The time span between when a credit sale takes place and when the cash is received also is part of the second revenue recognition issue. Accrual accounting assumes that there will be no serious difficulties with the collectibility of the amount due from the customer. If sufficient doubts exist about future collectibility, then alternative revenue recognition approaches should be used (installment sales or cost recovery).

Accrual accounting further assumes that the revenue earnings process is complete; that is, that the goods or services have been delivered to the customer. What if, as in long-term construction contracts, the earnings process is not complete but future delivery is all but guaranteed? In those cases, revenues should be recognized during the contract period and not deferred until the end of the contract. There are even very special cases to recognize revenues when products are ready to be sold but before an actual sale has taken place. In all of the various revenue recognition approaches, the goal is to determine the proper time period to measure and report the revenue in order to properly reflect profitability for that time period.

There are a number of other financial accounting issues that require management decisions in order to implement the related accounting standards. A good example is the depreciation of long-lived assets.[10] When such assets are acquired for use in the business, managers must answer three questions:

1.   What is the productive (useful) life of the asset in years?

---

9.   While it is beyond the scope of this work to discuss specific differences between GAAP and IFRS, two of those differences will be noted as they relate to accounting choice examples presented below.

10.   Unlike GAAP, IFRS will allow companies to restate long-lived assets at current value; an approach to asset valuation generally common outside of the United States.

2.   Should a residual value at the end of the asset's productive life be provided for?

3.   Which depreciation method should be used to allocate the cost of the asset over its productive life?

The answer to the first question is most often the shortest of the asset's physical life (how long can it be used before it must be replaced?), its economic life (how long before technological changes require the asset to be replaced?) or its legal life (how long before legal claims to the use of the asset expire?). The answer to the second question may be zero for an asset expected to have a relatively small residual value at the end of its useful life. However, determining this answer may be more complex for those assets expected to have a significant residual value.

The answer to the third question deals more directly with the implementation of the accounting standard for depreciation. There are a number of possible depreciation methods to choose from, including straight-line, units-of-production and various accelerated methods. Each has its own advantages and disadvantages when applied to particular assets. Straight-line is best when the asset's economic usefulness is approximately the same each year, and the accelerated methods are best when economic usefulness declines each year. The units-of-production method is best when the use of the asset can be measured (parts made, hours operated, miles driven, etc.).

Another example of an accounting implementation issue is the cost-flow assumption for inventory. The most common assumptions used are first-in, first-out ("FIFO"); last-in, first-out ("LIFO");[11] and average cost. Each has its advantages and disadvantages. FIFO prevents year-end purchasing decisions from manipulating cost of goods sold values on the income statement; however, it overstates profitability during periods of inflation. LIFO better measures profitability during periods of inflation, but can allow manipulation due to purchasing decisions at year-end. Average cost works best when the inventory items freely mix together (e.g., gasoline in an underground storage tank) or when prices tend to fluctuate within a relatively narrow band. Care should be taken to select the inventory model that leads to the highest quality of financial reporting for the company.

Within managerial accounting, most of the elections (management decisions) concern what accounting information to provide to managers and, in some cases, how that information will differ from its financial accounting counterpart in format, frequency, and the like. If this all sounds very open-ended, it is. Unlike financial accounting, which must follow specific rules (GAAP), managerial accounting is free to determine what information is needed to support managerial decision-making and how to provide that information to decision makers.

---

11.   IFRS will not allow the LIFO method of inventory valuation.

As an example, consider the computation of profitability—so near and dear to the hearts of managers. Under financial accounting rules, profitability (net income) is determined based on absorption costing (all costs are included). This method is appropriate for the company as a whole, but it falters when applied to subunits of the company, such as product lines. A typical managerial accounting approach to product line profitability includes only direct costs but not allocated overhead or other joint costs. The result measures the contribution to profitability of each product line and more effectively expresses the value of each product line to the company.

Consider, as another example, the difference between the GAAP rules imposed on financial accounting and the flexibility available to managerial accounting. An oft heard complaint from managers, particularly those in large, complex companies, is that the accounting department controls both the form and content of the information they receive and how they are evaluated based on that information. The source of this complaint is usually because strict financial accounting rules are being imposed on the flexible managerial accounting decision making process. This very often results in managers who "manage" the numbers rather than using the numbers to evaluate past decisions and/or to support future decisions.

Within both financial and managerial accounting there are certainly dozens, if not hundreds, of accounting elections (areas of managerial decision and/or judgment) that must be made for all companies. A well-informed manager is aware of most of those elections and, more importantly, how they affect the company's financial reporting. A less well-informed manager works with company accountants insuring that proper thought is given to the various electives. The well-advised manager also works with company accountants to understand how the choices affect the company's financial reporting for the quality of financial reporting is directly tied to those choices.

6.04   Financial Reporting

Financial reporting is, for many people, the most important aspect of the company's accounting function. It is how the company communicates to external users and it is the principal function of the financial accounting system. While financial reporting includes all sources of financial information provided by companies, it is primarily addressed by the three general purpose financial statements: balance sheets, income statements and cash flow statements.

The information provided by any one financial statement alone is not sufficient for most decisions about a company. However, the information provided by the set of all three financial statements (plus the notes to the financial statements and management's discussion and analysis) should provide sufficient information to make informed decisions about a company and its financial health, when evaluated in light of other factors. Other factors that should be integrated into the analytical process include both general and industry economic conditions, events that have occurred since the date of the financial statements, political events, current market conditions and anything else that might impact the company being analyzed.

A.   Balance Sheet

The balance sheet provides a snapshot of the company at a particular point in time; usually at the end of a defined time period such as a quarter or a year. It reports on the overall financial health (liquidity and solvency) of the company—is it lean and firm, or fat and flabby? Balance sheets should be evaluated at least annually to determine whether financial health (liquidity and solvency) is being maintained at levels appropriate for whatever environment the company is currently facing. Also, subsequent balance sheets should be evaluated for growth (improved health) or decline (reduced health) caused by any changes in profitability and/or cash flows over time.

1.   Assets

The major elements of the balance sheet are assets, liabilities and equity (owners' or stockholders'). Assets are defined in many ways but they essentially represent the tangible or intangible property owned by a company. The formal definition in *Statement of Financial Accounting Concepts No. 3* (SFAC 3) is more precise: assets are "probable future economic benefits obtained or controlled by a particular entity as a result of past transactions or events."[12] Assets provide future economic benefits because it is expected they will be used by the company to earn revenues in one or more future time periods. The future benefits are obtained (owned) or controlled (right of use) by the company and they are probable to indicate that the business environment is uncertain. Being the result of past transactions or events, assets are past costs that will be expensed against future revenues as the assets are physically consumed (or as their economic benefits expire).

The existence of many assets, and their future economic benefits, are obvious. The company purchases and owns many tangible (cash, inventories, building, equipment, etc.) and intangible (patents, copyrights, etc.) assets. There was a cost incurred to acquire those assets and that cost was incurred with the expectation of earning future revenues. A few assets are not so obvious. The company does not own assets held under capital leases; however, since the company enjoys the use of their economic benefits during the period of the lease, they are recorded as assets on the balance sheet.

---

12.   Statement of Financial Accounting Concepts No. 3 (Stamford, Conn.: Financial Accounting Standards Board, 1980), paragraph 19.

There are other potential assets acquired or developed by the company that are not recorded on the balance sheet, usually because the value of their future economic benefits cannot be objectively determined. For example, it has been decided by accountants that the future economic benefits of current research and development costs are so difficult to measure that all such costs are to be treated as a current period expense on the income statement rather than as an asset on the balance sheet. Similar problems (and prohibitions) exist for recording internally generated goodwill (changes in overall company value that cannot be objectively measured apart from actual exchange transactions) and employees (future benefits that neither can be objectively measured nor are under the control of the company) as company assets. When evaluating the financial health of a company, all of its assets—whether recorded or unrecorded—should be considered.

The current value of a company's assets is another problem that must be addressed on the balance sheet. All balance sheet assets start out being recorded at historical cost. This is the cost previously incurred by the company to acquire the asset. From that point on, asset values become more complicated. Some assets (e.g., land) usually remain recorded at historical cost, which can be far different from their current values. Other assets (e.g., long-lived tangible and intangible assets) have their historical cost allocated as an expense over time (e.g., depreciation, amortization, etc.). Thus, they are reported at book value (historical cost less depreciation or amortization), which also can be far different from their current values. A few assets (e.g., marketable securities) are actually reported at their current values, since those values are readily available from sources external to the company. Others (e.g., inventory) are regularly reported at the lower of historical cost or current market value (but, of course, higher market values are not reported). When evaluating the financial health of a company, the balance sheet valuation of its assets must be considered carefully compared to the estimated current values of those assets.[13]

2. Liabilities

Liabilities also are defined in many ways, but they essentially represent amounts owed to debt holders of the company. These obligations often arise from past transactions that provided economic resources to the company—economic resources used to acquire company assets—so, liabilities are claims against assets by nonowners. SFAC 3 more formally defines liabilities as "probable future sacrifices of economic benefits arising from present obligations of a

---

13.   As noted previously, IFRS will allow companies to restate assets to reflect current values.

particular entity to transfer assets or provide services to other entities in the future as the result of past transactions or events."[14]

As with assets, liabilities are probable because of the uncertainties inherent in the business environment. They are future sacrifices because the expected debt repayment is not until some time after the end of the current time period. They arise from present obligations because the debt exists currently; as opposed to a contingent liability in which the debt does not currently exist but may exist in some future time period. Liabilities result from past transactions or events because the debt is from company actions in the current or past time periods.

As with many assets, most liabilities are quite obvious. The company borrows money from financial creditors (e.g., bank loans and bonds), money that it is committed to repaying in the future. Also quite common, the company agrees to pay (in the future) for goods and/or services "borrowed" from suppliers (e.g., accounts payable). Some liabilities are commitments of future cash flows for the right to use assets (e.g., capital lease obligations). Other liabilities are commitments of future cash flows due to current expenses (e.g., pension obligations). Still, care must be taken to assess all possible liabilities. The existence of contingent liabilities (those that do not currently exist, but which may exist in the future) must be carefully evaluated.

Unlike assets, the balance sheet valuation of liabilities often appears less troublesome. Many liabilities (e.g., accounts payable, bank loans, etc.) are obligations to repay a specific sum of money to the creditor involved. In the normal course of business this sum does not change over time and, so, its current value is equal to its balance sheet value. However, for firms in financial difficulty, appropriate (or possible) changes in those amounts should be considered. Also, the current values of some liabilities (e.g., bonds and capital leases) can be market dependent (usually based on interest rates). While the balance sheet may accurately reflect their "maturity" values, it may not accurately reflect their current values. Finally, even the stated balance sheet values of some liabilities (e.g., warranties and pensions) are based on estimates and may not fully reflect the "true" value of those liabilities. Thus, as with assets, care must be taken both that all liabilities are properly considered and that their current values are fully evaluated.

3. *Equity*

Equity refers to the net worth of the company and represents the claims to the assets by the stockholders (owners) of the company. SFAC 3 defines equity as "the residual interest in the assets of an entity that remains after deducting

---

14.   Statement of Financial Accounting Concepts No. 3 (Stamford, Conn.: Financial Accounting Standards Board, 1980), paragraph 28.

its liabilities. In a business enterprise, the equity is the ownership interest."[15] Since equity represents the owners' residual claims to the net assets (assets minus liabilities) of the company, the proper valuation of both assets and liabilities is important to the evaluation of equity.

Equity in concept is a total value: assets minus liabilities equals net assets equals equity. The divisions of equity reported on by many modern corporations do not exist independently, but exist only as attempts to describe the source of certain equity elements. There are two primary sources of equity in corporations: contributed capital—equity provided directly by stockholders—and earned capital—profits of the company retained for use by the company. Contributed capital usually is not returned to stockholders except in partial or complete liquidation of the corporate entity. Earned capital can be returned to stockholders in the form of dividends.

Contributed capital often is divided into two elements: capital stock and additional paid-in capital. Capital stock most often represents the par or stated value of the common stock, and any preferred stock, issued directly by the corporation to its stockholders.[16] The par or stated value is a nominal amount selected by the board of directors for accounting purposes and is independent of the current market value of the stock. The market value is what a willing investor would pay for one share of stock on a secondary stock exchange, like the New York Stock Exchange. When a corporation issues capital stock, it may receive an amount greater than the stock's par or stated value, this excess amount is reported as additional paid-in capital. In some states, some or all of the additional paid-in capital may be returned to stockholders (in the form of a partial liquidation) without impairing the corporation's legal capital requirements.

Earned capital is most often represented by a single element: retained earnings. These are the earnings (profits) of the company not yet paid to stockholders as dividends. Most companies retain a portion of their annual earnings as an internal source of growth (increased financial health). This is good business practice as it helps the company maintain sufficient levels of cash on hand and/or increase inventory levels and/or replace long-term assets and/or acquire new assets. Thus, retained earnings is not a hoard of cash being kept away from stockholders. It is, rather, only one source of the net assets of the company. As such, in addition to retained earnings, the company needs sufficient cash on hand—not needed for some other purpose—in order to pay dividends to its stockholders.

---

15.   Statement of Financial Accounting Concepts No. 3 (Stamford, Conn.: Financial Accounting Standards Board, 1980), paragraph 43.

16.   Corporations only record the amount received from investors on the initial issue of stock to the public. Exchanges, like the New York Stock Exchange, exist to handle subsequent sales of stock between investors. Corporations neither receive funds from nor report the effects of those subsequent sales.

B.   Income Statement

The income statement provides a picture of the changes in the company due to operating activities over a particular period of time—annually, quarterly or monthly. It reports on changes in financial health due to profitability—the company's external sources of health. If the balance sheet is the body of the company, the income statement reports on the company's diet—is it eating right? Income statements should be evaluated to determine whether operating activities are increasing company health (creating profits) or decreasing health (suffering losses). Subsequent income statements should be evaluated for growth (improved health) or decline (reduced health) caused by any changes in profitability. Finally, are profits (or changes in profits) primarily related to customer inflows (revenues) or company outflows (expenses)?

1. Revenues

Revenues and expenses are the two major accounting elements reported on income statements. SFAC 3 states that "revenues are inflows or other enhancements of assets of an entity or settlements of its liabilities (or a combination of both) during a period from delivering or producing goods, rendering services, or other activities that constitute the entity's ongoing major or central operations."[17] This formal definition is too cumbersome for most people, who simply view revenues as the amounts received from the sale of products or services to customers.

   The accounting issues for revenues most frequently concern whether or not a sale has taken place and in which time period it should be reported. Care must be taken to insure that a sale has taken place—that is, that there has been a completed transaction with an external customer. Care also must be taken to ensure that sales are reported in the proper time period—that is, the correct month, quarter and year. Any violations of either principle will misstate profitability for the period being measured and, so, misstate the financial health of the company.

2. Expenses

SFAC 3 defines expenses as "outflows or other using up of assets or incurrence of liabilities (or a combination of both) during a period from delivering or producing goods, rendering services, or carrying out other activities that constitute the entity's ongoing major or central operations."[18] Most people

---

   17.   Statement of Financial Accounting Concepts No. 3 (Stamford, Conn.: Financial Accounting Standards Board, 1980), paragraph 63.
   18.   Statement of Financial Accounting Concepts No. 3 (Stamford, Conn.: Financial Accounting Standards Board, 1980), paragraph 65.

simply view expenses as the amounts spent to generate sales of products or services to customers.

The accounting issue for expenses most frequently concerns the application of the matching principle—that is, the expense should be matched with the time period in which its economic benefits have been consumed (used) by the company to generate revenues. Thus, as with revenues, any violation of this principle will misstate the measurement of profitability and, so, misstate the financial health of the company.

3. Gains and Losses

Additional, occasionally significant, elements on the income statement include gains and losses. They are essentially the same as revenues and expenses except that they are the result of company activities not associated with ongoing operations, for example, gains or losses on the disposal of long-term plant assets not held as inventory for sale to customers. The infrequent occurrence of gains and losses may make the evaluation of their impact on the company's financial health more difficult. Also, since the underlying transactions often are discretionary, care must be taken to insure that company management is not using the timing of gains and losses to influence the measure of profitability for a particular time period.

4. Articulation

Particular income statement accounts (revenues and expenses) are linked to particular balance sheet accounts (assets and liabilities); that is, there is articulation between the income statement and the balance sheet. By understanding the process of articulation (the linkages) it is possible to determine if balance sheet changes (e.g., this year compared to last year) are supported by the information reported on the income statement.

The most direct, and obvious, link is between net income (or loss) and retained earnings. Retained earnings is the balance sheet account (a part of equity) to which net income (loss) is added (subtracted) during the accounting closing process at the end of each year. So, articulation between the income statement and the balance sheet is directly accomplished through the retained earnings account.

There are many other linkages. Sales are linked to accounts receivable (credit sales) and cash (cash sales). Cost of goods sold is linked to inventory (what is available for sale to customers). Depreciation expense is linked to long-term assets, and amortization expense is linked to intangible assets. Common, recurring expenses (e.g., insurance, rent, etc.) may be linked to a current asset called prepaid expenses. Some recurring expenses (e.g., wages and salaries) may be linked to the current liabilities of wages payable or payroll taxes payable.

For all of the linkages, if unusual changes in the income statement accounts do not appear to be supported by expected changes in the balance sheet accounts (or vice versa), it may be necessary to conclude that the financial statements are not adequately reporting the correct financial condition of the company.

C.   Cash Flow Statement

Like the income statement, the cash flow statement provides a picture of the changes in the financial health of a company. Unlike the income statement, which is concerned with profitability (external sources of health), the cash flow statement is concerned with changes in cash (internal sources of health). It is the company's cardiovascular system and it demands not just a healthy diet (profitability) but also a healthy lifestyle, which includes the right kinds of exercise (positive cash flows). Like profitability, cash flows can be evaluated annually, quarterly or monthly. Cash flows are reported in three different areas: operating activities, investing activities and financing activities.

1.   Operating Activities

Operating activity cash flows restate net income from the accrual method of accounting to the cash method of accounting. This helps determine if profitability is actually benefiting the company. Profitability alone is not sufficient to maintain company viability; the company also must produce positive cash flows from operations. For example, selling all of its products on credit would produce a large level of profitability for the company, however, if the customers never paid their debt, the company would fail just as surely as if it had sold all of its products for free. High profit companies can fail and low profit companies can succeed; it all depends on the level of cash flow produced and what the company does with that cash flow.

For successful companies, it may be possible to use positive cash flows to increase the scope of its operations. It may be able to expand its customer base by offering more credit (increasing the size of accounts receivable). It may be able to expand its sales by offering more products (increasing the size of inventory). It may choose to expand its supplier base (increasing the size of accounts payable). Alternatively, companies in financial difficulty may use some of those techniques to artificially increase operating activity cash flows. A proper evaluation of this section of the cash flow statement can determine whether it is having a positive or negative effect on overall company health.

2.   Investing Activities

Investing activity cash flows primarily reflect a use of cash and they help determine if the company is maintaining (or increasing) its productive capacity to meet its future needs. Most of these cash flows are aimed at replacing long-term productive assets—buildings, equipment, etc. For growth companies, these cash flows also are aimed at increasing its productive assets. In addition, for high cash flow companies, this section reports on how the company is managing its idle cash in external investments—stocks, bonds, etc. For companies in financial difficulty, this section may reflect a source of cash as external investments and/or productive assets are sold off and not replaced.

3.   Financing Activities

Financing activity cash flows help determine if a company is properly employing debt and equity to meet its long-term financial resource needs. The financing activities section can be either a source of or a use of cash. It is often a source of cash whenever the company increases its financial resources by issuing its own debt or equity securities. It is often a use of cash whenever the company decreases its financial resources by repaying debt, paying dividends to stockholders or purchasing its own equity securities. Also, the net cash effect might be small, for example when the company refinances debt.

When financing activities are a source of cash (new debt or equity is issued), it is appropriate to consider two questions. First, why were the new financial resources needed and were they properly used? Did they support an appropriate increase in investing activities—new assets? Did they hide an unwelcome decrease in operating activities—negative cash flows? The former may reflect the actions of a successful company whereas the latter may indicate a company at or near the point of financial failure. Second, was the source of cash (bonds or equity) appropriate? Should the company have used that particular source at this time? What was the market impact of doing so?

When financing activities are a use of cash (debt is repaid or equity is purchased), two different questions are appropriate. First, where did the necessary financial resources come from—operating cash flows or the sale of investments or, in the case of refinancing, new debt or equity? Again, one particular source may reflect the actions of a successful company simply meeting the terms of its debt agreements whereas another source may indicate a company in severe financial difficulty. Second, particularly in the case of equity purchases or early debt payments, was that the best use of the company's current financial resources? Why weren't those resources used to expand the scope of operations with the expectation of increasing future profitability/cash flows?

D.   Quality of Financial Reporting

GAAP elections, estimates and other choices provide management with considerable discretion and can provide opportunities to manipulate the information presented in the company financial statements. Financial reporting should accurately reflect the company's financial health and should be useful to assess both past performance and future expectations. So, the closer that financial reporting is to financial reality, the higher the quality of information about the company's financial health. Because dishonest managers most often attempt to manipulate earnings (profitability), financial reporting quality is most often related to earnings quality. Figure 6B provides a checklist of some key items to consider when assessing earnings quality.

FIGURE 6B A CHECKLIST FOR EARNINGS QUALITY*		
1. Sales	4. Nonoperating Revenue and Expense	
A. Allowance for doubtful accounts	J. Sales of assets	
B. Price vs. volume changes	K. Interest income	
C. Real vs. nominal growth	L. Equity income	
2. Cost of Goods Sold	M. Loss on asset write-downs	
D. Inventory cost-flow assumptions	N. Accounting changes	
E. LIFO layer reduction	O. Extraordinary items	
F. Loss on inventory write-downs	5. Other Issues	
3. Operating Expenses	P. Number of shares outstanding	
G. Discretionary expenses	Q. Acquisitions and dispositions	
H. Depreciation/depletion/amortization	R. Reserves	
I. Pension accounting		
* Fraser, Lyn M. and Aileen Ormiston. *Understanding Financial Statements*, 6th edition (New Jersey: Prentice Hall, 2001). Page 220.		

1.   Sales

For companies that have significant credit sales, there should be a consistent relationship between sales, accounts receivable and the allowance for doubtful accounts. For all companies, determine if changes in gross revenues are the result of price changes or volume changes or a combination of the two. Also, determine how revenue changes have been impacted by inflation. For example, does the nominal (reported) growth remain a "real" growth after adjusting for inflation?

2. Cost of Goods Sold

For companies that sell significant amounts of merchandise inventory to customers, determine if the inventory cost-flow assumption selected by the company promotes earnings quality given the company's operating environment. For example, LIFO is viewed as promoting earnings quality for companies operating in an inflationary environment. If the company does use LIFO, determine whether or not reported earnings have been influenced by a reduction in LIFO layers from previous years. Determine if reported earnings have been adjusted for any write-downs due to the application of lower-of-cost-or-market rules to inventory valuations.

3. Operating Expenses

Companies can manipulate earnings by increasing or decreasing various discretionary operating expenses. Determine if major discretionary expense categories (such as research and development, repair and maintenance and advertising and marketing) are consistent both from year to year and with the company's long-term goals and strategies. Determine if both the cost allocation methods used (straight line, accelerated, etc.) and the estimates made (life and residual value) for depreciation, depletion and amortization are consistent with how the economic benefits of the underlying assets are consumed by the company. Pension accounting is based on various expectations, assumptions and estimates regarding the benefits that will be paid when employees retire and on the earnings (interest) from pension assets set aside to meet those future obligations. Determine if those expectations, assumptions and estimates are reasonable given both the mix of employees in the company and current (and expected) market conditions.

4. Nonoperating Revenue and Expenses

Determine if asset sales occurred in the normal course of business or were made to increase earnings and/or generate needed cash during the current reporting period. Because interest income is a nonoperating item and relates to the management of excess cash reserves, determine if the amount is reasonable given any changes reported in the company's cash reserves. Determine the extent to which earnings include an investor company's equity share of income from an investee company. This is income reported in the investor's earnings but not yet received from the investee company. As with inventory reductions above, determine whether earnings have been reduced for losses on write-downs of assets to lower-of-cost-or-market value. Determine the impact on reported earnings of any changes in accounting methods adopted by the company. Also, determine whether these changes appear to be reasonable for the company or were made primarily to increase earnings. Determine the impact on reported earnings of any extraordinary items reported by the company. Extraordinary items should be both infrequent (they do not happen very often) and unusual in nature (they do not normally occur within this company's operating environment).

5. Other Issues

Determine if there has been a significant change in the number of shares of company stock outstanding, particularly common stock. Such changes can greatly affect comparability from year to year. Other events that affect comparability are acquisitions, dispositions or other significant changes in major lines of business or subsidiaries of the company. In addition to the allowance for doubtful accounts and pension accounts (both discussed above), companies create reserves to cover known future costs. Determine whether the reserve amount is appropriate for the estimated future cost or whether the reserve is simply increased in good years and decreased in bad years in an attempt to smooth reported earnings.

6.05   Financial Statement Analysis

As discussed previously, an important aspect of the finance function is an analysis of the financial information produced by the company to improve the decisions that will impact the wealth of the company's owners. That is, the financial management system should take the output (financial statements) of the financial reporting system and use that information to make decisions aimed at increasing the wealth of company owners. Thus, effective financial statement analysis is at the heart of the financial management system.

Effective financial statement analysis uses three different, but related, analytical tools: horizontal analysis, vertical analysis and ratio analysis. Horizontal (trend) analysis is concerned with changes in financial statement elements over time. Vertical (common size) analysis is concerned with how various financial statement elements compare to a specified total. Ratio analysis is concerned with how related financial statement elements compare to each other.

A. Horizontal Analysis

Horizontal analysis determines by how much a particular financial statement amount has changed over time. The comparisons could be of end-of-period totals—this month's sales vs. last month's sales. This can help determine the overall trend in sales across time. The comparisons could be of like periods—this month's sales vs. the sales for the same month last year. This can help determine the trend in sales for similar times of the year. Horizontal comparisons always begin as dollar differences—the amount for this period minus the amount for last period. Dollar differences do measure the absolute magnitude of the change (a billion-dollar change is more significant than a million-dollar change). However, by itself, the dollar difference does not reflect the relative magnitude of the change (a ten-percent increase is more significant than a one-percent increase). The relative magnitude is best measured by the percentage change—the dollar difference divided by the amount for last period. The focus on relative, rather than absolute, amounts normalizes financial statement elements so that companies can be compared. This also is the focus of both vertical and ratio analysis.

B. Vertical Analysis

Vertical analysis determines how different financial statement elements compare to a specified (and related) total. It is a technique to determine the component makeup of the financial statements that is applied to the balance sheet and income statement.[19] On the balance sheet, each balance sheet item is compared to—is stated as a percentage of—total assets. On the income statement, each income statement item is compared to—is stated as a percentage of—net sales. This can provide important information about financial condition (balance sheet) or operations (income statement).

For example, on the balance sheet, management's liquidity strategy might be expressed in terms of the percentage of total assets held in cash, accounts receivable and inventory. Yet, the real question is, what is the appropriate percentage? Too much cash can indicate inadequate cash management. Too much in accounts receivable can indicate inappropriate credit policies and/or collection difficulties. Too much inventory can indicate obsolete products. The determination of the appropriate amounts in each area and their control over time become important aspects of the financial management system.

Also, on the income statement, management's profitability strategy might be expressed in terms of the percentage of net sales appropriate for cost of goods sold (or gross profit), marketing expenses, wages and salaries, rents and the like. Again, the question is, what is appropriate? Too low a gross profit and the company may not be profitable enough to survive. Too high a gross profit and the company may lose sales to competitors. Too little spent on marketing and customers may not be aware of the company's products. Too much spent and profits are reduced due to "wasted" marketing efforts.

---

19.   Vertical analysis tends not to be applied to the cash flow statement because it does not have a significant total that is directly related to all other items on the statement. Some have attempted to use the change in cash as the divisor for vertical analysis of the cash flow statement. However, doing so does not always produce satisfactory results.

C.   Ratio Analysis

Ratio analysis looks at how two related financial statement elements compare to each other. For ratio analysis to make sense, there must be a useful relationship between the financial statement elements being compared. For example, there is a relationship between current assets and current liabilities that helps measure a company's liquidity. There is a relationship between inventory and cost of goods sold that helps measure the speed at which inventory is being sold. There is a relationship between net income and stockholders' equity that helps measure the returns being earned by company owners.

Ratio analysis is often directed at relationships that can be divided into groups with a particular focus, including liquidity, cycle, solvency, profitability and equity. However, because the goal is to gain as much insight into the company as possible, and because of the articulation and interrelationships of the financial statements, it is important to consider more than one ratio within a group or even more than one group of ratios. Figure 6C provides a summary of many of the most common ratios used for financial statement analysis.

1.   Liquidity Ratios

Liquidity refers to the company's ability to meet its short-term debts as they come due. The liquidity ratios are designed to provide information to evaluate that ability. Short-term debts (current liabilities) are paid with cash obtained from revenues or from the conversion of assets into cash. Current assets generally exist to be converted into cash; unlike long-term assets, whose sale could disrupt the company's long-range goals and objectives. For this reason, liquidity ratios focus on the relationships between current assets, current liabilities and revenues. The common liquidity ratios (Current Ratio, Quick Ratio, Cash Ratio, Working Capital) measure the size of that relationship. In general, the larger the liquidity ratio, the larger the coverage of current assets available to meet current liabilities as they become due, and the more liquid the firm.

It does matter what form the current assets take. Holding large amounts of obsolete inventory or uncollectible accounts receivable may produce high liquidity ratios but they actually result in a lower level of liquidity. Thus, when evaluating the liquidity ratios it is important to consider the underlying assets and liabilities and whether their individual amounts are reasonable to meet the firm's operating needs. Also, too high liquidity results in nonproductive assets and a lower return to owners. Thus, the size of the liquidity ratios should be compared to the speed of the operating cycle to determine if firm liquidity is being properly managed.

2. Cycle Ratios

Where the liquidity ratios focus on the size of the operating cycle, the cycle ratios focus on the speed of the operating cycle. The operating cycle uses short-term debt (accounts payable) to acquire products (inventory) to sell to customers (accounts receivable) to generate cash. The amount of cash generated should be larger than the amount of cash needed to maintain the cycle (i.e., cash collections on accounts receivable are larger than cash payments on accounts payable). The excess cash (profitability) is used to meet other company needs (operating expenses, debt repayment, internal growth, etc.) and to provide a return to company owners (dividends).

Think of the operating cycle as a water wheel being turned by the river of business transactions that flow through the firm. The faster (or slower) the river, the smaller (or larger) the wheel needs to be to complete the work required of the operating cycle. Thus, as the cycle ratios become faster, the liquidity ratios can become smaller. Put another way, if the liquidity ratios are too large relative to the cycle ratios, the firm may be too liquid and may not be as profitable as it could be.

The turnover form of the cycle ratios measures relative levels of speed, and the higher the ratio, the faster that part of the operating cycle. The turnover form also measures the amount of work being done by that part of the operating cycle—in other words, the number of dollars of sales generated by each dollar of accounts receivable provided to customers. The number-of-days form of the cycle ratios measures absolute levels of speed—that is, just how fast that part of the operating cycle is moving. The overall speed of the operating cycle can be determined by the number of days in inventory plus the number of days in accounts receivable minus the number of days in accounts payable. This indicates the length of time the firm needs coverage for liquidity.

3. Solvency Ratios

Where the liquidity ratios focus on the short term, the solvency ratios focus on the firm's long-term debt-paying capabilities. In a very strict sense, some view solvency as simply the firm's ability to satisfy all of its debts in liquidation. That is, the firm has sufficient assets of a sufficient value so that if it should liquidate, all of its debts would be fully paid. This, of course, is never the firm's intent. Firms do not desire to liquidate as a means to pay their debts. As with liquidity, an important consideration for solvency is cash flows. To exist as a going concern, the firm needs to generate sufficient cash flows to meet both its short-term liquidity and long-term solvency needs. Payments on debt can take two forms: interest and principal.

Since interest payments are recurring they are often viewed from an income statement perspective because they are usually deemed to come from profitability. Two of the solvency ratios (times interest earned and fixed charge coverage) attempt to measure how well the firm can meet the recurring interest payments on its debt. Principal payments more often occur at specific points in time and, so, are often viewed from a balance sheet perspective because they usually come from assets set aside for that purpose. The cash flow adequacy ratio attempts to measure the firm's ability to set aside sufficient assets (cash reserves) to meet those future debt principal payments.

The debt ratios (debt to assets and debt to equity) look at how much of the firm has been financed with debt. Some amount of current debt (accounts payable) probably is necessary to support firm operations. Also, some amount of long-term debt often is desirable because (if it is used properly) it can generate financial leverage (additional profits) for firm owners. However, too much debt can lead to financial instability or distress or even insolvency. That is because, unlike equity, debt must be repaid to the lender at some specific point in time, and those eventual repayments put a financial strain on the firm. This is another example that a little of something can be good but too much can be bad.

4. Profitability Ratios

Profitability is an extremely important income statement concept and there are a number of ratios designed to measure the impact of the firm's operations on profitability. Because of the way in which accrual accounting works, profitability and cash flows are not necessarily correlated in the short run. As in the High Growth Company example shown in Figure 6A, high profitability can occur during periods of negative cash flows. However, in the long run, profitability does correlate with the firm's ability to generate sufficient cash flows to (a) support liquidity, (b) maintain solvency and (c) provide a return to firm owners.

The profitability ratios can be divided into two groups—those with an income statement orientation and those with a balance sheet orientation. The income statement group includes the gross profit margin, operating profit margin and return on sales (net profit margin). Each of those ratios looks at particular elements of the firm's operations and measures how each of those elements affect profitability. In effect, each measures how much of the revenue pie is left after taking out slices for each of the major expense categories. The profitability slice can be larger only by making the pie larger (increasing revenues) or making the other slices smaller (decreasing expenses); these ratios indicate the impact on the firm from those types of decisions.

Related to the net profit margin is the cash flow margin. Whereas the net profit margin follows accrual accounting conventions to measure profitability as a percent of revenues, the cash flow margin measures operating cash flows as a percent of revenues. A comparison of these ratios, particularly over time, can help determine the correlation, if any, between cash flows and profitability. The more divergent these ratios are, the more likely that current profitability actually represents future cash flows, and the more care that must be exercised to ensure the firm can maintain sufficient liquidity and solvency to be around to enjoy those future cash flows.

The balance sheet group includes return on assets, return on investment and return on equity. Unlike the income statement group, which measures the effects of revenue and expense decisions on profitability itself, this group measures the investment returns generated by the firm's capital and the benefit that profitability provides to the owners of the firm. The essential relationship is between return on assets and return on equity. Differences between those ratios represent the impact of financial leverage, which is the positive (or negative) effect of properly (or improperly) using debt in the firm's capital structure.

The simplest approach to evaluating the effects of financial leverage is to use the financial leverage ratio (one of the solvency ratios) to convert return on assets into return on equity as follows:

Return on Equity	=	Return on Assets	x	Financial Leverage
Net Income divided by Stockholders' Equity	=	Net Income divided by Total Assets	x	Total Assets divided by Stockholders' Equity

This approach is the most direct way to assess the impact of financial leverage on the firm. A second approach is to decompose return on assets as follows:

Return on Equity	=	Return on Sales	x	Asset Turnover	x	Financial Leverage
Net Income divided by Stockholders' Equity	=	Net Income divided by Net Sales	x	Net Sales divided by Total Assets	x	Total Assets Divided by Stockholders' Equity

This approach clearly shows that stockholder returns are a function of the relationship between profitability (return on sales), the operating cycle (asset turnover) and solvency (financial leverage). Also, this approach can be used to evaluate the association between risk (financial leverage) and reward (return on sales) compounded by the speed of the operating cycle (asset turnover).

As with the cash flow margin, the cash return ratios (cash return on assets and cash return on equity) remove the accrual accounting effects and focus on returns in terms of current cash flows. Also as with the profitability ratios, a comparison of the accrual return ratios and the cash return ratios aids in the evaluation of the time lag, if any, between profitability and cash flows.

5. Equity Ratios

The equity ratios (also called market ratios) help to evaluate of the firm's relationship with its stockholders (owners). Because the firm's common stockholders are its true owners, all of these ratios are computed only with respect to the income accruing to and the equity belonging to the common stockholders. In this way, any preferred stock issued by the firm is treated more like debt than equity.

The earnings per share and price to earnings ratios are probably the two equity ratios most often cited by financial analysts. Both must be evaluated with care. The computation of earnings per share (as shown in Figure 6C) appears simple, but it is deceptively so. The actual computation of earnings per share (by publicly traded corporations) includes the dilutive effects, if any, of stock options, warrants and rights and convertible bonds and preferred stock. This approach insures a conservative measurement for earnings per share and actual earnings per share—if there is such a thing—could be larger by some unknown amount. Thus, earnings per share should be viewed as a conservative measure of stockholder returns and not be confused with an actual measure of those returns.

Also, the dilutive effect can make valid comparisons of earnings per share across firms or across time difficult. For comparisons across time, care should be taken to insure that earnings per share for prior years have been restated for any dilutive effects in the current year. For cross-firm comparisons, care should be taken to evaluate the impact of any dilutive effects contained in the earnings per share of one firm that does not affect the earnings per share of the other firm.

The price-earnings ratio (P/E ratio) is commonly viewed as a benchmark that reflects the market's collective decision about the firm's future earnings power relative to that of other firms. From time to time the P/E ratio may indeed reflect the market's opinion about the firm's own future. That is, the firm's P/E ratio may be high (or low) as compared to other firms because it actually has higher (or lower) earnings potential than other firms. However, care must be taken to consider that the market's opinion (as reflected by stock prices) may be incorrect. In a bull (or bear) market all P/E ratios may be higher (or lower) simply because the market as a whole is higher (or lower). In such a market, while the firm's P/E ratio relative to other firms may be correct, the ratio may not well represent the actual value of the firm's future earnings. This can be particularly true in a bear market when all stock prices are depressed regardless of the firm's true earnings potential. P/E ratios also can be inflated (or deflated) because of investor infatuation (or disgust) with select firms and/or industry sectors—as the dot.com bubble of the late 1990s attests.

Several of the equity ratios measure either the amount of firm profitability paid out to stockholders (dividend payout ratio, dividend yield ratio) or the amount of profitability/cash flow kept by the firm to support internal growth needs (retained earnings ratio, retained cash ratio). These ratios are of little importance for firms at both ends of the maturity spectrum. Newer (less mature) firms generally must use all available cash flows to support their growth rates and, so, do not have sufficient cash resources to pay dividends. With no dividends, the ratios simply are not meaningful. Mature firms generally have consistent cash flows due to well-established profitability, and so they can support both their relatively modest growth needs and dividend payouts to stockholders. Their ratios, while meaningful, tend to be quite consistent from year to year and important mostly for selecting stocks for a retirement portfolio where current income is a primary goal of portfolio management. However, for firms in the middle ground, these ratios can provide useful information as firm management attempts to balance returns to stockholders with firm growth needs. This balancing act may cause these ratios to fluctuate from year to year and may provide an opportunity for investors to determine if the firm is making the best use of its financial resources.

Book value per share, like the P/E ratio, is often easy to comprehend but, just as often, difficult to evaluate. As noted in Figure 6C, book value per share is based on the accounting values of assets and liabilities on the balance sheet, and those values are based on the historical cost convention used in accounting. This convention requires that all assets and liabilities be valued at their historical cost; that is, at the exchange price on the date the assets and liabilities were acquired. While GAAP does require the revaluation (usually downward) of some assets and liabilities that have changed in value since their acquisition date, most assets and liabilities remain at their original, historical cost. The result is that, particularly for mature companies, book value per share can be very much out of date when compared to the true current values of the firm's assets and liabilities.

This is not to suggest that book value per share is always (even significantly) lower than the true value of the firm. While this may be true in the largest number of cases, the opposite also may be true—that book value per share may be (even significantly) higher than the true value of the firm. Care should be taken to assess the true value of the firm before conclusions about book value per share are reached. Just what are the true values of the firm's assets and liabilities? In an efficient market, the true value is the market price per share (actually, the total market capitalization) of the firm's shares. If it has been determined that the market has appropriately priced the firm's shares, then market value and book value can be compared to assess the firm's current worth relative to its historical cost. However, if the market has not appropriately priced the firm's shares, then market value is not an appropriate surrogate for the firm's true value. For example, when the market as a whole is severely depressed, market values may fall below a firm's true value and may approach (or even fall below) the firm's book value. Those are the times that warm the hearts, and line the pockets, of corporate raiders.

	FIGURE 6C	
	SUMMARY OF FINANCIAL RATIOS	
Liquidity Ratios		
Current Ratio	Current Assets divided by Current Liabilities	Measures the ability to pay bills as they become due.
Quick (Acid Test) Ratio	[Current Assets minus Inventory] divided by Current Liabilities	A more rigorous measure of bill paying ability. Removes inventory, usually the least liquid current asset.
Cash Ratio	[Cash plus Marketable Securities] divided by Current Liabilities	The most conservative measure of short-term liquidity.
Cash Flow Ratio	Cash Flow from Operations divided by Current Liabilities	A measure of the sufficiency of operating cash flows to support bill paying ability.
Working Capital	Current Assets minus Current Liabilities	Not a ratio but an absolute amount. Closely related to the Current Ratio. Another measure of bill paying ability.

	Cycle Ratios	
Accounts Receivable Turnover	Net Sales divided by Average Accounts Receivable	How many times, on average, that accounts receivable is collected during the year. It also measures the amount of sales generated by each dollar of accounts receivable.
# of Days in Accounts Receivable	365 divided by A/R Turnover	The number of days, on average, it takes to collect accounts receivable.
Inventory Turnover	Cost of Goods Sold divided by Average Inventory	How many times, on average, the entire inventory value is sold during the year. It also measures the amount of cost of goods sold (sales) generated by each dollar of inventory.
# of Days in Inventory	365 divided by Inventory Turnover	The number of days, on average, it takes to sell the inventory value.
Accounts Payable Turnover	Purchases divided by Average Accounts Payable	How many times, on average, that accounts payable is paid during the year. It also measures the amount of purchases created by each dollar of accounts payable.

# of Days in Accounts Payable	365 divided by A/P Turnover	The number of days, on average, it takes to pay the accounts payable.
Fixed Asset Turnover	Net Sales divided by Net Property, Plant and Equipment	The amount of sales generated by each dollar of fixed assets. It is a measure of the efficient use of fixed assets.
Total Asset Turnover	Net Sales divided by Total Assets	The amount of sales generated by each dollar of total assets. It is a measure of the efficient use of total assets.

Solvency Ratios		
Debt to Assets Ratio	Total Liabilities divided by Total Assets	Measures the proportion of total assets that are financed by debt.
Debt to Equity Ratio	Total Liabilities divided by Stockholders' Equity	Measures the proportion of total debt to total equity.
Times Interest Earned Ratio	Operating Profit divided by Interest Expense	Measures how many times interest expense on debt is covered by operating earnings.
Fixed Charge Coverage Ratio	[Operating Profit plus Lease Payments] divided by [Interest Expense plus Lease Payments]	A broader measure than Times Interest Earned. Treats lease payments as part of the debt coverage from operating earnings.
Cash Flow Adequacy Ratio	Cash Flow from Operating Activities divided by Average Annual Long-Term Debt Maturities	Measures how many times annual long-term debt maturities are covered by operating cash flows.
Financial Leverage Ratio	Total Assets divided by Stockholders' Equity	The amount of financial leverage (increase in returns to stockholders) provided by the use of debt in the firm's capital structure.

Profitability Ratios		
Gross Profit Margin	Gross Profit divided by Net Sales	Measures profitability after deducting cost of goods sold from sales.
Operating Profit Margin	Operating Profit divided by Net Sales	Measures profitability after deducting all operating expenses.
Return on Sales (Net Profit Margin)	Net Income divided by Net Sales	Measures profitability after deducting all other revenues and expenses.
Cash Flow Margin	Cash Flow from Operating Activities divided by Net Sales	Measures the ability to generate cash flows from sales.
Return on Assets	Net Income divided by Total Assets	Measures the efficiency of generating profits using all available assets.
Return on Investment	Net Income divided by [Long-Term Debt plus Stockholders' Equity]	Measures the efficiency of generating profits using all long-term sources of capital.
Return on Equity	Net Income divided by Stockholders' Equity	Measures the efficiency of generating profits using equity.
Cash Return on Assets	Cash Flow from Operating Activities divided by Total Assets	Measures the efficiency of generating cash flows from using all available assets.
Cash Return on Equity	Cash Flow from Operating Activities divided by Stockholders' Equity	Measures the efficiency of generating cash flows from using equity.

Equity Ratios		
Earnings per Share	Net Income divided by Number of Shares Outstanding	Measures return to common stockholders for each share owned.
Price to Earnings (P/E) Ratio	Market Price per Share divided by Earnings per Share	Measures the stock market value of the firm as a multiple of earnings.
Dividend Payout Ratio	Dividends per Share divided by Earnings per Share	Measures the percentage of earnings paid out to stockholders as dividends.
Dividend Yield Ratio	Dividends per Shared divided by Market Price per Share	Measures the return to stockholders from dividends.
Retained Earnings Ratio	[Net Income less Dividends] divided by Net Income	Measures internal growth potential as the percentage of earnings not paid in dividends.
Retained Cash Ratio	[Cash Flow from Operating Activities less Dividends] divided by Cash Flow from Operating Activities	Measures internal growth potential as the percentage of operating cash flows not paid in dividends.
Book Value per Share	Total Assets divided by Number of Shares Outstanding	The accounting (historical cost based) value of each share of common stock.

Financing a Business

Bruce F. Dravis
Downey Brand LLP
Sacramento, CA

Contents

CHAPTER *7*

Financing a Business

7.01   Preliminary Considerations

At some point, an emerging company will require outside financing to develop or extend its business. Whether the source is an equity investor, who shares in the ownership of the business, or a lender, whose return is measured by the interest rate on a loan, outside sources of funding expect compensation for the time and money they invest in the company.

The financing needs of companies vary according to each business's circumstances. Likewise, each investor, whether it supplies debt or equity, will have individual criteria for investment that will depend on the type of capital that the investor provides.

In seeking financing for a business, it is critical to evaluate which group of investors to target. Not all sources of capital are appropriate to every business. For example, the investment focus of venture capitalists is very different from that of commercial banks. If a company does not meet the investment criteria of the particular type of investor it is addressing, the company should not expect to receive funding from that source, regardless of the time, effort or money expended in trying to reach that source, and regardless of management's confidence that the business will prosper.

To evaluate which type of investor is right for an individual business, the client and its attorney must understand and integrate many factors, including the following:

- Different types of potential investors
- Key variables affecting each type of investor's decision to provide capital
- Business and industry of the company
- Company's prospects for growth

- Company's projected financial needs
- Stage of development of the company
- Business goals of the company's founders (for example, acquisition by a larger company)
- Investment instruments to be used
- Impact of state and federal laws regulating the offer and sale of securities

This chapter describes how these factors affect the financing decisions a company and its advisors must make.

7.02   Financing Sources

Before approaching a source of financing for an emerging company, the company must determine its cash needs, which can vary depending upon the nature of the business. For example, a software developer selling into an established market may have a short time horizon for product development and entry into the market, so the company's primary capital need will be to have cash to get through development and marketing phases of the software until it can generate revenues. By contrast, a biotech company may need cash or a source of cash to last the 9–14 years until the development, testing and regulatory hurdles to going to market have been crossed.

Once the business plan and the cash flow analysis have been done, the company can consider which of the many different types of financing is appropriate to achieve the company's success.

Set out below is a summary of different capital sources and different financial instruments or arrangements that emerging companies might use as a source of capital. Treatises have been written about each of the capital sources and instruments described herein; an overview such as this must necessarily omit nuances or details in favor of addressing major issues and themes.

A.   Venture Capital

1.   *Preliminary Considerations*

Venture capitalists ("VCs") are typically organized as investment partnerships that invest in emerging companies. The source of funds for venture capital firms are institutional public and private pension funds, endowment funds, foundations, insurance companies, banks, individuals, corporations and other investors who desire to include venture capital investment in a diversified portfolio.

A significant amount of the funds for venture capital investment comes from institutional public and private pension funds, although amounts have declined since the high point in 2000. During the 1990s, venture capital partnerships raised investment capital at increasing rates, reaching approximately $106 billion in the year 2000 alone. In the post-2000 environment, which included the bursting of the "dot.com" and real estate bubbles, the rate of investment in venture capital partnerships declined dramatically, to approximately $16 billion in the year 2009, according to the National Venture Capital Association ("NVCA"). While the venture capital firms continue to hold billions of dollars of capital for investment in emerging companies, VC investments have shrunk, and the returns to venture capital investors since the glory days of the 1990s can only be called dismal.[1]

Venture capitalists review thousands of business plans and proposals each year, yet invest in only a small percentage of the businesses. Their review will include consideration of the merits and feasibility of a proposed new technology and consideration of the business merits of the plan. VCs tend to invest in a portfolio of companies, permitting them to limit their investment risk with respect to any single investment.

A VC's objective is to invest in an emerging company before it has completely developed, with the expectation that the investment will have grown in value at a rate of 50% or more per year by the time of an "exit event." An exit event, such as an initial public offering ("IPO") of the company's shares or the merger or acquisition of the company by another company, is a transaction that permits the VC to convert its investment in the company back into cash. Most VCs look for an exit event within three to seven years after the initial investment. Not all investments by venture capitalists reach the target 50% annual rate of return, but VCs target that rate of return in order to permit the blended return from their successful and unsuccessful investments to achieve an actual return satisfactory to the VC fund investors. IPOs will be covered in more detail in Chapter 13 (Growing a Business).

Venture capitalists seek companies that target large and quickly expanding markets. Only those markets have the prospect of providing company growth that will generate high returns to VCs. Accordingly, companies that are likely to serve only niche markets, or to grow at a steady but undramatic rate, are not good candidates for venture capital financing.

VCs are not passive sources of capital, but will become actively involved in the management of the companies in which they invest. It is typical for a VC to require as a condition of investment that a member of the VC firm joins the portfolio company's board of directors. The VC firm's board member will actively participate in the company's management and strategic decision making.

---

1. Statistics on venture capital raising and investment performance can be found at the NVCA website, http://www.nvca.org/.

2.   *Factors Affecting Investment Decisions*

VCs will typically list a number of factors that affect their decisions to invest. Above all, they have to believe in the existence and strength of the market that the company is targeting, and they have to believe that the management and key employees in the company are capable of executing a business plan to succeed in that market.

As noted above, without a fast growing and broad market, a company cannot have the growth prospects that would provide a venture capitalist with the high rates of return needed to justify a VC investment. For a technology-based company, the high growth could come because the new technology creates an entirely new market, which is what occurred (in different eras) with personal computers, fax machines, wireless phones and smart phones.

The founders and management of an emerging company will identify target markets, including markets created or exploited by the company's new technology, and will create a business plan to capture the opportunity in those markets. A venture capital firm will have or retain individuals who can bring technology and business backgrounds to bear on the VC firm's review of the plan. If the VC agrees with the company's key assumptions and evaluation of the existence and scope of a target market, the company's chance of obtaining VC financing significantly improves.

Even if a VC believes a company has correctly identified a target market that would support VC investment, however, the VC will also need to have confidence that the company's management team has the talent and expertise to execute on the business plan and actually realize the opportunity. The technology expertise of inventors, and the business expertise and background of the nontechnical management team, will be critical to the VC investment decision. It would be unusual for a VC to entrust significant capital to an untried management team, even if the company's technology or new market represented a compelling opportunity. Founders, particularly if they are young or starting a company in an industry in which they have not previously worked, should be advised that they may need to recruit seasoned management in order to become eligible to receive venture capital.

Four other factors are very important to VCs: (1) the ability of the company to defend its product advantages, whether by patent, relationships with key players in the industry or otherwise, (2) the existence of high margins on product sales, which confirm the existence of a viable market and the lack of satisfactory substitutes, (3) existing sales and cash flow and (4) the industry or region.

The ability of a company to defend its position in a target market is a key factor in VC investment decisions. While being able to obtain a patent will not be reason enough by itself for a VC to invest, the *inability* to obtain a patent will likely be reason enough for a VC to avoid investing. If the VCs disagree with the company founders on the value of the target market, the company's ability to defend its position in that market is clearly of secondary importance. But where the market is valid and important, being able to erect "barriers to entry" to new competitors in that market means, at a minimum, that the opportunity is more valuable, both to the company and the VC, than if open entry by competitors was possible.

High margins on product sales are desirable in their own right, but for VCs the existence of high margins means that the product meets a compelling need for customers, such that customers are willing to pay a premium to have the need met. VCs sometimes refer to this as the distinction between "nice to have" and "need to have" or "solving a pain." It is not unusual for a VC to tell a company that its technology does everything the inventors claim, that the management team is good, that the product is protectable and that the market potential is good, and then decline to invest because the VC believes that customers may "want" the product but they do not "need" the product or that it does not "solve a pain" for buyers in the end market.

Finally, any individual VC investor will tend to limit itself to making investments in a particular industry or in a particular geographic region. The latter is particularly important to VCs that want to have all their investments in the same area so that they can regularly visit several in one day.

It is relatively rare for a full-blown venture capital fund to be involved with "seed" stage investments, in the $500,000 to $1,000,000 range. Investment in that size generally means that a company is at a very early stage and that the money will be spent to demonstrate the viability of a company's idea or to hit a key first milestone in corporate development. Many venture capital funds cannot profitably invest in smaller increments, because they have tens or hundreds of millions of dollars to invest, forcing them to evaluate a limited number of possible investments of $5 million or more rather than attempt to deploy the funds $1 million at a time. Initial-stage investments tend to come from other sources, such as the founders, their families and friends or individual "angel" investors, as is discussed below.

Venture capitalists typically invest in preferred stock, although they will also make investments in debt instruments or rights to purchase common stock in connection with other investments.

3. Advantages and Disadvantages

Since 2000, VCs have had less to invest, and have had poorer investment performance compared to the investments in the 1990s. The mediocre performance of the stock market generally during the 2000s, and changes in law, such as the adoption of the Sarbanes-Oxley Act in 2002, meant that high dollar IPO "exit events" were unlikely for VCs and their portfolio companies. Mergers and acquisitions have become the predominant exit vehicle for start-ups, but the eye-popping valuations of the 1990s are gone.

An emerging company that successfully meets the investment criteria for venture capital will find, nonetheless, that there are significant advantages to venture capital over other types of financing:

- VCs tend to be active, knowledgeable participants in the business. VCs invest in industries they understand. As participants in the boardroom, they will bring an understanding of the technological and commercial issues facing the company's industry. Very often, VCs have industry contacts through other portfolio companies or prior investments that can aid the emerging company in meeting its strategic or marketing goals.
- VCs are relatively long-term investors. VCs are not driven by a short-term need to realize a return. An emerging company will very typically have little or no revenues for a long time as a new product is being developed or sold. VCs may be willing to wait several years. The term depends on their area of investment, with technology investors typically looking for an exit after three years and biotech investors usually looking for an exit after seven years. VCs will, however, push an emerging company to meet these time frames.
- As equity stakeholders, VCs maximize their profits if the business grows significantly. This aligns their interests—mostly—with the interests of the founders. VCs generally invest in preferred stock, which will have additional rights over the common stock usually held by the founders and employees. VCs can provide access to underwriters and other professional or consulting help for the company. As a company succeeds, the ability to obtain access to such services increases in the normal course of events, but the VCs can provide additional points of contact for such services.

There are a number of disadvantages to venture capital as well:

- A great deal of time can be spent raising VC funding. First, it is very hard to get the attention of VC firms. They are inundated with proposals. Having a personal contact, who can be a friendly point of introduction within the VC firm, can help a company capture the VC's attention. Such personal contacts might arise through the company's industry contacts, law firm or accounting firm. Second, the negotiation process will likely consume a good part of management's time for three to six months, at a minimum. Many companies suffer from the distraction.
- The founders and the VCs may develop differences of opinion over company direction. Although the active participation by VCs in a company can be positive, there is also the potential for founders, management and the VCs to develop diverging interests, particularly if the company does not achieve success according to its business plan.
- In a negative business cycle, the VCs may require significant concessions in order to provide continuing funding to keep the company growing. Such concessions could take the form of highly increased equity positions or increased control over the management team. If the alternative is collapse of the company, there may be no meaningful choice for the founders or existing shareholder other than to take the funding on those terms.

- Venture capitalists often will want to invest with at least one other VC fund or corporate investor. Finding one enthusiastic VC for a company's venture usually will not be enough. The company (often with the VC's help) will have to locate a co-investor.

Historically, more companies wanted venture capital than were truly qualified to obtain it. The success of venture capital investing during the 1990s caused many entrepreneurs to believe incorrectly that venture capital was a prerequisite to success. If a company does not target the kind of high growth market that can provide a VC with its necessary rate of return on investment, it will not receive venture capital.

B.   Alternative Financing Sources

As discussed above, venture capital financing is appropriate for only a small segment of emerging companies. Other sources must be used for companies that are not yet ready for venture capital financing or will never be candidates for venture capital financing because they do not fit the venture capital financing model.

No source of capital is perfect for all companies. Each of the potential capital sources below will have advantages and disadvantages—from a legal perspective, an accounting perspective and an operational perspective. For example, a company that uses nonconvertible debt financing will not dilute the ownership stake of the founders and investors, but may find that balance sheet issues, interest payment issues or loan covenant restrictions on operating decisions impair its flexibility in dealing with future capital needs. It will be up to the management and the founders to determine, in the individual case, which capital source best suits the situation they face.

1.   Founders and Family Members

The initial source of capital, and a source of capital that brings the lowest risk of litigation, is the founding group for the company, including family members of that group. Obtaining either equity investment or loans from the founding group and their families has a number of advantages for the company: They are an identified group; they share the founders' goals; they have a stake in the founders' success; the resources and investment objectives of the founders and the family are more likely to be known or freely discussed than will be the case in negotiating with third-party investors; they may be more likely to offer favorable terms than a third party; and they are less likely to resort to litigation if things go wrong. Family members, depending upon the relation, may be accredited investors for purposes of the securities laws, as discussed in Chapter 2 (Preparing a Business Plan) and below.

The disadvantage of family money is that if things go wrong, the founder has to live with them. This could be an additional incentive to succeed, or an additional burden, depending on the founder's point of view. Founders should not take the decision to accept family money lightly. A business failure, disappointing in itself, can become a greater burden when family stress is added.

2. *Friends*

Friends of the founders are another early-stage source of capital. Friends as investors are likely to have the same advantages and disadvantages as family investors. Unlike family members, however, friends may not be eligible to receive securities law exemptions with respect to their investments in an emerging company, so the founders should be aware that additional documentation or other securities law compliance steps may be required.

3. *Angel Investors*

Wealthy individual investors, dubbed "angel" investors, are individuals who desire to invest in emerging companies. Typically, they invest when the company is not sufficiently mature as a business to be a credible candidate for venture capital, but needs more capital than the founders and their family and friends can provide.

The success of technology companies over the past 20 years has created a new generation of wealthy individuals who have the means and the experience with start up companies to be realistic sources of capital for founders. Angel investors often form regional groups, and networks of regional groups, to identify and evaluate potential investments within a geographic region.

Angel investors typically invest in an early-stage round, either as debt or preferred stock investors. They invest in the expectation that the capital they provide will be used to help the company hit a product development milestone, establish a proof of concept or develop an initial prototype that will increase the company's valuation in a future venture-capital round financing. That way, even if the angels are diluted by future rounds of venture capital investment, they expect that they will have purchased shares at the lowest price offered by the company to outside investors.

Under the securities laws, wealthy individual investors are "accredited investors" for whom the securities laws permit simplified investment disclosures. Assuming that the founders have a way to identify these individuals, limiting a capital search to angel investors or accredited investors can simplify the capital-raising task in two ways. First, the disclosures required by state and federal securities laws will generally not have to fit prescribed forms in order to receive exemption under the securities laws. Second, founders have a better chance of raising money from individuals who have ample money than from individuals whose means are more limited.

4.   *Corporate Partner/Investor*

A significant number of established technology companies will look to finance emerging companies, either through venture capital investment on terms similar to those offered to (and frequently side by side with) venture capital firms, or through loans, development agreements, licenses or other transactions.

An emerging company can provide a valuable service for a corporate partner or investor, by developing products or technologies that are complementary to the established company's product road map or marketing plans, but which the established company has determined not to develop itself.

Some corporations have established venture capital subdivisions that evaluate corporate investments in a fashion similar to that of other venture capital companies, but with a view to the objectives of the corporate parent. (Intel's venture capital arm, for example, is not a likely candidate for investment in a biotech startup, but could very well get involved with a semiconductor, software or hardware manufacturing startup.)

The availability of this type of capital can depend on the economic cycle. In boom times, corporations will have excess cash available for R&D and investment activities that is not available in more financially constrained times.

5.   *Public Shells*

Entrepreneurs seeking capital are sometimes approached by promoters who will offer them financial backing if they will merge their company into another, inactive company that already has shares that were registered for public trading (a "public shell"). The shares of a public shell will not be registered with the New York Stock Exchange or NASDAQ, but will trade in the "pink sheets" or a regional U.S. exchange, such as the Denver Stock Exchange, or a Canadian stock exchange, such as the Vancouver Stock Exchange.

The public shell promoter may claim (falsely) that the "public" status of the company will make fund-raising easier. The shell may have some cash left over from the last venture the company operated, and upon a merger that money would be available for operations of the merged company.

Public shell shares will trade for less than a dollar per share or for a low dollar amount and are sometimes referred to as "penny stocks." Penny stocks are prone to abuse by traders who use rumors, Internet postings or other market manipulations to generate buyer interest in the stock in a "pump and dump" scheme (in which the promoters pump up interest in the penny stock, then dump their shares on unsuspecting buyers).

Being publicly traded, in and of itself, does not provide additional capital to the company, nor does it make the capital raising process simpler for an emerging company. If anything, merging with a public shell makes the capital raising process for an emerging company more difficult, because it cuts off one potential exit strategy for the investors: the company cannot conduct an IPO because its shares are already publicly traded.

A company that is approached by a public shell promoter should scrutinize the situation very carefully, perform careful reviews of the ability of the promoter to deliver on any promised financing and investigate the background of the promoter and the promoter's affiliates. If not every public shell promotion is a fraud, so many of them are frauds that the transactions should be undertaken only if the company and its advisors use extraordinary care and due diligence. The circumstances in which a shell merger is a benefit to a company are exceedingly rare.

6. Grants

Some companies may be at a stage at which they are eligible for grant funding through a state or federal technology or business development grant program. Grants typically do not require a founder to give up equity in the company, but can require significant time before the grant application, review and award process is completed. Grants may also contain terms limiting how the technology developed under the grant may be used (for example, a mandatory license back to the government for government use). With the slowing of VC investment, many emerging companies turned to grants as a funding source.

7. Leasing Companies

There are a number of equipment leasing companies willing to work with an emerging company. Some are willing to provide leasing before the company has developed a significant venture capital relationship, although most want some level of investment money. Such infusion of capital provides some certainty to the lessor that the company will be afloat long enough to make the payments on the leased equipment. The leasing company is also able to rely indirectly on the due diligence process of the investors to give it assurance that there is an equity investor who believes in the markets that the company is targeting, the products and technology the company is developing and the ability of the management team to execute a winning strategy.

A leasing company generally will finance major equipment purchases for the lessee, permitting the cash raised through capital transactions to be conserved. The lease converts what would have been a large up-front cash payment on the company's part for equipment into a stream of monthly lease payments that do not strain the company's budget.

The lease payments are computed using the equipment purchase price and an imputed interest rate, as if the company were borrowing the money. While the company does not have a debt obligation on its balance sheet, it will have lease payments that affect the income statement in a fashion much like progress payments on debt.

Lease companies may exact, as compensation for extending the lease financing, additional compensation in the form of warrants to purchase common stock of the company. The purchase price per share is typically set at the price in the most recent venture financing. The number of shares that the lessor can purchase is determined by dividing the share price into a percentage of the total lease-financing amount (the "warrant coverage"). For example, a $2 million lease line with 25% warrant coverage would mean that the lessor would receive warrants to purchase $500,000 of the company's stock at the most recent venture financing price per share.

8. Banks

Banks generally will not finance emerging companies. The exceptions are banks that work with emerging companies that have received significant financing or banks that require the founders or executives of the company to provide personal guaranties for the loans. Banks that lend into ventures that have already received investor backing may also require warrant coverage as a condition of extending the loan.

Bank financing can provide a company with an immediate source of cash and leverage the company's assets. Unlike a lease, however, bank debt is a balance sheet liability.

If a bank requires a personal guaranty, the guarantor faces a difficult business choice. The ability to obtain financing, on any terms, may be the overriding consideration. However, if the company receives venture capital financing at a later stage, venture backers are likely to want their funds to go to new investment in the business, not to pay off old company obligations, so the guarantor would not be relieved of the potential liability until the loan is finally repaid.

See the additional discussion about loans below.

9. Other Methods of Raising Capital

a. Licensing

An emerging company with a promising technology may find that the technology has applications in markets it does not intend to exploit, or that it cannot immediately exploit. A proprietary fuel cell technology intended for electric cars, for example, might have applications for backup power generation or recreational use. In such cases, the company might permit a third party to license the technology in the noncompeting "field of use," providing a source of cash without compromising the company's ability to compete.

A company may find that the only parties interested in licensing its technology are firms that already operate in the industry, since they are in the best position to recognize the value that the new technology represents. This practice has been particularly common in the biotechnology industry.

A lump sum prepaid or fully paid license may provide an emerging company with the block of capital it requires to pursue its business plan. A license that generates an immediate and ongoing stream of royalties can provide an emerging company with a source of income.

The terms of the license cannot be so broad as to cut off the ability of the company to pursue profitably its own research and development for the products it intends to develop. It is important for the parties to negotiate completely at the term-sheet stage such issues as scope of the license, industry field of use, geographic area, term of the license, payment terms, ability of the licensor to make derivative products incorporating the licensed technology, ability of the licensee to sublicense, events of default and rights of the licensor on termination or default.

b. Development Agreements

Like a licensing agreement, a development agreement involves the emerging company using its technology to create a product or technology for the customer and using the cash to build staff, demonstrate technology or market feasibility or develop proprietary intellectual property.

Development agreements typically involve development of a specific product, or a customer-specific derivative of the emerging company's standard product. The parties define whose intellectual property is to be used in the development, who owns new intellectual property created in the course of development and how intellectual property rights are divided once the development is complete.

c. Sale of Discontinued Inventory, Equipment or Line of Business

A company may find that it has changed its business plan over time in response to technology or market changes. The sale of discontinued inventory or equipment may supply a source of cash to permit the company to pursue a new direction. A company may even have an ongoing operation or product line that is no longer part of the company's future plans. Finding a buyer for such a line can avert shut down costs and provide capital to the seller.

7.03   Financing Strategy

A.   Financial Needs

In connection with raising capital, a company must determine how much money it will need and how it expects to spend the money. The goal in capital raising is to obtain sufficient financing to carry the company through a period when it does not have sufficient cash to meet all its needs, and to reach a point where the company is self-sufficient. A company that seeks too little financing may not be able to achieve its goals, while a company that seeks more financing than it requires may find that it has sold a larger portion of the equity than was required.

It is typical for emerging companies, particularly companies that are candidates for venture capital financing, to raise capital in successive stages or "rounds" of financing. Using the proceeds of each round, the company would expect to achieve a new development stage that would justify another financing round, at a higher valuation. For example, successful completion of a prototype product could justify raising a financing round to mass-produce the product, or a successful regional marketing campaign could justify a financing round to market the product on a national basis.

As each development stage is achieved, the company's prospects for success should become better defined, permitting the company and its investors to set new (and hopefully higher) valuations on the company for the follow-on rounds of financing. The earliest financing rounds will be the most speculative. There may be issues about whether the technology concept will be successfully developed or whether the product can be mass-produced. As each problem is overcome, investment in the company becomes less risky for investors, justifying a higher company valuation.

The planning process for financing, therefore, should incorporate the concept of successive rounds of financing before the company reaches self-sufficiency. In the capital planning process it is critical that company founders bear in mind such key concepts as cash flow, burn rate and dilution, which are discussed below.

1.   Cash Flow

An emerging company must maintain adequate cash or it will fail. No matter how patient or forgiving a company's vendors, creditors or customers might be when times get tight, a company that runs out of cash will be unable to pay employees, tax authorities, landlords, utility providers or other third parties, and will reach a point where it cannot conduct operations.

Cash flow is related to, but is not the same as, revenue. For example, if a company sells goods on 30-day payment terms, the company would show revenue on its books from the date the goods were shipped to the customer, but the cash from the sale would not be available to the company until the customer pays its bills.

By contrast, a software company could sell a software license that included a year of customer support. The company would have the cash on hand from the sale immediately, but as an accounting matter would not reflect the full amount of the cash received as revenue, since the customer support portion would only be earned over the course of the ensuing year.

The cash that a company will have available to conduct its operations will equal the cash generated from sales plus cash generated from financing activities, either borrowing or selling equity. Buying on credit is the functional equivalent of receiving cash in financing: the company will have goods or services available to it, in exchange for a promise to pay in the future in cash.

2. Burn Rate and Dilution

For an emerging company, cash management is critical to success. Ideas, patent rights, business plans, services and hard assets may be crucial distinguishing assets that make a company succeed over its competitors, but the company also needs to have a supply of cash available, and needs to ration the use of the cash, in order to conduct operations.

Typically, an emerging company business plan will forecast an initial unprofitable period while the company is developing its product or establishing a customer base. Since the company in that period is spending more money than it is taking in, the company needs a source or reserve of cash to carry it into the period when it can operate profitably.

In the community of emerging companies, this negative cash flow, measured at a monthly, quarterly or annual pace, is the company's "burn rate"—the speed at which it is using up its supply of cash. The company needs to know its burn rate in order to calculate when it will need to be refueled with an infusion of new capital.

As discussed above, the source of cash may be the founders. Most often the source is an outside investor. An equity investor such as an angel investor or VC will exchange cash today for a certain percentage ownership stake in the company, in the expectation that the shares will increase in value in the future as the company succeeds. As founders sell a percentage of the company to outside investors, the ownership percentage of the founders is reduced, or "diluted."

The greater the percentage of the company's ownership the founders can retain for themselves, the greater their profit at the time the exit strategy is implemented, whether that consists of an IPO or the merger or sale of the company. For that reason, cash management is directly tied to the amount of dilution the founders sustain, which is directly tied to the founders' future wealth.

For example, if a company needs to raise relatively little cash before becoming profitable, the founders should need to sacrifice a relatively small percentage of the ownership to outside investors. In that case, the founders' initial 100%-ownership position would sustain relatively little dilution from the issuance of stock to subsequent investors.

If a company conducts a succession of rounds of fund-raising, it can use the money raised in one round to achieve a critical milestone toward future success, then sell the next round of shares at a higher price, resulting in less dilution of ownership percentage to the founders and the investors in the earlier rounds.

The chart in Figure 7A below shows a simplified version of this process at work:

FIGURE 7A			
DILUTION			
Company A and Company B each need $2 million to complete product development, $3 million to bring the product to market and $5 million to expand marketing and manufacturing as demand increases (a total of $10 million). By achieving these milestones, each company will be worth $100 million at the time of the exit event. The founders of Company A raise all $10 million at once, and Company B raises the money in series.			
Company A	**Shares**	**Percentage**	**$ Value**
A. Formation			
Founders' shares	5,000,000	100.0%	
B. Financing ($10m pre-investment company value; $20 million post-investment company value)			
Investors' shares ($2/sh)	5,000,000	50.0%	$10,000,000
Founders' shares	5,000,000	50.0%	$10,000,000
Total	10,000,000	100.0%	$20,000,000
C. Exit: Company worth $100m			
Investors' shares	5,000,000	50.0%	$50,000,000
Founders' shares	5,000,000	50.0%	$50,000,000
Company B	**Shares**	**Percentage**	**$ Value**
A. Formation			
Founders' shares	5,000,000	100.0%	
B. First Financing ($10m pre-investment company value; $12 million post-investment company value)			
Investors shares ($2/sh)	1,000,000	17.0%	$2,000,000
Founders shares	5,000,000	83.0%	$10,000,000
Total	6,000,000	100.0%	$12,000,000
C. Second Financing ($18m pre-investment company value; $21 million post-investment company value)			
Investors shares Round 1	1,000,000	14.3%	$3,000,000
Investors shares Round 2 ($3/sh)	1,000,000	14.3%	$3,000,000
Founders shares	5,000,000	71.4%	$15,000,000
Total	7,000,000	100.0%	$21,000,000
D. Third Financing ($35m pre-investment company value; $40 million post-investment value)			
Investors shares Round 1	1,000,000	12.5%	$5,000,000
Investors shares Round 2	1,000,000	12.5%	$5,000,000
Investors shares Round 3 ($5/sh)	1,000,000	12.5%	$5,000,000
Founders shares	5,000,000	62.5%	$25,000,000
Total	8,000,000	100.0%	$40,000,000

E. Exit: Company worth $100m			
Investors shares	3,000,000	37.5%	$37,500,000
Founders shares	5,000,000	62.5%	$62,500,000

By staging the investment in series, the founders of Company B sold fewer shares for the same amount of total capital investment compared to Company A. The Company B founders realize a better return using this method; the investors at each stage of the Company B investment process also benefit, because they are able to limit their investment risk. For this reason, an overwhelming number of venture capital investments are structured to occur as a series of investments, generally in preferred stock.

3. *Financial Projections*

Chapter 2 (Preparing the Business Plan) described how to draft a business plan. As noted, a critical component of the business plan is the financial section, including financial projections. It is important that the plan show cash burn rate and from that project the company's financing needs. The company's cash needs depend on such factors as the following:

- Amount of equipment needed to develop the product or service
- Whether financing is available for equipment or inventory, and on what terms
- How long the product development cycle is
- How long the company must wait for necessary regulatory approvals (for example, FDA)
- Length of the sales cycle (for example, a company may face a long selection process in connection with selling to a government agency)
- Size of the workforce required
- Whether sales can be conducted by using independent distributors or a captive sales force
- Profit margins once the product is manufactured and sold
- Amount of inventory the company must maintain

Once the founders have identified the key factors affecting the business, they need to quantify the cost of addressing those factors.

For each item in the plan, the founders should quantify the expected expense or revenue. In quantifying the line items, the founders should set out in writing their assumptions, so they can revise the work if new information becomes available later. Also, setting out assumptions on line items permits potential investors or financing sources to make their own evaluations or replace the founders' numbers with their own estimates, to generate numbers they either feel more comfortable with or prefer for negotiating purposes.

For many companies, management faces a trade-off between cash and time. Any given goal might be achieved more quickly by spending more cash on personnel, promotion or another factor that might generate sales. Management must decide whether cash or time is the most critical factor for the company's success. For example, if the founders of a software company estimate a development time of four man-years to develop a certain software code, the founders will have to decide, considering the market rate for the level of development experience the founders require, whether it is better for the company to have one employee working for four years or eight employees working for six months. If the company is developing a product that is in a highly competitive market, and time to market affects the ultimate ability to have successful margins or market share, using cash to accelerate the development process might be critical to the company's success.

On the other hand, if the company's product depends on the development of other devices or markets, time to market may not be as significant a factor in long-term success. In such a situation, the company could delay hiring or other costs and conserve cash. For example, if the existence of a critical mass of Internet users was a prerequisite to making an Internet business viable, being the first to market at a high cash burn rate would harm the company by reducing its cash supply ahead of the time that it could expect to achieve revenues.

In the cases in which a company cannot affect how quickly it gets to market, conserving cash is necessary to survival. For example, biotech or medical device manufacturers must develop a product, test it and then wait for FDA approval before marketing to the public. Those companies need to expend cash to stay in operation and maintain the workforce and other relationships in place while waiting for the FDA to act, but the expenditure of money does not by itself increase the speed of the FDA's approval.

Assuming that all stages of development are performed perfectly, the time and cash invested could be significant before a meaningful revenue stream commences; if you factor the additional expense or delay associated with the inevitable mistake, an error in initial assumptions or the need for experimental trial and error, as noted in Chapter 2 (Preparing a Business Plan), the necessary investment of time and cash only increases. The founders should, therefore, include a best case and a worst case of cash needs in their planning.

B.   Valuation

If a company uses debt financing, there are no issues of valuation. The value of the debt instrument is its principal amount and the primary consideration for the company and the investor is the ability of the company to pay interest and principal as they fall due.

For a company using equity financing, valuation is the key determinant of how much ownership interest the new investors take for any given level of investment, and how much ownership interest the founders and earlier stage investors must give up. For a privately owned emerging company, the valuation question has no clear-cut answer. It will be negotiated in each round of financing.

The value of companies whose shares are traded in the public market is easily calculated. Multiplying the stock price in the market by the number of outstanding shares will provide a "market capitalization" or calculation of the total market value of the firm. Within the public markets, company value is also calculated by measuring the stock price (and therefore the market capitalization) against other measurements of corporate performance, such as earnings or revenues.

Public company measurement techniques cannot be validly used for valuing private emerging companies. For one thing, the value of shares that are not freely tradable in the public market will always be less than the value of shares that can trade. For another, emerging companies typically are at an early stage of development and do not have earnings, and sometimes not even significant revenues, so a price-earnings ratio does not make a meaningful measurement.

One method of valuation routinely used by emerging companies starts by taking a point in the company's projected future when the company does have earnings and a growth rate, and then using those figures to determine a future valuation. For example, a company that estimates that it will have revenues in year four of its business plan of $20 million, $30 million in year five and $45 million in year six can point to a projected 50% growth rate once its goods are established in the marketplace. By looking to public companies with comparable growth rates, the company could estimate its market capitalization in some future year based on projected earnings and the price-earnings multiple for such high-growth companies.

Once the future valuation is calculated, the parties discount the projected future market capitalization to come up with a current valuation. For example, if the year 6 market value of a company with a 50% growth rate is calculated at $200 million, what percentage of that future $200 million would the investor need to have to justify an investment of $5 million today?

If the investor is looking to double the investment every two years (approximately a 50% compounded rate of return), the year six value of the $5 million investment would have to be $40 million, or 20% of the estimated year six value.

Obviously, this is a very rough cut into the valuation question. For example, if the investors say that they agree with the company's line of reasoning, but they think that the company's chance of achieving that $200 million value by year six is 50%, they would want to increase their investment percentage in the company to compensate for the risk that the future value might not materialize. Moreover, future dilution from later investment rounds will also affect the ultimate returns any investor achieves.

Using mathematical calculations on assumed revenues and projected profits to calculate a valuation is not science, and there is ample room for disagreement and negotiation. The process, while flawed, offers the parties a chance to test the likelihood that the company's assumptions will prove accurate, and to test the strength of the information they currently possess. The process is one of risk assessment: the company will be asked to withstand investor challenges to its assumptions concerning the size of the market, the ability of its personnel to invent the new product, the sales cycle for the product, the pricing the product would be likely to command and other factors that bear on future performance. If the company can answer the investors' concerns, it is removing risk for the investors, and as risk is removed, the valuation should increase.

Other methods of valuation may be used. If there is recent data concerning the prices paid by investors for investments in similar companies, the parties can extrapolate from that.

Even if the investor or the founders pick an arbitrary figure, the board is obligated to determine a value for stock in good faith as part of the offering process, so explanation for the valuation will be required.

Ultimately, however the valuation process is rationalized, the price and other terms will be acceptable to both investor and company, or no investment will take place.

C.   Debt vs. Equity

The key building blocks in corporate finance are debt and equity. The equity holders are the owners of the company; the debt holders are the company's lenders. This section discusses some of the typical variations in the debt and equity relationships that an emerging company may encounter. This summary is intended to acquaint the reader with key concepts that might affect business decisions, but readers are cautioned that the specific details of any loan or investment transaction could be critical to whether that transaction is good for the company.

1.   Equity

The value of stock rises and falls with the fortunes of the company. From a legal perspective, the stock represents the residual value of the company after the company's claims to others have been satisfied. A company can have obligations arising from borrowing relationships, trade relationships, employee relationships, the need to pay taxes or the need to satisfy judgments in litigation.

As a legal matter, as noted in Chapter 3 (Non-Tax Aspects of Forming and Organizing a New Business), the shareholders would be entitled to receive a distribution of the remaining assets once those obligations had been paid, if the company were liquidated. As a practical matter, the value of stock in a company is based not on the liquidation value, but on the value it has to an investor who expects the company's fortunes to prosper in the future. The shares of a company that is experiencing high growth, and is expected to have that growth continue, will command a higher price (calculated as a multiple of revenues or earnings, or forecast revenues and earnings) than will the shares of a company whose product demand is less robust.

The concept of exit strategy grows out of the investor's expectation that share valuation will be based on forecast revenues and earnings. A company that has established a foreseeable prospect for a significant revenue or earnings stream may be a good candidate to have its shares sold in a public offering, providing the founders and early investors with a liquid public market in which to convert their shareholdings to cash. Likewise, the potential buyers of a company consider the growth prospects of the company in the acquirer's hands in considering the price to be paid to shareholders.

As discussed in Chapter 1 (Starting a New Business), equity can be issued in the form of common stock or preferred stock. Preferred stock can be issued in multiple series, with each series bearing a set of rights different from the other preferred stock series. Common stock generally is issued in a single series, although there are rare exceptions.

a. Common Stock

Common stock has the lowest priority, meaning that in the event of a bankruptcy or dissolution of the company, the claims of creditors, which are senior to the claims of equity, would have the right to be paid first. Moreover, the claims of the preferred stock, while subordinate to the claims of creditors, are senior to the claims of the common stock.

The founders of the company typically issue themselves common stock at formation of the company. The company's stock option plan typically will be in common stock, as will warrants or other equity purchase rights issued to lessors, lenders, customers or advisors. The preferred stock will have the right to convert into the common stock. This right to convert into common stock is exercised at the time of an IPO, or in those acquisitions in which the value of the common stock is more valuable than the preferred stock.

Because the common stock is subordinate in rights to the preferred, the fair market value of the common stock, for purposes of tax calculations or valuing stock option grants, historically has been considered to be a discount of the preferred stock fair market value. Accounting rules require that the estimated value of a stock option granted to employees and officers of the company be shown on corporate financial statements as a compensation expense. Company auditors will require the board to make a determination of the discounted fair price for common stock when options are issued, as a condition of performing the audit.

b. Preferred Stock

There is significant flexibility in crafting the terms of a preferred stock. So long as the company and the investors do not run afoul of state-law limitations relating to the terms that can be included in a corporate charter, the preferred stock can contain economic and corporate governance terms that might otherwise be relegated to a contract, such as a right to receive dividends, the timing and payment amount of the liquidation preference or the right to elect members to the board of directors.

Venture capital investments, and many angel investor investments, take the form of preferred stock. A discussion of typical terms in venture capital investing, including the preferences accorded to the preferred stock, is set out below.

c. Options and Warrants

In addition to common stock and preferred stock, companies will sometimes issue equity-related instruments, such as stock options or purchase warrants, obligating the company to issue stock at a fixed price in the future. Stock options are generally used as an incentive for management, employees, advisors and consultants to the company. Warrants are issued to investors, lenders, lease finance providers, customers and other third parties.

Both warrants and options permit their holders to defer the risk of equity investment. By giving the option holder or warrant holder the ability to "wait and see" how the price of the underlying stock performs, these instruments provide the potential for holders to achieve gains at a point in time when the profit is certain.

A company will issue options to reward or motivate employees and advisors who provide services that the company needs to grow. Warrants provide an economic incentive to investors, lenders or other financial partners of the company to enter into financial arrangements with the company.

The company's board of directors must reserve, from the company's authorized but unissued stock, sufficient shares to permit the option or warrant holders to exercise the instruments in the future. This means that the reserved shares will not be available for future issuance by the company except upon exercise of the instruments. If the instruments expire without being exercised, the board can reverse the reserve.

Options and warrants confer on the holder a right to purchase shares for a fixed period of time. Options generally run no longer than 10 years, since the Internal Revenue Code imposes a 10-year time limit on incentive stock options. Warrant terms are frequently five years, but can vary.

The exercise price of an option or warrant should be set at or above fair market value of the stock on the date the instrument is granted. An option price significantly below market represents a transfer of value from the corporation to the instrument holder, giving rise to tax and accounting issues that benefit neither party. For an emerging company, the board must determine fair market value, often by reference to the price paid by investors in the company's most recent round of financing or on the basis of the company's achievement of business milestones that materially affect company valuation.

Employee options typically vest over a period of years. This means that the option is exercisable partly, or entirely, only after the employee has continued employment through the vesting term. The vesting is used as an employee retention tool, since the vesting ceases when the employee terminates. If the value of the shares underlying the option has risen during the vesting period, the employee has an incentive to remain with the company to collect the increased value of the shares that vest in the future.

Warrants may or may not have vesting terms, depending on the circumstances under which they were granted. Vesting terms might include the occurrence of particular conditions, other than simply the passage of time.

Outstanding equity instruments are treated as being fully exercised for purposes of calculating the company's equity ownership on a "fully diluted" basis. Calculation of a fully diluted capitalization is required to permit new equity investors to evaluate what their percentage ownership of the company would be assuming that all equity instruments were exercised. The fully diluted capitalization represents the worst-case percentage ownership for such new investors.

Equity instruments usually contain adjustment provisions so that holders retain the same economic position in the event of stock splits or dividends. For example, an option to purchase 1,000 shares at $1 would automatically become an option to purchase 2,000 shares for $ .50 if the company did a 2:1 split. Unlike preferred stock, options or warrants usually do not adjust the exercise price if there is a later issuance of shares at a lower price.

Even though the grant of an option does not, by itself, change a company's cash position, accounting rules require showing the grant as a noncash compensation expense affecting operating statements and profit-and-loss statements. The result is a decrease in a company's reported income.

d.   Convertible Debt

A company may issue debt that can be converted into equity in the company, in the form of a convertible promissory note. The lender of convertible debt generally will have the right, but not the obligation, to convert the debt into equity if the lender believes that such conversion is economically advantageous.

The conversion is generally calculated based on a conversion price per share. The debt holder will have the right to convert principal, and often accrued but unpaid interest, into stock at a fixed price during the term of the note. If the note is repaid, the conversion right expires as to the repaid portion.

A convertible note operates something like a prepaid, interest-bearing option. If the value of the company's stock rises above the conversion price, the lender can capture profits greater than would have been realized had it merely been repaid on the note. If the note holder does not convert, it still has the right to be repaid.

If a company issues convertible notes to a group of investors, the company may retain the right to prepay or call the notes after giving advance notice to the holders, or it may have the right to automatically convert the notes to equity upon approval of a specified number of investors (usually a supermajority of the debt amount outstanding).

As discussed below, debt holders have rights that differ from the rights of equity holders. An investor who wants to have the risk limitation of debt but the profit potential of equity may want to make a convertible debt investment.

2. Debt

Debt financing can be relatively straightforward: the company borrows money and promises to pay it back with interest in the future. Adding other terms to that basic structure will increase the complexity of the debt-financing instrument.

The basic elements of a debt instrument are the principal amount loaned, the interest rate, the repayment terms and (if the note is secured by assets of the company) the collateral. Depending upon the situation, it is possible to be highly flexible and creative with debt instruments in order to reflect the parties' perceptions of the risks they need to address in order for both to accept the economic terms of a proposed finance transaction.

The types of additional issues that the parties can define in a debt instrument include whether the debt will be secured or unsecured; if the debt is secured, which assets will be used to secure it; whether the debt will be convertible to equity, and if so, on what terms and by whose decisions; whether the debt can be prepaid and whether the debt will be senior to other debt obligations of the company or subordinate to them.

In its basic form, debt can offer significant advantages to an emerging company. Unlike equity, basic debt does not participate in the growth of the company, so the founders are not diluted by debt. The lender is compensated by receiving interest on the loan.

Some lenders will request warrants to purchase stock of the company in the future, or the right to convert the debt into equity either at a set price in the future or at a rate determined in a future financing round. This provides the lenders with the certainty of payment and return of basic debt, with a potential "upside" if the company succeeds. VCs, in particular, are likely to ask for warrant terms if they extend debt financing to a company in between equity rounds.

As a matter of corporate and bankruptcy law, the claims of creditors against the assets of the company have a priority over the claims of equity holders. Just as the claims of preferred stock will take priority over the claims of common stock in the event of a liquidation of the company, the claims of debt holders will be senior to the claims of all classes of equity, including preferred stock. Within the class of debt instruments, it is possible to construct a stratum of claims as well.

A more extensive discussion of debt obligations appears below.

7.04   Typical Venture Capital Financing Terms

The standard investing terms in venture capital transactions are well established. These standard terms include the following:

- Issuance of preferred stock to the venture investor
- Dividend preferences
- Liquidation preferences
- Right to convert the preferred stock to common stock in the future
- Anti-dilution protection for the VC
- Representation for the VC on the board of directors
- Information rights
- Registration rights

Depending on the circumstances for a particular company or the prevailing economic climate, the VCs may negotiate for additional terms. No exhaustive list of such additional terms can be prepared, since many terms arise only in individualized circumstances. Examples of some additional terms sometimes required by VCs are (a) founder's agreements, requiring the founders to offer their shares for repurchase by the company unless the founders stay with the company for a set period of time (in effect, reducing the founder's ownership of the company unless the founder participates for a set period of time); (b) co-sale agreements, giving one shareholder the right to participate in another investor's future sale of the shares; or (c) voting agreements, to ensure for investors that they are able to compel the outcome of corporate votes for directors, mergers and similar matters that the investors do not desire to have publicly disclosed as voting restrictions in the company's corporate charter.

There are no industry standard financing or valuation terms for investments. Every company's financing situation and valuation will be unique. However, the general economic climate can have an effect on the terms of a VC financing other than valuation. For example, in the late 1990s, when VCs competed among one another to invest in sought-after companies, the size of the liquidation preference and the terms by which it was calculated tended to be more generous to the company and the other investors.

The NVCA tracks evolving customs and changes in the investment practices in the venture capital industry. It also recognizes that there tend to be regional differences (East Coast vs. West Coast) in some of the terms that are negotiated in venture capital transactions.

The NVCA prepares and makes available on its website a public domain set of sample transactional documents for venture capital investments.[2] These documents are reviewed periodically by leading investors and law firms, in order to reflect legal developments and changes in practices in the venture capital investing community. At the time this chapter was prepared, the NVCA had posted model documents that included changes made during 2010. A number of these documents are attached as Exhibits to this chapter:

- Term Sheet, **Exhibit 7A**
- Stock Purchase Agreement, **Exhibit 7B**
- Certificate of Incorporation, **Exhibit 7C**
- Investor Rights Agreement, **Exhibit 7D**
- Voting Agreement, **Exhibit 7E**
- Right of First Refusal and Co-Sale Agreement, **Exhibit 7F**

A.   Initial Round

A company that has qualified for venture capital investment generally has achieved some key development using founders' money or capital from other sources, such as family, friends or angel investors. It may even have issued an initial series of preferred stock. The venture capital investor will require that its series of preferred stock take a priority over any existing common or preferred stock (and succeeding round investors will demand that their later series take priority over earlier series as well).

When the parties have agreed that the VC will make an investment in the company, they will generally prepare a term sheet setting out the key elements that will be included in the financing documents. Working from term sheet permits the parties to identify issues quickly and resolve potentially deal-breaking points before full documentation is prepared.

The bulk of the substantive terms for the investors will be embodied in the preferred stock provisions in the corporate charter. Other terms will be set out in the purchase agreement between the investors and the company, or in one or more separate investor rights agreements.

---

2.   The NVCA model documents can be found at the NVCA website at http://www.nvca.org/index. php?option=com_content&view=article&id=108&Itemid=136. The NVCA makes the model documents available with the following disclaimer: *"Disclaimer: Each document is intended to serve as a starting point only, and should be tailored to meet your specific requirements. The documents should not be construed as legal advice for any particular facts or circumstances."*

1. *Preferred Stock Terms in Corporate Charter*

The key preferences usually enjoyed by preferred stock are as follows:

a.   Dividend Preference

The preferred stock will receive cash dividends before any dividends are paid to the common stock. Dividends are usually set out in the company's corporate charter as a percentage of the original issuance price of the preferred stock. Dividend preferences may also exist among series of preferred stock; that is, the Series B dividend would be paid prior to payment of the Series A dividend, and both paid before any cash dividend to the common. This dividend preference term, if the dividends are paid, gives the preferred stock a right akin to a right to receive interest.

Sometimes dividends are payable only if they are declared by the board of directors. A company that needs to conserve its cash to grow would not want to siphon off the cash to pay investors. If the dividends are *cumulative*, the company's obligation to pay the preferred shareholder will mount with the passage of time and the accrued dividend obligation will be another priority that must be satisfied before the common stock can assert a claim on the company's assets. If the dividends are noncumulative, the decision of the company's board of directors in any year not to pay dividends will extinguish the preferred stock's right with respect to receiving dividends for that year.

b.   Liquidation Preference

The liquidation preference is an amount the preferred stockholders are entitled to receive at the dissolution of the company prior to the payment of amounts being paid to the common shareholders. The liquidation preference is calculated by reference to the original issuance price, sometimes as a multiple of that price. A "2x liquidation preference" for example, would mean a liquidation preference having two times the original purchase price.

For purposes of triggering the liquidation preference, a merger, acquisition of the company's shares or acquisition of the company's assets usually will be treated as a dissolution.

The terms and the size of the liquidation preference can have a significant impact on the return to the founders when a company is acquired. In some cases the entire preference amount must be paid before the common stock is entitled to any distribution. In other cases, the initial investment amount must be repaid before there is a distribution to common shareholders, and then the preferred and common share proceeds of the sale are distributed on a pro-rata basis until the entire preference has been paid to the preferred. In some cases, sale of the company above a preset amount may eliminate the company's obligation to make a preference payment, in which case the preferred converts to common and the shareholders take the proceeds ratably. Preferred stock that shares in the proceeds of the sale with the common after receiving some or all of its liquidation preference is called participating preferred stock.

c.   Election of Directors

The preferred stock as a class generally will be entitled to elect at least one member of the board of directors. In some cases, each series of preferred stock will be entitled to elect one or more board members. Depending on the number of investors in the class, the company may also be asked to grant board observation rights to other investors whose representatives do not sit on the board. Observation rights generally are covered in the investment contract, not in the corporate charter.

d.   Anti Dilution Protection

Preferred stock typically converts to common stock on a 1:1 ratio at the time of initial issuance. For example, a holder of 1,000,000 preferred shares would convert to 1,000,000 shares of common stock at the time of the IPO.

An anti-dilution right changes the conversion ratio to permit the preferred shareholder to receive a greater number of common shares upon conversion. The anti-dilution right is triggered if the company issues shares at a price lower than the price offered to the last round of preferred stock. The anti-dilution protection permits an investor whose ownership percentage was diluted by the sale of shares at a lower price to recapture some or all of that difference.

Anti-dilution rights generally are calculated either on a weighted average basis or on a "full-ratchet" basis. In the case of full-ratchet anti-dilution, the conversion ratio is calculated as if the original sale to the investor had occurred at the lower price.

> *Example:* The Company sells 1,000,000 Series A preferred for $1.00 per share, with a conversion rate of 1:1 to common and full-ratchet anti-dilution protection. The Company then sells 1,000,000 Series B preferred for $ .50 per share, with a 1:1 conversion rate. The Series A conversion ratio becomes 2:1, as if the first preferred shares had been sold at the same price as the later round. The Series A and B together would then convert to 4,000,000 common shares after the full-ratchet adjustment.

Weighted average anti-dilution adjustments do not bring the conversion ratio all the way down to the lower price, but use the total capitalization of the company or the impact of the lower-priced financing to adjust the conversion ratio.

> *Example:* The company sells 1,000,000 Series A preferred for $1.00 per share, with a conversion rate of 1:1 to common and weighted average anti-dilution

protection. The Company then sells 1,000,000 Series B preferred for $ .50 per share, with a 1:1 conversion rate. The Company has 2,000,000 shares of common stock outstanding.

Before the Series B sale, the Series A investors owned 33.3% of the company. After that round, before calculating the anti-dilution protection, the Series investors owned 25% of the company.

The weighted average anti-dilution formula would reduce the Series A conversion price to a fraction calculated by dividing (a) the common stock equivalents outstanding *before* the Series B offering (3,000,000 shares, giving effect to conversion of Series A at the 1:1 ratio) by (b) the common stock equivalents outstanding *after* the Series B offering (5,000,000 shares, converting Series A to 1,000,000 shares and Series B to 2,000,000 shares). In this example, the Series A conversion price would be adjusted to $.60 per share (.6 times the original $1/share conversion price). The anti-dilution adjustment would bring Series A back to a nearly 30% ownership position.

e. Redemption

A company may include the right to redeem the preferred stock at a preset formula price that takes into account accrued but unpaid dividends, the liquidation preference and the number of years the preferred stock has been outstanding (the greater the number of years, the greater the redemption price, in order to compensate the investors). A company that has sufficient cash to redeem shares would provide notice to the investors of the redemption. The shareholders would then have a period of time to decide whether to permit the redemption or to convert the shares to common stock. If a company has succeeded sufficiently to have cash available for a redemption, the common stock may be more valuable to investors than the redemption price.

f. Preemptive Rights

The company may or may not include a preemptive right in the corporate charter. The preemptive right permits shareholders to purchase shares in future equity offerings made by the company in an amount up to that investor's existing ownership percentage. Such rights may also be conferred in the investment agreement, rather than in the corporate charter.

g. Protective Provisions

A protective clause will require a supermajority vote of the preferred stock issued to the VC investor before the company undertakes any substantial transaction or transaction outside the ordinary course of business, such as the sale of substantially all of its assets or agreeing to merge with another entity, changing the terms of the preferred stock or creating a class of shares with equal or senior rights to the preferred stock, engaging in any business other than that presented to the VC investors at the time of investment, changing the number of directors on the board of directors, or redeeming any shares other than according to the terms of any repurchase agreement under an employee stock option or as set forth in the corporate charter.

2. *Purchase Agreement and Investor Rights Agreement Provisions*

In connection with venture capital financings, there are typically other rights granted to the preferred stock investors, such as registration rights, the rights to certain financial reports and rights to purchase, or participate in the sale of, shares of other shareholders who want to sell their shares of the company. Such rights generally are part of the purchase agreement, or a separate investor rights agreement, and not part of the corporate charter. Typical provisions include the following:

Company Representations and Warranties. These provisions concerning the nature of the company, its business and its assets are as thoroughgoing as the provisions of a merger or acquisition agreement. They will cover all material aspects of the company's business.

Some of the most critical representations relate to the capitalization of the company. The investors will want assurances that all shares, and all rights to purchase shares in the future, are fully and accurately disclosed. This permits the investor to calculate its ownership percentage interest, after taking into account all possible dilution from additional offerings.

For the company, the due diligence process of ensuring that it can disclose and document all key elements of its business should flush out any forgotten or neglected issues so that those issues can be resolved or, at a minimum, disclosed to the investor.

Registration Rights. Registration rights give the VC investors the right to cause the company to file a registration statement with the Securities and Exchange Commission to permit a public offering of the company's shares. These rights are rarely used in practice. They are not used to get a recalcitrant management group to conduct an IPO when the investors require; conducting an IPO when the investors and management agree is difficult, and conducting an IPO if the management did not agree would be impossible. These terms do guarantee that the investors will not be locked out of the post-IPO market forever and set guidelines on participation in such registration statements.

Monitoring Covenants. This provision identifies the internal financing reporting requirement of the company to the investors. Typically this provision specifies that the company management will prepare (a) an income statement, cash flow and balance sheet for a specified period (sometimes monthly, and at a minimum quarterly), accompanied by a report of the chief executive officer regarding the company's progress in the period, (b) an audited annual financial statement, together with a copy of the auditor's letter of management, (c) an annual budget, including projected income statement, cash flow and balance sheet and (d) a report identifying variations between the budgeted and actual results, with a discussion by the management on why the variations occurred.

Co-Sale and Other Share Restriction Agreements. Investors will sometimes include additional agreements relating to future sales of the stock by other investors. A co-sale agreement will require that an investor who, prior to the time of the company's IPO, determines to sell shares of the company and locates a buyer for those shares and will permit fellow investors to participate in the sale on a pro rata basis. This type of agreement would provide some protection to investors in the event that a major investor decided to sell to a third party on terms that might not be available to the minority shareholders.

Other stock restriction agreements that sometimes are used will require an investor who desires to sell shares to offer the shares first to the other investors at the same price and same terms. This permits the initial group to increase its investment if the situation arises and to exercise some control over who else becomes an investor in the company.

"Drag along" rights refer to an agreement under which other shareholders are required to vote their shares in favor of a corporate acquisition if a pre-determined majority of the preferred shareholders favor it. The goal of a "drag along" agreement is to provide the VC with assurance that the founders or other investors will not block an "exit event" that the VC wants to occur.

B.   Follow-on Rounds

Later-stage venture capital rounds are conducted in a fashion, and using documentation, substantially similar to the initial venture capital round.

However, in later rounds it is not unusual for additional venture investors to be recruited. The lead investor in the initial round very often will have one of its personnel on the board of the company, and the new investor may desire board participation as a condition of investment as well. Such an arrangement could require the company to amend its articles to increase the size of the board. Although the addition of another board member might also give investors increased numerical participation on the board, as a practical matter the investors exert significant control in the board room for the simple reason that a management decision made against an investor's wishes will cut off any future flow of funds from that investor.

The critical issue in every round is the calculation of the company's value. When economic conditions change, or if the market that the company counted on fails to materialize, or if the management fails to perform against the business plan and starts to run out of money, companies can find that VCs are not willing to extend new funding on valuations as favorable as they had in prior financing rounds. In those situations, many companies conduct "down rounds"—rounds of financing at a share price and company valuation that are lower than the price in the prior financing round.

The result of a down round is substantial dilution to common stock holders and prior round investors. However dismaying the dilution is, the alternative to a down round usually is having the company go out of business. This means an investor can (a) commit new money to maintain or increase the ownership percentage, (b) accept a diminished ownership stake at a diminished value, but hope for the company to turn around in the future and recapture the lost value or (c) have nothing if the company ceases to operate.

Management and employees, who have ownership stakes either through founders' shares or stock options, see the value of their potential gains diluted and diminished as well. In a down round, the VCs face a difficult task of imposing a dilutive valuation while preserving sufficient equity and motivational value to the non-investing employees who are ultimately the ones who will develop the products or services the company requires to succeed.

Because one or more existing investors supply the new money in a down round, this kind of financing has the potential to create issues of conflict of interest and self-dealing. When the alternative is the company's failure, the complaints are likely to be muted or nonexistent. If the company successfully turns around, there is the possibility that the fairness of the transaction would be reexamined by the shareholders who sustained significant dilution.

"Pay to Play" provisions in the corporate charter or investment agreements address the potential for the preferred stock investors to disagree on whether to participate in future financing rounds for the company. The "pay to play" provisions typically penalize a preferred stock investor who fails to invest in future offerings, such as by converting that investor to another series or class of stock with less advantageous economic terms.

7.05   Finding Investors: Securities Law Considerations

A.   Preliminary Considerations

As noted in Chapter 2 (Preparing a Business Plan), corporations that want to raise capital must comply with both state and federal securities laws. These laws will govern how the shares are offered, to what group of investors and with what specific disclosures concerning the business.

The chief laws for federal regulation of securities transactions are the Securities Act of 1933 ("1933 Act") and the Securities and Exchange Act of 1934 ("1934 Act"). The offer and sale of shares by a corporation is governed by the 1933 Act; the disclosures for companies whose shares are publicly traded are governed by the 1934 Act.

The key principle in state and federal securities laws is that they are focused on the protection of investors from companies or share promoters who might part unsuspecting investors from their money on terms that would operate as a fraud on those investors.

The federal scheme is based on disclosure; a company can sell its shares in a venture that intends to turn lead into gold, so long as the risks to the investors are fully disclosed. While some states have disclosure based securities laws, others regulate the substance of what is offered, so that a company that intends to turn lead into gold would not be permitted to sell its securities, regardless of the disclosure made, unless state authorities determined that the issuance of securities was fair to investors.

The federal securities law is structured to prohibit (at Section 5 of the 1933 Act) all securities offerings or sales that are not the subject of a registration statement that has been declared effective by the SEC. The federal law then sets out the numerous issuers, purchasers or transactions that are exempt from the registration requirements. State laws have essentially the same structure: a blanket prohibition, with numerous exemptions.

Registered public offerings are atypical for emerging companies offering securities. Securities offerings for new companies are more usually conducted as private offerings under the exemptions from registration created either by statute or regulation. A company that does not comply with the securities law requirements could be required to return the investors' money in a rescission action or on the basis of a securities fraud claim.

In this chapter we discuss nonpublic offerings that emerging companies are likely to make during their early stages. In Chapter 13 (Growing a Business), we discuss later stage offerings, including IPOs.

B. Federal Securities Laws

1. Private Offerings

If a company issues securities to a limited number of investors who, because of their wealth or financial sophistication were not in the class of investors Congress passed the 1933 Act to protect, the offering may qualify for an exemption from the 1933 Act registration requirements as a private offering.

Some of the private-offering exemptions have grown out of court interpretations of statutory exemptions. Other private-offering exemptions have been created by the SEC by regulations, pursuant to authority created under the 1933 Act.

One exemption to the 1933 Act's requirements of an effective registration statement and prospectus delivery is set out at Section 4(2) of the 1933 Act. Section 4(2) exempts transactions "not involving any public offering."

An offer or sale of securities to a limited number of parties who are not in the class of persons for whose benefit the 1933 Act was passed will qualify as a sale that does not constitute a "public" offering and, therefore, does not require registration under the 1933 Act. The person conducting the offering has the burden of proof that no public offering has occurred.

Factors that the courts and SEC look to in determining whether a public offering has occurred include the size of the offering (an offering to 5,000 investors is harder to justify as private than an offering to five), the sophistication of the investors, the ability of the investor to bear the risk of the investment, the access of the investors to the type of information that a registration statement would provide and the relationship of the investors to the company.

The SEC, in SEC Regulation D, developed the concept of the "accredited investor," an investor who is presumed, due to net worth or financial sophistication, not to need the prospectus delivery and registration effectiveness protections of the 1933 Act. Trusts, corporations and other entities can qualify as accredited investors, and all of the issuer's executive officers and directors are accredited investors as well. An individual who possesses a net worth of $1 million (excluding primary residence) or an annual income of $200,000 ($300,000 with spouse) for a period of at least two years and has a reasonable expectation of continuing income at that level in the current year is an accredited investor under Regulation D. However, the Dodd-Frank financial reform legislation of 2010 will require the SEC to review, and possible amend, that definition.

Congress created an exemption from registration at Section 4(6) of the 1933 Act for offers or sales to accredited investors, so long as that offering does not exceed $5 million.

The concept of accredited investor is important for the operation of the SEC's Regulation D, which provides exemptions from registration for offerings that are conducted according to its terms.

Accredited investors receive the full protection of the antifraud provisions of the securities laws. Any misstatement or omission of a material fact in connection with the purchase or sale of a security violates the antifraud protections of SEC Rule 10b-5 if it leads an investor, accredited or not, to be damaged in an investment.

As discussed above, angel investors tend to be wealthy individuals who are accredited investors. Venture capital investors qualify, on the basis of financial sophistication and ability to bear the risk of investment, for the private-offering exemption under Section 4(2) of the 1933 Act.

2. *Regulation D*

SEC Regulation D sets out "safe harbor" definitions and transaction requirements for transactions that will not be deemed to be public offerings.[3]

---

3.   17 CFR 230.501-508.

Regulation D is divided into eight rules, beginning with Rule 501 and ending with Rule 508.

- Rule 501 provides the definitions that are used in Regulation D. Of particular note are the definition of an "accredited investor" and the rules for meeting the purchaser limitation provisions of Regulation D.
- Rule 502 provides the conditions that must be met to qualify for an exemption under Regulation D. Of particular significance are the information requirements for purchasers who are not accredited investors.
- Rule 503 provides the notice filing requirements for exemptions under Regulation D.
- Rule 504 provides an exemption for the offer and sale of up to $1,000,000 of restricted securities in a 12-month period for companies that do not publicly solicit or advertise the offering.[4] Although a private offering of non-publicly traded securities does not require any special information disclosures, the issuer should disclose sufficient information to the prospective investor to avoid the antifraud provisions of the 1933 Act.
- Rule 505 provides an exemption for offers and sales of restricted securities totaling up to $5 million in any 12-month period to an unlimited number of "accredited investors" and up to 35 other persons who are not accredited investors who purchase the securities for investment and not for resale. As with Rule 504, no general solicitation or advertising may be used to sell securities under Rule 505. However, if any non-accredited investors are among the prospective purchasers, the issuing company must (a) give the non-accredited investors financial statement disclosure documents that contain the same information as used in registered offerings or on Form 1-A of Regulation A and (b) financial information required under Item 310 of Regulation S-B (for offerings up to $2 million) or under Form SB-2. In addition, if both accredited and non-accredited investors are included in the transaction, the company must provide the non-accredited investors with the same information provided to the accredited investors; and make management available to answer questions from prospective investors.
- Rule 506 provides exemption for offers and sales of an unlimited amount of restricted securities to an unlimited number of "accredited investors" and up to 35 other persons who are not accredited investors, if the prospective investors purchase the securities for investment and not for resale, and so long as no general solicitation or advertising is used to sell the securities. Unlike Rule 505, all non-accredited investors, either alone or with a purchaser representative, must be sophisticated—that is, they must have sufficient knowledge and experience in financial and business

---

4. "Restricted securities" are securities that may not be sold without registration or an applicable exemption from the registration process, which is in contrast to publicly traded securities that are freely tradable.

matters to make them capable of evaluating the merits and risks of the prospective investment. However, to the extent that any non-accredited investors are among the prospective purchasers, the issuing company must provide the same nonfinancial disclosure and financial disclosures as noted above regarding a Rule 505 offering, except that for offerings above $7,500,000 the financial statements must meet the requirements of the form the company would use to conduct a registered public offering.

- Rule 507 provides that if any issuer, its predecessors or affiliates has been subject to any order, judgment or decree enjoining that entity or person for having failed to file a Regulation D notice of sales, that entity or person may not use the Regulation D exemptions to sell securities.
- Rule 508 provides that a failure to exactly comply with a term or condition or requirement under Regulation D will not result in the loss of the exemption or necessarily result in a violation of the 1933 Act, if the failure did not pertain to a term, condition or requirement intended to protect the investor; the failure was insignificant; or there was a good faith, reasonable effort made to comply with the requirements of Regulation D.

The Regulation D offerings have certain common elements, specifically that (a) there must be no public solicitation of potential investors through newspaper ads or broadcast media, (b) a notice of the transaction must be filed with the SEC and (c) securities acquired in a Regulation D offering will be subject to the same restrictions on resale by the investors that would govern a resale of securities acquired in an offering conducted under the Section 4(2) exemption of the 1933 Act.

Regulation D specifies the disclosures that must be made to investors, but the specific disclosure requirements will vary by the dollar amount of the offering. In addition to the specific disclosures required to meet Regulation D's requirements, issuers must make disclosures sufficient to meet the antifraud standard (no misstatements or omissions of material facts). For offerings under $1 million, no specific disclosure to investors concerning the business or the financial status of the business is required under Rule 504. For offerings in excess of $1 million up to $2 million, the issuer must provide investors with financial information that includes an audited balance sheet not otherwise prepared in accordance with the SEC's accounting rules under Regulation S-X. For offerings above $2 million and below $7.5 million, the issuer must provide audited financial statements, unless such audited financial statements cannot be provided without unreasonable effort or expense, in which case only an audited balance sheet is required. For offerings above $7.5 million, the information that would be provided in a registration statement is required.

In a Regulation D offering, the required narrative description of the business varies according to the dollar level of the offering, but in all cases the discussion of the products, distribution methods, management and other operational information should be comprehensive, not only to ensure compliance with the Regulation D disclosure standards and the antifraud rules, but to ensure that management has thought through and communicated the essential elements of the business's success.

The requirement that there be no general solicitation of the offering means that a company must be particularly careful in the Internet era. A company should avoid advertising or posting fund-raising materials on its website, unless such materials are accessible only to persons previously known to the company or qualified as accredited investors. In considering whether a company has conducted a general solicitation, the SEC considers as a key factor whether the company had a preexisting relationship with a potential investor prior to the offering. The Internet has not changed the SEC's analysis on this point.

a. Number of Purchasers

An offering in excess of $1 million under Regulation D must also abide by the Regulation's limitation of 35 purchasers. For purposes of counting the number of purchasers in an offering, accredited investors (including corporate executive officers and directors) and their relatives are excluded.

State laws will often have limitations on the number of participants in an offering. The states are not uniform in their limitations on participants or in how participants are counted. For example, some states count only the participants in that state, while others look to the total number of participants in the offering. It is critical in a Regulation D offering that the issuer and its counsel review the laws of each state in which a potential investor resides to ensure that no state law violations occur.

b. Disqualification

Offerings for amounts below $1 million cannot be conducted by publicly traded companies under Regulation D. Offerings for amounts below $5 million cannot be conducted by companies that have committed securities- or wire-fraud violations, or whose officers, directors, promoters or 10% shareholders have committed securities- or wire-fraud violations.

c. Integration

Regulation D specifies the disclosures that are required to investors based on the dollar amount of the offering. To calculate that dollar amount, a company and its counsel must look backward in time to see if there is a prior offering whose proceeds must be "integrated" into the current offering amount.

In evaluating whether a prior offering will be integrated into a current offering, the company and its counsel should look into the following factors: Are the sales part of a single plan of financing? Are the securities in the same class? Are the sales made at about the same time? Are the sales made for the same general purpose? Is the consideration the same?

The SEC has set out a "safe harbor" of six months between the completion of one offering and the commencement of another to avoid integration. It is important, therefore, for the issuer and its counsel to track when an offering has been completed, in order to know when the six-month clock begins running.

One result of an integration of two offerings is that a prior offering that was compliant with Regulation D can become noncompliant after the fact, as the result of the integration. For example, suppose a company sells $700,000 of common stock for cash for general operating capital to a group of 25 investors using a disclosure document that does not include any audited financial information, in an offering that ends on January 1. On May 1, it sells another $1.5 million of common stock for cash for general operating capital to a group of 15 different investors, using documents that meet Regulation D requirements for offerings under $2 million.

Under the integration analysis, the two offerings would be treated as one single $2.2 million offering, to 40 investors. The documentation provided to investors in the original $700,000 would not meet Regulation D's requirements for a $2-million-plus offering, taking the first offering out of the Regulation D safe harbor for private offerings. The second offering, which standing alone would have been a valid Regulation D offering, is rendered invalid because the disclosure documents were not adequate for a $2.2 million offering and the number of investors exceeded the 35-person limit.

If the second offering had been commenced six months or more after the first offering had been completed, both offerings would have been valid. If the second offering had been for preferred stock, for the purpose of inventory acquisition, sold to a corporate investor who was providing the inventory and in the form partly of cash and partly of goods, the two offerings probably would have been sufficiently different, even if they were close in time, to avoid integration, making both offerings valid.

d.   Regulation D Is Not Exclusive

While Regulation D is a safe harbor regulation, it is not the only way for an offering to be deemed a public offering. An offering that does not meet all of the requirements of Regulation D might nonetheless receive the protection of the exemption for private offerings under Section 4(2) of the 1933 Act, if it meets the standards set out in the administrative and case law.

3. *Other Federal Exemptions*

a. **Regulation A**

The SEC's Regulation A sets out an exemption from registration for securities offerings of up to $5 million. Regulation A permits the offering to be conducted using a simplified disclosure form. Unlike Regulation D, Regulation A permits offerings to be advertised to the general public once the offering document has been filed for qualification with the SEC.

b. **Regulation S**

Regulation S exempts offerings that are conducted exclusively overseas. An issuer that conducts an offering to international investors must structure the transaction in order to qualify for the protection of Regulation S, by using disclosure documents and purchase and sale agreements that inform investors that the securities must not be offered or sold in the United States without a registration statement or valid exemption from registration, and ensuring that the securities are not sold for the account of any U.S. person. The issuer must include a legend on the securities restricting the transfer of the securities to ensure that the securities do not flow back into the United States.

c. **Intrastate Offerings**

The 1933 Act exempts from the registration requirements offerings of securities that are conducted by an issuer within a state to investors who are residents of that state, so long as no offers are made to residents in any other state. While such an offering would be exempt from federal regulation, it would be regulated by the laws of the state in which it was conducted.

C. State "Blue Sky" Securities Laws

In addition to the requirements of the federal securities laws, issuers must also comply with the requirements of the state securities laws—sometimes called "blue sky" laws because they were intended to regulate promoters who would sell investors nothing but blue sky—in any state in which they offer or sell securities.

As is true with the federal securities laws, the securities law structure for most states provides first for a permit or authorization process by which a company is permitted to sell securities after making appropriate filings and obtaining approval from the state, and then for a series of exemptions from that process for private offerings. In cases in which the company does not qualify for an exemption from state registration of the offering, the company must obtain any necessary permits or authorizations, as well as prepare any required offering documents.

A number of states have passed a variation of the Uniform Limited Offering Exemption ("ULOE"), which relates to the state regulation of private offers and sales of securities that are exempt from SEC registration.

Because each state has been free to pass ULOE with its own distinct variations, ULOE is not necessarily uniform from state to state. However, there are some consistent elements. Generally, a state will require a company to have a limited number of either offerees or purchasers; the states generally exclude accredited investors from the number calculation; the states often will not permit the payment of fees to underwriters or promoters if the ULOE exemption is being used; the states will often require a prior connection between the investor and the company or a level of financial and business sophistication by the investor; and the issuers cannot conduct general advertising of the offering.

The ULOE elements coordinate with the Regulation D elements, particularly on the limitation on participants and the ban on general advertising.

In some states, the participant limit is based on offerees, rather than purchasers. In some states, the participant limit is counted in terms of the entire offering, rather than just the number of participants in that state. In some states the issuer must file with the state to obtain the exemption before making any offers of the security; in some states the issuer must file with the state before making any sales; and in other states no filings are required until after the offering has been completed. New York and some other states have individual regulatory schemes that do not resemble ULOE.

Because there is so much variation among the states in the operation of their securities laws, an issuer and its counsel must—prior to conducting a securities offering—review the state laws of each state in which the issuer contemplates making an offer or sale of securities.

In 1996, through the National Securities Markets Improvements Act, the federal government preempted substantive state law restrictions on securities offerings conducted in accordance with the provisions of Rule 506. States can, however, continue to require the issuers in such offerings to make state required filings, and the states have the right to investigate and prosecute fraud claims in connection with such offerings.

D. Private Placement Memoranda

Issuers who have not identified a specific investor or group of investors, such as a corporate partner, venture capitalist or group of angel investors, may prepare a disclosure document to solicit potential investors who are identified during a fund-raising effort. As noted in Chapter 2 (Preparing a Business Plan), this disclosure document is usually called a private placement memorandum ("PPM"), since the objective is to locate investors whose purchase of securities will not trigger a public offering.

A PPM can be used in connection with any size offering, provided that the offering is conducted so as to be exempt from the need for a registration statement under the 1933 Act. Significant offerings of securities that are intended to be issued to institutional purchasers are conducted pursuant to offering circulars or PPMs.

For purposes of this section, the discussion of PPMs will focus on their uses as a vehicle to help an emerging company locate early-stage capital. A PPM will often be used in place of an angel investment or early-stage venture capital or corporate investment, to raise capital for the company to achieve a significant product or technology milestone that would justify a venture capital or later stage offering at a higher valuation.

An offering conducted using a PPM will usually be structured to comply with Regulation D's safe harbor provisions. Because the exact elements of disclosure under Regulation D will vary according to the dollar amounts raised, the first order of business for the issuer is to determine the size of the offering. This decision will depend upon the business objective the issuer is trying to achieve and the business plan forecast for the amount of money required to achieve it.

1. Minimum/Maximum Offerings

PPM offerings are often structured as minimum/maximum offerings. The minimum-offering amount is the amount that must be subscribed for by investors prior to the company conducting a closing. The maximum is the amount of securities that the company will issue if the offering is fully subscribed or oversubscribed. A company that is deciding what Regulation D disclosure requirements it must meet should prepare the offering document based on the maximum offering amount.

The minimum-offering limit provides a protection to the investors and to the company. A small amount of cash raised in a single subscription might be insufficient to permit the company to meet its milestone objective so that accepting money in less than a threshold amount would be unproductive for the company and defeat the investor's objective of making a return on the investment. Except in connection with raising a meaningful amount of capital, most companies avoid bringing in minority shareholders. Establishing a minimum-offering amount protects the company from taking in a minority interest for a negligible amount of capital. Finally, there are costs associated with closing an offering and conducting ongoing shareholder relations. If the offering is not successful in reaching the minimum amount, the company would prefer to avoid those costs.

A company conducting a minimum/maximum offering will provide investors with subscription documents that require investments to be sent to an escrow account. The escrow is broken and the closing on the securities occurs only once the minimum is achieved. Thereafter, the company may conduct closings on a periodic or ongoing basis until the maximum subscription is achieved or the offering is terminated.

The maximum offering limit also protects investors and the company. By establishing a maximum, the company ensures that the founders and the investors do not have their percentage ownership diluted at the price of the PPM offering. This is particularly of value if the company expects that it will conduct a future round of financing at a higher valuation, once the proceeds from the PPM offering have permitted it to achieve a business milestone. Investors can rely on their percentage ownership at the end of the offering not falling below the percentage created by a maximum offering amount.

2. Capitalization

Once the company has determined the amount of money it wants to raise, it needs to determine what securities it will issue and what percentage of the company it is willing to sell to investors in the offering (assuming the securities are equity securities). The issuer may decide to sell common stock, preferred stock, straight debt, debt with warrants, convertible debt or some combination thereof.

If the offering includes any equity component (stock, the right to purchase stock in the future or the right to convert debt to stock in the future), the issuer should calculate a capitalization table to show the investors what portion of the company their investment constitutes, assuming minimum or maximum proceeds in the offering. The capitalization table should be done on a fully diluted basis, to show the percentage ownership assuming the exercise of all options or warrants reserved for issuance by the company. An example is provided below in Figure 7B.

FIGURE 7B CAPITALIZATION TABLE				

A company wants to issue up to a maximum of 1,000,000 shares of Series A preferred stock for $2 per share in a PPM offering, with an offering minimum of 500,000. There are 4,000,000 shares of common stock outstanding to the founders as earlier investors and a stock option plan reserve of 1,000,000 shares.

The capitalization table would appear as follows:

Security	Min.	Percentage	Max.	Percentage
Common Stock	4,000,000	72.7%	4,000,000	66.7%
Option Reserve	1,000,000	18.2%	1,000,000	16.7%
Series A	500,000	9.1%	1,000,000	16.7%

In the example above, the company sets its pre-investment valuation at $10 million ($2 per share times 5 million shares outstanding and reserved under the option plan). The post-investment valuation would be $11 million at minimum or $12 million at maximum.

In establishing a valuation, the company should be aware of market comparables, including the price-earnings multiples of companies that are publicly traded. If the PPM offering price is set too high, potential investors may be driven away; if the offering price is set below market, the company's founders may have relinquished some of their own potential gain.

3.   Drafting the PPM

As noted in Chapter 2 (Preparing a Business Plan), the PPM should include all of the material discussion contained in the company's business plan. The PPM should include descriptions of the products, the manufacturing and distribution plans, the costs associated with the manufacture and sale of the products, the expected margins, the background and experience of the management team, risk factors associated with the proposed business, a discussion of the industry and the competitive landscape within that industry, the advantages that the company expects to have over its competitors and discussion of the company's financial position, backed, if required, with audited financial statements.

If there are any material contracts, those should be disclosed, as should be any material financial relationships between the company and the promoters, officers, directors or major shareholders. The company should disclose any pending or threatened litigation. In all events, the company should disclose any material facts, and should not omit any material facts, in order to avoid securities fraud liability.

A company that has developed propriety technology should not include the technical details of that technology in the PPM, since detailed disclosure, even in a PPM that is intended to be confidential, could adversely affect the company's intellectual property rights. The company should, however, include an overview of what the technology does, why it is technically viable or such other information a reasonable investor would require in order to understand the nature of the investment.

Initial drafting should be done by the company, to save on attorney time and expense. However, one of the purposes of drafting a PPM is to insulate the company from securities litigation in the event the company's plans go awry, so the company should expect significant input from the attorneys on each word in the PPM.

4.   Subscription Agreements

The investors in a PPM will be asked to sign and return to the company a subscription agreement and a qualification questionnaire that will establish that the investor is in fact qualified to participate in the PPM offering. An example of appears as **Exhibit 7G**.

The qualification questionnaire is particularly important. It permits the company to establish that the offering qualifies for an exemption from the registration requirements of the 1933 Act. The qualification questionnaire will solicit from the potential investor information about the investor's net worth, financial sophistication and ability to bear the risk of the investment for a indefinite period of time, and whether the investor is acquiring the securities for the investor's own account and not for distribution.

Qualification questionnaires also identify which investors are accredited investors. It is critical in a PPM to identify accredited investors and non-accredited investors, in order to keep an accurate count on the number of purchasers for Regulation D and state law compliance purposes.

The subscription agreement will identify the amount of securities the investor intends to purchase, include the name and address of the investor for the company's records and set out representations and covenants by the investor regarding the investor's investment intent.

The information and the agreements contained in the subscription agreement and the qualification questionnaire permit the company to create a record that it was reasonable in believing that the investors were appropriate participants in a private placement. The company must establish a record that it took reasonable steps to prevent the offering from being a public offering, so that it can withstand any challenge that the offering should have been registered with the SEC.

5. State Securities Law

Prior to circulating a PPM to any investor in any state, the issuer and its counsel must develop a list of the likely states in which the securities will be offered. Some states have requirements that must be met *before* an offering is conducted; an issuer that circulates a PPM in that state and then asks its lawyer to check the law will already not be in compliance.

As discussed above, state laws will vary in their requirements governing the offering and sale of securities. The company's PPM must include any disclosures or legends required by state law in the states in which potential investors reside. If the company does not qualify for an exemption from the state securities law provisions, it must obtain a permit or qualification to sell securities.

A company and its counsel will avoid cost and wasted time by reviewing and complying with state requirements before the offering is commenced.

6. Practical Considerations

The PPM should be prominently and plainly labeled as being confidential. The label should state that any investor who accepts the PPM accepts the obligation to maintain the information in the PPM as confidential. This labeling serves more than one purpose. First, it creates a record that the company is working to keep the offering private—authorizing the circulation of the PPM or publication of the information in the PPM is counter to the company's objective of keeping the offering private. Second, business or technical information contained in the PPM may be part of a trade secret maintained by the company, and the company does not want to compromise its intellectual property protection by an unqualified dissemination of such material. Third, potential investors may be reluctant to sign formal nondisclosure agreements with the company as a condition of receiving the PPM, but the label will be evidence, should the issue arise later, that the parties expected the information in the PPM to remain confidential.

The copies of the PPM should be numbered, and one person within the company should be charged with tracking the identity of each person who obtains a PPM. In this fashion, the company can establish a record of its efforts to ensure that the offering was not conducted as a public offering.

The company may not place ads relating to the offering or have any of the people who will distribute the stock make presentations at publicly advertised seminars. Widespread advertising of the offering ruins the Regulation D exemption.

The company counsel should review all the investor documents before a closing is conducted in order to ensure that the company does not sell securities to an investor who might adversely affect the private-offering exemptions.

7.   *Finders*

Many company officers and directors are uncomfortable with soliciting capital. This is not surprising; the founders start up the company with the goal of doing the things the company was formed to do, not to spend the time and energy required in fund-raising. The reality is that company management must be able to do both, achieve the company's substantive goals and solicit money, in order for the venture to succeed.

Often management will want to use a broker or a finder to do the money raising, or at least to identify target investors. The activities of brokers, who deal in securities, are regulated by state and federal authorities. Finders are persons who hold themselves out as merely bringing investors and issuers together, and not dealing in securities at all.

The ability of the company to use the Regulation D exemption can be compromised by the use of finders, because the company could run afoul of the regulation's "no general solicitation" requirement. A company that is considering using a finder or other unregistered placement agent for its PPM should consult first with counsel and should also request the finder to provide references and list successful experience, in order to see if the finder has a history of delivering on the promised performance.

States may also regulate the amount of compensation that can be paid to promoters, finders or placement agents. A company that does not conduct its own securities sales effort must be careful that anyone it has engaged to locate investors and offer securities on the company's behalf is qualified to do so under the laws of the state in which an offering occurs and does so on terms that are permitted by state law. In some cases, the payment of compensation in connection with a private placement will affect the company's ability to qualify for a state law exemption from the permit process.

7.06   Debt

Emerging companies tend not to be eligible for bank financing. Banks typically look to hard assets to collateralize a loan, and emerging companies are inclined to invest heavily into development of intellectual property assets and not in tangible assets. Banks also like to lend to established businesses with a track record that creates confidence of repayment; a company that is trying to develop a new product or sell into a new industry by definition cannot have a track record.

An emerging company may get a bank loan if the founders are deemed sufficiently creditworthy and they guarantee the corporate obligation. In that circumstance, the bank is not relying on the creditworthiness of the emerging company. Corporate funds will be used to repay the loan in the ordinary course of business, but if something goes dramatically wrong with the business, the bank will look to the individual assets of the founders for repayment.

Emerging companies may obtain loans from sources other than banks. The loan may come from early-stage investors, who would rather take a debt than equity position with the company. The loan may come from venture capitalists, who will often lend into a company to ensure that it has adequate cash flow pending an equity-financing round. The loan may come from a corporate partner, who wants the emerging company to continue a product development project on the partner's behalf. A company that has received significant venture capital financing may receive a bank loan from a lender that is specifically interested in lending to emerging companies and which understands (and prices the loan to reflect) the risks and rewards associated with working with emerging companies.

For the founders of an emerging company, debt financing can provide the same benefits that it provides to real estate developers or other industries in which debt financing is common: the founders use the cash from the loan to grow the company but do not have their equity ownership diluted. In a straight debt deal, the lender is repaid principal and interest, but does not participate in any increases in the value of the company's stock. While that arrangement limits the lender's profits, it also limits the lender's risk, since the lender does not participate in declines in the value of the company's stock.

A.   Warrants as Loan Condition

Lenders to emerging companies will often seek the ability to obtain equity at a favorable price as a condition of providing the financing. In such cases, the lenders will be entitled to be repaid principal and interest on the loan, and then will receive an additional instrument, typically a warrant, permitting the lender to purchase a set amount of the company's equity at a set price for a period of years.

The warrant agreement permits the lender to make additional profit without taking additional risk. If the company grows and share value increases, the lender can exercise the warrant to obtain shares at a price below the market; if the company does not succeed, the lender does not exercise the warrant.

Warrant arrangements are common in bridge loan and bank loan arrangements by companies that are venture capital backed. Corporate partners and angel investors may also seek warrants, depending on the issuer's individual circumstances.

B.   Secured vs. Unsecured Debt

A lender may request a security interest in some or all of the assets of the company as a condition of making the loan. The security interest permits the lender to obtain ownership of company assets following the company's default on the loan.

An unsecured loan requires the lender to rely solely on the borrower's solvency and ability to pay. If the company defaults, the lender cannot foreclose on the assets to collect its debt.

The security interest provides the lender with a mechanism for enforcing its claim against the company in preference to, and in priority over, the claims of other debt or equity claimants, to the extent of the assets covered by the security interest.

A company can grant a security interest in the same assets to more than one lender. As between the secured lenders, priority is established either by agreement among the company and the creditors or by one creditor being the first to file a public record of its perfected security interest, giving it the first-priority lien.

A company that grants a security interest should be cautious in doing so. The value of the assets should not be out of scale compared to the security interest granted ($1 million of assets securing a $1,000 loan, for example). There is a risk that the lender would acquire the assets if, for any reason, the company failed to meet its loan obligations.

The conditions that will trigger default on the debt can vary according to the specific situations of the lender and borrower. Failure to pay principal and interest when due will always be an event of default; provisions on grace periods, penalty payments and notice of default in the event of failure to pay will vary by transaction.

The borrower will generally make representations about the status of its assets and business at the time the loan is extended. It usually is an event of default if those representations are untrue when made, and sometimes if they become untrue with the passage of time. Provisions for notice and opportunities to cure the offending condition will vary by transaction.

The loan typically will include covenants that the borrower agrees to perform on a going-forward basis, the breach of which will constitute an event of default. Such covenants can include requirements on reporting of financial condition, maintenance of certain finance ratios (debt-to-equity, etc.), non-impairment of the assets that are the subject of the security interest, no material adverse change in business or business prospects or other specific requirements relating to business condition.

C.   Security Interest

In a secured lending transaction, the parties will enter into a promissory note, which sets out the principal, interest, maturity and repayment terms of the loan, and a security agreement, which identifies the collateral, grants the security interest to the lender, and describes the events of default. These generally, but not always, are separate instruments.

The lender's security interest attaches to the assets when the agreement is signed and the lender advances the value. The security interest is perfected when any filings under the Uniform Commercial Code have been made with appropriate state law authorities. The priority of one lien holder over any other lien holder is established by the security agreement and by the senior priority lien holder making appropriate filings prior to those made by other lienholders.

Where the security interest is in intellectual property, such as a patent, copyright or trademark, the parties will have to include additional documentation to permit the assignment of the property to the lender upon an event of default. The Patent and Trademark Office ("PTO") will continue to show the borrower as the registered owner of an intellectual property asset, unless the parties provide the PTO with an assignment agreement to transfer the property to the lender. The borrower in such a circumstance will also grant a power of attorney to the lender to permit the lender to execute documents that may be required in the name of and on behalf of the borrower.

D.   Subordination

An issuer and its lenders may agree among themselves that one lender will have rights to repayment that are senior to the rights of another lender. Such "senior" and "subordinated" debt arrangements are documented by a promissory note for each lender, setting out the repayments and other conditions of the loan, in the fashion of any other lending arrangement. Generally, there will be a cross-default provision that makes default on one obligation an event of default on the other.

There may also be an inter-creditor agreement, in which the two creditors arrange their relative rights and obligations toward one another when an event of default occurs (for example, an agreement governing when the subordinated creditor is entitled to foreclose on collateral if the senior creditor has not declared an event of default).

Technology and Intellectual Property Rights

Warner R. Broaddus

The General Counsel, LLC
San Diego, CA

Alan S. Gutterman

Gutterman Law & Business
Piedmont, CA

Dana M. Newman

Los Angeles, CA

Contents

Technology and Intellectual Property Rights[1]

8.01 Preliminary Considerations

Intellectual property can be *the* most important set of assets for today's emerging company. The same holds true for well-established companies. Under the Financial Accounting Standard Board's accounting standards, the value of a company's intangible assets should be accounted for in the company's financial statements. Many of today's most valuable publicly traded companies report relatively low levels of tangible assets when compared to their total market capitalization.

In order to enjoy the financial boost intellectual property can give to a company's bottom line, the intellectual property must first be identified. When you consider that intellectual property includes things such as brands, sub-brands, customer lists, computer programs, photographs, written works, new business methods and man-made or modified living organisms, identifying the parameters of each individual piece of intellectual property can be challenging. When you further consider that the federal statutes governing ownership of certain types of intellectual property require compliance with specific formalities, the issues concerning identifying intellectual property are usually compounded with the challenge of identifying who owns it.

After intellectual property is identified and ownership is confirmed, the company must be forever vigilant in protecting it. Without constant protection, what was once a valuable piece of intellectual property—a sizable asset on

---

1.   Pamela Winston Bertani, Dale C. Campbell, Scott M. Hervey, and Audrey A. Millerman were the authors of this chapter in the first edition of the *Guide*.

a company's balance sheet—can erode away to nothing. Trade secrets can fall into the public domain and into the hands of a company's competitors; trademarks can be encroached upon by infringers or turned generic; deadlines to file patent applications can be missed and copyrightable software can be misused by freeloading third parties. Inadequate policing of intellectual property not only chips away at its "value," but it also costs the company money. This is because each act of unchecked infringement represents an unexplored possibility to license the property.

The purpose of this chapter is to assist counsel for an emerging company identifying and protecting intellectual property. What follows is a discussion of the forms of intellectual property patents, copyrights and trademarks, trade secrets and the various methods of protection. A preview appears below in Figure 8A.

FIGURE 8A				
COMPARISON OF INTELLECTUAL PROPERTY PROTECTION				
Distinguishing Feature	**Trade Secret**	**Patent (Utility)**	**Copyright**	**Trademark**
Protected Interest	Business Information	Functional Inventions	Expression Embodied in Fixed Medium	Consumer Recognition & Related Goodwill
Requirements for Protection	Not Known; Valuable; Maintained As Secret	New, Useful, Nonobvious, Proper Subject Matter	Originality	Use in Commerce
Disclosure Required	No	Yes	Yes	Yes
Term of Protection	Potentially Indefinite if Information Remains Secret	20 Years from Application Date	Author's Life Plus 70 Years[2]	Potentially Indefinite if Mark Is Used Properly
Conduct Prohibited by Protection	Misappropriation	Making, Using, Importing, Selling, or Offering to Sell Invention	Copying or Substantially Similar Works	Creating a Likelihood of Confusion
Independent Development	Not Prohibited	Prohibited	May be prohibited	Prohibited
Reverse Engineering	Not Prohibited	Prohibited	Inapplicable	Inapplicable
Damages for Infringement	Compensatory and Treble Damages; Attorney Fees	Compensatory and Treble Damages; Attorney Fees	Compensatory and Statutory Damages; Attorney Fees	Compensatory and Treble Damages; Attorney Fees

---

2.   The term of copyright protection for corporations is 95 years after publication.

8.02   Patents

A.   Preliminary Considerations

Patents are personal property. A patent is a grant by the U.S. government to the inventor of the rights to exclude others from making, using or selling the invention in the United States, or importing the invention into the United States, for a period beginning on the issue date of the patent and ending 20 years from the filing date of the patent application. This grant is given in exchange for the inventor's disclosure of the invention to the public. Thus, patent law serves both to protect the patent owner's rights in the invention and to stimulate inventors to invent.

B.   Governing Law

Patents are primarily governed by federal statute. Article I, Section 8 of the U.S. Constitution provides: "The Congress shall have power . . . to promote the progress of . . . useful arts, by securing for limited times to . . . inventors the exclusive right to their . . . discoveries." Patent law is governed by Title 35 of the U.S. Code. The U.S. Patent and Trademark Office ("PTO") follows rules set forth in 37 Code of Federal Regulations and the Manual of Patent Examining Procedure ("MPEP").

Patent applications are submitted to the PTO, which issues patents after examining the applications, a process called patent prosecution. In most cases, any disputed decisions of the PTO are initially reviewed by the PTO's Board of Patent Appeals and Interferences and, from there, by the Court of Appeals for the Federal Circuit.[3] Litigation involving patents, such as patent infringement, or actions regarding the validity of a patent, must be brought in a federal district court, as the federal district courts have exclusive federal jurisdiction over patent matters.[4] The Federal Circuit has exclusive jurisdiction over appeals in these cases.[5]

C.   Types of Patents

There are three types of patents: (a) utility, (b) design and (c) plant. Most patents are utility patents, far fewer are design patents and even fewer are plant patents.

---

3.   The Court of Appeals for the Federal Circuit was created in 1982 for the purpose of providing uniformity in decisions of patent law.

4.   28 U.S.C. § 1338(a).

5.   28 U.S.C. §§ 1292, 1295.

Utility patents are provided for in 35 U.S.C. Section 101:

> Whoever invents or discovers any new and useful process, machine, manufacture, or composition of matter, or any new and useful improvement thereof, may obtain a patent therefore, subject to the conditions and requirements of this title.

Section 101 identifies five different classes of statutory subject matter, that is, types of inventions that can be the subject of a utility patent: (a) a process (also referred to as a method), (b) a machine, (c) an article of manufacture, (d) a composition of matter and (e) an improvement of an invention in one of the other four classes of subject matter. Process patents include patents for methods of doing just about anything, including some methods of doing business[6] and some computer software. Machine or apparatus patents include traditional types of machines as well as computer systems. Articles of manufacture are devices such as electronic components, pens or just about any non-machine. Compositions of matter include chemical compositions, genes and genetically engineered (nonnatural) living organisms, including bacteria, plants and animals.[7] Certain things are not patentable because they do not fit into one of the five classes of statutory subject matter, for example, pure mathematical algorithms that do not include the steps of a process, printed matter, natural compounds and scientific principles.

Design patents protect new, original, ornamental designs for articles of manufacture, such as chairs, dishes and glassware.[8] The patent protects only the appearance of the article, not any aspect of functionality. An article may be the subject of both a design patent and a utility patent, however, if it has function that satisfies the requirements for a utility patent.

Plant patents protect distinct, new varieties of asexually reproducible plants (i.e., plants that can be reproduced without seeds, such as by budding or grafting), including "cultivated sports, mutants, hybrids, and newly found seedlings, other than a tuber-propagated plant or a plant found in an uncultivated state."[9] Plants that may be patented under this section include certain types of roses, nuts, flowering plants and fruit trees. New sexually reproducible plants are protected by the Plant Variety Protection Act (7 U.S.C. §§ 2321 *et seq.*) through the U.S. Department of Agriculture.[10]

---

6. *But see* Bilski v. Kappos, 561 U.S. ____ (2010) *citing* State Street Bank & Trust Co. v. Signature Fin. Group, Inc., 149 F.3d 1368, 1375 (Fed. Cir. 1998). *State Street* initially opened the door to "business method" patents. While *Bilski* did not entirely close that door, a majority of the Court indicated in separate opinions that *State Street's* holding was too broad. Thus "business method" patents and perhaps software patents will likely be more limited in the future.

7. *See* Diamond v. Chakrabarty, 447 U.S. 303 (1980).

8. 35 U.S.C. § 171.

9. 35 U.S.C. §§ 161–164.

10. Both asexually reproducible plants and sexually reproducible plants can be protected by utility patents if the requirements are met. J.E.M. Ag Supply, Inc. v. Pioneer Hy-Bred Int'l, Inc. (2001) 122 S. Ct. 593.

D.   Practice of Patent Law

Only registered patent attorneys and agents can prosecute patent applications before the PTO. In order to be registered before the PTO, both attorneys and non-attorneys must have higher education in science or engineering and must pass a patent examination administered by the PTO.

Transactional work (e.g., licensing of patents) and litigation involving patents can be handled by a patent attorney or any other licensed attorney, as governed by state law. This work cannot be performed by patent agents, however, as they are not licensed attorneys and cannot practice law.

E.   Patent Rights

A U.S. patent is a grant to its owner of the right to exclude others from making, using, offering to sell and selling the patented invention in the United States, or importing the invention into the United States.[11] These rights are called exclusionary rights. Contrary to common assumption, however, a patent does *not* provide its owner with the rights to do these things. For example, an invention may be patentable but still infringe another patent. In such a case, the owner may have a patent on the invention, but cannot make or use the invention unless he or she obtains a license from the owner of the patent that is infringed.

Patent rights exist from the date of issuance of the patent through the end of the patent's term. The term of a utility patent is 20 years from the date of filing, or the earliest claimed priority date, for applications filed on or after June 8, 1995. For patents filed before June 8, 1995, and in force on that date, the term is the longer of 17 years from the date of issue or 20 years from the date of filing.[12] The term of a patent can be extended for specific reasons, including for delays due to the PTO's handling of the patent application[13] and for time spent in obtaining approvals of the Food and Drug Administration.[14] The term of a design patent is 14 years from the issue date.[15] The term of a plant patent is the same as that of a utility patent.[16]

Patent rights can be transferred to others by assignment or license. An example of an assignment appears as **Exhibit 8A**, while a general license appears as **Exhibit 8B**. An assignment is a transfer to another of all the patent rights (the right to exclude others from making, using, offering to sell and selling the invention in the United States, or importing the invention into the United States, for the entire term of the patent). If a patent is assigned,

---

11.   35 U.S.C. § 271.
12.   35 U.S.C. § 154(a)(2).
13.   35 U.S.C. § 154(b)(1).
14.   35 U.S.C. §§ 155–156.
15.   35 U.S.C. § 173.
16.   *See* 35 U.S.C. § 161.

the original owner, the assignor, retains no rights. The new owner, the assignee, holds all the exclusionary rights and has the right to sue others for infringement.

A license is a transfer to another of something less than all of the patent rights. The original owner, the licensor, retains the right to exclude others. The new owner, the licensee, obtains the right to infringe the patent without being sued for infringement (to make, use, sell, etc., the invention). A license may be for less than all of the exclusionary rights, (e.g., the right to use, but not make or sell, the invention), for a limited geographic area, or for a limited time period. An exclusive license means that the patent owner will not license the invention to anyone else, while a nonexclusive license means that the patent owner can license the invention to others.

F.   Requirements for Patentability

1.   Utility Patents

First, the invention must be useful.[17] If the invention does not work, or is illegal, it is not useful and not patentable.

Second, the invention must fall within one of the five classes of statutory subject matter: a process, a machine, an article of manufacture, a composition of matter or an improvement of an invention in any of the other four classes.

Third, the invention must be new. This requirement, referred to as novelty, means that the invention is different from what is known in the field (the prior art). There are six types of prior art or actions that constitute lack of novelty and, therefore, preclude patentability.[18] They are listed in the six subsections of Section 102. The six types fall within three categories: (a) those that occurred before the date of invention, (b) those that occurred more than one year before the date the patent application was filed in the United States and (c) those that do not relate to a date.

The date of invention is either the date the invention was conceived of by the inventor, as long as the inventor was diligent in later reducing the invention to practice, or the date that the invention was reduced to practice. Conception occurs when the inventor has a definite and permanent idea for the complete invention. If the inventor does not then abandon the invention, and is reasonably diligent in reducing the invention to practice, the date of conception is the date of invention. Alternatively, the date of invention is the date that the invention was reduced to practice. Reduction to practice may be either actual or constructive. Actual reduction to practice occurs when the

---

17.   35 U.S.C. § 101.
18.   35 U.S.C. § 102.

invention is made or performed.[19] Constructive reduction to practice is the date that a U.S. patent application is filed.

The first category of prior art that precludes patentability is prior art that occurred before the date of invention. This category consists of subsections (a), (e) and (g) of Section 102. Subsection (a) precludes a patent if the invention was known or used by others in the United States or patented or described in a printed publication anywhere in the world, before the date of invention. Under this subsection, patents issued in the United States or in any foreign country are prior art as of the date they are issued and publicly available. It does not matter if the patent has expired or been held invalid. A printed publication is prior art as of the date it is publicly available. A printed publication does not need to be actually "printed," nor must it be easily accessible or available to everyone; as long as a document is formally indexed, a single copy of the document located somewhere in the world is a printed publication within the meaning of the statute.

Subsection (e) precludes a patent if the invention was described in an issued U.S. patent to another person, which was filed before the date of invention, or described in an international patent application by another who has met certain requirements of filing the application in the United States before the date of invention. Under this subsection, a U.S. patent is prior art as of the date it was filed. This prior art is often referred to as "secret prior art," because an invention that is the subject of a U.S. patent is prior art as of its filing date, even though the application is initially kept secret by the PTO and, as such, is not available to the public.[20]

Subsection (g) precludes a patent if the invention was made by another in the United States before the date of invention.

It is important to note that the above rules for determining novelty and prior art are significantly different in the United States as compared to the rest of the world. All other countries follow a "first to file" system, meaning novelty and prior art questions are determined by the comparing the date of *filing* the patent application with the dates of other filings, publications, etc. In the United States, as discussed above, many of these questions turn on the date of *invention*.

The second category of prior art that precludes patentability is prior art that occurred more than one year before the date the patent application was filed in the United States. This category consists of subsections (b) and (d) of Section 102. These subsections are referred to as "statutory bars" or "time bars" because the inventor has one year from certain events or from taking certain action, in which to file a U.S. patent application. Subsection (b) precludes a patent if the invention was patented or described in a printed

---

19.   Actual reduction to practice is not required in order to obtain a patent; an inventor need not ever actually build the invention.

20.   U.S. patent applications are published approximately 18 months after their filing dates. 37 C.F.R. § 1.211.

publication anywhere in the world, or in public use or on sale in the United States, more than one year before the date the patent application was filed in the United States. Under this subsection, the effective dates of patents and publications as prior art are the same as for subsection (a). "Public use" includes commercial use, but also a private or hidden use if there is no effort made to keep the use confidential. "On sale" includes offers for sale, such as demonstrations at trade shows, sales that are secret and sales for consideration other than money.[21]

Subsection (d) precludes a patent if the invention was first issued as a patent in a foreign country, by the applicant, before the date an application was filed in the United States and if the foreign application was filed more than 12 months before the U.S. application was filed.

The third category of prior art that precludes patentability is prior art that does not relate to a date. This category consists of subsections (c) and (f) of Section 102. Subsection (c) precludes a patent if the invention has been abandoned. Subsection (f) precludes a patent if the inventor did not invent the invention (i.e., someone else was the true inventor).

The test for novelty is performed by looking at each element of the invention. If every one of the invention's elements is present in a single prior art reference (e.g., a single publication or patent), then the invention lacks novelty and is said to be anticipated by the prior art. The invention is not patentable.

If the invention satisfies the novelty test, the fourth requirement for a utility patent is that the invention must be nonobvious to a person having ordinary skill in the art.[22] The invention is obvious if the differences between the invention and the prior art are such that the invention, as a whole, would have been obvious, at the time it was made, to a person with ordinary skill in the art. Four items must be analyzed to determine obviousness: (a) the scope of the prior art, (b) the differences between the invention and the prior art, (c) the level of ordinary skill in the art and (d) other factors (called "secondary factors").[23] Unlike the test for novelty, the test for obviousness is not limited to a single prior art reference—any number of references can be combined to render an invention obvious. For obviousness to be found, every element of the invention must be present or suggested in the prior art, although not necessarily in the same reference, and there must be a suggestion to combine the elements into one invention.

---

21. An assignment does not constitute a sale.

22. 35 U.S.C. § 103.

23. These secondary factors include commercial success, a long-felt but unsolved need, identifying a problem, unexpected results, synergism, failed attempts in the past, failure of others, teaching away from the invention by people skilled in the art, disbelief by people skilled in the art, copying by competitors, and licensing activities. *See* Graham v. John Deere Co., (1996) 383 U.S. 1, 15 L. Ed. 2d 545 (1966).

2. Design Patents

The design for an article of manufacture is patentable if it is new, original and ornamental.[24] "Ornamental" means that the design is purely decorative and the patentability is based on the visual aspects (including surface ornamentation and shape). An article is not patentable if it is solely or primarily functional. Novelty under Section 102 and nonobviousness under Section 103 are also required. Many of the other rules pertaining to utility patents also apply to design patents.

3. Plant Patents

The Plant Patent Act of 1930, 35 U.S.C. Sections 161–164 ("PPA"), enacted in 1930 and recodified in 1952, provides patent protection for new, asexually reproducing plants (i.e., plants reproduced by methods such as budding or grafting which result in a plant that is genetically identical to its parent). A patent granted under the PPA (referred to as a plant patent) is narrower than a utility patent because a plant patent only grants its owner the exclusive right to asexually reproduce the plant. The requirements for obtaining the plant patent, however, are somewhat less stringent than those for a utility patent. To obtain a plant patent, the plant must be useful, new (novel) and nonobvious, as is required of a utility patent under Section 101, but the written description requirement is relaxed.

G. Who Can Obtain a Patent

The inventor is the person who conceives of the complete and operative manner of the invention.[25] A person who only helps reduce the invention to practice (i.e., helps make the invention), under the direction of the inventor is not an inventor. On the other hand, a person who makes an original contribution to the invention, as it is set forth in the claims, even if the contribution is small, is an inventor.

The person or persons who invent an invention own the invention. As noted above, an inventor may transfer ownership rights, by assignment or license, to another person or a business entity.

The transfer of ownership of an invention is governed by state law and involves issues of contract law and employment law. As noted in Chapter 1 (Starting a New Business), if an employer hires an inventor specifically to invent, the inventor is obligated to assign the invention to the employer. An employer may also enter into employment agreements with its employees or invention assignment agreements with its independent contractors, which

---

24.   35 U.S.C. § 171.
25.   The inventor must be a person; an entity such as a corporation cannot be an inventor.

set forth the rights and obligations of the parties with respect to inventions. Such agreements typically provide that the employer owns any inventions made in the scope of the work being performed and require the inventor to assign the invention to the employer and cooperate in the filing of any patent applications. These agreements should be in writing and should be required to be signed before the work is begun as a condition of hire; it is often more difficult to obtain an inventor's agreement after the work has been completed, as the inventor may no longer be employed or available.

If there is more than one inventor of an invention, each inventor owns an equal undivided interest in the invention and any patent on the invention. This is true regardless of the amount of the inventor's contribution. Each inventor can make, use, offer to sell or sell the invention in the United States, or import the invention into the United States, without the consent of the other inventors.[26] Thus, in order to transfer all of the rights to an invention, all of the inventors must sign an assignment.

In filing a patent application, each inventor must sign the oath or declaration.[27] All of the true inventors must be named as inventors, and the application cannot name a person who is not an inventor. For example, an inventor cannot be excluded because he or she is no longer employed by the company filing the patent application. Nor can a person who is not an inventor be named as an inventor as an acknowledgment or reward for working on the project. Errors in inventorship can be corrected by amending the patent application, as long as the error was unintentional.[28] It is crucial to make sure that the correct inventors are named, because a patent that issues with incorrect inventorship can be invalidated.

H. Patent Application

Pursuant to 35 U.S.C. Section 111, a utility patent application must have (a) a specification or disclosure,[29] (b) at least one claim, (c) a drawing, if necessary[30] and (d) an oath or declaration of the inventors.[31] Fees and other filing requirements are established by the rules of the PTO.

The specification is the text of the patent. The specification must satisfy three requirements. First, it must contain a detailed description of the invention. This description demonstrates that the invention was in the possession of the inventor. Second, the specification must enable a person with ordinary skill in the art, at the time the application is filed, to make and use the invention without the need for undue experimentation. This requirement ensures that

---

26. 35 U.S.C. § 262.
27. 35 U.S.C. §§ 116–118.
28. 35 U.S.C. § 116.
29. 35 U.S.C. § 112.
30. 35 U.S.C. § 113.
31. 35 U.S.C. § 115.

the inventor has fully disclosed the invention. Third, the specification must describe the best mode, at the time of filing the patent application, of carrying out the invention. This requirement precludes inventors from keeping secret the best way of using their invention. The specification need not state why the invention works, only how to make it work.

A patent application requires at least one claim.[32] The claims must contain the essential elements of the invention. It is the claims that set forth the patentable subject matter, and it is the claims that are used to determine whether there is infringement. The detailed description, enablement and best mode requirements must be met for each claim. Drawings are required if necessary to understand the invention.[33] The drawings must contain all of the elements claimed. The drawings may be sketches of a machine or article of manufacture or flow charts of the steps of a process or a method, for example, for a software patent. The drawings must satisfy a detailed list of standards, specifying items such as the size of the margins of the paper and the thickness of the lines.

The oath or declaration is a statement signed by the inventors, under penalty of perjury, that the inventors are the original, first inventors of the invention. The oath is an affirmation that the inventors did not derive the invention from someone else.

I.   How a Patent Is Obtained

Patent prosecution is the process of seeking to obtain a patent. Patent prosecution is conducted in writing between the applicant, usually through an attorney or agent, and the PTO examiner assigned to the application.

The process is begun by the filing of a patent application in the PTO. The patent application may be filed by the inventor, an assignee of the invention, a patent attorney or agent representing the inventor or the assignee or certain other representatives of the inventor.

After the patent application is filed, a patent examiner with knowledge in the field of the invention is assigned to the application. The examiner conducts a search of the prior art, including U.S. and foreign patents. The examiner then issues a written opinion or "office action" on the claims in the application stating whether the invention as claimed is patentable. The office action addresses issues of the sufficiency of the written description, the enablement and best mode requirements, novelty and nonobviousness. It can take two years or more after receiving the application for the PTO to issue the first office action.

It is common for patent applications to be rejected by the examiner, especially initially. In many cases, it may be prudent for the applicant to

---

32.   Design and plant patents can have only one claim.
33.   35 U.S.C. § 113.

file claims that are as broad as possible, so that a patent, when issued, will protect as much as possible. If the application is rejected, the applicant may argue for reconsideration of the claims or may amend the claims. This process can involve interviews with the examiner in order to determine what changes should be made to overcome the deficiencies. Further examination proceeds, and the examiner renders a final decision. If the decision is a rejection of some or all of the claims, the applicant may appeal to the PTO's Board of Patent Appeals and Interferences and from there, if necessary, to the U.S. Court of Appeals for the Federal Circuit.[34]

If the patent application is granted, the examiner sends a notice of allowance. An issue fee is due to the PTO, and the patent is then issued.

After a utility patent is issued, maintenance fees are due during the term of the patent. These fees are due at 3½, 7½ and 11½ years after the date of issuance.[35] If the maintenance fees are not paid on time, the patent is deemed abandoned.

The period of patent prosecution may take about three to four years or more, depending on factors like the type of technology and whether appeals or interferences are involved. The applicant can file a petition to make the application special (i.e., to speed up the prosecution process) in a number of situations. These include if the applicant is over 65 years of age or in poor health, if the invention falls within certain fields considered particularly significant (e.g., energy conservation, environmental quality and treatment of HIV or cancer) or if there is actual infringement, among others.[36] The patent application is maintained in secrecy by the PTO until it is published, which occurs about 18 months after the filing date.[37] Secrecy may be maintained throughout the entire prosecution process if the applicant requests it and certain conditions are met. If an application is issued as a patent, the entire PTO file (prosecution history) becomes publicly available.[38] During the prosecution of a patent application, a duty of candor (a duty to disclose) is owed to the PTO.[39] The duty is owed by the inventor, the patent attorney or agent and any assignee. A patent applicant is not required to conduct a search of the prior art before filing a patent application, but must disclose all known prior art that is material. Falsifying information or failing to disclose relevant information can invalidate the patent.

---

34.   28 U.S.C. § 1295(a)(4)(A).
35.   37 C.F.R. §§ 1.362, 1.378. No maintenance fees are due for design and plant patents.
36.   37 C.F.R. § 1.102.
37.   37 C.F.R. § 1.211.
38.   37 C.F.R. §§ 1.11, 1.14.
39.   37 C.F.R. § 1.56.

J.   Types of Patent Applications

1.   *Provisional Patent Applications*

A provisional patent application is a type of utility patent application that was created by statute in 1995.[40] A provisional application is not really a patent application, but a mechanism for allowing an inventor to obtain an earlier filing (priority) date.[41] A provisional application requires a specification and a drawing, but no claims or oath. The PTO never examines the application, and no patent ever issues directly from a provisional application.

An inventor has 12 months from the filing date of the provisional application in which to file a nonprovisional (or regular) utility patent application for the same invention, claiming the benefit of the earlier filing date of the provisional application. In order to claim the filing date of the provisional application, the provisional application must satisfy the written description, enablement and best mode requirements of a regular utility application. The provisional application is deemed abandoned 12 months after it is filed. If a patent issues from the regular application, its term begins on the filing date of the regular application, not the filing date of the provisional application.

A provisional application may be advantageous if the inventor needs to disclose the invention on short notice and does not have enough time to have a regular application prepared. In such a situation, the provisional application provides the inventor with an earlier filing date than might otherwise be obtained, as long as what is later claimed in the regular application was disclosed in the provisional.

2.   *Continuing Applications*

A continuing application is a patent application that claims the filing date of an earlier filed application.[42] In order to claim the earlier filing date, certain requirements must be met: continuity of disclosure, continuity of inventorship and continuity of prosecution. Continuity of disclosure exists if the earlier application discloses the same invention as the continuing application and satisfies the written description, enablement and best mode requirements. Continuity of inventorship exists if there is at least one common inventor between the original application and the continuing application. Continuity of prosecution exists if the continuing application is filed before the prosecution of the earlier application terminates, by the issuance of a patent, abandonment or otherwise.

---

40.   35 U.S.C. § 111(b).
41.   35 U.S.C. § 119(e).
42.   37 C.F.R. § 1.78.

There are several different types of continuing applications, including Continued Prosecution Applications ("CPAs") or Requests for Continued Examinations ("RCEs"), continuation-in-part applications ("CIPs") and divisionals. A CPA or RCE is not a different application, but merely a continuation of the prosecution of the earlier application.[43] A CIP includes some of the subject matter present in the earlier application, but also includes "new matter" not described in the earlier application.[44] The CIP may have two different filing dates, the filing date of the earlier application for claims that are supported by that application and the later filing date of the CIP application for claims that are based upon the new matter added in the CIP application. The term of a patent issued from a CIP application begins on the date the earlier application was filed. A divisional application is one that is divided out of an earlier patent application that contained more than one invention.[45] The divisional application carves out one invention from the earlier application for prosecution. A divisional application can arise from a requirement of the PTO that the applicant select a set of claims corresponding to one invention to be prosecuted first, or it can be a voluntary election. The other inventions are then prosecuted separately from the divisional.

3. Reissue Applications

A reissue application is a patent application seeking the reissuance of an issued patent that is wholly or partly invalid or defective.[46] Only the patent owner can file a reissue application. The invalidity or defect may be due to the scope of the existing patent (for example, the reissue application can seek to broaden or narrow the scope), defects in the drawings or the specification, incorrect inventorship or other matters. A broadening reissue application must be filed within two years of the issuance of the patent and no new matter can be added. A reissue application is treated by the PTO the same as any other patent application—it is fully examined. There is no presumption of validity; the claims that were previously allowed may not be allowed in the reissue application. If the reissue application issues as a patent, its term is the balance of the term left on the original patent.

K. Foreign Patents

Most foreign countries provide some patent protection. The law of each country governs the filing of patents, and a separate patent application has to be filed in each country. As noted previously, countries other than the

---

43. 37 C.F.R. § 1.53(d).
44. 37 C.F.R. § 1.53(b)(2).
45. 35 U.S.C. §§ 120, 121.
46. 35 U.S.C. §§ 251, 252.

United States follow a "first to file" priority system, rather than a "first to invent" system. The process has become simplified, however, by the Patent Cooperation Treaty ("PCT"), an international treaty among many countries entered into in 1978. The PCT does not create an international patent; it merely simplifies the process and minimizes the expense of filing multiple patent applications in foreign countries.

There are two phases for a PCT application: chapter I, during which an international search is performed and the application is published, and chapter II, during which an international preliminary examination of patentability is conducted. Chapter I concludes 20 months after the earliest filing date; while chapter II, which is optional, concludes 30 months after the earliest filing date. The end of either chapter I or chapter II represents the completion of the international stage. The applicant must then enter the national stage of the foreign countries in which a patent is being sought. The application is then governed by the law of the country in which the application is being prosecuted.

A PCT application is advantageous in that it allows an applicant to obtain a search, and a preliminary examination if desired, before spending the significant amount of money required to file a patent application in multiple foreign countries. Moreover, some PCT member countries may adopt the preliminary examination results obtained during the international stage and issue a patent with little or no additional examination.

L.   Miscellaneous Proceedings

1.   Reexamination

A reexamination is a process that can be initiated by the patent owner, the PTO or a third party to reexamine some or all of the claims of an issued patent.[47] The test is whether there is a substantial new question of patentability, based on prior art that was not originally considered by the PTO.[48] The only prior art that can be considered are patents, printed publications and admissions of a patent owner.

The decision to reexamine an issued patent is within the discretion of the PTO. There are two types of reexamination: ex parte and inter partes. These procedures differ in several ways, in particular, in the amount of involvement that a third party who requests the reexamination may have in the proceedings. The result of a reexamination is a certificate setting forth the status of all the claims.

---

47.   35 U.S.C. § 302.
48.   35 U.S.C. § 303.

2. *Interference*

Interference is a proceeding in the PTO before the Board of Patent Appeals and Interferences to determine who invented an invention that is claimed by two different parties.[49] Interference can be requested by the owner of a pending patent application, the owner of an issued patent or the PTO. Interference can be between two applicants, or an applicant and a patent owner, and can involve more than one patent.

In general, the inventor with the earliest date of reduction to practice wins the interference, unless the other party was the first to conceive of the invention and acted diligently until their (later) reduction to practice. In interference, the parties may submit evidence on the issue of the date of conception and other matters. A decision by the board results in a judgment and may include cancellation of a claim in an issued patent or a recommendation to the patent examiner on a pending application that a claim be rejected.

M. Patent Infringement

The number of patent infringement cases filed in the United States has increased dramatically over the last 10 years or so, and we can expect to see that trend continue. One reason is that the number of patents issued is increasing, and many of those patents, particularly business methods patents, are often quite broad and/or their scope and validity are in some doubt.[50] Another reason is that businesses are investing more time and money into intellectual property assets and the loss of those assets could cost the business greatly.

Anyone who makes, uses, offers to sell or sells in the United States, or imports into the United States, a patented invention, without authority from the patent owner, infringes a utility patent.[51] The prerequisite is an issued (not pending or expired) U.S. patent. No intent is required. The patent is infringed if any of the above acts are committed in the United States. An infringer cannot, for example, avoid liability by moving a manufacturing operation outside the United States if the patented product is then imported and sold within the United States. Likewise, a manufacturer of a patented product made in the United States infringes the patent even if the product is only sold outside the United States. The situation is somewhat different, however, for a patented process; performing a patented process in the United States infringes the patent, while performing the same process outside the United States does not, although the law also restricts importation of products

---

49.   35 U.S.C. § 135.
50.   *See* Bilski, *supra* note 5.
51.   35 U.S.C. § 271.

made by patented processes outside the United States, even if the product itself is not patented.[52]

There are three different ways a patent can be infringed: directly, by actively inducing infringement or by contributing to infringement.[53] Direct infringement occurs where the defendant itself makes, uses, sells, offers to sell or imports the infringing invention. Inducing infringement is essentially aiding and abetting infringement; it exists where the defendant knowingly induced another to infringe a patent and where the other did in fact infringe.[54] Corporate officers and directors can be personally liable for inducing infringement. Contributory infringement exists where the defendant sold or offered to sell a component of the patented invention where the component is not a staple item of commerce that has a substantial noninfringing use.[55] Neither inducing infringement nor contributory infringement can be found if there is no direct infringement.

Infringement is a two-step analysis. First, the claims of the patent are construed. The claims are the essence of a patent—the words of the claims define what is protectable. The particular invention that is described and disclosed in the patent's specification is not determinative; in fact, the claims of a patent are often broader than the invention that is disclosed. Claim construction is the interpretation, under certain rules and guidelines developed by the courts, of the meaning and scope of the claims. In an infringement action, claim construction is a question of law for the court.[56] Second, after the claims are construed, the claims are compared to the accused (allegedly infringing) device or method. Again, the invention described in the patent is not determinative—the claims set forth what is protected. In other words, infringement cannot be determined by comparing the invention that is disclosed in the patent to the accused device or method. For infringement to exist, each element (or its equivalent under certain circumstances) of the claim must be present in the accused device or method. Although a patent may have many claims, only one claim need be infringed for the patent to be infringed. In an infringement action, this second step is a question of fact.

The federal district courts have exclusive and original jurisdiction over patent infringement cases.[57] The Court of Appeals for the Federal Circuit decides the appeals.[58] Venue for a patent infringement claim is proper where the infringer resides or where acts of infringement have occurred and the

---

52.   35 U.S.C. § 271(g). Patent owners can collect damages and stop others from importing into the United States products made by a patented process, as long as such products are "not materially changed by subsequent processes."

53.   35 U.S.C. § 271.

54.   35 U.S.C. § 271(b).

55.   35 U.S.C. § 271(c).

56.   Markman v. Westview Instruments, Inc., (1996) 517 U.S. 370, 116 S. Ct. 1384.

57.   28 U.S.C. § 1338(a).

58.   28 U.S.C. §§ 1292, 1295.

infringer has a regular place of business.[59] There are two key defenses to patent infringement: noninfringement and invalidity of the patent.[60] Noninfringement is established if it is shown that the accused device or method does not contain every element of at least one claim of the patent. Invalidity may be based upon improper subject matter, lack of novelty, obviousness, the failure to satisfy all of the requirements for obtaining a patent, incorrect inventorship and inequitable conduct, among other things. Inequitable conduct claims usually arise from allegations that the owner/inventor lied to the PTO or withheld significant information while prosecuting the patent. Invalidity is difficult to prove because a patent is presumed valid and invalidity must be shown by clear or convincing evidence.[61] Both noninfringement and invalidity may be asserted as counterclaims. They can also form the basis of a declaratory judgment action brought by the alleged infringer against the patent owner.

A potential infringer can file an action for declaratory judgment of noninfringement, invalidity or unenforceability of the patent.[62] The federal district court has jurisdiction over such actions as long as there is an actual controversy, that is, there must be a reasonable basis for the potential infringer to believe that the patent owner would file a suit for infringement. A cease and desist letter from the patent owner, stating the intent to file suit if the infringing conduct is not stopped, is such an example. The advantages of filing a declaratory judgment action include that the potential infringer is the plaintiff, rather than the defendant, and that the available venue choices may be more favorable.

A successful plaintiff in a patent infringement case may obtain an injunction, compensatory damages, enhanced damages for willful infringement and attorneys' fees in exceptional cases.[63] Compensatory damages are awarded for the plaintiff's lost profits or in an amount at least equivalent to a reasonable royalty, for a period of time going back up to six years before the complaint was filed.[64] A condition to recovering damages, however, is that the infringer had to have had actual or constructive notice of the patent. If willful infringement is established, enhanced damages, up to treble the compensatory damages, may be awarded by the court. Willfulness depends on a number of factors, including whether the defendant intentionally copied the patented invention and whether the defendant obtained and relied in good faith upon an opinion of counsel on infringement and validity. Attorneys' fees may be awarded by the court to the prevailing party in exceptional cases, which may include cases of willful infringement.[65]

---

59. 28 U.S.C. § 1400(b).
60. 35 U.S.C. § 282.
61. 35 U.S.C. § 282.
62. 28 U.S.C. § 2201.
63. 35 U.S.C. §§ 283–285.
64. 35 U.S.C. § 286.
65. 35 U.S.C. § 285.

If the owner of a patent believes that patent is being infringed, the owner should obtain a legal opinion analyzing both infringement and validity. This analysis should always be conducted before filing a patent infringement suit. The filing of a suit without merit or where the patent is invalid may subject the patent owner not only to having the patent voided, but also to antitrust liability or to the defense of patent misuse. If the validity analysis suggests that there is a significant risk of the patent being held invalid, the patent owner must decide whether that risk is worth taking, as a finding of invalidity is binding on the patent owner in any subsequent action. If there is more than one potential infringer, the patent owner needs to consider who should be pursued (for example, perhaps the competitor, but not the customer). The patent owner may want to send a letter to the infringer to offer to license the patent or to put the infringer on notice of the patent, but such a letter must be carefully worded so that it does not trigger the filing of a declaratory judgment action by the potential infringer.

A potential infringer has a duty to exercise caution after having received notice of the patent. Notice may be actual or constructive. Examples of actual notice include where the infringer has become aware of the patent during licensing negotiations or has received a letter from the patent owner asserting rights under the patent. Constructive notice exists if the patent owner has sold products marked with the number of the patent.

The potential infringer has several alternatives; it can attempt to negotiate a license with the patent owner, it can stop the infringing conduct, it can try to design around the patent, or it can continue the conduct. If the potential infringer intends to continue the conduct, an opinion of counsel should be obtained. The opinion should analyze infringement, as well as validity and enforceability of the patent. A competent opinion should include a review of the patent's file history (the record of the prosecution of the patent in the PTO) because the file history may contain statements of the patent owner that affect the patent's scope and validity. The opinion should also include an analysis of the relevant prior art. Depending on the outcome of the legal analysis and financial cost/benefit considerations, the potential infringer should consider filing a declaratory judgment action against the patent owner for noninfringement and/or invalidity.

8.03   Copyright

A.   Preliminary Considerations

Copyright law can at times be very complex and its application to the business of an emerging company oftentimes remains unappreciated until a dispute arises. This section is intended to provide counsel for an emerging company with a no-nonsense understanding of basic copyright law so that copyright issues can be readily spotted and necessary steps can be taken to protect a client's copyright interests.

B. Copyright Protection

Copyright protection exists when an original work of authorship is fixed in any tangible medium of expression, now known or later developed, from which the work can be perceived, reproduced, or otherwise communicated, either directly or with the aid of a machine or device.

1. Original Works

The "originality" element for copyright requires only that the author independently created the work and that the work possesses at least a minimal degree of creativity. Selection, coordination and arrangement are elements of creativity.[66]

2. Work of Authorship

Copyrightable works must be works of authorship, and include books, musical compositions, multimedia works, original art, dramatic productions (including any associated music), motion pictures and other audiovisual works, sound recordings, computer programs, computer databases, Web pages and any other original expression that is fixed in some tangible medium.[67]

3. Fixed in Any Tangible Medium

The work of authorship must be fixed in a tangible medium of expression that may be perceived, reproduced or communicated either directly or with the aid of a machine or device.[68] A work is not fixed unless its embodiment in tangible form is sufficiently permanent or stable to permit it to be perceived, reproduced or otherwise communicated, for a period of more than a transitory duration. The understanding of a tangible medium is simple when the work is a writing fixed upon the pages of a book, a painting fixed on a canvas or a computer program fixed upon a compact disc. The mediums of paper, a canvas or a compact disc are obviously stable and non-transient. Likewise, it is easy to see how a fixed medium would not include transient reproductions such as a picture flashed upon a screen or on a television tube. However, the issue of a fixed medium becomes more difficult when computer fixations are considered. For example, placing a computer program or digital video in

---

66. *See* Matthew Bender & Co. v. West Publishing Co. (Hyperlaw), 158 F.3d 693 (2d Cir. 1998).

67. 17 U.S.C. § 102(a).

68. 17 U.S.C. § 102(a).

random access memory (RAM) creates a copy that is fixed enough to infringe a copyright, but it is unclear whether copies in RAM are fixed enough to be copyrightable.[69]

4. *Expression*

Most people would intuitively agree that Picasso's paintings, Steven Spielberg's movies or Tom Clancy's novels have enough requisite expression to be copyrightable. The visual representations, arrangement of dialogue or factual depictions carried by such famous works represent unique expression that would be per se copyrightable. However, what about the bland arrangement of names and addresses in a telephone directory or other compilations of factual information; are these works copyrightable?

In *Feist Publications, Inc v. World Telephone Services Company,*[70] the U.S. Supreme Court held that an alphabetical telephone directory of all people living in a particular area lacks sufficient originality and, therefore, was not copyrightable. In coming to its conclusion, the court understood the practical implications of its decision. The court stated:

> [This decision] inevitably means that the copyright of a factual compilation is thin, notwithstanding a valid copyright, a subsequent compiler remains free to use the facts compiled in another's publication to aid in preparing a competing work, so long as the competing work does not feature the same selection and arrangement.[71]

The *Feist* decision raises several important concerns for the developers of websites containing mainly content. Primarily, a third party may copy and freely use any factual information contained in the website, as long as the third party does not use the same selection and arrangement as is found on the website. A website owner's copyright protection will extend only to the copyrightable aspects of the compilation on the website. Thus, the facts that individually make up the compilation may not be protected; their arrangement and presentation *may* be protected.

The issue concerning the protection of the arrangement and presentation of factual compilations came to a head in *Matthew Bender and Company v. West Publishing Company.*[72] In this case the court addressed whether the changes West made to the text of federal judicial opinions, namely the "star pagination" feature, was copyrightable. The court found that the changes were insubstantial, unoriginal and uncreative and, therefore, not copyrightable. In

---

69.   *See* Mai Sys. Corp. v. Peak Computer Inc., 991 F.2d 511 (9th Cir. 1993); Cartoon Network, LP v. CSC Holdings, Inc., 536 F.3d 121 (2d Cir. 2008).

70.   Feist Publications, Inc. v. Rural Telephone Services Co., 499 U.S. 340 (1991).

71.   *Id.* at 349.

72.   *Matthew Bender*, 158 F.3d at 693.

coming to this conclusion, the court noted that most of West's choices were "inevitable, typical, dictated by legal convention, or at best, binary."

CDN v. Kapes,[73] dealt with the defendant's alleged infringement of the plaintiff's coin price guide. Kapes, who published on the Internet a retail coin price guide, used a computer program to determine these retail prices. In order to determine the retail price, Kapes had to input the coin's wholesale price that Kapes obtained from a wholesale coin price guide published by the plaintiff. Kapes acknowledged using CDN's wholesale price guide for the purpose of determining a coin's retail price. CDN alleged that Kapes infringed its copyright by using the wholesale prices found in its price guide as a baseline to arrive at retail prices.

In ruling on the cross-motions for summary judgment, the court found that the wholesale prices CDN established for various coins were sufficiently original compilations and therefore deserving of copyright protection. Comparing the matter to *Feist,* the District Court found that the prices in CDN's guidelines were not facts, but were "wholly the product of CDN's creativity." The court noted that, according to evidence submitted, CDN used its expertise and judgment to determine how a multitude of variables and factors would effect the bid and ask price for certain coins. It was this creative process, the court continued, which ultimately gives rise to CDN's "best guess" as to what the current bid and ask prices should be. The court made clear that it was not the "sweat of the brow" which created a copyrightable work; rather, it was the originality and creativity which CDN engaged in to come up with the prices. If CDN did nothing more than discover the prices paid by dealers in transactions throughout the country, the prices listed in CDN's wholesale price guide would not be copyrightable. However, because the prices listed were not actual prices paid, but CDN's best estimate of the fair value of the coins, CDN employed a process that satisfied the "minimal degree of creativity" required for copyright protection.

5. Subject Matter Not Capable of Copyright Protection

Copyright protection does not extend to ideas, procedures, processes, systems, methods of operation, concepts, principals or discoveries.[74] This is the case regardless of the form in which the idea, procedure, process, system, method of operation, concept, principal or discovery is described, explained, illustrated or embodied.[75]

"Functional" rather than "expressive" works cannot obtain copyright protection. However, while copyright protection may not be available for

---

73. CDN v. Kapes, 197 F.3d 1256 (9th Cir. 1999).

74. 17 U.S.C. § 102(b).

75. 17 U.S.C. § 102(b).

these functional categories of endeavor, many of these categories can obtain protection under the patent laws.[76]

a. Computer Programs

Computer programs are protected under the Copyright Act as literary works; however, they have many unprotectable aspects, and owners are progressively relying on patent law for greater protection. The Ninth Circuit held in *Apple Computer, Inc. v. Microsoft Corporation* that aspects of computer programs' graphical user interfaces are not copyrightable,[77] and the First Circuit soon followed with a ruling that software interfaces *per se* are "methods of operation" and thus are not covered by copyright law.[78]

C. Owners' Rights

1. Exclusive Rights

The copyright owner owns, subject to certain exceptions and limitations,[79] exclusive rights to the copyrighted material. The copyright owner's exclusive rights include the following:

- To reproduce the copyrighted work
- To prepare derivative works based on the copyrighted works
- To distribute copies of the copyrighted work to the public by sale or other transfer or ownership, or by rental, lease or lending
- In the case of literary, musical, dramatic and choreographic works, pantomimes, motion pictures and other audiovisual works, to perform the copyright work publicly
- In the case of literary, musical, dramatic and choreographic works, pantomimes and pictorial, graphic or sculptural works, including the individual images of motion pictures or other audiovisual works, to display the copyright work publicly
- In the case of sound recordings, to perform the copyright work publicly by means of digital audio transmission.[80]

While a copyright owner has the right to prepare derivative works based on the copyrighted work, under certain circumstances, a copyright holder's publication of a derivative work can substantially affect the holder's rights in

---

76.   35 U.S.C. § 101.
77.   35 F.3d 1435 (9th Cir. 1994).
78.   Lotus v. Borland, 49 F.3d 807 (1st Cir. 1995).
79.   The two most commonly litigated exceptions and limitations are Fair Use, 17 U.S.C. § 107, and the First Sale Doctrine, 17 U.S.C. § 109(a).
80.   17 U.S.C. § 106.

the original work. In the case *Batjac Productions v. Good Time Home Video Corp.*, the court addressed whether an owner of rights in a screenplay can claim infringement where the motion picture of the screenplay falls into the public domain.[81] The Ninth Circuit held that the publication of the derivative work, the motion picture, "published" the underlying literary material. Accordingly, when the motion picture went into public domain, the script also went to public domain.

Prior to this case, the general rule had been that publication of a derivative work also "publishes the underlying work." However, there had been some uncertainty when the derivative work was in a different medium from the underlying work. The rule set down in *Batjac* is applicable only where the copyright on the underlying material is common law copyright and not a statutory copyright and where the common law copyright and derivative work are held by the same entity.

All legal or equitable rights that are equivalent to the exclusive rights listed in The Copyright Act are subject to federal preemption.[82]

2.   *Limitations on Exclusive Rights*

The laundry list of limitations on the exclusive rights of copyright owners are catalogued in 17 U.S.C. Sections 107–119. Additionally, the Fairness in Music Licensing Act of 1998 ("Fair Music Act") also places limitations on copyrights. Those portions covering fair use, first sale doctrine, computer program copies and music licenses are the limitations of which emerging companies should be aware.

a.   Fair Use

Fair use is probably the most cited limitation on the rights of copyright owners. Fair use of a copyrighted work includes using the material for criticism, comment, news reporting, teaching (including making copies for use in a classroom), scholarship or research. Under 17 U.S.C. Section 107, whether an act of use or copying of a work constitutes fair use is determined by four factors:

1.   Nature of the use (commercial or nonprofit educational);
2.   Nature of the work;
3.   Amount and substantiality of the portions taken from the copyrighted work; and
4.   Effect on the potential market for the copyrighted work.

---

81.   Batjac Productions v. Good Time Home Video Corp. 160 F.3d 1223 (9th Cir.1998).
82.   17 U.S.C. § 301.

These highly fact-specific factors are weighed under an equitable "rule of reason analysis" to determine whether a particular use constitutes infringement.

Parody may also be claimed as fair use, even if the parody is commercial. The Supreme Court case *Campbell v. Acuff-Rose Music, Inc.* established that parodies fall under "fair use" and thus are excluded from the stable of exclusive rights granted to a copyright holder.[83] Accordingly, the crux of any parody defense is whether the work in question can be considered a parody.

For a work to constitute a parody under copyright law, the Supreme Court in *Campbell* stated, "the nub of the definitions and the heart of any parodist's claim to quote from existing material, is the use of some elements of a prior author's composition to create a new one that, at least in part, comments on that author's work."[84]

The Supreme Court continued to state that if "the commentary has no critical bearing on the substance or style of the original composition, which the alleged infringer merely uses to get attention or to avoid the drudgery in working up something fresh, the claim to fairness in borrowing from the another's work diminishes accordingly (if it does not vanish) and other factors like the extent of its commerciality loom larger." Accordingly, to be considered a parody, the work must, to some degree, comment on or criticize the original.

In *Dr. Seuss Enterprises, LP v. Penguin Books USA, Inc.*, the plaintiff brought, among other claims, a claim for copyright infringement against the author of an illustrated book entitled "The Cat Not In The Hat! A Parody by Dr. Juice."[85] This book was supposed to supply a "fresh new look" at the O.J. Simpson double murder trial. The book's rhymes, illustrations and packaging were designed to mimic the distinctive style of the family of works created by the author better known as Dr. Seuss.

The court considered the defendants' contention that, as to the elements that were incorporated into their book, their taking was excused under the fair use doctrine. The defendants did not argue that their book was a parody. Rather, they argued that all satirical uses are entitled to consideration under the fair use doctrine, not just parodies. In considering the defendants' argument, the court noted that the majority opinion in *Campbell* was silent on this issue. Despite a lack of guidance from the Supreme Court, the Central District applied the law as established by the Ninth Circuit and found that the fair use defense does not apply to satires, but rather, applies only to true parodies.[86]

A parody does not need to be funny to come within the fair use defense; commentary on and criticism of specific elements of the original work may still be protected, as found in a case involving a suit by the estate of *Gone*

---

83.   510 U.S. 569 (1994).
84.   *Id.* at 581.
85.   924 F. Supp. 1559 (S.D. Cal. 1996).
86.   *Id.* at 1567.

With The Wind author Margaret Mitchell over another writer's book titled *The Wind Done Gone.*[87]

The fundamental question in a parody defense is: where does the subject work fall on the parody/satire spectrum? A number of commentators have concluded that an individual with a fertile imagination or a literature degree could probably locate the necessary degree of commentary or criticism to turn a satire into a parody. However, Supreme Court Justice Kennedy's concurrence in *Campbell* cautions copyright defendants against taking refuge in the post-hoc testimony of literary critics.

The fair use defense has also been invoked to protect the intermediate copying of computer software via reverse engineering, where such copying is the only way to gain access to functional elements of the technology, and it's being used for a legitimate purpose, such as achieving interoperability or manufacturing competing hardware.[88] However, the Federal Circuit has upheld provisions in a "shrink-wrap" contract prohibiting software purchasers from engaging in reverse engineering.[89]

Despite claims that the copying was for research purposes, the fair use defense was rejected in cases involving TV news program footage[90] and articles from professional journals for distribution within a corporation.[91]

Google's use of thumbnail images of copyrighted photographs in its "Google Image Search" was ruled fair use, because it was transformative (the court found the use "fundamentally different" than that intended by the copyright owner), and it provided a significant public benefit.[92]

b. First Sale Doctrine

Another important limitation on the exclusive rights of copyright owners is the first sale doctrine, which holds that once a copy of a copyrighted work has been purchased, the purchaser can then resell or otherwise dispose of the copy without the consent of the copyright owner.[93] As long as the purchaser makes no unauthorized copies of the work, the copyright holder's rights in a particular copy of the work end once it has been sold.

---

87.   Suntrust Bank v. Houghton Mifflin Co., 268 F.3d 1257 (11th Cir. 2001).

88.   Sega Enterprises Ltd. v. Accolade, Inc., 977 F.2d 1510 (9th Cir. 1992), as amended, (Jan. 6, 1993); 17 U.S.C. § 1201(f)(1); Sony Computer Entertainment, Inc. v. Connextix Corp., 203 F.3d 596 (9th Cir.), *cert denied,* 531 U.S. 871 (2000).

89.   Bowers v. Baystate Technologies, Inc., 320 F.3d 1317 (Fed. Cir), *cert denied,* 539 U.S. 928 (2003).

90.   Los Angeles News Service v. Tullo, 973 F.2d 791 (9th Cir. 1992).

91.   American Geophysical Union v. Texaco Inc., 37 F.3d 881 (2nd Cir. 1994), order amended and superseded, 60 F.3d 913 (2nd Cir. 1994), *cert denied,* 516 U.S. 1005 (1995).

92.   Perfect 10, Inc. v. Amazon.com, Inc., 487 F.3d 701 (9th Cir. 2007), opinion amended on reh'g, 508 F.3d 1146 (9th Cir. 2007).

93.   17 U.S.C. § 109.

However, as to sound recordings or software, the buyer of these cannot rent, lease or lend them for commercial purposes.[94] In *Vernor v. Autodesk, Inc.*, No. 09-35969 (9th Cir. 2010), the Ninth Circuit considered whether a software purchaser could transfer (resell) software he had obtained under a standard end user license agreement. The Court held that a software user is a licensee rather than an owner of a copy where the copyright owner: (1) specifies that the user is granted a license, (2) significantly restricts the user's ability to transfer the software, and (3) imposes notable use restrictions. The Court found that Autodesk's end user license agreement satisfied all of these conditions, and thus Vernor did not own the software, but was merely a licensee, and could not transfer it freely to his customers under the first sale doctrine.

c.   Computer Copies

The Digital Millennium Copyright Act ("DMCA"), enacted in 1998, allows for the creation of a copy of a computer program if the copy is made solely by virtue of the activation of a machine that lawfully contains an authorized copy of the program, for purposes only of maintaining or repairing that computer, so long as the copies are destroyed after the service.[95]

In addition, the owner of a copy of a computer program may make another copy or adaptation of the program without liability where it is an "essential step" in the utilization of the program, or the copy is for archival purposes and kept only as long as possession is "rightful."[96]

The DMCA bars unauthorized circumvention of technological measures taken to limit access to protected works, with the following exceptions: (1) identifying and analyzing elements of a program necessary to achieve interoperability of an independently created computer program with other programs; (2) good faith encryption research; (3) intended and actual incorporation of a component or part in a technology, product, service or device for the sole purpose of preventing access of minors to Internet material; and (4) protecting personally identifying information.[97]

d.   Small Establishments, Nonprofit Organizations, Secondary Transmissions

Restaurants less than 3,750 gross square feet in space and other establishments less than 2,000 gross square feet do not have to pay royalties to music

---

94.   17 U.S.C. § 109(b).
95.   17 U.S.C. § 117(c).
96.   17 U.S.C. § 117(a).
97.   17 U.S.C. § 1201.

royalty clearing houses such as ASCAP or BMI for music played at their locations.[98]

While otherwise infringing, secondary transmissions by cable systems or satellite carriers to the public may be permitted subject to compulsory licensing.[99]

e.   Musical Works and Sound Recordings

Musical works may consist of either a written transcription of music and lyrics, or a physical recording of musical and lyrical sounds. Where the lyrics and music in a single work are written by different people, performed by singers and musicians and recorded by engineers, the copyright in the work may be shared by all of these different people.

Sound recording copyright owners' rights are limited to the rights to (1) reproduce the sound recording, including the right to duplicate it in the form of phonorecords or copies that directly or indirectly recapture the actual sounds fixed in the recording; (2) prepare derivative works based on the sound recording, in which the actual sounds fixed in the sound recording are rearranged, remixed, or otherwise altered in sequence or quality; (3) distribute copies by sale or transfer; and (4) perform the work publicly by means of a digital audio transmission.[100]

Sound recordings involving nondramatic musical works are subject to compulsory licensing under the Copyright Act, including the right to arrange the work to the extent necessary to conform it to the style or manner of interpretation of the performance involved, as long as the arrangement does not change the basic melody or fundamental character of the work.[101]

D.   Ownership of Copyright and Transfer

1.   *Initial Ownership*

Ownership of copyrighted material vests initially in the author or authors of a work.[102] Usually only the author, or those who derive the rights from the author, can claim copyright protection. Generally, the author is the person who physically creates the work. However, there are some exceptions to this rule: the work for hire doctrine, collective works and joint works.

---

98.   Fairness in Music Licensing Act of 1998 (Pub. L. No. 105-298, 112 Stat. 2827).

99.   17 U.S.C. §§ 111(c)–(d), 119.

100.   17 U.S.C. § 114.

101.   17 U.S.C. § 115; see 37 C.F.R. 201.19

102.   17 U.S.C. § 201.

2. *Works for Hire*

The work for hire doctrine addresses copyright ownership in a work created by an employee or a work commissioned from an independent contractor or other party. A "work made for hire" is a work

- Prepared by an employee within the scope of his or her employment; or
- Specially ordered or commissioned from an independent contractor for use in at least one of certain enumerated ways, provided that the parties expressly agree in a written instrument signed by them that the work constitutes a "work made for hire."[103]

Under the work for hire doctrine, the employer enjoys the copyright ownership in the prepared work of an employee. As noted in Chapter 1 (Starting a New Business), some states are reluctant to give employers the rights to works created by employees. Therefore, it is advisable to have employees sign an intellectual property acknowledgement, a sample of which appears as **Exhibit 10C**.

However, an employer who hires an independent contractor does not automatically own an exclusive right in any work created by the independent contractor. To obtain the exclusive rights to the copyrightable work created by an independent contractor, the work must be one of a specific type. It must be a work either specially ordered or commissioned for use as a contribution to a collective work, a part of a motion picture or other audiovisual work, a translation, a supplementary work, a compilation, an instructional text, a test, answer material for a test or an atlas.[104] Secondly, there must be a written agreement between the parties that specifically states the provider is acting as an independent contractor and that the work is made for hire. An example of such an agreement appears as **Exhibit 8C**. Another way for an employer to obtain the exclusive rights to a copyrightable work created by an independent contractor would be through an assignment, such as in **Exhibit 8A**.

The work made for hire issue should be considered whenever an emerging company is hiring an independent contractor to perform services. This includes writers, graphic designers, Web page designers and computer programmers. A company's independent contractor agreements should contain a clause which states that the work created by the independent contractor is considered a "work made for hire." The agreement should also contain a "back-up" clause that states that in the event the work is not considered a work made for hire, the independent contractor assigns all right, title and interest in the work to the company. A short-form work-for-hire agreement appears as **Exhibit 8D**.

At the very minimum, a company should have the independent contractor execute either a memorandum of understanding acknowledging that the work

---

103.   17 U.S.C. § 101.
104.   17 U.S.C. § 101.

created by the independent contactor is work made for hire, or an assignment agreement. A sample memorandum of understanding is included as **Exhibit 8E**. If a work is created by an independent contractor which does not fall within one of the specified categories, or it is covered by the statute but there is no writing confirming its status as a work for hire, the independent contractor will own the copyright to the work, unless there is a valid transfer.[105]

The distinction between an employee and an independent contractor under the Copyright Act is based on general common law principles of agency; the actual relationship between the individual creating the work and the party paying the creator controls, not the appearance of an employment or agency relationship.[106]

3. Collective Works

A collective work, such as a periodical, anthology or encyclopedia, is a work to which a number of contributions, all which constitute separate and independent works in themselves, are assembled into a collective whole.[107] Of the singular works made a part of the collective work, the authors, absent any express transfer of rights, maintain all rights to their individual contribution. The publisher of the collective work enjoys the right to use the various articles, essays or other composite works only as a part of the collective work.

The case of *New York Times Company v. Tasini*, involved six freelance writers who sued the New York Times and other publishers for copyright infringement.[108] Articles written by the plaintiffs, which had previously been published by the defendants, had been later included in certain electronic databases, such as Nexis, and CD-ROMs.

The main issue for the court was whether the use of the articles in the databases constituted a use of the works in a "revision" of the periodicals from which the articles were taken. Under Section 201(c) of the Copyright Act, there is a presumption that, in the absence of an express transfer of a right to use a work in a collective work, the original work may be used "in any revision" of that collective work. In their electronic form, the articles were individually retrievable and very little of the original collective work's copyrightable selection, coordination or arrangement was preserved. The court found that the databases did not constitute "revisions" of a particular collective work and therefore the publishers of periodicals could not relicense individual articles to databases under Section 201(c) of the Copyright Act.

In a subsequent Ninth Circuit case, a professional photographer who created thousands of photographic slides for a sporting goods maker sued

---

105.   BPI Systems, Inc. v. Leith, 532 F.Supp. 208, 210 (W.D. Tex. 1981).
106.   Community for Creative Non-Violence v. Reid, 490 U.S. 730 (1989); MacLean Associates, Inc. v. William M. Mercer-Meidinger-Hansen, Inc., 952 F.2d 769 (3rd Cir. 1991).
107.   17 U.S.C. § 101.
108.   New York Times Co. v. Tasini, 533 U.S. 483 (2001).

the company, alleging that it infringed his copyrights in his photographic images used by the company in collage-style online ads after the contract between them expired.[109] The court rejected the defendant's argument that the 24 images in the collage ads were privileged as collective works under § 201(c). Rather, the court found that they were derivative works because they transformed the plaintiff's original images into new promotional posters. The collective works privilege did not apply to the ads, and the defendant's displaying them online after its term of use had expired infringed the plaintiff's copyrights in the underlying images.

4. Joint Works

A joint work is where there is more than one author to a copyrightable work, where each author prepares the work intending their contributions to be "inseparable or independent parts of a unitary whole."[110] Under a joint work, both authors own the undivided copyright interests to that entire work equally. Each coauthor of a joint work has an independent right to use or license the copyright, subject to a duty of accounting to the other coauthor. A joint owner cannot be liable to a co-owner for a copyright infringement.

5. Community Property and Authorship

A nonauthor spouse in a community property state such as California may have a community property interest in the owner-spouse's work(s). In the case *In re Marriage of Worth,*[111] the court held that under California's community property law[112] a copyright could be transferred by operation of law from the owner-spouse to the marital community. The court rejected the owner-spouse's arguments based upon preemption of the federal Copyright Act by stating, "nothing is found in the Copyright Act which either precludes the acquisition of a community property interest by a spouse or which is otherwise inconsistent with community property law."[113]

It is unclear whether community property rights would apply to the renewal of a copyright term, depending on whether or not they were viewed as a contingent property right or a mere expectancy.[114]

---

109.   Jarvis v. K2, Inc., 486 F.3d 526 (9th Cir. 2007), motion granted by, in part, motion denied by, in part, request denied by, costs and fees proceeding, Jarvis v. K2, Inc., 2008 U.S. Dist. LEXIS 109310 (W.D. Wash. 2008).

110.   17 U.S.C. § 201(a).

111.   *In re Marriage of Worth,* 195 Cal. App. 3d 768 (1987).

112.   Other community property states include Arizona, Idaho, Louisiana, Nevada, New Mexico, Texas and Washington. In addition, the Commonwealth of Puerto Rico is a community property jurisdiction.

113.   *Id* at 777. *See also* Rodrigue v. Rodrigue, 218 F.3d 432 (5th Cir. 2000).

114.   1-6A Nimmer on Copyrights § 6A.02.

E.   Transfer of Ownership and Recording Transfer

1.   Transfer

The ownership of or one or more exclusive rights to a copyright may be transferred in whole or in part by any means of written conveyance or by operation of law.[115] Any signed document pertaining to a copyright is a valid means of conveyance.[116] Assignments, exclusive licenses or wills are such exemplary valid means of conveyance.

The requirement that a transfer be in writing operates as a statute of frauds. An oral agreement regarding a copyright transfer that is later confirmed in writing may satisfy the requirement, so long as the writing is "substantially contemporaneous" with the oral agreement and the product of the parties' negotiations.[117] It is unclear whether recent laws affecting electronic transactions and email signatures will translate in the copyright transfer sphere.

2.   Recordation of Transfers

The recordation of a transfer of ownership with the U.S. Copyright Office acts as constructive notice to the world of the transfer as long as two conditions are met: (a) specific identification of the work is made in the transfer, and (b) registration of a claim to copyright in the work is made with the Copyright Office.[118] Such a recordation allows the first transferee to have priority over any subsequent transfer so recorded. The first transferee is also allowed a one-month grace period (two months if the transfer was executed abroad) to record the transfer and prevail against a second transferee. Even without observing these time limits, the first transferee may prevail if it can be shown that the subsequent transferee knew of the first transfer, or where the second transfer was not otherwise in good faith, or where the transfer had not been taken for consideration on a binding promise to pay royalties.[119]

3.   Conflicting Transfers Involving Nonexclusive License

A difficult issue is brought up by nonexclusive licenses. The Copyright Act excludes such licenses from the definition of transfers of ownership. Nonexclusive licenses need not be in writing, much less recorded. But, whether recorded or not, written, signed, nonexclusive licenses prevail over

---

115.   17 U.S.C. § 201(d).

116.   17 U.S.C. § 204(a).

117.   *See* Eden Toys, Inc. v. Florelee Undergarment Co., Inc., 697 F.2d 27, 36 (2nd Cir. 1982); Konigsberg International Inc. v. Rice, 16 F.3d 355, 357 (9th Cir. 1994).

118.   17 U.S.C. § 205(c).

119.   17 U.S.C. § 205(e).

conflicting transfers if the license was taken either before the conflicting transfer or in good faith before the recordation of the transfer and without notice of it.[120]

F.   Duration of Copyright

A copyright in a work created by an author on or after January 1, 1978 (or prior to such date but not published or copyrighted until after January 1, 1978) endures for the life of the author plus 70 years.[121]

Under the 1909 Copyright Act, works published prior to January 1, 1978 had an initial copyright term of 28 years, with one renewal term of an additional 28 years; the 1976 Copyright Act extended the renewal term to 47 years, and the Sonny Bono Copyright Term Extension act further extended it to 67 years, so now the total years of protection may be 95 (28 plus 67).[122]

All copyright terms extend through the end of the year in which they expire.

1.   Joint Works

For a joint work, the copyright endures for the life of the last surviving author plus 70 years.[123]

2.   Works Made for Hire

Works made for hire endure for 95 years from the date of first publication or 120 years from creation of the work, whichever is shorter.[124]

3.   Termination of Copyrights

The Copyright Act allows authors, musicians and artists (and their heirs) to recapture the original copyrights in their creations by terminating a prior grant of the copyright. For the most part, these termination rights cannot be waived by contract, regardless of the terms of the assignment or license, provided that the artist and the artist's heirs meet the complex statutory termination requirements. Counsel involved in the creation, acquisition or exploitation of copyrighted works should be aware of the statutory right to terminate copyright grants.

---

120.   17 U.S.C. § 205(f).
121.   17 U.S.C. §§ 302(a), 303(a).
122.   Act of October 27, 1998, Pub. L. No. 105-298, 112 Stat. 2827, Sec. 101; 17 U.S.C. § 304(b).
123.   17 U.S.C. § 302(b).
124.   17 U.S.C. § 302 (c).

The provisions in the Act governing the right to terminate copyright transfers are at Sections 203 and 304 of the Act. The date that the grant was made determines which provision applies: grants made after January 1, 1978 are governed by Section 203, and grants made before January 1, 1978 are governed by Section 304.

There are several key exceptions to the right to terminate a grant. First, the grant must have been an *inter vivos* transfer by the author. In other words, the author had to have made the transfer during his or her lifetime. The statutes referred to here generally cannot be used to invalidate a transfer of copyrights under an author's will. Second, the termination right does not apply to a "work made for hire" under Section 201(b) of the Copyright Act. And third, the right to terminate a copyright grant does not apply to an authorized derivative work created after the grant by the grantee, but prior to termination of the grant. Thus, if an assignment of a copyright in a book included the right to create a film based on the book, the assignee may continue to reproduce and distribute copies of any such film created prior to the exercise of the termination right after the termination, but may not create a television series based on the book after termination of the grant.

G. Copyright Notice

1. Generally

Copyright notice is not required to be placed on publicly distributed copies of a work anymore. However, it is highly advisable to do so. If the copyright notice is omitted from the copies of a work, this could support an infringer's argument that he did not know the work was copyrighted and that the infringement was therefore in good faith, thereby leading to the possibility of the copyright owner obtaining only a minimal damage judgment against an otherwise willful infringer.[125]

2. Form of Notice

The form of copyright notice requires that the following three elements be included:[126]

1. The symbol © (the letter "C" in a circle), the word "Copyright" or the abbreviation "Copr." For sound recordings the symbol "p" inside a circle is required.

---

125. 17 U.S.C. § 401(a).
126. 17 U.S.C. §§ 401(b), 402(b); 37 C.F.R. § 202.2.

2. The year of first publication of the work. If the work is updated (such as chapter revisions in a textbook), then the years that the work was updated should also be included with the year of first publication.
3. The name of the copyright owner must be placed on the notice. Do not merely place the author's name on the notice unless the author is also the owner.

In certain circumstances, the year of first publication may be omitted,[127] and the owner's name may be abbreviated or a generally known alternative designation of the owner used.[128]

If a copyright notice is used, it is only effective if affixed to the copies of the work in such a manner and location as to give reasonable notice of the claim of copyright.[129]

H. Copyright Registration

1. *Preliminary Considerations*

Registration is permissive and may be done at anytime during the life of a copyright. Registration is done with the U.S. Copyright Office. There are many good reasons to register a copyright:

- Registration provides an official record of ownership. Recordation provides constructive notice to the public of the facts stated in the registration certificate.[130]
- If registration occurs within five years of first publication, this is prima facie evidence of the validity of the copyright and the information stated in the certificate.[131]
- Registration is required in order to be able to recover statutory damages (which require no proof of actual damages) and attorney's fees.[132]
- Registration is required in order to file a copyright infringement action in federal court.[133]

It is important to note that all Copyright Office registration records, including deposit materials, are generally publicly available. Accordingly, copyright registration will typically preclude confidential or trade secret status for the registered work.

---

127.   17 U.S.C. § 401(b)(2).
128.   17 U.S.C. §§ 401(b)(3), 402(b)(3).
129.   17 U.S.C. §§ 401(c), 402(c); 37 C.F.R. § 201.20.
130.   17 U.S.C. § 205.
131.   17 U.S.C. § 410(c).
132.   17 U.S.C. § 412.
133.   17 U.S.C. § 411.

2. *Application for Registration*

Applications to the U.S. Copyright Office for copyright registration may be completed in three ways:

The quickest and least expensive registration method for a basic claim for a single work (literary, visual arts, performing arts, including motion pictures and sound recordings) is online registration through the Electronic Copyright Office (eCO). Advantages of registering through the eCO include a lower filing fee, fastest processing time, online status tracking, secure payment by credit or debit card, electronic check (or Copyright Office deposit account), and the ability to upload some categories of deposits directly into eCO as electronic files. The eCO registration system is available at http://www.copyright.gov/eco/.

The next best registration option is with a Fill-In Form CO, which replaces Forms TX, VA, PA, SE, and SR. Using 2-D barcode scanning technology, the Copyright Office can process these forms much faster and more efficiently than paper forms completed manually. The user need only complete Form CO on their personal computer, print it out, and mail it to the Copyright Office with a check or money order and their deposit. The Form CO is available at www.copyright.gov, under "Forms." Form CO cannot be reused for subsequent registrations; the 2-D barcode it contains is unique for each registered work.

Finally, the old registration method via paper forms sent by U.S. mail is still available for some types of works. Paper versions of Form TX (literary works), Form VA (visual arts works), Form PA (performing arts works, including musical compositions and motion pictures), Form SR (sound recordings), and Form SE (single serials) are still available, but are no longer online; the Copyright Office will send them by U.S. mail upon request. Some applications are required to be submitted on paper and mailed to the Copyright Office with the appropriate fee and deposit, including Form RE for renewals of existing copyrights and forms for group submissions, including Form GR/PPh/CON (published photographs), Form GR/CP (contributions to periodicals), Form SE/Group (serials), and Form G/DN (daily newspapers/newsletters). These forms are still at www.copyright.gov. However for registrations of a TX, VA, SR, or SE work, the best options are using online registration through eCO or a fill-in Form CO.

After the correct online or paper form is completed, the applicant must pay the applicable filing fee and submit two complete deposit copies of the best edition of the published work as specimens of the work being registered, within three months after the date of first publication of the work.[134] Using the eCO method of registration allows for the ability to upload certain categories of deposits directly into eCO; however, for registrations of a published work,

---

134.   17 U.S.C. § 407(a).

a physical copy of the best published edition is required under Section 407 of the Act. A physical copy is not required for works that are published or distributed only electronically. Unpublished works require that one deposit copy be submitted.[135] The Register of Copyrights may make a written demand, including a "mandatory deposit notice," for the required deposit at any time after publication, and if the required deposit is not made within three months of the demand, the person or organization obligated to make the deposit is liable for a fine for each work plus the retail price of the copies; if the refusal to comply is willful or repeated, an added fine may be incurred.[136]

Most online registrations issue within six months of filing the application, while most Form CO and paper filers receive their certificates of registration within 8 to 22 months of filing. The effective date of registration is the day the Copyright Office receives a complete submission in acceptable form.

I. Copyright Infringement and Remedies

1. Infringement Basic Definition

Anyone who violates the exclusive rights of the copyright owner as enumerated in 17 U.S.C. Sections 106–118 is an infringer.[137] In the governing Supreme Court case, the court stated that two elements must be proven: "(1) ownership of a valid copyright, and (2) copying of constituent elements of the work that are original."[138] A copyright registration certificate constitutes prima facie evidence of a plaintiff's ownership.[139] With respect to copying, it is important to note that not every instance of copying constitutes copyright infringement; actionable copying requires appropriation of protected elements of the work.

It is unusual to be able to prove copying by direct evidence; in most cases, copying is usually inferred from proof of the defendant's access to the work and "substantial similarity" between the two works.[140]

The copyright owner must sue the infringer in federal court. State courts have no jurisdiction over federal copyright claims.[141]

---

135. 17 U.S.C. § 408.
136. 17 U.S.C. § 407(d).
137. 17 U.S.C. § 501; Feist Publications, Inc. v. Rural Tel. Service Co., Inc., 499 U.S. 340, 345 (1991).
138. Feist, 499 U.S. at 361.
139. 17 U.S.C. § 410(c).
140. Langman Fabrics v. Graff Californiawear, Inc., 160 F.3d 106, 115 (2d Cir. 1998).
141. 28 U.S.C. § 1338(a).

a. Direct Liability for Copyright Infringement

The Copyright Act imposes strict liability for infringement[142] and one can be held directly liable where he or she usurps any one of the various rights exclusively reserved for the copyright holder. Those rights include the right to reproduce or distribute copies of the copyrighted work, the right to publicly perform the work and the right to prepare derivative works.[143]

b. Contributory Copyright Infringement

Contributory liability is applied where anyone with knowledge of the infringing activity induces, causes or materially contributes to the infringing conduct of another.[144] The knowledge requirement is objective, and is established when the defendant knows or has reason to know of the infringing activity.[145]

- With respect to materiality, the law is inconsistent. The Ninth Circuit has held that providing the site and facilities for known infringing activity is sufficient.[146] However, some courts have required the participation to be "substantial," finding the mere fact that equipment or facilities may be used for copyright infringement is not determinative. In *Perfect 10 v. Visa International,* the court ruled that credit card companies were not liable for secondary copyright and trademark infringement (including contributory) as a result of payment transactions for infringing material on a website—the role of the companies was too attenuated from the infringing activity to be considered a "material contribution."[147]

c. Vicarious Liability for Copyright Infringement

Vicarious liability for copyright infringement may be imposed where the defendant (1) has the right and ability to supervise the infringing activity; and (2) has a direct financial interest in the activities.[148] Knowledge of the infringing conduct is not a requirement, and therefore lack of knowledge is not a defense; however, the absence of knowledge by the defendant may affect the plaintiff's available remedies.[149]

---

142.   17 U.S.C. § 501.
143.   17 U.S.C. § 106.
144.   Sony Corp. v. Universal City Studios, Inc., 464 U.S. 417, 435 (1984).
145.   *See, e.g.,* Sega Enters. Ltd. v. MAPHIA, 948 F. Supp. 923, 933 (N.D. Cal. 1996); Casella v. Morris, 820 F.2d 362, 365 (11th Cir. 1987).
146.   Fonovisa, Inc. v. Cherry Auction, Inc., 76 F.3d 259, 264 (9th Cir. 1996).
147.   494 F.3d 788 (9th Cir. 2007).
148.   Fonovisa, 76 F.3d 259 (9th Cir. 1996).
149.   3 Nimmer § 12.04[A][1].

2. Registration As a Prerequisite

The copyright owner must have an issued registration in hand prior to filing suit in federal court for copyright infringement.[150]

3. Copyright Infringement and the Internet

In general, copyright infringement on the Internet is treated in the same manner as infringement of works using other methods, except that the question of determining who is liable for infringement becomes more complex: is it the party who uses a computer to reproduce a protected work, the party who accesses the work thus reproduced, or the provider who maintains the network or server that makes such access possible?[151]

The Digital Millennium Copyright Act ("DMCA") was enacted in 1998 to provide, among other protections, safeguards from copyright infringement for online service providers. The second title of the DMCA is the Online Copyright Infringement Liability Limitation Act ("OCILL"), which added Section 512 to the Copyright Act. Section 512 does not change the copyright owner's right to proceed against the initial party who uploaded the owner's works online; rather, it only limits the owner's ability to make a claim of infringement against the "deep pocket" of the internet service provider. However, as it is often difficult to identify and/or serve the primary actor, or the actor may be judgment-proof, the limitations imposed by Section 512 greatly affect the copyright holder's ability to obtain relief in the event of an online infringement. In addition to the direct "copying" of infringing material onto the Internet, copyright disputes also grow out of linking and framing.

a. Uploading and Displaying

Online service providers face potential contributory infringement liability in the event they are on notice of an infringement, are able to take simple measures to prevent further infringements, and continue to aid the infringement. In 1995, in ruling on a motion for summary judgment, the District Court found that there was a triable issue of material fact as to whether Netcom engaged in contributory copyright infringement as a result of one of its users posting infringing material on a Usenet news group.[152]

The plaintiff argued that Netcom knew that its user, Erlich, was infringing their copyrights, at a very minimum, after receiving notice from the plaintiff's counsel indicating that Erlich had posted copies of the plaintiff's work through Netcom's systems. The court found that the evidence revealed a question of

---

150.   17 U.S.C. § 411.

151.   3 Nimmer on Copyright, § 12.B01[A][1].

152.   *See* Religious Technology Center v. NetCom Online Communication Services Inc., 907 F. Supp. 1361 (N.D. Cal. 1995).

fact as to whether or not Netcom knew or should have known that Erlich had infringed the plaintiff's copyrights after receiving the Plaintiff's letter. The court stated that because Netcom was arguably participating in Erlich's public distribution of the plaintiff's work, there was a genuine issue as to whether Netcom knew of any infringement before it was too late to do anything about it. If the plaintiffs could prove the knowledge element, the court concluded that Netcom would be liable for contributory copyright infringement.

Spurred on as a result of the court's decision in *Netcom*, Congress enacted the DMCA in 1998. Title II of the DMCA, the Online Copyright Infringement Liability Limitation section, immunized service providers from third party liability for damages, costs or attorney's fees due to claims of copyright infringement. The limitations or safe harbors are based on four categories of conduct by a service provider: (a) transitory communications, (b) system caching, (c) storage of information on systems or networks at direction of users and (d) information location tools.

The immunity provided to the service providers is predicated on the service provider's compliance with certain requirements set forth in the Title II. If the service provider fails to comply with these requirements, it may be held contributorily liable for copyright infringement.

i. *Eligibility for Limitations Generally*

A party seeking the benefit of the limitations on liability under Title II of the OCILL Act must qualify as a "service provider." For the purpose of transitory communications, a service provider is defined as "an entity offering the transmission, routing, or providing of connections for digital online communications, between or among points specified by a user, of material of the user's choosing, without modification to the content of the material as sent or received." For the purposes of the other three categories of conduct, a service provider is more broadly defined as "a provider of online services or network access, or the operator of facilities therefore."

In addition to meeting the definition of a service provider, to be eligible for any of the limitations or safe harbors, a service provider must meet two overall conditions. First, the service provider must adopt and reasonably implement a policy of terminating in appropriate circumstances the accounts of subscribers who are repeat infringers. Second, the service provider must accommodate and not interfere with measures used by a copyright owner to identify or protect copyrighted works that have been developed pursuant to a broad consensus of copyright owners and service providers in an open, fair and voluntary multi-industry process; are available to anyone on reasonable nondiscriminatory terms; and do not impose substantial costs or burdens on service providers.

ii.   Safe Harbor for Transitory Communications

In general terms, this safe harbor limits the liability of service providers in circumstances where they merely act as a data conduit, transmitting digital information from one point on a network to another at someone else's request. Immunity from liability as a result of transmitting, routing or providing connections to infringing material is available if the following are true:

- Transmission of the material was initiated by a person other than the service provider
- The transmission, routing or storage was carried out through an automatic technical process without the selection of the material by the service provider
- If the service provider selects recipients for the material it must be an automatic response to the request of another person
- No copy of the material is made by the service provider or the service provider's system in a longer period than is reasonably necessary for the transmission of the material
- The material is transmitted through the service provider's system or network without modification of its content

iii.   Safe Harbor for System Caching

This safe harbor limits the liability of service providers for the practice of retaining copies, for a limited time, of material that has been made available online by a person other than the service provider and then transmitted to a user at his or her direction. The practice of service providers retaining copies of online material is driven by the service providers' desire to reduce bandwidth requirements and the users' desire for a faster connection. A service provider is entitled to immunity from copyright infringement due to system caching where the following are true:

- Material is made available online by someone other than the service provider
- Material is transmitted from the above person through the system or network to the third party at that third party's direction
- Storage is carried out through an automatic technical process
- Content of the retained material is not modified
- Service provider complies with rules about "refreshing" material when specified in accordance with a generally accepted industry standard data communication protocol
- Service provider does not interfere with technology that returns "hit" information to the person who posted the material where such technology meets certain requirements
- Service provider limits users' access to the material in accordance with conditions on access imposed by the person who posted the material

- Any material that was posted without the copyright owner's authorization must be removed or blocked promptly once the service provider has been notified that, at the originating site, the material has been removed or blocked or ordered to be removed or blocked.

iv. Safe Harbor for Information Residing on System or Network at User's Direction

This safe harbor protects a service provider from liability due to the infringing material on websites hosted on their system. In order for the service provider to take advantage of this safe harbor, the service provider must meet the following conditions:

- Must not have actual knowledge that the material is infringing
- Must not be aware of facts or circumstances that would indicate the material is an infringement
- Upon becoming aware of the existence of such infringing material, must act promptly to remove or disable access to the infringing material.

In addition, in order to be entitled to copyright infringement immunity under this provision, the service provider must not receive a financial benefit directly attributable to the infringing material, where the service provider has the right and ability to control the placement of the infringing material on its system.

The user storage limitation is available only if the service provider has designated an agent to receive notification of claims of infringement. The service provider must make available on its website and provide to the U.S. Copyright Office the name, address, phone number and electronic mail address of the designated agent, and other contact information which the registrar of copyrights may deem appropriate. The Copyright Office has a suggested form for designating an agent and maintains a list of agents on the Copyright Office website.

In addition, a service provider must establish and implement a policy of terminating the accounts of repeat infringers, make users aware of this policy and accommodate and not interfere with "standard technical measures" in order to be entitled to immunity from copyright infringement.[153]

---

153. "Standard technical measures" are defined as technical measures that are used by copyright owners to identify or protect copyrighted works and (i) have been developed pursuant to a broad consensus of copyright owners and service providers in an open, fair, voluntary and multi-industry standards process; (ii) are available to any person on reasonable and non-discriminatory terms; and (iii) do not impose substantial costs on service providers or substantial burdens on their systems or networks.

v.   Safe Harbor for Information Location Tools

This safe harbor relates to hyperlinks, online directories, search engines and similar tools. Under this provision, a service provider's liability for referring or linking users to a site that contains infringing material by using information location tools is limited if the following conditions are satisfied:

- Must not have actual knowledge that the material is infringing
- Must not be aware of facts or circumstances that would indicate the material is an infringement
- Upon becoming aware of the existence of such infringing material, must act promptly to remove or disable access to the infringing material.

In addition, in order to be entitled to copyright infringement immunity under this provision, the service provider must not receive a financial benefit directly attributable to the infringing material, where the service provider has the right and ability to control the placement of the infringing material on its system.

vi.   Notification of Claimed Infringement

Title II also sets out procedures for third-party notification to the service provider of infringement and counter notification to the service provider's subscribers. When a notification that complies with the requirements of Title II is received,[154] a service provider must promptly remove or block access to the allegedly infringing content. In a case where a subscriber of the service provider posts the content, the service provider must take "reasonable steps promptly to notify the subscriber that it has removed or disabled access to the material."

Under Title II, a service provider is not liable to any person for a claim based on the service provider's good faith disabling of access to, or removal of, a material or activity claimed to be infringing based on facts and circumstances

---

154.   A notification of claimed infringement must be a written communication to the designated agent of a service provider which includes the following:

- A physical or electronic signature of the person authorized to act on behalf of the owner of an exclusive right to the material allegedly infringed;
- Identification of the copyrighted work being infringed, or in the case of multiple copyrighted works being infringed on a single site, a representative list of such works at that site;
- Identification of the material that is claimed to be infringing and information reasonably sufficient to permit the service provider to locate the material;
- Information reasonably sufficient to allow the service provider to contact the complaining party;
- A statement that the complaining party has a good faith belief that the use of the material in the manner complained of is not authorized by the copyright owner, its agent or the law; and
- A statement that the information and notification is accurate and made under the penalty of perjury.

in which an infringing activity is apparent regardless of whether the material or activity is ultimately determined to be infringing. This exception does not apply where the allegedly infringing material is moved based on receipt by the service provider's agent of a notification, unless the service provider notifies the subscriber that it has removed or disabled access to the material.

Where the service provider receives a counter notification[155] from the subscriber, the service provider must promptly provide the original complaining party with a copy of the counter notification. The service provider must then replace or restore access to the disputed content between the 11th and 14th business days after the date on which it received the counter notification, unless, within the first 10 business days, it receives notice from the original complainant that the complainant has filed suit to restrain the subscriber from engaging in copyright infringement. Where the service provider receives notification that a suit has been filed, the service provider must take no further action pending a ruling by the court.

While the DMCA may provide some immunity from copyright infringement for the acts of third parties, website owners may still be subject to direct liability.[156] Contributory liability for copyright infringement also still exists for persons and entities that do not fall under the definition of a service provider under Title II. In addition, contributory liability may exist where an entity falls under the definition of a service provider under Title II but fails to meet certain other threshold requirements set forth in Title II.

b.   Linking

In most cases, linking is unlikely to violate copyright law. In *Bernstein v. J.C. Penney Inc.,*[157] Gary Bernstein sued Elizabeth Arden Company ("Arden") and Perfumes International Ltd. for copyright infringement alleging that Arden and J.C. Penney were liable because Arden's Passion perfume was promoted on a J.C. Penney website that was hyperlinked to a website operated by

---

155.   A counter notification must be a written communication provided to the service provider's designated agent, which includes:
- A physical or electronic signature of the subscriber;
- Identification of the material that has been removed or to which access has been disabled;
- A statement under the penalty of perjury that the subscriber has a good faith belief that the material was removed or disabled as a result of mistake or misidentification;
- The subscriber's name, address and telephone number and a statement that the subscriber consents to the jurisdiction of the federal district court for the judicial district in which the subscriber is located or, in the case of subscribers outside the United States, in any judicial district in which the service provider may be found.

156.   *See* Bret Michaels v. Internet Entm't Group, 5 F. Supp. 2d 823 (C.D. Cal 1998). Michaels, the lead singer of the rock band Poison, filed a suit and sought a temporary restraining order prohibiting IEG from disseminating over the Internet portions of a homemade video which featured Michaels and actress Pamela Anderson Lee having sex. The court found that Michaels established a *prima facie* case of copyright infringement entitling him to a temporary restraining order.

157.   Bernstein v. J.C. Penney Inc., 50 U.S.P.Q.2d 1063, (C.D. Cal 1998).

Internet Movie Database that, in turn, linked to several other websites, one of which—the Swedish University Network—contained infringing copies of two of Mr. Bernstein's photographs of the actress Elizabeth Taylor, the spokesperson for Arden's perfume.

The court granted Arden's motion to dismiss with prejudice, finding that linking cannot constitute direct infringement because the computer server of the linking website does not copy or otherwise process the content of the two linked sites; multiple linking in the instant case could not constitute contributory infringement by Arden because there was no direct infringement in the United States to which Arden could contribute and linking is capable of substantial noninfringing uses; and multiple linking does not constitute substantial participation in any infringement where the linking website does not mention the fact that the Internet users could, by following the links, find infringing material on another website.

However, several courts have held that a hyperlink violates the law if it points to illegal material with the purpose of disseminating that illegal material:

- In a case brought by Universal City Studios against a party using DeCSS, a software program designed to circumvent the copying protections for the plaintiff's motion pictures on DVDs,[158] the court barred 2600 Magazine from posting hyperlinks to DeCSS code because it found the magazine had linked for the purpose of disseminating a circumvention device (a violation of the DMCA). The court ruled that it could regulate the link because of its "function," even if the link was also speech.

- In another case, *Intellectual Reserve v. Utah Lighthouse Ministry*,[159] a Utah court found that linking to unauthorized copies of a text might be a contributory infringement of the work's copyright. (The defendant in that case had previously posted unauthorized copies on its own site, and then replaced the copies with hyperlinks to other sites.)

c.   Framing

Framing allows a Web page designer to divide a Web page into multiple areas, each of which are scrollable and may operate independently of each other. Frames in a Web page may contain text, graphics, hypertext, links and even other imbedded frames. The most utilized application involving framing is a Web page containing a framed section that features links to other websites. These links allow the Web page viewer to view text, graphics and even entire websites without ever leaving the first Web page.

---

158.   Universal City Studios, Inc. v. Reimerdes, 111 F. Supp. 2d 294 (S.D.N.Y. 2000).
159.   75 F.Supp. 2d 1290 (D. Utah 1999).

One of the more well known cases dealing with liability for copyright infringement resulting from framing was handed down by the Ninth Circuit on February 6, 2002 in *Kelly v. Arriba Soft Corporation.*[160] Arriba operates an Internet search engine that displays its results in the form of small pictures, or thumbnails, rather than the traditional form of text. Arriba obtained its database of thumbnail pictures by copying images from other websites. When a user clicks on one of the thumbnail images, the user can view a larger version of the same picture framed within the Arriba Web page. The source for the larger picture, however, is not within Arriba's server. Arriba imports the image directly from the source website through a process called inline linking.

Kelly, a professional photographer, sued Arriba for copyright infringement as a result of discovering that his photographs were part of Arriba's search engine database. Arriba contended that the creation and use of the thumbnails in the search engine and inline linking to the source Web page was a fair use. The court found that fair use only provided a defense for Arriba with respect to the use of the thumbnails. Despite the fact that Arriba made exact replications of Kelly's images, the thumbnails were much smaller, lower resolution images that served an entirely different function than Kelly's original images. The court found Arriba's use of Kelly's images as thumbnails to be transformative and therefore noninfringing.

The court concluded differently when it came to Arriba's inline linking to and framing of Kelly's full-sized images. Although the process by which Kelly's images are displayed on Arriba's website did not involve copying, the court found that the process of inline linking and framing Kelly's images within Arriba's website infringed on Kelly's exclusive right to publicly display his copyrighted works. However, the Ninth Circuit later withdrew this portion of its opinion, leaving its reversal of the District Court's grant of summary judgment for the defendant based solely on procedural grounds, and this area of law unresolved.[161]

d. Copyright Infringement and P2P Networks[162]

Although most emerging companies do not need to understand the complete history of the recording industry's battle against music downloading, it is instructive to be aware of the U.S. Supreme Court's decision in *MGM v. Grokster.*[163] In that case, various record labels and motion picture studios brought copyright infringement action against distributors of peer-to-peer file-sharing computer-networking software. The U.S. District Court for the Central District of California granted partial summary judgment in favor

---

160.   Kelly v. Arriba Soft Corp., 280 F.3d 934 (9th Cir. 2002).
161.   336 F.3d 811 (9th Cir. 2003).
162.   P2P refers to peer-to-peer networks.
163.   545 U.S. 913 (2005).

of the distributors on issues of contributory and vicarious infringement.[164] On appeal, the Ninth Circuit upheld the district court's ruling, holding that Grokster and the other P2P distributors did not have knowledge of copyright infringement by users of the software, an element of contributory infringement, and that the distributors did not have the right and ability to supervise the direct copyright infringers who used their software, as required to impose vicarious liability. The court also acknowledged that peer-to-peer file-sharing computer-networking software was capable of substantial or commercially significant noninfringing uses.

The Supreme Court reversed, unanimously holding that the defendant P2P file sharing companies could be sued for inducing copyright infringement for acts taken in the course of marketing file sharing software.[165]

4. Civil Remedies for Infringement

a. Injunctions

Any federal court having jurisdiction over a copyright infringement suit may grant temporary and final injunctive relief to the copyright owner.[166]

b. Impounding and Disposition of Infringing Articles

At any time while a copyright infringement action is pending, the court overseeing the matter may order the impounding of all copies that have been made or used in violation of the copyright owner's exclusive rights.[167] Further, as part of the final judgment or decree, the court may order the destruction of all infringing copies.[168]

i. Actual Damages

The copyright owner may recover actual damages suffered as a result of the infringement, as well as profits earned by the infringer.[169]

ii. Statutory Damages

The owner of a registered copyright may elect, at any time up until final judgment, to seek statutory damages instead of actual damages. The statutory

---

164.   MGM v. Grokster, 259 F. Supp. 2d 1029.
165.   545 U.S. at 941.
166.   17 U.S.C. § 502.
167.   17 U.S.C. § 503(a).
168.   17 U.S.C. § 503(b).
169.   17 U.S.C. § 504(b).

damage option provides the copyright owner with a level of certainty in obtaining damages. Often, in copyright cases, evidence of actual damages is difficult to discover and may have been destroyed by the defendant. In such a case, statutory damages provide a secure fall back option for the copyright owner.

Statutory damages range between $750 and $30,000 per infringement in the court's discretion, where the infringement was non-willful. The maximum of $30,000 for non-willful infringement may be raised to $150,000 per infringement in cases where willful infringement is proven. Where a court decides that an infringement was completely innocent and the accused infringer had no reason to believe its acts were infringing, the $750 minimum may be lowered to $200 in the court's discretion.[170]

The DMCA also heightens the penalties for copyright infringement on the Internet. In addition to the power to grant equitable and monetary remedies similar to those under Section 504, Section 1203 provides for statutory damages of not less than $200 or more than $2,500 per act of circumvention, device, product, component, offer, or performance of service, as the court considers just, and the sum of not less than $2,500 or more than $25,000 for each violation of Section 1202 (providing or distributing false copyright management information, or removing or altering such information).

c.   Costs and Attorneys' Fees

In any civil action under the Copyright Act, the court in its discretion may allow the recovery of full costs by or against any party other than the United States or an officer thereof. The court may also award reasonable attorneys' fees to the prevailing party.[171]

5.   *Criminal Remedies for Infringement*

In addition to civil penalties, an infringer can be liable criminally. While civil practitioners will likely never encounter a criminal proceeding for copyright infringement, it is important to be able to counsel clients on the possibility of criminal penalties attaching should they continue to undertake infringing activities. Most often, federal authorities will only pursue criminal copyright cases that have the potential to severely damage commerce. Criminal prosecution is often pursued in cases of repeat counterfeiters or foreign knockoff artists who disperse their products into the U.S. commerce channels to the detriment of major corporate copyright owners. In these cases, money damages are not enough and the added criminal penalty is needed to fully

---

170.   17 U.S.C. § 504(c).
171.   17 U.S.C. § 505.

prevent these pirates from damaging commerce. The Copyright Act provides for the following criminal penalties:[172]

- Forfeiture and destruction of infringing articles
- Fine for fraudulent copyright notice
- Fine for fraudulent removal of copyright notice
- Fine for false representation on copyright application

In addition, violating Section 1201 or 1202 of the DMCA willfully and for purposes of commercial advantage or private financial gain is a criminal offense: under Section 1204 penalties range up to a $500,000 fine or up to five years imprisonment for a first offense, and up to a $1,000,000 fine or up to ten years imprisonment for subsequent offenses.

6.   Limitation on Actions

a.   Criminal Actions

Criminal copyright actions must be commenced within five years after the cause of action arose.[173]

b.   Civil Actions

The statute of limitations for copyright infringement is within three years after the claim "accrued."[174] However, where there is a series of infringing acts, one line of authority holds that only the last act need take place within the three-year limit for there to be liability for all of the infringing acts.[175] However, in *Gaste v. Kaiserman* the court rejected this view by limiting monetary recovery to damages that accrued within the three-year period immediately preceding the filing of the lawsuit.[176] *Gaste* remains the majority view.

7.   Limitation on Civil Remedies Due to Nonexisting Registration

There can be no award of statutory damages or attorney's fees as provided in Sections 504 and 505 of the Copyright Act for any infringement of copyright in an unpublished work commenced before the effective date of registration.[177] Also, there can be no award of statutory damages or attorney's fees for any

---

172.   *See* 17 U.S.C. § 506.
173.   17 U.S.C. § 507(a).
174.   17 U.S.C. § 507(b).
175.   Taylor v. Merrick, 712 F.2d 1112 (7th Cir. 1983).
176.   Gaste v. Kaiserman, 669 F. Supp. 583 (S.D.N.Y. 1987).
177.   17 U.S.C. § 412(1).

infringement of copyright commenced after the first publication of the work and before the effective date of the work's registration, unless the registration is made within three months after first publication of the work.[178] This limitation acts as an incentive for copyright owners to register their works. By failing to undertake the relatively minimal expense of registering a work, a copyright owner with a valuable work may be forfeiting the cheap remedy of statutory damages. The copyright owner who has lost out on statutory damages will still be able to avail itself of actual damages, but at the higher added costs of paying attorney fees and having to prove up such damages, which would now be unreimbursable.

J.   Client Interview Checklist

A client checklist is attached as **Exhibit 8F**. While not an exhaustive list of all copyright issues to be encountered by the practitioner, it is provided as a useful tool to properly interview a client and collect the most important information regarding a client's copyright situation.

8.04   Trademarks

A.   Preliminary Considerations

Trademarks perform a number of important functions. They are consumer road signs; they tell consumers which products to buy. They are a company's public persona; they epitomize all the positive (and negative) qualities of a company or a product. Lastly, trademarks represent a solemn promise to the purchasing public that the products or services branded with a company's mark will meet certain standards. By now, it can be seen that trademarks are more commonly referred to as "brands."

Trademarks can be one of the more valuable assets a company owns. Trademarks generate brand equity based on the amount a consumer will pay for a branded product as compared to a nonbranded product. For some companies, brand equity can make up a substantial portion of the companies' value.

In business, branding comes as second nature. In order to survive in a competitive environment, a business must separate itself and its products from the pack and summarize these differences in a concise and succinct manner. This is even more important for emerging companies that are new to the field and in competition against established businesses with market share.

---

178.   17 U.S.C. § 412(2).

Given the important function of trademarks, it is imperative that an emerging company select available marks, analyze whether the marks are strong or weak and then protect the stronger marks from infringement, dilution and becoming generic due to public misuse. Registration is not required to create or maintain a trademark, yet there are important benefits to be gained by registering a trademark with the U.S. Patent and Trademark Office: prima facie evidence of ownership and the exclusive right to use the mark throughout the U.S. in connection with the goods and services identified in the registration.

B.   Identifying and Choosing Strong Trademarks

1.   What is a Trademark

A trademark functions to identify a source of goods or services and to assure purchasers of the standard of quality associated with that source. According to the Lanham Act, the Federal law that deals with trademark issues, a trademark can be a word, a saying or a logo.[179]

A trademark can consist of a sound (NBC's chimes, Intel's chord sequence), color (pink for Owens Corning fiberglass insulation[180]), shape (Coco-Cola bottle) or a smell (plumeria blossoms on sewing thread). As long as the proposed mark meets the essential purpose of functioning as a trademark, that is, it serves to identify the manufacturer of the goods or provider of the services, it can properly be categorized as a trademark.[181] The proposed mark must mentally trigger an association between the mark owner and the goods or services bearing the mark, otherwise it is not a trademark.[182]

2.   Types of Marks: Trademark, Service Marks, Certification Marks, Collective Marks and Trade Dress

a.   Trademark

The term trademark is more commonly used to refer to all of the different classes of marks. However, in a technical sense, a trademark is a mark used in connection with goods.[183] A common synonym for a trademark is a brand name. The Lanham Act defines trademark as "any word, name, symbol or

---

179.   Brooks Bros. v. Brooks Clothing of California, Ltd., 60 F. Supp. 442 (D. Cal. 1945) (Nicknames); *In re* E. Kohn's Sons Co., 343 F.2d 475 (CCPA 1965) (Slogans); Federal Glass Co. v. Corning Glass Works, 162 U.S.P.Q. 279 (TTAB 1969) (Symbols).

180.   *In re* Owens-Corning Fiberglass Corp., 774 F.2d 1116 (Fed. Cir. 1985) (Color).

181.   Self-Realization Fellowship Church v. Ananda Church of Self-Realization, 59 F.3d 902 (9th Cir. 1995).

182.   Procter & Gamble Co. v. Keystone Automotive Warehouse, Inc., 191 U.S.P.Q. 468, 474 (TTAB 1976).

183.   15 U.S.C. § 1052.

device or any combination thereof" either used, or made the subject of an application for federal registration with a bona fide intent to be used, to "identify and distinguish a person's goods, including a unique product, from those manufactures sold by others and to indicate the source of the goods, even if the source is unknown."[184] An example of a trademark that identifies goods is "LEVI'S" for jeans.

A "trade name" is defined by the Lanham Act as an individual's name and surname; a name of an entity, such as a corporation, partnership, or limited partnership; or a firm name used by individuals or entities to identify their business, vocation, or occupation.[185] Trade names are to be distinguished from trademarks, which are the names or symbols that identify a business's goods. Although trade names and trademarks may be the same or very similar (i.e., XEROX Corporation makes XEROX brand copiers), a name that functions only as a trade name is not registrable as a trademark.

b. Service Marks

A service mark is a mark that identifies and distinguishes the service of one company from the services of another.[186] Under the Lanham Act, a service mark is defined as any word, name, symbol, device or any combination thereof used to identify and distinguish the services of one person, including a unique service, from the services of others and to indicate the source of the services, even if that source is unknown.[187] "FEDEX" is an example of a service mark, for delivery services.

c. Certification Marks

A certification mark is any word, name, symbol, device or any combination, used or intended to be used, in commerce with the owner's permission by someone other than the owner to certify regional or other geographical origin, material, motive, manufacture, quality, accuracy or other characteristics of someone's goods or services, or that the work or labor on the goods was performed by members of a union or other organization.[188] The "GOOD HOUSEKEEPING SEAL" is a well known certification mark.

---

184.   15 U.S.C. § 1127.
185.   15 U.S.C. § 1127.
186.   15 U.S.C. § 1127.
187.   15 U.S.C. § 1127.
188.   15 U.S.C. § 1054; *see also* Roquefort v. William Faehndrich, Inc., 303 F.2d 494 (2d Cir. 1962).

d. Collective Marks

A collective mark is a trademark or service mark used, or intended to be used, in commerce, by the members of a cooperative, an association or other collective group or organization, including a mark that indicates membership in a union, an association or other organization.[189]

e. Trade Dress

The Lanham Act provides broad protection—no mark may be refused registration and protection "on account of its nature."[190] Accordingly, the shape of a product, packaging for goods, and devices used in connection with goods and services may all be protectable and registrable as trademarks similar to any other nonword mark. As a category, these types of marks are generally referred to as trade dress. Trade dress has been expanded to include product designs, such as the appearance of a puzzle,[191] a book cover,[192] or a restaurant motif.[193]

In order to obtain trade dress protection, the configuration or shape of the product design cannot be functional.[194] A feature is functional if it is "essential to the use or purpose of the article or if it affects the cost or quality of the article."[195]

In 1992, the Supreme Court decided *Two Pesos, Inc. v. Taco Cabana, Inc.*,[196] a case of trade dress infringement brought by the owner of a restaurant with a particular Mexican theme in its décor and atmosphere. In that case, the Court held that trade dress that is inherently distinctive (i.e., arbitrary, fanciful, or suggestive) and nonfunctional is entitled to protection without proof of secondary meaning.

However, in *Wal-Mart Stores, Inc. v. Samara Brothers, Inc.*,[197] the Supreme Court recognized a presumption that an unregistered product design could not be inherently distinctive, such that proof of secondary meaning is required for unregistered designs to be eligible for trade dress protections under the Lanham Act. In *Wal-Mart*, the plaintiff, Samara, designed and manufactured a line of children's clothing. Defendant *Wal-Mart* contracted with another of its suppliers to manufacture outfits based on photographs of Samara's garments. After discovering that *Wal-Mart* and other retailers were selling Samara knockoffs, Samara brought suit for infringement of its unregistered

---

189. *Id.*
190. 15 U.S.C. § 1052.
191. Ideal Toy Corp. v. Plawner Toy Manufacturing Corp., 685 F.2d 78 (3rd Cir. 1982).
192. Harlequin Enterprises Ltd. v. Gulf & Western Corp., 644 F.2d 946 (2nd Cir. 1981).
193. Two Pesos, Inc. v. Taco Cabana, Inc., 505 U.S. 763 (1992).
194. *See, e.g.*, Tie Tech, Inc. v. Kinedyne Corp., 296 F.3d 778 (9th Cir. 2002).
195. Traffix Devices, Inc. v. Marketing Displays, Inc., 532 U.S. 23, 33 (2001).
196. Two Pesos, Inc. v. Taco Cabana, Inc., 505 U.S. 763 (1992).
197. Wal-Mart Stores, Inc. v. Samara Brothers, Inc., 529 U.S. 205 (2000).

trade dress. The Supreme Court distinguished *Two Pesos*, finding that that was more akin to a product packaging case and therefore had no bearing on a product design case. The Court then opined that product packaging can be inherently distinctive, but not product design. Secondary meaning must always be established in a product design case.[198] The Court indicated that it would have very little sympathy for the product innovator who cannot prove secondary meaning, and noted that design patent and copyright protection are always available.

Shortly after the Supreme Court gave its decision in *Wal-Mart*, the Court was given another opportunity to further define what constitutes protectable trade dress in *Traffix Devices, Inc. v. Marketing Displays, Inc.*[199] There the plaintiff sought to protect a spring-like mechanism for keeping portable signs erect in high winds. The mechanism had previously been covered by a utility patent that, at the time the defendant put into use a similar mechanism, had expired. The court found the fact that the mechanism had previously been subject to a utility patent was prima facie evidence that the mechanism was merely a functional feature. Without evidence of secondary meaning, the court found that trade dress protection was not available.[200]

After *Traffix*, the Ninth Circuit addressed trade dress issues that presented an interesting twist on *Two Pesos*. In *Clicks Billiards, Inc. v. SixShooters, Inc.*[201] the court considered whether elements that made up the interior décor of a pool hall were protectable trade dress. While these elements may be functional when considered in isolation, the court determined that if the particular integration of these elements leaves a multitude of alternatives to competitors that would not prove confusingly similar to its trade dress, then the overall look and feel is not functional as a matter of law.

3. Selecting a Mark

a. Availability

In addition to the practical considerations of choosing a trademark that is memorable and easy to pronounce and spell, the legal issues include selecting a mark that is distinctive, eligible for registration, and not likely to cause confusion, mistake or deception in connection with another mark (which would be trademark infringement).[202]

Companies are well-advised to perform a trademark search *before* adopting a mark to ensure that they do not inadvertently infringe on a prior mark. Trademark searches can be done quickly and at relatively little cost by

---

198.   *Id* at 216.
199.   Traffix Devices, Inc. v. Marketing Displays, Inc., 121 S. Ct. 1255 (2001).
200.   *Id.*
201.   Clicks Billiards, Inc. v. SixShooters, Inc., 251 F.3d 1252 (9th Cir. 2001).
202.   15 U.S.C. § 1114(1).

organizations specializing in such services, or intellectual property lawyers who practice in the area of trademark law. The PTO and most international trademark offices also maintain online public databases of trademark registrations. It is well worth the investment to conduct a search in advance of adopting a new trademark in order to avoid the expense and business interruption caused by having to respond to legal claims or to change a trademark after it has already been in use.

b. Fanciful Marks

The category of trademarks that provides the strongest protection are those that are fanciful or coined words, having no intrinsic meaning; for example, "KODAK" for film, "STARBUCKS" for coffee and "EXXON" for gasoline.

Because such coined marks are inherently distinctive, no proof of secondary meaning is necessary before a court will protect the trademark rights of the first user of such marks.[203]

c. Arbitrary Marks

Words that are arbitrarily used in the identification of unrelated goods or services also serve as strong trademarks that are inherently distinctive. Some examples of arbitrary marks are "AMAZON" for an online store, "APPLE" or "SUN" for computers, "BLACKBERRY" for mobile phones or "GREY GOOSE" for vodka.

d. Suggestive Marks

Suggestive marks are the third type of trademark registrable on the Principal Register without proof of secondary meaning. Suggestive marks are those that, while not really descriptive of the product's qualities, nevertheless suggest some benefit or property of the product.

An example involves the trademark "ROACH MOTEL" for insect traps, in which this mark was enforced against an infringer using "Roach Inn." The Court explained,

> We do not find the mark ROACH MOTEL® to be a merely descriptive mark. While roaches may live in some motels against the will of the owners, motels are surely not built for roaches to live in. Hence, the mark is fanciful on conception. Indeed its very incongruity is what catches one's attention.[204]

---

203.   Secondary meaning is established through showing that through long and exclusive use in the marketplace, the public has come to recognize the term as signifying the goods or services as coming from a particular source, and thus the mark is distinctive of those goods or services in commerce. Union Carbide Corp. v. Ever-Ready Inc., 531 F.2d 366, 380 (7th Cir. 1976).

204.   American Home Products Corp. v. Johnson Chemical Co., Inc., 589 F.2d 106 (2d Cir. 1978).

Other suggestive marks include "7-11" for a store that is open from 7:00 a.m. to 11:00 p.m., or "MUSTANG" for a fast car.

e. Descriptive Marks

One step down from suggestive marks, but miles away as far as protectability goes, are descriptive marks. Marks that describe the intended purpose, function or use of the goods, the size of the goods, desirable characteristics of the goods, the nature of the goods or the end effect upon the user are considered merely descriptive and are not registrable absent establishing secondary meaning.[205] For example, "NICE 'N SOFT" for bathroom tissue or "PARK 'N FLY" for off-airport auto parking services are descriptive marks. The same is true with respect to marks that identify the place in which the goods or services originate and therefore are geographically descriptive.[206] The major reasons for not protecting marks that are merely descriptive is to prevent the owner of a mark from inhibiting competition in the sale of particular goods and to maintain freedom of the public to use language that naturally describes the goods or services, thus avoiding the possibility of harassing infringement suits by the registrant against others who use the mark when advertising or describing their own product.[207]

Marks that are merely self-laudatory and descriptive of the alleged merit of a product are regarded as being descriptive.[208] Laudation does not per se prevent a slogan or mark from being registrable. Like other descriptive marks, a mark that is self-laudatory may be registrable on establishing secondary meaning. However, courts have refused registration even on the Supplemental Register of marks that are so highly laudatory and descriptive of the alleged product that they are incapable of functioning as a trademark.[209]

The determination of whether a mark is suggestive or merely descriptive, and therefore not registrable absent evidence of secondary meaning, has always been a challenging task. *In re Wilderness Group Inc.*, the Trademark Trial and Appeal Board (the quasi-judicial body responsible for adjudicating issues that arise concerning the registration of a trademark) opined that there is "a thin line of demarcation involved in making a determination as to whether a term or slogan is suggestive or merely descriptive and, apropos, thereto, when a term stops suggesting and begins to describe the goods in connection with which it is used, it is, at times, a difficult question to resolve."[210] The Board suggested that in determining whether a mark has crossed the threshold from suggestiveness to descriptiveness, the following factors should be

---

205. Two Pesos, Inc. v. Taco Cabana, Inc., 505 U.S. 763 (1992).
206. 15 U.S.C. § 1052 (a).
207. Estate of P.D. Beckwith, Inc. v. Commissioner of Patents, 252 U.S. 538 (1920).
208. *In re* Boston Beer Company, 53 U.S.P.Q.2d 1056, 1058 (Fed. Cir. 1999).
209. *Id.* (Registration sought for the mark THE BEST BEER IN AMERICA).
210. *In re* Wilderness Group Inc., 189 U.S.P.Q. 44 (TTAB 975).

analyzed: (a) is the mark used in a trademark sense and not in a descriptive manner to describe the goods; (b) is the mark an expression that would be or is commonly used to describe the goods; (c) does the mark possess some degree of ingenuity in its phraseology; (d) does the mark say something at least a little different from what might be expected from a product, or say expected things in an unexpected way; and (e) does the mark possess more than a single meaning, namely, a double entendre, that imparts to it a degree of ingenuity and successfully masks or somewhat obscures the intended commercial message.

f. Generic Names

A generic name is a term that was once a brand name of a single manufacturer, but has since come to be understood as the name of the product or service itself. Examples include aspirin, cellophane, escalator, videotape and shredded wheat. Because they serve primarily to describe products rather than identify their sources, generic terms are incapable of becoming trademarks, at least in connection with the products that they designate.[211]

In order to avoid having a brand name become generic, it is important for trademark owners to use the name in such a way that identifies the source of the product, and does not become the name by which the public identifies the product itself. Using the words "brand" or "trademark" with the name, or using the brand name in association with the name of the general type of product involved, for example, "KLEENEX tissues," are both ways to do this. Xerox Corporation created "trademark awareness" ads to prevent its brand from becoming a generic noun or verb, including statements such as "You can't make a Xerox."

g. Marks Prohibited by Statute

Although a trademark can be anything, not everything can and should be a trademark. This is a very important distinction, which goes back to the basic requirement that a mark must fundamentally function as trademark.

There are certain marks that will be denied protection as a trademark. Marks that consist of immoral, deceptive or scandalous matter or of matter that disparages any person (living or dead), institutions, beliefs or national symbols are not registrable or protectable.[212] Neither are marks which resemble flags, coat of arms or other insignias of the United States or of any state or municipality or of any foreign nation, or marks that utilize the name, portrait or signature of a particular living individual without that individual's consent.[213]

---

211. *See* Park 'N Fly, Inc. v. Dollar Park & Fly, Inc., 469 U.S. 189, 193-94 (1985).
212. 15 U.S.C. § 1052 (a)–(b).
213. *Id.*

Also, marks that consist or comprise of a portrait of a deceased president of the United States are not registrable during the life of the president's widow except by written consent of the widow.[214] In addition, certain organizations, by acts of Congress, have been granted exclusive rights to use certain marks. For example, the U.S. Olympic Committee has been granted exclusive right to use a number of "Olympic" symbols, marks and terms.[215]

C.   Protecting Trademarks

1.   Creating Trademark Rights

Trademark rights arise from either: (a) actual use of the mark in connection with goods or services in commerce, or (b) the filing of an application to register a mark in the PTO stating that the applicant has a bona fide intention to use the mark in commerce.[216] Neither federal nor state registration is required to establish rights in a mark or to begin using a mark in commerce.[217] Common law trademark or service mark rights are enforceable in the geographic area where the user of the mark sells the goods or services. Federal or state registration can secure benefits beyond the rights acquired by merely using a mark. For example, the owner of a federal registration is presumed to be the owner of the mark for the goods and services specified in the registration and to be entitled to use the mark nationwide.[218]

Trademarks rights are based on priority of use; thus, the first person to adopt and use a mark generally has priority to the exclusive right to use that mark over another party who subsequently began using the same or a similar mark for the same or similar goods or services.[219]

2.   Federal Registration

After a trademark has been identified, the first step in protecting it is to register it with the U.S. Patent and Trademark Office. Registration with the PTO is beneficial for a number of reasons. First, registration of a mark provides constructive nationwide notice of the existence of the mark and the owner's claim. Second, the registration of a mark is concrete evidence of ownership of the mark and priority of use. (This type of evidence can be very handy when a party is seeking an order restraining a third party from infringing its mark). In addition, registration of a mark with the PTO can serve as the basis for registration of the same mark with foreign countries

---

214.   15 U.S.C. § 1052(c).
215.   36 U.S.C.A. § 380(c).
216.   15 U.S.C.A. § 1127.
217.   Allard Enterprises Inc. v. Advanced Programming Resources, Inc., 249 F.3d 564 (6th Cir. 2001).
218.   15 U.S.C. § 1115.
219.   New West Corp. v. NYM Co. of California, Inc., 595 F.2d 1194, 1200 (9th Cir. 1979).

and the registration can be filed with the U.S. customs office to prevent the importation of infringing foreign goods.

a. Basis for Application

The Registration process begins with the application. An applicant who has already commenced using a mark in commerce may file an application based on use (a "use" application).[220] An applicant who has not yet used the mark may apply for registration based on a bona fide intention to use the mark in commerce (an "intent-to-use" application) ("ITU").[221] In addition, an applicant filing an intent-to-use application may, under certain circumstances, claim the benefit of its first filed prior foreign application.[222]

For a mark used in connection with goods, use is established when the mark is "placed in any manner on the goods or their containers or the displays associated therewith or on the tags or labels affixed thereto, or if the nature of the goods makes such placement impracticable, then on documents associated with the goods or their sale, and ... the goods are sold or transported in [interstate] commerce."[223] For a service mark, use is established when the mark is "used or displayed in the sale or advertising of services" made in interstate commerce.[224]

"Affixation" of the mark on goods, containers, or displays means physically placing the mark on these items. This requirement has been expanded over time; mere use of a mark in promotion or advertising before the product or service is actually provided on the mark on a normal commercial scale does not qualify.[225] It is sufficient to use the mark in close association with images of the goods, such as in a mail order catalog, television infomercial, or website, through which a customer can identify the products they want to purchase and order them.[226]

For the purpose of obtaining federal registration, commerce means all commerce that may lawfully be regulated by the U.S. Congress.[227] This includes interstate commerce, as well as commerce between the United States and another country. The use in commerce must be a bona fide use in the ordinary course of trade, and not made merely to reserve a right in a mark. In addition, use of a mark in purely local commerce within a state does not

---

220.   15 U.S.C. § 1051(a).
221.   15 U.S.C. § 1051(b).
222.   15 U.S.C. § 1126(d).
223.   15 U.S.C. § 1127.
224.   *Id.*
225.   Daltronics, Inc. v. H.L. Dalis, Inc., 158 U.S.P.Q. 475 (TTAB 1968); Lucent Information Mgt. Inc. v. Lucent Technologies, Inc., 980 F. Supp. 253 (D. Del. 1997); Cullman Ventures, Inc. v. Columbian Art Works, Inc., 717 F. Supp. 96 (S.D.N.Y. 1989).
226.   *See* McCarthy on Trademarks §§ 16:27 to 16:32.2 (4th ed.).
227.   15 U.S.C. § 1127.

qualify as "use in commerce."[228] If an applicant files an application based on a bona fide intention to use in commerce, the applicant will have to use the mark in commerce and submit an allegation of use to the PTO before the PTO will register the mark.[229]

b. Registration Process

Trademarks may be registered at the state level, with the federal government, or both. State registration usually involves submitting a form to the state's department of commerce.

At the federal level, registering a trademark is accomplished by filing an application (based on either use of or intent to use the mark in commerce) with the PTO to register the mark on the Principal Register. Electronic application forms are available through the PTO's "Trademark Electronic Filing System" or "TEAS" website at www.uspto.gov. Paper forms are also available by request; however, electronic filing is encouraged and will result in a faster application processing time. At the time of this writing, the filing fees, per class of goods or services, are currently $325 for electronic applications (or $275 for "TEAS Plus" applications, in which the applicant agrees to certain concessions including describing the goods and services in accord with the Office's "Acceptable Identification of Goods and Services Manual"), and $375 for a paper application.[230]

For applications based on use, the owner will also need to submit a specimen with the application. A specimen is a real-world example of how the mark is actually used on the goods or in the offer of services: labels, tags, or containers for the goods are acceptable specimens of use for a trademark, while advertising, such as magazine advertisements or brochures, is acceptable for a service mark.

Once filed, the application is assigned to an attorney at the PTO who will examine the application for technical compliance with the provisions of the Lanham Act and the various sections of the Code of Federal Regulations dealing with the registration process.

In order for a trademark or service mark to be federally registrable, the mark must distinguish the goods or services of the applicant from those of others.[231] For a mark to be registrable on the Principal Register, the mark may not be merely descriptive of the quality or characteristics of the goods or services to be covered by the mark and may not be merely geographically descriptive

---

228. *In re* G.J. Sherrard Co., 150 U.S.P.Q. 311 (TTAB 1966); *but see* Coca-Cola Co. v. Fanta, 155 U.S.P.Q. 276 (TTAB 1967) (registration granted for applicant located in California but who performed services for out-of-state customers).

229. 15 U.S.C. § 1051.

230. 37 C.F.R. §§ 2.6(a)(1), 2.22 to 2.23.

231. 15 U.S.C. § 1052.

of the goods or services (i.e., incorporation of a term denoting a generally known geographical location or indication of the place of origin).[232]

In addition, in order for a trademark to be accepted for registration, the mark may not conflict with another registered mark to such an extent that, when used on or in connection with the intended goods or services, it would be likely to cause confusion.[233] The test the PTO conducts in deciding whether to accept or reject a trademark application based on likelihood of confusion can be generally stated as the following question: Considering the relative similarity of the mark in appearance, sound and meaning to one already in use, coupled with the similarity of the goods or services to which each mark is applied, are prospective consumers of the goods or services likely to be confused as to their source?[234]

The Examining Attorney will examine the mark in order to determine whether it conflicts with another registered or prior pending trademark application to such a degree so as to create a likelihood of confusion as to affiliation or relationship between the two mark owners among a group of relevant consumers.[235] If the examining attorney determines that the application has technical defects or if there is some basis for refusing registration of the mark on the Principal Register (e.g., the mark is merely descriptive or would tend to create a likelihood of confusion with a registered or prior pending application), the Examiner will issue an Office Action.[236]

If the Examiner has determined that the application is technically deficient, usually the Examiner will detail the deficiency in the Office Action and may even suggest an acceptable approach to cure the problem. Most of the time, the Examiners suggestions can be implemented without any prejudice. However, there are times when the Examiner's proposed "cure" would seriously impact an applicant's rights. For example, an Examiner may try to limit and narrow a broad, but acceptable, recitation of services. The applicant has the right to argue against any position taken by the Examiner in an Office Action.[237]

Responding to an Office Action should be treated in the same fashion as responding to a motion in litigation. The response should be well researched and advocate the broadest possible protection of the applicant's mark. Where the applicant has a colorable claim in support of its position, a well-written response to an Office Action can sometimes mean the difference between a refusal and a registration. An applicant has six months from the date of notification is mailed to respond to an Office Action; if no response if filed within this period, the application is deemed abandoned.

---

232.   15 U.S.C. § 1052(e).
233.   15 U.S.C § 1052(d).
234.   This is also part of the analysis a court will apply when determining a claim for infringement. *See E.I. duPont de Nemours & Co.,* 476 F.2d 1357 (C.C.P.A. 1973).
235.   15 C.F.R. § 2.61.
236.   *Id.*
237.   37 C.F.R. § 2.62.

When the applicant files a response to the Examiner's Office Action, the application will be reexamined in light of the arguments made by the applicant.[238] The Examiner can either issue a final refusal based on the issues raised in the first Office Action[239] or allow the application to go forward to registration.

After the application completes the examination phase, the Examiner will pass it along for publication in the Official Gazette of the Patent and Trademark Office. During the publication phase, any member of the public may challenge registration by showing a likelihood of being harmed by registration of the mark.[240] Such a challenge is called an "opposition" and is most often instituted by one with a similar mark engaging in the sale of more or less similar goods or services. Oppositions must be filed within 30 days after the date the mark is published in the Official Gazette, unless an extension is obtained. An opposer need not have a registered mark to challenge the registration of a pending mark—common law rights are sufficient.[241]

After the publication period, if there were no oppositions brought or if they were resolved in the applicant's favor, a trademark registration certificate is issued to the applicant.

An ITU application follows the same examination process up to the point of registration, allowing the applicant an opportunity to assess whether there are any issues with the mark before investing in using it in commerce. The registration on an ITU application will not issue, however, until the applicant files a declaration of actual use, which is due within six months from the date a "Notice of Allowance" is sent from the Office. Extensions of time to file the verified statement of actual use are available, up to 36 months for good cause.[242]

3.   Maintaining a Registration

a.   Notice

Notice of a trademark registration may be provided in three ways: (a) "Registered in U.S. Patent and Trademark Office;" (b) an abbreviated form of this notice, "Reg. U.S. Pat. & Tm. Off.;" or (c) the letter "R" enclosed in a circle ("®").[243] Notice must be displayed with the mark, and is usually done through the letter "R" enclosed in a circle placed just above and immediately after the trademark. If the owner of a registered trademark does not use the above methods to give notice of the registration, "no profits and no damages

---

238.   37 C.F.R. § 2.63.
239.   37 C.F.R. § 2.64.
240.   15 U.S.C. §§ 1063,1067; 37 CFR § 2.101.
241.   15 U.S.C. § 1125.
242.   15 U.S.C. § 1051(d); 37 CFR § 2.89.
243.   15 U.S.C. § 1111.

shall be recovered under the provisions of [the Act] unless the defendant had actual notice of the registration."[244]

b. Duration of Registration and Renewals

A trademark registration certificate remains enforceable for 10 years, but will be canceled by the commissioner unless the registrant files an affidavit of use under Section 8 of the Act ("Section 8 Affidavit") (1) between the fifth and sixth year following registration, and (2) within the year before the end of every ten-year period after the date of registration. The registrant may file the affidavit within a grace period of six months after the end of the sixth or tenth year, with payment of an additional fee. The Section 8 Affidavit must show that the mark is still in use, or is excused from any nonuse due to special circumstances and not any intention to abandon the mark.[245] The registrant must also file a Section 9 renewal application within the year before the expiration date of a registration, or within a grace period of six months after the expiration date, with payment of an additional fee.

Assuming that an affidavit of use is timely filed, registrations granted *prior* to November 16, 1989 have a 20-year term, and registrations granted on or after November 16, 1989 have a 10-year term. This is also true for the renewal periods; renewals granted *prior* to November 16, 1989 have a 20-year term, and renewals granted on or after November 16, 1989 have a 10-year term.

c. Incontestability

After five years following registration of the mark has passed, and within one year following five consecutive years of continuous use of the mark on or in connection with the goods and services in the registration, an affidavit may be filed under Section 15 of the Act which provides the registrant "incontestable" status for the trademark.[246] The Section 15 Affidavit is usually combined with the Section 8 Affidavit, and makes the grounds for cancellation of the registration more limited.

---

244.   15 U.S.C. § 1111.
245.   15 U.S.C. § 1058(a).
246.   15 U.S.C. § 1065.

d. Cancellation

Any person who believes that they will be damaged by a continuation of a trademark registration may file an application for cancellation of the mark's registration. In most cases, the application for cancellation must be filed within five years of the registration date.[247] A petition for cancellation may also be filed at any time when a registered mark becomes the common descriptive name of an article or substance (generic) or has been abandoned, or if the registration was obtained fraudulently or unlawfully.[248]

Petitions for cancellation are prosecuted through the Trademark Trial and Appeal Board. An answer must be filed within 30 days of the mailing of the notice of the petition, which may contain any defense as well as a request for affirmative relief via cancellation of a registration pleaded in the petition.[249]

e. Abandonment

Rights in a trademark can be lost through nonuse, which is referred to as abandonment. There must be an intent not to resume use, which may be inferred from the circumstances. Nonuse for two consecutive years constitutes prima facie evidence of abandonment of the mark under the Lanham Act.[250] Abandonment may be complete, or limited to specific geographic areas.[251]

Apart from nonuse, a trademark may be abandoned through the failure to control the quality of goods or services sold under the mark by licensees,[252] assigning rights in the mark apart from the goodwill associated with the mark,[253] or causing or failing to prevent the mark from becoming generic for the goods or services.[254]

D. Protecting Against Infringement and Dilution

After a trademark has been adopted, the owner should take steps to ensure that the mark is not being infringed or diluted by third parties. This is the case whether or not the mark has been registered. Although registration with the PTO is a very important component of protecting a mark owner's rights, a mark owner should always be on the lookout for infringers. (Likewise, it is equally important to understand exactly what infringement entails so as to avoid committing infringement of another party's mark.)

---

247. 37 C.F.R. § 2.111(b); 15 U.S.C. § 1065.
248. 15 U.S.C. § 1064.
249. 37 C.F.R. § 2.114.
250. 15 U.S.C. § 1127.
251. Shiela's Shine Products, Inc. v. Sheila Shine, Inc., 486 F.2d 114, 124 (5th Cir. 1973).
252. *See, e.g.,* Shiela's Shine Products, Inc. v. Sheila Shine, Inc., 486 F.2d 114, 124 (5th Cir. 1973).
253. *See, e.g.,* Golden Door, Inc. v. Odisho, 646 F.2d 347 (9th Cir. 1980).
254. *See, e.g.,* 15 U.S.C. § 1127.

1. Elements of Infringement

Under Section 43 of the Lanham Act, infringement occurs when the use by one party of a mark is likely to cause confusion, to cause mistake or to deceive as to the affiliation, connection or association of such person with another person, or as to the origin, sponsorship or approval of his or her goods, services or commercial activities by another person.[255] Only a likelihood of confusion is required to obtain injunctive relief, but proof of actual confusion is necessary to obtain damages.[256]

Under the Ninth Circuit's ruling in *AMF Incorporated v. Sleekcraft Boats*,[257] the determination of "likelihood of confusion" is made by examining the following factors: (a) the strength of the mark; (b) the proximity of the goods; (c) the similarity of the marks; (d) the evidence of actual confusion; (e) the marketing channels used; (f) the type of goods and the degree of care likely to be exercised by the purchaser; (g) the defendant's intent in selecting the mark and (h) likelihood of expansion of the product line.[258] This line of analysis is similar for most jurisdictions.

a. Strength of the Mark

Generally, arbitrary and fanciful marks are entitled to wide protection, while marks that are suggestive are entitled to a restricted range of protection. Where a suggestive mark is the subject of a suit, infringement will be found only if the marks in question are very similar and the goods are closely related.[259]

b. Proximity of the Goods

For related goods, the danger is that the public will mistakenly assume there is an association between the producers of the related goods, even though no such association exists. Where the goods are complementary and the public is more likely to make such an association, the marks need to be less similar in appearance to support a finding of likelihood of confusion.[260]

c. Similarity of the Marks

Similarity of the marks is tested on three levels: sight, sound and meaning. Each must be considered as they are encountered in the marketplace. Although

---

255. 15 U.S.C. § 1125.
256. *See, e.g.*, AMF Inc. v. Sleekcraft Boats, 599 F.2d 341 (9th Cir. 1979).
257. AMF Inc. v. Sleekcraft Boats, 599 F.2d 341 (9th Cir. 1979).
258. *Id.* at 349.
259. *Id.* at 350.
260. *Id.*

similarity is measured by the marks in their entirety, similarities weigh more heavily than differences.[261]

d.   Evidence of Actual Confusion

Evidence that the use of the two marks has already resulted in consumer confusion is persuasive proof that future confusion is likely.[262]

e.   Marketing Channels

Convergent marketing channels increase the likelihood of confusion.[263]

f.   Type of Goods and Purchaser Care

In assessing the likelihood of confusion, the standard used by the courts is the typical buyer exercising ordinary caution. When the buyer has expertise in the field, a higher standard is proper though it will not preclude a finding that confusion is likely. Similarly, when the goods are expensive, the buyer can be expected to exercise greater care in his purchases.[264]

g.   Intent

When the infringing party knowingly adopts a mark similar to another's, reviewing courts presume that the defendant can accomplish his purpose, that is, that the public will be deceived. Good faith is less probative of the likelihood of confusion, yet may be given considerable weight in fashioning a remedy.[265]

h.   Likelihood of Expansion

Inasmuch as a trademark owner is afforded greater protection against competing goods, a "strong possibility" that either party may expand his business to compete with the other will weigh in favor of finding that the present use is infringing. When goods are closely related, any expansion is likely to result in direct competition.[266]

---

261.   *Id.* at 351.
262.   *Id.* at 352.
263.   *Id.* at 353.
264.   *Id.* at 353.
265.   *Id.* at 354.
266.   *Id.*

2. *Protecting Against Dilution of Your Trademark*

Under the Federal Trademark Dilution Act ("FTDA"), the owner of a "famous mark" is protected "against another person's commercial use ... of a mark or trade name, if such use begins after the mark has become famous and causes dilution of the distinctive quality of the mark."[267] The FTDA defines dilution as the lessening of the capacity of a famous mark to identify and distinguish goods and services, regardless of a presence or absence of competition between the owner of the famous mark and other parties, or likelihood of confusion, mistake or deception.[268] There is protection available under many state anti-dilution laws as well.[269]

A mark must have some amount of national renown to obtain protection against dilution under the Act, not just distinctiveness based on secondary meaning.[270] In addition, a plaintiff must establish a higher degree of similarity between the marks to obtain injunctive relief based on dilution claims.[271]

In *Mosely v. V Secret Catalogue, Inc.*,[272] the Supreme Court held that a senior trademark holder had to prove actual dilution in order to prevail on a dilution claim under the FTDA. However, in 2006 the Trademark Dilution Revision Act ("TDRA") was enacted, which eliminated this requirement.[273]

The changes made by the TDRA include the following:

(a) The applicable standard is "likelihood of dilution."
(b) Dilution may be blurring or tarnishment, which are defined in the TDRA.[274]
(c) Six non-exclusive factors are provided for courts to use in determining the likelihood of dilution by blurring.[275]

---

267.   15 U.S.C. § 1125(c)(1).

268.   15 U.S.C. § 1127.

269.   *See, e.g.*, Yahoo! Inc. v. La Ligue Contre Le Racisme Et L'Antiesemitisme, 433 F.3d 1199 (9th Cir. 2006) (registration of a famous mark as a domain name in order to sell the name to the owner violates both federal and California anti-dilution statutes).

270.   I.P. Lund Trading ApS v. Kohler Co., 163 F.3d 27 (1st Cir. 1998).

271.   Jet, Inc. v. Sewage Aeration Systems, 165 F.3d 419 (6th Cir. 1999).

272.   537 U.S. 418 (2003).

273.   See 15 U.S.C. §§ 1125(c), 1127.

274.   15 U.S.C. § 1125(c)(2) (defining "blurring" as an impairment to distinctiveness, and "tarnishment" as an impairment to reputation); *see also* Starbucks Corp. v. Wolfe's Borough Coffee, Inc., 559 F. Supp. 2d 472 (S.D.N.Y. 2008).

275.   15 U.S.C. § 1125(c)(2)(B) lists the six factors as:
    (i)   The degree of similarity between the mark or trade name and the famous mark.
    (ii)   The degree of inherent or acquired distinctiveness of the famous mark.
    (iii) The extent to which the owner of the famous mark is engaging in substantially exclusive use of the mark.
    (iv)   The degree of recognition of the famous mark.
    (v)   Whether the user of the mark or trade name intended to create an association with the famous mark.
    (vi)   Any actual association between the mark or trade name and the famous mark.

(d) Four factors are provided for assessing whether a mark is "famous" enough to obtain protection against dilution; the TDRA clarifies that "niche fame" is not enough.[276]

3. Trademark Infringement Remedies

A plaintiff in a trademark infringement suit may seek injunctive relief, damages for past infringement, or both.[277] While punitive damages are not recoverable,[278] treble damages may be awarded in the court's discretion and are mandatory in cases of intentional infringement by a "counterfeit" mark. Statutory damages or actual damages and profits may be elected for infringing use of a counterfeit mark;[279] statutory damages are not less than $500 or more than $100,000 (except where the use is willful, in which case they can go up to $1,000,000) per counterfeit mark for each type of goods or services sold, offered for sale, or distributed.[280]

Criminal penalties are not available for trademark infringement under the Lanham Act but are provided for the knowing use of a counterfeit mark under 18 U.S.C. § 2320(a).

4. Protecting Against Infringement on the Internet

Trademarks can be infringed or diluted on the Internet via website text or graphics, due to meta tag misdirection, in banner advertisements, on gripe or fan sites, through spam or in domain names (see Section E.3.a. below). The same legal analysis is relevant to determining the existence of trademark rights, priority of use and likelihood of confusion of trademarks on the Internet. Courts will typically examine whether there is a likelihood of confusion between a plaintiff's mark and a defendant's use of its domain name, trademarks or service marks, and may also look at defendant's website to determine if its design makes confusion likely.

---

276.   15 U.S.C. § 1125(c)(2)(A) provides that a mark is famous if "it is widely recognized by the general consuming public of the United States as a designation of source of the goods or services of the mark's owner. In determining whether a mark possesses the requisite degree of recognition, the court may consider all relevant factors, including the following:

(i)   The duration, extent, and geographic reach of advertising and publicity of the mark, whether advertised or publicized by the owner or third parties.

(ii)   The amount, volume, and geographic extent of sales of goods or services offered under the mark.

(iii)   The extent of actual recognition of the mark.

(iv)   Whether the mark was registered under the Act of March 3, 1881, or the Act of February 20, 1905, or on the principal register."

277.   15 U.S.C. § 1117.

278.   *See* Getty Petroleum Corp. v. Bartco Petroleum Corp., 858 F.2d 103 (2nd Cir. 1988).

279.   15 U.S.C. §§ 1117(a), (b).

280.   15 U.S.C. § 1117(c).

a. Infringement Factors

In *Goto.com Inc. v. The Walt Disney Company*,[281] the Ninth Circuit addressed whether Goto.com, Inc.'s website logo was infringed by Disney's Go Network logo. More importantly, in this case the court addressed whether the same factors should be utilized in determining trademark infringement online. Ordinarily, infringement is determined by an analysis of the eight factors set forth by the court in *AMF, Inc. v. Sleekcraft Boats*. The *Goto.com* court, referring to its holding in *Brookfield Communications, Inc. v. West Coast Entertainment Corp.*,[282] stated that the *Sleekcraft* test is a "pliant" one in that "some factors are much more important than others." The court found similarities between the two competing movie/entertainment industry websites due to the fact that each site maintained a searchable database. From this, the court stated, "undeniably then, the products are used for similar purposes."

Relying on its holding in *Brookfield*, the Court held that, in the context of the Web in particular, the three most important *Sleekcraft* factors are (1) the similarity of the marks, (2) the relatedness of the goods or services, and (3) the parties' "simultaneous use of the web as a marketing channel." This rule is referred to as the Ninth Circuit's "internet trinity" of confusion factors.[283] Under this line of cases, the analysis of whether and to what extent the goods and/or services of two marks are similar will focus on whether the consuming public is likely to associate two services or products with the mark owners. The Ninth Circuit made clear that the differences in principal lines of business should not be over emphasized (e.g., whether one site focuses on information services while another site focuses on communication services). The Court noted that these distinctions are lost on the ordinary user of the Internet.

b. Meta Tags

Meta tag misdirection, which is the use of another party's trademark in the meta tags of an unaffiliated website, in order to lure a person performing an Internet search to that site, was initially another area in which trademark infringement cases arose. Search engines such as Google generally do not index websites based on their meta keywords tags anymore; however, when meta tags were known to affect search engine results, several courts found a likelihood of confusion due to use of competitor's trademarks in meta tags even though the competitor's marks were totally invisible to the consumer and did not make an appearance in the website description in search engine results. These courts relied on a theory that the use of the marks in meta tags

281. Goto.com Inc. v. The Walt Disney Co., 202 F.3d 1199 (9th Cir 2000).

282. Brookfield Communications, Inc. v. West Coast Entertainment Corp., 174 F.3d 1036 (9th Cir. 1999).

283. Interstellar Starship Services v. Epix, Inc., 304 F.3d 936, 64 U.S.P.Q.2d 1514 (9th Cir. 2002) (finding no likelihood of confusion between EPIX and epix.com). *See also*, SMC Promotions, Inc. v. SMC Promotions, 355 F. Supp. 2d 1127, 1135 (C.D. Cal. 2005).

was likely to cause "initial interest confusion," meaning that search engine users would be drawn in to the defendants' sites believing them to belong to the plaintiffs, whether or not the search engine users ultimately discovered their error before making a purchase.[284]

While for the most part meta tag cases have decreased, the Eleventh Circuit recently upheld a finding of infringement based on the use of a competitor's trademarks in meta tags. The trademarks were not visible to visitors to the site, nor did the site mention the plaintiff or its marks in visible text. The issue was that a Google search for the plaintiff's marks led to search results listing Axiom, the trademark owner, first, and North American Medical, the competitor, second. On the search results list, the short description of the defendant's website included Axiom's trademarks.

The Eleventh Circuit found that the defendant intentionally "included the terms within its meta tags to influence Internet search engines" and concluded that use of those marks in the description of the website listed in Google search results created a likelihood of confusion.[285] The court in *North American Medical* did not rely on initial interest confusion; rather, it found a straightforward likelihood of confusion as to source, because the plaintiff's trademarks appeared in the description of defendant's website in Google's search results, which would mislead consumers into believing that the parties were connected.

The use of another company's marks in one's meta tags does not always cause consumer confusion. Such use may be deemed "fair use" where the defendant needs to use the marks to convey the content of its website. In order to avoid a claim of infringement, companies should only use a competitor's trademarks in description meta tags if the marks are also mentioned on the website for the purposes of a product comparison. If it is essential to use a competitor's marks in description meta tags, it should be expressly stated that those marks belong to another party and that they are only used for comparison, in order to avoid any confusion.

E.   Trademark Law and Domain Names

1.   Generic Top-Level Domains

Like trademarks, domain names are valuable business assets. Not only can a domain name reflect a company's brand, it also serves as the address for

---

284.   *See* Venture Tape Corp. v. McGills Glass Warehouse, 540 F.3d 56 (1st Cir. 2008); Australian Gold, Inc. v. Hatfield, 436 F.3d 1228 (10th Cir. 2006); Promatek Indus., Ltd. v. Equitrac Corp., 300 F.3d 808 (7th Cir. 2002); Brookfield Communications, Inc. v. West Coast Entertainment Corp., 174 F.3d 1036 (9th Cir. 1999). *But cf.* Eli Lilly & Co v. Natural Answers, Inc., 233 F.3d 456, 465 (7th Cir. 2000) (holding that, while use of another party's trademark as a meta tag is evidence of an intent to confuse, it is not evidence of actual confusion).

285.   North American Medical Corp. v. Axiom Worldwide, Inc., 522 F.3d 1211 (11th Cir. 2008).

the company's online location. Originally, a company seeking to propel itself into cyberspace could only choose between three generic top-level domains ("gTLDs"): .com, .net and .org. Since that time, country codes and other restricted and unrestricted use gTLDs have been established by the Internet Corporation for Assigned Names and Numbers ("ICANN"), a nonprofit corporation that manages the Internet domain name system. The gTLDs .com (commercial enterprises), .biz (for use by businesses), .info (unrestricted) and .name (for registration by individuals), are the least restricted and most open to registration by the general public.

In 2010, ICANN began a program to dramatically expand the number of gTLDs available online. Organizations may apply for both standard character gTLDs as well as Internationalized Domain Names, which contain one or more characters other than the letters A to Z, digits 0 to 9, and a hyphen. The number of new gTLDs that can be added under this new program is unlimited, and ICANN also plans to launch additional gTLD application rounds after the 2010 round, with a goal of beginning the next round within one year after the application submission period for the first round is over. This new program is still being developed; refer to www.icann.org/en/topics/ new-gtld-program.htm for the most up-to-date information.

Naturally, the addition of more domain names creates more opportunities for cybersquatters to attempt to register others' trademarks. ICANN is working on various safeguards for trademark owners, two of which are a proposed Trademark Clearinghouse (which would maintain a centralized database of validated trademark rights), and the Uniform Rapid Suspension System, to provide a fast procedure for stopping clear cases of bad faith registration. A problem with the database concept is that it's limited to domain name registration of only the identical trademark that appears in the database; cybersquatters typically register domain names with slight typographical differences or the addition of other terms. The proposed Uniform Rapid Suspension System, however, would be very beneficial for trademark owners.

2.   Registering a Domain Name

Currently, domain names may be registered with any of the over 150 registrars accredited by ICANN. These registrars are required to implement and follow ICANN's Uniform Domain Name Dispute Resolution Policy ("UDRP"). ICANN requires the gTLD registries to implement policies and procedures to reduce the potential for cybersquatting and allow trademark owners the ability to protect their intellectual property rights.

Basically, anyone can register a domain name in the .com, .info, .net or .org gTLDs, as long as the domain name is not identical to a previously registered domain name. Domain name registration operates on a first-come, first-served basis. Registration is inexpensive, usually about $35 a year. Registrars require applicants to sign contracts including terms required by ICANN.

Registering a domain name is separate from a trademark registration in the PTO. One can register—as a domain name—descriptive or generic terms that would not be registrable in the PTO, like computers.com or furniture.com, and there is no examination as to potential infringement. Thus, registering a domain name with a registrar does not confer trademark protection.[286]

The PTO will register domain names as trademarks if they meet all of the legal requirements for registrable trademarks or service marks. If a domain name is used solely to indicate an Internet address, and not to identify the source of goods and services, the PTO does not recognize it as a trademark and will not issue a registration.

In order to determine whether a certain domain name has already been registered, perform a search of the WHOIS database on the site of any accredited domain name registrar or on one of the other WHOIS databases, such as allwhois.com or uwhois.com.

3. Domain Names and Trademark Disputes

Since the commercialization of the Internet, lawyers, the courts and trademark owners have attempted to find effective ways of dealing with domain name disputes. Presently, there are a number of different claims a plaintiff may make in this situation. A plaintiff may claim trademark infringement, in which case the court will engage in an analysis of likelihood of confusion. A plaintiff may also make a claim under either state or federal anti-dilution laws, or may bring suit under the Anti-Cybersquatting Consumer Protection Act, as discussed below. Lastly, an aggrieved party may take advantage of the domain name dispute resolution procedures established by ICANN.[287]

a. Trademark Infringement

As with all questions of trademark infringement, the ultimate issue will focus on the likelihood of confusion. Thus, a trademark owner will only be able to raise an infringement claim where a competitor or purveyor of closely related goods or services is using the domain name at issue. Similar to traditional trademark disputes involving common law marks, the court must go through the analysis of determining which party has priority over the other. In *Brookfield* the court addressed the issue of priority with respect to a domain name. The court held that the registration of a domain by itself

---

286.   Newborn v. Yahoo!, Inc., 391 F. Supp. 2d 181(D.D.C. 2005).

287.   One situation facing many trademark owners that is not covered by the ACPA or UDRP is cyberpiracy involving foreign registries and ccTLDs (e.g., brandX.uk, for the United Kingdom). If the domain name registrant can be found and has some presence in the United States, an *in personam* action may be possible, though an *in rem* action would be unlikely to succeed as the foreign domain name registry is not within the territory of any United States district court. Foreign registries are not ICANN-accredited and most do not follow its UDRP.

does not establish use sufficient for ownership of a trademark. Further, the limited use of a domain to exchange a few e-mails with customers and attorneys similarly is not sufficient to establish use sufficient to support a claim of trademark ownership.[288]

While registration of a domain is not sufficient to establish priority of use, registration similarly does not constitute "commercial use" for the purpose of establishing liability for trademark infringement.[289]

Use of a trademark in the post-domain path of a URL (everything to the right of the gTLD) is generally not considered trademark infringement. The Sixth Circuit has held that the post-domain path does not typically signify source and thus "it is unlikely that the presence of another's trademark in a post-domain path of a URL would ever violate trademark law."[290]

b.   Trademark Dilution

Trademark owners may utilize both the federal dilution law[291] and the federal anticybersquatting law[292] to protect their marks from dilution on the Internet. Under the TDRA, a famous mark is likely to be blurred or tarnished (the two forms of dilution) by the use of another mark as part of a domain name where there was commercial use of the mark.[293] If the owner of a famous trademark can show that a domain name holder had a bad faith intention to profit from its mark, it can also use the provisions of the Anticybersquatting Consumer Protection Act (ACPA) to claim dilution (see below).

There is an important difference in proof between these two statutes. The ACPA requires proof that the defendant has registered, trafficked in, or used a domain name that is *dilutive* of the plaintiff's famous trademark.[294] Federal dilution law, however, allows a plaintiff to show merely that the defendant's use of its mark is *likely to dilute* the plaintiff's famous mark.

Hasbro, Inc. v. Internet Entertainment Group[295] involved the use of the domain "candyland.com" for a pornography site. Hasbro successfully claimed that their mark "candy land" is usually associated with a children's game, and that this domain diluted or tarnished that association.

Use of a trademark owner's famous mark in a domain name and website may cause blurring in violation of the ACPA where the defendant uses the mark to create an association between the site, and both the mark *and* this use is found to harm the mark owner by reducing the selling power of its

288.   174 F.3d at 1053.
289.   *See* Lockheed Martin Corp. v. Network Solutions, Inc., 985 F. Supp. 949 (C.D. Cal. 1997).
290.   Interactive Prods. Corp. v. A2Z Mobile Office Solutions, Inc., 326 F.3d 687 (6th Cir. 2003).
291.   15 U.S.C. § 1125(c).
292.   15 U.S.C. § 1125(d).
293.   15 U.S.C. § 1125(c).
294.   15 U.S.C. § 1125(d)(1)(A)(ii)(II).
295.   Hasbro, Inc. v. Internet Entm't. Group 40 U.S.P.Q.2d 1479 (W.D. Wash 1996).

mark. For example, a defendant who operated a website at peta.org under the name "People Eating Tasty Animals" was found to have diluted plaintiff's mark "People for the Ethical Treatment of Animals" by blurring.[296]

c. Anti-Cybersquatting Consumer Protection Act

The ACPA, signed into law on November 29, 1999, prohibits registration of, trafficking in, or use of a domain name with a bad faith intent to profit from the goodwill of another's trademark. The ACPA adds Section 43(d) to the Lanham Act with a cause of action against cyberpiracy and cybersquatting, protecting trademark owners from infringement and dilution of their marks by domain name holders acting in bad faith. The ACPA was codified at 15 U.S.C. Section 1125(d).

The ACPA establishes a cause of action where a "cybersquatter" had a bad faith intent to profit from the mark and engaged in actionable conduct, such as the registration, trafficking or use of a domain name that is identical or confusingly similar to, or dilutive of, the registered trademark of another. "Bad faith" is established by showing a variety of factors, including an offer by the cybersquatter to sell the domain name to the owner of the registered mark and the existence (or lack thereof) of any independent rights to use the mark or name at issue. There is no bad faith where the defendant had a reasonable belief that the use of the domain name was fair use or otherwise legal.

The ACPA provides for statutory penalties in lieu of actual damages in an amount no less than $1,000, but as high as $100,000 per domain name. In addition, the ACPA provides for the cancellation or transfer of the offending domain.

d. ICANN Dispute Resolution

As of January 2000, all of the domain name registrars who register .com, .net, .org, .biz, .info and other ICANN-approved gTLDs are required to agree to abide by the ICANN Uniform Domain Name Dispute Resolution Policy. This policy permits the owner of a mark to initiate an administrative complaint against an alleged cybersquatter. A dispute may be resolved under ICANN's policy only if it involves a bad faith registration of a domain name; that is, registration of the domain name with the intent to profit commercially from another's trademark.

Under ICANN's policy, the complainant is required to prove the following elements: (a) that the challenged domain name is identical or confusingly similar to a trademark or service mark in which the complainant has rights,

---

296.   People for the Ethical Treatment of Animals v. Doughney, 113 F. Supp. 2d 951 (E.D. Va. 2000), *affirmed on other grounds,* 263 F.3d 359 (4th Cir. 2001).

(b) that the respondent (domain name holder) has no rights or legitimate interest in the subject domain name, and (c) that the domain name has been registered and is being used in bad faith.

ICANN's policy requires that the subject domain name has been registered and is being used in bad faith. The policy provides the following examples, which constitute evidence of bad faith registration and use:

- The alleged cybersquatter registered or acquired the domain name primarily for the purpose of selling, renting or otherwise transferring the domain name registration to the complainant who is the owner of the trademark or service mark, or to a competitor of that complainant, for consideration in excess of documented out-of-pocket costs directly related to the domain name;
- The alleged cybersquatter registered the domain name in order to prevent the owner of the trademark or service mark from registering a corresponding domain name, provided that the cybersquatter has engaged in a pattern of such conduct;
- The alleged cybersquatter has registered the domain name primarily for the purpose of disrupting the business of a competitor; or
- The alleged cybersquatter has, by using the domain name, intentionally attempted to attract, for commercial gain, Internet users to its website or other online location, by creating a likelihood of confusion with the complainant's mark as to the source, sponsorship, affiliation or endorsement of the alleged cybersquatter's website or location or of a product or service on its website or location.

There are currently four active ICANN-approved administrative dispute resolution service providers: the World Intellectual Property Organization (WIPO), the National Arbitration Forum (NAF), The Czech Arbitration Court Arbitration Center for Internet Disputes and the Asian Domain Name Dispute Resolution Centre.[297] As of March 1, 2010, parties are required to file their UDRP submissions (complaints and responses) electronically. Nevertheless, to help ensure receipt, providers will send each respondent a written notice in hard copy that a UDRP complaint has been filed against it, as well as an electronic copy of the complaint. A complainant must pay fees usually starting at approximately $1,500 to institute proceedings for one domain name.

The panel that decides the dispute is made up of either one or three individuals. Usually, there are no in-person, teleconference, videoconference or web conference hearings, so decisions are made entirely based on the documents submitted. Decisions are made in most cases by the panel within 14 days of appointment, and are published on ICANN's website (www.icann. org). Remedies are limited to cancellation or, as is more common, transfer of the contested domain name.

---

297.   For the most current list of providers, see www.icann.org/udrp/approved-providers.htm.

A federal court may overrule a UDRP panel decision.[298]   Unless the respondent provides the domain name registrar with proof of the initiation of a federal suit within 10 business days of the panel's decision, the registrar will implement the decision of the panel. By enacting the ACPA, Congress provided a cause of action to overrule UDRP decisions and established that a declaratory judgment of compliance with the ACPA trumps a UDRP panel's finding of cybersquatting.

4.   *Developing an Online Trademark Plan*

New businesses should implement a preventative, cost-effective Internet strategy to protect and enforce their trademark rights online, including defensive domain registrations and monitoring the web through alerts or a commercial watch service. When issues arise, it's best to approach them from a practical perspective; not all online battles can or should be fought.

The first thing to do upon learning of a possible infringement is to search one of the WHOIS databases to determine who registered the domain name and to obtain that person's contact information. Perform a background check of the domain name holder through Internet and corporate intelligence sources as you would on any other potential defendant. In addition, it is critical to preserve evidence early on because websites can be changed within minutes; print out the website's pages, preferably with a color printer, and download them to save an electronic copy as well.

Companies are advised to be cautious before immediately firing off a strongly worded cease-and-desist letter, because it very well may be posted on the offending website and elsewhere on the Internet. It could also trigger a declaratory judgment action, and in some countries (including the United Kingdom) it could serve as the basis for a threatened litigation lawsuit. Strident, bullying claims can easily backfire and result in a public relations debacle for the rightful trademark owner. Instead, consider crafting a cease and desist letter as simply a warning or request for information or assistance, rather than a demand for immediate action; some offending site owners may not be aware of their transgression, and sending a letter puts them on notice of your trademark rights and deprives the cyberpirate of its claims of innocence or acquiescence.

If litigation is unavoidable, in general, using the UDRP system will be far quicker than pursuing a cyberpirate or cybersquatter through federal court. Under the UDRP's rules, a panel must decide the case within 14 days of being appointed. However, it is important to note that even though the UDRP procedures are completed more quickly, the status quo is maintained during the proceedings, meaning that the domain name holder can keep using the domain name throughout that time. If a trademark owner needs immediate

---

298   Sallen v. Corinthians Licenciamentos LTDA, 273 F.3d 14 (1st Cir. 2001).

emergency relief against a currently operating site—for example, a competitor's site that is taking away prospective customers—the mark owner may want to file a lawsuit and seek a TRO in federal court under the ACPA rather than, or prior to, filing a UDRP complaint.

UDRP administrative proceedings are also generally less expensive than litigating in federal court. Filing fees for the service providers range from $750 to $2500 for one domain name, depending upon whether there is a one-member panel or a three-member panel. Beyond attorneys' fees for preparing the complaint and exhibits, there are few other expenses to proceed under the UDRP. Federal court cases involve far more attorneys' fees, for hearings on injunctive relief, discovery, motion practice, and trial.

Another important factor is the remedy sought: if the trademark owner seeks damages or attorneys' fees, they will need to go to federal court, as the remedies under the UDRP process are limited to the cancellation or transfer of the domain name at issue.

8.05   Trade Secrets

A.   Uniform Trade Secrets Act

A growing number of U.S. businesses are electing to protect commercially valuable information via state trade secret law, particularly in light of the substantial number of patent applications that are rejected and issued patents that are subsequently invalidated by the courts.[299] Recognizing the growing commercial importance of state trade secret law to interstate business and the law's uneven development in various states, in 1979 the National Conference of Commissioners on Uniform State Laws approved the Uniform Trade Secrets Act, which was last amended in 1985 ("UTSA").[300] To date, 46 states and the District of Columbia and the U.S. Virgin Islands have adopted UTSA in some form.[301]

UTSA codifies the basic principles of common law trade secret protection while preserving the essential distinctions between trade secret protection and other forms of intellectual property protection, particularly patent protection.[302]

---

299.   ULA Trade Secret References & Annotations, Uniform Trade Secrets Act References & Annotations.

300.   *Id.*

301.   ULA Trade Secret References & Annotations, Uniform Trade Secrets Act References & Annotations (UTSA has been adopted in every state except Massachusetts, New Jersey, New York and Texas, all of which either continue to apply the common law to trade secret issues or have adopted separate statutes).

302.   ULA Trade Secret References & Annotations, Uniform Trade Secrets Act References & Annotations. The long line of decisions that make up the common law of trade secrets was originally incorporated into the Restatement of Torts (1939), which remains an important influence on the definition of a trade secret and the rights of a trade secret owner even in those jurisdictions that have adopted the UTSA.

For instance, under both UTSA and common law trade secret principles, more than one person may be entitled to trade secret protection for the same information, and it is permissible to reverse engineer a lawfully obtained product to discover a trade secret.[303] Conversely, under patent law an invention can only be patented once, and reverse engineering a patented invention in most cases will constitute infringement.[304] These and other distinctions, as more fully set forth below, have helped to define the types of information most suitable for trade secret protection and the most appropriate remedies for trade secret misappropriation.

Pursuant to the UTSA, a "trade secret" is information, including a formula, pattern, compilation, program, device, method, technique or process that "(a) derives independent economic value, actual or potential, from not being generally known to, and not being readily ascertainable by *proper means* by other persons who can obtain economic value from its disclosure or use, *and* (b) is the subject of efforts that are reasonable under the circumstances to maintain its secrecy."[305]

Pursuant to the UTSA, *misappropriation* means:

(i)   acquisition of another's trade secret by a person who knows or has reason to know that the trade secret was acquired by improper means; or

(ii)   disclosure or use of another's trade secret without express or implied consent by a person who:

    (A)   used improper means to acquire knowledge of the trade secret; or

    (B)   at the time of disclosure or use, knew or had reason to know that his knowledge of the trade secret was:

        (I)   derived from or through a person who had utilized improper means to acquire it;

        (II)   acquired under circumstances giving rise to a duty to maintain its secrecy or limit its use; or

        (III)   derived from or through a person who owed a duty to the person seeking relief to maintain its secrecy or limit its use; or

---

303. ULA Trade Secret References & Annotations, Uniform Trade Secrets Act References & Annotations. *See also,* Bestechnologies, Inc. v. Trident Environmental Systems, Inc., 681 So. 2d 1175 (1996) (under the statutory trade secret definition, the fact that several competitors independently used a process that each competitor had independently discovered did not preclude trade secret protection for this undisclosed information).

304. ULA Trade Secret References & Annotations, Uniform Trade Secrets Act References & Annotations.

305. ULA Trade Secret S.1, Uniform Trade Secrets Act § 1 (emphasis added).

(C)   before a material change of his [or her] position, knew or had reason to know that it was a trade secret and that knowledge of it had been acquired by accident or mistake.

Under the UTSA, a prima facie claim for trade secret misappropriation requires the plaintiff to demonstrate (1) the plaintiff owned a trade secret, (2) the defendant acquired, disclosed or used the plaintiff's trade secret through improper means and (3) the defendant's actions damaged the plaintiff.[306] "Improper means" includes theft, bribery, misrepresentation, breach or inducement of a breach of a duty to maintain secrecy, or espionage through electronic or other means.[307] Since improper use is an element of the plaintiff's prima facie case (as opposed to an affirmative defense), the plaintiff bears the burden of proving improper use.[308] Proof that the defendant's use resulted from reverse engineering or independent derivation is evidence that the defendant did not use the trade secret via improper means.[309] The defendant does not have a "burden of proof" to make this showing, but the defendant acts at its peril by failing to present evidence rebutting the plaintiff's showing.[310]

Thus, establishing trade secret protection for certain proprietary information does not necessarily preclude the subsequent discovery and use of that *same information* by another who gains knowledge of the trade secret by *proper means*. According to UTSA, *proper means* include discovery by independent invention, discovery by reverse engineering, discovery under a license from the trade secret owner, observation of the information or item in the public domain and obtaining the trade secret information from published literature.[311] On the other hand, improper means include obtaining trade secret information via theft, bribery, misrepresentation, breach or inducement of a breach of a duty to maintain secrecy, or espionage through electronic or other methods.[312]

From a practical standpoint, a clear, crisp definition of what qualifies as a protectable trade secret simply does not exist. Rather, the circumstances under which a dispute over trade secret ownership arises will determine whether the information will be protected as a trade secret.[313] As a general rule, trade secrets derive their value from the fact that they are not disclosed to those who may use them for the purpose of creating value or gaining a competitive advantage in the relevant market.[314] Thus, commercially valuable information that has been scrupulously kept confidential will be considered a trade secret, and the trade secret owner will be entitled to protection and relief against those who have misappropriated the trade secret or improperly

---

306.   Sargent Fletcher, Inc. v. Able Corp., 110 Cal. App. 4th 1658, 1665 (2003).
307.   *Id.* at 1666.
308.   *Id.* at 1669.
309.   *Id.*
310.   *Id.*
311.   ULA Trade Secret S.1, Uniform Trade Secrets Act § 1, *Comment* 1990 Main Volume.
312.   *Id.*
313.   Stephen Elias, Patent, Copyright & Trademark 14 (1st ed. 1996).
314.   *See* Pillsbury, Madison & Sutro v. Schectman, 55 Cal. App. 4th 1279 (1997).

disclosed the trade secret information.[315] "The secrecy requirement is generally treated as a relative concept and requires a fact intrusive analysis."[316] Even publication over the Internet does not necessarily destroy the secrecy element of a trade secret if the publication is brief, relatively obscure or otherwise limited so as not to become generally known to competitors or become part of the public domain.[317]

The categories of commercially valuable information that may constitute a trade secret are broad, and the list of potentially protectable categories provided in UTSA is nonexhaustive. According to UTSA Section 1, information potentially protectable as a trade secret includes formulas, patterns, compilations, programs, devices, methods, techniques or processes that derive independent economic value from not being generally known and are subject to reasonable efforts to maintain their secrecy.[318] In essence, practically any kind of information that a business may wish to protect as a trade secret could be subject to protection under trade secret law. Some of the more common types of information that have received trade secret protection include customer lists, business plans, business methods, financial information, technical processes and related know-how information and blueprints.[319]

It should be noted that definitions of trade secrets have also been prescribed or judicially developed in relation to various federal statutes such as the federal Trade Secrets Act, the Freedom on Information Act, the Toxic Substances Control Act, the Economic Espionage Act of 1996, the Computer Fraud and Abuse Act, the National Stolen Property Act, federal mail fraud and wire fraud statutes, and the Racketeer Influenced and Corrupt Organizations Act. Reference should also be made to state statutes that impose civil and criminal liability for theft of property, including trade secrets.

---

315. ELIAS, *supra* note 233, at 14.

316. DVD Copy Control Ass'n Inc. v. Bunner, 116 Cal. App. 4th 241, 251 (2004), citing 1 MILGRIM ON TRADE SECRETS § 1.07[2], at 1-343, 1-352 (2003).

317. *Id.* at 251, 253.

318. ULA Trade Secret S.1, Uniform Trade Secrets Act § 1.

319. *See* ALTA Analytics, Inc. v. Muuss, 75 F. Supp. 2d 773 (S.D. Ohio 1999) (technology, design and marketing features of insurance and financial fraud detection software were trade secrets and properly suitable for protection under Ohio law); Basic American, Inc. v. Shatila, 992 P.2d 175 (Idaho 1999) (manufacturer's method of introducing certain additives to potatoes that had been processed in a certain way was neither generally known nor readily ascertainable by competitors, and thus qualified for trade secret protection under the Idaho Trade Secrets Act); TDS Healthcare Systems Corp. v. Humana Hosp. Illinois, Inc., 880 F. Supp. 1572 (N.D. Ga. 1995) (computer programs are protectable trade secrets under the Georgia Trade Secrets Act); Reingold v. Swiftships, Inc., 126 F.3d 645 (5th Cir. 1997) (under the Louisiana Trade Secrets Act, a portable female fiberglass boat mold was not precluded from qualifying for trade secret protection); ABBA Rubber Co. v. Seaquist, 235 Cal. App. 3d 1 (1991) (a company's customer list was appropriate for trade secret protection); Capital Asset Research Corp. v. Finnegan, 160 F.3d 683 (Ga. 1998) (a unique combination of publicly available information, which adds value to the information, may qualify as a trade secret under the Georgia Trade Secrets Act); Revere Transducers, Inc. v. Deere & Co., 595 N.W.2d 751 (Iowa 1999) (business information that may constitute a protectable trade secret includes customer lists, supply sources, confidential costs, price data and figures, customer information, financial information, information regarding manufacturing processes and product composition information).

B.   Comparing Trade Secrets with Other Forms of Intellectual Property

While trade secret protection may be available for a wide range of information, it is important to consider the distinctions between trade secret protection and other forms of protection for intellectual property. Such distinctions will undoubtedly influence the scope and enforceability of available protection for different types of proprietary information.

As discussed above, the Patent Act of 1952 governs patent rights and the PTO grants patents for new, useful and nonobvious inventions, which must be fully disclosed in a patent application.[320] The PTO grants patents after patent applications have been examined and determined to satisfy the statutory requirements for obtaining a patent as set forth in Title 35 of the United Stated Code.[321] Generally speaking, patent owners are entitled to exclude others from practicing the patented invention for a maximum term of 20 years from the date the related patent application was filed, with the exception of design patents, which are limited to 14 years of exclusive protection.[322]

The Lanham Act, which is discussed above, is the federal statute governing trademark rights.[323] In addition, states employ their own statutes and common law to ensure that trademarks serve their intended functions—to identify the origin of goods and services, assure the quality of those goods and services and symbolize accumulated goodwill acquired in association with the goods and services.[324] Trademark laws protect the distinctive names, designs, logos, slogans, symbols, colors, containers and any other devices that businesses use to distinguish their goods and services in the marketplace.[325] Similar to trade secret protection, trademark protection can potentially last indefinitely.[326]

Federal copyright law protects an author's original writings, which may include not only books, but also computer programs, phonorecords, plays, television broadcasts and jewelry designs.[327] Copyright law protects only tangible expressions of ideas rather than ideas in the abstract.[328] Copyright protection lasts for a finite period of time—the life of the author plus 50 years thereafter.[329] When the author is a corporation, the term of protection is 75 years from first publication or 100 years from first creation, whichever

---

320.   Siegrum D. Kane, Trademark Law, A Practitioner's Guide § 1:1.5, at 1–6 (3d ed. Practicing Law Institute 1999).

321.   Id.

322.   Id.

323.   Id. § 1:3, at 1–11 & fn. 25. The 1946 Act has been amended several times; the most comprehensive revision was the Trademark Law Revision Act of 1988.

324.   Id. § 1:3, at 1–11.

325.   Elias, supra note 233, at 3.

326.   Elias, supra note 233, at 3.

327.   Kane, supra note 240, § 1:1.5, at 1–6.

328.   Id.

329.   Id. § 1:1.5, at 1–7.

expires first.[330] As with patents, federal law exclusively governs copyright protection and states are prohibited from granting protection which conflicts with federal law.[331]

With this brief synopsis of intellectual property protection in mind, consider the primary factors that distinguish trade secret protection from other forms of intellectual property protection. Those most notable are summarized below in Figure 8A.[332]

C. *Reasonable Efforts* to Keep Secret

A trade secret is protectable only so long as it is kept secret. UTSA requires that trade secret information be "the subject of efforts that are reasonable under the circumstances to maintain its secrecy."[333] Absolute secrecy is not required. Only reasonable efforts, not all conceivable efforts, must be taken to maintain its secrecy.[334]

Courts consider numerous factors in determining whether or not reasonable efforts have been taken to protect trade secrets. "Reasonableness" is a question of fact and no one set of criteria is dispositive.[335] The weight to be given any one particular safeguard depends on the nature of the trade secret. For instance, what constitutes reasonable protective measures differs depending on whether the claimed trade secret is confidential customer information, a product formula or a manufacturing process.[336]

Following is a list of protective measures that courts have examined in the context of employment relationships to evaluate the reasonableness of protective measures:

- Are employees required to execute nondisclosure agreements?
- Are employees regularly reminded that certain information is considered a trade secret and should not be disclosed?
- Is access to trade secret limited on a "need-to-know" basis?
- Is access to sensitive areas of the production facility limited on a "need-to-know" basis?
- Is confidential information stored in locked file cabinets?
- Is the sharing of confidential information between branch offices limited to a "need-to-know" basis?
- Are documents claimed to be confidential marked confidential?

---

330. *Id.*
331. *Id.*
332. *See* TRADE SECRETS PRACTICE IN CALIFORNIA Appendix C, at 589–91 (CEB 2d ed. 1996).
333. ULA Trade Secret S.1, Uniform Trade Secrets Act § 1(4)(ii).
334. Meadox Medicals, Inc. v. Life Systems, Inc., 3 F. Supp. 2d 549 (D.N.J. 1998); E.I. duPont deNemours & Co., Inc. v. Christopher, 431 F.2d 1012, 1017 (5th Cir. 1970).
335. Surgidev Corp. v. Eye Technology, Inc., 828 F.2d 452, 455 (8th Cir. 1987).
336. *See* Rockwell Graphic Systems v. DEV Industries, 925 F.2d 174, 178–80 (7th Cir. 1991).

- Is the manufacturing facility located in an isolated area to preserve secrecy?
- Is public access to the facility limited to nonsensitive areas?
- What is the degree and type of other internal controls imposed by the company, including the use of visitor logs, sign-out sheets for proprietary documents and a document-destruction policy?

The foregoing list is not exhaustive and certainly not all of these measures must be adopted to demonstrate that reasonable steps were taken to preserve secrecy.

While the reasonableness of efforts to maintain secrecy is a question of fact, all courts that have considered the question of "reasonable efforts" place great weight on whether a company utilizes confidentiality or nondisclosure agreements.[337] Employees must be told that the proprietary information is secret and that information must be kept secret. Third party vendors or suppliers should execute confidentiality or nondisclosure agreements if trade secret information must be disclosed during the course of the relationship.

Once a company adopts formal measures to protect its trade secrets, care must be taken to continue to follow those procedures. If confidential documents are to be marked with a cautionary notice, all confidential documents should bear the seal. Otherwise, the company will risk an argument that the unmarked documents are not confidential or that the company was sloppy in its efforts and therefore did not take reasonable precautions to protect the trade secrets.[338] If employees are required to execute a nondisclosure agreement, the nondisclosure agreement must be consistently enforced. Lack of consistent enforcement and failure to comply with internal procedures may result in a loss of trade secret protection.

---

337.   MAI Systems Corp. v. Peak Computer, 991 F.2d 511, 521 (9th Cir. 1993); Hollingsworth Solderless Terminal Co. v. Turley, 622 F.2d 1324, 1334, fn. 7 (9th Cir. 1980); Courtesy Temporary Service v. Camacho, 222 Cal. App. 3d 1278–88 (1990); Structural Dynamics Research Corp. v. Engineering Mechanics Research Corp., 401 F. Supp. 1102, 1117 (E.D. Mich. 1975).

338.   *In re* Providian Credit Card Cases, 96 Cal. App. 4th 292, 306–8 (2002); *Rockwell,* 925 F.2d at 176, 177.

D.   Practical Examples of Trade Secrets

UTSA provides a list of items that may qualify as a trade secret, including "a formula, pattern, compilation, program, device, method, technique or process."[339]

1.   Formulas and Processes

A wide variety of formulas and processes have been found to warrant trade secret protection. These trade secrets include production processes as well as formulas for final products. Product formulas are frequently found to be protectable trade secrets so long as the other elements set forth in UTSA are satisfied. Formulas and processes have not been afforded trade secret protection if it is determined that the formula or process is "readily ascertainable" or is a result of a failure to prove that the process or formula has independent economic value because it is not generally known to competitors.[340]

2.   Patterns, Programs and Devices

Patterns, programs and devices may also qualify as protectable trade secrets if the information is not readily ascertainable. Product patterns and design features are not protectable if the alleged secret is fully disclosed once the product is built and marketed. Trade secret protection will not be afforded if the design or device can be readily reverse engineered from the product itself. In that case, the owner of the design or device must seek other forms of intellectual property protection such as patent or copyright protection, as described above.

3.   Methods and Techniques

A "method" or "technique" may also qualify as a trade secret under UTSA.[341] UTSA adopted the terms "method" and "techniques" to incorporate concepts that courts have protected at common law prior to the adoption of UTSA known as "know-how" secrets.[342] "Know-how" trade secrets are methods or processes regarding how to achieve certain results. The steps to obtain the results must not be known to others in the industry. However, a "know-how" trade secret need not rise to the level of "novelty" required for patent protection.

---

339.   ULA Trade Secret S.1, Uniform Trade Secrets Act § 1(4).

340.   Kewanee Oil Co. v. Bicron Corp., 416 U.S. 470, 476 (1974).

341.   Lamb-Weston, Inc. v. McCain Foods, Ltd., 941 F.2d 970, 975 (9th Cir. 1991).

342.   Vacco Industries, Inc. v. Van Den Berg, 5 Cal. App. 4th 34, 49–51 (1992); Surgidev Corp. v. Eye Technology, Inc., 648 F. Supp. 661, 687, fn. 8 (D. Mass. 1986), *aff'd* 828 F.2d 452 (8th Cir. 1987).

Trade secret protection is not available for general knowledge.[343] However, "know-how" trade secrets may consist of a unique combination of many components that individually may exist in the public so long as the end product is not generally known in the industry.[344]

"Know-how" trade secrets may also include negative know-how so long as the negative know-how has independent economic value.[345] For example, a company may invest years of research investigating alternative methods and processes to perform a certain task. During this process, the company eliminates dozens of possible methods through trial and error. This knowledge has independent economic value to competitors who would not have to invest the same time and effort to duplicate the research and will be provided trade secret protection.

4. Competitive Pricing and Marketing Strategy

Production costs and pricing information can be trade secrets. This can include pricing, profit margins, costs of production, discounts, advertising costs, rebates, customer concessions and payment terms if not generally known to competitors. The production costs and pricing information may not be merely "general methods of doing business." General methods of doing business are not protectable trade secrets. The information must be such that it would be valuable to a competitor for setting prices to meet or undercut prices set by the holder of the privilege.[346]

Marketing strategies and plans may also qualify as trade secrets. Potentially protectable information includes marketing research, advertising strategy and marketing techniques. Marketing research can be a trade secret only if it "explores the needs of numerous, diverse buyers." Such information is not protectable if it "relates to a single prominent buyer that is presumably aware of its own needs."[347]

---

343. Rohn & Hans Co. v. Adco Chemical Co., 689 F.2d 424, 431 (3d Cir. 1982).

344. Imperial Chemical Industry v. National Distillers and Chemical Corp., 354 F.2d 459 (2d Cir. 1965); *see also* Computer Care v. Service Systems Enterprises, Inc., 982 F.2d 1063, 1074 (7th Cir. 1992) (combination of known marketing techniques does not qualify as a trade secret because the final product was generally known in the industry); Self Directed Placement Corp. v. Control Data Corp., 908 F.2d 462, 465 (9th Cir. 1990).

345. *Courtesy Temp. Serv.*, 222 Cal. App. 3d at 1278; Morton v. Rank America, Inc., 812 F. Supp. 1062, 1073 (C.D. Cal. 1993); *see also* legislative comments by the California legislation in adopting UTSA (Comment to California Civil Code Section 3426.1):

> The definition of "trade secret" . . . includes information that has commercial value from a negative viewpoint, for example the results of lengthy and expressive research which proves that a certain process will *not* work could be of great value to a competitor.

346. Whyte v. Schlage Lock Co., 101 Cal. App. 4th 1443, 1455 (2002), citing *Courtesy Temp. Serv.*, 222 Cal. App. 3d at 1288 (billing and mark-up rates "irrefutably" of commercial values); SI Handling Systems, Inc. v. Heisley, 753 F.2d 1244, 1260 (3d Cir. 1985); Lumex, Inc. v. High Smith, 919 F. Supp. 624, 628–30 (E.D.N.Y. 1996).

347. *Whyte*, 101 Cal. App. 4th at 1456, citing *SI Handling*, 753 F.2d at 1259; and Metro Traffic Control, Inc. v. Shadow Traffic Network, 22 Cal. App. 4th 853, 863–64 (1994).

5. *Customer Lists*

Customer lists are not specifically mentioned in UTSA but may be considered a trade secret under proper circumstances.[348]

The initial question in considering whether a particular customer list is a protectable trade secret is whether the information in the list is known or accessible to others in the trade or general public. The courts must also balance the employer's right to protect its confidential information against, for instance, an employee's right to make a living. The question of whether customer information is sufficiently confidential possibly to constitute a trade secret depends on various factors, including the following:

- Nature of the business
- Whether the information was known or readily ascertainable to others in the industry
- Whether the disputed information is available from public records sources
- Whether the former employee and the customers at issue developed a personal relationship during the former employee's prior employment[349]
- Whether the list included information about customer preferences
- Whether the relevant industry was broadly competitive and customer relationships were usually not exclusive
- Whether the process of compiling the information was sophisticated
- Whether the disputed information was compiled through a difficult and time consuming process

Courts consider these and other factors in determining whether a customer list is entitled to trade secret protection. The case of *American Paper and Packaging Products v. Kirgan* was one of the first California cases to rule that customer information *may* qualify as a trade secret under UTSA.[350] In *American Paper*, the employees set forth detailed declarations describing how they formulated and updated their customer list, which included visiting communities in their sales area, visiting areas zoned for industry in those communities and making cold calls to potential manufacturing companies. The former employees also pointed out that due to the highly competitive nature of the business, emphasis was placed on price, speed and product quality; long term relationships between manufacturers and shipping supply companies did not exist; and manufacturers generally did not order all their shipping supplies and containers from any one company. Consideration of

---

348. *See* American Paper & Packaging Products v. Kirgan, 183 Cal. App. 3d 1318 (1986), for the proposition that a customer list may constitute a protectable trade secret under UTSA; *see also* Hollingsworth Solderless Terminal Co. v. Turley, 622 F.2d 1324, 1332 (9th Cir. 1980).

349. Moss, Adams & Co. v. Snelling (1986) 179 Cal. App. 3d 124, 128–29; Klamath-Orleans Lumber, Inc. v. Miller, 87 Cal. App. 3d 458, 464 (1978).

350. *American Paper*, 183 Cal. App. 3d at 1318.

these factors ultimately weighed against granting trade secret protection for the disputed customer list.

On the other hand, cases that have afforded trade secret protection to customer lists and related information have involved circumstances where

- The former employer provided relatively unusual services
- The former employer established that customer information was specialized and was compiled over a period of years with great effort
- Customer identities were not generally known in the industry
- The former employer imposed reasonable efforts to maintain the secrecy of customer identities and related confidential information
- The customer list included additional information concerning pricing and knowledge of a particular customer's needs

A trade secret claim is strengthened if the customer list contains not only the customers' identity but additional information concerning the customers' requirements and preferences.[351] But the mere fact that this additional information is part of a customer list does not assure its status as a protectable trade secret. Customer requirements, preferences and specifications can be disclosed by the customer to any competitor including a former employee. Moreover, specific customer needs are commonly disclosed by those customers in trade publications, requests for proposals and goods specifications.[352] The question of whether a customer list is protectable is a fact intensive inquiry that varies from industry to industry.

The factors listed above are essential in determining whether or not a customer list is potentially a protectable trade secret, but they alone are not enough. A customer list, to be protectable, must also have independent economic value to a competitor. In determining whether a customer list is valuable, it is important to remember that courts do not consider whether the information has value to the owner, but rather whether the information has value to competitors.[353]

Lastly, the owner of a customer list must take reasonable measures to maintain the secrecy of its list. Such measures should include the use of employment agreements and employee handbooks to inform employees that customer information is confidential and a trade secret.[354]

One final consideration in cases involving the alleged misappropriation of a customer list concerns whether or not the former employee has "misused"

---

351. ABBA Rubber Co. v. Seaquist, 235 Cal. App. 3d 1, 19 (1991); *see also Courtesy Temp. Serv.* 222 Cal. App. 3d 1278 (1990) (temporary employment agency's customer list included specific type of temporary services those customers would use); and Morlife, Inc. v. Perry, 56 Cal. App. 4th 1514 (1997) (a customer list compiled by a roofing company concerning unusual roofing services, as well as particular roofs and customer roofing needs, constituted a protectable trade secret..

352. *Metro Traffic*, 22 Cal. App. 4th at 863.

353. *ABBA*, 235 Cal. App. 3d at 19.

354. Continental Car-Na-Var Corp. v. Moseley, 24 Cal. 2d 104 (1994).

the list. UTSA only prohibits the misuse of another's trade secret.[355] Misuse of a customer list occurs when a former employee "solicits" customers on a former employer's customer list. Courts have distinguished solicitation, which is actionable under UTSA, from announcing a job change, which is not actionable. Merely announcing a change in employment, without more, is not solicitation. Also, a former employee is not prohibited from discussing business with a party listed on a former employer's customer list when approached by that customer. The law does not prohibit a former employee from receiving business from his former employer's customers—the former employee can only be prohibited from soliciting that business.[356]

E.   Trade Secret Conflicts Involving Employers and Employees

Cases involving the use of trade secrets frequently arise in the context of a departing employee. A variety of tools exist whereby a company can seek to protect its trade secrets from a departing employee.

1.   *Employment and Nondisclosure Agreements*

Employment agreements, which are discussed in more detail in Chapter 10 (Human Resources), containing confidentiality or nondisclosure provisions are enforceable. The employment agreement should preclude the employee from disclosing to others or using for himself the protectable trade secrets of the employer. However, the protectable trade secrets are only those trade secrets that are protectable under UTSA. The employer cannot create a protectable trade secret when it otherwise would not exist.[357]

The confidentiality or nondisclosure provision should attempt to define and limit the legitimate trade secrets of the company. An employment agreement cannot preclude an employee from using basic acquired skills to persons in the trade.[358]

2.   *Covenants Not to Compete*

A covenant not to compete often provides that a departing employee may not work for a competitor for a specified period of time and within a specified geographical area. Many companies utilize a covenant not to compete to limit a departing employee's ability to capitalize on trade secrets learned as

---

355.   Imi-Tech Corp. v. Gagliani, 691 F. Supp. 214 (S.D. Cal. 1986).

356.   AETNA Building Maintenance Co. v. West, 39 Cal. 2d 198, 204 (1952), American Credit Indemnity Co. v. Sacks, 213 Cal. App. 3d 622, 636 (1989).

357.   *American Paper*, 183 Cal. App. 3d at 1325.

358.   *S.I. Handling,* 753 F.2d at 1262.

an employee. However, employment agreements that contain a covenant not to compete are illegal and unenforceable in many states.[359] Employers with employees located in multiple states must carefully modify their employment agreements to comply with the laws of each state. On the other hand, covenants not to compete included within an employment agreement are enforceable in many states. However, the state law may have unique limitations concerning the permissible scope of time or geographical territories.

3. Statutory Protections of Trade Secrets

State law provides additional protections for an employer's trade secrets. For example, California Labor Code Section 2860 provides:

> Everything that an employee acquires by virtue of his employment, except the compensation due to him from his employer, belongs to the employer, whether acquired lawfully or unlawfully, or during or after the expiration of the term of his employment.

This provision has been successfully used to preclude a departing employee from utilizing trade secrets that were either learned or developed by the employee during the term of his employment. If the employee is hired specifically to improve or develop new products, anything that the employee invents or develops while employed belongs to that employer. It does not matter if the employee contends that the improvements or developments were made on the employee's own time away from the work place, so long as the invention or improvement relates to the business of the employer.[360] However, if the employee is not hired principally to develop or invent new improvements or products for the employer, inventions developed on the employee's own time may remain his own.[361] As noted, **Exhibit 10C** is an employee intellectual property acknowledgement that can be used to confirm that the company owns any work done by the employee.

F.   Inevitable Disclosure

The doctrine of inevitable disclosure has experienced a recent renaissance, but is now coming under close scrutiny as a result of cases such as *Electro Optical,* decided in California in April 1999.[362] The doctrine bridges the gap

---

359.   *See* Cal. Bus. & Prof. Code § 16600, which states that covenants not to compete are only enforceable if included as part of a sale of a business.

360.   Daniel Orifice Fitting Co. v. Whalen, 198 Cal. App. 2d 791 (1962) (in which the court rejected the employee's argument that improvements of the products should remain his since they were developed in his own time away from the work place.)

361.   Standard Parts Co. v. Peck, 264 U.S. 52, 68 (1924); *but see* Marshall v. Colgate-Palmolive-Peet Co., 175 F.2d 215, 217 (3d Cir. 1949) (employee not originally hired to invent, but job responsibilities changed such that the invention belonged to the employer.)

362.   *See* Electro Optical Industries, Inc. v. White, 76 Cal. App. 4th 653 (1999).

between trade secret law and covenants not to compete, allowing jurisdictions that find noncompete covenants void for reasons of public policy not to extend the ban to the protection of legitimate trade secrets.[363] The inevitable disclosure doctrine extends traditional trade secret misappropriation principles to cases where there has been no *actual* or *threatened* misappropriation, allowing a court to issue an injunction to prevent an employee from working for a competitor even where there is not a noncompetition agreement.

Although the inevitable disclosure doctrine represents a significant departure from existing law, the courts have applied it in only certain circumstances.[364] The following factors are relevant: the honesty of the former employee in dealing with his or her employer, the scope of the proposed injunction (whether it would completely prohibit the former employee from accepting a new position or would be limited in scope or time), whether the former employee would be compensated for any period in which he or she could not work, the degree of competition between the two businesses, the extent of the former employee's knowledge of highly sensitive information, the similarity between the former employee's new job and previous job, the existence of a noncompete agreement and the ability of the new employer to develop the trade secret information on its own.

The doctrine allows an employer to prevent or restrict former employees from assuming tasks in a new setting where they will inevitably disclose trade secrets of the prior employer. The employer must prove that irreparable harm will result if the employee is allowed to assume the new position. Such a burden may be met with a showing that (a) the former and current employers are competitors, (b) there is significant overlap in the employee's duties at both the new and old companies and that performing these duties will make it inevitable that the employee will use or disclose the former employer's trade secrets and (c) that the current employer had not taken adequate steps to prevent any misappropriation from occurring.[365]

1. PepsiCo *Era*

The Seventh Circuit decision, in *PepsiCo, Inc. v. Redmond*, seemed to indicate that a limited showing of actual or threatened misappropriation was enough

---

363. *See* Cal. Bus. & Prof. Code § 16600 (West 1997); Scott v. Snelling & Snelling, Inc., 732 F. Supp. 1034 (N.D. Cal. (1990) (holding that California employer cannot restrain former employee from conduct other than that which would constitute unfair competition or use of trade secrets).

364. The following states have applied the doctrine under certain circumstances: New York, Illinois, Massachusetts, North Carolina, Florida, Texas, Washington, Oregon, Arkansas, Wisconsin, Michigan, Iowa, Utah, Alabama, Arizona, Indiana, Pennsylvania, Texas, Missouri, Minnesota, Connecticut, New Mexico, Ohio, Rhode Island, North Dakota, Colorado, New Jersey and Louisiana.

365. *See* Lawrence I. Weinstein, *Revisiting the Inevitability Doctrine: When Can a Former Employee Who Never Signed a Non-Compete Agreement nor Threatened to Use or Disclose Trade Secrets Be Prohibited from Working for a Competitor?* 21 Am. Jur. Trial Advoc. 211, 212 (1997).

for the court to apply the doctrine.[366] There, the court greatly expanded the range of trade secret misappropriation by upholding an inevitable disclosure injunction absent a noncompete agreement where it found that the defendant would inevitably disclose his former employer's trade secrets to his new employer.[367]

2.   Post–PepsiCo *Era*

Since the *PepsiCo* decision, the inevitable disclosure doctrine has not been applied as broadly as some commentators feared it would. For example, some litigants have obtained injunctions where a party uses confidential information for purposes other than those for which it was disclosed.[368] In contrast, courts have refused to grant injunctions in several cases where subsequent activities did not involve the subject matter of the confidential information.[369] Similar to these decisions, commentary about the inevitable disclosure doctrine has also been very mixed.[370]

A number of cases have been decided under the doctrine of inevitable disclosure on facts similar to that of *PepsiCo*. The majority of these cases have involved existing covenants not to compete.[371] The doctrine has been applied

---

366.   *See* PepsiCo, Inc. v. Redmond, 54 F.3d 1262, 1263–64 (7th Cir. 1995).

367.   The *PepsiCo* case is unlike a traditional trade secret misappropriation case because there was no claim that the former employee actually took a trade secret (e.g., a customer list) when he left PepsiCo. Instead, the case is based on the "threat" of misappropriation. The evidence was that the employee had received PepsiCo's confidential strategic plan, pricing structure, and marketing plans and that, in his new job, he would be performing similar duties for Quaker Oats. Also, because the employee had been dishonest in connection with his resignation from PepsiCo, the court did not believe the employee's testimony that he would not use PepsiCo's trade secrets in his new position. As a result of these factors, the court concluded that the employee would not be able to perform his duties at Quaker Oats without using the PepsiCo trade secret information. The court described its theory as "inevitable disclosure," meaning that the former employee would "inevitably" rely on PepsiCo's trade secrets in his new job.

368.   *See* Southwestern Energy Co. v. Eickenhorst, 955 F. Supp. 1078 (W.D. Ark. 1997); Ackerman v. Kimball International, Inc., 652 N.E.2d 507 (Ind. 1995); La Calhene, Inc. v. Spolyar, 938 F. Supp. 523 (W.D. Wis. 1996); Neveux v. Webcraft Technologies., Inc., 921 F. Supp. 1568 (E.D. Mich. 1996); Uncle B's Bakery, Inc. v. O'Rourke, 920 F. Supp. 1405 (N.D. Iowa 1996); Lumex, Inc. v. Highsmith, 919 F. Supp. 624 (E.D.N.Y. 1996); Branson Ultrasonics Corp. v. Stratman, 921 F. Supp. 909 (D. Conn. 1996); Merck & Co., Inc. v. Lyon, 941 F. Supp. 1443 (M.D.N.C. 1996).

369.   *See* Campbell Soup Co. v. Giles, 47 F.3d 467 (1st Cir. 1995); Glaxo Inc. v. Novopharm Ltd., 931 F. Supp. 1280 (E.D.N.C. 1996); FMC Corp. v. Cyprus Foote Mineral Co., 899 F. Supp. 1477 (W.D.N.C. 1995).

370.   *See* 74 N.Y.U. L. Rev. 575, *The Legal Infrastructure of High Technology Industrial Districts: Silicon Valley, Route 128, and Covenants Not to Compete* (Ronald Gilson compares the relationship between high-tech industrial districts such as the Silicon Valley, where noncompetition agreements are not enforced, and Massachusetts's Route 128, where they are enforced. He persuasively argues that the legal rules governing employee mobility influence the dynamics of high-technology districts by either encouraging rapid employee movement between employers to start-ups or discouraging such movement. Gilson argues that these knowledge spillovers have allowed Silicon Valley firms to thrive while Route 128 firms have deteriorated.). *See also* Brenda Sandberg, *After Uproar, Cal Supremes Depublish Trade Secrets Ruling* (wherein critics of the doctrine say that companies are trying to block start-ups or make it too expensive for them to set up shop).

371.   *See, e.g.*, Bridgestone/Firestone, Inc. v. Lockhart, 5 F. Supp. 2d 667, 680–82 (S.D. Ind. 1998) (refusing to grant an injunction in the presence of a covenant not to compete where there was no evidence

only a handful of times where no noncompete agreement was in place.[372] As these cases illustrate, where the employee has not signed a covenant not to compete, courts have been unwilling to grant an injunction on a theory of inevitability alone. Rather, they have required evidence, such as position similarity, competition between current and former employers and willingness of the employee to disclose, tending to show that misappropriation of trade secrets is more than simply "inevitable." In doing so, courts have struck an effective balance between the employee's right to choose his profession and the employer's right to protect its intellectual property, trade secrets included. Explicit guidance is needed, however, to ensure that this balance is maintained.

3. *California Snuffs Inevitable Disclosure Doctrine*

California law is typically very favorable of employees' rights to pursue their careers. On the other hand, in the briefly heralded case, *Electro Optical,* the California Court of Appeal for the Second District took a huge step by expressly adopting the inevitable disclosure doctrine, making it much more difficult for employees to roam between competing companies.[373] This was the first California jurisdiction to allow a trade secret owner to use the inevitable disclosure doctrine as a basis for proving a trade secret misappropriation, even though courts in other jurisdictions applying California law and some superior courts in California had found that the inevitable disclosure doctrine was recognized under the California Trade Secret Act.[374] Within months,

---

that the employee had or would disclose sensitive information.), and *see Lumex,* 919 F. Supp. at 625, 636 (granting an injunction where the employee signed a "Technical Information and Non-Competition Agreement").

372. *See Merck,* 941 F. Supp. at 1457, 1460–61; DoubleClick, Inc. v. Henderson, 1997 WL 731413, at 6 (N.Y. Sup. Ct. Nov. 7, 1997).

373. Electro Optical v. White, 90 Cal. Rptr. 2d 680, 685, ordered not to be officially published by Electro Optical Industries v. White, 2000 Cal. LEXIS 3536 (April 12, 2000) (The defendant in *Electro Optical,* Stephen White, was a sales manager for the company ("EOI"). White had held his position for 15 years and was a key contact between the company and its customers. White answered an advertisement placed by a competitor. This competitor, Santa Barbara Infrared ("SBI") hired White to create a list of potential customers for SBI and to develop a profile of SBI's competitors, and point out their strengths and weaknesses. After White resigned from EOI, the company filed a complaint contending that White would inevitably disclose EOI's confidential information in his new job. The appellate court affirmed the lower court's denial of EOI's request for an injunction on two grounds. First, much of the information did not constitute a trade secret. For example, the customer list did not qualify as a trade secret because there were only about 100 entities worldwide that purchased infrared test equipment and it would not be difficult to discover their identities. Additionally, EOI did not show that SBI could use this information or that White had the ability to disclose it. Second, EOI had not proven that it would suffer the requisite degree of harm if the injunction was not issued. In balancing the harm to each party, the court found that White would be unemployed for a period of time if the injunction were granted, but there was no evidence EOI would suffer any harm if the injunction were withheld.).

374. *See* Surgidev Corp v. Eye Technology Inc., 648 F. Supp. 661, 679 (D. Minn. 1986). The court apparently did not consider whether the doctrine conflicts with Cal. Bus. & Prof. Code § 16600, as the federal courts in California have held for sometime. Prior to the *Electro Optical* case, the California courts followed the traditional requirements for proving a misappropriation of trade secrets. The trade secret owner

however, the Supreme Court ordered the decision depublished, snuffing out the opportunity for companies to more easily block their employees from working for competitors.[375]

In the shadow of *Electro Optical* have come two recent decisions from the federal courts in California—decisions outrightly rejecting the theory of inevitable disclosure. *Danjaq LLC v. Sony Corp.*[376] involved an allegation of actual misappropriation of trade secrets relating to a "James Bond" motion picture. The court stated in footnote one, "Lacking proof of actual disclosure and actual use, the Plaintiffs fill-in the gaps in the record with the 'inevitable disclosure doctrine' articulated in *PepsiCo.* Plaintiffs' reliance on the inevitable disclosure doctrine is misplaced. *PepsiCo* is not the law of the State of California or the Ninth Circuit."[377] The Court of Appeal in *Whyte v. Schlage Lock Co.* confirms, "the inevitable disclosure doctrine cannot be used as a substitute for proving actual or threatened misappropriation of trade secrets."[378]   Other jurisdictions outside of California have also been hostile toward the inevitable disclosure doctrine.

4. Conclusion: The Great Debate

Some commentators view the inevitable disclosure doctrine as a blessing to businesses by allowing them to proactively protect their confidential information before the information is disclosed.[379] However, opponents assert that the doctrine's harmful effects, primarily that it restricts employees from freely changing jobs, outweighs the benefit.[380] The expansion of the inevitable disclosure doctrine involves costs and benefits similar to the enforcement of the noncompetition agreements for emerging businesses. The doctrine's application impedes the flow of new talent to these budding businesses. The implications are even greater when applied to start-up companies founded by technology workers. With the pace of innovation in the market, a constraint of even limited duration can prevent a start-up company from delivering an

---

had to prove that the alleged infringing party was in wrongful possession of its trade secrets and also had the capabilities to exploit the information. *See* Bayer Corp. v. Roche Molecular Systems, Inc., 72 F. Supp. 2d 1111, 1120 (N.D. Cal. 1999).

375.   As a result of the depublication, the opinion cannot be cited in California as authority that the inevitable disclosure doctrine is the law, and the order cannot be cited as authority that it is not. Cal. Rules of Ct., 977 and 979 (e).

376.   Danjaq LLC v. Sony Corp., 50 U.S.P.Q.2d (BNA) 1638 (C.D. Cal. Mar. 12, 1999).

377.   *Danjaq* was followed in Computer Sciences Corp. v. Computer Associates Int'l, Inc., 1999 U.S. Dist. LEXIS 21803, 1999 WL 675446, 16 (C.D. Cal. Aug. 12, 1999) (reiterating that inevitable disclosure doctrine "is not the law of the State of California or the Ninth Circuit").

378.   Whyte v. Schlage Lock Co., 101 Cal. App. 4th 1443 (Ct. App. 2002). *See also*, Bourns, Inc. v. Raychem Corp., 331 F.3d 704 (2003).

379.   At best, the trade secret owner can recover the information, suffering only the diminution of value for the time it was used by the competitor. At worst, the trade secret can be lost forever, since once the information is disclosed it disperses immediately into the public domain.

380.   *Supra.*

innovative and competitive product during that window of time when its idea is novel and potentially profitable. Somewhat problematic for the emerging company is that it may actually benefit from the protections of the inevitable disclosure doctrine once it begins to compete within the marketplace. In an industry heavily reliant on the intellectual capital of its workforce, a company's greatest strength and point of vulnerability is its employee base. Once the emerging company begins to compete in the marketplace, it feels the same need to protect its proprietary information and valuable human capital from hungry competitors. Thus, the inevitable disclosure doctrine offers a bittersweet choice for a company of the new millennium.

G. Remedies for Misappropriation

1. Damages

According to Section 3 of UTSA:

(a)   Except to the extent that a material and prejudicial change of position prior to acquiring knowledge or reason to know of misappropriation renders a monetary recovery inequitable, a complainant is entitled to recover damages for misappropriation. Damages can include both the actual loss caused by misappropriation and the unjust enrichment caused by misappropriation that is not taken into account in computing actual loss. In lieu of damages measured by any other methods, the damages caused by misappropriation may be measured by imposition of liability for a reasonable royalty for a misappropriator's unauthorized disclosure or use of a trade secret.

(b)   If willful and malicious misappropriation exists, the court may award exemplary damages in an amount not exceeding twice any award made under subsection (a).

Monetary recovery for trade secret misappropriation is appropriate only for the period in which information is entitled to trade secret protection.[381] Section 3(a) adopts the principle of a line of trade secret cases allowing for recovery of both a trade secret complainant's *actual losses* and the misappropriator's *unjust benefit* resulting from misappropriation.[382] However, UTSA strictly

---

381.   ULA Trade Secret S.3, Uniform Trade Secrets Act § 3, *Comment* 1990 Main Volume.

382.   *See* Tri-Tron International v. A.A. Velto, 525 F.2d 432, 437 (9th Cir. 1975) (in formulating UTSA, the National Conference of Commissioners on Uniform State Laws adopted the principle of *Tri-Tron* and other then recent cases, which held that the measure of damages for trade secret misappropriation was not limited to the misappropriator's profits, but also included the victim's loss that might in no way be related to the benefits accruing to the misappropriator. Citing the 9th Circuit's prior decision in Clark v. Bunker, 453 F.2d 1006 (9th Cir. 1972), the *Tri-Tron* court went on to say that the proper measure of damage is not limited to either plaintiff's loss or defendant's benefit, but includes a combination of both where the circumstances call for such in order to make the plaintiff whole. *Accord* Telex Corp. v. International Business Machines Corp., 510 F.2d 894, 931 (10th Cir. 1975) (analyzing *Bunker*). *See also* Reingold v. Swiftships Inc., 210 F.3d 320, 323 (5th Cir. 2000) (The Louisiana Uniform Trade Secrets Act (LUTSA) damages remedy provision is a replica of the original 1979 UTSA Section 3. Both UTSA and the LUTSA adopt the principle of cases that

prohibits double counting (i.e., counting the same item as both a complainant's loss and a misappropriator's unjust benefit).[383]

If a court finds that willful and malicious misappropriation exists, UTSA Section 3(b) authorizes the court to award a complainant exemplary damages, in addition to actual recovery under Section 3(a), in an amount not exceeding twice that recovery.[384] Thus, where compensatory damages are sought and awarded for trade secret misappropriation, courts in jurisdictions that have adopted this provision of UTSA are empowered to award punitive damages.[385]

As an alternative to all other methods of measuring damages caused by a misappropriator's past conduct, a complainant has the general option of requesting that damages be based on a demonstrably reasonable royalty for a misappropriator's unauthorized disclosure or use of a trade secret instead of actual damages.[386] In order to justify this alternative measure of damages, the amount of a reasonable royalty must be demonstrated by competent evidence.[387] Section 4 of UTSA provides that if (a) a claim of misappropriation is made in bad faith, (b) a motion to terminate an injunction is made or resisted in bad faith or (c) willful and malicious misappropriation exists, the court may award reasonable attorney's fees to the prevailing party.[388]

2. *Injunctive Relief*

Under Section 2 of UTSA:

(a)   Actual or threatened misappropriation may be enjoined. Upon application to the court, an injunction shall be terminated when the trade secret ceased to exist, but the injunction may be continued for an additional reasonable period of time in order to eliminate commercial advantage that otherwise would be derived from the misappropriation.

(b)   In exceptional circumstances, an injunction may condition future use upon payment of a reasonable royalty for no longer than the period

---

allow recovery of both a complainant's actual losses and a misappropriator's unjust benefit resulting from misappropriation. Likewise, both UTSA and the LUTSA adopt an express prohibition against counting the same item as both a loss to a complainant and an unjust benefit to a misappropriator.).

383.   ULA Trade Secret S.3, Uniform Trade Secrets Act § 3, *Comment* 1990 Main Volume.

384.   ULA Trade Secret S.3, Uniform Trade Secrets Act § 3(b).

385.   In sustaining a $75,000 punitive damages award, the *Tri-Tron* court noted that the district court correctly awarded punitive damages because appellants obtained appellee's trade secret by abusing appellee's confidence in them with respect to negotiations to sell appellee's device; appellants wrongfully appropriated appellee's trade secret to their own use; and in dealing with appellee, several of the appellants misrepresented their intent and were conniving and underhanded. *Accord, Clark*, 453 F.2d at 1009–12. Roton Barrier, Inc. v. The Stanley Works, 79 F.3d 1112 (Mo. 1996) (competitor's misappropriation of manufacturer's trade secret did not justify punitive damages award because competition, rather than malice against the manufacturer, motivated competitor to devise a plan for entering the market).

386.   ULA Trade Secret S.3, Uniform Trade Secrets Act § 3, *Comment* 1990 Main Volume.

387.   *Id.*

388.   ULA Trade Secret S.4, Uniform Trade Secrets Act § 4, *Comment* 1990 Main Volume.

of time for which the use could have been prohibited. Exceptional circumstances include, but are not limited to, a material and prejudicial change of position prior to acquiring knowledge or reason to know of misappropriation that renders a prohibitive injunction inequitable.

(c)   In appropriate circumstances, affirmative acts to protect a trade secret may be compelled by court order.

Injunctions are frequently sought to restrain future use and disclosure of misappropriated trade secrets and the moving party must satisfy the requirements for obtaining injunctive relief.[389] The general principle of UTSA Sections 2(a) and (b) is that an injunction should last for as long as is necessary, but no longer, to eliminate the commercial advantage or lead time with respect to good faith competitors that a person has obtained through misappropriation.[390] Accordingly, an injunction should terminate when a former trade secret becomes either generally known to good faith competitors or generally knowable to them because of the lawful availability of products that can be reverse engineered to reveal the trade secret.[391] In the proper circumstances, monetary relief may be appropriate in addition to a grant of injunctive relief.[392] However, if a *person charged with misappropriation* has materially and prejudicially changed position in reliance on trade secret knowledge acquired in good faith and without reason to know that the trade secret was actually misappropriated by someone else, the same considerations that may justify denial of injunctive relief may also justify denying monetary relief.[393]

Section 2(b) contemplates the special situation in which a misappropriator's future trade secret use will damage the trade secret owner, but an injunction against future use is nonetheless inappropriate in light of exceptional

---

389.   ULA Trade Secret S.2, Uniform Trade Secrets Act § 2. *See* Litton Systems, Inc. v. Sundstrand Corp., 750 F.2d 952, 955, 958–59 (Fed. Cir. 1984) (One seeking a preliminary injunction to impede use of an allegedly misappropriated trade secret has the burden of demonstrating either (a) a combination of probable success on the merits and the possibility of irreparable injury or (b) that serious questions are raised and the balance of hardship tips sharply in favor of issuing the desired injunction. The moving party must carry its basic burden of pleading and showing facts to establish the existence of subject matter capable of protection as a trade secret in the manner provided for in the requested injunction. Ordinarily, a preliminary injunction will not issue in a trade secrets case until the alleged trade secrets have been identified with sufficient particularity. Matters of broad public knowledge or of general knowledge in an industry cannot constitute a trade secret.); Ciena Corp. v. Jarrard, 203 F.3d 312, 322 (4th Cir. 2000) (In entering a preliminary injunction, a court must consider (1) the likelihood of irreparable harm to the plaintiff if the preliminary injunction is denied, (2) the likelihood of harm to the defendant if the requested relief is granted, (3) the likelihood that the plaintiff will succeed on the merits and (4) the public interest.).

390.   ULA Trade Secret S.2, Uniform Trade Secrets Act § 2, *Comment* 1990 Main Volume. *See* Lamb-Weston, Inc. v. McCain Foods, LTD., 941 F.2d 970, 974 (9th Cir. 1991) (An injunction in a trade secret case seeks to protect the secrecy of misappropriated information and to eliminate any unfair head start the defendant may have gained. Thus, a worldwide injunction in this case is appropriate because it places the defendant in the position it would have occupied if the breach of confidence had not occurred prior to public disclosure of the trade secret.).

391.   ULA Trade Secret S.2, Uniform Trade Secrets Act § 2, *Comment* 1990 Main Volume.

392.   ULA Trade Secret S.3, Uniform Trade Secrets Act § 3, *Comment* 1990 Main Volume.

393.   *Id.*

circumstances.[394] Such circumstances may include those where an overriding public interest requires the court to deny a prohibitory injunction against future use, or a situation in which someone reasonably and in good faith relies on their acquisition of a misappropriated trade secret, without reason to know that the trade secret's prior misappropriation would result in an injunction against future use thereof.[395] In such cases, courts have discretion under Section 2(b) to grant an injunction conditioning future use of a disputed trade secret on payment of a reasonable royalty rather than issue an injunction prohibiting future use of the trade secret at issue.[396]

With respect to royalty awards, it is important to distinguish a royalty order injunction under Section 2(b) from the reasonable royalty alternative under Section 3(a).[397] Most notable in this regard, the Section 2(b) royalty order injunction is appropriate only in exceptional circumstances; whereas a reasonable royalty measure of damages under Section 3(a) is a general option.[398] Also, a Section 2(b) royalty order injunction regulates a misappropriator's future conduct; Section 3(a) damages, including a reasonable royalty grant, are awarded for a misappropriator's past conduct.[399] Thus, both remedies cannot properly be awarded for the same conduct.[400] Moreover, if a royalty order injunction is appropriate (e.g., because a person materially and prejudicially changed position before knowing that its trade secret was acquired from a misappropriator), then damages should not be awarded for conduct that occurred before the person seeking relief knew that he or she acquired a misappropriated trade secret.[401] Finally, Section 2(c) authorizes *mandatory* injunctions to require that a misappropriator return the fruits of its misappropriation to the aggrieved party.[402]

---

394. ULA Trade Secret S.2, Uniform Trade Secrets Act § 2, *Comment* 1990 Main Volume.

395. *Id. See* Republic Aviation Corp. v. Schenk, 152 U.S.P.Q. 830 (N.Y. Sup. Ct. 1967) (illustrating the public interest justification for denying prohibitory injunctive relief).

396. ULA Trade Secret S.2, Uniform Trade Secrets Act § 2, *Comment* 1990 Main Volume.

397. *Id.*

398. ULA Trade Secret S.3, Uniform Trade Secrets Act § 3, *Comment* 1990 Main Volume.

399. *Id.*

400. *Id.*

401. *Id.*

402. ULA Trade Secret S.2, Uniform Trade Secrets Act § 2, *Comment* 1990 Main Volume.

Product Development and Distribution

Robert L. Brown

Greenebaum Doll & McDonald PLLC
Louisville, KY

Alan S. Gutterman

Gutterman Law & Business
Piedmont, CA

Contents

Product Development and Distribution

9.01 Preliminary Considerations

In this chapter, we deal with the development and distribution of a company's products. We describe agreements for the development, manufacture, sale and distribution of products. We also touch on the legal issues of these agreements.

9.02 Development Agreements

Emerging companies have a number of options in developing their technology.

A. Founder

First, to the extent that the founder has already undertaken some or all of the development before the start-up was formed, the founder should contribute the technology to the company. This will be covered by the shareholders agreement (if a corporation), operating agreement (for limited liability company) or partnership agreement.

B. Internal

Second, and most obvious, the company may bear all the expense of development and keep the development inside. In this case, the only development agreements are with the employees who will be doing the work. Such agreements should include explicit statements that any work developed by the employee is owned by the company. They should also include statements that the employee will assist the company in filing any reports or applications needed to show that the company owns the technology. As a precaution or fallback if courts do not uphold these statements, the agreement should give the company the right to use the technology at no charge. Counsel should review employment agreements, since, as noted in Chapter 1 (Starting a New Business), some states do not recognize blanket assignments or put severe limitations on what they will accept. **Exhibit 10B** is an example of an employment agreement providing such protections for companies.

C. Research and Development

Third, some or all of the development could be outsourced to outside parties. Research and development arrangements usually involve a separate contractual agreement between the party providing funding for the research, sometimes referred to as the "sponsor," and the researching party with responsibility for conducting the research project. The research project may focus on the development of existing technology owned by one or both of the parties. It may also include one or more additional agreements relating to various aspects of commercializing the technology or products being developed.

Such research and development arrangements can take a variety of forms. In some cases, the research agreement is simply a "fee-for-service" arrangement that calls for the sponsor to pay a fee to the researching party to conduct specified work over a fixed period of time. **Exhibit 9A** is an example of a development agreement. In other situations, the research agreement is one of several agreements in a much more complex set of economic relationships between the parties. The following list provides examples of different fee-for-service agreements:

- A private sponsor may provide funding to a university for basic research in areas of mutual interest. The university receives fee income for the research work and, in some cases, royalties from the commercialization of products derived from the research work. The private sponsor gains access to "cutting-edge" basic research in new areas and to the skills of researchers in the academic community.
- A larger firm engaged in the distribution of technology-based products may enter into a research agreement with a smaller firm to provide funding for the smaller firm to develop new products that can be incorporated into the large firm's product line. The smaller firm will receive a research fee and revenues from the sale of the products to the larger firm.
- Joint venture arrangements may include a program of research activities that are to be jointly engaged in by the joint venturers for the benefit of the joint venture and each of the participants. For example, both parties may

conduct research to develop products that will be marketed by the joint venture in a specified geographic territory. In addition, the joint venture might license the technology to each of the joint venturers for use in areas that fall outside of the joint venture's mission.

- A large firm may make an investment in a smaller firm to permit the smaller firm to continue its existing research and development activities. In addition, the smaller firm may enter into a specific research agreement with the larger firm to develop products of specific interest to the larger firm, with the larger firm providing any required additional financing in the form of loans or advances against projected royalties.

In negotiating research and development arrangements, the parties must consider the following issues: scope and content of the research program; budget for conducting the research program; manner in which the research program will be staffed by the researching party; contributions of technology, services and materials that may be made by the parties to complete the research program; and any other arrangements regarding further work relating to the commercialization of the technologies and products created during the research program.

Of particular importance is the allocation of ownership and usage rights with respect to the technology developed during the research program. On the one hand, the sponsor will want to own any work performed by the subcontractor. On the other hand, the researcher will want to retain ownership of any technology it has already developed or is using for other clients. The biggest hurdle will be determining who owns technology resulting from improvements to the researcher's technology that falls within the scope of what is being developed for the sponsor. Both sides will lay claim to this technology. This is an important battle for the emerging company to win. Otherwise it may prove difficult for the emerging company to claim ownership to the technology on which its product is based.

D.   R&D Partnership

A fourth strategy is the research and development partnership, or "R&D partnership." As noted in Chapter 4 (Tax Aspects of Forming and Organizing a New Business), an R&D partnership uses capital contributed by outside investors to finance research work by a firm ("start-up") usually with previously developed, similar technology. A typical R&D partnership is arranged in the following manner:

- The start-up contributes the base technology to the R&D partnership.
- Investors contribute capital as limited partners.
- The start-up performs research work for the benefit of the R&D partnership that approximates in value the amount contributed by the investors.
- Investors receive a return on their investment from royalties on the sale of products using the technology developed in the research program

The start-up generally has a right to "buy-out" the interests of the investors at a set price—either fixed or based on a formula. R&D partnerships provide start-ups with the opportunity to finance development work without using their own funds. The risk that the development work will be unsuccessful is shifted to investors.

E.   R&D Subsidiary

In response to some of the drawbacks associated with R&D partnerships, some companies have used a fifth approach—contributing the base technology to a new wholly owned subsidiary. Capital is raised by a public offering of "units" that consist of callable shares of common stock of the new subsidiary and warrants to purchase shares of common stock of the sponsor. The start-up performs the development work on behalf of the subsidiary. The shares of the subsidiary's common stock, it is hoped, appreciate in value on completion of the development work. The "call" feature allows the start-up to repurchase the technology from the subsidiary at a fixed price. Investors share in the success of the technology, however, through the warrant component of the investment.

9.03   Manufacturing, Supply and License Agreements

After developing the product, the next task for an emerging company is to get its product manufactured. Its choices fall into two categories: internal and external.

A.   Internal Manufacturing

If manufacturing is done internally, little documentation is required other than the development team providing the manufacturing team with detailed specs. The sales department may also be involved in creating a time schedule for meeting customer needs. If raw material suppliers are involved, their obligations to provide specified materials on certain dates should be well documented.

B.   External Manufacturing

Another approach is to have manufacturing done externally. If so, a detailed agreement requiring the manufacturer to keep confidential anything it learns from the emerging company is important. The agreement should also state that the technology provided by the start-up is owned by it, with the manufacturer releasing any rights or claims. As with supplier agreements, detailed specs and delivery terms should be included. **Exhibit 9B** is an example of a manufacturing agreement. It can also be adapted to a supply agreement.

Many start-ups look to their suppliers and manufacturers for more than production; they also obtain significant financial assistance from them. For example, a vendor willing to accept net 30, 60 or 90 day payment is a valuable ally, particularly if the emerging company has a quick turnaround on its products and gets paid net 15 or 30 days. Delayed vendor terms allow the emerging company to use supplier credit instead of debt or equity. The producer in essence pays for the financing. Some suppliers are willing to accept such terms if they believe the emerging company has a good chance of success and that they will be able to grow with it.

C.   License

A third approach is a non-exclusive license that is granted by the party that developed the products and the accompanying technology (the "developer") to a larger company (the "senior party") that allows the senior party to manufacture the products and then sell the products to end users. The developer would be entitled to a royalty on sales made by the senior party. The developer would remain free to manufacture the products itself and the senior party will usually be obligated to purchase some materials from the developer over the term of the agreement.

Royalties received by the developer from sales made by the senior party can be used for the development of new products, as well as to allow the developer to "ramp up" its own manufacturing capabilities. Also, use of the senior party as a manufacturer allows the developer to have a sufficient volume of products available to permit it to begin to construct its own distribution network. Moreover, the senior party becomes a guaranteed purchaser for some number of products over the term of the agreement. Finally, the solid relationship with a larger company enhances the credibility and reputation of the developer and allows it to gain access to new financing. Some of the key terms of a license agreement are discussed below.

1.   Products

As with any form of licensing or distribution arrangement, careful consideration must be given to defining the products that are to be the subject of the agreement. The process begins by defining the basic type of product, such as a 5-¼" half-height Winchester technology based disk drive, and then describing how any new or improved versions of the basic product are going to be included in the arrangement. For example, the parties may define licensed products to include any version of the basic product as to which commercial production commences within a specified time period following the date of the agreement. In other cases, the parties may include newer models to the extent that they continue to fall within a specified range of performance characteristics.

2. *Manufacturing Activities*

In order for the senior party to commence and continue manufacturing the licensed products, the agreement must provide for a license of the developer's patents and other intellectual property rights to the senior party for the purposes described in the agreement. It should also include the actual transfer of technical information, such as trade secrets, needed to build and manufacture the products. In addition, the developer should agree to provide some training to the senior party's engineers regarding the use of the technical information. The parties will also attempt to work together to minimize the costs of raw materials and other inputs in the manufacturing process.

a. Transfer of Technical Information

The agreement should obligate the developer to transfer to the senior party all of the technical information that the senior party needs to manufacture the licensed products on the scale contemplated by the parties. Among the items that may be delivered are the following:

- Specifications of the developer's prototype of the products that are to be manufactured
- Assembly drawings and parts drawings
- Purchase specifications of parts and components
- Bill of materials
- Assembly, manufacturing and test instructions
- Test and inspection standards
- Test and operational software, including both object and source code
- Part and component sourcing
- Die and tool drawings

The developer will usually be asked to provide some representations and warranties to the senior party regarding the technical information. For example, the developer may represent to the senior party that the technical information is in sufficient detail to allow an experienced manufacturer of items similar to the licensed products to be able to manufacture, install, maintain and operate the products or any modified, improved or derivative versions thereof.

b. Training and Assistance

The transfer of the technical information should also be facilitated by additional training and assistance that will be provided by the developer to the senior party. For example, the developer may agree to provide training to a reasonable number of engineers and technicians of the senior party, as well as ongoing technical assistance during the term of the agreement. Some of the training and assistance may be provided free of charge or at the developer's cost.

Since both parties will be involved in the manufacture of the licensed products, it makes sense for them to seek out ways in which they can cooperate in reducing the costs of the various raw materials, manufacturing facilities, maintenance and other items that are important to the manufacturing process. As such, the parties should agree to cooperate in the exchange of data, the development of joint procedures, and the joint purchasing of supplies, equipment and raw materials. Also, if one party is in a position to best satisfy the supply requirements of the other party, the price of such supplies should generally be kept to an amount that is no greater than the cost to the supplier plus any reasonable handling charges.

3. Scope

The developer will grant the senior party a non-exclusive license to use the developer's patents and technical information to manufacture, use, lease and sell the licensed products in a specified territory. In turn, the senior party will generally grant the developer the right to use senior party's patents as they relate to improvements or enhancements that the senior party might make to the licensed products during the term of the agreement. As noted above, the senior party would be required to pay a royalty to the developer based on a specified percentage of the net sales price of products sold by the senior party. The senior party's license to the developer is usually royalty-free.

4. Senior Party's Obligations

In addition to the royalties received from the sale of products by the senior party, the developer will be able to receive income from the sale of products to the senior party. The parties should specify the number of products that must be purchased, the price to be charged for the products, the manner of payment and any requirements as to forecasted purchases or minimum orders.

a. Pricing

The price that the senior party will be charged for the products will generally be established by reference to the prices that the developer is charging to similar customers for any like amount of products at the time of delivery. For example, the agreement may state that the purchase price for the products shall be the developer's original equipment manufacturer list price for comparable quantities at the time of delivery. In most cases, the senior party will receive the benefits of a "most favored customer" clause that obligates the developer to charge the senior party the best price offered to any customer, irrespective of discount.

b. Payment

Payment for products purchased under the agreement will usually be in two stages. The senior party will usually agree to pay a portion (e.g., 50%) of the total dollar amount ordered for a particular month at the time that the order is given to the developer, which is generally 60 to 90 days prior to the delivery date. The amount paid in advance will be based on the purchase price as it would have been if the products were delivered on the date of the order. The balance will be due within a specified number of days (e.g., 30, 45 or 60) following delivery and will be adjusted to reflect the actual price at the time of delivery. The developer will retain a security interest in the products until the senior party makes full payment.

c. Forecasts

The parties should agree on an order forecast to permit proper planning by the developer. Forecasted orders should be laid out in monthly increments, although the senior party will generally have the right to delay or accelerate shipments within specified limitations. For example, the agreement might provide that the senior party will have the right to reschedule any forecasted order by giving 90 days' written notice, provided that the delay or acceleration of shipments in any calendar quarter does not exceed 25% of the amounts specified in the original forecast for delivery during any three month period.

5. Senior Party's Obligations

The developer will also have the right to purchase products from the senior party. For example, the agreement might provide that the developer shall have the right to purchase from the senior party, under the developer's own private label, products manufactured by the senior party pursuant to the license. The developer would be entitled to the best price, including all discounts, terms and conditions on which the senior party offers such products to any other customer, irrespective of quantity.

D. OEM

A fourth alternative is an OEM (original equipment manufacturer) relationship. The principal will agree to sell goods to the distributor who, in turn, will add some "value" to the goods, such as enhancements or additional applications, and then sell the "value-added" products to its customers. An OEM agreement usually involves detailed negotiations regarding the specific requirements of the OEM with regard to the products, as well as the terms on which the products will be sold to the OEM. Properly structured, an OEM relationship can provide smaller firms with a significant customer for its products at a time when it may be struggling to develop its own distribution network and stable of customer accounts.

An OEM relationship combines elements of three distinct strategic business arrangements: a manufacturing and supply agreement wherein one party, the "manufacturer," actually makes products that are to be supplied to the other party, the "OEM"; a product purchase agreement, which includes the terms that will govern the sale of the products by the manufacturer to the OEM; and a distribution agreement under which the OEM distributes the products purchased from the manufacturer as part of the line of products otherwise sold by the OEM. The parties to any form of OEM arrangement must deal with most of the issues that exist in separate product purchase and distribution relationships. In addition, the parties must deal with the unique considerations that arise when the products are to be customized to the special needs of the OEM. In the following paragraphs, we cover some of the key terms in OEM agreements.

1. Product Specifications

One of the key threshold issues in an OEM relationship is reaching agreement on the specifications of the products that are to be produced and sold by the manufacturer to the OEM. The process begins with the OEM's submission of design requirements, which are used by the manufacturer to develop a prototype version of the anticipated product. While the manufacturer will often agree to assume the costs of developing the prototype, it will require reimbursement from the OEM for any additional expenses relating to subsequent adaptations or changes that might be made in the original specifications. In some cases, the OEM may even be required to pay for the cost of the original prototype if it fails to purchase a sufficient volume of products.

As with any form of distribution arrangement, the OEM generally bargains for the right to sell all of the current and future products of the manufacturer. Obviously, there will be a good deal of reluctance on the part of the manufacturer to grant such broad rights to the OEM. One compromise is to include certain specified enhancements as part of the original agreement, but provide that any other products will only be covered by a "right of first negotiation" that obligates the manufacturer to negotiate in good faith with the OEM regarding a new agreement on additional products.

2. *Product Manufacture and Acceptance*

Once the product design has been agreed on, the parties must then agree on the procedures that are to be followed as to manufacture of the products and acceptance of the finished items by the OEM. The agreement will set out the requirements with respect to production, inspection and testing of products, as well as the rights of the OEM to audit the quality control procedures utilized by the manufacturer. The manufacturer may seek limitations on the OEM's ability to delay acceptance of products by requiring that delivered products that have not been rejected within a specified period will be deemed to have been accepted.

The OEM may demand a license to manufacture the products itself in the event a substantial amount of the manufacturer's products fail to conform to the specifications established by the OEM. The manufacturer will be reluctant to grant such a license in situations other than bankruptcy or insolvency; however, it may be necessary to grant the OEM a non-exclusive license that comes into effect on the occurrence of certain events. For example, a non-exclusive royalty-bearing license may be granted if the manufacturer is unable to adhere to the quality control standards relating to the products. If the manufacturer is not able to meet its commitments due to a cessation of its business activities, the manufacturing license may be royalty free. In most cases, the license only extends to the manufacture of the number of products that were originally contemplated by each of the parties and terminates at the time that the agreement would have otherwise expired.

3. *Pricing and Ordering*

The issues relating to pricing and ordering in any OEM relationship are similar to those in any other type of product purchase arrangement. The OEM will seek retroactive discounts based on the volume of products purchased, and both parties will seek adjustments in the purchase price to take into account any increases or decreases in the cost of components. Firm orders will be placed in accordance with an agreed-on monthly or quarterly schedule, and forecasts will be used in order to manage the long-term production schedule and allow the manufacturer to take advantage of volume purchases of components. Cancellations and changes in delivery dates are handled in the same manner as in any distribution agreement.

4. *Spare Parts*

The OEM may have legitimate concerns about any price increases for spare parts that may occur during the term of the relationship, since they may have an effect on the OEM's net profit margin for the products that it eventually sells to its customers. In some cases, the OEM may want to negotiate a cap on the prices for spare parts, perhaps in the form of a covenant that the total price of the material for spare parts, proprietary parts and components that may be required to actually build the manufacturer's product will not exceed a specified percentage of the current price charged by the manufacturer for the finished product.

5. Product Warranties

Warranty issues in the OEM area may be somewhat complicated if the products are incorporated into other goods that are manufactured or assembled by the OEM. For example, manufacturers will be unwilling to assume any responsibility for the components or parts that may be supplied by the OEM. Also, the obligations of the manufacturer with respect to infringement claims by third parties will not extend to components, specifications, modifications or designs supplied by OEM, unless approved by the manufacturer.

When the manufacturer's products involve software, it is generally customary for the manufacturer to provide the OEM with updates, which are mandatory engineering changes made to correct errors that lead to product failure, at no extra charge. On the other hand, if the manufacturer develops software enhancements that are not required to prevent product failure, but do result in increased functionality or improved performance, the OEM will usually have the right to purchase the enhancements at a price that is to be negotiated when they are available. In some cases, the pricing of the enhancements may be made subject to a "most favored nation" clause.

6. Confidentiality

In an OEM relationship, both parties may have access to certain proprietary technical and design information relating to the other's products. Accordingly, it is important for the OEM agreement to contain the usual covenants on maintaining confidentiality of each party's trade secrets. For its part, the manufacturer will want the OEM to agree to cause its agents, subcontractors and customers to adhere to the confidentiality provisions. In no event, however, will the parties be required to protect any information known by it at the time of the agreement, any information rightfully received by it from a third party, information developed by the party independently of the other party, or information that generally becomes known to the public other than as a result of a breach of the agreement.

One area of specific concern to the manufacturer in the OEM relationship is the possibility that the OEM might attempt to "reverse engineer" the products by inspecting or analyzing those products of the manufacturer that are otherwise available in the marketplace. Reverse engineering is generally considered to be a permissible exception to protectable trade secret interests. As such, the manufacturer may seek an additional covenant from the OEM that restricts the OEM from reverse engineering the products supplied by the manufacturer.

7.   Termination

Termination issues in the OEM area are unique in that the manufacturer's products usually are an essential feature of other products or services provided by the OEM to its end users. The OEM will want to be sure that it has some access to the products, service and technology provided by the manufacturer prior to the date of termination, assuming that the termination is not due to a material default by the OEM. The parties often agree that the manufacturer will continue to provide some support for a minimum period of time following termination, including field services, spare parts and software updates. If, due to bankruptcy or some other event that results in the cessation of the manufacturer's business activities, the manufacturer is unable to provide all of the required support, the OEM will be given a license to manufacture the required products and spare parts.

9.04   Sales Contracts

From a downstream perspective, some customers may be willing to prepay a portion or all of a purchase price. They may even pay a non-recurring research and development fee that will enable a start-up to develop a product they need. Emerging companies may even persuade customers to purchase all their requirements. If so, a long-term commitment (particularly from a prominent company) may encourage lenders and investors to provide financing. In some cases, a prominent customer may want to invest in a start-up. Many have sophisticated investment departments looking for such opportunities.

Another downstream or customer approach is for an emerging company with a single or narrow product selection to contract with a larger company with an established line of products and a strong distribution network. Under such a strategic partnering, the established company could purchase and resell goods manufactured by the smaller company. In order to gain greater access to the smaller company's technology and provide additional capital that the smaller company can use, the larger company might make an equity investment in the smaller company, on terms similar to those in venture capital investment transactions. In some cases, the larger company may receive an option to acquire the smaller company at a later date.

Regardless of whether the sales contract uses one of the above financing techniques, it should set out the obligations of the emerging company as seller and its customer as buyer. The most important terms are what is being sold, for how much and when. The biggest arguments are usually over specifications, which may be attached or referred to, and warranties that the seller gives about the quality of its products. The seller will want to limit its representations and warranties about the products, its covenants on what it will do in the future if the goods turn out to be defective, and its indemnities to reimburse the buyer for injuries or damages suffered by the buyer or the buyer's customers. Some sales contracts may be short documents that incorporate standard sales terms, such as **Exhibit 9C**. Others, such as **Exhibit 9D**, may be more detailed.

A. Commercial Laws Governing Sale of Goods

In the United States, transactions that involve the sale of goods are subject to the provisions of the Uniform Commercial Code ("UCC"), which is a model act that has been adopted with certain variations in all of the states except Louisiana. Article Two of the UCC applies to the "sale" of "goods." A sale occurs whenever title to goods passes from the seller to the buyer for a price. Goods are defined as "all things" movable at the time the contract is formed, a definition broad enough to include transactions involving all tangible objects and chattels, including raw materials, work-in-process, building materials, standard as well as specially manufactured goods, farm products, inventory items, consumer goods and equipment.[1] Other articles of the UCC will apply to various aspects of a sale transaction, including Article Six relating to "bulk sales" and Article Nine relating to "secured transactions."

Article Two of the UCC deals with all of the fundamental issues that arise in a sale of goods transaction, including the following:

- Formation of the sales agreement, which can occur by using standard forms setting out the basic terms of the transaction, through negotiations leading to an agreement that is customized to the needs of the parties, and by oral discussions and negotiations that ultimately create an enforceable contract.[2]
- The time or event when the risk of loss or destruction of the goods passes from the seller to the buyer. If the parties have not reached their own agreement regarding the risk of loss, the default rules in the UCC will apply, and, as a general rule, the UCC provisions place the risk of loss on the party who was in the best position to have prevented the loss, on the party who was at fault, or on the party with the broadest insurance coverage.[3]
- The general obligations of the seller under the contract of sale, including the seller's obligations to tender the goods in the manner provided in the contract and to provide goods that conform to the specifications in the contract.
- The warranty obligations of the seller, including warranties of title, non-infringement, merchantability and fitness for a particular use, and the

---

1. UCC § 2-105(1).

2. However, UCC § 2-201(1), which is the UCC's "statute of frauds" provision, states that any contract for the sale of goods "for the price of $500 or more is not enforceable . . . unless there is some writing sufficient to indicate that a contract has been made" and which is signed by the party against whom enforcement is sought.

3. See UCC §§ 2-509, 2-510 and 2-319.

manner in which the seller might disclaim or otherwise limit any warranty that is otherwise provided for under the UCC.

- The general obligations of the buyer under the contract of sale, including the obligations to pay the purchase price when it becomes due and to accept goods that conform to the specifications in the contract and that are tendered in the manner agreed by the parties.
- The remedies for breach of the contract of sale. For the seller, these might include the right to receive from the buyer adequate assurances of performance, the right to retain a security interest in the goods, the right to sue for the contract price, the right to receive damages for nonacceptance or repudiation and the right to resell any conforming goods that were not accepted by the buyer. For the buyer, remedies include damages for non-delivery, the right to reject nonconforming goods, and the right to purchase substitute goods and recover from the seller any additional costs incurred due to the need to purchase such substitute goods.

In addition to the UCC provisions, sales transactions, including the activities of sales agents and distributors, will be subject to federal and state statutes that proscribe the use of deceptive acts and practice in the sale of goods. For example, the Federal Trade Commission, acting pursuant to Section 5 of the Federal Trade Commission Act, has the authority to identify and regulate unfair acts or practices, deceptive acts or practices or false advertising. Comparable, and often overlapping, authority has also been given to the federal Food and Drug Administration and the Federal Communications Commission.

B.   Standard Contract Terms

Each of the relationships described in this chapter is, to some extent, based on the purchase and sale of products between the parties. A distribution agreement is essentially an agreement by the distributor to purchase products from the manufacturer at a specified discount for resale to end-users. An OEM agreement is based on the manufacturer's ability to produce a sufficient amount of products for sale to the OEM so that the OEM can use the products as part of its other product offerings. Finally, a manufacturing and distribution license often includes provisions for the sale of products by the licensor to the licensee, as well as for distribution by the licensee. Therefore, it is important to summarize some of the standard terms of any product purchase arrangement:

1.   Acceptance

The agreement should set out the basis for acceptance of orders by the seller. As a general rule, the seller will be unwilling to accept orders that do not incorporate the terms and conditions of the seller's standard form of purchase order.

2.   Change Orders

The agreement should cover the rights of the parties in the event that the buyer wishes to make any changes in the product specifications, volume of products, time and place of delivery or method of transportation. If the buyer is allowed to make any changes, some equitable adjustment should be made to the purchase price to take into account any increase or decrease in the cost of the products resulting from such change. In order to mitigate the effect of any changes, the buyer may insist that the seller not purchase any materials, or make material commitments or production arrangements, in excess of the amount, or prior to the time necessary to meet the buyers original delivery schedule.

3.   Cancellation

In the event that the buyer cancels the order, the seller will be entitled to receive some compensation in relation to the amount of work done in connection with the order. For example, the cancellation charge might be set as a percentage of the order price reflecting the percentage of the work performed prior to the notice of termination, provided that if cancellation occurs too close to the delivery date, the buyer will be obligated for the entire amount of the purchase price.

4.   Pricing

Pricing is generally based on prices that are published by the seller from time to time. The seller may be willing to provide discounts from published prices for orders that exceed a certain dollar amount and, in some cases, buyers will negotiate for the "most favored customer" clauses.

5.   Terms of Payment

The agreement will provide for payment within a specified period of time following the date that the products are shipped or delivered to the buyer. The payment period determines the amount of "credit" that the seller is willing to provide to the buyer. Most agreements provide for a "service charge" equal to a specified percentage of the purchase price in the event that the buyer is late in making payments. The seller will retain a purchase money security interest in the products until payment is made.

6.   Shipping Terms and Risk of Loss

The agreement should specify the shipping dates for the products and the time that the risk of loss is to pass to the buyer. Shipping instructions must be set out in the agreement, including the manner of shipment.

7. *Nonconforming or Defective Shipments*

The buyer will have the right to inspect the products received from the seller and may reject any nonconforming or defective goods. The seller will be obligated to replace or repair any nonconforming or defective goods and the buyer will be entitled to reimbursement for the expense of returning such goods to the seller. The buyer must complete the inspection within a reasonable period of time after delivery of the goods.

8. *Warranties*

The seller will provide standard warranties with respect to the products and will agree to repair or replace any goods that do not conform to the warranty for a specified period of time following sale. However, the seller will disclaim any other express or implied warranties, including any warranties of merchantability or fitness for a particular purpose. Also, the seller will insist that it not be liable for any incidental or consequential damages.

9. *Indemnification*

Although the seller will seek to limit its liabilities to the buyer to the scope of the warranty provision, there may be situations where the buyer may require the seller to indemnify it against certain claims arising out of buyer's purchase and use of the products, including intellectual property infringement claims made by third parties, the failure of the goods to comply with specified performance characteristics, and defects in the design of the products.

10. *Force Majeure and Excuse*

As a general rule, the parties will agree that the seller's performance will be excused by the occurrence of specified events, such as war, terrorism, fire, explosion, flood, riot, labor dispute, shortage, accident, act of God, regulation, law, or other event or circumstance beyond the seller's reasonable control that prevents or delays the seller's performance.

11. *Default*

Should the seller fail to deliver the purchased products in a timely fashion, or deliver substantial amounts of nonconforming or defective goods, the buyer will have the right to terminate the agreement for cause. In such cases, the parties may provide for some sort of liquidated damages.

12. Choice of Law

The parties should include a choice of law provision that determines how the terms of the agreement will be interpreted and the legal rights of the parties apportioned. In the United States, this requires the selection of that version of the UCC that has been adopted by the state chosen by the parties. As to international sale agreements, the parties must not only select the governing law, but must decide on the application of international treaty provisions, such as the United Nations Convention on the International Sale of Goods.[4]

9.05   Distribution Agreements

When considering how to distribute a product, emerging companies have several options. The basic distribution schemes are through employees, sales representatives, agents, brokers, consignees or distributors. **Exhibit 9I** summarizes the different distribution methods to be discussed below.

A.   Employee and Salesperson

Employee is a frequently used term, and in the context of marketing means what most people think it does. Basically, it includes anyone (the employee) working for another (the employer) and who is subject to the control and direction of the employer, not only as to the result to be achieved, but also as to the details and means by which the result is accomplished. Thus, an employee *is subject to close supervision*, and it is this criterion that distinguishes it from agents and brokers. Salesperson is usually a synonym for an employee. The only possible difference that may exist between the two is that an employee may perform any function, while a salesperson devotes his or her attention to sales. As noted above, an example of an employment agreement appears as **Exhibit 10B**. The same style can be used for sales people.

B.   Sales Representative

On a scale measuring their relative independence, sales representatives fit between employees and agents. A sales representative has more control over

---

4. The United Nations Convention on the International Sale of Goods, which was prepared by the United Nations Commission on International Trade Law, is an attempt to provide a "neutral" body of sales law that can be applied to sales transactions between parties whose "places of business" are in different countries. A number of countries, including the United States, have ratified the Convention and the Convention may apply to international sales contracts involving parties from the United States unless the parties specifically agree *not* to have the Convention apply or to vary the Convention's provisions in the sales agreement.

the way it operates than an employee does. Furthermore, a sales representative will generally not have an office in its principal's place of business. An employee will. In this sense, a sales representative is very similar to an agent. In fact, much of what is mentioned in the next section on agents is also applicable to sales representatives. Unlike an agent, however, a sales representative will almost always be an individual, whereas an agent can be an individual, partnership or corporation. In addition, although a sales representative has more autonomy than does an employee, it must still make more reports to its principal than an agent must. Appearing as **Exhibit 9E** is an example of a sales representative agreement.

C. Agent and Broker

Through an agency, a manufacturer or wholesaler, known as the principal, gives to another (the agent) the power to solicit orders from potential buyers. The principal must accept the orders before they are binding. The principal then usually sends the goods directly to the buyer. Normally, the sales agent does not *receive* possession at any time. The difference between an employee and an agent is that the agent is only controlled as to the result to be achieved, and not as to means chosen. A broker is essentially an agent, with little if anything to distinguish the two terms. Therefore, this summary will treat both as being equivalent. An example of a sales agent agreement appears as **Exhibit 9F**.

D. Consignment

In a consignment, the person seeking to sell goods (the consignor) entrusts the possession of those goods to a consignee, who endeavors to sell them to potential buyers. If the consignee is successful and finds a buyer, in the usual case, title to the goods passes directly from the consignor to the buyer. Thus, the consignee only receives possession, and not title. However, there is a variation of this pattern involving a consignee who does take title once the buyer is arranged. Prior to such time, title remains in the consignor even though the goods have been delivered to the consignee. In either case, *delivery of the goods to the consignee does not cause title to pass.* This is the key difference between consignment and distributorship. **Exhibit 9G** is an example of a consignment agreement.

E. Distributor

In a distributorship, the holder of goods (the manufacturer or wholesaler) actually sells the goods to the distributor, thereby giving the distributor both *title and possession*. It is then up to the distributor to sell the goods to others, assuming all risks until it does so. **Exhibit 9H** is an example of a distributorship agreement.

The distribution agreement should enumerate all of the products that are to be made available to the distributor for resale, terms on which spare parts and supplies relating to the main products are to be stocked by the distributor, the treatment of enhancements and improvements to the main products that might be developed by the manufacturer during the term of the agreement, and, in some cases, extension of the arrangement to cover new products that might be developed by the manufacturer in the future. In the following sections, the key issues of distributor agreements are discussed.

1. Products

The distribution agreement should clearly describe the product or products that are to be covered by the arrangement, including the exact names of the products and any specifications. Specificity is particularly important in those cases where the manufacturer has a broad line of products and the distribution arrangement is to be limited to a certain subset of the available items. In many cases, the parties will simply attach a schedule to the agreement that lists and describes the products to be covered, including items that are manufactured by third parties and sold by the manufacturer, thereby permitting the parties to amend the agreement during its term to add any new products or delete products that are no longer in the manufacturer's product line.

2. Parts and Supplies

The basic products to be offered under the terms of the distribution arrangement will often need to be supplemented by the availability of spare parts, supplies and accessories. The manner in which parts and supplies are to be treated depends, to some extent, on the party that will be producing the items. If the manufacturer is planning on manufacturing or otherwise selling the parts and supplies, the procedures for ordering and pricing can be drafted in a manner that is essentially similar to those governing the basic products. However, if parts and supplies are to be provided to the distributor through third parties, the parties should clearly understand how relations with third party suppliers are to be conducted, and the manufacturer may impose various requirements on the distributor with regard to ordering and stocking additional items from such suppliers.

One common provision imposes an obligation on the distributor to maintain an inventory of spare parts that, in the reasonable judgment of the manufacturer, is sufficient to permit the distributor to perform maintenance and repair on the products sold to the distributor's customer base. The manufacturer would have the right to inspect the distributor's inventory in order to be sure that the requirements are being satisfied. In turn, the manufacturer would be obligated to sell all of the required spare parts to the distributor at normal and usual prices and to ship all of the ordered parts to the distributor in accordance with any reasonable instructions provided by the distributor. Also, distributors may negotiate for accelerated delivery of the spare parts, including provisions for emergency orders.

3. Enhancements and Improvements

During the term of the distribution relationship, the manufacturer will usually develop new products that modify, update or even replace the original products. The agreement should contemplate ongoing communication between the manufacturer and the distributor with regard to the perceived needs of the customer base and the types of enhancements and improvements that might facilitate the sale of additional products. However, it is usually important for the manufacturer to retain ultimate control over product changes, including the right to modify, replace, update or cease to manufacture any of its products on delivery of reasonable notice to distributors. In turn, the distributor will want to ensure that proper provision is made for existing inventory in the distribution channel, including the risk that any product changes will make any existing inventory items obsolete, and that parts remain available to repair and replace "old" products.

4. Rights to New Products

One of the most important issues with respect to the definition of products relates to whether or not the distributor will have the right to distribute any new products that may be developed by the manufacturer in the future. In some cases, the manufacturer may wish to reserve the right to directly distribute future products or to utilize different distribution channels. If the distributor is not to be given the right to distribute future products, it may seek a "right of first negotiation," which requires that the manufacturer must at least discuss any possible distribution arrangements with the distributor before granting new distribution rights to a third party.

5. Scope of Appointment

As with licensing agreements, distribution agreements raise various issues regarding the scope of the appointment. It will be necessary for the parties to define the geographic, market or customer limitations that will be imposed on the activities of the distributor. In addition, the agreement should set out the expectations of the parties regarding the distributor's use of subdistributors and dealers to assist in the sale and marketing of the products in the specified market. Finally, whether or not the appointment is to be exclusive is a crucial question that must be resolved by the parties.

a.   Geographic Limitations

It is quite common for the scope of the distribution arrangement to be limited to a specified geographic territory, such as one or more countries, states, counties, cities or any part thereof. Geographic limitations generally arise from the desire of the manufacturer to control the distribution function by retaining the ability to either sell goods directly into a given territory or engage a distributor with proven experience in that area. From the distributor's perspective, its ability to sell products may be restricted by the significant costs associated with working with distributors in other territories.

b.   Market or Customer Limitations

In addition to, or in lieu of, geographic limitations on the scope of the distribution arrangement, the parties may specify that the rights of the distributor will be limited to one or more markets or types of customers. For example, the manufacturer may retain the right to distribute its products directly to certain major customers, commonly referred to as "national accounts." In those cases, the manufacturer will usually be attempting to develop its own skills and capabilities with respect to marketing products to, and servicing the needs of, a particular customer base. Distributors will be used to service those markets or channels of distribution that do not fit the specific resources of the manufacturer or as to which the distributor may have certain strategic advantages.

c.   Subdistributors and Dealers

A distributor may be given the right to appoint one or more subdistributors or dealers to develop the distribution channels in the specified territory or market. In some cases, the distributor may even be *required* under the terms of the distribution agreement to appoint a minimum number of subdistributors in order to ensure geographic coverage of the territory, although it may simply be sufficient to impose some sort of "best efforts" obligation on the distributor with respect to any of its activities. Whenever the agreement contemplates the appointment of subdistributors or dealers, the manufacturer may insist on qualifications as to the identity, skills and course of conduct of the appointees.

d.   Exclusivity

A distribution arrangement may be either "exclusive" or "non-exclusive." Exclusive rights provide the distributor with the sole legal right to resell the products in the specified territory or market to be covered by the agreement. On the other hand, the rights of any non-exclusive distributor will exist side-by-side with those of the manufacturer or any third party distributor or dealer who may be given identical or similar rights to distribute the products in a manner that might compete with the efforts of the distributor.

The choice between an exclusive distribution arrangement and the use of two or more non-exclusive distributors, as well as any direct sales by the manufacturer, will depend on a number of factors. An exclusive distribution arrangement amounts to a total delegation of the responsibility for the sale and marketing of the products in the specified territory and, as such, carries a good deal of risk to the manufacturer. On the other hand, while the use of two or more non-exclusive distributors in a specified territory or market clearly reduces the degree of risk associated with depending on the efforts of a single distributor, excessive competition among distributors or dealers may actually reduce the level of overall sales and may well lead to substantial discontent among the various distributors and dealers if they experience any significant erosion in their own margins.

Assuming that the manufacturer is willing, or required, to grant exclusive rights to the distributor, it should ensure that the distributor evidences sufficient experience, organizational skills and financial resources to fulfill all of the obligations that may be necessary for it to adequately penetrate the specific territory or market. Any exclusive distribution arrangement should contain strict standards of distributor performance, such as minimum sales requirements and various commitments with respect to the level of promotion of the products. For its part, the manufacturer should undertake to assist the distributor in fulfilling its various obligations under the agreement, such as by referring any inquiries received from potential customers in the territory to the distributor.

6.   *Pricing and Payment Terms*

Generally, a distribution arrangement involves a sale of products by the manufacturer to the distributor, along with an agreement by the distributor to pay for the products within a specified number of days following delivery of the products. As such, the parties enter into a credit arrangement under which the manufacturer, in effect, extends credit to the distributor on the terms provided in the agreement. The distribution agreement must describe the manner in which the products will be priced for sale to the distributor and the terms of payment following delivery of the products.

a.   Pricing of Products Sold to Distributor

The pricing element of any distribution agreement must take into account the actual costs and expenses to be incurred by both parties, the desired level of profitability for both parties, and the anticipated pricing of competitive or substitute products in the target marketplace. The manufacturer begins the process by analyzing each component of the costs and expenses associated with the product, including manufacturing costs, delivery expenses and marketing and promotional expenditures. In addition, some consideration should be given to the recovery of "sunk" costs, such as research outlays in the course of developing the product, and the need to establish a reserve to cover the cost of repairing and servicing products under any warranty obligations.

Once the manufacturer has adequately estimated the costs and expenses relating to a particular product, attention turns to establishing a price, or range of prices, at which the product can be sold to end-users. This price, which is often characterized as a "suggested retail" price, follows from an analysis of a number of factors, such as the pricing of competitive or substitute products, the functionality of the product, the durability of the product and the need to supplement the product through the use of allied goods and services. In some cases, the price may simply be a multiple of the costs and expenses of the manufacturer.

The price of the products to the distributor is usually established as a fixed percentage of the suggested retail price, although the percentage may vary depending on the volume of purchases made by the distributor and other factors. For example, the distributor may receive a larger discount if it orders a greater quantity of products during a specified ordering period. In any case, the "discount" afforded to the distributor should be sufficient to allow it to realize an appropriate "profit," after taking into account all of its own costs and expenses with respect to promoting, stocking and shipping the products within its own distribution channels.

b. Payment Terms

The terms of payment and credit that are established in any distribution arrangement reflect a balance between the desire of the manufacturer to accelerate the realization of cash flow from the sale of the products and the needs of the distributor to defer payment until such time as it may have had the opportunity to sell the products to the eventual end users and, hopefully, collect the purchase price from the consumer. As such, the payment terms will usually call for payment by the distributor within a period fixed in the distribution agreement. If the products are sold prior to the date that payment is due, the distributor will have the right to use the proceeds until the payment date. However, in the event that the distributor is unable to sell the products on or before the payment date, it will be obligated to remit the purchase price and continue to bear the risks of resale and the costs of holding the products in inventory.

Since deferred payment arrangements such as those that are generally provided for in distribution agreements are essentially an extension of credit by the manufacturer, the first concern of the manufacturer should be the overall financial strength of the distributor. Such strength can be ascertained by reviewing the financial statements of the distributor and its history of payments to other suppliers. Assuming that the manufacturer is satisfied with the results of this review, it is then left to each of the parties to negotiate the terms of payment, including any "downpayment" or deposit on placement of any order, and the period of time following receipt of the invoice (e.g., 30 days) that the distributor will have to pay for the products. A manufacturer may sometimes be able to negotiate a shorter payment period in return for a larger discount on the sales price.

c. Security for Performance of Payment Obligations

The manufacturer generally retains a security interest in products delivered to the distributor pending full payment for the goods. Also, in international distribution agreements, payment for the orders placed by the distributor are often secured by and effected through an irrevocable letter of credit that is delivered to the manufacturer together with the order. Each such letter of credit will provide for payment in full of the amount of the manufacturer's invoice plus the cost of insurance and freight on presentation of the manufacturer's invoice and airway bill or bill of lading.

d. Pricing Adjustments for Unsold Inventories

Sometimes the manufacturer and its distributor may overestimate the anticipated level of sales or underestimate the rapidity of any technical or competitive changes that may lead to obsolescence of the products that were originally specified in the agreement. As such, the distributor may be left with significant levels of unsold inventories and may be reluctant to stock new products without some guarantee that the manufacturer would be willing to repurchase any unsold products or exchange such products for new products. In the event that inventory problems are created by slow sales, rather than the introduction of new products, the manufacturer may be forced to "reprice" inventory held by distributors in order to avoid massive returns and distributor dissatisfaction.

7. Ordering and Shipping Procedures

Ordering and shipping procedures are key elements of the planning process in the distribution relationship, particularly in the case of new products where the manufacturer will be gradually "ramping-up" its production capabilities to meet the demand that may be generated through the activities of its distributors. The distribution agreement should establish guidelines for placement of orders, allocating the burden of any scarcity of products among the manufacturer's distribution partners and the procedures for shipping the purchased products.

a.   Ordering Procedures

The manufacturer will deliver products to the distributor in accordance with written orders that will be delivered from time to time during the term of the distribution arrangement. It is extremely important for the agreement to provide for the delivery of order estimates by the distributor to the manufacturer in order to permit the manufacturer to properly plan for actual orders in future periods. Also, the manufacturer should negotiate for a sufficient period of "lead time" to fill actual orders, realizing that distributors are usually reluctant to carry any substantial amount of inventory until it has actually received orders or solid indications of interest.

The distribution agreement will contain provisions relating to the placement of firm orders and delivery of estimated orders for future periods that can be used for planning purposes. For example, the agreement might provide that the distributor must place firm orders for its requirements of products for a calendar quarter at least 45 or 60 days prior to the commencement of that quarter. In addition, at the time the distributor delivers each firm order, it should also provide the manufacturer with estimates of the amount of products that it expects to order during the following calendar year, realizing that the estimated orders are not binding on the distributor.

Forecasts of future orders are not intended to be binding on the distributor; however, they do serve as a basis for the manufacturer to plan production schedules and order the parts and components required to fulfill the indicated volume of orders. Moreover, the manufacturer will usually be obligated to fill any firm order for a period if the volume is within the forecast that was previously provided by the distributor. Accordingly, if the distributor changes a forecast, such as by rescheduling delivery of a certain amount of products to another period, it is common for the agreement to provide for some penalty, unless the change is made sufficiently far in advance of the actual order date so that the manufacturer is not materially disadvantaged.

The manufacturer will also be concerned about any requests from the distributor to cancel or reschedule fixed orders or to deliver an amount of products that exceeds the prior forecasts for the period. While the manufacturer will usually be willing to provide the distributor with some degree of flexibility as to the delivery of orders, significant variations will or could cause material financial and production problems for the manufacturer. Canceled orders may result in a cancellation charge that is set in inverse proportion to the number of days prior to shipment that the cancellation occurs. In turn, fulfillment of orders that exceed the forecasted amount may be conditioned on the payment of a specified premium to compensate the manufacturer for any additional costs incurred to meet the schedule.

b.   Product Availability

One of the primary objectives of any distributorship arrangement is to generate sufficient demand for the products in one or more territories or markets that may have previously been unavailable to the manufacturer. However, the manufacturer must understand that any anticipated success of the distribution effort may create pressures on the ability of the manufacturer to make and ship a sufficient number of products to meet the requirements of its various distributors as well as the needs of its own direct sales activities. Accordingly, the agreement should contemplate how the parties will manage any shortage of products for use by the distributors.

If it is anticipated that the manufacturer will be unable to satisfy the demands of all its distributors for the products, a provision might be included that will allow the manufacturer to "allocate" supplies among distributors in times of shortage in proportion to a predetermined formula, perhaps on a *pro rata* basis among distributors in proportion to purchases in prior periods. However, if necessary, the manufacturer may reserve the right to make larger allocations to distributors in certain territories and to include new distributors and dealers in any allocation, even when they have few or no purchases in the prior period.

c.   Shipping Procedures

The agreement should describe the manner in which the products will be shipped and delivered, as well as the allocation among the parties of the costs and risks associated with shipping the products to the distributor. The parties must consider the methods that will be used to ship the products, such as by air, truck or railroad, as well as the point at which the products will be turned over to the distributor. If products are to be delivered by the manufacturer to the distributor's place of business, the price should reflect the shipping charges. On the other hand, if the delivery will be "F.O.B." the manufacturer's facilities, there is no need for the manufacturer to exact any additional charges for shipping. The agreement should also describe when title to, and ownership of, the products is to pass to the distributor, as well as any other matters relating to the risk of loss during the course of shipment and insurance needs.

d.   Manufacturer's Failure to Deliver on a Timely Basis

The agreement should cover the consequences associated with the manufacturer's failure to deliver products on a timely basis. From the distributor's perspective, late delivery should allow it to recover liquidated damages or some other form of penalty. If the manufacturer is repeatedly unable to meet the requirements of the distributor, the distributor may have the right to terminate the agreement and, possibly, exercise a right to manufacture the products itself. While the manufacturer will generally agree to pay some amount if it fails to meet the delivery dates, it will expressly disclaim any liability for lost profits, loss of use, or consequential or incidental damages that might be suffered by the distributor as a result of late delivery.

8. Resale Pricing

As noted above, the distributor's net income from the relationship is derived from the "spread" between the price at which the distributor is able to resell the products to its customers and the total costs, including the price of purchasing the products from the manufacturer, incurred by the distributor with respect to acquiring, storing and marketing the products. Since the manufacturer's profit is not directly related to the resale price charged by the distributor, given that the parties will agree on a fixed transfer price, there will usually be no limitations placed on the right of the distributor to determine the prices or terms at which the products may be resold; however, the suggested retail price prescribed by the manufacturer may have a significant impact on the price that the distributor may be able to reasonably charge to consumers.

One area of particular concern to the distributor results from the fact that the manufacturer may need to vary the amount of the suggested retail price from time to time during the term of the distribution agreement as costs and competitive factors change and the financial objectives of the manufacturer with respect to the product evolve. Any change in the suggested retail price will have a significant economic impact on a distributor, particularly if the manufacturer reduces the suggested retail price at a time when the distributor still holds a significant amount of inventory that was purchased at higher prices. In some cases, distributors may demand some form of protection against the adverse effects of price decreases and in almost all cases the manufacturer must provide the distributor with prior notice of any price changes.

9. Product Warranties

Distributors will, on behalf of themselves and their end users, request a variety of warranties and guarantees from the manufacturer regarding various aspects of the products that are to be the subject of the distribution agreement. For example, in almost all cases, the manufacturer will be required to provide some warranties with respect to the design and functionality of the products, although the scope of the warranties will generally be quite restricted and the remedies of the distributor and end user limited to repair of the defective products provided that a claim is made during the specified "warranty period." In other cases, the manufacturer may be asked to provide representations and warranties regarding the integrity of the legal rights that may underlie the specified product, such as a statement that the products do not infringe the intellectual property rights of any third parties.

a.   Express Performance Warranties

The distribution agreement should cover any warranties that are to be provided by the manufacturer with respect to the design and functionality of the products. As might well be expected, the distributor will seek a fairly broad warranty to the effect that the products meet applicable specifications and are free from any defects in design, material and workmanship. Moreover, the distributor will want the manufacturer's warranties to extend for as long as possible. In turn, the manufacturer will want to limit the warranties to exclude any responsibilities with respect to various performance specifications, such as mean time between failures, which will necessarily vary among individual units. In addition, the manufacturer will not only want a shorter warranty period, but will also want the warranty period to begin on the date of manufacture or, at the latest, the date of delivery to the distributor.

After some negotiation, the parties will usually settle on fairly typical limitations on the scope of the warranties that are to be supplied by the manufacturer. For example, one common type of "short-form" warranty might read as follows:

> Seller warrants to [original] Buyer for a period of [number of days/months] from the [specify date] that the Products will be free from defects in materials and workmanship and shall conform to the specifications set forth on [the attached Schedule]. The foregoing warranty is subject to proper operation and maintenance of the Products in accordance with the operating instructions set forth on [the attached Schedule]. Warranty claims shall be made by Buyer in writing to Seller at [specify address]. Seller's sole obligation under the foregoing warranty is, at Seller's option, to repair, replace or correct any such defect that was present at [specify date], or to remove the Products and to refund the purchase price to Buyer.

The above warranty allows the parties to establish the duration of the warranty period, the date on which the warranty period commences (e.g., date of delivery to the distributor), the exact specifications that the manufacturer is willing to guaranty and the exclusive remedies that are to be available for warranty claims. When repairs are required, the distributor will generally pay the freight charges for sending the products to the manufacturer, and the manufacturer will bear the expense of sending the products back out to the distributor or the end user. If "on-site" warranty repairs are to be made, the costs will be subject to negotiation between the parties. In some cases, if the record of warranty claims seems to indicate that the same defect is appearing in a number of units, the distributor may seek some additional compensation from the manufacturer.

b.   Implied Warranties and Disclaimers

In addition to any express warranties that might be required from the manufacturer, there may be a number of so-called "implied warranties" that might also be imposed on an unwitting manufacturer. For example, if the manufacturer knows that the products are to be used for a particular purpose and that the user is depending on the manufacturer's skills and judgment in designing the products to achieve that purpose, an argument can be made that the manufacturer is actually providing an implicit warranty that the products will be fit and suitable for that particular purpose. Also, any merchant also implicitly warrants that goods will be "merchantable," which means that they will be fit for the ordinary purpose for which they are intended.

The manufacturer will want to limit its obligations with respect to warranties to those express statements that are set out in the agreement. As such, it will bargain for a clause that effectively disclaims any other warranties, including any implied warranties, and limits its prospective liabilities to those set out in the agreement. The usual provision will read something like the following:

> THIS WARRANTY IS EXPRESSLY IN LIEU OF ALL OTHER WARRANTIES. THERE SHALL BE NO LIABILITY ON THE PART OF THE MANUFACTURER FOR ANY GENERAL, SPECIAL OR CONSEQUENTIAL DAMAGES ARISING OUT OF THE SALE, MANUFACTURE OR USE OF ANY PRODUCTS SOLD HEREUNDER. MANUFACTURER MAKES NO WARRANTIES, EXPRESS OR IMPLIED, (INCLUDING, BUT NOT LIMITED TO, ANY WARRANTIES OF MERCHANTABILITY OR FITNESS OF THE PRODUCTS FOR ANY PURPOSE) WITH RESPECT TO THE PRODUCTS COVERED BY THIS AGREEMENT, EXCEPT AS OTHERWISE EXPLICITLY PROVIDED.

The above all-capitals print size is required under most Uniform Commercial Code rules.

c.   Intellectual Property Warranties

If the products are technologically advanced, warranties concerning patent and other infringements may be extremely important to the distributor and the ultimate end-users. Under the Uniform Commercial Code, every merchant implicitly warrants that the goods shall be free from any claim for infringement of patent or trademark.[5] Although the manufacturer may desire to disclaim such intellectual property warranties, many distributors will insist on some warranty in this regard. In cases where a warranty against infringement is to be given, the manufacturer will usually retain complete control over any infringement proceeding and will have the right to minimize its exposure by demanding the return of the goods for credit. If the agreement contemplates any modification of the basic products to meet the specifications of the distribution, the distributor should agree to indemnify the manufacturer for infringement claims resulting from the specifications or other actions by the distributor.

---

5.   UCC § 2-312(3).

10. Technical Support and Service

Technical assistance is an important part of the entire distribution relationship. Technical assistance may take the form of on-site consultation involving manufacturer personnel, as well as telephone "hotline" service staffed by persons who can provide advice and answer questions relating to the use of the products. The agreement should cover the types of assistance that the manufacturer will make available and the cost, if any, to the distributor of such services. Generally, telephone support will be provided free of charge, while trips to the distributor or its customers are made on a "cost plus" basis, perhaps with some "free" time at the beginning of the relationship.

a.   Training Classes

A manufacturer will often organize or otherwise provide training classes for the personnel of distributors generally with respect to the products and their use, maintenance or operation. If that is the case, the manufacturer may require that the distributor enroll a reasonable number of its employees in at least one of the training classes provided by the manufacturer each year, with the distributor paying the cost of their transportation to and from the places of instruction, their respective salaries and social benefits and all costs incurred in connection with attendance at such training sessions. The location and expense of any additional training will be subject to negotiation between the parties.

b.   Documentation

The distributor will request copies of the manufacturer's hardware, software and support documentation, including all of the information necessary to enable the distributor to prepare technical and service manuals and end-user documentation. If the manufacturer agrees to provide any of this information, it will do so only if the distributor specifically agrees to protect the trade secrets and proprietary information of the manufacturer that is included in the documentation. Moreover, in most cases, the manufacturer will *not* agree to supply the distributor with copies of source code or circuit designs.

c.   Service

The parties must agree on how service and repairs will be performed on the products. Among the issues to be considered are which party is to perform the specified service obligations, the duration of any service obligations, and the locations at which the service and repair work is to be performed. In those cases where the distributor is to assume some responsibility regarding service and repairs, the parties will need to provide for any training, service manuals or technical information that might be needed by the distributor.

The decision as to which of the parties is to have the primary responsibility for servicing and repairing the products will depend on a number of factors. If the manufacturer has an existing network of service centers throughout the area in which the distributor will be active, it may make sense to have all of the work done by the manufacturer's representatives. However, in some cases, the distributor may want to take responsibility for all technical support obligations following completion of basic training. If this is done, there may be some agreement as to reducing the distributor's purchase price, since presumably the manufacturer will be relieved of the expense of maintaining additional service capabilities for the products.

Service and repairs during the warranty period will be performed at no cost to the end user. After the warranty period has expired, customers may still require service and repairs to be provided from time to time, perhaps under the terms of some type of maintenance contract. If the parties are to offer any ongoing service agreements to customers, decisions must be made regarding pricing, including expenses, as well as the scope and timing of the services to be provided. Sometimes, maintenance arrangements will be subcontracted to third parties; however, if this is done, either the manufacturer or the distributor must remain obligated to supervise and guarantee the performance of the third party.

If the distributor is to assume responsibility for service and repairs, the manufacturer should be able to train, advise and assist the distributor with establishing and maintaining the technical skills of the service force. Among the measures to be considered would be training seminars, either in the field or at the manufacturer's facilities, detailed service manuals and a telephone "hot-line" that allows each service representative to consult with engineers and technicians dedicated to training and "trouble-shooting" at the manufacturer's facilities. Also, the manufacturer should agree to sell to the distributor all of the tools and testing equipment that might be required to install and repair the products, perhaps at a price that reflects only the costs of such tools and equipment to the manufacturer plus a nominal amount to cover overhead.

11. Duties of the Distributor

While the manufacturer is certainly interested in making a profit on sales made to the distributor, it will also want to be sure that the distributor is able to successfully penetrate the specified market, thereby assuring the manufacturer of enhanced sales over the term of the arrangement. Accordingly, the parties will include various covenants and agreements by the distributor to ensure that it uses its best efforts to develop the full sales potential of the products within the territory. Among the items that are typically included are the following:

- Distributor will agree to promote the products, identifying them by their correct names as products of the manufacturer. The distributor will also agree to maintain a qualified sales force and distribution organization, although it may be necessary for the manufacturer to supply appropriate training with respect to the uses and functions of the products.

- Distributor will maintain a staff of trained technicians and a stock of spare parts and technical literature adequate to provide technical support and service to its customers. Once again, it may be necessary for the manufacturer to provide training in the appropriate service techniques, particularly when concerns exist regarding the overall quality and reputation of the product offerings.

- Distributor will establish and maintain a place or places of business in areas throughout the territory adequate to provide good customer support and marketing coverage.

- Distributor will agree not to sell or distribute products that are competitive with the products that are produced by the manufacturer.

- Distributor will be obligated to maintain an inventory of products sufficient to satisfy customer orders on a timely basis; however, the obligations of the distributor in this regard must be made subject to any other agreement covering the allocation of limited products supplies among other distributors.

- Distributor should provide the manufacturer with periodic reports regarding product sales, competitive goods and prices and additional information relating to the markets in which the distributor's activities are being conducted.

- Distributor will be obligated to conduct its business in a manner that will reflect favorably on the manufacturer and will agree not to engage in any deceptive, misleading, illegal or unethical business practices. It is important to understand the importance of local regulations and customs regarding the sale and distribution of goods, particularly if they differ materially from those that might exist in the home market of the manufacturer.

- Warranty obligations with respect to the products should be clarified, as should the allocation of the costs and responsibilities associated with any warranty repairs. The distributor should agree to promptly inform the manufacturer of any complaints regarding the products.

12. Promotional Activities

One or both of the parties to a distribution arrangement may take on various responsibilities with respect to promoting and marketing the various products. For example, both the manufacturer and the distributor may develop an advertising budget, promote products at industry trade shows and engage in "point-of-sale" promotion and merchandising. It is important for the parties to agree on the appropriate mix of promotional activities and to allocate duties between them in a manner that is the most cost-effective and that capitalizes on the particular skills and experience of the parties. An agreement may sometimes contain a commitment by one or both of the parties to undertake a certain minimum amount of advertising or to expend a fixed amount of money for promotional activities.

The relative duties will depend, to some extent, on the resources of the manufacturer and distributor. For example, if the distributor has a large national distribution network, it is likely that it will take on responsibility for developing and managing a significant amount of promotional activity. For its part, the manufacturer may commit to supplying the distributor with reasonable quantities of any technical, promotional and advertising photography, artwork and literature (including but not limited to, catalogues, leaflets and posters) relating to the products that may be developed by the manufacturer, as well as any technical information that may be required for the proper installation, operation and maintenance of the products.

13. Trademarks and Goodwill

Whenever a manufacturer enters into a distribution agreement, it effectively transfers to the distributor all the benefits that may be associated with, and the duties with respect to the protection of, its valuable goodwill and business reputation. An established manufacturer will want to protect and promote the value of the goodwill and reputation in the course of any arrangement. When the manufacturer is new to the market, as is the case when it is involved in the introduction of its first line of products, it will be eager to build goodwill and trust through its distribution decisions. As such, it is important for the parties to clearly establish the manner in which the distributor will be allowed to use the name, trademarks, logos and other manifestations of the manufacturer, as well as the requirements that will be imposed on the distributor with respect to the integrity of its activities.

The distribution agreement will usually provide that the name, trademarks and logos of the manufacturer may not be utilized by the distributor in its advertising or point of sale activities, or on signs or letterheads, without the written consent of the manufacturer. A distributor may be granted a license to use the manufacturer's trademarks, which often will be accompanied by specific requirements designed to control the manner in which the rights are utilized, as well as the quality of the distributor's promotional activities. Quality control and advance approval is particularly important when the manufacturer does not yet have any extensive product literature or advertising copy relating to the products. In such cases, the manufacturer will be particularly dependent on the decisions of the distributor with respect to the use of licensed trademarks in promoting the products.

14. Distributor Review

One of the fundamental goals and objectives of any form of distribution arrangement is to generate revenues from sales of products and, in turn, to build and maintain market share. While in some cases the obligation of a distributor under the agreement will be limited to the use of its "best efforts," it is generally most desirable for the manufacturer to impose various standards under which the performance of the distributor will be measured. However, the ability of the manufacturer to effectively monitor the performance of the distributor will depend on a number of factors, including the relative size and experience of the parties and the consequences attached to any failure by the distributor to meet the expectations of the manufacturer.

Performance criteria can take a number of different forms, such as sales quotas, minimum inventory purchases, levels of staffing, shelf or floor space requirements, number and geographic coverage of dealer appointments, warehouse locations and the amount of expenditures on promotional activities. Whatever the form of criteria, it is important to provide ongoing incentives for the distributor and to take into account anticipated changes in market conditions and in the various strategic objectives of each of the parties. One method for ensuring that a distributor will diligently attempt to meet any performance measures is to condition any ongoing right of exclusivity on the achievement of the objectives. If the distributor does not attain the goals set forth in the agreement, the manufacturer may have the right to engage other distributors and, in some cases, to terminate the entire relationship.

In addition to any objective performance measures, the agreement may include a number of other procedures calculated to build and reinforce communication between the parties regarding the conduct of the relationship. For example, it generally makes sense to provide for periodic financial and marketing reports, on-site inspections of distributor facilities, training sessions and other meetings or telephonic conferences between representatives of each of the parties. Ongoing contact of this sort will give the manufacturer a good sense of the distributor's commitment to the relationship and the feasibility of expanding the scope of the arrangement into other areas.

15. Term and Termination

Although each of the parties may certainly contemplate that the distribution arrangement will continue for a long period of time, it is necessary to give careful consideration to the term of the arrangement, any conditions with respect to renewal of the arrangement, and, most importantly, the circumstances under which it will be possible for one or both of the parties to terminate the arrangement prior to the end of any specified term. Also, the agreement should describe the effect of any termination of the agreement, as well as any procedures that may be established to regulate the resolution of disputes among the parties with respect to their respective rights following any termination of the agreement.

a. Initial Term and Renewals

Although many times the parties will not agree on a fixed term for the agreement, preferring instead to allow the term of the agreement to run until one party elects to terminate or the parties agree on a revised arrangement, it may well be useful to include a fixed term of some sort in the agreement. The length of any fixed term should take into account a number of factors, including the sales goals of the manufacturer, the breadth of the territory to be covered by the distributor and the period that might reasonably be required by the distributor to properly promote the new products. If a fixed term is used, the parties may provide that the agreement is automatically renewed unless one of the parties notifies the other of its election to terminate the agreement. In some cases, the agreement may require discussions between the parties as a condition to renewal or extension of the agreement, a process that forces the parties to formally assess the relationship.

b. Early Termination

Every distribution arrangement should specify the terms on which one or both of the parties might elect to terminate the agreement prior to the end of its stated term. While termination "events" should be tailored to the needs of the parties, the most basic provisions would cover the following items:

- Termination without cause: Either party would have the right to terminate the agreement, without cause, on delivery of notice to the other party no less than a specified number of days or months prior to the date of termination. The ability of a party to terminate the agreement in this manner will alleviate any concerns regarding the definition of those events that might give rise to the right to terminate the agreement as a result of any alleged "default" by the other party.
- Termination for cause: In the event that either party refuses to perform its obligations under the agreement, or commits an act or omission that constitutes a material breach of the agreement, the other party would have the right, on notice to the breaching party, to terminate the agreement "for cause." As a general rule, a party that is alleged to be in breach would have a specified period of time to "cure" any deficiencies, although such a right may not be appropriate in some instances. Termination provisions of this type are particularly difficult to administer, given the lack of a clear definition of "material." In some cases, the agreement may recite those areas of concern that may give rise to a right to terminate, such as failure to make timely payment, breach of warranty or service obligations or, in the case of the distributor, failure to meet its sales objectives or fulfill its covenants relating to promotion of the products and services.
- Bankruptcy, insolvency or lack of credit worthiness: Bankruptcy or insolvency of one party generally might lead to an automatic termination of the

agreement, subject to any constraints that might be imposed by law. In some cases, the manufacturer may be allowed to terminate the agreement if the credit of the distributor becomes impaired or unsatisfactory to the manufacturer.

Although the manufacturer will, and should, insist on some rights to terminate the distributor, it may not always be the most prudent means of managing the relationship. Before electing to terminate the arrangement, the manufacturer must consider how it intends to cover the designated territory, either directly or with the assistance of other distributors. Also, in those cases where the termination is to be made "for cause," the manufacturer needs to be mindful of the risks of costly litigation surrounding the circumstances for termination, including the possibility of counterclaims by the distributor. Accordingly, the manufacturer may need to tolerate certain technical breaches of the agreement in some instances and should concentrate its efforts on building and maintaining a trusting and long-term relationship.

c. Legal Consequences of Termination

Termination of the distribution agreement may expose the terminating party to potential claims with respect to damages that might be suffered by the other party due to termination of the relationship. While both parties will attempt to limit their exposure with respect to such claims by including disclaimers of any liability for damages or restitution arising out of any decision to terminate the agreement, such provisions may not be effective under the laws of various nations. Also, termination generally does not affect the rights of the parties to receive payments that may be owed as a result of activities that occurred prior to the date of termination.

A number of countries now have laws that provide various protections for local agents and distributors on termination of an international distribution relationship. For example, it may be possible for the terminated distributor to obtain compensation for the value of the goodwill that may have been developed with respect to the manufacturer's products, for the loss of expected profits during the remaining term of the agreement, for the value of capital investments that the distributor may have made in the course of marketing the products and, in some cases, for the cost of employee severance benefits paid to those employees that the distributor needs to lay off as a result of the termination of the distribution agreement. The manufacturer can avoid liability if the termination is "justified;" however, most laws contain a very narrow definition of "just cause," limiting it to criminal acts and gross incompetence.

The distribution agreement should provide for settling outstanding accounts and payment obligations between the parties. For example, subject to any agreement that the parties might have regarding the repurchase of inventory held by the distributor at the time of termination, the distributor will remain obligated to remit to the manufacturer any amounts that might be due for products purchased prior to termination. In turn, the distributor may have the right to "set off" against any amounts due to the manufacturer any expenses for which it might be entitled to reimbursement by the manufacturer, such as for copies of promotional materials.

d.   Post-Termination Obligations and Procedures

Since termination will generally occur while the parties are still involved in various activities relating to the arrangement, the more difficult issues usually arise out of the need to ensure that existing customers are properly serviced, that outstanding orders are filled, that existing inventories are accounted for and that warranty obligations are satisfied. In some cases, "termination" of the agreement actually commences a period of "winding-down," in which both parties seek to properly allocate ongoing obligations to customers within the territory.

- Outstanding orders: The distributor may have outstanding orders at the time of termination. The willingness of the manufacturer to fill any such orders depends on its ability to ensure that the items will be paid for on a timely basis, as well as the need to ensure that products continue to be delivered into the market until the manufacturer is able to make any alternative distribution arrangements. As a general rule, it is probably better practice for the manufacturer to continue deliveries to the terminated distributor in order to permit the distributor to fill previously accepted customer orders, rather than exposing the distributor to any potential liabilities for failure to deliver products to existing customers. Also, the manufacturer will have an interest in satisfying outstanding orders in order to maintain overall product "goodwill."
- Distributor inventories: Termination may come at a time when the distributor has a significant level of inventory. In some cases, a manufacturer will be required to repurchase any inventory, although the repurchase price may be set at some appropriate discount from the price originally paid by the distributor. However, the manufacturer will generally want to keep the inventory repurchase right optional and any repurchased products will be subject to a right of inspection in order to ensure that the products are unused, new and not obsolete. If the manufacturer is not able to repurchase the inventory, it may either arrange for the goods to be transferred to, or "purchased" by, another distributor or allow the distributor to have some limited rights to continue to sell the balance of any products remaining in inventory.
- Manufacturer's products on distributor's premises: If the manufacturer should have any of its own products or assets, such as samples, demonstration products or consigned inventory, on the distributor's premises, the agreement should provide for delivery of such products and assets to

the manufacturer on termination of the agreement. Usually, the manufacturer should retain ownership of, or a security interest in, any such products and assets.

- Customer service and warranty claims: It may be difficult, if not impossible, to expect a terminated distributor to adhere to its obligations with respect to service and warranty claims. The manufacturer should insist that the distributor provide some minimal level of assistance in phasing out service obligations and the distributor will usually be required to turn over to the manufacturer all of its customer information and service records. However, the manufacturer must be able to provide viable service alternatives, such as "in-house" service facilities, other distributors or an independent service organization.

- Trademarks and marketing literature: If the distribution arrangement contemplates the use of trademarks, names and logos of the manufacturer by the distributor, the agreement should provide that the rights of the distributor to use such items will cease on any termination of the agreement. Product books, technical information and marketing literature and materials should be returned to the manufacturer, although the parties may need to negotiate the manner in which any costs associated with such returns are to be allocated between the parties.

- Confidentiality obligations: Any obligations of the parties to preserve the confidentiality of trade secrets or proprietary information exchanged or acquired during the relationship should survive termination of the agreement. The distributor is usually required to return to the manufacturer copies of any proprietary information regarding the products and should agree not to use any confidential information that it may have received regarding the products in future business dealings.

F.   Antitrust Laws

Having analyzed the different types of distribution methods, the next step is to understand how the antitrust laws regulate them.

1.   The Laws

Even before the end of the nineteenth century, the United States attempted to control big business. Since then, it has enacted a strenuous antitrust program designed to encourage competition and prevent unfair means of doing business. The substantive provisions of the antitrust laws are few and brief; they are contained in seven sections taken from three statutes—the Sherman Act of 1890, and the Clayton Act and Federal Trade Commission Act of 1914.

The Sherman Act of 1890 contains two main prohibitions:

Section 1: "Every contract, combination in the form of trust or otherwise, or conspiracy, in restraint of trade or commerce among the several States or with foreign nations, is hereby declared to be illegal..."

Section 2: "Every person who shall monopolize, or attempt to monopolize, or combine or conspire with any other person or persons to monopolize any part of the trade or commerce among the several States, or with foreign nations, shall be deemed guilty of a misdemeanor..."

The Clayton Act of 1914 declares illegal four specified types of restrictive or monopolistic practices:

- Price discrimination (Section 2)
- Exclusive-dealing and tying contracts (Section 3)
- Acquisitions of competing companies (Section 7)
- Interlocking directorates (Section 8)

All these sections are qualified by various exceptions (some more elaborately defined than others) to the general effect that the practice concerned becomes unlawful only when its "effect may be to substantially lessen competition or tend to create a monopoly." The section dealing with price discrimination was revised in the Robinson-Patman Act of 1936, and that dealing with acquisitions in the Celler-Kefauver Act of 1950.

The Federal Trade Commission Act of 1914 is concerned largely with setting up the Commission and the mechanics of its operation. Section 5 of the Act, however, contains one important substantive provision, which reads (as amended by the Wheeler-Lea Act of 1938): "Unfair methods of competition in commerce and unfair or deceptive acts or practices in commerce are hereby declared illegal."

2. Application of Laws to Distribution Agreements

The following discussion concentrates on the effect of U.S. antitrust laws on agency, consignment and distributorship agreements. Since by nature they are similar, any comments made in reference to agents and consignees should also be understood to apply to employees, sales representatives and brokers. **Exhibit 9J** summarizes the key portions of this antitrust summary.

a. Price Fixing

As quoted above, Section 5 of the Federal Trade Commission Act proscribes all unfair methods of competition. Along with Section 1 of the Sherman Act, this has been held to condemn price fixing and maintenance. Generally, these terms refer to agreements between competitors (a horizontal agreement) and between those on different levels of distribution, such as a manufacturer and a wholesaler (a vertical agreement), whereby the parties agree to either set a new price or to maintain a present one.

A principal and its agent, and a consignor and its consignee are essentially single entities, because in each case the principal-consignor so dominates and controls the agent-consignee, that the latter cannot really be said to be independent, or distinct. Inasmuch as the *antitrust laws of the U.S. basically apply when two or more persons are involved*, this means the former can set the price of the latter without violating the antitrust laws, since two legally distinct parties are not involved. However, a seller cannot set or maintain the price that a distributor charges, since a distributor is an independent party. However, a seller can recommend (without requiring) the price that it believes a distributor should charge. Such a recommendation is known as a suggested retail price.

b. Price Discrimination

As indicated above, the Robinson-Patman Act prohibits price discrimination that adversely affects competition. Price discrimination has been held to be the same seller charging competing buyers different prices. As before, the existence of an agent or consignee is ignored. Therefore, the price charged by a principal-consignor and its agents-consignees must be the same. This means the principal-consignor must set the price charged by its agents-consignees who sell to competing buyers, and that such prices must be the same as those charged by the principal-consignor. As to distributors, sellers must equalize the prices they charge to their distributors and to those in competition with such distributors.

There are exceptions to this requirement of equal prices charged to competitors for permissible discounts. What this means is that a seller (either directly or through an agent or consignee) can give buyers quantity discounts for volume purchases, discounts necessary to meet (not beat) competition, and functional discounts to those performing different services or on different levels of distribution.

c. Market Division

Section 1 of the Sherman Act prohibits, among other practices, any horizontal or vertical division of a market whether by allocating territories or customers. A horizontal division occurs when companies on the same distribution level agree among themselves to restrict competition. A vertical division is one imposed by someone on a higher distribution level on someone lower down (usually by a principal, consignor or seller on an agent, consignee, or distributor).

The old rule was that in order to violate this section there must also be a plurality of actors. This meant a principal-consignor could limit an agent or consignee to a specific territory or group of customers, but could not so limit a distributor. However, a seller could grant to a distributor a recommended territory for which the distributor has chief responsibility. Known as an area of primary responsibility, the effect was that the seller expressed its hope the distributor would concentrate only on that area, but did not mandate such a limitation. However, in a 1977 decision involving GTE Sylvania, this rule was changed. Under that decision a seller can now restrict a distributor's sales territory, store location or customers, if the effect of such restrictions is not to adversely affect competition. Where such adverse effects are likely to occur, a seller may be able to give a distributor an area of primary responsibility. Although even areas of primary responsibility may be held to result in improper restrictions adversely affecting competition, this is less likely to occur than with territorial restrictions. Therefore, it is advisable that areas of primary responsibility be granted in lieu of territorial restraints to distributors. The old rules concerning the ability of a principal or consignor to limit the activities of an agent or consignee remain. An agent or consignee may usually be limited to a certain location or territory if such a limitation does not seriously affect competition adversely.

A word of caution: The above rules also apply to distributor sales outside the United States. At one time, U.S. antitrust laws were not concerned with market restrictions outside the country. This is no longer the case, since the federal government now recognizes that such export restrictions indirectly limit production within the United States.

d. Exclusive Dealing

Section 3 of the Clayton Act prohibits restrictive methods of distribution including exclusive dealings whereby the recipient of goods agrees to deal only in the goods of the seller, principal or consignor.

This statute prohibits exclusive dealings in so many instances it is difficult to indicate when such dealings are valid. For instance, exclusive dealings affecting a significant amount of commerce either between states or between the United States and a foreign country are probably illegal. This effect can occur under the following circumstances:

- One of the parties has a sizable market share, sells or buys a large volume of goods either in quantity or dollar value, or earns a large percentage of its gross income from interstate trade.
- The exclusive dealing requirement may have a significant affect on someone who falls into one of the above categories.
- Similar arrangements are used by competitors, and the arrangements taken together are significant.

About the only instance when such dealings may be valid is when the arrangement can be justified as protecting goodwill and has a short duration.

Originally, requirements that an agent deal exclusively with its principal were deemed not to violate Section 3, as before, on the theory a plurality of actors was required. However, recent Supreme Court decisions appear to indicate this is no longer true and that agency, consignment and distributorship agreements containing exclusive dealing clauses could violate this statute. However, contrary to the Supreme Court, lower courts continue to allow an exclusive dealing clause in a true agency or consignment.

e. Exclusive Sales Outlet

Section 1 of the Sherman Act also restricts the assignment of a sales area solely to one sales outlet. Such an appointment is referred to as an exclusive distributorship, consignment or agency. Whereas, in exclusive dealing the buyer agrees to buy from only one seller, in this case the seller agrees to sell to only one buyer.

The courts have been considerably more lenient towards exclusive distributorships, consignments and agencies than they have been towards exclusive dealings. So long as similar goods are available to competing buyers in the same region, the appointment of an exclusive sales outlet does not violate Section 1 of the Sherman Act. Although all three are valid appointments, exclusive consignments or agencies would appear to be safer again because of the lack of plurality of actors.

3. Application to Accompanying Agreements

In accordance with the thoughts expressed above and leading cases in this area, the accompanying agency agreements serve the following functions:

- To give the agent the authority only to solicit orders
- To reserve title in the principal
- To have the agent quote prices established by principal
- To limit the agent to certain territories or customers
- To require the agent to deal exclusively with principal
- To disqualify the agent for sales outside its territory

Although clauses can been drafted to give greater flexibility, consignment agreements basically do the following:

- Reserve title in consignor
- Give consignor a security interest in the proceeds (accounts receivable) resulting from any sale of the goods consigned to consignee
- Defer payment of the purchase price to consignor by consignee until resale of the product to the ultimate purchaser

- Have consignor set prices to be charged by consignee
- Make consignor responsible for sales taxes due on transactions between consignor and consignee if any are assessed
- Limit consignee to certain territories or customers
- Require consignee to deal exclusively with consignor
- Adjust for any sales by consignee in the territory of another consignee

For the most part these provisions, though found in the agency and consignment agreements, are either lacking or negated in the case of the distributorship agreement:

- Distributor not made agent of seller
- Distributor takes title to the goods
- Payment to seller must be made within a certain number of days after delivery of the goods to distributor
- Seller does not fix prices charged by distributor, only those charged to distributor
- Taxes to be paid by distributor
- There is no article requiring distributor to deal exclusively with seller
- Distributor is not required to share its profits on sales made in another distributor's sales area

Human Resources

George J. Miller
Wyatt, Tarrant & Combs, LLP, Lexington, Kentucky

Contents

Human Resources[1]

10.01   Preliminary Considerations

One of the critical issues facing any new company is hiring the right people for the right positions. As discussed in Chapter 2 (Preparing a Business Plan), many investors are more concerned with the quality of the management team than with any other element of the business plan. Many lenders will have the same preference. Similarly, potential customers are more likely to be interested in a rollout product by a start-up if they feel there is a strong management team behind it. Even after the team is in place, the need for strong human resources does not end. Retaining important members becomes a critical issue. This chapter will address both issues—hiring and retaining employees—as well as what happens when it is time to let them go.

10.02   Hiring

Generally, an emerging company may hire whomever it desires, as long as its decision does not discriminate on the basis of protected characteristics, such as age, national origin, race, color, sex, religion, disability or any other characteristic protected under federal or state law. Employers must ensure that their hiring/selection process does not eliminate certain groups of persons from employment consideration on the basis of a protected characteristic. Even if employers' hiring process is not discriminatory, employers must still ensure that the individuals administering the hiring system do not discriminate when

---

1.   Philip C. Eschels and Robert L. Brown were the authors of this chapter in the first edition of the *Guide*.

dealing with a particular candidate. Employers must also ensure that, even if the hiring process is not intentionally discriminatory, the process does not have an unintended, adverse impact on persons of a particular race, color, religion, sex, national origin, or on persons over the age of 40 years old or any other protected group. There are also various protections afforded individuals under state law, which must always be considered. Finally, employers must be aware of child labor laws and minimum age limits for engaging in certain kinds of work. In conjunction with and in addition to the above, the following is a brief, non-exhaustive overview of some of the issues to consider when employers begin hiring employers' employees.

A. Recruiting

The goal of the recruiting process is to provide employers with the opportunity to attract and assess the best available candidates. Naturally, the people selected as recruiters need to be (a) intimately familiar with employer's needs and (b) proficient in evaluating candidates' abilities consistent with those needs. Recruiters should additionally be well versed in federal and state employment laws. The aim of these laws is to encourage employers to select individuals on the basis of their abilities and potential to perform successfully, rather than on the basis of protected characteristics. Recruiters may utilize one of several different methods of recruiting. The following are some of the more common methods:

Word-of-Mouth Recruiting. For this type of recruiting, recruiters orally inform either current employees or other individuals that the employer has openings. The employer's goal is to have these current employees or other individuals let the employer know of individuals they think would be good candidates for the positions the employer wishes to fill. Employers must be careful that when informing current employees and other individuals of the openings, the people they are informing reflect the racial, ethnic, or sexual composition of the relevant labor market. Otherwise, exclusive use of word-of-mouth recruiting could perpetuate an unbalanced pattern of employment.

Newspaper, Internet and Campus Advertising. Obviously, advertising in any one of these types of venues is a terrific way to recruit new employees. However, there are a few pointers that employers must keep in mind when advertising:

The language of employers' advertisements must be carefully worded. Employers should avoid describing the open positions in a way that tends to exclude individuals of a protected characteristic.

Example: "We are seeking qualified salesmen . . ."

This advertisement tends to exclude women.

Example: "We are seeking recent college graduates . . ."

This advertisement could be found to exclude individuals based upon their age.

Employers should avoid placing job advertisements in publications that are specifically geared towards members of one protected class (i.e., geared towards one gender, one race, etc.). Otherwise, even a neutral advertisement may appear discriminatory.

> *Example:* If the publication is labeled as "Classified ads for women," then any job advertisement placed in the publication may be deemed discriminatory towards men (if the position could theoretically be filled by either men or women).

> *Example:* If the publication is a local Chinese newspaper, then any job advertisement placed in the publication may be deemed discriminatory towards all non-Chinese individuals (as long as the position could technically be filled by persons of any nationality).

At the bottom of all job advertisements, employers should state that they are Equal Opportunity Employers.

B.   Employment Applications

All of the questions employers ask prospective employees should be job-related. Because the job requirements are presumably different for each type of position, employers have one of three choices with respect to employment applications: (a) employers may choose to have different applications for the different employment positions; (b) employers may utilize the same application for all prospective employees, but then instruct prospective employees to answer only those questions that are related to the job for which they are applying; or (c) employers may utilize the same application for all prospective employees, have the prospective employees answer all of the questions contained therein, but then only consider responses to the questions that are related to the job in question.

The reason that employers must only use questions in an employment application or job interview that are job-related is that any that are unrelated to the job for which a person is applying can form the basis of a discrimination claim. In deciding whether to include a particular question on an employment application or job interview, it is advisable that employers think about the following three questions: (a) Does this question tend to have a disproportionate effect in screening out minorities or women? (b) Is this information necessary to judge this individual's competence for performance of this particular job? (c) Are there alternate, non-discriminatory ways to secure this information?

Briefly, questions regarding the following topics should generally not be asked on an employment application or in a job interview unless the answer to such question is directly related to whether the applicant will be able to perform the functions of the job:

- Age, including date of birth
- Race, religion and national origin
- Physical traits and disabilities
- Education (obviously, when the performance of a job requires a particular level of education, applicants may be questioned about educational background, schools attended, degrees earned, etc., but if a job does not require a particular level of education, questions of this nature may be evidence of discrimination against minorities, for example)
- Sex, marital and family status
- Arrest and conviction records (although inquiries concerning whether an applicant has ever been convicted of a felony are usually proper)
- Prior history of garnishment

C. Interviewing

Interviewers (particularly, if different from recruiters) should be educated on how to conduct an interview. They should know precisely what they can and cannot promise applicants. Interviewers should, for example, refrain from promising "permanent employment" or "employment that will last as long as the job is satisfactorily performed." In other words, they should not promise anything to applicants that can later be used as evidence of an implied contract of employment. Rather, interviewers should specifically mention in the interview that the applicant, if hired, will be employed at-will and can be terminated with or without cause.

Interviewers should be provided with written instructions listing what they should and should not discuss during an interview. It is also advisable that they be provided with a list of specific questions to ask each applicant. The best kinds of questions are performance-based or behavioral questions, which ask applicants to describe in detail past successes and how they dealt with difficult workplace situations. Past job performance is the best predictor of future job performance. After an interview, the interviewer should document all points covered during the interview and evaluate the applicant in writing. Documentation of the interview should specifically reflect that the employment-at-will status of all employees was covered.

D. Testing

Employers may decide that they want to use certain aptitude, general ability, or other type of tests in hiring employees. Because there is a chance that such tests may be deemed discriminatory towards a protected class of employees, employers should make certain that testing is actually necessary. Employers should examine the job descriptions and identify their critical requirements before they select tests to screen applicants. Further, employers should make sure to avoid utilizing tests that are based on knowledge, skill, or behavior that can be acquired in a brief orientation on the job.

If employers decide to utilize a testing procedure, they must ensure that the test accurately predicts work behavior or other criteria of employee competency, the content closely duplicates the actual duties performed in a particular position, and the test identifies general mental and psychological traits employers believe necessary to the successful performance of the job in question.

E.   Reference Checks

Reference checks are frequently used by employers to screen applicants. The legal considerations involved in references pose difficult legal dilemmas and risks on the one hand. Information asked or given must not violate discrimination laws, indicate retaliation or otherwise violate the law. As discussed below in connection with firing, there is a possibility of being sued as a result of giving truthful, but harmful, information about former employees, in responding to reference requests. On the other hand, negligent hiring claims may arise if initial information is not obtained for individuals hired into certain positions, such as maintenance personnel with access to apartments or people who work with young people in isolated locations. As a result, many employers refuse to give references about former employees, or are careful in giving out any information beyond employment dates, salary history and promotions.

F.   Offers of Employment

When offering employment to individuals, it is advisable to make the offer in writing. Attached as **Exhibit 10A** is an example of such an offer. The offer should cover the critical issues, such as who is being extended the offer, the position and salary offered, where the work will be performed, and, if appropriate, a brief description of what work will be required. The offer should also specify a deadline by which the offer must be accepted. The offer should also designate any preconditions for employment, such physicals and presentation of proof of ability to work, as discussed below.

1.   Pre-Employment Physicals

The Americans with Disabilities Act ("ADA") prohibits employers from making inquiries of applicants that would require them to reveal a disability—including requiring them to undergo a physical examination—until *after* making an offer of employment. However, before making an offer, employers may ask applicants to describe or demonstrate how they would perform job-related functions. Tests for the presence of unlawful use of controlled substances are also permitted before a job offer is made, because they are not considered medical inquiries.

After employers have offered employment to prospective employees and prior to their commencement of employment, employers are permitted to require the employees to undergo a medical examination in order to do the following:

- Determine whether they have the physical attributes necessary to perform the essential functions of the job in question and, if not, whether there are reasonable accommodations that would allow it.
- Sensitize the new employees to their physical limitations so that they can avoid activities leading to injury or illness.
- Place the new-hire employees in positions where they are least likely to sustain occupational injury.
- Ascertain the general health of the prospective employees, and establish a record of injuries or other medical conditions present at the time of hire that may be useful in any subsequent worker's compensation case.
- Screen out persons who use controlled substances.

The ADA allows employers to condition an offer of employment on the results of a required medical examination (or on information revealed on a medical history questionnaire) as long as: (a) they require, as noted, the potential employee to undergo the examination only *after* offering a position; (b) employers require all entering employees in the same job category to submit to medical examinations (regardless of disability); (c) employers maintain medical information on separate forms and in separate files; and (d) employers maintain the confidentiality of medical records.

2. Immigration Reform and Control Act

The Immigration Reform and Control Act of 1986 prohibits employers from employing "unauthorized aliens," penalizes employers if they do hire unauthorized aliens, and requires employers to check whether each of their employees is legally entitled to work in the United States. Employers are required to verify the employment eligibility and identity of every employee they hire. This means that each employee must provide documents that establish the employee's identity (e.g., a driver's license, voter registration card or a school identification card) and that establish the employee's employment eligibility (i.e., birth certificate or social security card). Certain documents establish both identity and employment eligibility, such as a U.S. passport, a resident alien card, an alien registration card or a certificate of naturalization or U.S. citizenship. After examining the appropriate documents for each employee, employers and employees must then complete an Employment

Eligibility Verification (INS Form I-9). Employers must complete their part of the I-9 form within three business days of hiring the employee.

In carrying out the requirements of this law, employers must take care not to discriminate against job applicants because of their citizenship status, national origin, race, ethnicity, and the like. However, this type of information would be revealed to employers by their birth certificates, driver's licenses and other documents employers must inspect in order to comply with the immigration law. Thus, it is advisable to consider requesting the necessary documentation only *after* making a job offer to a job applicant. The offer, then, should be conditioned on proper documentation of identity and employment eligibility.

G. Alternative Arrangements

1. Independent Contractor

Rather than hiring individuals as employees, one alternative is to retain them as independent contractors or consultants if circumstances permit and this relationship meets the requirements for this status. Since many of the protections discussed in this chapter are only applicable to employees, employers may be able to reduce their legal obligations and risks by engaging contractors. In such case, the independent contractor agreement attached as **Exhibit 8C** can be used. Prudent employers should obtain legal advice concerning such relationships, as fines, penalties and damages may result if done in error.

Recognizing that many employers may be tempted to recast employees as independent contractors for this reason, state and federal labor departments and the courts will look beyond what the position or agreement is called to determine the work involved and the independence of the employee and the other factors that are analyzed in making this determination.

2. Telecommuting

According to a pilot program in California, telecommuters accomplished 10–30% more than office workers. In this new century, employers may want to consider including, as a portion of employers' workforce, telecommuters. Telecommuters are employees who perform some significant portion of their work at some fixed location other than their employers' central office or plant—typically at their home. Telecommuters may also work at a satellite office or telework center located near their home or on the road or at a hotel. Why would employers want to hire telecommuters? There are several advantages to telecommuting:

- Employers can avoid labor shortages by retaining employees who might otherwise leave

- Employers may see increased employee productivity. Telecommuters can focus on the task at hand without interruption from co-workers, phones and meetings
- Employers' real estate costs will be cut because employers will not need as much office space
- Employers' other overhead expenses will be reduced
- Employee morale and quality of life may increase as their stress, commuting time and transportation costs decrease
- Employee turnover can be reduced by as much as 18%

Many employers will have a dramatically increased hiring pool for two reasons: (a) employers will not have any geographical restraints; and (b) employers' offer of a telecommuting position will be very attractive to a wider range of prospective employees. Telecommuting clearly will not work for some job positions. In deciding whether to approve a telecommuting relationship with some or all employees, employers should consider the adaptability of the work to be performed, the impact of the arrangement on other employees and the applicant's work history and characteristics. Factors to be considered include the following:

Length of Service. New employees may not make good candidates for telecommuting because they are not familiar with the employers' business and culture, their co-workers and their own individual job responsibilities. Most telecommuting consultants recommend that an employer require the employee to work for a short period of time in the office before telecommuting or to receive training prior to working off site.

Job Content. Not every job or position is suitable for telecommuting. Positions that are well-suited for telecommuting include jobs that can be measured by results, such as jobs involving sales, marketing, customer service positions, computer-related work or information-based jobs (e.g., researchers, writers, editors, transcribers, analysts).

Job Performance and Work Habits. Telecommuting is most successful for employees who are organized, self-disciplined, self-motivated and self-directed. Should employers decide to include telecommuters as part of their workforce, employers must understand that there are several practical and legal issues that are involved, which have not been discussed here. These can include recording hours worked for purposes of complying with wage and hour laws, while at the same time ensuring that the employees have actually performed work during the hours recorded. Employers should consult an attorney, who can help them draft a clearly defined telecommuting policy that addresses these practical and legal considerations in detail under the state and local statutes, ordinances and regulations that may apply. Additionally, employers should consider executing individual written telecommuting agreements with each telecommuter at the commencement of the arrangement.

3.   Temporary Employees

Many employers obtain a significant part of their workforce from temporary employment agencies. Such employees are sometimes referred to as "leased" employees. Usually leased employees are not eligible to participate in a company's employee benefit plans, such as the health insurance plan, but that is determined by the wording of the benefit plan documents. The leasing agency provides the employees to its client, which in turn pays the agency a fee. The leasing agency pays the employees and withholds the taxes and other legally required withholdings. In this sense, the leased employees are employed by the leasing agency, not the client. However, for purposes of some employment laws, such as the Family and Medical Leave Act and Title VII of the Civil Rights Act of 1964 (discussed later in this chapter), these employees may be considered employees of both the leasing agency and the client company and have the right to bring claims against the client company for violations of these laws.

10.03   Employment Contracts

Employers should consider the use of detailed employment agreements, especially for managers and executives, who may have confidential, propriety and trade secret information in their possession. Consequently, in the discussion below, we pay particular attention to the issues relevant to them. Attached as **Exhibit 10B** is an example of an employment agreement.

A.   Description of Duties

The agreement should specify the position to be occupied by the employee within the company, and the duties and obligations associated with the position. Reporting relationships can also be described. Obviously, the description of duties is fact-specific and must be tailored to the structure of the company and the understanding of the parties. When the employee is serving in an executive capacity, a general description of the position instead of the tasks to be done is more appropriate. On the other hand, when an agreement is used for a mid-level manager, the best practice is to include a reasonably detailed description of the anticipated duties, perhaps with a list of actions that the manager is not authorised to take without first obtaining approval from senior managers or executives. Restrictions may also be imposed on approving transactions that involve sums in excess of a specified amount.

In addition to the description of duties, the agreement should generally include language describing the expected standard of performance, as well a statement of the amount of time and effort that the employee is expected to spend on behalf of the company. A common requirement is that the employee must devote substantially all of his time to the affairs of the company. Alternatively, the company may seek to restrict the employee from any other business activities during the term of employment. In any case, consideration should also be given to including prohibitions against any direct or indirect form of competition with the company, including ownership of stock in rival companies.

Several other issues may be addressed under the general topic of employee duties. For instance, the agreement could explicitly state that the employer has the right to do the following:

- Change the duties or hours of the employee and to transfer the employee to another position, group, or affiliated company, although employees may demand restrictions on material changes in duties, or the location at which they will be stationed, without their consent. Such an inclusion will reduce the likelihood of a successful claim for constructive dismissal or a claim for breach of contract
- Supplement the general description of duties by referring to internal regulations and existing job-related rules and regulations, such as the company's personnel handbook
- Discharge the employee for any lawful reason with or without notice or cause
- Enforce a non-competition, confidentiality, or non-solicitation agreement in court. This should, of course, be reviewed with counsel before entering the agreement because state laws and court decisions vary among the states

B.   Compensation and Expenses

Compensation is a key element of any employment relationship and the parties should always try to carefully lay out the elements of the employee's remuneration for services to be provided to the company. While the employment agreement should include a general outline of the compensation package, certain benefits may actually be provided under the terms of separate plans or agreements (e.g., stock options).

Salary.   The cornerstone of the compensation package will generally be the base salary. The agreement should include the initial amount of salary, typically expressed as an annual or monthly amount, and the frequency of payment (e.g., weekly, semi-monthly, or monthly). In a contract for a lengthy period (e.g., in excess of 12 months), provision is generally made for periodic review of the salary amount.

Commissions.   Commissions are generally used as a means to pay compensation that is directly proportional to employee productivity. The agreement should make it clear when a commission on sales will be payable. While the company will want to delay commission payments until the purchase price has actually been collected from customers, the employee will want payments made when the order is booked. In most cases, the parties can reach a compromise by providing for advances against earned commissions in order to allow the employee to cover expenses. The agreement should provide clear terms for how and when commissions are earned, especially when employment is terminated. Federal and state wage and hour laws must be carefully considered to avoid violations.

Incentive and Retirement Plans. For executives and senior managers, the base salary is typically supplemented with a variety of additional compensation elements. For example, the employee usually will be eligible for incentive compensation, which includes all forms of compensation for which the amount that may be earned is tied to attaining certain performance goals. In addition, employees may participate in equity-based incentive compensation programs, including stock option plans, as described below.

Discretionary bonuses are certainly the simplest and most direct form of incentive payment. Bonuses may be paid to all, or to a limited number of, employees, and may be based on several factors, such as individual performance, recommendations from supervisors, or performance of the entire company or a particular operating unit. Profit-sharing plans may be used to distribute bonuses to employees out of company profits. Target performance plans might award participants on the basis of company profits, profits of a division or other operating unit, revenues of an operating unit, or some other measure deemed appropriate by senior management or the board of directors. Employees may also be allowed to participate in any retirement plan that the company has established. Because there are many pitfalls under various federal and state laws, receiving legal counsel is critical.

Fringe Benefits. Companies often offer various fringe benefits to their employees, including disability and health insurance benefits, life insurance, meals and lodging, educational benefits, automobile use, club memberships, reimbursement of moving expenses, and discounts on purchases of company products. This area is highly regulated by laws such as ERISA and, therefore, seeking legal advice should be considered.

Expenses. Employees will often ask employers to agree to reimburse the employee for certain expenses incurred in connection with the job. As a general rule, employers are required to reimburse their employees for any costs that an employee necessarily incurs as a direct consequence of discharging his or her duties on behalf of the employer. The items that may be covered by this reimbursement obligation will vary depending on the employee's position, and may include travel and entertainment expenses, professional dues and other licensing fees, legal and accounting fees, training expenses, equipment costs, and parking expenses. Often an employer and an executive employee will negotiate for reimbursement of the costs associated with business and social club memberships for the executive. Employers may also be willing to consider reimbursing certain employees for all or a portion of their relocation expenses when the employee is moving from another area to take the position.

Leave.   Companies must comply with statutory requirements that regulate how employers provide paid vacation and sick leave to employees. We describe the various types of leave in more detail below in the discussion of personnel policies and applicable employment laws.

C.   Term

Unless employers choose otherwise, employees will be employed on an at-will basis. What does this mean? It means that employers may discharge employees for any lawful reason, or no reason at all, without incurring liability. It is highly recommended that employers maintain an at-will employment relationship with all employees. With certain important exceptions (discussed later in this section), employing employees on an at-will basis provides employers with the freedom to terminate employees without limitation.

Although employing employees on an at-will basis allows employers great flexibility in terminating employees (and will allow employers to avoid breach of contract claims for such terminations), there are certain exceptions to the at-will rule that may give a terminated employee a legitimate potential lawsuit. The most common exceptions are statutory and include the following:

Federal or State Employment Discrimination Statutes.   These rules prohibit, for example, any termination that is motivated by discrimination against a protected group (including race, religion, color, national origin, sex and disability) and also prohibit an employer from terminating an employee in retaliation for exercising his rights under the acts.

State Worker's Compensation Statutes.   These statutes may specifically prohibit an employer from terminating an employee because he or she has exercised rights to claim worker's compensation benefits.

In addition to statutes limiting the employment at-will doctrine, most, if not all, state courts have held that at-will employees may have a legitimate wrongful discharge lawsuit if they were terminated in violation of public policy. Although different states' courts apply different criteria, generally a terminated at-will employee has a legitimate wrongful discharge claim for violation of public policy if the employee can show the following:

- Discharge is expressly prohibited by legislative enactment
- Reason for discharge was failure or refusal to commit an unlawful act in the course of employment
- Reason for discharge was as a result of an exercise of rights conferred by state law

As indicated at the outset, employees will automatically be at-will employees *unless employers choose otherwise.* How can employers alter employees' at-will status? The most obvious is by agreeing with employees that the employment relationship will continue for a definite period. In other words, employers can alter employees' at-will status by entering into contracts of employment that contain specified periods of employment. In some states, even oral assurances of a definite length of employment can, in some circumstances, alter at will status.

If the parties decide to include a specific term in the employment agreement, it may be subject to separate provisions relating to renewal or termination prior to the end of the stated term. If no term is included in the employment agreement, the employment relationship will generally be deemed to extend for an indefinite period unless and until such time as the parties elect to terminate the agreement in accordance with its terms. Employment for an indefinite period of time is generally considered at-will employment. Even if an employment agreement provides for an initial term with the possibility of renewal, the parties must carefully consider the conditions for extending the contract. For example, the agreement may provide for automatic renewal unless one of the parties gives notice within a specified period of time that he or she objects to the renewal. On the other hand, the employment agreement may require that one or both of the parties must affirmatively elect to renew the relationship, or that automatic renewal will be conditioned on satisfaction of one or more objective conditions. If a renewal provision is included in the employment agreement, the parties will need to discuss what, if any, other provisions in the agreement (e.g., salary) will be changed if the relationship continues beyond the initial term.

D. Termination

While it is sometimes difficult to think about the end of the employment relationship before the employee has even started working, it is important for the parties to take the time to consider what should happen in the event there is a need to part ways in the future. Given that statutes and case law now provide employees with substantial protection against termination of the employment relationship under a number of theories, it is important for employers to establish specific termination procedures in the agreement to avoid costly and time-consuming litigation. When drafting termination provisions, distinctions are often made between involuntary events that render the employee unable to perform his duties (e.g., death or disability), a voluntary decision by the employee to terminate the relationship, and termination by the company for cause or otherwise.

Death or Disability.   The death of the employee may not terminate the company's obligation to pay compensation and benefits to the employee's estate. In addition to payment of all amounts that have accrued through the date of death, the estate of executives and senior managers may sometimes be entitled to receive additional sums based on the anticipated value of compensation that might have been payable in the future. Also, the estate or beneficiary will generally have some period of time to decide whether or not to exercise any stock options that the employee may have held at the time of death. An employee's inability to perform the agreed services due to some type of physical or mental disability during the term of employment should also be addressed in the agreement. The key issues in this area include the definition of what constitutes a "disability" and the scope of the company's right to terminate or reduce the compensation payable to a disabled employee.

Termination by Company "For Cause." Employment agreements with executives and senior managers generally include provisions that allow the company to terminate the relationship "for cause." If such a provision is used, the definition of "for cause" must be carefully drafted, and the definition will depend on the business of the company, the position of the employee, and any other applicable policies adopted by the company. Typically, the company will be allowed to terminate the agreement if the employee willfully breaches the agreement or habitually neglects (or refuses to perform) the duties of his position for reasons other than disability. Other grounds may include breach of a fiduciary duty to the company or of company policy, or commission of a felony, fraud, or misrepresentation. Termination by employers is discussed in a later section on firing.

Termination by Company for Other Reasons. Companies often want to reserve the right to terminate employees without "cause." If so, the agreement should address this. This type of termination is also covered in a later section on firing.

Voluntary Termination by Employee. While the agreement generally focuses on the rights and duties of the parties when employment is terminated by actions of the company, voluntary termination by the employee prior to the end of the agreed term should also be addressed.

Severance Benefits. For executive employees, some of the most important benefits that can be provided are the benefits promised on termination of employment prior to retirement. Common types of benefits provided during an agreed "severance period" include salary continuation, health insurance benefits, life insurance benefits, out-placement services, and office space and support. The severance benefits provided to executives are often memorialised in a formal contract or agreement. One common, and often controversial, arrangement is the "golden parachute," which provides for severance payments and other benefits in the event of a change in control (e.g., merger or acquisition) of the company that results in termination of the executive's employment within a specified period of time.

Post-Termination Duties.   Employment agreements should also cover other post-termination duties that the parties may have to one another. For example, the company will want assurances that the employee will return all company property, including manuals, records, customer lists, keys, credit cards and other proprietary information. The employee may also have continuing obligations under nondisclosure, nonsolicitation, and noncompetition covenants included in the employment agreement or a separate agreement.

E.   Additional Terms

The employment agreement can give the employer rights in addition to the basic requirements explained above:

- To set conditions that must be complied with in the case of illness, such as providing a doctor's certificate or informing the company by telephone before a specified time
- To have employees medically examined periodically during employment (seek legal counsel first)
- To restrict holidays when necessary to reduce disruption
- To search employees' desks, lockers, bags, etc.
- To enforce noncompetition, nonsolicitation and confidentiality agreements, as discussed below under personnel policies
- To intercept telecommunications, as discussed below under privacy

F.   Changes

Changes in the contract of employment are possible as a matter of right during the term of the contract only if they are provided for in the contract itself. In addition, the contract can be changed by consent, which may be implied by the actions of the parties (e.g., if the hours worked are modified and the employee works the amended hours without complaint).

The company should proceed carefully in enforcing a variation in the terms of employment without the consent of the employee, since an enforced serious variation may amount to a repudiation of the contract, entitling the employee to leave the employment and make a claim for constructive dismissal. Such a claim may, however, be defeated if the company can show it acted reasonably and can show some substantial reason for the change, such as economic necessity.

10.04   Personnel Policies and Strategies

A.   Employee Handbooks

One of the most important documents that employers maintain is the employee handbook. If the handbook is *properly drafted and implemented*, it can be extremely useful by reinforcing the employment at-will doctrine; informing employees of their duties, responsibilities, and benefits to which they are entitled; incorporating desirable statements concerning equal employment opportunity and anti-discrimination; improving employee loyalty and performance; reducing the probability and severity of lawsuits and administrative actions, and reducing the potential for employees to seek union representation. The key here is that employee handbooks must be properly drafted, they must be regularly updated, and they must be followed by management. A poorly drafted or out-of-date handbook, or one which management routinely ignores, can be worse than no handbook at all and can lead to a confused or resentful workforce or, worse yet, lawsuits alleging violations of the handbook's terms.

In order to have a properly drafted employee handbook, employers must take particular care to ensure that the handbook is not inadvertently converted into a contract of employment. Employers do not want employees to have the right to sue for breach of contract in the event that employers' actions are at odds with the language contained in the handbook. Thus, to ensure that the employment relationship remains at-will and is not converted into a contractual relationship, employers must refrain from including language that indicates that employers or employees will be *bound* by the handbook's terms. For example, employers should not require employees to acknowledge in writing that they will abide by the terms and conditions of the handbook. Otherwise, the acknowledgment may be used as evidence by a court to support a finding that the handbook should be treated as a contract. Instead, the certification they sign should be limited to acknowledging receipt of the handbook. Further, employers should include a disclaimer in the handbook. This disclaimer should be clear and conspicuous, making clear that the handbook is not a contract of employment and that employees are employed at-will.

> *Example:* Nothing stated in this handbook constitutes a contract, express or implied, between the Company and its employees or any individual employee. Nothing contained in this handbook constitutes a guarantee of continued employment, but rather employment with the Company is on an "at will" basis. Either you, as the employee, or the Company, may terminate the employment relationship at any time for any reason not expressly prohibited by law. Any verbal or written representations (in this handbook or outside of this handbook) to the contrary are invalid and may not be relied upon by any employee. The policies in this handbook are subject to change without prior notice.

B.   Standard Policies

In addition to containing language indicating that it is not a contract of employment, the employee handbook should also contain certain key provisions in order to be as valuable a human resources tool as possible. The following are some of the more important provisions that employers should include:

- Employment policies such as equal employment opportunity, open door/ grievance policy, smoking, conflicts of interest, attendance, and drug and alcohol testing
- Compensation policies, including regular workweek, regular and overtime hours of work, employment classifications (e.g., full-time vs. part-time employees, exempt vs. non-exempt)
- Insurance and related benefits
- Time off benefits (e.g., vacation, family and medical leave policy, etc.)
- Standards of conduct, such as attendance and punctuality, health and safety standards, and grooming standards
- Disciplinary action, including a progressive discipline policy, as discussed below under firing

General Non-Discrimination Pledge.   For employers operating in more than one state, employers must ensure that this pledge covers the various protected groups in all of those states. For example, marital status, while not protected by federal law, is protected in some states and not in others.

> ***Example:*** It is the Company's policy to provide equal employment and advancement opportunity to all persons without regard to race, color, religion, age (40 and above), national origin, sex, sexual orientation, or disability. In addition to recruitment, employment, transfers and promotions, this policy of nondiscrimination applies to all aspects of the employment relationship— including (but not limited to) compensation, benefits, layoffs, recall, training, discipline and dismissal. Employees who feel that they have been discriminated against on these grounds are urged to report such incidents to their supervisor, the President, or the Human Resources Office immediately.

Harassment.   Employers' EEO policy should include a specific provision on harassment, in addition to employers' general nondiscrimination pledge. Among other things, this specific provision must define and express employers' strong disapproval for all forms of harassment.

Complaint Procedure.   Employers must establish a credible complaint procedure by which employers' employees can inform management of their concerns about, or complaints of, unlawful discrimination, including harassment. The procedure must allow employees to bypass the supervisor, because a supervisor may allegedly be engaging in the objectionable conduct.

Leaves of absence.   Employers need to have a general leave of absence and return to work policy, indicating when and under what circumstances employees may take this leave and if they need documentation upon their return to work. Types of leave include the following:

- Leaves pursuant to the Family and Medical Leave Act: employers should describe in detail the different types of leave under this law
- Funeral leave: employers should have a separate funeral leave policy if they choose to provide this type of leave
- Jury duty leave: employers should have a separate jury duty leave policy if they choose to provide such leave—state law may apply
- Worker's compensation leave: employers need a worker's compensation leave policy that complies with state laws
- Time off without pay: employers may decide to have this type of leave, so long as it is approved and scheduled in advance
- Vacation: employers should have a vacation policy indicating how many vacation days a year to which employees are entitled

This is a non-exhaustive list of what to include in employee handbooks. While many of these provisions are important to include in employee handbooks for any type of business, employers may find that the type of business they run requires different provisions as well.

Regardless of the content of the provisions that employers include in employee handbooks, remember to be clear that the provisions contained in the employee handbook are not promises to employers' employees regarding benefits, hours, wages, and the like. Employeree handbooks should speak in terms of coverage and not in terms of particular benefits. Handbooks should also explicitly state that all statements of coverage are subject to the terms, conditions, restrictions and other eligibility requirements set forth in the particular benefit plans. Finally, employers should make sure to reserve their right to modify, amend, or terminate any benefit plan at any time and for any reason.

C. Intellectual Property

As discussed in Chapter 1 (Starting a New Business), it is important to confirm that the employer owns intellectual property developed by employees during the course of their employment. While there is a presumption of such ownership in most states, there are limits to the doctrine. For instance, in California, a business may not require the employee to transfer or assign inventions that are created outside of the scope of employment without the use of materials owned by the business entity.[2] The acknowledgement can be included in the employee handbook, employment agreement or in a separate document. A sample form of stand-alone acknowledgment is included as **Exhibit 10C.**

---

2. Cal. Labor Code Section 2780; *see also* Nev. Revised Statute 600.500.

D. Non-Competition

Whether contained as a provision in the employee handbook or maintained as a separate agreement between employers and employees, non-competition agreements (typically including a section regarding confidentiality) are a must in highly competitive industries. These types of agreements provide a shield of protection for employers' trade secrets and valuable information, such as customer files, customer lists, marketing, financial or sales records, data, plans and surveys, as well as any other information relating to the present or future product or service of employers' business. With the expansion of the information age, these agreements have become increasingly popular among employers seeking to prevent employees with knowledge of company trade secrets from using such secrets against them.

Non-competition agreements generally prevent employees from going to work for a competitor of their employer for a specified time in a particular place. Most State courts have developed laws regarding the enforceability of non-competition agreements entered into between employers and their employees. Those decisions must be closely analyzed before requiring employees to sign a non-competition agreement or seeking to enforce such agreements in court. As a general rule, many courts will find a non-competition agreement enforceable if the following criteria are met:

- Employers can prove that employers have a legitimate business interest by restricting employees' right to compete against employers
  Examples of legitimate business interests recognized by several courts: highly specified training given to employees, pricing lists, customer lists, goodwill, bidding strategies, profit margins and other confidential information.
- The scope of the restriction on competition is reasonable in relation to the interests that employers seek to protect
- In evaluating whether the scope of the restriction on competition is reasonable, state courts consider the following factors:

  - Length of time of the restriction (during employment and one to two years after termination of employment is generally deemed reasonable, although even longer restrictions have been upheld)
  - Geographic scope of the restriction, which can be stated in terms of a mileage radius from the employer's business locations, or in terms of the city, county, or state where competition is prohibited. In some instances, even nationwide restrictions have been upheld where the employer conducted business on a nationwide basis
  - Breadth of the activities prohibited. It will generally be deemed reasonable if the only activities prohibited are those that were performed by the employee at the employer's place of business, although sometimes any work for a competitor, even if different from the work previously done, can be sufficiently harmful to be prohibited

- The non-compete agreement is supported by consideration—that is, employees received something in exchange for having had to sign (and be bound by) the agreement. Many courts will consider an employer's promise to provide an employee with confidential information and trade secrets sufficient consideration to support the employee's promise not to compete. Each state's laws must be analyzed

E.   Employee Use of Voice Mail, E-mail and Internet

Voice mail, e-mail and the Internet are not as private as people may think. An employee forwarding a sex-charged joke could prompt a colleague to allege sexual harassment, and a employee's innocent exchange of proprietary information could give competitors a leg up. Electronic mail continues to win widespread praise as the means of speedy communication, but the technology's inherent informality is also a litigation time-bomb for companies that fail to monitor its use by employees.

There are also business implications that result from failing to monitor, such as wasted time and resources. Employees may spend a good part of the day looking busy while they exchange personal e-mail both within and outside the company. Monitoring is, therefore, a valuable tool to protect against potential litigation and to support legitimate business interests in meeting demands for maximum cost efficiency, productivity and quality imposed by global competition. Thus, although employers must consider the constitutional, contractual, judicial and statutory privacy implications of doing so, employers should consider implementing an electronic monitoring and communications policy, such as included in **Exhibit 10D**.

There are many privacy implications to such policies, including the following:

Constitution.   Both the U.S. Constitution and state constitutions provide individuals with zones of privacy protected from government intrusion. They also provide individuals with protection against unwanted searches and seizures by the government. Therefore, employees working for entities that are not federal, state or local governmental entities have no constitutional protection from employers' implementation of an electronic monitoring/ communications policy.

Contract.   Obviously, employers may voluntarily provide safeguards to employee privacy via employers' policies or contracts, either express or implied. Should employers do so, employers must make sure that employers' communications policy does not violate the employee privacy policy or any contract that employers may have adopted.

Judicial.   Courts have created a common law right to privacy that encompasses two different areas, including security from intrusion into his or her seclusion, and security from disclosure of facts that one deems private. An employee suing under either of these theories has a relatively high burden of proof: that he or she must have a reasonable expectation of privacy under the circumstances, and management's intrusion or disclosure must be deemed highly offensive to a reasonable person. Courts will weigh the level of privacy expectation against legitimate business reasons for the intrusion or disclosure.

State Statute. The state in which employers conduct employers' business may have a wiretapping or eavesdropping statute which employers must abide by.

Federal Statute. One of the most important federal statutes in this area is Title III of the Omnibus Crime Control and Safe Streets Act of 1968, as amended by the Electronic Communications Privacy Act of 1986 ("Federal Electronic Privacy Statute").[3] This statute prohibits the intentional interception, use or disclosure of a wire, electronic or oral communication, and prohibits the intentional use of an electronic, mechanical or other device to intercept an oral communication. The statute also makes it unlawful to access intentionally and without authorization an electronic communication storage facility or to knowingly to divulge the contents of a communication stored by that service, such as e-mail messages. There are, however, three exceptions to this rule, which open the door for employers to monitor employees' communications under certain circumstances:

- Extension telephone exception: under this exception, employers are allowed to monitor wire and electronic communications within the ordinary course of business from telephone equipment furnished and used in the ordinary course of business. Thus, monitoring business-related calls, voice mail or e-mail is appropriate. However, monitoring the content of personal calls, voice mail or e-mail is prohibited, even if the employee is violating a policy against personal phone calls or is abusing a privilege permitting such calls. Generally, employers may monitor employees' calls, voice mails or e-mails up to the point employers determine that they are personal. At that point, employers must cease
- Employee consent: if an employee consents to being monitored, then employers may listen to calls or voice mail and employers may read e-mails, regardless of whether they are business-related or not. Most courts equate consent to actual notice or acknowledgment of a clearly-defined monitoring policy. Thus, if employees are made aware of the specifics of employers' monitoring and communications policy, employers should be permitted to monitor calls, voice mail and e-mail without regard for whether such communications are business-related or personal. Disclosure of the contents of such a call, voice mail, or e-mail is permis-

---

3.   Title III of the Omnibus Crime Control and Safe Streets Act of 1968, as amended by the Electronic Privacy Act of 1986, 18 U.S.C. §§ 2510–2521 and 2701–2711.

sible under this exception only if the employee consented to disclosure as well as monitoring

- System provider exception: the prohibition against access to stored communication does not apply to the person or entity providing a wire or electronic communications service. Thus, if employers provide for voice mail on an internal telephone system that the employers own, or e-mail on an internal electronic mail system that employers own, then employers are arguably the "provider" of these wire communications services and can access any communications stored on them

This statute is quite complex and must be closely analyzed. Further, there has been very little case law to date regarding the monitoring of e-mail and Internet usage and, thus, courts may analyze these exemptions differently than expected. Employers should learn the particulars of this statute before implementing a communications policy.

Employers' policy should be clearly communicated to employees. This will put them on notice as well as reduce the chances for costly lawsuits and any adverse impact on employee morale. In addition, employers should do the following in their communications policy:

- State that telephones, computers, and software are the property of the employer and are provided for business activities, and that excessive personal use of this equipment is prohibited. Employers should define expected use of Internet capability and surfing limitations
- Warn users to avoid inappropriate references in their telephone and electronic communications, including material or comments that could be construed as discriminatory, hostile or suggestive, or that might violate other company policies, such as non-solicitation and harassment
- Advise that the contents of voice mail and e-mail communications should be disclosed only on a need-to-know basis. Employers should caution voice mail and e-mail users about the dangers inherent in forwarding communications of others and that they should assume someone other than the intended recipient may become a party to the communication
- Expressly reserve the right to monitor communications and the right of access to business-related information and materials
- Define the types of monitoring that may be utilized and describe how it will be done. This includes defining the circumstances of monitoring, including frequency and duration
- Identify legitimate business purposes, such as training, productivity standards, quality control, network overload, security performance management and marketing research
- Declare that employees do not have a right to personal privacy with respect to their telephone and e-mail communications or the contents of their work areas. The employer should also explain that passwords are designed to minimize unauthorized access only

- State that workplace documents and communications are business records subject to possible review by the employer as well as outside parties. The employer should explain that e-mail and computer files are backed up to tape or disk and retained as business records (including deleted records).
- Expressly state that violations of the policy should be considered in performance evaluations and can be a basis for disciplinary action
- Have an acknowledgment page, which states that the employee has read the policy, understands it, and accepts it as a condition of employment or continued employment. This acknowledgment should be signed and dated by the employee

F.   Social Networking

In the last few years the popularity of Internet blogging and social networking sites such as Facebook, Twitter, and Linked-In has exploded. Hundreds of millions of people now use blogs and social networking sites to communicate with each other and, indeed, the whole world. Businesses have also started using these new media as a means of communicating with the public and their customers, promoting their brands, and improving their business. They are also a quick and easy source of information about competitors and others. Another advantage is that they are free.

This phenomenon thus has numerous potential business applications. But there are also serious pitfalls associated with the instantaneous international publication of information for those unprepared for its consequences. Careful planning and training, along with a general awareness of the legal implications of social networking, will help place your business on the right track.

With respect to the employer/employee relationship, social networking can create the following issues:

- Employees inappropriately depicting an employer's property or workplace on the internet
- Employees making derogatory comments about the employer, its management, employees, or products
- Employees divulging confidential or proprietary company information
- Employees wasting time while at work
- Employees harassing or defaming others
- Computer system security problems, such as hackers and viruses
- Employers using these sites to gather information about current or prospective employees that they might be prohibited by law from asking for in an interview or on an application (e.g., age, disability, genetic information, marital status, sexual orientation)
- Employers violating federal laws such as the Stored Communications Act by accessing employee accounts, particularly if the accounts are password protected

- Potential for employers to be sued for slanderous or harassing statements made by their employees about others (including other employees), particularly if the statements are posted during working hours

For these reasons, employers should either adopt a separate social networking policy or include rules for use of social media in their internet and email policy, as discussed above. The purposes of doing so are to protect company confidential information, trade secrets, trademarks, brands and logos, prohibit discrimination and harassment of others, and address the proper use of company time and resources. Employees should be trained on the policy, compliance should be monitored, and violations should be addressed consistently. A sample policy is in **Exhibit 10E.**

G. Arbitration

In order to avoid employment-related lawsuits, employers should consider implementing a mandatory arbitration agreement that covers employment disputes. Employers who prefer arbitration may avoid employment litigation for several reasons: (a) employers that lose court cases may have to pay larger verdicts, (b) employee lawsuits are resulting in huge settlements, and (c) employers are spending significant sums to defend employment lawsuits.

Arbitration is a "simple proceeding voluntarily chosen by parties who want a dispute determined by an impartial decision-maker of their own mutual selection, whose decision, based on the merits of the case, they agree in advance to accept as final and binding."[4] Arbitration is particularly advantageous for employers because (a) arbitration is a much friendlier forum than the courtroom, where employers run the risk of being in front of a hostile jury capable of rendering a "runaway" verdict, (b) it is unlikely that arbitration will result in the "jumbo" settlements that have become commonplace in employment lawsuits, and (c) the arbitration process is generally more expedient and less expensive for employers.

Arbitration is not a panacea and is not necessarily the best option for every employer. Before implementing mandatory arbitration, employers should review their experience in litigation to determine if they would be better off in arbitration. Employers that have never been sued or have been sued infrequently may not need mandatory arbitration. For one, employees who might not otherwise file a lawsuit may demand arbitration, particularly if they are not required to bear any of the cost. So mandatory arbitration could end up increasing the number or frequency of formal employment disputes. In addition, unless they are settled, arbitration cases almost always end up in a hearing before the arbitrator. The arbitration hearing is essentially a trial

---

4.   Elkouri & Elkouri, *How Arbitration Works* at 2 (4th Ed. 1985), *quoting* Chapell, *Arbitrate . . . And Avoid Stomach Ulcers,* 2 Arb. Mag. Nos. 11–12, pp. 6–7 (1944).

without a jury and can last for days. Witnesses must testify and are subject to cross-examination by the opposing party or opposing attorney. While an arbitration case usually, though not always, takes less time, effort, and expense to prepare for trial than a case in court, a substantial investment of resources must still be made in order to increase the chances of a successful outcome. In contrast, many employment cases filed in court, particularly in federal court, are dismissed by the judge before trial.

Arbitration agreements (as long as they are valid and enforceable) are lawful under the Federal Arbitration Act ("FAA").[5] If employers intend to draft such an agreement, in addition to closely scrutinizing both the FAA and state law, they should draft and implement such an agreement in conjunction with legal counsel. The following pointers are intended as a guide with recommendations only:

- To ensure that employees have knowingly agreed to arbitrate statutory employment claims, the agreement should reference the major statutes by name. The agreement should, however, also include broad "catch-all" language, such as, "any and all claims, including statutory claims, arising out of employers' employment or cessation of employment, including but not limited to . . ."
- Employers should require new employees to sign an arbitration agreement as part of the application process or following a job offer, but prior to their start dates. Applicants and new employees can be advised that their refusal to sign will disqualify them from employment
- Advise all current employees of employers' decision to implement an arbitration procedure, but do not require them to sign an agreement. The problem with requiring employees to sign an agreement to arbitrate is that many may balk. This puts the employer in the position of having to terminate anyone who refuses (this would likely beg a response from the Equal Employment Opportunity Commission). By implementing without a signed agreement, the employer avoids this pitfall. Moreover, several courts have indicated that a signed agreement is not necessary for enforcement. Employers can argue that the employees agreed to arbitration by continuing to work
- Require employees to pay filing fees equivalent to what they would have to pay in federal court. This would serve as a sort of "earnest money," ensuring that employees incur some cost before pursuing their claims
- Appoint arbitrators through the American Arbitration Association ("AAA"). This is advisable because: (a) using a universally acknowledged neutral third party addresses many potential due process concerns employees may have and (b) the AAA is getting fairly adept at handling

---

5. See U.S. Supreme Court decision, Circuit City Stores v. Adams, 535 U.S. 1112 (2002), in which the Court held that employment claims, including statutory employment claims, can be subject to mandatory arbitration.

employment law disputes, so that any fears concerning traditional labor arbitrators may not be realized

- Require a transcript of the arbitration hearing, give both parties the opportunity to submit pre-hearing briefs, and require the arbitrator to issue a written opinion containing findings of fact and conclusions of law. To the extent that judicial review of the arbitration occurs, it will only be meaningful if the parties and the reviewing court are provided with the factual and legal rationale behind the decision and a record of the proceedings, including a transcript and at least the opportunity to brief the issues

- Provide for confidentiality. One of the primary advantages of private arbitration is that, unlike litigation, it is not a matter of public record

- Deny the binding effect of arbitration results on subsequent arbitrations involving different employees (with similar claims). Although this might have the effect of denying employers a defense that employers would otherwise employ in court, it has the salutary effect of avoiding an avalanche of "me-too" claims following a successful arbitration. Employees are much less likely to choose to endure the time and trouble of arbitration if they have no certainty of success

- Unless all parties agree, do not permit class action or joint claims to go to arbitration. The risk of a substantial damage award may be unacceptably great by giving a single arbitrator the power to decide such claims. Of course, in appropriate circumstances (particularly where the damage exposure is limited), employers may agree to class or joint claims, as it may be more efficient to resolve all such claims in one proceeding

- Include a severability clause that allows a court to "blue pencil" portions of the arbitration agreement should the court find any provision unlawful. Doing so will allow the remainder of the agreement to stand and be enforceable, despite the fact that certain provisions were unlawful. With severability, unlawful provisions will be stricken

10.05   Stock Option Plans

There are two types of stock option plans: incentive stock options ("ISOs") and nonqualified stock options ("NQOs"). While ISOs offer favorable tax treatment to employees, as well as being favored by them, they are more expensive from a tax standpoint for employers. NQOs offer the reverse situation. Both plans offer employees (and other parties in the case of NQOs) the opportunity to purchase shares in the employer (or the third party issuing the option in the case of NQOs). The option recipient has the right under both plans to purchase the shares represented by the option at some point in the future, but at a price fixed at the time of the grant. This allows the recipient to pay in future dollars when money may be more available, such as at the time of a public offering, but to pay a price based on present (and presumably much lower) value. Such plans were a driving force during the dot.com era of the late 1990s.

A. Incentive Stock Options

The requirements for an ISO are as follows:

- Option term cannot exceed 10 years, unless the optionee owns more than 10% of the voting power of the issuer, in which case the term cannot exceed five years
- Option price must not be less than the fair market value of the stock on the date of option grant, or not less than 110% of the fair market value if the optionee owns more than 10% of the voting power of the issuer
- Optionee must be an employee at time of grant and within three months of the time of exercise, except for disability, when the three-month period is extended to one year. There is no limitation on the exercise period in the event of death (but the issuer normally sets this period at one year)
- Shareholders must approve the option plan within 12 months before or after the plan is adopted by the board of directors
- If the aggregate option price of the stock that first becomes exercisable by an optionee during any calendar year under all ISOs exceeds $100,000, the excess amount is treated as an NQO. For example, if in year one the optionee may exercise the option for $150,000 of stock (1500 shares at an option price of $100, 500 shares would be NQOs; but if the optionee could only exercise 750 shares in the first year and 750 in the second year, all would constitute ISOs even if 1500 shares were exercised in the second year)

The tax attributes of an ISO are as follows:

- No income is recognized by the optionee at the time an ISO is granted, nor is the issuer entitled to a deduction
- Upon exercise of the option, the optionee does not recognize any income, nor is the issuer entitled to a deduction. This is one of the two major advantages to employees
- The difference between the option price and the fair market value of the stock on the date the option is exercised is treated as income to the optionee for purposes of the alternative minimum tax ("AMT")
- Upon sale of the stock by the optionee (unless the sale is a "disqualifying disposition," which essentially means a sale of the stock within two years from the date of grant or within one year of the date of transfer of the stock upon exercise), the optionee recognizes long-term capital gain or loss equal to the amount realized on the sale, less the option price. This is the other great advantage of ISOs to employees—increase in value is treated as a capital gain

- Upon sale of the stock (unless the sale is a "disqualifying disposition"), no deduction is allowed to the issuer. This is why ISOs are not beneficial to employers
- If the sale is a disqualifying disposition, the optionee will be taxed as follows:
  - Ordinary income in an amount equal to the difference between the option price and the lesser of (a) the fair market value of the stock on the date the option is exercised or (b) the amount realized from the disqualifying disposition
  - Capital gain equal to the amount, if any, by which the amount realized upon the disqualifying disposition exceeds the fair market value of the stock on the date the option is exercised
  - In addition, if the disqualifying disposition occurs in the year the option is exercised, the AMT is limited to the gain on the disposition of the stock; if the disqualifying disposition occurs in another year, there are no AMT consequences
- Upon a disqualifying disposition, the issuer is entitled to a deduction equal to the amount of ordinary income the optionee recognizes by reason of the disqualifying disposition
- In Notice 2001-14 (2001-61 RB), the Internal Revenue Service announced that it will no longer follow an old Revenue Ruling which exempted ISO exercises from Federal Insurance Contributions Act ("FICA") and Federal Unemployment Tax Act ("FUTA") taxes, and withholdings on disqualifying dispositions, effective January 1, 2003

The accounting treatment of ISOs is that stock options are expensed for financial reporting purposes at the time of the grant in an amount equal to the amount by which the option price is less than the fair market value of the option stock. Consequently, as ISOs must be granted at fair market value, there is no charge to earnings either at the time of grant or at the time of exercise. From time to time, however, there have been proposals to require companies to value options granted at fair market value and to set forth that value in a footnote to the financials, or take a charge against earnings for their value.

In issuing ISOs, employers should consider the following tax planning considerations:

- The major advantage to the optionee is that ISOs permit the deferral of gain until disposition of the stock. Capital gains are now taxed from 20% to 28%, while most optionees will be taxed for federal income tax purposes from 31% to 39.6% on ordinary income. To the extent the ordinary income tax rate increases, the tax benefits of an ISO should increase
- The major disadvantage is the AMT on the spread between the option price and the fair market value on the date of exercise

- To the extent indebtedness is incurred to buy the stock, interest may not be deductible unless the stock pays dividends or the optionee has other investment income
- The option price may be satisfied with previously owned issuer stock

B.   Non-Qualified Stock Options

There are no stated tax requirements for NQOs. Thus, the option can be granted to non-employees, the term can exceed 10 years, the option price can be less than fair market value, there is no restriction on the number of shares that can be subject to option, and no shareholder approval is necessary (unless required by state law—although there are no such requirements, for instance, in Delaware—or by a stock exchange; for example, the NYSE requires shareholder approval of an employee stock option plan).

The tax attributes of NQOs can be summarized as follows:

- Unless an NQO is determined to have a readily ascertainable fair market value, the optionee recognizes no income upon grant of the option. Essentially, the position of the Internal Revenue Service is that unless options in the issuer's stock similar to the NQO are traded on a recognized exchange, NQOs do not have a readily ascertainable fair market value
- Upon exercise, an optionee who is not subject to liability under section 16(b) (short-swing profits) of the Securities and Exchange Act of 1934 with respect to a sale of the stock will recognize ordinary income in an amount equal to the excess of the fair market value of the stock over the exercise price. This is the main disadvantage of NQOs over ISOs for recipients
- If the optionee is subject to liability under section 16(b), has an unrelated purchase of stock within six months of the exercise of the NQO and does not file a special election, it is likely that income will be recognized six months after the date of the unrelated purchase in an amount equal to the difference between the exercise price and the fair market value of the stock as of that date
- The issuer is entitled to a deduction equal to the amount of the "deemed income" (which is the spread) of the optionee in the taxable year of the employee when the option is exercised which ends in or with the issuer's year. This is the advantage of NQOs over ISOs to issuers
- A subsequent sale of the stock results in capital gain or loss treatment, assuming one of the required holding periods is met
- The optionee's basis in the option stock is increased by the income recognized upon exercise of the option

The accounting treatment of NQOs is the same as for ISOs, unless the option is granted at less than fair market value. When this occurs, there is a charge against earnings based upon the spread between the option price and the then fair market value of the stock on the date of grant. This charge is spread over the period for which the compensation is being earned, which generally is the vesting period, and, if the option is immediately exercisable, the charge would be recognized in the period in which it was granted. Some firms do, however, reflect this charge in their footnotes, not in the income statement.

C.   See-Saw Options

A "See-Saw" option is an NQO where the option price decreases as the value of the stock increases. The purpose of a See-Saw option is to provide the same economic results to the issuer as an ISO. Because a See-Saw option is an NQO, the difference between the option price and the exercise price is deductible by the issuer and is income to the optionee at the time of exercise. The result of a See-Saw option is that the issuer will receive, through the option price and the tax deduction, an amount equal to the fair market value of the stock at the date of grant. For example, if the value of the stock at the date of grant is $10.00, and the value of the stock at exercise is $20.00, the adjusted option price would be $3.33 if the issuer is in the 40% tax bracket. At an option price of $3.33, the issuer would receive a tax deduction of $16.67, which at a 40% rate would save it $6.67 in taxes, which, together with the $3.33 option price, would give it $10.00, the initial option price. The tax attributes of see-saw options are the same as those of NQOs.

Because of the variable nature of the stock price, even NQOs granted at fair market value have accounting consequences. To the extent that there is a difference between the option price and the fair market value of the stock under option, that spread is reported as a charge against earnings for accounting purposes each year. Thus, as the spread widens as the stock increases in value, greater sums are reported as a charge against earnings for accounting purposes. (This accounting treatment does not have any affect on the tax treatment.) Requiring a vesting period for the option may reduce this charge, so only a small piece of the spread is included each year.

A stock option plan covering both ISOs and NQOs appears as **Exhibit 10F**. A sample stock option agreement, which covers both types of options, is included as **Exhibit 10G**.

10.06   Firing

A.   Preliminary Considerations

While employment lawsuits arise out of many circumstances, the primary source of employment litigation is a discharge or involuntary termination of employment. As a result, employers must be increasingly sensitive to the laws governing terminations. It is frequently advisable to engage in "termination planning" before an employee is actually fired.

B. Training

Because the manner in which a termination is handled can be critical, it is important that all individuals having authority to discharge employees be given sufficient training to know what is lawful and unlawful in their state. These individuals should also be instructed as to when legal advice should be sought in connection with a termination. In-house seminars or training sessions may be beneficial to ensure that managers and supervisors understand the risks and potential liabilities in this evolving area of employment law.

C. Progressive Discipline

1. System

Non-union employers increasingly use progressive discipline in dealing with employee problems. Such a system imposes progressively greater disciplinary measures upon an employee whose performance continues to be unsatisfactory. Such systems are usually committed to writing and appear as part of the employee handbook. Documentation of all disciplinary actions, especially when they may result in termination, is critical.

2. Employer Education

Employers using a system of progressive discipline must educate their managers and supervisors about the consequences of improperly handling disciplinary matters. If supervisors and managers are not properly trained in connection with this system, disgruntled employees may have a stronger basis for a wrongful discharge claim than if the system had never been used.

Supervisors and managers must be even-handed, consistent and thorough in dealing with disciplinary situations. Supervisors should review employees' personnel files to confirm what, if any, prior discipline has been imposed. In order to ensure consistency, all disciplinary actions, including verbal warnings, should be documented in writing and placed in the employee's personnel file as soon as possible after the discipline is imposed. Unless an employee's conduct warrants immediate and severe discipline or discharge, the supervisor should follow all progressive disciplinary steps prior to discharging the employee.

To ensure consistent application of the employer's disciplinary procedure, an internal review system should be implemented, requiring senior management, the human resources manager, and/or legal counsel to review all termination decisions. Special consideration should also be given to ensure consistent treatment of all individuals. Exceptions made for individuals not in protected groups, even where mitigating circumstances exist, can make it more difficult for an employer to justify the subsequent termination of a similarly-situated individual in a protected group.

D. Peer Review System

In recent years, a growing number of non-union companies have developed various types of peer review systems. Traditionally, non-union employees have had no way to formally resolve problems they encounter at work. Thus, an employee could be suspended, disciplined or even terminated without the opportunity to have the decision reviewed by persons other than the supervisor making the decision. Peer review systems have been developed to allow employees to appeal adverse employment decisions.

Typically, peer review appeals are limited to terminations. The appeal board normally consists of both management and hourly employees (peers). Under most systems, the board does not have the authority to change company policy. The board can, however, decide whether the facts support management's decision and make recommendations as to whether the termination should be upheld. Management generally retains the final authority to terminate or retain an employee; the peer review panel's recommendations, although persuasive, are not binding.

Employers utilizing such systems must be careful not to "dominate" or interfere with the formation or administration of any labor organization or contribute financial or other support, which is prohibited by Section 8(a)(2) of the National Labor Relations Act ("NLRA" or "Act"):[6]

> It shall be an unfair labor practice for an employer --
>
> . . .
>
> (2) to dominate or interfere with the formation or administration of any labor organization or contribute financial or other support to it.

The term "labor organization" is defined in the Act as: "[a]ny organization of any kind, or any agency or employee representation *committee* or plan, in which employees participate and which exists for the purpose, in whole or in part, of dealing with employers concerning grievances, labor disputes, wages, rate of pay, hours of employment, or conditions of work."

An employee committee that is established, at least in part, for the purpose of "dealing with" the employer regarding conditions of employment constitutes a labor organization under the Act.[7] The "dealing with" requirement can be met where an employee group makes proposals, recommendations or suggestions

---

6.   29 U.S.C. §158(a)(2).
7.   Electromation, Inc., 309 NLRB No. 163 (1992).

to the employer regarding working conditions, even if no recommended action is proposed.[8] In *Uarco, Inc.*,[9] the National Labor Relations Board ("NLRB" or "Board") found that an employee committee which met with company officials to discuss employee complaints concerning terms and conditions of employment was a "labor organization" under the Act. Because the committee met with the employer "to present and discuss complaints and conditions of employment," the employer violated Section 8(a)(2) of the NLRA in dealing with it.

Likewise, in *Keeler Brass Automotive Group*,[10] the NLRB found that a grievance committee was a labor organization unlawfully dominated by the employer. The committee was deemed a labor organization because it was comprised of elected employees and existed in part for the purpose of dealing with the employer on the subjects of grievances and terms and conditions of employment. The committee "dealt with" the employer because it proposed a less severe disciplinary action for an aggrieved employee, discussed another policy, and functioned in a bilateral way in the sense that the committee and management went back and forth until they reached an agreement. The committee was "dominated by" management because, although its members were elected by the employees, management set the criteria for membership, modified the structure and function of the committee, paid committee members for their time, and supplied the meeting room and secretarial support.

In *Sparks Nugget, Inc.*,[11] however, an employer established a committee consisting of one rank-and-file employee, one management official and a third individual selected by the other two. The committee conducted ad hoc meetings to discuss employee grievances. It did not, however, file grievances, propose changes to employment terms and conditions, or advocate employee interests. The Board concluded that the committee performed a "purely adjudicatory function" and did not interact or deal with the employer who, therefore, did not violate the Act.

Properly established and administered employee involvement programs can lead to increased productivity and a more satisfied workforce. If implemented incorrectly, however, such programs may result in a myriad of legal problems. In order to avoid potential violations of the Act, employers should proceed carefully and consult with legal counsel before taking such actions.

E.   Pre-Termination

Where employee agreements or handbooks contain procedures for termination, they should be reviewed before the termination occurs to make sure that the employer is acting in compliance with its own procedures. The employee's

---

8.   Memphis Truck & Trailer, 284 NLRB 900, 901 (1987).
9.   286 NLRB 55 (1987).
10.   317 NLRB 1110 (1995)
11.   230 NLRB 275 (1977), enforced, 623 F.2d 571 (9th Cir. 1980), *cert. denied*, 451 U.S. 906 (1981).

personnel file should also be reviewed to ensure that adequate documentation exists to support the termination. Investigate the events surrounding the termination to make sure that you have the facts straight. Be sure to get the employee's version of the incident before making a final decision. If the conduct of an employee requires immediate action before an investigation can be completed, consider suspending the employee, with or without pay, until an investigation can be conducted. If the employer discovers circumstances that mitigate or eliminate the basis for termination, it can return the employee to work without having exposed the company to potential liability.

During an investigatory interview, a bargaining unit employee in a unionized company has a right to request the presence of a co-worker or union representative if the employee reasonably believes the investigation could result in disciplinary action, such as termination. This right, often called a *Weingarten* right, arises from the NLRA. Between 2000 and 2004, the NLRB extended this right to non-union employees.[12] In 2004, the NLRB reverted to its previous interpretation of the law that non-union employees do not have *Weingarten* rights.[13]

Once the investigation is complete, the employer should carefully consider the circumstances of each case and evaluate the possibility of a discrimination, wrongful discharge, or retaliation claim resulting from the termination decision. How old is the employee? Is the employee pregnant? How many minority employees remain with the employer? By whom will the employee be replaced? How long has the employee been with the employer? Does the documentation in the personnel file support termination? Was the employee hired away from a long-time employer? Has the employee filed a workers' compensation claim or any other type of claim with a federal or state agency? Has the employee made any internal or external complaint about allegedly unlawful practices? Has the employee participated in any internal investigation of workplace practices (e.g., has the employee been interviewed as part of a sexual harassment investigation)? Have other employees been discharged (or alternately, been retained) who committed similar infractions in the past?

In addition, employers must evaluate the practical considerations of termination (although some of these can have legal implications as well). If the termination is challenged, can the employer afford adverse publicity? To what extent has the employer failed the employee? Assuming that the employee is not terminated and the problem does not improve, can the employer stand continuation of the problem? Is the employee the kind of person who is likely to file suit? What impact would terminating, or failing to terminate, have on employee morale and employer credibility? What has been the immediate supervisor's history in terms of having problems with his or her people? Does the employee have potential for success working in

---

12.   Epilepsy Foundation of Northeast Ohio v. NLRB, 268 F.3d 1095 (D.C. Cir. 2001).

13.   IBM Corp., 341 NLRB 1288 (2004).

a different job or under another supervisor? Are there any non-job-related problems that have created or added to the employee's problems at work? Has the employee tried to improve? Even if the termination is legally defensible, is it a wise decision to terminate? Test the tentative decision by letting an independent source evaluate it. Seek legal advice concerning terminations where serious liability may result from the discharge.

F. Termination Conference

The final and most critical step in the termination process is the termination conference. Problems often arise from improper handling of a termination conference. The termination conference may generate litigation if an employee becomes angry, hostile and intent on filing suit because the termination was not handled properly. In this regard, the following guidelines should be considered:

- Choose the right person for the job
- Prepare a written script to follow. This could be helpful evidence in the event of a dispute about what the employee was told in the meeting
- Rehearse what will be said and how the situation will be handled
- Choose a neutral, private site, such as a conference room
- Make sure there is another managerial employee present during the meeting
- Within the first few minutes of the interview, tell the employee that he or she is being terminated. Do not beat around the bush or be overly-blunt. Rather, be up-front and candid
- Tell the employee why he or she is being terminated. Don't try to avoid hurting the employee's feelings by saying something untruthful, such as saying that it is a "restructuring," when in fact the reason is the employee's poor performance. If you later have to defend the decision in court, and you testify that the reason was poor performance, the inconsistency will be used against you. Even telling the employee that he or she is just not "a good fit," is not advisable when the true reason is something else
- Review the employment history briefly, commenting on specific problems that have occurred and the attempts on the part of the employer to correct those problems
- Do not argue with the employee in an effort to justify the decision
- Avoid counseling at this point; it should have already been done
- Do not be so complimentary of the employee in an effort not to hurt his or her feelings that the employer sounds like there is really no reason for termination
- While employers are not obligated to provide employees with written reasons for termination, if the employer chooses to do so, the responsibility should be delegated to upper management or human resources in conjunction with legal counsel. If the employer chooses to provide reasons,

always give an accurate, truthful and complete explanation for the termination; never lie to an employee in an attempt to soften the blow

- Explain any benefits, including COBRA, that the employee is entitled to receive and, if the employee is not going to receive certain benefits, explain why
- Give the employee an opportunity to respond, and pay close attention to what is said. Be careful about what is said, because the termination conference may become relevant to or cause a subsequent employee claim or lawsuit
- When terminating an employee who is in a protected class (minority, over 40, pregnant, etc.), the potential for a subsequent claim or lawsuit is obvious. It is, therefore, essential to avoid referring to anything that could be considered evidence of discrimination
- Avoid any reference to sex, age, race, religion, disability, color or national origin
- Be organized and prepared for the interview and give the impression that the employer is confident that the right decision has been made
- Attempt to obtain the employee's agreement that he or she has had problems on the job or that job performance has not been satisfactory
- Take notes during the meeting; after the meeting, type them, but keep the handwritten notes
- Be as courteous to the employee as possible. Remember that the employer is not merely trying to win a potential lawsuit, but trying to prevent one
- The termination conference should be well documented, including a summary of what the employee was told, what the employee said and whether the employee disputed the basis for the discharge; both the person conducting the conference and the management witness should sign the final documentation
- Try to follow the same procedure utilized in previous discharges, while also trying to make improvements

G. Release and Severance Agreements

If an employer feels certain that an employee will sue upon termination, if there are problems involved with terminating an employee in a protected group, or if there is a major dispute between the employer and the employee, the employer should consider asking for a written release from the employee. In such an agreement, the employer agrees to provide the employee with some additional benefits (e.g., severance pay or a favorable reference) in return for the employee's agreement to release the employer from any claims that the employee might have against the employer. The employer's attorney should prepare such an agreement, and the employee should be allowed to review the agreement with his or her attorney. This kind of agreement is certainly not right for every situation and should not be used without careful consideration and legal advice.

Courts have upheld the validity of release agreements that are entered into knowingly and voluntarily. In determining whether the knowing and voluntary requirements are met, courts will consider the following factors:

- Employee's experience, background and education
- Amount of time the employee had to consider the waiver, including whether the employee had an opportunity to consult with a lawyer
- Clarity of the waiver
- Consideration for the waiver
- Totality of the circumstances

The Sixth Circuit Court of Appeals cast doubt on an employer's ability to have an employee waive future claims he might have against his or her employer through a release entered into knowingly and voluntarily. In *Adams v. Philip Morris, Inc.*,[14] the employer offered an enhanced severance and benefits package to employees affected by a layoff. In consideration for the benefits, employees were required to sign a release "settling all claims which I ever had or may have with the company" and agreeing to waive any claim or demand for employment with the company.

A year later, Adams responded to an advertisement for his or her former position. He brought suit against the company for age and reverse race discrimination after discovering that a young black male was awarded the position. The Court of Appeals concluded that the release Adams signed was effective to bar any claims that arose prior to signing the release. The Court further concluded, however, that despite the clear language of the release, a fact issue remained regarding whether the parties intended to release claims that had not yet arisen and whether the parties intended that Adams be forever barred from Philip Morris' labor pool. The Court determined that an employment agreement that attempts to settle prospective claims of discrimination could violate public policy unless the acts were the continuing or future effects of past discrimination or the parties contemplated an unequivocal, complete and final dissolution of the employment relationship.

In 1990, Congress enacted the Older Workers' Benefit Protection Act, which contains specific requirements when obtaining waiver of employees' rights under the Age Discrimination in Employment Act. This issue is discussed later under the Age Discrimination in Employment Act minimum requirements.

H. Post-Termination

After termination, the employee should be informed of any COBRA benefits within the required time period. In addition, all wages or benefits owed to

---

14.   67 F.3d 580 (6th Cir. 1995).

the employee should be paid promptly. Some states require employers to pay all earned salary or wages not later than the next normal pay period after the dismissal or voluntary termination of employment, or within 14 days of termination of employment, whichever is later. It is often advisable to pay the employee accrued salary and benefits at the time of termination, however, in order to minimize the terminated employee's future contact with the employer's other employees. Failure to pay wages and benefits promptly will add to the employee's feeling that he or she is being treated unfairly.

What is stated to the employee as the reason for termination can be of great importance if litigation occurs. In some cases, failing to state the true reason for the termination, or stating reasons that are inconsistent with those later stated, has been held to be evidence of bad faith or discrimination. Before a separation notice is completed, an employer must consider how the notice will affect the employer if subsequent litigation arises. It is possible to say too little or too much, depending upon the circumstances, so careful consideration should be given to the completion of the separation notice. If the termination involves a controversial or complicated matter, it is a good idea to obtain legal advice in drafting the separation notice.

An employer should have a policy concerning what information will be released about a former employee when a job reference is requested, including limiting the individuals with authority to disseminate information to prospective employers. Most employers are no longer willing to give the full story on former employees. Unless personnel employees are well-trained, it is probably advisable to only provide information about former employees' past or present employment, dates of employment, and job titles or positions held. If the policy limits the information to be given to prospective employers, it should also be specified that the employer to whom the reference is being given should not take the limitation of information to be a positive or negative statement, but that this is simply the policy of the employer.

Employers should also pay careful attention to the handling of unemployment compensation claims filed by former employees. What the employer states as the reason for the termination to the unemployment office is important. Similarly, what the former employee states as the reason for his or her termination can be of great significance in a subsequent legal proceeding. It may be possible to discredit a former employee with statements he or she made to obtain unemployment compensation if the employee later claims something different in court. An unemployment compensation hearing can be a useful tool to find out precisely what the former employee's position is. Further, an unemployment compensation decision that is favorable to the employer may be of value in persuading the employee not to pursue other claims.

However, keep in mind that an unemployment hearing is also an opportunity for the employee to obtain information from the employer and to cross-examine the employer's witnesses. So if the employer anticipates that the employee may later file a lawsuit over the termination, or if the employee will be represented by an attorney at the unemployment hearing, then the employer needs to be very well prepared for the hearing.

Finally, employers should pay special attention to replacing a terminated employee. It is always important to find the most qualified replacement regardless of the individual's protected status. An employer should be mindful, however, that replacing an employee with another person of the same race, sex, national origin or age will better insulate the employer against a charge of discrimination.

I.   Facility Closure

If the employer is shutting down a facility that will affect 50 employees or more, the Worker Adjustment And Retraining Notification Act[15] ("WARN Act") will apply. This law requires covered employers to give 60 days' advance notice of (a) plant shutdowns that affect at least 50 employees, and (b) mass layoffs lasting greater than six months that affect at least one third of the employees at the site of employment, provided that at least 50 employees suffer a job loss. Employers are covered under the WARN Act if they employ 100 or more employees excluding part-time employees or if they employ 100 or more employees who, in the aggregate, work at least 4,000 hours per week (excluding overtime). If employers are covered under the WARN Act, except under a very finite list of exemptions and exceptions, employers must comply with the WARN Act's particularized notice requirements whenever employers shutdown employers' offices or do a mass layoff affecting the requisite number of employees.

10.07   Employment Laws

There are many federal and state statutes, as well as state common laws (i.e., law created by the courts) that directly affect employment decisions made by employers, including hiring, promotion, demotion, discipline, and firing decisions. It is critical for employers to know and understand the laws affecting the employment relationship in order to avoid potential liability. In order to familiarize employers with laws affecting the workplace, the following is a very general overview of several federal employment-related statutes. Although we have discussed many of them already, this section is intended to be a handy reference of the main employment laws. The laws are listed alphabetically, followed by common law doctrines.

Keep in mind that this section simply seeks to put employers on notice about some of these laws and how they may impact the decisions employers

---

15.   29 U.S.C. § 2101 *et seq.*

make regarding employers' employees—it is by no means a comprehensive analysis of these laws. Furthermore, defenses to employees' claims under these laws are not addressed here, but are critically important and must be studied very carefully. Also, although state employment statutes will not be discussed here, employers must make sure to pay heed to employers' state's employment-related laws as well.

A.   Age Discrimination in Employment Act of 1967

The Age Discrimination in Employment Act of 1967[16] ("ADEA") prohibits discrimination in employment because of age. This statute applies to all employers engaged in an industry affecting commerce, who employ 20 or more employees each working day in each of 20 or more calendar weeks in the current or preceding calendar year. If employers are a covered employer under the ADEA, employers are prohibited from discriminating against job applicants or employees with respect to hiring, firing, compensation and other terms and conditions of employment because such job applicant or employee is 40 years of age or older.

1. Enforcement

Like Title VII, the provisions of the ADEA can be enforced against employers by the filing of a charge with the EEOC or by the filing of a private action (for which, again, the individual must first file an EEOC charge of discrimination). And, as with Title VII, there are very specific timeliness rules employers' human resources personnel should know with respect to filing the EEOC charge of discrimination and filing suit under the ADEA.

2. Proof

Proof of discrimination under the ADEA follows the same general procedures outlined under Title VII, although there is a difference in how disparate impact claims against employers are handled. Thus, claims under the ADEA may follow disparate treatment, disparate impact, or class-wide discrimination theories. With respect to disparate treatment cases, however, the Supreme Court has made a distinction between proof needed to establish Title VII and ADEA claims. Traditionally, all discrimination plaintiffs had been required to show that individuals outside the protected group were treated more favorably than the complaining individual. Under this analysis, an ADEA plaintiff was required to show that an individual under 40 received more favorable treatment. But the Supreme Court has held that an ADEA plaintiff need

---

16.   29 U.S.C. § 621 *et seq.*

not show that he or she was disfavored as compared to a person under 40. Rather, the proper inquiry is whether the plaintiff was disfavored because of his or her age.

3. Employer Defenses

There are certain specific defenses set forth in the ADEA that may relieve employers of liability. Some of the more important ones follow:

- Bona fide occupational qualification: the ADEA specifically provides that it is not unlawful for employers' company or business to take actions that would otherwise be prohibited under the ADEA where age is a "bona fide occupational qualification reasonably necessary to the normal operation of the particular business...." Although this exception has been narrowly construed, it has been held to permit age limitations for the performance of certain types of jobs (e.g., public safety personnel, airline pilots)
- Bona fide seniority or employee benefit plan: in addition, the ADEA specifically provides that it is not unlawful for employers to "observe the terms of a bona fide seniority system or any bona fide employee benefit plan such as a retirement, pension, or insurance plan, which is not a subterfuge to evade the purposes of [the ADEA]...." Thus, an employment decision mandated by bona fide seniority systems may be held lawful although it impacts primarily upon persons age forty and over.

4. Remedies

As under Title VII, successful claimants who have sued employers' company or business under the ADEA are entitled to preliminary injunctive relief, back pay, front pay and other equitable relief (such as reinstatement, promotion or awards of seniority). Further, the ADEA specifically provides for awards of "liquidated damages" where the employer's violation is shown to have been willful. A willful violation of the ADEA occurs when an employer has actual knowledge or shows "reckless disregard" for whether federal law prohibits its conduct.

5. Lilly Ledbetter Fair Pay Act

On January 29, 2009, President Obama signed the Lilly Ledbetter Fair Pay Act ("Act"), which addresses the issue of discrimination in compensation. The Act amends the ADEA, the Americans with Disabilities Act, Title VII, and the federal Rehabilitation Act, to state that, "... a discriminatory compensation decision or other practice that is unlawful under such Acts occurs *each time* compensation is paid pursuant to the discriminatory compensation decision or other practice, and for other practices." The statute's effective date was retroactive to May 28, 2007, the day before the U.S. Supreme Court's decision in the case of *Lilly Ledbetter vs. Goodyear Tire and Rubber Co., Inc.*, in which the Court held that a new violation of the law does *not* occur each time an employee is paid following a discriminatory compensation decision. The Act effectively overrules the Supreme Court's decision and allows claims for discrimination in pay to be go forward that would otherwise have been barred by applicable statutes of limitations because the original, allegedly discriminatory compensation decision was made outside the limitations period.

6.   Other Amendments

The Older Workers' Benefit Protection Act (the "OWBPA") amends the ADEA to prohibit age discrimination in employee benefit programs. In addition, the OWBPA establishes minimum standards for employees to waive their rights under the ADEA. Among other requirements, if employers ask employers' employees to waive their rights under the ADEA (via some sort of release of claims agreement), employers must advise the employees in writing to consult an attorney before signing such a release agreement, must give them at least 21 days (or 45 days in the case of a group reduction in force or exit incentive program) to consider such an agreement, and an additional seven days in which to revoke the agreement after signing.

The OWBPA also prohibits employers from including any language in a waiver agreement that would require the employee to agree not to file any charge of discrimination against the employer with the EEOC or participate in any investigation or proceeding conducted by the EEOC. Further, employers cannot require employees to pay back the monetary consideration for the waiver as a condition precedent to filing a charge with the EEOC.

B.   Americans with Disabilities Act

The Americans with Disabilities Act[17] ("ADA") prohibits discrimination in employment because of a disability. This statute applies to all employers, engaged in an industry affecting commerce, who employ 15 or more employees in each of 20 or more calendar weeks in the current or preceding calendar year. If employers are a covered employer under the ADA, employers are prohibited from discriminating, with respect to hiring, firing, compensation and other terms and conditions of employment, against otherwise qualified job applicants and employees who have disabilities or who become disabled. In addition, employers are prohibited from conducting pre-employment medical examinations as well as inquiries as to whether a job applicant has a disability.

---

17.   42 U.S.C. §12101 *et seq.*

An individual with a disability is defined as one who has a physical or mental impairment that substantially limits one or more of the individual's major life activities, has a record of having such an impairment or is perceived to have such an impairment. This statute is particularly complex and can be difficult to comprehend. The key to both understanding and complying with the ADA rests in understanding the meaning of the key terms in this statute (i.e., "physical or mental impairment," "substantially limits" and "major life activities").

1. Examples

Disabilities covered by the statute include, but are by no means limited to, cosmetic disfigurement, psychological disorders, learning disabilities, infectious or communicable diseases (including AIDS), and persons recovering from serious illness, such as cancer or heart disease. While alcoholism is considered a disability under the ADA, the ADA excludes from its coverage current alcoholics who cannot adequately perform their job duties or whose employment presents a threat to the safety or property of others, as well as current illegal drug users.

2. Enforcement

As with claimants under Title VII, claimants may file a charge of discrimination with the EEOC, alleging that the company or business violated the ADA. Consistent with the provisions of Title VII, individual ADA claimants will also be entitled to file suit in state or federal court to enforce the provisions of the ADA, provided they first file a charge of discrimination with the EEOC. Again, claimants will be required to abide by specific timeliness requirements with respect to filing EEOC charges or filing suit.

3. Remedies

A prevailing ADA complainant is entitled to recover from employers its attorney's fees, limited compensatory and punitive damages, as well as equitable relief in the form of backpay, frontpay, reinstatement and promotions.

4. Specific Employer Defenses

Employers must demonstrate good faith efforts, in consultation with the disabled individual, "to identify and make a reasonable accommodation that would provide such individual with an equally effective opportunity as any employee and would not cause an undue hardship on the operation of the business." However, employers can be insulated from an award of damages in an ADA action if employers can demonstrate they did make the above good faith efforts, that they offered a reasonable accommodation, or that any possible reasonable accommodation would cause the employers' business undue hardship.

5. Recent Amendment

The Americans with Disabilities Act Amendments Act (ADAAA) became effective on January 1, 2009. Its purpose is to expand the ADA's coverage by effectively overruling two decisions of the U.S. Supreme Court that had limited the ADA's coverage. In addition, in September 2009 the EEOC issued proposed amended regulations implementing the ADAAA. Public comments about the proposed regulations were due in November 2009. At this time, the date of implementation of the regulations is unknown.

Together, the amended statute and proposed regulations provide for a broader definition of "disability," provide that an impairment need not "severely" or "significantly" limit a major life activity in order to be a disability, and expand the list of major life activities to include major bodily functions. In addition, except for eyeglasses and contact lenses, mitigating measures that cure or keep conditions or disease in check are not to be considered in determining whether an individual has a disability.

C. Civil Rights Act of 1964, Title VII

Title VII of the Civil Rights Act of 1964[18] ("Title VII") prohibits discrimination and harassment in employment because of race, color, sex (including pregnancy), national origin and religion. This statute applies to all employers engaged in an industry affecting commerce who employ 15 or more employees each working day in each of 20 or more calendar weeks in the current or preceding calendar year. If employers are a covered employer under Title VII, employers are specifically prohibited from discriminating against any job applicant or employee with respect to hiring, firing, compensation, terms, conditions or privileges of employment because of such applicant's or employee's race, color, sex, national origin or religion.

1. Enforcement

An applicant or employee can enforce the provisions of Title VII in one of two ways: (a) by the filing of a charge with the Equal Employment Opportunity Commission ("EEOC") against the employers' business or (b) by the filing of a private action against the employers' business in state or federal court (in federal court, the individual must first file an EEOC charge of discrimination;

---

18.   42 U.S.C. § 2000e *et seq.*

this is not always required for state courts). Employers should ensure that their human resources staff is mindful of the specific timeliness rules associated with when an individual can file an EEOC charge or a private lawsuit.

2. Proof

An employee or applicant may try to prove that the employers' company discriminated against him or her in violation of Title VII in one of three ways: (a) disparate impact; (b) disparate treatment; or (c) class-wide discrimination.

3. Disparate Impact

An employee or applicant who utilizes this theory of proof will have to show that one or more of the employers' facially neutral employment practices or selection criteria excludes a disproportionate number of minorities, women or other protected group. In utilizing this theory of proof, the complaining individual need not prove the employers' business engaged in any intentional discrimination. Rather, the individual would need to show, first, that the challenged employment practice, although neutral on its face, has the effect of discriminating against members of a protected group. The individual would then have to establish that he or she has been adversely affected by the policy or practice in question in order to be entitled to relief. An employers' company or business may defend against a disparate impact claim by showing the policy is justified as a business necessity in that it is a predictor or a determinant of job performance.

4. Disparate Treatment

An employee or applicant who utilizes this theory of proof has to show that he or she received treatment from the employers' business different from that afforded to other similarly-situated individuals because of the individual's status as a member of a protected class; in other words, persons outside the protected group received more favorable treatment than the individual did. The individual in a disparate treatment case bears the burden of proving that his or her employer engaged in intentional discrimination. Employers may defend their employment actions by showing that these actions were based upon legitimate, non-discriminatory reasons. The claimant then has the opportunity to rebut the employer's showing if he or she can prove that employer's stated reason is merely a cover-up, or pretext, for discrimination.

5. Class-Wide Discrimination

Where discriminatory conduct impacts upon a large group of individuals, class-wide actions may be pursued. Class-action employees or applicants must establish that discrimination was the employer's standard operating procedure, rather than an isolated or accidental act, or be based on a disparate impact theory of recovery. Statistical evidence is frequently utilized in proving class-wide discrimination.

6. Harassment

It is extremely important to keep in mind that harassment on the basis of any protected status is also unlawful under Title VII and state law. Harassment law is particularly complicated and must be analyzed quite carefully.

7. Remedies

If an employer's business is found liable for Title VII discrimination, it faces the possibility of having to provide preliminary injunctive relief, back pay, front pay, recovery of costs, attorney's fees and other equitable relief (such as reinstatement, promotion, etc.). An employer's business may also face the possibility of having to pay compensatory and punitive damages if it is found guilty of intentional discrimination. These latter two damage categories are capped under Title VII, however, depending on employers' company or business size.

D. Employee Polygraph Protection Act of 1988

The Employee Polygraph Protection Act of 1998[19] ("EPPA") prohibits employers (EPPA applies to most private employers) from using lie-detector tests to screen job applicants or to test current employees unless employers reasonably suspect that the employee was involved in a workplace theft or other incident causing economic loss to the employer. Further, EPPA prohibits employers from disciplining, discharging, discriminating against, or denying employment or promotions to job applicants or current employees solely on the basis of polygraph test results. Additionally, the EPPA prohibits employers from taking any retaliatory action against an employee who has filed a complaint or proceeding under the EPPA, testified in such a proceeding, or otherwise sought to exercise rights afforded by the EPPA. Subject to very limited exceptions (of which employers' human resources staff should be aware), the EPPA effectively eliminates the use of polygraph testing with respect to either applicants or employees. EPPA does not preempt any state or local law or collective bargaining agreement that is more restrictive regarding the use of lie-detector tests than EPPA is.

---

19.   29 U.S.C. § 2001 *et seq.*

E.   Employee Retirement Income Security Act of 1974

The Employee Retirement Income Security Act of 1974[20] ("ERISA") governs the defined-benefit and defined-contribution pension and retirement plans employers provide for employers' employees. It is specifically designed to ensure that employees' pension rights are protected and their retirement plans are securely funded by establishing: (a) a number of pension-plan rules and standards that employers must observe, including minimum participation, funding, and vesting standards; (b) reporting and disclosure requirements and (c) fiduciary standards. Employers' plans must, among other things, meet non-discrimination requirements designed to make sure they do not unduly favor certain groups, such as top management officials.

F.   Equal Pay Act of 1963

The Equal Pay Act of 1963[21] ("Equal Pay Act") prohibits most employers from discriminating on the basis of sex in the payment of wages. It is important to note that employers will not violate this law if they have wage differentials between men and women in comparable positions that are based on: (a) a seniority system, (b) a merit system, (c) a system which measures earnings by quantity or quality of production or (d) a differential is based on any factor other than sex.

1.   Enforcement

As under Title VII, the provisions of the Equal Pay Act can be enforced either by the filing of a charge with the EEOC or by the filing of a private civil action in either state or federal court. Once again, claimants must be mindful of timeliness requirements for filing EEOC charges or lawsuits under the Equal Pay Act, as should employers' human resources personnel.

2.   Proof of Discrimination

Courts have established a "substantially equal" test as the standard for judging the comparability of jobs under the Equal Pay Act. To be substantially equal, jobs need not be identical, but must require similar skills, effort and responsibility. In addition, such jobs must be performed under similar working conditions. In determining whether jobs are substantially equal for purposes of Equal Pay Act analysis, courts look beyond job classifications, job titles and job descriptions and examine the actual work performed by the claimant and any comparable employees. A wage differential will be justified only

---

20.   29 U.S.C. § 1001 *et seq.*
21   29 U.S.C. § 206(d).

if it compensates for a significant variation in skill, effort, responsibility or working conditions between otherwise comparable work activities. As noted above, however, the Equal Pay Act permits the payment of different wages for equal work if those payments are made pursuant to a bona fide seniority or merit system or a system that measures earnings by quantity or quality of production. In addition, wage differentials will be upheld if based upon factors other than sex (i.e., job performance, education, or experience).

3. Remedies

Under the Equal Pay Act, a successful claimant may recover from employers back pay, front pay, attorney's fees and, in some cases, liquidated damages. If the court finds that the employers' company or business acted in good faith and had reasonable grounds for believing that it was not violating the Equal Pay Act, the court may limit or deny liquidated damages.

G. Fair Labor Standards Act of 1938

The Fair Labor Standards Act of 1938[22] ("FLSA") is a federal law that requires employers to pay non-exempt employees of covered employers a minimum hourly wage ($7.25/hour) and overtime at one-and-one-half times the regular rate of pay for all hours worked in excess of 40 hours in one work week. However, employers in certain industries, such as agriculture, are completely exempt from this federal law. There are many industry exemptions, so employers should consult their attorneys to see if they are exempt.

In addition, certain employees of covered employers are exempt from the minimum wage and overtime provisions of the law. The most common exempt employees fall under the "white collar" exemptions for executive, administrative, professional, computer professional, and outside sales employees. Such employees must be paid a salary of at least $455 per week and must have the requisite primary duties in order to be exempt.

H. Family and Medical Leave Act of 1993

The Family and Medical Leave Act of 1993[23] ("FMLA") requires that covered employers provide eligible employees with up to 12 weeks of unpaid, job-protected leave each year to care for a newborn child or newly placed adopted or foster child; to care for a child, spouse, or parent who has a serious health condition; or because of the employee's own serious health condition. Employers are covered under the FMLA if they are engaged in an industry affecting commerce and employ 50 or more employees for each

---

22. 29 U.S.C. § 201 *et seq.*
23. 29 U.S.C. § 2601 *et seq.*

working day during each of 20 or more calendar weeks in the current or preceding calendar year.

A "serious health condition" is defined under the FMLA to mean an illness, injury, impairment, or physical or mental condition that involves: (a) inpatient care in a hospital, hospice, or residential medical center or (b) continuing treatment by a health care provider for a condition which incapacitates the employee for a period of more than three consecutive, full calendar days.

1. Eligibility

In order to be eligible for leave under the FMLA for one of the above reasons, an employee must have (a) worked for the employer for at least 12 months and (b) worked at least 1,250 hours during the 12 - month period. All hours worked under the federal wage and hour guidelines will be counted toward the 1,250-hour requirement. Salaried employees who are exempt from the minimum wage and overtime provisions of the Fair Labor Standards Act are presumed to have met the 1,250 hours of work requirement if no records of hours worked have been kept.

2. Consecutive vs. Intermittent Leave

An entitled employee may take twelve weeks of consecutive leave within a 12-month period or may take his or her twelve weeks within a 12-month period intermittently. "Intermittent leave" is leave taken in separate blocks of time for a single illness or injury and may include leave periods from an hour or more to several weeks at a time. While there is no limit on the size of a leave increment of an intermittent or reduced schedule leave, employers may limit such leave increments to the shortest period of time used by the payroll system to account for absences or use of leave.

When an employee takes intermittent or reduced schedule leave, only the amount of leave actually taken may be counted toward the twelve weeks of leave entitlement.

Finally, where it is foreseeable that an employee will need intermittent leave or leave on a reduced leave schedule for planned medical treatment, employers may require the employee to temporarily transfer to an available alternative position that affords equivalent pay and benefits to assist employers' business to better accommodate recurring periods of leave than if the employee remained in his or her regular position.

3. Protections

With certain exceptions, an employee who takes leave under FMLA is entitled, on return from leave to be restored to (a) his or her former position or (b) an equivalent position with equivalent employment benefits, pay and other terms and conditions of employment. In addition, FMLA provides protection for employees against retaliation once he or she has filed a suit, claim, or otherwise participated in any proceeding or investigation under the FMLA.

Where the leave is due to the employee's own serious health condition, employers are permitted under the FMLA to require the employee to report periodically on his or her status and intent to return to work. In the event the employee unequivocally states that he or she will be unable to return to work, the employee's entitlement to rights provided for under the FMLA, including continuing leave and maintenance of benefits, ceases.

The requirement that employers maintain benefits accrued prior to the leave does not require that the employee be eligible for benefits to which she otherwise would have been entitled if she had remained continuously employed. Thus, seniority does not accrue during the period of leave.

4. Enforcement

The U.S. Department of Labor is responsible for administering, investigating and resolving any complaints for alleged violations of FMLA. The Secretary of Labor is permitted to bring actions against employers on behalf of aggrieved employees. An employee is permitted to bring a suit against employers for violations in any federal or state court of competent jurisdiction. As with all of the above statutes, individuals who wish to file lawsuits under the FMLA are required to abide by certain timing requirements that may be found in the actual act or the FMLA regulations.

5. Remedies

A successful claimant in an action under FMLA may recover the following: attorney's fees; expert witness fees and other costs incurred in the action; damages equal to the amount of wages, salary, employment benefits or other compensation denied or lost by reason of the FMLA violation; and, in some cases, liquidated damages. Where wages, salary, employment benefits or other compensation have not been denied or lost, an employee can recover any actual monetary losses sustained as a direct result of the violation, including the cost of providing care, up to a sum equal to twelve weeks of wages or salary for the employee. If employers' business can show that the violation of FMLA was committed in good faith and that there were reasonable grounds for believing that it was not in violation of the FMLA, the court may, in its discretion, determine that liquidated damages will not be assessed.

Where the action is brought by the Secretary of Labor, damages are limited to recovery of actual damages, issuance of an injunction and other equitable relief such as employment, reinstatement and promotion.

This statute and its regulations are particularly complex and can be difficult to understand. The key to both understanding and complying with FMLA rests in understanding and retaining a copy of the regulations. Please also note that FMLA does not supersede state or local laws providing greater family or medical leave rights.

6. *Recent Amendments*

The FMLA was amended in 2008, 2009 and 2010. In addition, the U.S. Department of Labor implemented amended regulations in 2009. The major change brought about by these amendments was to introduce two new forms of qualifying leave: qualifying exigency leave (QE leave) and military caregiver leave (MC leave). QE leave allows an eligible employee to take leave when a family member of the employee is deployed abroad in the military. However, QE leave is limited to time off for specific events or reasons, such as short notice deployments (up to seven days off), attending military events and ceremonies, urgent child care and school activities of the family member's children under age 18, financial and legal matters, and counseling.

MC leave allows an eligible employee to take up to 26 weeks of leave in a single twelve month period to care for a spouse, son, daughter, parent or next of kin who has a serious health condition that was incurred in the line of active duty in the military.

The amendments also made numerous changes to provisions relating to the original four types of leave allowed by the law. Among the changes are that employees who are under continuing treatment by a healthcare provider must have visited the provider two or more times in the first 30 days of the employee's incapacity, or have made at least one visit which resulted in a regimen of continuing treatment. Employees who take leave due to chronic conditions must now visit their provider at least twice a year. Employees who need to take unforeseeable leave (leave taken less than 30 days from the time the need for leave is known) must notify the employer as soon as practicable, which means the same day or the next business day after learning of the need for leave.

I. National Labor Relations Act

The National Labor Relations Act[24] ("NLRA") prohibits employers from discriminating against, disciplining, or discharging their employees for engaging in union activity or for engaging in protected concerted activities for mutual aid or protection. Most employers will not likely have unionized facilities and, thus, need not be concerned about employees engaging in union activity. However, employees may engage in a wide variety of activities ("protected concerted activities"), done outside the union context, that are also protected by NLRA. Protected concerted activities in the non-union context are usually activities that involve two or more people and that are pursued

---

24.   29 U.S.C. § 151 *et seq.*

to improve the terms and conditions of employment for all employees or to otherwise improve their lot as employees. However, a single employee acting on behalf of, or in the interest of, other employees can also be protected. Because protected concerted employee activities are protected by NLRA, employers must refrain from discriminating against any employees in their terms and conditions of employment for engaging in such activities.

J.   Occupational Safety and Health Act of 1970

1.   Federal law. As discussed in Chapter 3, the Occupational Safety and Health Act of 1970[25] ("OSHA") imposes upon employers (all private employers engaged in a business affecting interstate commerce) a general duty to provide employees with a place of employment that is free from any recognized hazards that are likely to cause death or physical injury. In addition to this general duty under OSHA, employers are also required to comply with specific safety and health standards promulgated by the Secretary of Labor. Employers must ensure that employees are aware of and comply with any specific safety and health standards that may apply to their business. If employers do not, OSHA inspectors, who are empowered to inspect employers' premises to determine compliance with such standards, may issue employers citations for violations thereof.

OSHA provides for an Occupational Safety and Health Review Commission to act as a quasi-judicial court system, designed to decide any cases arising as a result of the issuance of citations for alleged violations of OSHA.

2.   State Plans. Approximately half the states in the United States have their own, federally approved plans to enforce health and safety standards in workplaces. In addition to a state statutory general duty clause, they may also have their own regulations. For the most part, these states have adopted the federal regulations, but some states have different standards on certain subjects. For example, Kentucky has different standards for fall protection and lockout/tagout. In states with their own plans, state officials inspect workplaces and issue citations as appropriate. A state Review Commission hears cases that are contested by employers.

K.   Uniformed Services Employment and Re-Employment Rights Act

The Uniformed Services Employment and Re-Employment Act[26] ("USERRA") provides eligible employees, who enter military service, with the right to re-employment with the pre-service employer if they properly inform the

---

25.   29 U.S.C. § 651 *et seq.*
26.   38 U.S.C. § 4301 *et seq.*

pre-service employer of their intent to return to work. Also, under USERRA, employers are prohibited from discriminating against job applicants and employees with regard to hiring, firing or other terms and conditions of employment based on the individual's past, present or future military service.

USERRA specifically provides, however, that employers are not required to re-employ an individual if his or her employment prior to military service was for a brief, non-recurrent period and there was no reasonable expectation that the employment would continue indefinitely.

USERRA permits a person to accumulate a total absence from his or her job of five years by reason of voluntary or involuntary military service. Additionally, service beyond five years to complete an initial period of obligated service is also allowable under USERRA.

1. *Position to Which Employee Entitled upon Re-Employment*

An individual with fewer than 91 days of military service must be re-employed promptly in the position that he or she would have attained if continuously employed, unless proven not to qualify after reasonable efforts have been made by the company or business. If not qualified for that position, the person would be re-employed in the position he or she left.

If the employee has over 90 days of military service, employers may reinstate the returned worker to the position he would have held if continuously employed by them or employers have the additional option of offering a position of like seniority, status and pay. If the reinstated employee fails to demonstrate he is qualified for the position after reasonable efforts made by the business or company, the individual must be re-employed in any other position of lesser status and pay for which he or she is qualified, with full seniority.

2. *Rights and Benefits of Returning Employee*

Upon re-employment, a person is entitled to the seniority, and other benefits determined by seniority, that the individual had at the beginning of the military service, plus any additional seniority and benefits the individual would have attained, with reasonable certainty, had he or she remained continuously employed.

Employees are entitled to non-seniority-based rights and benefits, established by a contract, practice, policy, or agreement, effective at the beginning of the period of service or implemented while the individual is performing service. However, a person is not entitled to any benefits for which a person would not be entitled if he or she were on leave of absence.

An employee re-employed in accordance with USERRA may not be discharged, except "for cause," within a one-year period after commencing re-employment if the employee had been in military service for more than 180 days, or for a period of six months if the employee's service was more than 30 days but less than 181 days.

3. Enforcement

An employee denied rights under USERRA may file a complaint with the Secretary of Labor. If the complaint is found meritorious, the Secretary of Labor will seek to remedy the complaint. If the efforts at remedying the complaint are unsuccessful, the Secretary shall notify the employee, who is entitled to request that the Secretary refer the complaint to the Attorney General. The Attorney General may commence an action in federal district court against the employer. In the alternative, an employee is entitled to bring a suit individually.

4. Remedies

Courts have broad remedial powers to ensure full vindication of violations of USERRA including granting re-employment, back pay, and attorney's fees. If employers' business or company's failure to comply with USERRA is found to be willful, employers may have to provide liquidated damages (in addition to the other types of remedies) to the employee.

L. Worker Adjustment and Retraining Notification Act

The Worker Adjustment And Retraining Notification Act[27] ("WARN Act") requires covered employers to give 60 days' advance notice of (a) plant shutdowns that affect at least 50 employees and (b) mass layoffs, lasting greater than six months, that affect at least 1/3 of the employees at the site of employment, provided at least 50 employees suffer a job loss. Employers are covered under WARN Act if they employ 100 or more employees excluding part-time employees or if they employ 100 or more employees who, in the aggregate, work at least 4,000 hours per week (excluding overtime).

M. Genetic Information Non-Discrimination Act

This federal statute went into effect in November 2009 and applies to employers of at least 15 employees. It prohibits employers from using genetic information about employees or applicants in decisions concerning hiring, firing, or other

---

27.   29 U.S.C. § 2101 *et seq.*

terms and conditions of employment. It also prohibits employers from limiting, classifying, segregating, or retaliating against employees based upon genetic information. Prohibited use of genetic information also includes using such information about family members to the fourth degree of relationship to employees, (i.e., family history). Thus, for example, an employer could not fail to hire an employee because her uncle had a known genetic abnormality or condition resulting from it.

Genetic information is information from tests that detect genotypes, mutations, and chromosomal changes, including tests of DNA, RNA, chromosomes, metabolites, and proteins. With some exceptions, employers are prohibited from purchasing, requesting or otherwise acquiring such genetic information. Exceptions include wellness programs, FMLA leave requests, and law enforcement. Any genetic information that is lawfully acquired must be kept confidential and cannot be used to discriminate against employees.

N. State Common Law

In addition to federal and state employment-related statutes, there are also state common law claims that employees often make against their employers. Employers should be aware of these potential claims as well. Again, the following is simply an overview. It is not intended to be a comprehensive analysis of these claims.

1. Wrongful Discharge

These types of claims were discussed in the employment at-will vs. contracts of employment section of this chapter.

2. Breach of Contract

As described in several sections above, employers may be held liable for wrongful discharge based on breach of contract if the terminated employee can show that employers violated a written or oral promise regarding job security or other terms and conditions of employment. Again, this is why it is very important that employers advise managers and supervisors to refrain from making verbal or written assurances of continued employment, that the employee handbook contains no promises of employment for a definite duration, and that the employee handbook includes a disclaimer.

3. Breach of the Covenant of Good Faith and Fair Dealing

Several states have implied a covenant of good faith and fair dealing into the employment relationship that may give rise to liability for wrongful discharge. Although the elements that one must prove for this cause of action may vary from state to state, the crux of this claim generally requires a showing that (a) the employee and his or her employer were parties to a contract under which the employee reasonably expected to receive certain benefits; (b) the employer engaged in conduct that injured the employee's right to receive some or all of those benefits and (c) when committing the acts by which it injured the employee's right to receive benefits it reasonably expected to receive under the contract, the employer was acting in bad faith.

Employers likely will not have to worry about this type of common law claim if they ensure that they and their employees have not entered into a contract of employment and that, instead, employees are employed at-will.

4. Defamation

Defamation is an available common law claim in most, if not all, states. Employers may be liable to an employee for defamation if the employee can show that employers (via one of employers' managers or supervisors) uttered a false and defamatory statement about the employee, the statement was communicated to other people (published), and that, as a result, the employee's reputation was injured. Typically, if employees sue employers for defamation, they will do so because one of employers' managers or supervisors made (a) certain statements in connection with post-employment referrals; (b) derogatory statements when evaluating the employee's job performance; (c) certain statements during a pre-discharge investigation or (d) certain post-discharge communications to the employee's co-workers or others.

It is important to note that if the statements were true (and employers can prove that the statements were true), employers will not be held liable for defamation. Similarly, if any of the statements were internal communications between management relating to employee job performance or other employment-related activities, then they were most likely privileged and employers will not be held liable for defamation, unless the employee proves that the employer's internal communications were made maliciously.

5. Invasion of Privacy

There are actually four different kinds of invasion of privacy: (a) unreasonable intrusion upon one's seclusion, (b) appropriation of one's name or likeness, (c) unreasonable publicity given to one's private life and (c) publicity that unreasonably places one in a false light before the public. In reality, only the first, third, and fourth types of invasion of privacy would apply in the employment context.

With respect to the first type of invasion of privacy claims, employers may be held liable if the employee can show that the employer intentionally intruded, physically or otherwise, upon the employee's solitude or seclusion or his private affairs or concerns and that this intrusion would be highly offensive to a reasonable person. With respect to the third type of invasion of privacy claim, an employer could be held liable if the employee could show that the employer publicly disclosed information regarding him or her that (a) would be highly offensive to a reasonable person and (b) is not of legitimate concern to the public. Finally, with respect to the fourth type of invasion of privacy claim, an employer could be held liable if the employee could show that the employer placed him or her in a false light, the false light in which he or she was placed would be highly offensive to a reasonable person, and the employer had knowledge of or acted in reckless disregard as to the falsity of the publicized matter and the false light in which the employee would be placed.

6. Negligent Hiring

In a number of states, employers may be held liable for negligent hiring to a non-employee who was injured by one of their employees. In order to be held liable for negligent hiring, the non-employee would have to show that the employer failed to conduct a thorough background check on the employee before hiring, and had employer conducted an adequate background check, the employer would never have hired such employee.

> *Example:* A company was liable to a customer who was allegedly molested by an employee because of the company's failure to discover the employee's prior record of sex crimes.

> *Example:* An apartment owner was liable for negligent hiring to a tenant who was allegedly burglarized by an employee. The apartment owner was liable because he failed to discover prior burglary convictions of the maintenance employee.

Although the negligent hiring theory is used frequently in the courts, it is unlikely that employers will be required to conduct a detailed background investigation on all of employers' employees, particularly on employees who will have very little contact with the public.

7. Intentional Infliction of Emotional Distress

This common law claim is available in most states. Again, although the particular elements may vary slightly from state to state, generally speaking, employers may be liable to a current or former employee if the employee can show: (a) certain conduct employers engaged in was intentional or reckless, (b) the conduct was so outrageous and intolerable that it offended generally accepted standards of decency and morality, (c) there was a causal connection between employers' conduct and the employee's emotional distress and (d) the distress was severe. Generally, intentional infliction of emotional distress is a hard claim to prove in court because the conduct that is complained of must be extreme and intolerable. Employers will not be held liable for intentional infliction of emotional distress based on an employee's complaints of petty insults, minor indignities, or impolite trivialities.

8. *Promissory Estoppel*

Where an employer makes a promise to an employee on which the employee relies to his detriment, the employee may have a cause of action for the damages incurred, even if no enforceable contract was formed. The elements of promissory estoppel are the following: (1) a promise, (2) which the promisor should reasonably expect to induce action or forbearance on the part of another person, (3) which does induce such action or forbearance, and (4) injustice can be avoided only by enforcement of the promise. For example, in one case a job offer was made to an applicant who lived thousands of miles away and who, in reliance on the offer, quit his current job and sold his house, but then was fired before beginning the new job.[28] In another case, an employee was told by his employer that one of his employer-provided benefits was group life insurance coverage provided by the employer. In reliance, he did not procure his own coverage. During the course of his employment, the employer allowed the group life insurance policy to expire but failed to tell the employees it had expired. When the employee died and his widow was told by the employer that there was no coverage at the time of death, she sued and won.[29]

---

28.   Sheppard v. Morgan Keegan & Co., 218 Cal. App.3d (Cal. App. 1990).
29.   McCarthy v. Louisville Cartage Company, Inc., 796 S.W.2d 10 (Ky. App. 1990).

Internet and Online Business Activities

William Tolin Gay
Luce Forward
Irvine, CA

CHAPTER **11**

Contents

Internet and Online Business Activities

11.01   Preliminary Considerations

Over the past two decades, the Internet has been transformed, largely through the development of the World Wide Web, from a military and educational tool to an indispensable communication medium for businesses. No longer do books and articles on the subject begin with a litany of historical and projected exponential growth statistics; the pervasive nature of the Internet is now taken for granted, as is the perceived need for most businesses to establish and maintain a suitable presence in cyberspace.

However, the move to the Internet presents a host of legal challenges to a business, both initially and with ongoing operations. As will be discussed below, many of these can be viewed as applications of existing legal principles; others involve extension by analogy; yet a few represent entirely novel concepts that have no counterpart in "carbon-based reality." These challenges may be encountered in varying combinations or sequences, depending on a number of factors, including the manner in which the business moves to the Internet, the purpose and type of site and the features and functionalities offered to viewers. This discussion follows a typical sequence; others are possible.

11.02   Online Business

A.   Establishing an Online Presence

1.   Domain Names

For most businesses, the process begins with obtaining a unique domain name (e.g., www.yourbusiness.com), as discussed in Chapter 8 (Technology and Intellectual Property Rights) in the context of trademarks. This is usually included in the bundle of services provided by professional web designers or can be done easily online; however, obtaining a domain name actually involves a rather complex process that warrants a brief description.

Every computer that is connected to the Internet is assigned a unique Internet protocol ("IP") address, consisting of four numbers, each ranging from 0 to 255, in the format 123.456.789.10. These numbers are referred to as Uniform Resource Locator, or "URL." This system is unwieldy for business purposes, and an intelligently selected domain name has greater mnemonic value.

The Internet Corporation for Assigned Names and Numbers ("ICANN") is responsible for the accreditation of registrars. An accredited registrar is authorized to issue domain names. Not surprisingly, many of them also offer site hosting and other services. An American domain name is selected from the end first; the suffix extension is called the generic top level domain, or "gTLD," and is ".com" for most commercial enterprises. Other possible extensions are ".net" (networks), ".gov" (government, except military), ".edu" (educational), ".org" (organization), ".int" (international organizations), ".mil" (military), ".biz" (business), ".pro" (licensed professionals) and ".info" (informational). A number of additional gTLDs have been proposed and are gradually being adopted, including ".shop," ".web," ".arts," ".rec," and ".nom." Although this proliferation of extensions was intended in part to relieve a glut that was beginning to occur as all simple and obvious domain names were gradually taken, the effect has been the opposite. Now, businesses are well advised to reserve their gTLD with as many extensions as are potentially useful (e.g., www.mybiz.com, www.mybiz.net and www.mybiz.biz). In addition, sites in foreign countries end in the gTLD for that country (e.g., "ca" for Canada or "jp" for Japan). For more information on ICANN and gTLD choices, see Chapter 8 (Technology and Intellectual Property Rights).

The second level domain immediately precedes the gTLD extension. This is often the name of the company or an approximation of it. The process of selecting the second level domain should be done with great care and thoroughness; a well thought-out URL can enhance, rather than dilute, an established mark, as discussed in Chapter 8. The links www.disney.com and www.cocacola.com leave little doubt as to where they will lead, whereas

The Law Offices of Joseph Blow, Esq. may be relegated to www.blowlaw. com. (One of the more unfortunate examples is that of The Lumberman's Exchange, whose URL, www.lumbermansexchange.com, admits of more than one reading.) The Coca-Cola Company has also reserved www.coke.com, which automatically transfers to the main site.

In the early years of commercialization of the Internet, gTLDs were granted on a first-come, first-served basis, with little or no regard to any proprietary rights. This gave rise to a land-rush mentality, and instances of "cybersquatting" and auctions at exorbitant prices were common. This trend has since given way to civil litigation sounding in trademark law, including the adoption of the "Anti-Cybersquatting Consumer Protection Act," which provides for punitive damages for predatory taking of gTLDs derived from registered trademarks or service marks. Again, this issue is discussed in more detail in Chapter 8 (Technology and Intellectual Property Rights).

Once a site name has been selected, the next step is to determine availability. The most obvious method—typing in the URL and hitting the "Enter" key—is, unfortunately, not foolproof, as it may produce the same result for untaken names as for names that have been reserved but for which a site has not yet been developed. Most of the major registrars, such as Network Solutions and VeriSign, have name availability functions on their sites. These are generally reliable but may not be entirely up to date. The only sure way to secure the availability of a name is to reserve it online, at which time the owner will receive an e-mail acknowledgement from the registrar.

An alternative approach is to obtain a subfolder within an existing provider, which may take the form www.yeehaw.com/~yourbusiness, where "yeehaw" is the Internet Service Provider ("ISP"). This "tilda site" format is generally disfavored from an image standpoint, as it suggests that the business was unable or unwilling to obtain its own domain name and gives the impression that the site was set up at a discount or even for free.

2. *Transferring Domain Names*

The need to transfer ownership of a registered domain name may arise when a business is sold or changes its name or under other circumstances. This process is also effectuated through accredited registrars. It is relatively simple, but care must be taken to comply with specific requirements relating to signatures, addresses, notarial acknowledgements, and the like. These are laid out in the specific registrar's registrant name-change documents. At this point a distinction should be drawn between transfer of ownership of a domain name, which is intellectual property, and transfer of a website from one host to another. The former is comparable to giving up your trade name to your competitor; the latter is comparable to moving your offices from one building to another. Many registrars also provide web-hosting services, either directly or through affiliate relationships, and make it easy to transfer a site from its current location to their servers.

Some domain name transfers are not voluntary. ICANN has developed a Uniform Domain Name Dispute Resolutions Policy, which can be accessed from www.internic.net/udrp. Practitioners should consult this site prior to commencement of any action over a URL, even when the URL appears to be protected by some other body of law, such as trademark.

3. Developing Site Content

The threshold issue for a business that wishes to establish a web presence is the purpose of the website. A site can be informational and non-interactive or the converse—it can exist to solicit views from customers or observers. A site can have a sales and marketing focus or can actually make online sales. A site can exist to satisfy a statutory or regulatory requirement or to promote investment in the company.

In fact, most sites have multiple purposes. A site may, for example, sell products directly, offer viewers an opportunity to sell products and earn profits through an affiliate program, provide user or expert reviews of products, elicit customer response through a feedback form or e-mail link, offer shares of the company either directly or through a broker, and provide investor relations information for online reading or download. Few sites spring into being fully formed, but rather grow from an initial purpose. Identifying the purposes of the site, both initially and as they arise in the future, is a critical step in site design. Doing so will help dictate site design, enable the site to flow from one page to another, and facilitate functionality on each page.

a. Internal Development versus Outsourcing

The next issue for a site owner is whether to develop the site internally or to commission outside developers. In this analysis, it is useful to divide content, albeit somewhat arbitrarily, into two parts: technical and artistic. In most cases, a combination emerges whereby the company and its employees produce textual content, logos and ideas relating to design and functionality, and professional developers encode the "heavy lifting," including animation, interactive features and e-commerce operations.

It is natural for this relationship to develop over time, as employees who understand certain aspects of the Internet are tapped to assist on the project while outside developers familiarize themselves with the company and its business. It is helpful for management to think ahead to when the site is operational and make staffing decisions based on future expectations. As the project develops, and as the scope of the site becomes apparent, decisions can be made as to the extent to which outside assistance will be required on a continuing basis.

A second dichotomy may emerge with respect to the artistic aspects of a site, or the words and pictures. Although it is not difficult to find enough material to set up a site initially, many site owners find that it soon becomes quite a challenge to create sufficient material to keep the site fresh in order to keep viewers coming back for more. As a result, many sites will solicit contributions from customers, purchase content from professional or freelance sources or exchange content with other sites. In every case, the site owner should observe the same formalities as with any printed medium. This includes obtaining some kind of warranty of ownership from the source and making independent verification if warranted by the facts or circumstances. Perhaps most importantly, the site should include a procedure for handling viewers' infringement complaints. This could include a written disclaimer on the site, a readily visible e-mail link to collect complaints and a practice of promptly removing allegedly infringing material until the dispute can be resolved.

b.   Ownership of Assets

Whether elements of the site are produced internally or externally, the site owner should remain alert to issues of ownership of site assets. The analysis should begin with the Copyright Act, which generally provides that ownership of copyrightable material belongs to its author. This fact comes as a surprise to managers at many companies, who assume that the company owns the work that it commissioned.

As initially discussed in Chapter 1 (Starting a New Business) and in Chapter 8 (Technology and Intellectual Property Rights), in the context of intellectual property rights in general, with employees, the "work for hire" or "assignment of inventions and work product" provision included in most employment agreements, such as contained in **Exhibit 10B**, should suffice. For greater protection, it is advisable to have the employee execute assignment agreements for specific works. (See **Exhibit 8A** for a general assignment agreement and **Exhibit 11A** for a copyright assignment agreement.) If an independent contractor ("IC") is used, the IC agreement should specify that all products of the engagement are "work for hire" and expressly owned by the principal. **Exhibit 8C** is an independent contractor agreement containing such wording.

With outside developers, the issue is complicated by the prevalence of reusable code in most development tools. For example, clicking on the "Contact Us" button on many commercial websites will bring up a pre-addressed e-mail window in the user's browser. The code behind this process is simple; however, it only makes sense for developers to write it once, save it in a library and copy and paste it into each project as needed. This saves time and, equally importantly, reduces the chance of error. Developers maintain libraries of such code snippets and much, if not most, of any given project will involve stitching them into a cohesive whole held together by original code that is specific to the project.

The difficulty is obvious. If the site owner insists on a copyright assignment or exclusive license, the developer will effectively be out of business. On the other hand, no commercial site owner will wish to pay full fare for an original site only to have the developer offer an identical site, perhaps at a discounted rate, to that owner's competitors. The solution is not simple, but is fact specific and involves a meticulous articulation of those site elements that are original, which are then assigned to the owner with express carve-outs for reusable libraries and other code that the developer requires for other projects. This approach can sometimes be coupled with an exclusivity arrangement within the site owner's industry or scope of business. Such an agreement may preclude the developer from developing a site for a competitor of the current customer for a specified period of time, which site incorporates specific elements of the current project combined in a certain order.

c. Specification Sheet

A specification or spec sheet, such as **Exhibit 11B** will typically be appended to the content development agreement. Although it is difficult to generalize, some of the items that should be covered here, or in the body of a formal agreement itself, are as follows:

Number of Pages. How many web pages will the site feature? What, in general, will be contained on each page? Although some layout decisions may be left to the designer, some preliminary thought should be given to this aspect of the site. It is technologically possible to present all information on a single page; however, the result would likely be unsightly, unwieldy to navigate and slow to load.

Features and Functionality. These can often be stated in general terms, such as, navigation tools, e-mail, java applet or flash support, or cookies.

Browser Support. By most accounts, the browser war is over and Microsoft has won. As of this writing, however, many Internet users eschew Internet Explorer in favor of Netscape Navigator, Mozilla or others. Setting aside the fact that some websites have intentionally been set up so that some features are unavailable in certain browsers, it has always been the case that some sites simply look better with one browser than with another. Some website home pages give the user a choice—in effect setting up two or more sites that only differ in the way they appear to different browsers. At an initial page, the user indicates which browser is being used—or it is detected automatically—and is redirected accordingly.

A separate but related issue deals with functionality and bandwidth. Some users like media-rich sites and have incorporated audio and video add-ins into their browsers from such companies as Macromedia and RealAudio. Other users prefer speed and would like a static, or even text-only, experience. The choice may be driven by hardware considerations—a user on a 28.8 modem may not wish to wait for what would be a nearly instantaneous transfer to a user on a T1 line.

d. Timetable

Website development should be viewed as an engineering project and, hence, subject to inexplicable delays. No matter how experienced a developer may be—or claim to be—each project is unique, and there is no way to predict with certainty that all parts, hardware and software, will function together properly until completion. Companies may wish to take an approach that is common with contractors in other industries and build in positive financial incentives for early completion and penalties for lateness.

e. Testing

When the project is finally complete, there should be an opportunity to test the site offline in advance of "going live." Every function should be tested, including e-mail, downloading, streaming, and the like, and all links, especially navigational links, should be tried. It is not practical, however, to try every possible keystroke or mouse-click combination. Thus, no release should be given until the developer has provided some kind of warranty.

f. Support and Training

Every developer should stand behind its work product, and, as suggested above, bugs might not appear until the site has been subjected to some level of online usage. Moreover, the company should update the content on its site from time to time, and technological advances may give rise to the need for a facelift. Finally, the company may at some point elect to bring much of the website maintenance in-house. These factors and others necessitate some degree of ongoing support following the completion and posting of the site. Not only should this be provided for in the initial development agreement, the cautious owner should also make contingency plans in the event the original developer becomes unavailable.

g. Legal Notices

It is good practice to place a copyright notice at the bottom of each page of the site. Similarly, all trademarked terms or logos should bear the trademark or service mark symbol. Protected work that is licensed to the site should bear appropriate credits. The site should provide an easy way for the webmaster to be contacted, and internal controls should exist within the company for prompt removal of copyrighted material in the event a viewer of the site recognizes that some item posted on it belongs to someone else and so notifies the webmaster.

Assuming that some variant of the Uniform Commercial Code ("UCC"), which is discussed in Chapter 9 (Product Development and Distribution), will govern transactions carried out through a website, it may be advisable to insert any disclaimers or other limitations at appropriately visible locations on the site's pages. In addition, jurisdictional or privacy notices may be posted, although, as is discussed below, their enforceability is yet open to question.

4.   Website Hosting

A website, once developed, must be hosted on a server. "Host server" may be defined as a computer connected to the Internet as a node on which the data files and applications that comprise a website are stored. Even as simple a definition as this, however, invites challenge due in large measure to the "cyber" nature of the Internet—an e-mail sent to a website may be instantly forwarded to another address; links on a site may direct a web surfer to another site; or pointers contained within the code of a website may open other, remote websites within "frames." At any given time, it is difficult to pin down exactly what is occurring and where. Nevertheless, the principal elements of a website—those features that define its identity and from which its functionality flows—must be "put" somewhere, and site hosting agreements are the mechanisms for taking up tenancy on the Internet. An example appears as **Exhibit 11C**.

a.   Onsite or Outsource

The initial question for a site owner is whether to set up and maintain the host server or to hire someone else to do it. This is usually an easy choice. Continuous connectivity is best ensured by full-time host maintenance. Host maintenance should only be undertaken by companies whose business is, or includes, website hosting or which are sufficiently large to devote full-time resources to it. All other businesses, especially smaller businesses, should outsource their web hosting, often to an ISP.

b.   Virtual Web Servers and Colocation

These are two terms that may be heard in connection with outsourced web hosting. In the normal case, a website is stored on the hard drive of a single machine, together with any number of other websites. It is possible, however, to divide the hard drive of a machine into two or more "virtual web servers," each of which operates with relatively little software interaction with the others. Each virtual server can host one or more websites in relative isolation from the sites on the other virtual servers. This can result in some performance enhancement, but it is important to remember that any hardware bottlenecks or constraints will affect all virtual servers on the same machine.

Colocation is the practice of entrusting a machine, with one or more websites on it, to a company that provides physical shelter, climate control, security and, in some cases, backup and some level of maintenance. It is often used by ISPs for the protection of their machines. In this type of arrangement, the ISPs tend to become little more than a sales force.

c. Platform

As with desktop computers, web servers have an operating system, the two most common of which are Microsoft Windows and UNIX in its various distributions, including the freeware Linux. Basic websites, which are written in Hypertext Markup Language ("HTML"), as well as various software enhancements, are platform independent, and, as a general matter, it is not necessary to consider platform when developing site content. However, various host servers may have or lack extensions to their particular platform, which will affect the operation of some of the more sophisticated functionality that may be built into a site. A skilled developer will know what extensions are necessary to make a particular site operational.

d. Performance

Website developers may go to great lengths to script sites that load quickly onto a user's machine; however, their efforts are wasted if the site is then hosted on a slow server. A server's performance, that is, speed, is a function of server response time, connection speed and bandwidth. The last of these also affects how much traffic a server can handle. Traffic is in turn a function of the number of simultaneous users and the size of files that are transferred. In short, much depends on who else is sharing your server.

e. Reliability

As with all statistics, those relating to web server reliability should be evaluated critically. Many host companies boast an uptime in excess of 99 percent; a few claim over 99.9 percent. However, this usually refers only to unscheduled downtime (i.e., system crashes), rather than periodic maintenance, which is usually scheduled during low usage hours and for which a "temporarily down for maintenance" page is displayed. It should be noted that even 99.9 percent still leaves nearly nine hours per year of unscheduled, unwarned disappearance into ether. A site's users will have no clue as to what has happened to the site, nor will they know for how long the site will be down, and they will have no alternative but to check back periodically. Consider also the fact that many crashes occur as a result of system overload, the result of which is an increased likelihood that the site will go down during a crucial period, such as the holiday season. To put it in concrete terms, imagine having a commercial website that sells toys, and being told by your ISP that your site will be unavailable for a total of nine hours at some time, or at various times, most likely during the month of December. That's 99.9 percent reliability.

Some providers offer backup, often in the form of mirror sites, to which a user's browser will be referred if the principal site is down. This is significantly more expensive to maintain but should be considered in critical cases. A related issue, then, is service and support. If a server crashes, will there be anyone there to hear (read: repair) it? The hosting agreement should address this issue, and a site owner is well advised to make independent confirmation of the host company's reliability in this area.

f.   Security

Website hosts can provide varying levels of security for hosted sites. There are two common security protocols that are used for certain data transfers, such as credit card information. The first is SHTTP, or Secure Hypertext Transfer Protocol, which encrypts data one page at a time between the user's machine and the server. Such sites have "https" headings, rather than the familiar "http," and a tiny padlock or similar icon is highlighted in a corner of the user's browser. The second is SSL, or Secure Sockets Layer, which encrypts data between applications and the Internet itself. If it is contemplated that sensitive information will be transferred through the site, one or the other protocol should be made available by the host.

g.   Termination and Transfer

Termination of a hosting arrangement may be subject to early termination charges or other fees; however, the most important point is ease of transfer of the URL to another host. So long as the URL is properly registered in the owner's name with the name registrar, this should be a simple matter. The owner should also take steps to ensure that the site, and all of its assets, is removed from the previous host's machines so as to avoid the possibility of misappropriation. This can often be done by the owner with the website development and file transfer protocol software that is used to maintain and modify the site.

h.   Cost

Hosting agreements usually have a term of at least one year, payable monthly or quarterly. Discounts are usually available for prepayment or for committing to a longer term. Costs may vary from one host to another, and some features, such as mirroring and backup, may vary as well, but the single most important determinant in cost will be the size of the website. This is measured in terms of two parameters, both expressed in megabytes. The first is the actual size of the site, including all files that are stored on the server. The second is traffic, that is, how many megabytes of data are transferred per month. Data is transferred every time someone views any page of the site, as well as any time someone downloads something from it or sends it an e-mail message, and so on. Both parameters employ server resources; the first uses physical storage on the server's hard drives, and the second uses bandwidth.

Entry-level sites may retail at $10–$20 per month, and many plans provide for unlimited disk space and traffic. In plans where traffic is limited, additional capacity can be added as needed at an additional charge. If so, it is important to know whether the hosting agreement provides that such capacity will be added automatically, and the customer billed for it in arrears, or that capacity will only be added upon request. The former is preferable, as the latter may lead to dropped connections.

5. *Electronic Commerce*

Some site owners elect to use the web simply for promotion or for dissemination of product or company information. The web can serve this purpose beautifully. However, most wish, if possible, to use the web to its full commercial potential—a round-the-clock, international storefront where products or services can be bought at any time. This requires additional work beyond what has thus far been described.

a. Merchant Account

A number of entrepreneurs have tried implementing various forms of cyberspace money, but no such method has found as much widespread acceptance as online use of credit cards. Issuing banks have overcome their initial reluctance to open accounts for online businesses, and online accounts are now commonplace, if not expected. With substantial legal safeguards, few consumers are overly concerned about providing credit card information over the Internet. Filling out an online form at the website of a respected retailer is arguably safer than entrusting it to a perfect stranger in a restaurant for several minutes. However, there is a substantial risk of dishonor or nonpayment to the merchant, which many merchants simply accept as a cost of doing business online.

b. Fulfillment

By this point, it should come as no surprise that even processing orders, maintaining inventory and mailing out merchandise are functions that can be outsourced. This presents the site owner with the opportunity to make the business almost entirely "virtual." Costs should be weighed against benefits, and the reputation and reliability of the fulfillment house should be thoroughly investigated.

c.   Electronic Content

Computer software, written materials and digitized visual and audio products are unique in that the Internet can be the method of distribution through download from a commerce server. It then becomes the buyer's responsibility to commit the content to hard copy, whether by printing it out or burning a compact disk or the like. This can be tremendously profitable, as variable costs approach zero. Of course, the bane of digital media, compared to analog media, is that it can be copied repeatedly without any degradation of content. However, many download sites offer the capability to assign a unique license number to each download, and the vendor can require that the buyer provide registration information, in some cases verified through a credit card, before the download commences.

d.   Terms of Use and Policies

All sites have terms of use, whether intentional or not, such as in **Exhibit 11D**. This issue comes most sharply into focus on commercial sites, where some form of the UCC will govern domestic sales. Most sophisticated commercial site owners take a proactive approach and attempt to articulate the terms of use and other policies that best serve their interests.

Many of the terms of use parallel the boilerplate section of a written contract, such as governing law, choice of forum, mandatory arbitration, and so on. If a site is interactive, the owner may adopt a policy that bars users who post information that is defamatory, offensive or commercial in nature. These terms should not only be clearly spelled out in writing, but should also be made readily visible and accessible to the user. In addition, a site owner should consider archiving and dating old terms of use as they are modified.

6.   *Jurisdiction*

In order to appreciate fully the gravity and complexity of jurisdictional issues in cyberspace, it is helpful to recall the origins of the Internet. In 1962, the Advanced Research Projects Agency ("ARPA") commissioned the Rand Corporation to develop a communications system that could survive a nuclear attack. Rand developed the concept of "packet-switching," whereby information is broken into discrete packets and sent from origin to destination in such a manner that if any packet is lost or disrupted, it can be resent. In 1969, ARPANET was unveiled as the first network, operating among four university campuses, to use packet-switching. Three years later, the first e-mail was sent.

Structurally, the concept behind ARPANET was survivability through redundancy; if one route were destroyed, the network would automatically select another. Indeed, the course that a given message takes from source to destination bears little relationship to geographical economy, but rather is usually determined by current loads on the system. A message sent from one person to another within the same state could, at least hypothetically, be routed around the earth. Although this fact may be of little consequence under U.S. jurisdictional principles, the laws of other countries may lead to less predictable results.

Traditional principles of jurisdiction, as articulated in *International Shoe Co. v. Washington*[1] and its progeny, seek to establish the existence of "minimum contacts" with the host forum, based on purposefully directed activities or transactions. Furthermore, there should be some relationship of the subject claim to those activities or transactions, all against a backdrop of "fair play and substantial justice."

In addition, in order to establish general jurisdiction, there must be systematic and continuous contacts with the forum state, such that the defendant might reasonably anticipate defending any claim there.

These concepts, which seemed apt in the era of mail order catalogs and the growth of large corporations, are decidedly anachronistic when applied to cyberspace. Recall that web images are retrieved from the server on which they reside, which could be located anywhere. Does this act of retrieval, which is performed by the customer, constitute a "contact" by the seller? Given that setting up a website provides instant worldwide exposure, does it follow that all site owners reasonably anticipate defending any claim anywhere in the world? In the near future, when intelligent agents and "bots" will be able to perform comparison shopping and make purchases while their owners sleep, will the consumer protection overtones of these traditional notions be as compelling as they were in the past?

Some new concepts are emerging. The sliding scale approach looks at the nature of the website. For passive sites, there is no jurisdiction. For information exchange sites, this approach looks to the sites' other contacts, if any, with the forum. For sites involved in buying and selling, there may be jurisdiction.

None of this should suggest that sellers are powerless in the process. One approach is to limit sales to buyers who are resident in a certain jurisdiction and to post a notice to that effect. Another slightly less certain approach is to post terms of sale, including a choice of laws and forum provision. Among other difficulties, this approach may be subject to the enforceability of such "click-wrap" agreements in the buyer's forum.

On the international level, it is difficult to generalize other than to say that most countries that have addressed issues of jurisdiction in cyberspace have adopted a broader approach than the United States. In addition, some countries have fashioned rules that are uniquely suited to them; for example, courts in The Netherlands hold that if a website is in Dutch, the site has

---

1.   326 U.S. 310, 66 S. Ct. 154, 90 L.Ed. 95 (1945).

voluntarily submitted to Netherlands jurisdiction. The logic behind this holding is unassailable but would be wholly inapplicable to a less indigenous language such as English and useless to courts of the 50 separate state jurisdictions of the United States.

B. Conducting Business Online

1. Privacy

a. Customer Information

With many commercial websites, a social contract is formed when a customer makes an initial purchase. "In order to serve you better," a site will solicit valuable demographic information. To encourage responsiveness, the site may promise not to disclose this information to other parties. The enforceability of such "contracts" is challenged in bankruptcy, when a company's customer list may be its most valuable asset, and the trustee or receiver is legally charged with maximizing the value of the estate. The Federal Trade Commission has stated that privacy, meaning non-transfer of information promises, takes priority over bankruptcy courts' desire to sell assets and raise money.

A separate issue is whether companies actually observe their own privacy policies. Many website owners believe that they are observing their policies if they simply refrain from selling or leasing their customer lists. They may be unpleasantly surprised to learn how much confidential information is routinely and necessarily disclosed to credit card companies, fulfillment houses and other business partners. In the ordinary course of online business, these partners are not bound by the owner's privacy policy.

To protect themselves, website owners should take three actions. First, owners, working with their site developers, should take steps to anonymize data or otherwise limit the scope of disclosure to their business partners to the minimum level necessary to do the job. Second, they should require business partners to become parties to the site's privacy policy. Third, they should revise their privacy policy to indicate that some information may be disclosed to the owner's partners. Sample privacy policies appear in **Exhibit 11E**.

Moreover, some companies may inadvertently adopt a privacy policy. An expression such as, "Use our commerce server; it's confidential and secure" may be intended to mean that the server is difficult to hack into, but the plain meaning of "confidential" could reasonably be construed as "not to be disclosed."

A related area involves information gathering that may operate invisibly to the consumer. Cookies, clickstreams and web tracking are all software techniques that can reveal much about a user's identity or activities. Some privacy policies expressly eschew the use of such techniques. Several states have legislation that requires written disclosure, on the site, of the nature and use of such techniques. Best practices dictate that this disclosure should be made in all cases.

b.   Employee Relations

A separate area of privacy law is in employee relations and deals with employee use of e-mail and the World Wide Web, as well as use of computer storage space for personal purposes, and the employer's right to monitor all of this. Although the current law in most jurisdictions holds that an employee has no reasonable expectation of privacy in this realm, employers are well advised to provide specific notice of this fact, for example, by articulation of a "computer usage policy" that can be included in the employee handbook. This issue is discussed in more detail in Chapter 10 (Human Resources).

2.   *Advertising and Marketing*

Online advertising is subject to the same regulatory framework as offline advertisement, with the Federal Trade Commission taking a leading role at the federal level in concert with various state agencies. Most Internet advertising takes the form of banner ads, which are graphic images placed on a web page, and interstitial ads, which are ads that pop up unexpectedly, often in a separate window, when a user attempts to move from one page to another. Both kinds of ads are usually subject to an agreement between the advertiser and site owner. Pricing is based on some measurement of how much traffic the site experiences. In addition, software is available that can rotate a given banner ad space among several pages.

Some users might construe such advertisements as endorsements. A site owner can exercise caution in a number of ways, short of an express disclaimer. First, observe truth-in-advertising laws in one's own promotional material, whether displayed on one's own site or elsewhere. Second, clearly demarcate other parties' advertising as not one's own. Third, do not accept ads from sites that engage in activities that are illegal in one's own jurisdiction. Fourth, visit the sites that wish to advertise with you, both before accepting the contract and from time to time afterwards. If such sites appear to be engaging in false advertising or are unseemly or have annoying features, consider whether the advertisement is worth accepting. Fortunately, many Internet advertising agreements are for short periods, such as three months, and can simply not be renewed.

3.   *Sales*

Successful advertising leads to sales for which the commercial website owner should be prepared. The process of an online purchase can be divided into a number of discrete steps.

First, the buyer peruses on online catalog. Prices should be kept up to date or at least at a level the seller is willing to honor. Although this seems like an obvious point, a surprising number of sellers that have both a real world and an online presence do not actively take steps to ensure that prices are consistent. When this occurs, it should be intentional rather than accidental, that is, pursuant to a conscious policy to drive buyers to, or from, the web.

Second, the buyer selects one or more products. This is often done by means of a virtual "shopping cart" into which items may be placed and in which they are stored until the buyer is ready to finalize the purchase. A well-designed shopping cart has the following characteristics: First, it is easy to navigate—the user can easily understand how it works, and getting around doesn't require excessive keystrokes or mouse-clicks. Second, as items are added, the option to "continue shopping" is as easy to follow as the option to "check out." Finally, a "refresh" button allows for the possibility that a buyer will *right*-click on each item of interest and open a new window for each one.

Third, the buyer begins the checkout process, and enters credit card information or makes other payment arrangements. By this stage, the site should have switched to a secure status employing one of the methods described above. Credit card information and an authorization are transmitted to the bank with whom the seller maintains its merchant account. Credit is verified, the account is charged and a thank-you notice with the transaction number appears on screen. In addition, an e-mail message with this and more information is sent to the buyer's e-mail address. If the item is shipped by FedEx or United Parcel Service, the e-mail may include tracking information.

Fourth, the order is sent to the fulfillment center and processed. Another e-mail message may be sent to the buyer when the item is shipped or if a stock outage or other problem occurs.

Each of these steps may be further subdivided. The significance for the seller is that each of these processes, except for credit card processing, may be either done internally or outsourced, and the seller must make a decision with respect to each. Few sellers will want to internalize the entire process; however, every outsourcing decision involves an increase in risk of various kinds. An outsource partner may be dilatory, become insolvent or fail to perform in a timely manner for a variety of reasons. It may misappropriate customer information, be acquired by a competitor or be hacked or have a technological failure. Anything that could happen to the seller itself could befall an outsource partner. With outsourcing, therefore, the seller's responsibility becomes one of supervision, maintaining contact and anticipating and managing any breakdown.

4. Procurement

This is the flip side of sales. The Internet can provide an attractive and inexpensive means for a buyer, especially a large wholesale buyer, to obtain quotations, bids and offers from suppliers. Usually, the buyer will post its requirements, with specifications, and solicit bids from suppliers. In doing so, the buyer should consider the following:

Method of Notification.   Although the request for proposal ("RFP") or similar action can and should be posted on the site, the effectiveness of the site can be enhanced if an e-mail notification is sent to former and current suppliers as well. This notice should be in the form of a blind copy so that each supplier is not able to determine who else received the notice.

Open or Closed System.   Most buyers prefer a closed system accessible with a password by authorized users and not by the general public. If this method is used, and new vendors are welcome, the site should feature a sign-up process or at least clear instructions on how to apply to become an authorized provider.

Method of Response.   The simplest form is by e-mail; however, a more foolproof method, and one that helps to ensure that standards and specifications are observed, is to provide for a response through the site itself. Variable features, quantities and the like can be entered through form elements, such as radio buttons, check boxes and drop-down menus, and user error can be minimized through the use of mouse-clicks, rather than keystroke entries.

Confidentiality and Other Ground Rules.   Whatever process is used for selection, the ground rules should be made clear to all participants. Nothing can undermine a procurement process, online or off, faster than a perception among participants that the process is somehow unfair or even unclear. Vendors will simply stop participating. One issue is whether the method should be a "silent auction," whereby each bidder is unable to see other bids. There are good business—and antitrust—reasons not to share this information, but where it is warranted, it can be anonymized (i.e., price, but not bidder's identity, can be shown). Once the selection is made, submitters of losing bids should be notified promptly.

5. *Sweepstakes and Contests*

A highly visible give-away is immediately attractive to many website owners as a means of attracting customers and, if possible, eliciting demographic information. Care should be taken, however, to ensure that such activities do not fall into the legal classification of a lottery, which is illegal in most states. The distinguishing characteristics of a lottery are that (a) a prize is awarded, (b) based on chance to a person chosen among contestants (c) who have paid some consideration for the privilege to compete. In order to reduce the likelihood of classification as a lottery, a contest should entail some degree of knowledge or skill and limit anything, including elicitation of information that could be construed as consideration. A more cautionary approach is to make the contest expressly unavailable to users in states that present problems. When faced with the risks, and the somewhat alienating effect of carving out entire states, many site owners opt not to use contests at all.

6. Spam

As late as 1995, the Internet was considered by some to be a preserve of academia and computer developers and overtly commercial activities were not welcomed. The temptation was difficult to resist—through the use of listservs and other devices, an e-mail message could be sent by a single mouse-click to an enormous number of recipients.

The market for qualified, "live," e-mail addresses has grown rapidly and remains active today. A few states have responded with statutory restrictions on mass e-mailing. As spammers seldom have any idea of the state of residency of their multitudinous addressees, they are forced to comply with the most restrictive provisions of the various state acts. One example of such a restriction is the requirement that all spam include a toll-free telephone number that recipients can call to be removed from the mailing list. Another is the requirement that the subject line of unsolicited commercial e-mail begin with the letters "ADV," for "advertisement."

A quick survey of one's own daily e-mail will quickly reveal that these regulations are of little effect. In fact, most spammers rely on the anonymous and fluid nature of the Internet to avoid any attempt at regulation. For home-based, multilevel marketing Internet schemes, which tend to have a lifespan measured in months, at most, this approach may be satisfactory. For established businesses, it is not. Such businesses should comply with any applicable spam regulations if they even determine that spamming is consistent with the professional image that they wish to project.

7. Children

The Children's Online Privacy Protection Act of 1998 ("COPPA")[2] provides a higher level of review of online solicitation of information from persons under the age of 13. Pursuant to COPPA, the Federal Trade Commission has promulgated guidelines relating to collection and disclosure of information and requiring prior consent of parents. Although COPPA has been attacked as unconstitutional, it remains good law in most parts of the country.

8. Online Contracts

Contracts in cyberspace can take many forms. Perhaps the easiest example is an orderly exchange of e-mail (i.e., where no communications have crossed

---

2.   15 USCA 6502.

or been superseded). Questions arise when the extent of human input is reduced. For example, is a mouse-click on an onscreen button that says "I Accept" sufficient to create a binding contract? Does it matter whether the default is "I Accept" or "I Refuse"? What happens if the exchange is entirely automated and occurs pursuant to a program in which a buyer has entered an acceptable price range?

Practitioners who have been in practice for more than 20 years may recall similar questions that arose when facsimile correspondence became commonplace. However, electronic communication presents additional problems. What happens if an electronic message is garbled or lost in transmission? What if the intended recipient's e-mail server misidentifies the message as spam or a virus and fails to deliver it?

On October 1, 2000, the federal Electronic Signatures in Global and National Commerce Act ("E-Sign") became effective. It provides, in general, that a signature will not be denied enforceability merely because it is electronic in nature. E-Sign is permissive and allows contracting parties ample opportunity to provide otherwise contractually. Significantly, it defines "electronic signature" as follows:

> The term 'electronic signature' means an electronic sound, symbol, or process attached to or logically associated with a contract or other record and executed or adopted by a person with the intent to sign the record.

Interestingly, E-Sign also provides that it may be superceded by state law under narrowly defined circumstances. At the time of its promulgation, an immediate need for uniform legislation was recognized at the federal level. Nevertheless, the drafters were mindful of the fact that the National Conference of Commissioners on Uniform State Laws ("NCCUSL") was addressing the same subject matter. Because so many industries that require signatures, including insurance, real estate, and the like, are regulated at the state level, the drafters wished to defer to those states that chose to draft their own laws on the subject. Thus, E-Sign was by its nature a stop-gap measure.

NCCUSL's product was the Uniform Electronic Transactions Act ("UETA"), which covered much the same territory as E-sign. As of this writing, it is finding acceptance in most states.

NCCUSL's far more ambitious project was the Uniform Computerized Information Transactions Act ("UCITA"), which would provide a legal framework for transactions involving software, databases and other forms of digital and electronic information. In this respect, it was intended as a kind of extension of Article 2 of the UCC to transactions involving computerized information. UCITA has only been adopted in Maryland and Virginia, and Iowa has enacted its own "anti-UCITA." Although several of its provisions are contentious, especially for commercial licensees, it does provide a roadmap of the issues that must be addressed in some fashion in the near future.

The first of these issues is the use of mass-market licensing agreements, especially of the online or "click-wrap" variety. In many cases, the licensee is unable to read the license agreement prior to use of the software. In other cases, the licensee may make a counteroffer that the licensor is unable to read prior to first use. Section 209 of UCITA provides for the enforceability of mass-market licenses in general, subject to subsequent rights of rescission.

The next issue involves the use of electronic agents in purchasing transactions. Electronic agents are defined as "a program, or electronic or other automated means, used by a person to initiate an action, or to respond to electronic messages or performances, on the person's behalf without review or action by an individual at the time of the action, or response to a message or performance." Section 207 provides that a person that uses an electronic agent that it has selected for making an authentication, performance or agreement, including manifestation of assent, is bound by the operations of the electronic agent, even if no individual was aware of or reviewed the agent's operations or the results of the operations.

Consider the following hypothetical. Buyer "B" has been in e-mail negotiations with Seller "S" to purchase S's car. Negotiations are ongoing, with B currently offering $15,000, but B is going on a vacation. Buyer programs his e-mail to respond as follows:

If "From:" = Seller S; and

> If "Message" contains "car" or "auto" or "automobile"; and
> If "Message" contains "$0 – $17,500"
> Then respond: "I accept."
> Else respond: "Sorry, that's too much. No deal."

B's intention is to accept any counteroffer from S up to $17,500 and to reject anything over that amount. Consider the following four possibilities:

- S writes: "Okay. I'll sell you my car for $15,000."
- S writes: "Okay. $15,000 it is."
- S writes: "Received your $15,000 offer for my car. Make it twenty thousand, and it's yours."
- S writes: "Tell you what. Even though we both know my car is worth $32,000, I'll let you have it for half that much."

Each of these is a plausible response, but only the first effectuates B's intention. In the second case, B rejects his own offered amount because S's e-mail did not contain the word "car" or "auto" or "automobile." In the third case, B accepts a $20,000 counteroffer that merely references his $15,000 offer, because the counteroffer price was expressed in words, not numbers. In the fourth case, B rejects a counteroffer of $16,000, which was within his range, because the only numerical value that appears in S's communication is $32,000.

In the latter three cases, it is probably B's fault for programming his e-mail too restrictively. UCITA would hold B accountable for this fact.

Section 405 of UCITA introduces a new warranty: an implied warranty of system integration. If an agreement requires that the licensor provide or select a system consisting of computer programs and goods, usually hardware and software, and if the licensor has reason to know that the licensee is relying on the licensor's skill or judgment in selecting the system components, there is an implied warranty that the components provided or selected will function together as a system.

Sections 811 through 816 of UCITA provide a limited right of self-help, including the possibility of "remote disabling," whereby the licensor disables the licensee from further accessing the subject database or other information by means of directly contacting the licensee's hardware, for example, through the Internet. This right has been widely criticized as disproportionately favorable to licensors but is subject to a number of limitations. First, the licensee must assent in advance to a term authorizing the licensor's use of self-help. Second, the term must provide for notice of exercise by the licensor, with the name of the person representing the licensee, place and manner of notice specified. Third, the licensor must provide at least 15 days prior notice, which notice must include a description of the alleged breach, and the name, title and contact information of a person with whom the licensee may communicate about the breach. Finally, UCITA provides for direct and incidental damages for the wrongful use of electronic self-help.

A separate complaint is that the implementation of a mechanism whereby a licensor can employ self-help will by its nature compromise the security of the licensee's site. It necessitates the creation of a back door—the concern is that if the licensor can use it, hackers can find it. The UCITA has been amended twice to restrict the use of electronic self-help in licenses to consumers or as a default provision. Not surprisingly, opponents have regarded these developments as cynical attempts to dilute opposition to this provision, and progress on passage in most states has stalled. Nevertheless, UCITA has several good provisions and provides guidance on issues that should be addressed in licensing agreements relating to computerized information.

11.03 Document Retention Policies

A. Background

Document *retention* policies, or "DRPs," are something of a misnomer, as they are principally concerned with the timely and systematic *destruction* of documents. However, in the era when "document" was commonly understood to mean what is now referred to as a "hard copy," physical storage actually was an economic consideration, destruction was the norm and companies had to make a conscious decision to keep, and pay for the storage of, paper documents. Today, by contrast, one recent estimate is that 93 percent of all business documents are created electronically, and only 30 percent are ever printed to paper.

B. Purpose

In most cases, the purpose of a DRP is to protect the company against disclosure of potentially harmful information in the course of an adversarial proceeding. Typically, the potential harm is inflicted by the other side in the proceeding; generally, confidential information can often be shielded from third parties by protective orders and other measures.

However, the stated purpose of the DRP should be something more innocuous; remember, you'll have to present this in court. Judges will not take kindly to something like: "To keep it out of the hands of jerks like these." Some thought should go into developing a purpose that is plausible and in line with the business purposes of the enterprise. There is an analog to asset protection or tax planning schemes here; the DRP should have a separate, legitimate business purpose that can stand on its own. In short, the objective is to be able to demonstrate that documents are unavailable for production because they were intentionally destroyed pursuant to a legitimate document management system.

Also, remember that "gone" means gone for all purposes, including defensive. In this context, the question of statutes of limitations often arises. Although this is not the driving force behind DRPs, some California statutes of limitations are as follows:

- Verbal contract: 2 years
- Written contract: 4 years
- Tort: nonviolent, 3 years; violent, 2 years
- Products Liability: 4 years from completion, or injury, or reasonable discovery

C. Design

Design considerations should include several matters in addition to purpose. First, the program should be effective; that is, it should carry out the purpose. Second, it should be clearly understandable. It is not necessary that every employee understand all aspects of the policy, but everyone should understand that there *is* one in place and what it requires of them. Third, it should be enforceable. Enforceability has two aspects: the policy must be realistic, and there must be some method of monitoring compliance, including some procedure for dealing with infractions. Fourth, the DRP creates its own set of documents, including a log of destroyed documents. Some thought should be given to the characteristics of this log, especially in terms of identifying destroyed documents in a manner that does not itself assist adverse counsel.

Finally, the "retention" aspect of DRP should not be overlooked. If the norm is to delete, there must be some procedure for retention.

D. Implementation

In some respects, the technological phase of implementation is the easy part; by and large, machines will continue to do what you tell them to, so long as you say it in a language they understand.

Employees, however, are another matter. Unless they are directly involved in litigation or regulatory enforcement actions, they may not appreciate the importance of the DRP. The policy needs to be communicated to the rank and file, preferably by senior management, and reiterated from time to time, at least annually. This explanation needs to be presented in concrete terms, including examples of infractions, and even then it may not sink in until someone actually loses a document that is needed.

E. Enforcement

Expect breaches and leakage. Employees will install second hard drives, move files to new folders and subfolders, e-mail documents to their homes, and copy them onto flash drives. It is simply not possible to ensure a high level of compliance without impairing the effectiveness of the company's IT.

By and large, courts understand this. A company should take its DRP seriously, which means taking reasonable measures to enforce it, and treating known infractions seriously. Here there is an analog to confidentiality policies and agreements. If it is demonstrated that the company does not take its own DRP seriously, then why should the court?

F. Subject Matter

There are various kinds of documents, and each should be considered separately. They include the following:

- Data files, including word processing documents, spreadsheets, etc. Treat each version separately.
- E-mail, where a different holding period may be applicable to sent and received communications
- Calendars
- Hard copies
- Metadata
- Items in various "deleted" folders

G. When Disaster Strikes

Several things happen when the corporation is investigated by a government agency or is sued. First, a duty to preserve evidence arises, such that those aspects of the DRP that bear on the lawsuit or investigation must be immediately suspended. This does not necessary mean the entire program and all employees, but it certainly applies for those persons and documents that are involved in the subject matter of the suit or investigation. The general rule is, when in doubt, overcompensate. Mistakes will be construed against the company.

At some point in the lawsuit or investigation, the company may be called upon to defend its DRP. Defensibility will depend in large measure on the factors described above (purpose, feasibility, enforcement, etc.).

Inevitably, there will be breaches in the system. These fall into two general categories: those that bear directly upon the subject matter of the suit or investigation, and those that do not. The first category does not present much of a legal issue; the DRP has failed, and the opposition gets the smoking gun. The second category goes to the issue of defensibility: opposing counsel will look for as many such breaches as possible, preferably with no monitoring of, or disciplinary consequences for, the perpetrators, in order to try to discredit the DRP itself.

A court that finds that a company has improperly destroyed documents can impose a number of sanctions. In a case involving Philip Morris, these included adverse findings of fact, disallowance of testimony, and monetary sanctions. In an extreme case, it can include a directed verdict.

H. Recent Legal Developments

The Sarbanes-Oxley Act contains two provisions that bear directly on DRPs. Section 802 is an amendment to federal obstruction-of-justice statutory law, and provides that persons who knowingly alter, destroy, mutilate, conceal or falsify any document or tangible object with the intent to impede, obstruct or influence proceedings involving federal agencies or bankruptcy proceedings may be fined, imprisoned up to twenty years, or both.

Second, this section imposes on accountants an obligation to retain certain corporate audit records and review work papers for a period of five years from the end of the fiscal period during which the audit or review was concluded.

Section 1102 of the Act amends the provisions of the federal obstruction-of-justice statute that prohibits witness tampering. Under the new provision, acting or attempting "corruptly" to alter or destroy a record or other object "with the intent to impair the object's integrity or availability for use in an official proceeding" is punishable by fines or imprisonment of up to 20 years.

Zubulake v. UBS Warburg is an employment discrimination case brought in the Southern District of New York. It is notable for a number of holdings relating to when the duty to preserve evidence arises. The *Zubulake* rulings start from the premise that the "obligation to preserve evidence arises when the party has notice that the evidence is relevant to litigation or when a party should have known that the evidence may be relevant to future litigation."[3] This duty can arise long before a lawsuit is filed, as the *Zubulake* court found that the defendant's duty to preserve was triggered four months before the plaintiff filed her EEOC complaint and ten months prior to the filing of her civil complaint.[4] The court based its conclusion on a series of recovered e-mails indicating that "key players" in the defendant company recognized the possibility that the plaintiff might sue even before she filed her EEOC complaint. A client who is concerned enough about a claim to retain outside litigation counsel may be deemed to be on sufficient notice to trigger the duty to preserve electronic evidence.

The *Zubulake* court held that upon reasonable anticipation of litigation, a party must suspend routine document retention and destruction policies (assuming such policies exist) and institute a "litigation hold."[5] The duty to impose a "litigation hold" runs to both the client and its attorneys, as "counsel must oversee compliance with a litigation hold, monitoring the party's efforts to retain and produce relevant documents."[6] According to the *Zubulake* court, simply notifying the client and its personnel of the litigation hold is not sufficient; instead, counsel should issue the litigation hold to the client and its personnel at the outset and repeat it periodically thereafter.[7]

Under the latest *Zubulake* ruling, imposing a "litigation hold" is only the beginning. "Counsel must become familiar with their client's document retention policies, as well as the client's data retention architecture." To do so, the *Zubulake* court says, the lawyer must speak with information technology personnel about the client's backup procedures and must also communicate "with the 'key players' in the litigation, in order to understand how they stored information."[8]

In addition, the lawyer "must also make sure that all backup media which the party is required to retain is identified and stored in a safe place."[9] This may also involve a suspension of the client's existing document retention policy if allowing that policy to remain in effect would result in the destruction of relevant and unique evidence or documents.[10] However, it may not be necessary to preserve all backup tapes unless there is unique relevant evidence

---

3. "Zubulake IV", Zubulake v. UBS Warburg, 220 F.R.D. 212 (S.D.N.Y. 2003).
4. *Id.*
5. *Id.*
6. "Zubulake V", Zubulake v. UBS Warburg, 2004 WL 1620866 (S.D.N.Y. July 20, 2004).
7. *Id.*
8. *Id.*
9. *Id.*
10. Zubulake IV.

on the tapes. Some computer and electronic data systems "overwrite," and thus destroy, older data on a periodic or even perpetual basis, thus putting a premium on preserving such data if it does not exist in some other form elsewhere.

Defense counsel in *Zubulake* narrowly escaped sanctions (though their client was not so fortunate) for the failure to preserve electronic evidence in that case. But the *Zubulake* rulings and other recent commentary about them sound an ominous tone: "parties and their counsel are [now] fully on notice of their responsibility to preserve and produce electronically stored information."[11] As one commentator observed, "there will be repercussions for those who fail to preserve at least one copy of the unique, electronic data of the key players in a dispute after the duty to preserve such data attaches."

11.04   Taxation

There is a story, perhaps apocryphal, about the invention of the telephone. Following a demonstration of the new device, a government official, it is said, admitted that he found it intriguing, asking Alexander Graham Bell, "But what use is it?" Bell replied, "Perhaps some day you will find a way to tax it." Policymakers today have shown no such lack of ingenuity; the most common forms of Internet taxation, currently in effect or proposed for the future, are the following:

A.   Income Taxes

Some things even the Internet can't change. State and federal income tax liabilities are incurred based on traditional source rules. Attempts to move the commerce server or the corporate entity offshore are generally ineffective so long as the business activities remain in the forum state.

B.   Sales and Use Taxes

State sales taxes are assessed against resident purchasers and withheld by vendors. They are collected only if the buyer is resident in the state where the sale occurs. As Internet sales are generally regarded as occurring in the state of the seller's residence, sales taxes are only due when buyer and seller are resident in the same state. It should be noted, however, that some sellers, and even some buyers, may be deemed to be resident in more than one state.

Use taxes are an attempt by states with sales taxes to recoup the tax revenue that would otherwise be lost when a resident makes a purchase outside the state.

---

11   Zubulake V.

In the past, use taxes have frequently been applied to mail order purchases. With increasing regularity, they are applied to online purchases as well.

C.   Internet Access and E-commerce Taxes

Like the telephone, the Internet has proven irresistible to legislators, many of whom have sought to tax access itself or at least any transactions occurring in cyberspace. The Internet Tax Freedom Act imposed a three-year moratorium on such taxes and was renewed for additional three-year terms upon its expiration on October 1, 2001 and 2004, and for a seven year term in 2007.

11.05   Raising Money Online

As described in Chapter 7 (Financing a Business), the primary federal body of law governing initial offerings of securities is the Securities Act of 1933 ("1933 Act") and related regulations. As a general matter, the 1933 Act requires registration of all securities that are publicly offered. The federal system is structured as a disclosure system, rather than a merit system, meaning that the competent regulatory agencies, chiefly the Securities Exchange Commission, will not inquire into the value of securities, or the price charged for them, so long as they are fully and accurately described in the disclosure documents. States, on the other hand, vary between disclosure and merit systems; however, if a security will qualify for listing on the New York Stock Exchange or American Stock Exchange immediately upon completion of its initial public offering, the state registration requirements are largely pre-empted.

The Internet, as an efficient medium of information exchange, meshes nicely with the concept of a disclosure system. It can, potentially, play two broad roles in corporate finance. The first is as a tool for the issuance of securities, either directly by the company or through underwriters. The second is as a conduit of information disclosure, both to the SEC and to shareholders, as required by law.

These roles have been treated together by the SEC. In a series of Interpretive Releases, the SEC has gradually moved from a posture of initial mistrust of this new medium to recognition that it portends the future of shareholder relations. It articulated four criteria for determining whether an issuer and its underwriter have, by use of the Internet, satisfied their disclosure requirements:

First, unlike written communications, the recipient must have consented to electronic delivery, which consent may be revoked at any time. Such consent may be in writing, including electronic writing or recorded telephone conversation.

Second, any notices must be adequate and timely. In this context, "adequate" argues in favor of e-mail, rather than mere posting on a website, although such a posting, followed by an e-mail or regular mail notification of the posting, should suffice.

Third, investors must have effective access to electronically available information. Adobe Acrobat, or "PDF" format, is commonly used for downloadable text and graphic communications. This has been determined to be "effective access," provided issuers or intermediaries inform investors of the format in advance, and provide them with necessary software and technical assistance free of charge.

Fourth, there must be reasonable assurance of delivery. This can be satisfied through such means as e-mail return receipt or confirmation, faxed acknowledgement of receipt, investor's traceable access of a web hyperlink or investor's use of forms that are available only by accessing the document.

11.06   Conclusion

In less than two decades, the Internet has been transformed from an obscure military communications link and academic playground to an indispensable tool for businesses of all sizes. The first question every business owner should ask before throwing up a website is, "What role do I intend a web presence to play in my business?" A website for its own sake, or out of perceived peer pressure, is a mistake. Once a business determines the function of its planned website, whether it be promotional, informational, elicitation of customer feedback or online sales, then a number of design and function considerations will become clear.

The next question is, "How much web?" The cost of a website ranges from zero to millions of dollars; the issue should be treated like the establishment of a new market. The business owner should be ever mindful of the fact that a website must be constantly updated in order to sustain interest.

Finally, the business owner should ask, "To what extent should the company be involved in its new web presence, both initially and continuously?" Some involvement is necessary and good; the website should in part be a cyberspace manifestation of the company and should reflect its distinct personality. This can only be achieved with significant input from company insiders. Moreover, company employees, especially those dealing with customers, should be up to date on what is on the website. Few things are more embarrassing than to be educated about your own organization by a perfect stranger. In addition, some familiarity with the technical aspects of the website is desirable. This facilitates the updating process, and provides some protection in case of the designer's disappearance.

However, the Internet and web technology are very seductive. Basic authoring tools are very easy to learn, and early results can be impressive. It is vital to remember that, despite all its capabilities, for most people the Internet is only a tool, a medium and a market channel. It is not a business in itself. A company's commercial success or failure will be determined only in part by its facility with such tools and, ultimately, by its commitment and ability to deliver value to its customers.

Marketing and Public Relations

Dawn Yankeelov

ASPectx
Louisville, KY

Contents

Marketing and Public Relations

12.01   Preliminary Considerations

The leaders of most new technology-driven companies assume that everyone wants to know about their new product and service. Usually, they believe that, by some mysterious force of will, clients, customers and other interested parties will find them. As a result, a marketing professional for an emerging company is initially valued at the bottom of the feeding chain where proposals collect dust waiting for signoff. It is only when "nothing happens," even though the product has been available for several months, and the door has not been battered down with orders or service inquiries, that things change. The savior salesperson may cry out (largely from frustration), "We need a marketing person on this!" adding, only slightly later, "Some good PR might help too. No one understands what we do here."

Indeed, the salesperson is generally correct. Marketing supports sales, and proper public relations gets the word out in a meaningful way about what is being sold, whether product or service. Economic downturns cannot be used as a bellwether for a drop in marketing and public relations efforts because spending may be increased in marketing and public relations to achieve profitability objectives. For example, U.S. marketers spend over $200 billion on direct response advertising each year, according to the Direct Marketing Association. This includes the distribution of offers, the creation and production of direct marketing materials, and advertising placement. And, each year it increases, despite economic downturns.

A.   Marketing

Marketing and public relations activities are to a sales team what massage is to chronic back pain. No emerging company should live without it, and delivered to the right targets, everyone relaxes. In a crisis situation, this plays out quickly and is certainly more obvious.

Marketing is loosely defined as "the action or business of bringing or sending a commodity or service to market," according to the Oxford English Dictionary.[1] Alternatively, we can take the definition from a popular textbook: "Marketing is the process of planning and executing the conception, pricing, promotion, and distribution of ideas, goods, services, organizations, and events to create and maintain relationships that will satisfy individual and organizational objectives."[2] The big picture of marketing today for emerging companies can be simply defined as finding the right target audience and sending messages in an understood fashion for a desired result—namely, to generate attention or sales for products or services.

B. Public Relations

Public relations become a trusted component to a "proper marketing mix," a term that came into vogue in the late 1960s in classrooms studying economics. It can encompass media relations to establish credibility, or it can be broadened to include actions that talk to several types of audiences, including investors, vendors, value-added resellers and the general public. For example, public speaking engagements at trade shows can be very useful public relations.

Do not confuse a marketing team as the replacement of the sales force. In fact, marketing and sales are joined at the hip in a solid, well built organization poised for growth. All the marketing support materials, process planning, deliverables and credibility that come with public relations cannot make up for a knowledgeable sales professional closing the sale with a client. Marketers can buzz all day long about electronic communications patterns that now include e-commerce, e-mail, texting, instant messaging, interactive television, live video conferencing, real-time surveillance, telematics and wireless devices. The reality is that first-time sales over $2,500 often require people to be in direct communication—the higher the ticket item, the more likely a personal sales call will be required to close the contract deal—still sealed with a handshake.

C. Research

No one tactic will deliver to the target audience information in the form they wish to receive it. At an emerging growth company, the executive team must devise a number of approaches to push their presence into the marketplace. As listed later, these tactics may include using technology solutions: customer relationship management tools, e-commerce with personalization

---

1. www.oed.com.

2. Boone & Kurtz, Contemporary Marketing Wired (Dryden Press, 1998).

or any number of specific marketing blitzes mixing pop-up ads, web banner ads, texting and video e-mail. More traditional marketing tactics continue: direct mail; print, radio or television advertising; billboards or other forms of advertising, including sponsorships of events or giveaways; video news releases; promotional deals; subscription services; media relations; trade show activity and sales training kits for distributions channels. Doubtlessly, inventive, web-based delivery mechanisms of information will continue to emerge.

Before finding tactics, startups and established firms alike must do research to determine their real clients. Defining the demographics of a target audience is the beginning of a proper marketing strategy.

12.02   Marketing Strategy and Program

Developing the marketing strategy for a growing company is no easy task. In general, it is best to begin by analyzing the following questions:

- What are the market trends in the industry today?
- What are the demographics of the target audience? Buying motives? Consumption patterns? Are there up-sell opportunities not being tapped?
- Where will the core market be in the next six to nine months?
- What is the hottest potential market in the next six to nine months related to the target audiences?
- Is product or service pricing on target and packaged well? Does this match the market's needs and wants? What do surveys say?
- What are the available resources for the marketing department (in-house or outsource)? Evaluate staff, money, time/production schedule requirements and technology tools available or budgeted. What needs to be outsourced?
- Name the distribution channels for the products or services. Is this strictly a direct sales company? What actions can the marketing department take in the next 90 days to move more products/support services into the various distribution channels?
- What strategic alliances can marketing turn to for cooperative interaction (internal or external)?

With preliminary answers in hand, the marketing team can then consider the following building blocks as they put together the actual marketing program:

- **Use competitive intelligence:** Do the research or spend the money to have it done, and know the target opportunities intimately. This may include focus group studies, surveys and white papers written by others in the field. Be aware of the competition, and study their value propositions.

For more information, consider attending events by the Society of Competitive Intelligence Professionals (www.scip.org). Focus and fortitude pay off.

- **Determine the demographics of the target audience:** There is a finite world of buyers in given categories. Look at the vertical industry opportunities and the horizontal, broader markets. Determine the priorities. Some targets are easier to define, access and close than others are. Avoid wasting time with a shotgun approach.

- **Think timeliness, uniqueness and value:** Use a journalist's approach to measure what steps to take. Consider whether the timing of products or services will work, and determine the window of opportunity. Define the value proposition early, and know how to answer the "why to buy now" question.

- **Create a budget and generate an action plan to meet objectives:** Written documentation creates a measure to weigh the efforts and determine how to move forward. Record the plans, execute from a process, and learn from the potential clients and signed accounts.

- **Assign resources to marketing and public relations:** Internal or external staffing is required to support sales efforts. These are not secretarial duties to be done between other critical assignments. Marketing responsibilities are never more critical than prior to and during product launches.

- **Develop a marketing mix:** Decide what media outlets to use in getting the word out and developing a brand. Do not exclusively rely on risky one-media-outlet strategies, for example, just web-based transactions or just television marketing. A marketing mix is just as important for a business-to-business enterprise as for the retail operation.

- **Evaluation and reassessment:** Sometimes it is difficult to measure marketing directly; however, companies that eliminate marketing entirely in economic downturns often suffer the consequences within three to six months. This is because every marketing and public relations step is critical to the business. Survey, formally and through dialogue, the key accounts to find out what was supporting the messages best in the sales cycle. Remember that marketing remains important to retain clients as well as to land them.

Perhaps the best advice in marketing is follow-through. This means that every marketing campaign is tied to every other action supporting sales. A trade show is an opportunity to develop a database. A database is an opportunity to develop a newsletter. A newsletter is an opportunity to do media relations. Media relations create an opportunity to show who in the organization is an expert on what. Expert status is an opportunity to send out invitations to a tailored seminar and so on.

The devil remains in the details because, if mailing labels are never printed, then direct mail pieces wait and no communication occurs. If signoff does not occur on proofs for the new ad campaign, then the magazine continues to run the old campaign. When no one loads the new mailing lists into the primary database for the newsletter, then the new prospects are not in the loop. There is really no excuse for failing to get organized in the early days of the company. Even no-budget startups with only sweat equity can use web-based tools available to provide digital calendars, address books and synchronized data from wireless devices. For example, free tools can be found at Yahoo! or through the offerings listed on Freewareandstuff.com. It is often the simple steps that are overlooked as all departments rush forward to build a company. Solid marketing ties internal communications to external actions of value.

Additionally, marketing campaigns and solid public relations do not end after a launch phase. They are a regular part of business development.

12.03   Defining the Niche

The more electronic clicks "simplify" our lives each day, the less we absorb communication. More advertising, more e-mail, more text messages and more instant messaging leads to multitasking with less time to process what is received as a manager, client or consumer. Therefore, targets must be well defined each financial quarter and attacked with vehemence—over and over if necessary to get their attention. It also means that messages from the emerging company must target a defined demographic group in order to achieve a meaningful result. As a company looking for growth, the marketing team must define its niche in terms of product or service and customers.

In some cases, the definition emerges from early research that leads to a new product being developed for a particular customer. For example, a regional company selling specialized web development and integration with self-administration features decided to work through industries in its region via affiliations with trade groups. The firm had handled industry-specific middleware issues for several trade associations, merging complex systems from different vendors. This led to an opportunity to market to the trade association membership with a combination of e-mail, direct mail, endorsements from the local trade association and seminars held with the local trade associations.

In another instance, a two-year-old, venture-backed firm with a new real-time news feed product for a specific industry was able to secure new clients by evaluating the top 25 players in a given limited market. Each sale represented closing $500,000 annual subscriptions, so booking this revenue became more important in the beginning than pursuing many ancillary forms of lower sales. A layered, target funnel for the next three years to attack this market was developed, and public relations efforts were begun to build within the target audiences on the table, according to the business plan.

Larger corporations, even those with known brands, constantly spend money on marketing research because customer awareness and buying publics change. They age, economic conditions shift, fads fade, competitors enter the arena, and what is known about a particular product or service may be altered with more information. Following the 2008 global financial crisis, "gone bust" signs reaffirmed the value of targeting the market, offering a value and building on existing sales. The same principle applies to emerging companies. Its marketing plan should be a work in progress that is constantly re-evaluated.

12.04 Market Intelligence and Research Sources

There are many advisors and agencies willing to assist in developing marketing strategies and programs and in defining a niche. Each will be known for a particular expertise area. It is always a good idea to check references or enter the agency name into a search engine to briefly research them. One key agency choice can be successful if the agency is to manage all your strategic and creative efforts, some of which may require subcontractors or other affiliate agencies. However, different agencies are often hired for specific types of work. For instance, many advertising agencies are not in the habit of determining demographics through competitive intelligence gathering, but rather define a specific print, radio or television advertising campaign, for example, to appeal to an identifiable demographic market. Similarly, a newly hired graphic design firm, and even a newly hired public relations firm, may expect to be told a company's demographic targets. Graphic designs firms, for example, may be widely credited with producing beautiful, four-color magazine ads, but the firm may be able to offer no counsel on what magazines to put it in.

Marketing consulting firms or independent marketing consultants, however, are usually specialists in assisting with the strategy that must come before the tactics—this will include competitive intelligence and market planning. If an emerging company has the money to spend on a marketing consultant, it is probably worth it.

12.05 Managing Marketing Dollars

As with any important business function, marketing should be driven by a tight and detailed budget. When setting the marketing budget, consider the following issues:

- Has a budget been accepted or has marketing quantified its needs formally in documentation?
- What media outlets must be used and, correspondingly, what is the scope of the efforts? What specific regions (local, regional, national or international) must be considered? Have media representatives been contacted to give estimates on coverage possibilities?
- Have all vertical and horizontal plays been considered in this budgeting process?
- Does the budget have a marketing mix? Use the following checklist as a possible review step. Rank the following and other marketing expenditures in order of importance and plot them on a timeline for the next six to nine months
  - Direct mail
  - Connect with the press through media relations, tours, etc.
  - Corporate outreach through trade shows, speaking engagements, etc.
  - Television, such as programming, sponsorship, infomercials and advertising
  - Online advertising, including website, banners, pop-up ads, search engine and advertising
  - E-marketing through texting, e-mail opportunities and e-newsletters
  - Audio and video opportunities, such as tapes, specialized e-mail or demo presentations
  - Print advertising, including newspapers, magazines and books
  - Outdoor advertising, such as signage and billboards
  - Radio
  - Affiliate or co-op advertising
  - Analytics, which includes surveys, backend tracking of product purchases and website activity
  - Competitive intelligence (that is, original research)

The rules of thumb for how much of the budget should be spent on marketing has widely varied in the last 10 years from round percentages beginning at seven percent to double that in the dot-com era. Broad, sweeping statements about how much should be spent may be misguided given that objectives are so varied and niche marketing has become more important. With web-based tools and other technologies, a non-marketing professional will often be expected to pinch hit in marketing as the company grows. Do-it-yourself guerilla marketing tactics can be quite useful when managing the marketing dollars.

Trends in advertising, marketing and public relations must be monitored to maximize marketing dollars. For instance, technology continues to strongly impact marketing and public relations choices. For example, marketers have worried for years about ad-zapping technologies affecting television commercials, but the threat has been relatively abstract. That is changing with the advent of TiVo and its competitors ushering in the generation of the personal video recorder ("PVR"). Market watchers indicate that television ad dollar spending will drop when these PVRs spread to 30 million U.S. households. General Motors, Procter & Gamble, and Coca-Cola have already indicated that they are concerned and will expect to shift marketing dollars to sponsorships, product placement in movies and more content creation.

12.06   Web-Based Marketing and PR

"Send more messages" becomes the mantra for seasoned executives using the e-marketing approach to garner leads or build brand. Low-budget options exist in this category from opt-in e-mail boxes taking names on the corporate website to using a bulk e-mail firm that has compiled lists of individuals in the target audience needing products or services. There are good list-management firms now offering to do an entire marketing campaign. PostMasterDirect.com, for instance, has lists ranging from accountants to woodworkers. Fees start under a quarter per name, which includes e-mail delivery. For media relations, emerging companies can rent lists through Bacon's MediaSource (www.cision.com) with selections from about 65,000 media outlets and 450,000 editorial contacts. The cost is about one dollar per name with minimum purchase requirements.

Forrester Research estimates that more than $6 billion is spent on e-mail marketing. This represents more than a 40-fold increase in per-user message volume; however, the value of e-marketing might offer diminishing returns in the years ahead. More messages may equate to more deletes if potential clients are not carefully chosen. E-mail disadvantages include issues surrounding privacy, talking to potential customers that are not listening and communicating too often without offering real news.

For those looking to build a campaign with existing customized lists, online firms like www.explorecommerce.com have built-in templates to walk viewers through a process that includes pre-set subscription costs and custom-designed campaign charges.

Companies interested in wireless handheld access for media relations done by text, e-mail and phone, as well as investor relations or government relations should investigate www.vocus.com, which offers a complete turnkey relationship management system for an annual fee of under $5,000 for the individual user.

With the advent of the national CAN-SPAM Act of 2003 signed into law in December 2003, a crackdown on deceptive spamming began. This supercedes at least some of the provisions in 37 state laws enacted to improve e-mailing practices. Companies based in the United States must now adhere to new policies and procedures. For example, the law restricts transmission of certain e-mails that do not include proper disclosures regarding their nature or origin. Commercial e-mails are now required to do the following:

- Include an opt-out mechanism. Recipients of e-mail must have the opportunity to opt-out of certain types of commercial e-mail.
- Opt-out requests must be honored within 10 business days. The Federal Trade Commission ("FTC") reviewed this rule, and all companies are encouraged to work with this guideline.
- A valid physical postal address must be present, along with an operative return address. This must be true for up to 30 days after a message is sent.
- Each e-mail must provide a clear notice that it is an advertisement when sent as one. There are no recommendations on what form this must take.
- Misleading e-mail transmissions are not permitted in subject lines. This heads off deceptive practices of getting e-mail opened.

According to Chip House, VP for Deliverability and Abuse Management at ExactTarget, an interactive marketing provider:

> "What is the most important item to remember as a commercial business about sending email today? The most important aspect of email today is that we must have permission from our audience to communicate with them. Marketers should never cut corners with the permission process and should make every effort to provide value to each subscriber in return for their email permission."

House also cited a recent study by NFO WorldGroup showing that most customers will provide their e-mail address to you if they see a potential benefit. A full 24 percent in that study reported that they provide their e-mail address to receive order confirmations by e-mail, and 22 percent said they provide it to receive special offers, coupons or discounts on future purchases. Finally, 17 percent said they register online to receive newsletters or in-depth information to which they otherwise would not have access. _

The Federal Communications Commission ("FTC") is establishing requirements regarding promotions to cell phones and other wireless devices, so it is wise to check with your marketing firm or area marketing consultant on what is possible as legislation emerges.

In October 2003, the marketing and advertising industry released its own guidelines for legitimate e-mail marketing practices. Participating associations included the American Association of Advertising Agencies ("AAAA"), the Association of National Advertisers ("ANA") and the Direct Marketing Association ("DMA").[3]

Some e-marketing firms are holding free "webinars" (web-based seminars) on topics that involve e-mail compliance, optimization and deliverability. Sessions are free from Indianapolis-based ExactTarget at www.exacttarget. com, for example.

---

3. For more information, go to www.aaaa.org or call for the "Guide to E-mail Marketing" at 212-682-2500.

Media relations are useful for a company of any size because a news article offers a level of credibility to the reader that an advertisement does not. Contrary to popular belief, solid public relations involve knowing how to talk to reporters directly, not finding ways to send a press release. In a recent survey done by www.workinpr.com, 73 percent of PR professionals said having a personal relationship with a reporter provides the best response from a news outlet and is better than direct e-mail pitches and unsolicited press releases.

A related approach is using news services to publicize emerging companies' operations, products and progress. PR Newswire (www.prnewswire.com) and BusinessWire (www.businesswire.com), two competing news services, offer a broad variety of services that go beyond straightforward media communications.

ProfNet, a service of PR Newswire, allows experts within an organization to participate in offering comment for various stories. ProfNet links the in-house spokesperson with journalists seeking comments and interviews. It has three platforms:

- ProfNet Search: Reporters tell the information/expertise they need, and ProfNet professionals relay the queries to their members via e-mail (four times a day). If members have an expert or information that meets the reporter's criteria, they respond directly to that reporter.
- ProfNet Experts Database: Reporters can profile the in-house expert in a database searchable by the media.
- ProfNet Leads: Reporters can proactively alert other reporters to experts who can comment on timely and newsworthy subjects. In addition, Prof-Net users/subscribers receive daily reports on their industry news from the perspective of both public relations and investor relations professionals.

12.07   Establishing Credibility and Expert Status

In an effort to garner attention, many entrepreneurs take out expensive advertising in local publications or pay to sponsor a mix of local venues in their field in the hopes that the information will trickle up to the national or international marketplace. At times, there is wisdom in this approach— especially if the company has limited competition or the local event is the national convention in a category. Local business journal articles can lead to international inquiries from time to time.

However, a more targeted approach may be to carefully review the events in the region, nation and on the international scene relevant to the profession or targeted buying audience. Two to five speaking engagements in a year on select programs can go far to qualify an entrepreneur as an expert on key topics related to the company's sales objectives. These speaking engagements are generally available at least one year in advance of the opportunity, which means proper planning is essential. The entrepreneur, for instance, may have to ask for the opportunity at this year's conference to be part of next year's panel of experts.

A related approach to establishing credibility is the trade-show circuit. If establishing a brand name or new invention is important, the standard trade show can reach many people and leave a memory to be built on with direct mail and e-marketing or straightforward follow-up sales calls. Although many business people question the value of trade shows, the reason companies do not get value out of trade show activity may be that they do not track or make use of the database generated. Most trade show participants collect business cards and leads but leave them in the corporate sales department where they become cold leads within 90 days.

Another easy approach to establish expert credibility is publishing a newsletter where the entrepreneur offers tips, insights or steps on how to take care of specific matters related to products or services. Electronic or paper, the recipient is generally receptive to receiving this form of communication because it is not a pure sales piece and offers real news that can be of use immediately.

Finally, for high-ticket items, be it consulting or packaged goods, turn back to the contact databases in the company and look for individuals who may give personal recommendations. When a potential customer receives a referral from a trusted colleague or peer, he or she is more willing to learn and entertain an informational interview. This in turn can be a wonderful opportunity for some hands-on market research or survey work in the context of an introduction.

12.08   Evaluation Process and Smart Steps

Once the company has made its marketing moves, the evaluation cycle must be kept in gear to determine the best course of continuing action. Today's e-marketing is conducted with real-time analytics available in most cases—every click-through can be tracked. Feedback opportunities from the analytics in the form of buying decisions, comments and surveys should be documented and reviewed periodically. With customer relationship management toolkits on the desktop and virtual communities for every type of transaction, the tracking of market interactions has become more instantaneous. This is a double-edged sword because the marketing team is now required to provide quick turnaround on decision-making to best the competition.

Another effective method of evaluating the marketing function is to ask the following questions on a regular basis, no less frequently than every six months:

- What expenditures drove the most results in credibility, overall brand recognition, client awareness of products/services, sales channel improvement and sales?
- What client requests could be useful in marketing strategy? Are corporate value propositions correct for the target audiences served?
- Do potential clients understand key messages in documentation received and read?
- What do analytics in online activity indicate about website activities?
- Is a focus group of potential or existing clients in order for new products or services entering a test phase?
- Is the marketing mix really a mix? Is more needed in a given media outlet to achieve objectives?
- What objectives call for a change in marketing activity? How will they be handled?
- Have internal communications been considered in planning to show marketing tie-in corporate wide?

12.09   Crisis Management

A.   Preliminary Considerations

Recognizing the consumer crisis of confidence in everything from national security to economics affected by corporate financial and pollution debacles, it is not advisable to avoid crisis-response planning. Worldwide terrorism, environmental disaster, and the financial collapse of top corporations have fueled fear of the unknown in recent years.

Public relations play a meaningful role in this area. PR is now seen as the keeper of perceptions and expectations of an organization's stakeholders and is charged with enhancing the organizational reputation through socially responsible practices.

Crisis management begins with proper governance. Determining an ethical code of conduct has always been critical in the planning process. This continues to gain corporate acceptance as the first step in knowing what should happen next. Acknowledging the trend to publicize corporate policies and procedures for crises, the Public Relations Society of America launched a new professional interest section for its members called Strategic Social Responsibility. Its aim is to bring together members from the corporate, nonprofit and government sectors practicing in the areas of business ethics, corporate governance, human rights and work-life issues.

As the types of crises expand, many organizations providing public relations have had to expand the services they offer. Many now have crime-fighting and social-welfare capabilities. The Conference Board, a leading global business organization, for instance, offers programs on crisis management and corporate security. Large entities have added security officers to their staffs.

B. Approach

Today's concerns relating to crises are not new. Public relations was forced to address crisis communications 20 years ago during the Tylenol tampering case when unknown individuals added cyanide poison to the popular pain killer. Johnson & Johnson executives contend even today that the simple lessons they learned still hold true in crisis:

- Take a positive action to serve the public interest
- Have a timely response ready
- Tell the truth

The Center for Risk Communication, directed by Dr. Vincent Covello at Columbia University, calls for establishing only three messages in a crisis response plan to ensure credibility. Who delivers the message is also important and should be decided in advance for each type of crisis. In crisis, nonverbal queues represent more than 50 percent of the communicated information. The challenge is in boiling down messages to their most simplistic form.

Another lesson is the importance of advance planning because it is easier to secure third-party support before a crisis than during. For example, Monsanto spent several years building a network of health-care experts before launching a genetically engineered hormone that makes cows produce more milk. When they needed third parties to counter opposition from biotechnology activists and small dairy farmers, the company was prepared. In addition, before a crisis strikes, research can be done on what stakeholders think. Surveys and interviews with targeted opinion leaders add value, and fewer than 100 interviews can provide meaningful information on how stakeholders will react to a crisis and what they expect from a company.

Exhibit 12A is a crisis communications audit for companies to evaluate how prepared they are for a crisis and **Exhibit 12B** provides crisis planning checklists on how to handle a crisis before, during and after it occurs.

C. Lessons from Enron and BP

The financial collapse of Enron in 2001–2002 and BP's 2010 oil rig disaster in the Gulf of Mexico can be revealing exercises on how to evaluate what steps must be taken before and during a crisis. The lessons can be applied to crises less horrific than the Enron and BP stories. They apply to employee layoffs, financial results below expectations, poor employee morale, product defects, technology mistakes and sudden death of an executive who is key to running the company. Even the loss of a major account can create a crisis in how to generate the necessary revenue and deal with potential customers' uncertainty about corporate stability.

Enron's executives and its accounting firm ignored Johnson & Johnson's three lessons—even after the federal investigations began. Specifically, tales of its financial questioning appeared in the media beginning in January 2001 with a *Fortune* article by Bethany McLean. Enron executives did not assess their own vulnerabilities, prepare a timely response or tell the truth. By October 2001, when the shredding of documents was revealed, steps were still not taken to prevent a public crisis of greater magnitude.

On the other side, Eron's accounting firm, Arthur Anderson, failed to have a timely response ready. Instead, it tried pointing the blame at Enron as late as January 2002. The finger pointing did little more than create an even darker perception of Arthur Andersen's culpability.

BP's response to the explosion of its Deepwater Horizon drilling rig and subsequent oil spill into the Gulf of Mexico is similarly full of errors and misjudgments.

Possibly the greatest failure was Enron's and BP's inability to adopt the first rule of Johnson & Johnson—take a positive action to serve the public interest. Perhaps the best public relations and marketing tactics begin with caring about people and being fair-minded. As the chair of Unilver stated during the early Enron crisis:

> On the one hand, companies plead for liberalized markets.... but this must be accompanied by accountability, by transparency, business principles, environmental policy, and by corporate social responsibility.[4]

12.10 Conclusion

The characteristics that contribute to successful marketing and public relations strategy include the following:

- Management participation
- Knowledgeable marketing professional support and experience
- Centralized decision-making
- Communication from internal teams, target audiences and sales teams
- Coordination of efforts to support company-defined objectives

By educating the entire company about the value of marketing and public relations, management can build confidence and cooperation throughout the entire organization. In addition, integrating creative marketing strategy into operations can increase revenue and profits.

---

4. Anthony Burgmans, Chairman of Unilever, *Bangkok Post* (Jan. 26, 2002).

Growing a Business

Robert L. Brown
Greenebaum, Doll & McDonald, PLLC
Louisville, KY

Alan S. Gutterman
Gutterman Law & Business
Piedmont, CA

CHAPTER **13**

Contents

Growing a Business[1]

Once the business entity is formed and financed, that entity should consider alternatives to assist in the growth of the business. Growth can come in many different forms, including joint ventures, strategic alliances, corporate partnering and development initiatives. As growth is occurring, the business entity should also consider where its new markets are located, that is, is it time to go global, and when should this expansion occur? While growth and development are occurring for the business entity, the entity should carefully keep its goals in sight to ensure it is well prepared to achieve them.

13.01 Joint Ventures and Other Strategic Alliances

In the past, an entity seeking new markets, innovation or new technology would have looked to traditional acquisitions or mergers. However, new relationships in the form of joint ventures and other strategic alliances now provide these business entities with alternatives encompassing much more flexibility and results similar to acquisitions or mergers without much of the risk.

A. What are Joint Ventures?

Joint ventures are a form of strategic alliance that can generally be described as a collaborative effort which may take the form of (i) a legal entity, i.e., a corporation, partnership or limited liability company or (ii) a contractual relationship without the use of a separate entity. More specifically, a joint

---

1.   Anna Capelle, Lars Johansson, and Eunice J. Paik were the authors of this chapter in the first edition of the *Guide*.

venture is a commercial collaboration of two or more persons, which may include individuals as well as corporations, partnerships, trusts and limited liability companies, that carries out a single business enterprise for profit. Parties enter into joint ventures for different reasons, such as sharing the cost and risk of a specific project, improving access to financing resources or gaining entry into a new market. The elements common to joint ventures include the following: (1) community of interest in the subject of the undertaking, (2) sharing in profits and losses, (3) equal right or right in some measure to direct and control the conduct of each other and of the joint venture and (d) fiduciary relation between or among the parties. These entities are often narrowly focused in their direction and purpose with one or more of the participants operating the joint venture. For example, a software company may enter into a joint venture with a computer manufacturer to create and market a new operating system to run on the manufacturer's new electronic device in a new market, combining the expertise of the software company and the computer manufacturer.

B.   Types of Joint Ventures

Joint ventures are organized as distinct legal entities separate from the entities of the participants. A joint venture may take (i) any form of entity that the parties choose, including corporations, general partnerships, limited partnerships or limited liability companies or (ii) the simple form of a contractual relationship without the use of a separate entity, generally referred to as a strategic alliance. In the absence of a formal relationship between the parties, a joint venture will, from a legal standpoint, be treated as a partnership and will generally be governed by the Uniform Partnership Act with the participants serving as partners in the partnership. The main difference between a typical partnership and a joint venture organized as a partnership is that a partnership usually relates to the conduct of general business activities continuing over time, whereas a joint venture relates to a single specific transaction and is therefore more limited in scope and duration.

A corporate joint venture is established in the same manner as a corporation with the shareholders as participants in the joint venture. To continue the above example, the software company and the computer manufacturer would both be shareholders in the corporation. The charter documents, such as the articles of incorporation and bylaws, would provide the overall management structure of the joint venture with a shareholders' agreement providing for the participants rights and obligations.

C.   Key Components of Joint Ventures

Once the type of entity for joint venture is chosen, it is important for the participants to document the relationship as a joint venture between the participants in order to assign the responsibilities, establish ownership and distribution principles, and protect the assets of the participants. An example of a joint venture agreement appears as **Exhibit 13A.** Key components to document in a joint venture agreement include the following:

Purpose.   The purpose of the joint venture should be described in detail in the joint venture agreement. Preparing and drafting the purpose of the joint venture will assist the participants to critically evaluate both the goals of the joint venture and the difficulties that the joint venture may face. If the joint venture is formed for a single project, a contractual structure as opposed to a separate legal entity structure may be sufficient.

Duties and Contributions.   The duties and contributions of the participants in the joint venture should be clearly specified. In this section of the joint venture agreement, the exact responsibilities of the participants should be described in sufficient detail so that other participants are satisfied with the duties and the timing of performance of such duties throughout the duration of the joint venture. Along with the duties, the actual contributions required of the participants should be fully outlined. Such contributions may include capital, intellectual property or other forms of property, services or time, or some combination thereof. The participants in the joint venture should agree upon the value of such contributions.

Ownership of Venture Property.   During the life of the joint venture, it will likely acquire or develop property. The joint venture agreement should specify how the title to such property should be held. Normally, the property would be held in the name of the entity that was formed for the joint venture; however, title to the property could be held with one of the participants or an individual as trustee for the joint venture. The particular ownership interests in the venture property should also be designated on behalf of each of the participants. To continue the above example, which participant will own the intellectual property rights of the operating system or the device? Will there be licensing arrangements following the creation of the system and the device? What will happen to the intellectual property assigned or developed by the joint venture when the venture is terminated?

Management Structure.   The joint venture can be managed in various ways (e.g., management board, independent managers). How the management of the joint venture is structured depends on who the participants are and the level of involvement in the joint venture they desire. The structure of the management will likely reflect the choice of form of the entity for the joint venture. The approval process by the participants should also be established, including the percentage of interest required to approve transactions or decisions and the types of transactions and decisions that will require approval by the participants.

Dispute Resolution. To avoid confusion and unnecessary future expense, the participants should include in the joint venture agreement how disputes or deadlocks will be resolved, be it through arbitration or mediation, along with the procedures for such dispute resolution. The choice of law and venue should also be clearly stated.

Duration and Dissolution. The participants should consider whether to include a termination date for the joint venture. Where no termination date is fixed by agreement, the venture remains in full force until its purpose is accomplished or it is established that the purpose cannot be accomplished. The parties may terminate the venture by mutual consent, but the participants may prefer to know that the joint venture will not continue indefinitely. See the discussion on liability below. Further, dissolution provisions are applicable to joint ventures depending on the type of entity chosen for the joint venture.

D. Taxation of Joint Ventures

Joint ventures are not recognized as a distinct form of entity for either legal or tax purposes. For tax purposes, a joint venture will normally be taxed as a partnership.

E. Potential Liabilities of Joint Ventures and Participants

Typically, the rights and liabilities of participants in joint ventures, as between themselves and as to third parties, will be governed by the same rules and principles governing the type of entity in which the joint venture is formed. Torts committed by one participant in the joint venture in the course of the enterprise are imputable to all participants of the venture. This is a reason why the choice of participants in the joint venture should be carefully considered. The sophistication and experience level of the participants in the venture should be reviewed prior to forming the venture. Part of this review should include a discussion of whether the participants are considered equals. For example, do the participants have management talent, sufficient cash, quality products and the ability to sustain the risk of a joint venture?

F. Strategic Alliances

If the business entity is looking for further flexibility and has an ability to adapt to a changing mission or goal with its participants, then the entity should consider forming one of many types of strategic alliances. Strategic alliances are essentially cooperative efforts by more than one participant working toward agreed-upon goals. The cooperative effort can take several forms and can be comprised of any or all of the following: technology licensing arrangements, research and development agreements, manufacturing relationships, sales and distribution agreements and equity investments. A strategic alliance may take on the form of a joint venture by forming a separate distinct entity, but typically strategic alliances are created through contractual arrangements.

G. Advantages and Disadvantages of Joint Ventures and Strategic Alliances

The creation of a joint venture or other strategic alliance can open new opportunities for any business that is looking to expand and grow. However, with these new opportunities can come additional burdens and risks that should be considered.

1. Advantages

a. Access to New Technologies

Access to state-of-the-art technologies is particularly important to companies looking to grow their business and enter into global markets. A joint venture or other strategic alliance can provide a growing business with technology from a participant that it may not otherwise be able to develop due to costs or time constraints. The right new technologies can provide a growing business with a springboard into new markets and products.

b. Cost Reduction

Usually, it is not possible for one company to do it all, but a joint venture or other strategic alliance may be able to provide a growing business with the technology, manufacturing or distribution capabilities that it could not otherwise afford. This sort of partnership allows the combination of collective strengths that makes it more likely for participants to succeed. At the same time, an alliance may also free up capital for use in other markets and activities.

c. Learning Opportunities

Forming an alliance permits the participants to work with other businesses in the same or related industries. This provides participants with the opportunity to learn from each other's successes and mistakes. It may also lead to a regular transfer of information, business practices, operational processes and technology.

2. *Disadvantages*

a. Loss of Competitive Advantage

An alliance with an actual or potential competitor, as is often the case with alliances, may jeopardize the cooperative advantage that a business might otherwise have developed in the absence of the relationship. The growing business must determine before entering into an alliance whether such opportunities and goals can be achieved without the assistance of competitors or whether the price of such opportunities and goals is excessive in light of the overall business objectives of the entity.

b. Lack of Control

No matter how the alliance is structured, participants inevitably will lose some aspect of control over the project. In order for participants to gain, they must also give something up, which is usually control of some aspect of their business. It is, therefore, important that participants simultaneously (1) structure the management of the alliance in such a manner as to retain as much control as possible without stifling the project and (2) conduct due diligence on the participants to ensure a level of trust amongst them.

c. Governmental Relations

Alliances may be formed with foreign entities that can lead to substantial opportunities for a growing business, but such business must also be mindful of local regulations and governmental review procedures that may impact the activities of the participants. For example, the European Union strictly regulates joint ventures for possible antitrust violations.

13.02 Corporate Partnering

A business entity considering a strategic alliance may want to evaluate corporate partnering as an alternative to seeking traditional financing. For example, an emerging technology company typically has a plan to sell or license its technology but often lacks the funding necessary to bring the technology to market. In order to get to the point where technology can be marketed and distributed as a product or licensed to third parties for a fee, the company will be required to invest in research and development of the technology. The emerging company may seek financing from institutional investors or venture capital firms who typically invest in the company through the purchase of convertible equity securities. However, the emerging company may find partnering with a larger, established company to be an attractive option. By creating a relationship with a corporate partner, the emerging company may be able to come up with various alternatives to issuing large amounts of equity securities, which will potentially dilute the equity interests of the founding shareholders. Additionally, a relationship with an established company with its name in the market can provide credibility and a reputation to an emerging company.

The established company may finance the emerging company in exchange for a combination of equity securities, the right to license the developed technology, the right to distribute the products developed, or research to be performed by the emerging company. In general, corporate partnering relationships involve an ongoing arrangement between a large, established company with the ability to develop, manufacture, market and distribute products and a small, entrepreneurial technology company without the resources to bring its products to market. The parties to the corporate partnering relationship may agree to any combination of the following:

- Established company makes an equity investment in the emerging company
- Established company engages the emerging company to conduct a research and development project for a fee and/or royalty arrangement related to the technology development through the project
- Established company agrees to distribute the emerging company's products
- Established company funds the emerging company's development of products incorporating the emerging company's technology and agrees to buy the products
- Established company negotiates an option to purchase the emerging company at a future date

A. Finding Corporate Partnering Opportunities

If the management of an emerging company believes that a corporate partnering arrangement is desirable, the next step is to find an appropriate partner. An emerging technology company should seek out an established corporate partner that fits its technology, product or service. Ideally, the relationship should create a synergy so that the corporate partnering relationship is mutually beneficial.

The emerging company may look to its service professionals for information about potential corporate partners. The emerging company's legal counsel or accountants may know of established companies that are looking for the opportunity to engage in a corporate partnering relationship. Lastly, industry events, such as conferences and seminars, can provide a forum for meeting and developing relationships with corporate partners.

B.   Types of Investment Instruments

Many corporate partnering relationships involve some form of debt or equity investment in the emerging company by the established company. The parties to the corporate partnering relationship must decide what type of investment instrument to use based on certain factors affecting both entities and the industry.

The appropriate investment instrument in a corporate partnering relationship will depend on various factors. The established company should consider the financial risk it is willing to take, the need for liquidity of its investment, other outstanding financial obligations of the emerging company, the amount of control it wishes to have over the emerging company, the maturity of the emerging company and the emerging company's current and future financing needs. The emerging company should examine the amount of control over its business that it would be willing to concede, its ability to repay its debts in the future, the terms of any outstanding agreements with investors or lenders, and the emerging company's current and future financing needs. Generally, the established company will invest in the emerging company through a form of convertible preferred stock, but the investment may also take the form of common stock, convertible debt or nonconvertible preferred stock or debt.

1.   *Common Stock*

Common stock is not typically issued in a venture capital or corporate partnering investment, especially when the financing occurs in the formative stages of the emerging company. If the established company took common stock, it would not obtain the benefit of liquidation or dividend preferences in relation to the other shareholders. Additionally, the sale of common stock to the established company would set the value of the common stock at a price that will likely be higher than the emerging company would like for any stock option plans, which will make it more costly for employees to become equity owners.

2.   *Convertible Preferred Stock*

Convertible preferred stock is the preferred method of investment for venture capitalists and others who invest in the emerging company at the early stages of the company's development. The convertible preferred stock typically will have liquidation and dividend preferences, anti-dilution protection, and it will grant the holders the right to approve certain transactions. In addition to these protections, the established company that purchases convertible preferred stock will also have the opportunity to participate in the company's success through its ability to convert the preferred stock into common stock.

3.   Convertible Debt Securities

Convertible debt securities provide the investor with certain protections, such as a fixed rate of return and priority with respect to equity holders in the event of the company's liquidation. However, although convertible preferred stock likely will have the right to vote on certain corporate transactions, the holders of convertible debt securities in most cases must separately contract for these rights.

The emerging company's management may prefer to avoid issuing convertible debt securities to the established company because the securities will appear as debt on the company's financial statements, which will affect the company's ability to obtain credit from third parties. Additionally, the company could be obligated to pay interest periodically, even if the company is not profitable.

4.   Nonconvertible Equity or Debt Securities

Nonconvertible equity or debt securities are generally not issued in early stage investment in emerging companies because they usually obligate the company to repay nonconvertible debt and redeem nonconvertible securities. Similarly, an established company would not find nonconvertible equity and debt securities attractive investments compared to the other methods of investment that give the established company the opportunity to share in the potential growth of an emerging company.

C.   Documenting the Relationship

After selecting the type of investment instrument, the parties should negotiate the obligations of the emerging company with respect to the operation of its business once the investment has been consummated, as well as any other agreements between the parties relating to other arrangements that require documentation, for example, contract-based research that the emerging company agrees to perform for the established company.

Many of the terms that an established company in a corporate partnering scenario will negotiate are the same types of terms that venture capitalist investors will demand. Most of the key terms and issues are established to protect the investor's investment in the emerging company.

Participation in Management.   The established company may require that it be entitled to have a certain number of representatives on the emerging company's board of directors. By having representatives on the board, the established company has access to information about the emerging company's operations and has the ability to participate in management decisions.

Information Rights. The established company may require the emerging company to provide it with financial information on a regular basis. The financial information usually consists of the company's financial statements prepared in accordance with generally accepted accounting principles, including the balance sheet and income statement. There may be an additional requirement that the financial statements be audited.

Registration Rights. As discussed in Chapter 7 (Financing a Business), the securities acquired by the established company will likely have been issued in reliance on an exemption provided by Section 4(2) of the 1933 Act or Regulation D (Rules 501–508) adopted by the Security Exchange Commission. Therefore, the securities will be restricted and cannot be freely transferred by the established company. The securities can be transferred if the requirements of Rule 144 of the 1933 Act are met or if the securities are registered under the 1933 Act. The established company may negotiate for registration rights that require the emerging company to register the established company's securities so that the securities can be resold.

Right to Participate in Subsequent Financings. The established company may bargain for the right to participate in subsequent financings of the emerging company so that it can maintain or increase its percentage equity interest in the emerging company. By acquiring a right of first offer, the established company will have the right to purchase a certain amount of any new securities issued and thereby maintain or increase its percentage equity interest. The emerging company should negotiate certain exceptions to the established company's right to purchase new securities, such as issuances of securities to employees, directors and third-party vendors and issuances of securities upon conversion of convertible securities. The parties can determine when the right to participate in subsequent financings will terminate.

Conduct of Business. The established company may require that the emerging company agree to certain covenants. In this manner, the established company can control the business of the emerging company and require that the emerging company obtain the established company's consent or waiver with respect to any of the designated actions. For example, the emerging company may covenant to use the proceeds of the investment for certain purposes, to continue to conduct its business as it currently is doing or other similar requirements that assure the established company that the emerging company is maintaining "good" business practices. The established company may prohibit the emerging company from taking certain corporate actions, such as effecting a merger, consolidation or sale of its business or assets.

D. Corporate Partnering Advantages

Corporate partnering can be an attractive opportunity for an emerging company with the technology to create a marketable product but without the resources to bring the product to market. By engaging in a relationship with a larger, established company, the emerging company can take advantage of the established company's experience and greater resources and may be able to obtain financing without giving away as much control as in a typical venture capital financing.

13.03   University Relationships

Another form of strategic alliance that may be attractive to an emerging company is a partnering with a university or similar educational facility. Many universities have discovered the benefits of partnering with the private sector to commercialize technology developed by the university's student and faculty researchers. As a result, universities have allocated resources to specifically handle the transfer of technology from the university to private industry. The private sector can take the technology and knowledge generated by academics and put it to practical use to create a commercially viable product. Private industry can also leverage the commercial value of university-developed technology.

Universities may also obtain funding from federal and state agencies to perform research that would not otherwise be possible. A university can benefit financially by licensing its technology to private entities, by obtaining funding for research projects from third parties or by hiring out its researchers to third parties. However, because the general philosophy in academia is to freely disseminate knowledge, and the general philosophy in the marketplace is to capitalize on it, there is an inherent tension in university/private sector relationships. A private business entity that enters into a relationship with a university for the purpose of developing technology should determine whether the rights it will receive to the resulting technology will be adequate for its needs.

A.   Organization of University Technology Development Activities

Universities that engage in research and regularly commercialize the results of their research will typically have in place policies and procedures for the technology transfer of their intellectual property to third parties. Many universities actively solicit relationships with private entities and provide detailed information on the types of arrangements that can be established with the university.

Depending on the size of the university and the amount of commercially exploitable research conducted, the university may designate a single person or an entire staff to handle the dissemination of the university's technology transfer policy and procedure, its intellectual property portfolio and any arrangements with third parties relating to the university's intellectual property.

A university involved in regular technology transfer with third parties will likely have a policy in place relating to intellectual property owned by the university. In general, although the development of relationships with industry is encouraged and the benefits to both the university and society are acknowledged, universities are concerned with for-profit activities that will prohibit researchers from engaging in open discussions about research results or publishing research results or with activities that will interfere with the researcher's responsibilities to students of the university. Most universities will require that all potentially patentable inventions conceived or developed while employed at the university be assigned by the researcher to the university. If the invention is developed pursuant to a university-approved consulting agreement with a third party, any resulting patent rights would not be required to be transferred to the university.

B. Government-Sponsored Research Activities and Funding

Federal and state agencies play an important role in funding research at universities, but grants from such agencies typically come with some "strings" attached. State or federal governments usually will have an interest in knowing that the funds are being used in an agreed upon manner, and the university will be responsible for providing an accounting to the agency at issue.

1. Federally Sponsored Research

There are many federal agencies that sponsor research in various fields. For example, the National Institutes of Health ("NIH") is a federal agency that contributes funding to a number of private and public entities, including universities. NIH allows universities to maintain title to the technology that is developed though a research project but requires that the university grant it certain non-exclusive rights to the technology. To perfect its ownership rights to any technology that results from an NIH-sponsored research project, the university must follow the procedures provided by NIH, which include providing notice and copies of any patent applications filed on the subject technology. Another example is the National Science Foundation (NSF) which is a federal government agency that supports fundamental research and education in all the non-medical fields of science and engineering.

2. State-Sponsored Research

Some states have provided funding for university researchers to attract high-technology businesses. States have created various forums for the collaboration of university researchers with private industry, including the establishment of research centers that are affiliated with universities, working groups that are made up of both academics and industry professionals, and sponsorship of university programs focused on technology with the potential for commercialization.

C.   Licensing University Technology to Third Parties

Discoveries made in the university's laboratory may have great potential for commercial development and application, which can be tapped when licensed by a private entity. The license may be structured in a variety of ways, but generally the license will enable the licensee to market and distribute the technology or use the technology to create a product that will then be marketed and distributed. The university will receive a fee for the license grant, which can take the form of royalties based on the revenues generated by the licensee's sale of the technology/products. The university may share some of the proceeds with members of the research team that developed the licensed technology.

The license granted to the private entity by the university will typically be an exclusive license to make, use and sell any products covered by the license. The licensee will also be granted the right to sublicense the technology. In some cases, however, the license granted will not be exclusive, depending on whether the university retains a right to the technology or whether funding of the technology by a non-profit entity entitles that non-profit entity to license rights as well.

In most cases, a license agreement between a university and a third party will be analogous to a license agreement between two private parties. However, universities usually have a strict policy prohibiting use of the university's name in connection with commercialization of the product.

D.   Research Agreements with Third Parties

A private individual, entity or group might provide funding to a university for the purpose of executing a specific research project. The research agreement between the university and the third party may provide that the personnel, equipment, facilities and research capabilities of the parties will be shared. The agreement must specify the research project to be performed. The project could be one entirely new to the university, in which case the third party will negotiate to own any resulting technology rights, or the project could relate to technology already licensed from the university, in which case the ownership of any new technology likely will belong to the university.

The research agreement should delineate the scope of the project and the university research staff that will work on the project. Generally, the research staff will be obligated to provide updates on the project and may even be required to perform additional research as the developed product goes to market. The cost of the project should be agreed upon, as well as ownership of any technology that is developed through the project. Universities will bargain for the right to present and publish research results to the academic community. The research sponsor may agree to allow for this, provided that the sponsor's prior approval is obtained.

E. Individual Consulting Agreements with Research Sponsors

Some universities have recognized that their researchers are highly sought after by private industry and have compromised by allowing their researchers to enter into consulting agreements with private sponsors. This type of consulting arrangement can be very lucrative for a university researcher and enable the researcher to conduct research that would otherwise not be funded. Oftentimes private firms will require that a consulting agreement be put in place with the chief researcher because the success of the research project is highly dependent on the individual.

The consulting agreement will generally provide for the services to be provided by the researcher (or consultant) and the compensation to be paid to the researcher-consultant. The researcher-consultant will typically agree to assign any rights to technology developed in the course of the consulting relationship to the research sponsor.

13.04   Going Global

In addition to, or in combination with, strategic alliances, growing companies should consider the possibilities and opportunities of taking their business to a global scale. In an increasingly competitive world economy, more companies find themselves adopting a strategy for international expansion. Such expansion can take various forms. A company simply may consider entry into new customer markets or it may seek to create a joint venture with a foreign business partner. The potential rewards of succeeding internationally are great but so are the pitfalls and the risks.

A. Globalization: Need for an International Outlook

Growing through international expansion can be an enormous task, burdening the domestic operations as well as exposing the company to new risks overseas. It is therefore critical that a company seeking to go global carefully evaluates its goals and alternatives.

1.   *Reasons for Going Global*

International trade takes many shapes and forms, and the reasons companies seek international expansion vary among industries and over time. Mainly, however, companies seek new markets for services and goods, lower production costs, risk diversification, access to new technologies or access to foreign capital. With international trade, there is increased competition in domestic markets, which forces domestic companies to adopt an international outlook early on, if not from inception.

Entrepreneurs in small countries normally will adopt a strategy for international expansion if not at the time of inception, soon thereafter. The domestic customer markets in small countries are too small to support substantial research and development of products. In contrast, the U.S. customer market is sufficiently big to provide most emerging companies with enough customer demand for a sustained period of time, and the typical U.S. company seeking international expansion is a mature business that has proven its business model domestically. Nonetheless, foreign markets such as the European Union, China or the emerging economies in East Asia present significant market opportunities for U.S. businesses.

There are several advantages to going international at a later stage: the company has a proven business model, revenue, and greater ability to finance migration and expansion into new geographic areas. A disadvantage can be that the company culture and the business have developed in light of and in response to domestic concerns and issues. The challenges involved in going international may indeed be drastically different and may require a different skill set in the management team.

Many companies, especially in high-technology industries, seek international expansion in order to gain access to new technologies or a larger pool of knowledge and in order to lower the cost of production. Although, historically, companies would seek raw materials not available or more expensive at home, or source production in a country where labor costs were cheaper, in today's economy, a company may locate its headquarters in the United States, source research and development in India or in the United Kingdom, while sourcing production in China or Taiwan. A company that develops a strategy for international expansion early on will have many opportunities to take advantage of the giant knowledge pool that makes up the world economy and the flexibility to source development and production of its products where the cost is the lowest.

2.   *Where to Go Global*

Unless the company seeks to export products that are easily promoted all over the world, such as Coca-Cola, it must focus on a geographic area. Although it is a daunting task to research and determine which countries present the best economic opportunities for the company, in reality the geographic area of focus will be more or less determined by the industry in which the company operates, the reasons for its international expansion and, most importantly, the contacts the company has established or will be able to establish in a particular geographic area.

If the company is seeking to become a domestic exporter, operating mainly domestically but exporting its goods or services, the analysis of where to expand internationally will be based on market demand for the particular good or service. The market research is critical and may be done in-house or by a consultant. Typically, the company will decide on a few test markets to see whether it can develop appropriate distribution channels and whether its current production facilities can support such expansion abroad.

If the company is seeking to become an international company with operations domestically and abroad, variables like cultural affinity, language barriers or access to human capital will be the main determining factors. The international type of company is becoming increasingly common especially in the high-tech industries where research and development is sourced in a country or continent different from the primary place of production or the company's headquarters. The legal structure of the company, whether organized as one entity or with one parent company with subsidiaries in foreign countries, is largely determined by the flexibility of the legal systems in the countries where the company plans to conduct business. It is also an issue determined by tax considerations. When structuring an international company, it is important to find a structure that makes the most economic sense from a global perspective, including the preferences of investors (that it makes sense), tax treatment under various domestic laws (to avoid any double taxation or litigation), as well as local regulations (many countries regulate foreign corporations).

One element to determine where to go can be the country incentives. Often countries provide significant incentives to entice foreign businesses. The incentives can take many different the forms including tax exemptions, loans, use of property or subsidies. The Company seeking to become international should research and evaluate which foreign country provides the best incentives in its particular industry. The local consulate or chamber of commerce are good resources to initiate such research.

B.   Exporting Successful Businesses

There are substantial challenges involved in going international, and solutions that may work in the domestic customer markets or in employment relationships at home may not work abroad. The qualities sought in a management team about to take a company international may also be different from those looked for in the domestic context. This section will discuss some of the challenges involved.

1.   Challenges in Going Global

One of the lessons from the last ten years concerns the difficulty in exporting highly successful business models. The greatest barrier to a foreign market is not the language barrier, cultural differences, legal issues or government regulations. It is the difficulty in establishing and gaining access to a business network with the necessary depth. For example, foreign businesses that move to Silicon Valley may join various business networks but fail to gain access to the necessary expertise available in Silicon Valley. The consequence, here and abroad, is that the foreign company has difficulty finding the right personnel, the right offices and ultimately the cost-efficient solutions to small everyday issues that inevitably come up and which, domestically, might be resolved with a telephone call to a neighbor or business partner.

In migrating or expanding a business abroad, it is critical that the corporate structure or legal arrangement be the most cost effective, taking into account both U.S. and foreign laws and regulations. The reason is that a company seeking to establish presence in several markets may inadvertently become a subject of several tax jurisdictions. Setting up representative offices abroad may be easy enough, but getting out of them may be difficult, especially where employees are involved. The labor laws of many countries make it difficult to terminate employees; the standards for terminating employees are often very different from standards in the United States.

It can be difficult to obtain the legal expertise needed to find a solution that reconciles the legal differences to the company's advantage. Because the nature of law practice is geographically limited, the perspective of legal professionals is often more narrow than that of the business people. The most common solution to this difficulty is to engage a local firm that has offices in the jurisdictions where you want to expand your business. This solution will be more efficient than retaining two separate firms. Most of the value provided by the international firm will come from its ability to efficiently cross over information with its foreign offices and optimize your entry in the local market.

2.   Different Ways to Go Global

The manner in which a company decides to go global is largely a function of the maturity of the company, its resources and the type of industry. There are several ways in which a U.S. company can structure a business relationship with a foreign entity. It may export, open a representative office of the company overseas to prospect the markets, acquire a local business or enter into a strategic relationship with a local company.

The company may export its products directly, in which case it would retain all operations, including manufacturing, in the United States. In deciding whether to export its goods, a company should consider the adaptability of its products to the applicable international standards, relevant export laws of the

United States and any foreign laws governing international trade. This will be particularly true if the company's products include new technologies or any technology that can be used for military ends. Before exporting goods, the company typically will engage a consulting firm to conduct market research of target markets. Unless the company has its own channel of distribution, it must engage an intermediary who will sell the goods in the foreign market.

If a company merely wants to establish a presence in the foreign market, the company may consider engaging a local sales representative or enter into an arrangement with a local business partner. The sale representative normally would be compensated based on volume sold. It is important to be careful in entering into a distributor agreement in that it may be more difficult to terminate such agreements under foreign laws, especially if the sales representative is deemed an employee. In Chapter 9 (Product Development and Distribution), the types of distribution agreements that can be used are described.

Acquiring a local business is often expensive. Significant due diligence must be conducted to avoid assuming any unwanted liabilities, and managing a foreign entity is likely to be more difficult and burdensome than anticipated. Corporate organizations have a very different look and feel from one country to another, and there are many pitfalls in running a foreign business. In many countries, unions have statutory rights and are entitled to participate in certain decision-making processes.

One way to overcome the lack of a solid business network and familiarity of the local culture and market is to enter into a partnership with a local company where the U.S. company will seek to leverage the network of the local company. Although this may seem straightforward, in reality it could be a costly proposition if the wrong partner is chosen.

However, when a U.S. company seeks to expand abroad or develop new products at lower costs overseas, it will eventually need a significant business partner. In partnering up with a foreign entity, the first decision will be the form of cooperation: a non-equity joint venture in the form of a contractual relationship consisting of license, production and distribution agreements; one unitary agreement; or an equity joint venture where the parties form a business entity under the local laws with both parties contributing capital. The best form of relationship will be a function of the practicalities of doing business in foreign markets, the personal relationships of the parties and legal realities.

Entering into a strategic relationship often requires extended negotiations between the parties regarding the purpose of the joint venture, the control and termination provisions and the legal structure of such relationships. These negotiations may be difficult due to language and cultural differences that impact the approach of the parties to such negotiations.

Global expansion of any magnitude will be extremely difficult, if not impossible, without great familiarity with the local markets and sufficient knowledge of the culture in order to reduce unnecessary mistakes based on cultural differences. By creating a joint venture, the company may obtain the critical cultural affinity, and if structured correctly, the incentives of the domestic and foreign parties should be well aligned. The U.S. company would, however, lose control over operations and may suffer from teaming up with the wrong partner.

Licensing technology can potentially allow the company to create a presence in new markets while generating income without engaging in the distribution or marketing of its products. There are many considerations to keep in mind when entering into a license agreement including foreign anti-trust regulations that may prohibit certain geographic limitations and exclusivity provisions. Licensing technology is remote partnering, and when business objectives change or the licensor must protect its intellectual property, it must act locally but remotely, in what may be hostile territory and under foreign laws.

Because many companies are unwilling to spend the capital necessary to acquire another business or enter into a strategic relationship before it has entered the foreign market, the most common approach is perhaps to open representative offices to prospect the market opportunities for the company.

3. Advantages and Disadvantages of Going Global

Developing an international strategy for the company may be important to increase sales revenue, establish early market presence or attract new capital or a potential acquiror. For example, the new integrated market of the European Union is one of the biggest markets in the world, with an overall well educated and sophisticated customer base. It presents any manufacturer with great potential for operations of scale and increased sales. A well-executed, international strategy will position the company not only in international markets but also domestically. By diversifying its customers, the company will minimize its dependence on existing markets. In this high-technology era, where some countries have technological advantages in certain areas but not all, going global might also mean gaining access to new technologies and know-how.

However, the risks can be substantial, and any expansion will take time away from other endeavors and may cause a loss in focus in domestic operations. Expansion into global markets also means that the company must spend time and money away from its present core activities. The company might lose focus and find itself spread too thin. Products and packaging might require modification to be in compliance with foreign regulations. Regulatory compliance and the legal costs involved in finding the appropriate structure for a joint venture or a licensing agreement may force the company to raise additional capital.

C.   Operational and Corporate Complexity in an International Context

As soon as a company expands overseas, it will add a layer of complexity to its corporate structure. This will become an issue if the company is positioning itself for a domestic IPO or as a target company in a merger. It is critical for any potential investor, for example, that the existence of a licensing agreement does not expose the company to any claims of joint ownership of its proprietary information or weaken the claims to its intellectual property rights.

If the company enters into a joint venture, the legal structure must make sense not only from an overall business standpoint but also from a corporate legal perspective so that the company will not risk any unnecessary liabilities.

In the event the company decides to create a wholly owned subsidiary, it will be important to comply with corporate formalities in the applicable jurisdictions to avoid any piercing of the corporate veil. For tax purposes, the company may also want to consider formalizing the relationship between the parent company and the subsidiary through some type of service agreement to avoid the two entities being treated as one entity by tax authorities. It is also important to ensure that the foreign subsidiary of the U.S. company complies with all applicable U.S. laws and in particular the Foreign Corrupt Practices Act of 1977, which has been the object of a recent surge in enforcement activity by federal authorities.

The management skills required overseas might be very different than in the United States, so it is important that the international company have a corporate structure and culture flexible and tolerant enough to allow for different styles of management. Managers in international organizations must also be more flexible. Managers in a foreign subsidiary must be able to not only manage the local work force but to translate the business model and the company's core values into his or her management style as well.

D.   Bridging Cultures

In negotiating international agreements, whether joint ventures or simple distribution agreements, the drafting attorney must be sensitive to the fact that the reader may not be familiar with U.S. legal customs or native to the English language and that his or her attorney may be used to agreements only a fraction in length of the typical U.S. contract. An agreement that is overly burdened by legalese and longwinded phrases may threaten the creation of business relationship. It is also important to keep in mind that, in many countries where business are less regulated than in the U.S., business people do not have ongoing relationships with attorneys, and it may be the business person who first reads the agreement.

13.05   Preparing for IPO

Conducting an initial public offering ("IPO") is often seen as an important milestone for a successful growing business. In the course of the growth of a company, at some point the private equity markets will not be sufficient to fund further growth. The company may need to seek capital from a wider network of potential investors in which case the exemptions from registration of securities available for private offerings, as discussed in Chapter 7 (Financing a Business), would no longer be available. Early investors may also push for an initial public offering as an exit strategy and a way to make their investments liquid. For whatever reason, if a growing company decides to conduct an IPO, there are things that it can do to be well prepared for an IPO. An agenda for an IPO appears as **Exhibit 13B,** and a schedule of events and responsibilities for an IPO appears as **Exhibit 13C.**

A.   Reasons for Conducting IPO

Going public through an IPO enhances the corporate image, and many newly public companies benefit from the increased attention and publicity associated with a public offering. A public offering gives access to additional capital that often cannot be raised in private equity transactions. It provides for a source of additional capital in the future. Other benefits include an improved debt to equity ratio, which enables the company to borrow money from financial institutions on better terms than those available prior to the public offering. Another benefit of becoming a public company is that it will be easier to acquire privately held companies, including their technologies.

B.   Due Diligence

The goal of due diligence should be not only to gather information regarding the issuer, its officers, directors and shareholders, but to document such due diligence so that in the event the offering is challenged in the future, the company can obtain a pre-trial summary judgment. Because the issuer and its control persons can also be exposed to substantial liabilities under the 1933 Act following an offering, generally the due diligence is conducted in a cooperative spirit.

In positioning itself for an IPO, it is important that the company document all transactions of significance, employment relationships, and ownership of intellectual property, as well as the availability of private offering exemptions for previous prior debt or equity offerings.

The company should also preserve a corporate structure as simple and transparent as possible. A simple structure adds credibility and will facilitate any due diligence in connection with an IPO. Make subsidiaries wholly owned and make sure that all intellectual property is vested in or under the control of the parent company.

From inception, a company planning for a potential IPO must be careful to avoid any unnecessary liabilities. A well-advised company will minimize its exposure to expensive litigation. It will most likely achieve its growth at a lower cost than a company that goes through extensive due diligence for reasons related to actions taken by a management not guided by the company's lawyer. Naturally, not every entrepreneur will understand or take the time to understand the importance of issuing securities in compliance with securities laws or the potential liability of employment related conflicts. However, the feasibility or success of an IPO may depend on the credibility of the company in the eyes of the underwriters who will do extensive due diligence on the history of the company.

In positioning a company for an IPO, it is important that it attract members to the board and human capital that will give credibility to the prospects of the company. It is advisable that the company run a background check on board members, as well as key officers. Underwriter investors will run a background check on key executives, and if anything questionable shows up that may affect the credibility of the IPO, the entire underwriting process will be jeopardized.

In many of the new technology industries where innovation is critical, there is a desire to attract entrepreneurial skills and spirit to the management of companies. Entrepreneurs, generally seen as driving forces behind economic progress, receive compensation packages with a view toward making them better agents of the corporation by aligning their interests with those of the shareholders. Another important objective may be to induce managers to become less risk averse. It is important that these compensation packages not be extraordinary nor place the company in breach of any securities laws, particularly if equity awards are part of the package, and that they be tailored to statutory legal requirements.

C. Level of Commitment

To assist in the due diligence process and prepare for the IPO, a growing company must look to its management and employees for assistance. In deciding whether to go public, a growing company must consider the internal human resources that are necessary to successfully complete an IPO. The company, for instance, will have to call on its key management and other employees to assist with due diligence, conduct interviews and participate in road shows. Although exciting and worthwhile to the company, all of these activities are time consuming and distract members of management and key employees from doing what they do best—growing a successful business. Therefore, a company must carefully consider the internal implications of going public and the impact that it can have on a growing business.

D.   Selection of Underwriters

Underwriters often focus on certain industries, and a particular underwriter may develop a reputation in a particular field. Some underwriters focus on certain sizes of offerings or sizes of companies, and they may have other relevant criteria like minimum time of operations or patentable technology. Certain underwriters focus on IPOs, others on secondary offerings.

A company will be associated with the underwriter of the offering, which means that the reputation of the underwriter is critical to the success of the offering. Some underwriters are known for putting together strong syndicates, which is another factor to look for in selecting the underwriter. Because the public offering process lasts six months or longer, it is also important that personalities mix well.

In selecting the underwriter, consideration should also be given to the underwriter's ability to continue to give "aftermarket support market-making ability," research capabilities, as well as continuing advice and support. Finally, the issuer should conduct due diligence on the underwriter and follow-up on previously underwritten offerings.

E.   Alternatives to IPO

The alternative to an IPO really depends on whether the company has previously raised outside capital, in which case the investors are looking for an exit or an event that will give them liquidity. The only alternative to an IPO as an exit strategy is to become acquired by a public company or a company that will do its own public offering.

Some entrepreneurs prefer to grow internally by reinvesting the company's capital or by acquiring technology through mergers and acquisitions, which can be difficult if the company does not plan on becoming a public company in the foreseeable future.

13.06   Distressed and Troubled Companies

A growing business will face many challenges and disappointments as it continues to grow and expand. Hopefully, the path that the growing business takes will lead to success with the business achieving its goals. Inevitability, most growing business will have some bumps along the way to success. Some of the more common types of "bumps" are described below.

A.   Pace of Growth

As a growing business continues down its path toward success, the path should be well planned and scheduled. This plan should be followed as carefully as possible so that the growing business is able to weather any problems or downturns in the economy. Growing businesses are often faced with too much success or opportunities at one time, which can distract a growing business and management from its plan. Although this situation can be appealing to a growing business, it is necessary for the business to focus on its plan and to follow the planned pace of growth. Otherwise, the business can find itself over-committed to an uncharted path. Once the business goes down an uncharted path outside of its plan, then the business is more likely to face problems or difficulties that result from making a hasty change in the plan or unforeseen circumstances. Of course, a growing business must be flexible, but at the same time growth must be planned and that plan followed.

B.   Thinking Long Term

For many growing businesses, it is difficult to envision the business in the future at a time when the growing business is concerned with present events such as meeting payroll or getting product to market. With this perspective, many growing businesses tend to take actions in the present that, unfortunately, affect the long-term growth of the business. These actions can include general sloppiness or cutting corners when it comes to following internal procedures or legal review of substantial transactions. For example, in a technology business, it is important for the business to set an internal policy regarding the development, documentation and ownership of technology. Often in a shortsighted business, this procedure is either not established or more likely not followed. This lack of attention to an internal procedure can lead to expensive mistakes; at some point in the future the business will have to unwind such technology to determine how it was developed and who owns the technology. Usually, this review will occur at a critical time, such as before an acquisition or financing. A growing business revisiting issues, such as the basis for its technology, can be extremely expensive to reconstitute after the fact due to fading memories, departing employees and legal expenses.

Another example of short-sightedness is a growing business that is facing economic hardship in the short term and decides to cut corners with their legal counsel by not having counsel review substantive transactions or agreements. Although the business may save cash in the short term, in the long term this cost cutting measure can be extremely dangerous to the health of the business and, inevitably, becomes more expensive. Most frequently, this type of shortsightedness can affect future financings of the growing business if agreements and transactions have not been reviewed by legal counsel, who often will be required to opine in a financing that the existing agreements do not conflict with the terms of the financing. Legal counsel will not be able to give such an opinion without a substantial review of the growing business' agreements and transactions. At the very least, it is expensive and time consuming for legal counsel to go back after the fact and review the agreements and transactions. The worst-case scenario is legal counsel uncovering problems or conflicts in unreviewed agreements or transactions that must be revisited or unwound, which could derail or kill a financing.

C. Finding and Making Connections

So much of a growing business' success depends on finding and making connections, whether for financings, strategic alliances or partnerings. However, finding and making those connections can be difficult for new, growing businesses. These businesses find themselves with a great product and great management but no purchasers of their product or industry contacts because of the lack of connections. This is where a growing business cannot just sit back and wait for investors or partners to come to the business. Instead, the business must go and seek out the connections that make the business grow. The first place for the business to start is with current professional service providers such as legal counsel and accountants. Both attorneys and accountants can be excellent sources of connections for a growing business just based on their respective clients alone. A growing business also should get involved in the target industry by attending conferences and trade shows in the community and by reaching out to other growing or established businesses in the industry for guidance and connections.

D. Financial Distress

One of the challenges of any growing business is facing some level of financial distress. This distress can come in the form of difficulty in finding financing to avoid bankruptcy.

1. Reasons for Financial Distress

To paraphrase Leo Tolstoy's opening lines from Anna Karenina, successful companies are successful for the same reasons (high productivity, good management, significant revenues), whereas each unsuccessful company is unsuccessful in its own way.[2] It is critical that managers of a company become aware of its financial problems as soon as possible and that they be able to identify the sources of the company's problems so that they can adopt an appropriate remedy and position the company for either an out-of-court workout or, if appropriate, file for bankruptcy proceedings.

Bankruptcy proceedings are disruptive and expensive. A so-called Chapter 11 reorganization could cost from $200,000 to several millions of dollars. By early detection of financial troubles and appropriate intervention, a

---

2. Leo Tolstoy, *Anna Karenina* (New York: Random House, Inc.), 1965, pg. 3.

troubled company increases its chances of avoiding bankruptcy. It is important that a company in financial distress adopt a business plan that is realistic and tailored to the financial problems. In order to execute such a business plan, management may want to seek shareholder approval and an extension of pending maturity dates on outstanding debt obligations.

a. Internal Control Procedure and Early Detection

Both seasoned companies and newly formed entities should adopt internal control procedures that ensure early detection of financial distress of the company. Such control procedures should focus on both financial and non-financial information. The control procedures should be formal in nature and involve employees and officers of the company in different areas of management. Naturally, the necessary remedial action will be very different if the company is experiencing problems because it had set unrealistic goals or has problems relating to collections and budgeting.

b. Remedial Action Plan

Any remedial action must be tailored to the overall goals of the company. For example, if the company is positioning itself for a sale, management must be careful to avoid any contingent liabilities that may limit its ability for a successful sale. In order to increase a company's structural flexibility in negotiating a sale, management may seek to recapitalize the company, which may take the form of an out-of-court workout agreement among all security holders of the company. In this type of situation, management of the company must be sensitive to its capitalization structure, as well as to the rights of any creditors and their position, whether secured or not.

c. Business Considerations

If a sale is unlikely but the company wants to continue its business operations in the face of financial distress, management must focus on quickly raising funding to continue its business operations. In raising additional capital, management of the company may have to reconsider the terms and conditions of earlier investments, such as what approvals are needed by the board of directors and shareholders, security interests granted and dilution impacts on current investors from any new funding. The company should adopt a remedial plan that goes beyond the company's immediate survival. Such plan should address specific issues like productivity, employee performance, inventory and sales of the company's products. The management should also examine its accounts payable and prioritize among its creditors and may want to seek to renegotiate the terms of its trade debt as well. In some cases, trade creditors are willing to convert their claims into equity or prolong the repayment of debt if it will insure that they are able to recoup some of their initial investment or insure some repayment over none. Usually, both trade creditors and other creditors have an incentive to find a solution beneficial to all parties because pursuing their claims through bankruptcy or foreclosure proceedings is expensive and time consuming.

d. Avoiding Contingent Liabilities

In managing a company in financial distress, management will face tough and difficult decisions involving reduction in force and downsizing business operations. In this process, which is typically swift and accomplished under pressure from existing investors and creditors of the company, it is important that management navigate the company with assistance of its legal counsel through this difficult time so as to avoid any unnecessary liabilities, including potential employment-related claims.

2. *Out-of-Court Workouts*

Filing for bankruptcy is not only expensive, it essentially involves a transfer of the management and control to a bankruptcy court and a trustee appointed by the court. Before taking the drastic step of pursuing bankruptcy, a company in financial distress may want to seek an out-of-court workout arrangement with its main creditors.

a. Process

The form of workout available to a troubled company depends on the timing of the negotiations and whether outstanding debt obligations have matured or are about to mature. A workout can be a simple negotiation resulting in one agreement among the troubled company and its creditors. It can also result in lengthy and more complicated individual negotiations with each creditor resulting in a comprehensive recapitalization of the company.

A workout is not unlike a financing or acquisition; the company makes itself available for due diligence to be conducted by the creditors and the parties negotiate terms and conditions for the restructuring of the company in order for the company to be better able to repay its debts. Often management of the company will send a letter to the company's creditors advising them of the current situation and, if preliminary negotiations have been undertaken with principal creditors, an outline of the general understanding. Such letters of understanding should be addressed to all creditors and shareholders of the company since the company may need to seek the approval of the shareholders at some point, and it generally is difficult to reach an agreement with creditors unless all creditors agree to the terms. A creditor who does not agree to the terms may seek to enforce his or her claims through a bankruptcy or insolvency proceeding, which may jeopardize the company's ability to reach a workout arrangement or fulfill its obligations pursuant to a workout. The letter should also make it clear that, although the parties are discussing a possible reorganization, including a restructuring of the company's obligations to the creditors, each creditor will still retain all its rights during the negotiations.

b.   Purpose of Workout

The goal of a workout is to maximize the value of the various claims to the company's assets, although primarily the company's creditors are also its shareholders. The workout is negotiated in light of the alternative of bankruptcy or foreclosure proceedings, both of which are expensive to both the companies and its creditors.

3.   *Reconciling Various Creditors' Interests in Workout*

A company in financial distress will have more flexibility in negotiating a potential workout the earlier such negotiations begin, which is why it is important that the company identify and adopt a plan of action as soon as possible. Entering negotiations for a workout when outstanding debt has matured or is about to mature can be very complicated, which also means the earlier started the better.

Typically, the main creditor or a representative of the creditors initiates a due diligence investigation of the company's business operations to assess the reasons for the financial distress. It may also be the first time a creditor really examines the legal documentation underlying the loans or similar debt instruments extended to the company. The due diligence is often very detailed and goes beyond the legal relationships of the company. The creditors will often want to know the company's strengths and weaknesses in the marketplace as well as its competition to determine if agreeing to a workout is worth the trouble. Although less expensive than bankruptcy proceedings, any workout negotiations are disruptive to the management of the company and divert management's attention from its core duties.

If the principal lenders, which may be the largest creditors or the secured creditors, are willing to negotiate a workout with the company, they, jointly with the company, will approach the other creditors to determine whether all creditors are willing to restructure their claims. On the one hand, one unwilling creditor may jeopardize the entire workout. On the other hand, all creditors have an incentive to find a solution because the alternatives—bankruptcy or foreclosure proceedings—are too costly. A workout may be the result of direct negotiations between the company and its creditors, but it often involves a neutral third-party consultant.

4. Workout Agreements

If the company and its creditors agree to a workout, the parties normally will enter into one or a series of agreements. As in standard financing documents, such agreements typically will contain covenants by the company to undertake certain actions, such as closing unprofitable parts of its business, reducing the number of employees, and other actions that will lower costs and increase the profitability of the company. The creditors may also demand changes in management; however, it is important for creditors to remain creditors and not assume roles as quasi–equity holders, which may jeopardize their preferences as creditors under the "equitable subordination" doctrine.

Other agreements common for a workout are extension agreements, where creditors agree to an extension of repayment of a debt without reducing the company's obligations, composition agreements that reduce the amounts of the claims but seek to ensure collectibility of the remaining claims, liquidation agreements that create a framework for an orderly liquidation of the company, and settlement agreements that may include terms relating to extension, composition and liquidation but are used to settle pending litigation.

5. Advantages and Disadvantages of Workout

A workout is usually faster and cheaper than either a bankruptcy or an assignment for the benefit of creditors. Except as required by the creditors and as specified in the workout agreement, existing management continues to make business decisions according to the plan, and there is no loss of control of the company. Any scrutiny that is required by the parties to a workout agreement is less onerous and burdensome than the scrutiny experienced in a bankruptcy case. Moreover, a composition agreement, when legally effective, can completely discharge the company and its sureties or guarantors from their original obligations. A discharge in bankruptcy will only be available for the debtor, not its sureties. In addition, there is no stigma of bankruptcy.

The benefits of an out-of-court workout depend largely on the company's ability to obtain the support of its creditors. Although there is no legal requirement that all of the company's creditors participate in a proposed composition, there are clear risks in relying on an arrangement that does not include at least all the major creditors. Any collection action brought by a non-agreeing creditor may prevent completion of the composition agreement by depleting the company's funds below a level necessary to meet its composition obligations.

A common feature in many workout agreements is to prohibit the company from filling a bankruptcy proceeding. However, such provisions generally are not enforced unless the court was to find that the company entered the agreement in bad faith, and the subsequent filing was made in bad faith. Most likely, a court would be persuaded to find that the post-workout bankruptcy filing was made in good faith if unanticipated circumstances had occurred after the workout that precluded the performance of the workout terms, and the debtor has a realistic chance of reorganizing under bankruptcy.

E.   Duties of Board of Directors

1.   Fiduciary Duties of Board of Directors

The general rule is that the members of the board of directors owe their fiduciary duties to only the shareholders, not the creditors of the company.[3] The board of directors does not owe a specific duty to debt holders of the company, such as note holders, when the company is in good standing. For example, note holders are afforded the protection of the terms of their notes and certain statutory provisions that make directors directly liable to creditors for unlawful distributions of assets.[4] However, when a corporation approaches insolvency, creditors may arguably claim that they hold an interest in maximizing the value of such corporation and that the board of directors' duty should shift to the creditors. The Delaware Supreme court addressed this issue in the Gheewalla case[5] and decided that "the creditors of a Delaware corporation that is either insolvent or in the zone of insolvency have no right, as a matter of law, to assert direct claims for breach of fiduciary duty against its directors." In the Gheewalla case, the Delaware Supreme court considered that creditors are already afforded protection through contractual agreements, fraud and fraudulent conveyance laws, implied covenants of good faith and fair dealing, bankruptcy law, general commercial law and other sources of creditor rights.

2.   Duties in Bankruptcy Proceedings

In a so-called Chapter 11 reorganization, the duty of care of the board of directors becomes a duty to "protect and conserve property in [the debtor's] possession for the benefit of creditors . . . [and to] refrain . . . from acting in a manner which could damage the estate or hinder a successful reorganization of the business."[6] There is an affirmative duty of a debtor in possession to "maximize the value of the estate."[7]

---

3.   *See* Revlon, Inc. v. MacAndrews & Forbes Holdings, Inc., 506 A.2d 173 (Del. Super. Ct. 1985); In re Stat-Tech Int'l Corp., 47 F.3d 1054 (l0th Cir. 1995); Hartford Fire Ins. Co. v. Federated Dep't Stores, Inc., 723 F. Supp. 976 (S.D.N.Y. 1989); Metropolitan Life Ins. Co. v. RJR Nabisco, Inc., 716 F. Supp. 1504 (S.D.N.Y. 1989); *see also* Del. Code Ann. tit. 8, § 141.

4.   *See* Sections 316, 506 and 2009 of the California General Corporation Law.

5.   *See* North American Catholic Educational Programming Foundation Inc. v Gheewalla, 930 A.2d 92, 2007 WL 1453705 (Del May 18, 2007).

6.   In re Sharon Steel Corp., 86 B.R. 455, 457 (Bankr. W.D. Pa. 1988), aff'd, 871 F.2d 1217 (3d Cir. 1989).

7.   Equitable Life Assurance Soc'y v. James River Assocs. (In re James River Assocs.), 156 B.R. 494, 498 (E.D. Va. 1993).

F.   Financial Strategies for Troubled Companies

A trouble company may avoid a workout agreement or bankruptcy by raising additional capital in the private markets. Raising capital for a troubled company may prove difficult and expensive. New and old investors generally will conduct a detailed due diligence and will be in a position to demand rights, preferences and privileges that may affect the rights of earlier investors. If the valuation of the company has declined and the company is negotiating a so-called down round, the company's board of directors must be sensitive to its current investors whose interests most likely will be severely diluted. Yet the company may not have much flexibility because of its desperate need for additional capital.

1.   Down Round

When the valuation of a company declines between two financings, as described in Chapter 7 (Financing a Business), the subsequent financing is typically described as a down round. The most immediate effect of a down round is a lower per-share price of the stock that may cause dilution of the interests of previous investors. The company may find itself negotiating with both new investors and its existing investors whose interests will be affected by the new terms and conditions in the down round. The capital raised in a down round is usually considered expensive capital and the process more burdensome than a regular financing.

In structuring a down round, the company must also be concerned with avoiding any potential liabilities. With potentially disgruntled previous investors, it is important that the company proceed carefully. The company may also need the approval of such disgruntled investors in order to amend its charter documents.

2.   Debt Financing versus Equity Financing

In order to better protect their interests when contributing capital to a troubled company, investors may structure a financing as a debt financing instead of an equity financing because it gives them preference in the event of bankruptcy. Such interest is voidable, however, for a period of 90 days. If the company were to file for bankruptcy within 90 days of funding, the creditors may loose their preference in the bankruptcy proceedings. For insiders, members of the board of directors or owners of 20 percent of the voting equity of the company, the relevant time period is 12 months.

The benefit to the company of a debt financing is that it does not need to price its equity at a time when the valuation normally would be in decline, and the new investors have an interest in the survival of the company for 90 days or twelve months, until their bankruptcy preference has been perfected.

3. Secured Debt Financings

Debt financings, especially of troubled companies, are often combined with a security interest. Collateralizing its debt obligations may be the only way a company may raise additional capital. However, the company should be careful in structuring the security interests so that it does not jeopardize its ability to negotiate a sale of the company. For example, it is important that the term of the debt obligations not be too short so that the company has an ability to remedy its financial troubles without losing its assets.

CHAPTER 14

Purchasing and Selling a Business

Robert L. Brown

Greenebaum, Doll & McDonald, PLLC
Louisville, KY

Alan S. Gutterman

Gutterman Law & Business
Piedmont, CA

Contents

Purchasing and Selling a Business

In this chapter, we describe the negotiation process and issues that are likely to arise when selling a business or buying another. Because the chapter is built around negotiations, the approach in this chapter is a different from prior chapters. Rather than general discussions of issues, we describe the main agreements likely to be encountered in purchasing and selling a business and analyze the main provisions in terms of their effect on a buyer and seller.

14.01   Preliminary Considerations

Purchases and sales of businesses begin, end and are ultimately based on negotiations. This means explanation and exhortation. Negotiators must consider both aspects.

First, effective negotiators must be able to explain needs and concerns. Rather than saying "no," for instance, an good negotiator describes why "no" is appropriate. It is possible that the other side may agree with a position if the background is explained.

Second, effective negotiators are prepared to persuade the other side to accept their position. Although explanations tend to be objective, this is where the negotiator becomes subjective, mustering the arguments in its favor and laying them before the other side in the most effective way possible.

Although some negotiators prefer a demanding tone, from our experience the best deals are those that are based on discussions rather than arguments. By "best deals," we mean deals that stand the test of time in that the parties continue to work through issues as they develop over time. If, for instance, a negotiator is selling a business and never expects to do business with the buyer or anyone else on the other side again, a belligerent tone may work. When forming a joint venture, it will not. The success of a long-term relationship is based on mutual trust and support—not domination.

Many books have been written on the negotiation process. Two of the better ones are Herb Cohen's, *You Can Negotiate Anything*[1] and Roger Fisher and William Ury's *Getting to Yes.*[2] Both are well worth the time it takes to read them, and the information provided could be the difference between closing a deal and not.

For the balance of this chapter, we apply some of these general principles of good negotiation to the following negotiation opportunities typically encountered in the purchasing or selling process:

- The negotiation and execution of a confidentiality agreement under which the parties agree not to disclose their negotiations to others.
- The negotiation and execution of a term sheet covering the basic deal points.
- The conduct of due diligence, particularly by a buyer who wishes to investigate the seller's business and assets.
- The negotiation and execution of detailed agreements covering the purchase or merger.
- Obtaining approvals from directors (usually conducted behind closed doors without public disclosure).
- Obtaining approvals from shareholders (inevitably public).
- Obtaining third parties' approvals (such as banks, suppliers, customers and government agencies).
- Closing, where the assets are transferred and money is received.

14.02   Confidentiality Agreement

Whether acting as a buyer or seller, negotiators will be discussing privileged information during the course of their negotiations. They should be certain that the information will not be disclosed. Therefore, before entering into substantive discussions, they must be certain any confidential information disclosed will not be made public.

The best protection is to rely on a confidentiality agreement, also known as a nondisclosure agreement. **Exhibit 14A** is a unilateral nondisclosure agreement covering instances where only one party, such as seller, will be providing information. If buyer will also be revealing confidential information, for instance when the purchase price is dependent on the acquired business's future performance, a mutual nondisclosure agreement, such as **Exhibit 14B,** should be used. Alternatively, each party could request the other to sign a unilateral agreement.

Let's review some of the major components of the unilateral confidentiality agreement.

---

1. Bantam Books, 1982.
2. Penguin Books, 1991.

The second full paragraph of the agreement contains a fairly detailed description of confidential information. If the disclosing party can foresee any other type of information that may be revealed, it should include that information in this paragraph. Although the phrase "and other subject matter pertaining to the business of Disclosing Party" should pick up anything discussed, it is safer to include other forms of specific information in the definition.

Section 1 is the obligation to keep the information confidential. It is the heart and soul of the agreement.

Section 2 contains the purpose of the disclosure. In the appendix, the description is to be included, so don't forget to do so. Sellers should keep the definition as narrow as possible, whereas buyers want it as broad as possible. A seller should insist on retaining the last sentence so that it is not obligated to provide information unless it wishes to do so.

Section 3 is the negative version of Section 1. It prohibits the recipient from disclosing received information to any other person. It includes a specific statement that the Disclosing Party owns the information and is not granting a license to the Receiving Party.

Section 4 authorizes Receiving Party to disclose the Confidential Information to its officers, agents and similar parties. The section also contains limits on such disclosures. Recipients must need the information and must have agreed in writing to keep it confidential. The section also imposes a further obligation on Receiving Party to advise its recipients that they cannot use, reproduce, publish or disclose such information.

Section 5 imposes a further burden on Receiving Party. It must take all necessary action to protect the confidentiality and Disclosing Party's ownership of the information.

Section 6 contains the exclusions from Confidential Information. It excludes information that the Disclosing Party cannot reasonably claim. Such information includes information publicly known at the time of disclosure or subsequently becoming known other than through recipient's actions, information required by a court order to be disclosed or information that becomes known to recipient from an authorized source.

In many cases, the disclosure of information may cause damage that monetary awards cannot adequately compensate. Section 7 addresses this problem by giving Disclosing Party another remedy. It can seek an injunction to prevent the recipient from disclosing the information.

What happens to information provided to the recipient at the end of the agreement? Under Section 8, the recipient must return it to the disclosing party.

Section 9 states that recipient's obligations are binding on its successors and assigns. Similarly, Disclosing Party's successors and assigns can enforce the agreement against the recipient.

Sections 10 and 11 contain general legal provisions, such as entire agreement, no amendment except in writing, governing law and recovery of attorneys' fees by the prevailing party in a dispute.

This completes the discussion of confidentiality agreements. With it in hand, negotiators can begin to disclose information while negotiating the letter of intent.

14.03   Letter of Intent or Term Sheet

The letter of intent (or term sheet) summarizes the deal. It has three purposes:

- It describes the key issues and makes certain the parties have agreed on them. (Once the parties have reached a consensus on the big-ticket items, detailed agreements can cover the issues in more detail.)
- It points out issues that have not been agreed on and need further negotiation. (This is important to remember. The letter of intent does not need to resolve all issues. Although the key issues should be addressed and resolved to minimize ensuing negotiations, even this is not necessary.)
- It sets the timetable and assign responsibilities in the next stage. (This may be limited to describing when government approvals will be obtained and how due diligence will be conducted, but it is important to cover them.)

A.   Contents

A letter of intent for a typical acquisition appears as **Exhibit 14C**. Let's review the key elements.

Section 1 is the heart and soul. It describes the contemplated transaction—seller will sell, and buyer will buy, seller's business and assets. This letter is for an asset purchase. In the case of a stock purchase or merger, necessary changes must be made to the letter. This section describes the assets being purchased by referring to seller's balance sheet but excludes assets it needs to sell in the ordinary course of business. Assets being sold include cash, notes receivable, raw materials, works-in-process, finished goods, machinery, real property as well as seller's intellectual property.

Section 2 covers what it is going to cost buyer, and when buyer must pay seller. This section allows some cash at closing, with the balance by promissory note.

Section 3 describes the liabilities of seller that buyer will assume. It is the counterpart of Section 1 describing what assets buyer gets. For both parties' sake, it is important to carefully describe the liabilities being assumed. The section also provides that all other liabilities remain with seller. It is important to consider this section carefully. A little time spent on this section will greatly shorten negotiations later over the detailed agreement.

After the assets are purchased, buyer does not want seller turning around and starting up another operation that will compete with the business that buyer has acquired. Section 4 prohibits seller, its key officers and shareholders from doing so. This section must be carefully reviewed in light of local rules. States vary greatly on how much they are willing to enforce such noncompete clauses. There are differing rules on the following:

- Duration (the range being from about six months to two years in many cases)
- Geographical area (local, state or national)
- Business

It is important, therefore, to check the prevailing rules to draft a provision that the courts will enforce. Provisions that violate allowable state limits may be stricken completely or narrowed to fit the acceptable limits.

We will discuss Section 5 in part B of this section.

Section 6 sets the deadline for a closing—the date when assets will be transferred and payment made. Be certain that the deadline is far enough in the future to obtain financing and government approvals, such as under the Hart-Scott-Rodino Anti-Trust Improvements Act ("HSR Act"). Alternatively, the section can be redrafted to state that the closing will be held on the later of a certain date or 10 days, for instance, after receiving HSR Act approval.

Section 7 requires the parties to pay their own expenses. An exception appears for HSR Act filing fees, which are to be split equally. Oftentimes, buyers will demand that sellers pay such fees.

In section 14.04, below, we will discuss the due diligence that buyer will be conducting to ensure the assets are worth what is being paid. Section 8 of the exhibit requires seller to give buyer access to records and information buyer needs to value the business.

Section 9 will be discussed below.

Section 10 states that the previously discussed confidentiality agreement remains binding. This is intended to eliminate any argument that the letter of intent cancels or supercedes any separate confidentiality obligations. In some cases, the letter of intent will contain the confidentiality provisions; therefore, a separate confidentiality agreement will not be executed.

B.   Binding Nature

In this draft, **Exhibit 14C**, the agreement is couched as a non-binding letter. For instance, it is called a "letter of intent" and refers to a "Contemplated Transaction." In Section 5, the letter explicitly states that the legal obligations of the parties will be covered by a "Definitive Agreement."

Following Section 10 is a paragraph that states the purpose of the letter is to memorialize the parties' expression of interest and to outline the basic terms and conditions. It also provides that the letter is only based on information through the date of the letter. It goes on to state that, other than a few stated exceptions, the parties' legal obligations will only be contained in the Definitive Agreement.

The net effect of these provisions is to create a road map without obligating the parties to take the road.

A party is not prohibited in subsequent negotiations from trying to change the terms reflected in the term sheet or letter of intent. Unless there has been a change of circumstances, however, such a position will antagonize the other side, which may walk away from the deal.

C.   Lock-Up

If, however, one party wants to make the other party take the road mapped out for it in the letter, it can take a more aggressive approach.

In some ways, the parties will want the letter to be binding. The letter, for instance, specifically provides that Sections 7 (expenses), 8 (access to information for due diligence) and 10 (confidentiality) are binding.

Additionally, a buyer who wants a unique asset owned by seller may be particularly interested in tying the hands of seller—particularly in a rising market. On the other hand, if seller believes the market has peaked or will drop, it may want to force buyer to take the asset if certain conditions are met.

Section 9 of the letter addresses this issue by prohibiting seller from shopping the deal to others. Specifically, seller is prohibited from the following:

- Soliciting or accepting other offers
- Negotiating or discussing other agreements
- Disclosing

There is a 90-day limitation from execution of the letter on the first two items. There is no time limit on the last.

Many states dislike no-shop or no-talk clauses. They feel such clauses violate the director's duty of care by preventing directors from making an informed decision. In response, some letters of intent contain a fiduciary-out clause that allows the board to deal with a third party if the board determines the third party's proposal is superior.

D.   Remedies

What happens if the other side violates the no-shop or no-talk limitation?

1. Breach

The most likely argument is that seller has breached its contractual obligations and is liable to buyer. The problem is that courts have been reluctant to find meaningful damages in such cases.

2. Tortuous Interference

Another argument used by buyers is to sue the successful bidder that has beaten it. The legal theory is tortuous interference with a contract. Again, the problem is that most buyers have been dissatisfied with the damages awarded to them under such a theory.

3. Break-Up Fees

A more successful approach has been to agree in advance on what the damages will be.

Some agreements take an even more aggressive approach by requiring seller to pay a break-up fee to buyer if it does shop the deal or talk to others. The courts have applied different standards in evaluating the acceptability of such fees. Delaware has applied a liquidated damages test, rather than a business judgment rule. Under the liquidated damages test, the fee must be reasonable and the damages uncertain or difficult to determine. The courts have not been willing to accept exorbitant or punitive fees. Fees of one to three percent (perhaps up to five percent with such other compensation as lock-up options) of the value of the deal are likely to be accepted by the courts.

E. Disclosure Effect

For securities law purposes, if a letter of intent is signed, it probably means that negotiations have progressed to a point that an announcement may be necessary by publicly traded companies. Such an announcement has several disadvantages.

First and most important, the announcement lets others know about a pending deal before it is closed. For buyer, the announcement may encourage other bidders to come forward. For seller, it may cause a momentary or permanent drop in sales. Customers may wait for the deal to close before placing long-term orders or may go elsewhere if they feel uncertain about the new owner.

Second, if the transaction is not finalized after such an announcement, it can cause embarrassment to the two companies and could affect their stock prices. For a seller, it could mean other buyers of its assets will be less willing to negotiate with it, and the price it can obtain may be reduced.

For these reasons, many companies prefer not to enter into a letter of intent but to move directly to the main agreement. Such a solution may not be sufficient. The U.S. Supreme Court has held that preliminary negotiations even before execution of a letter of intent may be sufficient to require a public announcement.

14.04   Due Diligence

Due diligence refers to the pre-closing period during which buyer and seller evaluate each other.

A.   Purpose

The main purpose of due diligence is to give buyer a chance to look for the bad news. Buyer is usually given 30–60 days to review seller's records, access senior managers and ask questions. During this period, it has a chance to confirm that the price it is paying is appropriate. If the news is better than expected, buyer will be pleased and anxious to close. There is no renegotiation of the price. If the news is as expected, again, the price stays the same and closing proceeds. If the news is not as good as expected, buyer is likely first to try to renegotiate the price, unless the news is so materially adverse as to negate the true value of the deal. Failing a price reduction, buyer will withdraw.

Due diligence, however, can serve other purposes:

* Allow seller to understand buyer and ensure that buyer will be able to pay the purchase price and perform its obligations
* Permit seller to confirm that buyer is an appropriate person to take over the business. This is a more likely a concern when seller is a closely held business and the owners want to make certain buyers will continue or grow the business.
* Help buyer to understand seller's business and what its obligations are likely to be
* Lay the foundation for integrating buyer's and seller's operations
* Identify warranties, representations and covenants that buyer will want from seller in the main agreement
* Identify third-party consents that must be obtained
* Identify agreements that will be required
* Prepare a timetable for consents and closing

Sellers should keep a copy of all written information disclosed and notes about oral information conveyed to buyers during this phase. In case of a dispute as to what was disclosed, such evidence can be the best evidence for seller.

B.   Timing

With all the work that must be done during due diligence, it is important for buyer to have a plan on what it is looking for. The plan should assign responsibilities for who will be doing what and when their work must be accomplished. Tasks will usually be split up among outsiders and insiders. Outsiders will include lawyers, accountants and investment bankers. Insiders will include individuals from many departments in the two companies. For instance, buyer's IS people will discuss issues with seller's IS people. Similar matching will occur for human resources, accounting, credit, research, purchasing, production, marketing and distribution.

One difficult issue is when to get different departments involved. For integration purposes, sooner is better. There are several reasons, however, why this is neither possible nor advisable.

1.   Confidentiality

From a confidentiality standpoint, seller will not want to turn over trade secrets until closing. Even with a non-confidentiality agreement, such information should not be released. The more people with access, the more risk it will be released.

2.   Antitrust

From an antitrust standpoint, certain types of information cannot be disclosed before closing. Otherwise, if buyer and seller are in the same business, such disclosures may be treated as a sharing of information between competitors—an activity that is a per se violation of the antitrust rules.

To reduce the risk of disclosures during the due-diligence period violating the antitrust laws, there are several rules or policies that should be followed by buyer and seller. The more their businesses overlap and compete, the more important these rules become:

- Remain competitors during the pre-merger phase. Regardless of how well the negotiations are proceeding, something may happen to prevent a closing—including the government deciding the deal is not advisable. Anticipate the worst: that the deal will not close. Do not give the government and competitors the chance to argue that, during the due diligence period, the seller and buyer coordinated their businesses. This may enable the government to argue that lessons learned during this period permitted the seller and buyer to align their activities and that the entire proposed acquisition was just a sham to allow them to exchange information. Even if the deal closes, a competitor who loses market share during the due diligence period may argue that the loss was the result of illegal coordination during that period.

- Exchange only what is necessary. Although some information is important to evaluating the other party and the risks and liabilities being transferred, draw the line at what is essential to that purpose.
- Exchange only when necessary. Defer disclosing information until as late as possible, with closing being the ideal time.
- Limit who gets information. Only those individuals who need the information at the time of disclosure should be given access to it. It should not be available to anyone involved in day-to-day operations. Most importantly, it should not be turned over to anyone setting prices for competing products or services.
- Avoid joint meetings with customers.

To make certain these rules are met, it is safest to have antitrust counsel present when information is being exchanged and to have documents passed through them.

C. Checklist

An example of a due diligence checklist appears as **Exhibit 14D**. It covers most of the topics and issues that are likely to arise in an asset acquisition and the types of information the parties likely want or have to disclose. The form is drafted as a certificate to be signed by an officer of seller. This encourages seller to take what is being disclosed seriously.

It also provides buyer with a misrepresentation argument if the information is not accurate. Such a representation will be eliminated in the main agreement, which will contain a statement that it is the entire agreement with all of seller's representations, and all other agreements and representations are replaced by it. If the main agreement is not executed, however, the representation in the checklist remains effective and can be grounds for buyer recovering costs.

In the following discussion, we describe the disclosures from the standpoint of buyer.

Starting with the basics, as reflected in Section 1, buyer will want copies of seller's corporate records. This allows buyer to confirm the number of shares outstanding and who owns them. Buyer will also want to review board minutes to make certain they are in order, proper actions have been taken, prior securities and agreements have been approved, and proper procedures for approval of the transaction are followed.

In this area, buyer will look for evidence of securities law violations, including registration and periodic filings, shareholder meetings and reports, insider trading, self-dealing and fraud.

Buyer will also be concerned with whether seller is qualified in the states where it is doing business. This will be addressed at closing by good standing certificates from each state where it does business. Such certificates are issued by the secretary of state. Be careful of the fatal four (Arkansas, Alabama,

Mississippi and Vermont), where transactions prior to qualification are invalid and cannot be cured by subsequent registration.

Section 2 addresses references. If buyer is in the same business, this is less important. If seller is publicly traded or has a well established market, it may similarly not be important. It can be very important, however, if seller is closely held and is an emerging company. Personally, we are not big fans of references. Most people can produce a few people willing to vouch for their wisdom. With employment rules becoming stricter, what former employers are able to disclose is becoming narrower than before. On the other hand, it is amazing what one can sometimes learn.

Section 3 covers seller's financial statements. These may be the most important disclosures because they are the most objective reflection of seller's business. Buyer should be clear on what it needs in terms of financials, make certain it receives all that it needs and reviews the information carefully. Buyer's financial team must be well qualified and able to understand someone else's financials. For this reason, someone from buyer's credit department may be particularly helpful.

Section 4 addresses seller's accounting procedures. Buyer should consider how seller recognizes revenue and its accounting policies. It should make certain they are consistently applied.

Sections 5 and 6 ask for information on seller's existing products and services and those in development. If buyer is in the same business, it is probably already aware of the existing products and services. From an antitrust standpoint in such case, buyer probably cannot ask for those in development.

Having information on seller's products and services, the next issue is what is the market. Related to that is seller's market share. Buyer will be interested in the market, seller's share at present and how it is changing. These issues are covered in Section 7.

In Section 8, the emphasis is on seller's customers. How does seller market and sell? Related questions are who is it selling to, who are the important customers and what new customers are there?

Section 9 looks at seller's competitors—who they are, how they compete and how strong they are.

In Section 10, we look more carefully at seller's property, plant and equipment. Critical areas are a description of the property seller owns and leases and liens on such property. For owned real property, buyer will want copies of title reports. For owned personal property, buyer will need copies of tax and Uniform Commercial Code ("UCC") state and local filings to see what liens have been recorded.

Sections 11 and 12 focus on contracts that are important to seller. Under this category, buyer will also be interested in seller's material agreements. Buyer should review the documents that are keys to seller's business. In particular, it should look for the following:

- Agreements requiring consents to the purchase (Seller, on the other hand, will be concerned with its post-closing obligations and liabilities once the contracts are assigned.)
- For purchase obligations, how secure important sources are
- On the sale side, how firm major customer contracts are and the type and severity of warranties
- Most loan agreements contain negative covenants prohibiting share and asset sales without lenders' written consent. If the asset being transferred has been pledged or a lender has a security interest, that lender's approval must be obtained
- Leases traditionally require consents to asset and stock sales, so pay particular attention to these. Also look for extensions and options
- Be certain key employees are under contract to seller. Even if they are, look for change-of-control provisions that allow them to leave with golden parachutes containing options and bonuses. Any such benefits exceeding three times the employee's average compensation over the prior five-year period are non-deductible by seller

Section 12 considers distribution agreements—agency, distributor and reseller. These can be important because they represent how seller gets its products to the marketplace.

Section 13 considers seller's inventory. What is there, how long has it been there, how many of them are returned goods, are any obsolete and what is seller's inventory accounting practices?

In Section 14, the issue is warranties given to customers. What are the representations and warranties, and how expensive have they been to seller in the past (as measured by damages paid)?

The next two sections look to the people inside seller. Section 15 asks questions about its officers. Who are they, how much are they paid, what are their employment agreements and how reputable are they?

In Section 16, buyer asks for information on seller's employees, starting with an organizational chart and job descriptions. In this section, when buyer asks for a list of fired employees, it is really looking for leads. Disgruntled employees are more likely to give buyer bad news about seller. Similarly, buyer wants to know how good seller's relations are with employees and unions and whether there have been any problems (lawsuits or strikes) in the past. In this area, buyer will be asking for information on pension benefits and the adequacy of their funding.

Section 17 turns to seller's intellectual property. This checklist is more focused on a hi-tech company with limited manufacturing. The questions on seller's IP are, therefore, extensive. The questions address seller's software, hardware and Internet presence. If, on the other hand, manufacturing is a critical function for seller, questions on its manufacturing operations must be added. They should focus on life expectancy of equipment, expansion capabilities, quality control, inventory control and just-in-time supplier relations.

Section 18 asks about seller's litigation experiences. Is it presently involved in any cases or arbitrations? Has it been? Are any threatened?

In Section 19, seller is asked to provide information about its insurance policies. This includes the policies, risks covered, maximum amounts covered, deductibles and pending claims.

Section 20 covers sellers' regulatory compliance. Seller should have business licenses issued by government agencies for the business it conducts. Unfortunately, many licenses may not be transferable. Buyer may have to seek new ones once the transaction closes. Seller is also asked about noncompliance with governmental rules and any government reports it files. Such reports likely will give buyer great insight into seller's business. Environmental compliance is very important. Under the Comprehensive Environmental Response, Compensation and Liability Act ("CERCLA" or "Superfund Act"), owners and operators of facilities (including lessees) are strictly liable for remedial costs if hazardous wastes or materials are discovered. Therefore, it is important to review all existing and prior uses of property. An indemnity in the main agreement may not be sufficient if seller ceases to exist after the transaction closes.

Section 21 looks at seller's financing arrangements. It requests copies of all its financing agreements, including loans, mortgages, liens and capitalized leases. Information on defaults, collateral and guarantees is also requested.

Section 22 considers seller's tax structure. It requests copies of its national, federal and state filings for the past three years. To evaluate future risks for past activities, the section asks for information on current tax audits. In this area, buyer should consider whether any taxes are likely to arise on assets being transferred to it.

In Section 23, seller is asked to provide information on its bank accounts. Buyer should be looking for financial controls and location of accounts.

Finally, Section 24 is a catch all covering any other relevant information, such as management or consultant reports on seller. They can be a gold mine of information.

14.05   Main Agreement

The type of transaction will determine the documents required. In stock purchases, seller as a shareholder of a business must sign a document transferring the stocks it owns in that business. This will usually be a stock power. In mergers, the controlling document is the merger plan filed with the appropriate state agency. All assets and liabilities are transferred, the disappearing entity is dissolved and shares are converted without further action.

Assets purchases are more difficult. Each asset must be transferred. Although there will be one master agreement covering, summarizing and acting as a blueprint for the entire transaction, there will be individual transfer agreements covering different types of assets and the filing required to implement them. For example:

- Patents and trademarks will be covered by one or more assignments filed with the U.S. Patent and Trademark Office.
- Real property will be covered by separate conveyances filed with the county clerk's office where the property is located.
- Personal property will be covered by a bill of sale that may be filed with a local county clerk's office.
- Leases will be covered by separate assignments, with a copy provided to each lessor.
- Vehicles may be covered by individual bills of sale filed with the state department of motor vehicles.

For a major company, identifying each asset to be transferred and preparing the appropriate form is a tremendous task. Because of the complexity of documenting an asset purchase and the preference for them, in the remainder of this section we focus on asset transactions. Most of the comments, however, are equally applicable to stock purchases and mergers.

Our comments follow the form of the asset purchase agreement appearing as **Exhibit 14E**. It is keyed to the acquisition of a high-tech business.

A.   Deal Provisions

The first part of the agreement contains the main points of the deal (first paragraph, recitals and Section 2) and definitions (Section 1). The most important issues are parties, transaction, price and payment method.

1.   Parties and Transaction

The transaction must be described in detail. What is being acquired—stock or assets? If the latter, will any liabilities be acquired? These issues are covered in Section 2.

2.   Price and Payment

The price can be fixed or dependent on future events. Fixed prices can be measured in cash, stock or other asset. For instance, the price may be $1 million, one million shares of buyer's common stock or one parcel of land. In **Exhibit 14E,** the price is paid in common stock of buyer (Section 2.7).

In some cases, the price can be a combination of fixed and dependent. For instance, fixed assets may be transferred at a fixed price, but current assets, at their price current at closing. In such case, a mechanism should be established to allow an adjustment in the price for changes in current asset values.

There are two types of changes that can be made to price. First, the price may be adjusted for business changes between signing and closing. These are usually adjustments based on a multiple of earnings or changes to working capital, book value or price of asset being used as consideration.

Problems often arise if the calculation of earnings, working capital or book value is made on a closing day that does not coincide with the end of a financial period for seller—for example, a closing in the middle of a month rather than at the end of a fiscal month. In such cases, interim adjustments must be made with difficult decisions based on interim allocations and accruals. For instance, should year-end bonuses or other once-a-year expenses be accrued or charged as an expense when expended?

These calculation difficulties arise whether income statements (such as adjustments for earnings) or balance sheets (such as adjustments for book value) are used. Adjustments may require shifting income, expense or asset. For instance, if seller reports an annual charge such as property tax when the bill is received rather than during the period covered, a large increase in the current period's bill may not be reflected in the interim income statement. The same problem can exist if an asset has been acquired but not yet included on seller's balance sheet.

Second, the price may be adjusted for performance. The performance could be between signing and closing or even after closing. This second type of price change is called an earn-out and ties the price to how well the assets or acquired company does in the future. The better the performance, the higher the price paid. In some cases, the price can be a combination of fixed and earn-out. A certain amount is paid at closing, with seller entitled to an additional amount or bonus depending on future performance.

Earn-outs raise two issues. First, seller should establish in detail what buyer can and cannot do with the assets acquired. Buyer, on the other hand, will want great autonomy in its handling of the acquired asset, such as being able to act in its best judgment without any fiduciary duty to seller. Second, instruments reflecting an earn-out obligation are not a security that must be registered under the Securities Act of 1933 so long as the deferred payment rights are granted to seller "not as an investment, but as an integral part of the consideration for the sale."

If the purchase price is not fixed but adjusted at closing or some date after closing, a mechanism for handling adjustment disputes should be established. A common approach is to have seller's accountants prepare the calculations, buyer's accountants review them, and a mutually agreed-upon third set of accountants resolve any differences between the first two.

Payment is a key part of the deal. Will the price be paid at closing or in installments? If in installments, is there interest? If not, will tax authorities impute an interest factor? When paid, how will payment occur—wire transfer or bank cashier's check?

If payment is delayed, as with an earn-out, seller will have to conduct its own due diligence on buyer's ability to make future payments. It will also want to strengthen buyer's representations regarding its financial condition and any events likely to affect its ability to pay in the future.

Seller should also address the question of what happens if buyer is unable to make a future payment. Unwinding a merged asset is usually quite difficult. Even the U.S. Supreme Court has recognized the impossibility of having two monopolists undo their merger. Seller may want to insist on some security, such as in the assets transferred or a pledge of the stock that buyer is acquiring. Another approach is a letter of credit or guarantee from buyer's stockholders, affiliates or banks.

B.   Representations and Warranties

Each party to the transaction must make certain representations about its business and the transaction. Such representations serve three purposes:

- Establish a base line for what the parties believe and are relying on
- Enable either party not to close if any representation or warranty is not true at closing
- Enable either party to recover under the indemnity provision for a breach

The most important are reflected in Sections 4 and 5. They cover due incorporation, qualification to do business, approval of the transaction by necessary parties, receipt of regulatory approvals and third-party consents, compliance with generally accepted accounting principles, accuracy of financial statements and absence of material adverse change in seller's business.

The financial statements receive great attention in the representations. Some of the issues likely to be addressed include the following:

- Accuracy of financial statements as a whole
- Accuracy of information on particular assets
- Collectability of accounts receivable (If this is a material issue, an allowance for bad debts should be included.)
- Value and obsolescence of inventory
- Usability and value of assets, including pre-paid items
- Lack of undisclosed liabilities
- Product warranty liability and customer claims (The parties should discuss how to handle post-closing claims. Seller will not want such claims, arguing that they are expenses of the business acquired. Seller will also argue that buyer has no incentive to resist such claims if it can treat them as adjustments to the purchase price or reduce its earn-out payment.)
- Tax liabilities, including those arising on the transaction (The parties should establish a mechanism on how to handle post-closing tax claims. There is likely to be different perspectives as with claims. Seller will want to resist all claims, whereas buyer will be more inclined to concede and charge back the amount to seller.)

- Compliance with laws (This provision is usually a blanket statement that seller is in compliance with all laws, regardless of how unlikely the statement is. Our favorite example is of an executive on her way to a closing who received a speeding ticket and arguably caused the company to be in breach of the provision. A limitation to material violations of material laws should be logically included, but is usually rejected.)
- Description of pending, threatened and unasserted claims

It is important to describe carefully what representations each party is liable for. For instance, oral statements by a lower-level employee should probably not constitute a representation. For this reason, most agreements specify what representations a party is liable for. This will usually be written statements. Oftentimes it will only be those by designated individuals or contained in specific documents provided in due diligence. Representations in other agreements may be excluded and not superseded by the main agreement.

Another question that should be addressed is whether the representation is based on actual condition or knowledge? Is the representation an absolute statement that must be true or can it be based on maker's knowledge? If knowledge-based, whose knowledge is relevant? As with statements, knowledge of lower-level employees should not be the trigger. It is more common to designate the individuals or class of officers whose knowledge is important.

What happens if one party, buyer for instance, knows a representation is false at the time of signing? Can it later sue on grounds of misrepresentation? This is called sandbagging and is permitted unless the agreement provides otherwise. It is wise, therefore, to include an anti-sandbagging provision that no liability applies to a statement that buyer knew or had reason to know was false at the time of signing.

1. Seller

In an asset sale, the selling company makes seller's representations. In a stock sale, representations are made by individual shareholders selling their shares. In **Exhibit 14E,** they appear in Section 4.

As due diligence progresses, the types of representations by seller will become more fleshed out and specific. When buyer identifies an issue that it feels uncomfortable about, it will try and insert a representation from seller about it. In **Exhibit 14E,** Sections 4.9 and 4.12 reflect issues that are likely to arise during due diligence. For this reason, it is important that the team conducting the due diligence be the same as, or work closely with, those drafting the main agreement.

On the other hand, if the purchase price represents a significant discount, seller may be able to insist on minimal representations.

Because seller is taking buyer's stock as payment in **Exhibit 14E,** securities representations appear in Section 4.15. These representations state that seller is acquiring the payment securities for its own account. These representations mean that buyer is less likely to have to register its common stock as a result of such payment.

2. Buyer

In **Exhibit 14E,** buyer's representations appear in Section 5. Because buyer is paying the purchase price by issuing its common stock, Section 5.2 should be included to make certain buyer's stock is valid and to confirm the percentage of ownership that it represents.

3. Survival

Representations are a snapshot of the present. Seller or buyer describes what the condition is at present. This raises two problems: First, if closing occurs after the agreement is signed, new representations should be made as of the closing date. This is called a bring-down certificate, and the delivery of one should be required in the agreement.

C.   Covenants

The second problem is that one party may want to limit the other's actions in the future. In other words, it may want to change the snapshot of buyer as reflected in the purchase agreement into a motion picture. This is achieved by covenants, which can regulate the other party's actions between signing and closing or even after closing. Covenants control actions during the entire period, whereas representations only describe conditions at fixed times—such as signing or closing. There are usually two types of covenants: those involving the conduct of business and those that facilitate closing.

1. Conduct of Business

Covenants concerning the conduct of business regulate how the parties will operate their business. They are usually limited to the interim period between signing and closing and require seller to conduct its business in the ordinary course. Seller cannot, for instance, sell off assets other than as it normally does. In **Exhibit 14E,** these appear as Sections 6 (especially Section 6.2 for seller) and 7 (for buyer).

Covenants can also apply during the post-closing period. In **Exhibit 14E,** they appear as Section 8. On seller's side, such covenants can, for instance, limit for a fixed period seller's ability to re-enter the business being sold, compete with buyer, solicit buyer's employees or contact buyer's customers (Section 8.8). On buyer's side, they can be important, for instance, when an earn-out payment provision applies. Buyer could be obligated to conduct the acquired business diligently in order to achieve the earn-out levels. In **Exhibit 14E,** because buyer is paying the purchase price in its common stock, Section 8.6 limits buyer's ability to dilute the value of that stock by issuing additional shares.

2. Facilitate Closing

The parties may be obligated to take specific actions to make certain the closing occurs. This can include filing government reports, seeking third parties' consents and obtaining director and shareholder approvals. In **Exhibit 14E,** seller must give buyer access to information it needs for due diligence (Section 6.1), and both parties must use their best efforts to close (Section 6.5 and Section 7.1). The agreement also includes limitations on seller's ability to market the assets or stock to other potential buyers and how it can respond to such inquiries between signing and closing (Section 6.4).

D. Conditions

Conditions set the ground rules for when the parties must close the transaction. Extensive lists are prepared for both parties on what must happen before they are obligated to complete the deal. In **Exhibit 14E,** they appear as Section 9 (for buyer's obligation to close) and Section 10 (for seller's obligation). The most important conditions follow:

- Accuracy of representations
- Obtaining tax ruling
- Expiration of any pre-merger notice period
- Compliance with securities law requirements
- Approval by boards of directors and shareholders
- Execution of related agreements, such as employment agreements and agreements not to compete
- Absence of any pending, threatened or unasserted claim

A deadline for the closing is usually established, subject to extension by mutual agreement. In **Exhibit 14E,** the issue is covered by the closing (Section 3) and termination provisions (Section 11).

In some agreements, a separate description of what actions must be taken at the closing is also included. It lists what each party must bring and deliver at the closing and can be a handy checklist. **Exhibit 14E** contains such a provision. Section 12.1 lists what seller must provide, with Section 12.2 listing what buyer must deliver.

E.   Indemnification

Indemnification is important in two cases:

- When the deal does not close because of one party's actions, such as failure to obtain necessary consent or refusal to close
- When the deal closes, but one party does not get what it bargained for because of the other's actions, such as misrepresentation or breach of covenant

In either case, the damaged party will seek reimbursement for its out-of-pocket expenses and losses. In the first example, break-up fees are an example. Damages are an example of the second.

Sellers will usually seek to limit their liability in three ways: notice, time and amount. They want to require notice of claims and the right to handle third-party claims rather than allowing buyer to settle them. They also want a deadline by which indemnity claims must be made and possibly a separate deadline by which the basis of the claims must arise. Sellers also want to exclude claims that only shift liabilities between post-closing periods and request a maximum liability or cap. The cap can be tied to the purchase price (for instance, no more than 50 percent or 100 percent of the purchase price). Sellers may also want minimum levels and aggregation (for instance, no liability until claims reach $100,000, with buyer aggregating claims until they reach that amount).

In **Exhibit 14E,** the indemnification provision appear in Section 13, with Section 13.1 describing seller's indemnity, and Section 13.5 covering buyer's indemnity.

F.   Miscellaneous

These provisions are usually called the boilerplate because the format reappears over and over in agreements. Most business people begin to skim the agreement when they get to this point. Nevertheless, some of these provisions are dependent on the transaction. Therefore, it is important to recognize them, review their terms and tailor them to the circumstances.

1.   Choice of Law

When buyer and seller are in the same state, particularly if all the assets being purchased are located there, that state's law will usually be selected as governing law. When the parties and assets are in different states, the choice is a bit more difficult. If one party is dominant, its local law will most likely be chosen. If the two are of equivalent negotiating position, a neutral state, such as Delaware, may be chosen.

As the desk sergeant used to say in *Hill Street Blues*, "Be careful out there." Be selective when agreeing to a particular state's governing law. Check to be certain that actions being undertaken, or the way business is conducted, do not violate the state's laws. Also look to see what a party may be liable for in case of a breach. Does local law allow consequential damages? What about punitive damages?

2. *Dispute Settlement and Consent to Jurisdiction*

A related question is how and where disputes will be handled. Regarding how, disputes can be subject to mediation, arbitration, litigation or a combination of the three. Recent preference is to mandate non-binding mediation, which, if unsuccessful, becomes arbitration. Many parties have not been completely satisfied with their arbitration experiences, particularly what they feel is the tendency of arbitrators to split the parties' differences. As a result, in some agreements, parties appoint their own arbitrators with instructions not to split.

As to where, the settling of disputes does not have to be the same as the place of the governing law. For instance, the parties could have Delaware as governing law but agree to have the dispute handled in another jurisdiction. Whatever the choice, if the parties are relying on arbitration, be certain there are adequate and trained arbitrators in the location. Even in the 21st century, bias for local companies can be strong. This is something to consider when agreeing on a dispute-resolution place.

Whatever jurisdiction is chosen, make certain jurisdiction exists over the other party. This is best accomplished by having both parties specifically agree that they will submit any dispute to a specific arbitration tribunal or court and that they will be subject to its jurisdiction. Particularly when the dispute is handled by arbitrators, take it one step further and have the parties agree on what courts can enforce any decision.

3. *Fees*

Agreements usually include two provisions on fees. First, each party agrees to pay its own expenses and fees, with possibly some sharing of any pre-merger filing fee. Second, there will be a representation by each party as to whether it used any brokers and, if so, who it used. In **Exhibit 14E,** these appear as Sections 4.13 and 5.6. If any brokers were used, the agreement then provides who pays their fees. In case of a breach of the representation, the party breaching will be liable for the broker's fees.

G. Exhibits and Schedules

Many issues requiring a great deal of space, as well as lists, will be turned into separate exhibits and schedules. One advantage is that materials from other sources can be attached without inputting them into the main agreement. Additionally, revisions in those external-source documents can be made easily by substituting pages, even up to closing, without having to go back and change the main agreement.

14.06 Approvals

Many approvals will be required before the transaction can be finalized. The four main categories of approvals are boards of directors, stockholders, government and third parties.

A. Boards of Directors

Whether board approval is required depends on the type of transaction.

Stock Purchases: Seller's board must approve if the transaction is material to it. Seller's board must approve if it is a party to the acquisition.

Asset Purchases: Seller's board usually must approve the sale of substantially all of its assets and sales not in the ordinary course of business. Buyer's board must approve if the acquisition is material to it.

Mergers: Seller's and buyer's board must approve. In forward and reverse subsidiary mergers, board approval of the parent will also be required if it is a party to the transaction or issues securities.

Share Exchanges: Seller's and buyer's board must approve.
    Examples of the standards that board members must adhere to when voting to approve or reject are:

Duty of Care: Directors have a duty to inform themselves prior to making a business decision of all material information reasonably available to them. Having informed themselves, they must act with requisite care. In some states, this is close to the ordinary prudent person test.

Duty of Loyalty: Directors have an affirmative duty to protect the interests of the company and an obligation to refrain from conduct that would injure the company or deprive it of a profit or advantage. This usually means directors must be independent and disinterested. Therefore, only outside directors should vote on acquisitions.

Business Judgment Rule: Directors are presumed to have acted on an informed basis, in good faith and in the honest belief that the action was taken in the best interest of the company. This is the reverse of the duty of care and places the burden of proof on the plaintiff.

Enhanced Business Judgment Rule: A variation of the previous rule, this one places the burden of proof on the board in hostile tender offers.

Fair Auction Test: If seller decides to conduct an auction sale of its assets, directors cannot favor one bidder. The auction must be conducted fairly and is subject to the business judgment rule.

Intrinsic Fairness Test: Directors are not required to conduct an auction but, if they do, it must be fair.

Exhibit 14F is an example of a resolution by a seller's board of directors approving a sale or merger. It contains extensive recitations on the actions taken by the board in an attempt to confirm that they have met their legal obligations.

B.   Stockholders

The need for a stockholder approval depends on the type of transaction.

Stock Purchases: No approval by seller's stockholders is required because buyer is purchasing directly with them and they indicate their approval by selling their shares. However, some states have adopted control share acquisition statutes that prohibit buyers from voting acquired shares over a certain percentage unless the acquisition has been approved by a majority of the disinterested stockholders.

Asset Purchases: Approval of seller's stockholders is required if substantially all assets are sold.

Merger: The majority of buyers' and sellers' shareholders must approve. In some states, two-thirds approval is required. Exceptions may apply to companies with supermajority requirements.

Share Exchanges: Approval of seller's stockholders is generally required.

In addition, many stock exchanges have rules that may modify the above requirements. Many obligate companies listed by them to obtain stockholder approval.

Exhibit 14G is an example of a shareholder's consent signed by one or more shareholders holding a majority of seller's shares. Following its execution, notice is given to other shareholders, and a mailing receipt is signed that confirms such notice.

C. Government

Governmental approval of stock and asset purchases and mergers is often required. The most important government approvals are for regulated industries, antitrust and securities.

1. Regulated Industries

If seller or buyer is in a regulated industry, some governmental approvals may be necessary. Examples are companies in alcohol, aviation, banking, communications, insurance, transportation and public utilities.

2. Antitrust

Under the HSR Act, mergers and acquisitions in excess of a certain size must be reported to the Department of Justice and Federal Trade Commission. After the filing, buyer and seller must wait for 30 days (15 days in a stock purchase by a cash tender offer). The waiting period can be extended for another 20 (or 10) days by either agency if it requests additional information.

3. Securities

In many cases, reports must be filed with the Securities and Exchange Commission ("SEC") or state securities agencies. These filings parallel the disclosures for new offerings described in Chapter 7 (Financing a Business). No closing can occur until the filings are made and the applicable waiting period is over.

Following are the most common securities filings:

- Registering securities under the Securities Act of 1933
- Qualifying an indenture under the Trust Indenture Act of 1939
- Filing a proxy or consent statement in connection with obtaining shareholder approval under the Securities Exchange Act of 1934
- Obtaining shareholder approval of a merger under state law (In some states, the timing is reversed with the agreement signed first and then submitted to shareholders for their approval.)

It can take several weeks to compile the necessary information and another 30–60 days to complete the SEC review process. A typical example of the time involved is depicted in Figure 14A.

FIGURE 14A—SECURITIES ISSUES TIME SCHEDULE

Day	Activity
1	All Hands Meeting to Organize Offering
25	Review Officers and Directors Questionnaires
40	Distribute First Draft of Registration Statement
45	All Hands Meeting to Revise Registration Statement
50	Distribute Revised Draft of Registration Statement
55	All Hands Meeting to Revise Registration Statement for SEC Filing
60	File Registration Statement with SEC
61	Mail Red Herrings to Proposed Underwriters
65	Road Show Begins
100	Receive SEC Comment Letter
114	All Hands Meeting to Revise Registration Statement to Reflect SEC Comments
115	Effective Date
120	Closing

As indicated in the chart, the total time involved can easily be four months.

D. Third Parties

The approval of many other persons may be required in the case of changes of control, mergers and sales of substantial assets. Examples include the following:

Unions: Collective bargaining agreements may require approval of the union.

ESOP Trustees: If buyer insists on purchasing a minimum percent of seller's shares, and some of its shares are held under an employee stock ownership plan, then the approval of the trustees of the plan may be required to meet the minimum.

Creditors: Most bank loans require approval of the lender for sale of assets.

Lessors: Most lessors require their consent to assignment of their leases. In some cases, they require the assignee to execute a new lease. If so, the purchase agreement should require that the original lessee be released.

14.07   Broker Fees

Two basic payments will be made at the closing. Buyer will pay the agreed upon purchase price, and Seller, on the other hand, will usually pay broker fees to investment bankers. The usual fee will be set in the agreement between seller and its investment banker. It is usually a range of five percent to one percent based on the value of the transaction. A full five percent may be paid on the first million, four percent on the second, etc., with one percent on anything of $5 million and over. A modified version starts at six percent and works its way down to one percent.

At times, more than one investment banker may be involved. For instance, seller and buyer may each have retained brokers. Seller may have sought an advisor to help it sell an asset or its business. Buyer may have retained an advisor to help it identify acquisition targets. In such cases, each party will be liable for its own broker, with the fees negotiated in advance at the time the broker is retained.

Payments are usually made by wire transfer.

As noted, the agreement may include representations as to who each party's brokers are (see Sections 4.13 and 5.6 in **Exhibit 14E**), covenants that they will pay their own broker's fees and indemnities to the other party if they do not. Second, there will be a representation by each party as to whether it used any brokers and, if so, who it used.

14.08   Closing

The closing depends on two issues: timing and documents produced.

A.   Timing

In its simplest form, the closing is when the main agreement is signed, stock or assets are transferred, and the money is paid. This is usually called a simultaneous closing. There are many variations, however.

In other cases, the parties may sign the main agreement, and while at closing, the stock or assets are transferred but not all consideration is paid. Instead, some part of the purchase price is delayed. Such deferral could be a mandatory payment, such as a note covering future, required payment. Alternatively, it could be conditional, such as an earn-out dependent on the acquired business achieving certain sales levels.

In some cases, the parties may sign the main agreement but postpone closing until certain events occur. Once those events occur, the stock or assets are transferred, and the money is paid. This is usually called a deferred closing. The most obvious examples of factors deferring closings include the following:

- Arranging financing
- Obtaining board and shareholder approval
- Obtaining government approvals

The larger the transaction, the more government approvals likely are required. In the previous section, we discussed some of the more important ones:

- Regulated industry
- Antitrust pre-merger notice
- Securities compliance

In addition, a closing may depend on obtaining a favorable tax ruling.

In a deferred closing, representations and warranties should be updated or restated. A new certificate delivered at the deferred closing can accomplish this by confirming that the representations and warranties are still true.

B.   Deliveries at Closing

In addition to the main agreement, many other agreements will be signed and exchanged at closing.

1. Transfer Documents

As noted earlier, in an asset purchase, many documents will be needed to transfer title to the various assets:

- Deeds for real property, which are filed with the county clerk's office where the property is located
- Assignments for leases, which must be given to and, depending on the lease terms, approved by the appropriate lessor
- Assignments for patents and trademarks, which are filed with the U.S. Patent and Trademark Office
- Bills of sale for personal property, which are filed with the local county clerk's office
- Bills of sale for automobiles, which are filed with the state department of motor vehicles

2. Payment

Possibly the most important issue is payment. Payment can be in the form of money, stock or other consideration. The closing will usually be confirmed and documents released only when payment is received.

In the case of money, for large transactions, payment will usually be by wire transfer to a bank account designated by seller. Lesser amounts may be by bank cashier's check.

In the case of stock, properly endorsed certificates will be delivered. If there are many sellers, a guarantee of signatures may be required.

3. Certificates

Seller and buyer will also exchange a number of certificates. Examples include the following:

Good-Standing and Tax-Clearance Certificates: Issued by secretary of state and state taxing authorities certifying that the company is in good standing (meaning it continues to exist as a company and has paid its annual filing fee) and has filed its state tax return.

Articles of Incorporation and Bylaw Certificates: Signed by corporate secretary attaching and certifying copies of current articles of incorporation and bylaws.

Secretary Certificates: Signed by corporate secretary of each party certifying that the necessary board of directors (and, where appropriate, shareholder) approval has been obtained.

Bring-Down Certificates: Signed by officers confirming that the representations and warranties in the main agreement, which related to the date it was signed, are still true on the closing date.

Update Certificates: Used in deferred closings, signed by officers that bring up to date disclosure schedules, representations and warranties to reflect changes between execution of main agreement and closing.

4. Legal Opinion

Each party's law firm will be asked to issue opinions stating the following:

- Its client is duly organized, validly existing and in good standing. This opinion means the party was properly formed, adopted its bylaws, appointed its officers, has not dissolved or ceased to exist and has paid its taxes and annual state filing fees.
- Its client is qualified in all jurisdictions where the failure to be qualified would have a material adverse effect on its business. Although it is easy to get good standing certificates from each state where the client says it must qualify, the hard part is ensuring that the company has qualified in each state where its business requires.
- Its client has the requisite power to own its properties and conduct its business. Before giving this opinion, counsel will review the client's

organizational documents to make certain the company is not limited in the type of business it can conduct.

- Its client has the requisite corporate power to enter into the closing agreements.
- Closing agreements have been duly authorized by all necessary board and shareholder approvals and have been duly executed and delivered. In granting the opinion, counsel may rely on corporate secretary certificates.
- Closing agreements are valid, binding and enforceable in accordance with their terms, except as limited by equity and bankruptcy. This opinion means that the client has the legal capacity and power to enter into the agreements; the agreements have been duly authorized, executed and delivered; the agreements are binding and are not invalid under any specific statute or contrary to public policy; and remedies are available to the other party for breach.
- Property being transferred is as described. In some cases, title insurance rather than the opinion may cover this.

When stock is being issued as part of the transaction, counsel may also be asked to opine on additional issues:

- The amount of authorized and outstanding shares
- That new shares are duly authorized and validly issued
- That new shares were issued for proper and sufficient consideration and are fully paid and non-assessable

Typical opinions also contain the following provisions:

- Date that information is as of
- Person to whom opinion is issued, with an attempted disclaimer that only that specific person is allowed to rely on the opinion
- Description of transaction
- Relationship of attorney to transaction
- Client's scope of engagement of counsel
- Statutory and contractual requirements of the opinion
- Key definitions
- Scope of counsel's review, including records inspected, persons interviewed and certificates relied on
- Assumptions such as conformity of copies to originals, facts stated in representations and certificates, legal capacity to execute documents and due execution of documents if not observed by counsel
- Limitations such as materiality, limitation to particular state laws plus federal law and enforceability exceptions for bankruptcy, equity, usury, choice of law, penalties and public policy.

Standard forms of opinions have begun to evolve over the past several decades, beginning with the 1989 Silverado Conference sponsored by the

American Bar Association's Business Law Section. Nevertheless, opinions are still influenced by the parties' bargaining positions (including, whether opinions are required at all) and their needs (such as requirements of law that they be provided and address certain issues).

Attorneys can be liable if their opinions are not accurate. In specialized areas such as tax, they will be held to a higher standard of prudent expert. As a result, their opinions only address legal issues and documents reviewed by them. Frequently, the issues and documents are listed in the opinion. For these reasons, the opinions may incorporate by reference opinions issued by other law firms on local law issues and factual backup statements signed by officers of the client.

5. Accountant Opinion

In two cases, seller's accountants may be asked to provide an opinion. First, if seller does not have audited financial statements, its accountants may be asked to give a comfort letter confirming that seller's financial statements appear to be accurate. Second, if the transaction requires a proxy statement with the SEC or involves a registration statement under the Securities Act of 1933, a comfort letter may be requested to show due diligence. In light of the Enron situation and the audits of its accountants, there may be less reliance of such opinions and more emphasis on buyer's own due diligence.

6. Investment Banker Opinion

Many boards require investment bankers involved in a transaction to issue fairness opinions. The opinions state that the price being received is fair to seller and are designed to reduce the potential liability of seller's board members for failure to meet their obligations.

7. Other Documents

At the closing, a number of related documents may be executed that do not involve the transfer of assets or stock. Examples are covenants not to compete, releases, employment agreements, consulting agreements and leases.

8. Press Release

Although not exchanged between buyer and seller, a press release agreed upon by the parties (and their attorneys who review it for securities law compliance) usually will be released summarizing the transaction.

Estate Planning for the Corporate Owner

John S. Lueken

Greenebaum Doll & McDonald PLLC
Louisville, KY

John R. Cummins

Greenebaum Doll & McDonald PLLC
Louisville, KY

Jeremy P. Gerch

Greenebaum Doll & McDonald PLLC
Louisville, KY

Contents

CHAPTER **15**

Estate Planning for the Corporate Owner

§ 15.01 Preliminary Considerations

Corporate owners may find themselves overwhelmed by the seemingly endless number of tax and organizational decisions involved in the formation of a business. While the average corporate owner is usually diligent in completing the basic steps of his or her business formation process (i.e., filing articles of incorporation and adopting bylaws), important estate planning opportunities are often overlooked. As a general rule, more than 70% of those persons controlling businesses fail to effectively transfer their business to the next generation. In most cases, this loss is attributed to a failure to plan. Many clients working on a limited budget and a dream only seek planning advice after they hit the top. Ironically, certain estate planning techniques, if implemented properly and early in the business formation process, can shelter businesses and a significant amount of their value from taxes and creditors.

While the planning objectives for the corporate owner are the same as for any other individual, the issues encountered in estate planning for the corporate owner involve many unique considerations. The assets of the typical corporate owner differ from those of other individuals in that they consist predominantly of interests in a closely-held business. This means that their estates are generally non-diverse and largely tied to the economic well being of their business. Although the distribution of assets according to the corporate owner's wishes is his or her primary goal, wealth preservation and liquidity for the corporate owner's estate upon his or her death is of critical importance.

The estate planning challenges of corporate owners are many. Because it is difficult to value a closely-held business, it is difficult to estimate the amount of death taxes that might be due upon the death of the corporate owner, and this raises various issues. For instance, will the estate need to sell a significant portion of the business assets to meet its estate tax needs and other administration expenses? If so, how? A partial interest in a closely-held business is virtually non-marketable. And, assuming a sale is feasible, at what price will the business interest be sold? Will the business have enough capital to continue operation, particularly if business funds must be used to pay the deceased owner's death taxes? If the business is providing significant support to the corporate owner's family, how will that support be replaced after the corporate owner dies?

This chapter will address some of these considerations, and discuss several effective planning techniques to appropriately deal with them. These issues must be addressed as early in the development of a business as possible. This chapter will not attempt to give a comprehensive estate planning guide for individuals, but will focus primarily on those issues relevant to closely-held business issues. This chapter will discuss (1) the use of different types of business entities in the context of estate planning (and techniques to gift interests in such entities), (2) annual exclusion gifting with Crummey Gift Trusts, (3) the use of buy-sell agreements and their critical role in the estate plan of the corporate owner, (4) valuation of the corporate owner's business and estate, (5) the use of life insurance in the estate planning context, (6) the use of Grantor Retained Annuity Trusts and installment sales as effective planning tools for estate freezing and/or reduction, and (7) the use of trusts in the operation and sale of a business to reduce state income taxes.

The Tax Relief, Unemployment Insurance Reauthorization, and Job Creation Act of 2010 ("Tax Relief Act") brought significant changes and clarification to the federal estate, gift and generation skipping transfer tax regimes. However this Tax Relief Act only applies with respect to 2010-2012, after which lowered estate and generation skipping tax exemption levels and higher marginal rates are reinstated. The Tax Relief Act provides that for decedents dying in 2010 only, each estate has a choice. It can be subject to the federal estate tax with a $5 million exemption and a full basis "step up" for all estate assets (which is the default position). Alternatively, each estate of 2010 decedents will be able to elect out of the federal estate tax and choose a modified carryover basis system. While there would be no federal estate tax under the modified carryover basis system, there is also not a full "step up" in basis of assets at a person's death to their then current fair market values. Rather, upon a person's death, his or her beneficiaries will receive the same basis in the asset received as the decedent possessed, subject to a total $1.3 million general limit on basis step-up for appreciated assets left to any beneficiary and another $3 million basis step-up in assets passing to a surviving spouse. This means that even though there is a choice to have no federal estate tax in 2010, an estate must weigh the factors carefully as there may be significant income tax costs with business owners who died in

2010 and who had grown a business over their lifetime, but had a low basis in that business.

One of the most significant changes under the Tax Relief Act is the "portability" of the estate tax exemption amount for 2011-2012. This means that if a business owner died in 2011 or 2012, made the election to be subject to estate tax and only had a taxable estate of $4 million, the remaining $1 million of estate tax exemption could be later utilized by the business owner's surviving spouse, at least if the surviving spouse dies before the end of 2012. The surviving spouse would then have the ability to shelter $6 million from estate tax. While this new portability of estate tax exemption amount has many advantages, the Tax Relief Act provides that the surviving spouse may only use the remaining unused estate tax exemption of the most recent spouse to die, which ensures that there is no doubling up of unused estate tax exemption amounts of predeceased spouses. Also, the portability only applies for 2011-2012, which means that traditional estate planning techniques are still useful in the event that portability ceases to apply after 2012 and is not later reinstated.

The following schedule shows the amount exempted from estate and generation-skipping taxes under current law, as well as the top marginal bracket for 2010-2013:

FIGURE 15A TAX RELIEF ACT TAX RATE AND EXEMPTIONS		
Year	Maximum Estate Tax Rate	Estate Tax Exemption
2010[1]-2012	35%	$5 million
2013	55%	$1 million

The exemption for gift taxes was $1 million in 2010, but is increased to $5 million for gifts made in 2011 and 2012, thus unifying the estate and gift tax credits for these years. However, the Tax Relief Act sunsets after 2012 and the gift tax exemption is lowered to $1 million in 2013 and beyond under current law. The top gift tax rate is 35% for 2010-2012, and is then limited to the top estate tax rate in 2013 and later years. Regardless of the changes to the federal estate and gift tax laws and the new sunset of them in 2012, the gifting techniques discussed below will remain useful for many business owners. If anything, the two-year increase in the federal gift tax exemption creates a great incentive for large gifts in 2011 and 2012, to seize what could be a one-time opportunity.

---

1.   In addition to the election out of the estate tax for decedents dying in 2010, there is also an applicable generation-skipping tax rate of 0% for generation skipping transfers occurring in 2010 as well as a new $5 million GST exemption for 2010-2012.

§ 15.02 Use Of Entities

Many businesses, by default or for purposes of simplicity, function initially as sole proprietorships. As these businesses get off the ground, their owners may wish to include another person or persons in the ownership of the business. Accordingly, the business needs to be restructured, whether it is by incorporating the business (as a C corporation or as an S corporation), or by changing its form to that of a partnership or as more commonly seen, a limited liability company.

The corporate owner must keep in mind that there are several estate planning issues involved in determining which type of entity to use. Among them are the degree of control that the corporate owner desires to maintain, transfer tax considerations and the corporate owner's desire regarding continuation of the business and successor ownership following the owner's death. In the estate planning context, the business entity of choice is typically the limited liability company, unless an S corporation is desired and able to be used. The S corporation option is not available, for example, where several classes of stock beyond voting and non-voting common are desired.

A. Corporations

The use of a regular C corporation will generally result in greater taxes on the corporation and its stockholders than if a limited liability company or S corporation were used – as noted in Chapter 3 (Non-Tax Aspects of Forming and Organizing a New Business) all are, or can be treated as, pass-through entities for income tax purposes. However, for tax years beginning after December 31, 2002, qualified dividends paid to stockholders by a domestic corporation or a qualified foreign corporation are taxed at capital gains rates through December 31, 2012. After December 31, 2012, unless the capital gains treatment is further extended, dividends will be taxed as ordinary income, and at a higher level than currently taxed. Particularly advantageous in the estate and business planning context, the C corporation enables the issuance of multiple classes of corporate stock, and allows the corporate owner to gift corporate stock with limited voting rights, while retaining full control of the business.[2]

In the case of an already existing C corporation, these same estate planning objectives can be accomplished by a "recapitalization" of the corporation, whereby new classes of stock are created for transfer purposes. A "recapitalization" is a type of tax-free corporate reorganization that generally occurs whenever a stockholder transfers his or her stock to the

---

2. An S corporation is permitted to have multiple classes of stock that have different voting rights, but all classes of stock in an S corporation must have the same distribution and liquidation rights.

issuing corporation in exchange for a different kind or class of stock in that corporation. Once a class of stock with limited (or no) voting rights is created, shares of such stock can be gifted to family members. Shares of stock in a closely-held corporation are generally discounted for gift tax purposes due to their lack of marketability, lack of control and the imbedded corporate taxes on any unrealized asset appreciation. If the C corporation non-voting stock is given away through a limited liability company structure as discussed below, a greater tax discount may be available.

An S corporation is generally not subject to the corporate tax, but extra requirements for S corporation status often make the election impractical for many businesses.[3] Lifetime transfers of S corporation stock are accomplished in the same manner as transfers of C corporation stock. However, one must be sure that the S corporation stockholder requirements are met, due to the fact that a transfer that results in S corporation stock being held by an ineligible stockholder will terminate the S election.[4] S corporations are typically used as the general partners of limited partnerships, to shield the stockholders of the general partner from partnership liability. An S election might also be made if the stockholders of a C corporation want to convert to a pass-through entity and determine that it would not be economical to liquidate the C corporation and form a partnership or limited liability company. Even then, a tax on the built-in gain at the time of the S election must be paid if the corporate assets owned at the time of the S election are sold within 10 years. Companies with LIFO inventory may find this tax cost prohibitive.

B.   Limited Liability Companies

The limited liability company ("LLC") essentially can combine the best features of both partnerships and corporations, such as flow-through taxation, operational flexibility and limited liability for all its members, although it favors partnerships. If an LLC is formed for estate planning purposes, it will usually resemble a partnership, rather than a corporation. For example, the LLC provides the same opportunity to make gifts of non-voting interests and the value of such interests can be discounted for lack of marketability and minority characteristics. Recent cases suggest that discounts are also available if the asset portfolio lacks diversification or if the assets have unrealized capital gains that will generate income tax for the LLC owners. Generally, all the advantages provided by a partnership can likewise be provided by the LLC.

There are some states in which the LLC statute is not conducive to estate planning. The IRS has rules that prohibit discounts for features of an LLC that are more restrictive than applicable state law. Where state law does not

---

3.   Section 1361 of the Code.
4.   Section 1361 of the Code.

have the desired restrictions on LLC equity transfers or has other undesirable features, the discounts allowed for gift and estate tax purposes may be smaller than if another form of business entity were used.

Once the LLC has been formed, the business interests are transferred to the LLC. However, if the business interests are stock in an S corporation, an LLC is not desirable because once an LLC owns stock in an S corporation, the S election is lost and the corporation reverts to a C corporation unless the LLC **also** elects to be taxable as an S corporation.[5] The best strategy when utilizing a corporation and an LLC is to recapitalize the corporation into voting and non-voting stock prior to the transfer of stock into the LLC. Once the corporation has been recapitalized, only non-voting stock should be transferred to the LLC. This strategy maximizes the potential valuation discounts which may be obtained and also minimizes any estate inclusion arguments by the IRS under Code section 2036.

Once the business interests are transferred to the LLC, the LLC interests can be given away over time to the children of the corporate owner, or other individuals, utilizing the annual gift tax exclusion ($13,000 a year per donee[6]) and/or the estate tax applicable exclusion amount of the corporate owner and spouse (which is $5 million per person in 2011-2012). It is generally advisable to postpone the first gift for some reasonable time period after the LLC is formed. Assuming the LLC interests are non-voting, the value of these LLC interests may be discounted for both minority interests and lack of marketability, thereby maximizing the estate tax benefit[7]. Using this technique, the corporate owner could at some point reduce his or her interest in the LLC through gifts to as little as 1% of the value of the LLC, while still retaining full management and control.

An already existing LLC or S corporation may need to be recapitalized in order to achieve the results and benefits that an owner desires. In either case, the use of non-voting or restricted voting equity interests can be very useful.

Here's an example of how gifting with an LLC really works:

> *Example:* A husband and wife own a business worth roughly $2 million that they want to give to their three children. The annual exclusion and spousal gift-splitting would permit an annual gift of $26,000 to each child ($13,000 from the husband, $13,000 from the wife), or an aggregate of $78,000 of stock each year without gift tax consequences. Alternatively, the parents can contribute all of their non-voting closely-held stock to an LLC (initially established with each spouse owning a 1% voting interest and a 49% non-voting interest) and give the children non-voting LLC interests.

---

5. Section 1361 of the Code.
6. Section 2503(b) of the Code.
7. *Clarissa W. Lappo v. Commissioner,* T.C. Memo 2003-258; *Peter S. Peracchio v. Commissioner,* T.C. Memo 2003-280.

If a valuation discount of one-third can be justified for the LLC interest gifts, a 1.95% LLC interest could be given to each child each year, which is equal to $39,000 of LLC assets (1.95% of $2 million). Therefore, the $39,000 of underlying LLC assets would have a $26,000 gift tax value. Thus, by gifting LLC interests, the husband and wife could gift $117,000 in underlying LLC interests (or stock) valued at only $78,000 for gift tax purposes, and therefore fully covered by the gift tax annual exclusion. All future appreciation on the gifted LLC interests is removed from the parents' estates, eliminating estate tax liability on the appreciation. Furthermore, the income attributable to the LLC interests given as gifts will not become part of the parents' estates, also reducing the ultimate estate tax liability.

The LLC offers the corporate owner several other important planning opportunities as well: (a) LLCs can generally be formed without any adverse tax consequences; (b) they can provide protection against creditors' claims; (c) they can be modified by amendment to the LLC's operating agreement in the event business circumstances change; and (d) they enable transfers of interests in family assets without the burdensome formalities of a corporation.

C. Use of Trusts with Transfers of Business Entities

A trust can be useful in achieving a business owner's goal in transferring interests of the LLC or other entity out of his or her estate. However, remember that when utilizing a trust with respect to S corporation stock, the trust must meet certain requirements in order to be considered an eligible stockholder. One of the most common goals in transferring interests in a business is to maintain some level of control over the business. The use of a trust serves this goal well. With a trust, all of the transferred interests are maintained collectively and can be managed by a single trustee. This also serves to minimize inter-family disputes over the business interests and decisions associated with the ownership interests.

These trusts are most often structured as "Crummey"[8] gift trusts. A Crummey gift trust is a trust where certain beneficiaries of the trust (most often the spouse and descendants of the business owner) are permitted to withdraw assets that are transferred or gifted to the trust. This power of withdrawal is limited by the gift tax annual exclusion (currently $13,000). This power of withdrawal must be exercised within a specified period of time, usually 30 days, after which time, any assets not withdrawn remain in the trust and are excluded from the donor's gross estate. Crummey gift trusts are also very useful with non-business interests, such as cash or other liquid assets, because future income and growth are removed from the donor's gross estate.

Using the example in Section 15.02[B] above, the gifting process would be very similar. Assume that the husband and wife established the same

---

8. *Crummey v. Commissioner*, 379 F.2d 82 (9th Cir. 1968).

LLC, but also established a Crummey gift trust of which their three children are the beneficiaries. The husband and wife would simply transfer a 5.85% (1.95% x 3) LLC interest to the trust. Then each child would have 30 days to withdraw his or her respective portion of the 5.85% transferred. After the lapse of the 30-day period, the Crummey gift trust would own the 5.85% interest and the husband and wife would have effectively transferred $117,000 worth of underlying assets, along with all future appreciation and income associated with that 5.85% interest, out of their collective estates.

While this yields the same gift and estate tax result as the above outright gifts, suppose that each of the three children had two minor children of his or her own. Not many business owners are willing to make outright gifts of business interests to minors or even individuals under the age of 25. With a Crummey gift trust, these individuals can be utilized as potential withdrawal beneficiaries, in order to maximize the gifting potential. In our example, there would now be nine withdrawal beneficiaries, which equates to a total of 17.55% (1.95% x 9) of the LLC interests able to be gifted to the trust each year and the underlying asset value of that interest gifted would be $351,000.

The amount of assets able to be transferred has increased dramatically due to the use of a Crummey gift trust. Furthermore, there is no concern about passing assets directly to individuals who may not be suitable to have control over those assets. Another benefit to the trust is that all 17.55% of the LLC gifted would be retained by the trustee of the trust, who is then able to vote the LLC interests, eliminating the potential for intra-family disputes over the voting of the business interests.

As noted above, cash and other liquid assets can also be utilized with Crummey gift trusts. However, the ability to obtain valuation discounts may be limited.

§ 15.03 Buy-Sell Agreements

The principal goals of the typical corporate owner include preserving wealth, ensuring liquidity for his or her estate, and maintaining continuity and control among the remaining owners of his or her business. As mentioned in Chapter 3 (Non-Tax Aspects of Forming and Organizing a New Business), an effective tool for achieving these goals is a buy-sell agreement. Generally, buy-sell agreements restrict the transfer of stock in a closely-held business and give either the corporation or the other stockholders the option to purchase the stock of a deceased, disabled or otherwise departing stockholder before the stock can be sold to an outside party. In this way, the buy-sell agreement effectively prevents any unwanted outsider from becoming a stockholder. A buy-sell agreement also creates a market for closely-held business stock, virtually guaranteeing the estate liquidity with which to pay estate taxes and administrative expenses.

One of the most attractive features of a buy-sell agreement is that it can establish the price of the stock of a closely-held business for estate and gift tax purposes, as well as for other situations where stock valuation is a priority.[9] Thus, a buy-sell agreement can minimize the problems and uncertainty associated with the valuation of closely-held stock. For this to occur, (a) the stock price must be fixed in the agreement by either a formula or a definitely determinable number, (b) the estate must be obligated to sell the stock at such a price upon death of the corporate owner, (c) the obligations must be binding upon the stockholder during his or her lifetime and upon his or her estate, and (d) the agreement must be a bona fide business arrangement.[10]

There are generally two types of buy-sell agreements: (a) redemption agreements; and (b) cross-purchase agreements. A redemption agreement, such as in **Exhibit 15A**, is an agreement between the business and its owners under which the owners agree to sell, and the business agrees to buy, the interests of the owners if certain events occur. These "triggering events" can include events such as death, disability or the lifetime conveyance of the ownership interest. A cross-purchase agreement, such as in **Exhibit 15B**, is one among the corporate owners in which each owner agrees to sell his or her interest to the other owners, or purchase the interest of the other owners, upon the occurrence of the specified triggering events.

Perhaps the most critical issue when entering into a buy-sell agreement is determining how the purchasing party or entity will obtain the funds to purchase the deceased corporate owner's interest. One of the most common ways to fund the purchase obligation under a buy-sell agreement is through insurance on the life of the individual whose stock is to be purchased, unless age or health concerns make it impractical. Other businesses opt to generate the necessary funds from the business over time, via the use of an installment purchase.

Where the triggering event is the departing stockholder's retirement or disability, the utility of life insurance obviously decreases. Depending upon how much cash has accumulated within the policy, which in turn depends upon the type of insurance purchased, it may be more advisable to fund the purchase obligation with a life insurance policy that would have considerable cash value, such as a whole-life insurance policy or a universal life insurance policy. It is also possible to obtain disability buy-out insurance from some insurers.

A redemption agreement is funded either by the acquisition of life insurance on the life of the corporate owner, or by setting funds aside prior to and after the owner's death. When life insurance is used to fund the redemption, the business is the applicant, owner and beneficiary of the policy, and the business pays the premium. If the life insurance is payable to or for the benefit of the

9.   Rev. Rul. 59-60, 1959-1 C.B. 237.
10.   Treas. Regs. section 20.2031-2(h) and section 2703 of the Code.

business, the life insurance is excluded from the decedent's estate for estate tax purposes. The premiums paid by the business are non-deductible.[11] The receipt of life insurance proceeds is not taxable as income to the corporation; however, in the case of a C corporation, the alternative minimum tax may be applicable since 75% of the insurance proceeds are an adjustment item for purposes of adjusted current earnings. (S corporations are not subject to the corporate alternative minimum tax.) This means that if a corporation is subject to the alternative minimum tax, 75% of the death benefit proceeds received by the corporation are included in adjusted current earnings and taxed at a 20% rate. For example, if a corporation received $500,000 in life insurance proceeds, the alternative minimum tax liability associated with the proceeds would be $75,000 (or 20% of 75% x $500,000). Also, the redemption of the stock is non-deductible by the corporation. The redemption can be free of income tax for the deceased owner's estate if it qualifies as a "complete termination" under the Code.[12] If the estate beneficiaries are also stockholders, family and entity attribution rules apply, making complete termination much harder to accomplish. With proper planning, the desired "complete termination" result can still be obtained in some cases.

A redemption agreement is often easier than other buy-sell agreements to fund with life insurance from a practical standpoint. For example, if there are five stockholders, there would have to be only five life insurance policies, all of which are owned by the corporation, and all premiums are paid by the corporation. In contrast, 20 policies would be required for a cross-purchase agreement, with each stockholder individually owning life insurance policies on all the other stockholders. A practical advantage of the redemption agreement is that funding arrangements and payment of life insurance premiums are handled by the business, and not left up to the individual stockholders. Also, the corporation can include the cash value of the life insurance as an asset on its balance sheet.

If life insurance is used to fund a cross-purchase agreement, then the life insurance will be owned by a corporate owner or stockholder with a separate policy on each of the other owners or stockholders, typically in an amount sufficient to cover the purchase obligation under the buy-sell agreement. Since the insured will have no incidents of ownership in these policies on his or her life, the proceeds will not be included in the estate of the decedent, and likewise, because the corporation is not part of the transaction, there are no tax consequences to the corporation. For stockholders or other owners, the policy premiums are non-deductible, the death proceeds are received income tax free, and the surviving stockholders or other owners will have a new stepped-up basis in the business interest that they acquire equal to the price paid.

---

11. Section 264(a)(1) of the Code.
12. Section 302(b)(3) of the Code.

§ 15.04 Valuation

For obvious reasons, when determining the value of the deceased corporate owner's estate for estate tax purposes, the value of the estate's interests in closely-held corporate stock must be determined. As discussed above, a mechanism for determining the value of the stock may be set forth in a buy-sell agreement that meets the IRS standards. The IRS standards are more stringent when the buy-sell is between a senior generation business owner and his or her children. Therefore, particular care must be taken to demonstrate that the valuation process is commercially reasonable in the industry. In the absence of a qualifying buy-sell agreement, fair market value is standard.

If a buy-sell agreement provides a method to determine the value of stock for estate tax purposes, the agreement usually calls for the use of one of three basic approaches: (a) fixed price; (b) formula price; or (c) appraisal.

A. Fixed Price

This is the most basic method, by which the parties simply negotiate a fixed price that will be paid upon the occurrence of a triggering event. If the fixed price method is used, the buy-sell agreement should provide for periodic adjustments of the fixed price to account for increases or decreases in the corporation's value after the agreement is executed.

B. Formula Price

The parties may agree upon a formula for establishing the purchase price. Generally, the formula involves the use of value-related factors such as the capitalization of earnings, asset book values, and a multiple of gross and net income. The formula may also be used to determine the value of goodwill.

C. Appraisal

The business owners may decide to select an independent appraiser to determine the price of the stock at the appropriate time. Typically, when the triggering event occurs, the parties will then agree on an appraiser, and the standards that the appraiser is to use.

If there is no buy-sell agreement, then for estate tax purposes the fair market value of the closely-held stock is used. The fair market value is generally determined based on the price a willing buyer would pay a willing seller, neither being under any compulsion to buy or to sell, and both having reasonable knowledge of relevant facts.[13] The problem with this general approach is that the stock in a closely-held business is by definition owned by a relatively small number of stockholders, and is not typically traded in the marketplace – meaning that there is simply no established market for such stock. Consequently, there is no clearly ascertainable basis for determining its fair market value.

Under the IRS Regulations, when market valuation techniques do not apply, value is generally determined based on a company's net worth, prospective earning power, dividend paying capacity and other significant factors. In an effort to give further guidance on this issue, the IRS issued Rev. Rul. 59-60[14] regarding the general nature of the valuation process with respect to closely-held stock.

Revenue Ruling 59-60 provides an additional framework for the analysis of a closely-held stock's value. It sets forth eight "intrinsic factors" that must be considered in determining value, the weight to be accorded each of the various factors in establishing a value, the various capitalization rates used in arriving at a value and the effect of restrictive agreements on the valuation of closely-held stock. These factors include: (a) the company's history; (b) industry-wide economic projections; (c) book value and financial condition of the business; (d) the company's earning capacity; (e) the company's dividend paying capacity; (f) enterprise goodwill; (g) recent sales of the stock being valued; and (h) comparable sales within the industry.

Revenue Ruling 59-60 also suggests that where no market exists for closely-held securities, the selling price for stock in companies engaged in the same or similar lines of business that are traded on a free and open market may provide the best measure of value.

It is important to note that there have been legislative and executive proposals which would eliminate much of the valuation discounting able to be done in an estate planning setting.[15] However, currently, no such restrictions or eliminations have been enacted.

§ 15.05 Life Insurance

Life insurance can be an effective tool in the estate planning process. It can be used by decedents with modest estates to ensure adequate funds for the survivors, or for larger estates to provide liquidity to pay estate taxes and expenses, potentially avoiding a forced sale of valuable, illiquid assets. Life insurance may also provide a needed source of funds for the decedent's

---

13.   Treas. Regs. section 20.2031-1(b).
14.   Rev. Rul. 59-60, 1959-1 C.B. 237.
15.   See the General Explanations of the Administration's Fiscal Year 2010 Revenue Proposals; See also H.R. 436, Certain Estate Tax Relief Act of 2009.

surviving family members during the interim period of estate administration. In addition, life insurance proceeds may be used to fund purchase obligations under buy-sell agreements.

In the estate and business planning context, the corporate owner must consider two important questions with respect to life insurance: (a) should the corporate owner transfer his or her presently existing policies (where the corporate owner is the insured and owns the policy); and (b) should new policies be obtained on the life of the corporate owner and, if so, what types of policies should be acquired and how should they be purchased and issued? The answers to these questions are of course dependent on the business and personal objectives of the corporate owner, but a general overview of these issues may be helpful.

A.   Transfer of Life Insurance Policies

If a corporate owner owns a life insurance policy or his or her life, then at his or her death, the entire amount of the insurance proceeds will be included in his or her federal taxable estate, assuming the federal estate tax is applicable. A simple way to avoid having life insurance included in one's estate is to give it away. Generally, to transfer ownership of a life insurance policy, (a) the policy must be given to another person or persons or (b) the policy must be transferred to an irrevocable life insurance trust ("ILIT").

An ILIT can be an extremely valuable estate planning tool for holding life insurance policies and receiving the proceeds thereof at the death of the insured. Proceeds under a policy can be paid to a trustee at the time of the insured's death, providing substantial flexibility to the trustee in investing the proceeds received from the insurer. An ILIT can also coordinate the collection, investment and distribution of the proceeds of several policies, as well as the management of other assets, such as securities, which are part of the principal of the ILIT after the death of the insured, or which pass to the ILIT under the insured's will. This ILIT can be used for the same purposes as any other trust (e.g., sprinkling income and principal, generation-skipping and marital deduction provisions,). An ILIT can also help avoid the expenses and delays of probate administration, and the proceeds can avoid potential exposure to the creditors of the beneficiary of the trust.

An ILIT can be created and the ownership of insurance policies can be irrevocably transferred to the ILIT. The ILIT may be otherwise unfunded or may be funded with other financial assets. An otherwise unfunded ILIT is ordinarily created by the transfer to an ILIT of only the ownership of the life insurance policies. The trustees will have no funds with which to pay the premiums and those premiums must be paid by another person (e.g., the grantor). The funded ILIT is created by a transfer of insurance policies on the life of the ILIT grantor, plus sufficient funds to be used to satisfy (or to generate income to satisfy) the premium payment requirements.

Some important estate and gift tax considerations are involved in the formation of an ILIT. The transfer of the life insurance contracts to an ILIT will be a gift for federal gift tax purposes, and if the ILIT is funded with cash or similar assets to enable subsequent premium payments, the fair market value of these other assets transferred to the ILIT will also be transfers for gift tax purposes. If an ILIT is unfunded and the grantor makes gifts to pay the premiums on policies owned by the ILIT, these payments will constitute additional gifts when made. In these situations, the ILIT must be structured to take advantage of the annual gift tax exclusion (remember, a person can make $13,000 worth of gifts during each taxable year to each donee without incurring any gift taxes) by giving the beneficiaries Crummey withdrawal rights, particularly if the ILIT is unfunded and annual transfers are necessary to maintain the policy in effect.

Since an irrevocable transfer will have been completed during life, no estate tax liabilities should attach upon the death of the grantor, provided the life insurance policy is transferred to the ILIT more than three years before death or is acquired directly by the ILIT. The grantor must also be careful not to retain any "incidents of ownership" in the life insurance policies held by the ILIT and insuring the grantor's life or any beneficial life interest from the ILIT itself. For example, if the ILIT directs the trustee to pay debts and taxes of the estate of the decedent from policy proceeds, the funds required for such purposes are includible in the decedent's gross estate.

B. Types of Insurance

For estate planning purposes, there are essentially two types of life insurance: (a) term, which provides insurance for a set period of time and (b) some form of "permanent" insurance, which is effective as long as the premiums are paid. Over time, permanent insurance will build a cash value that produces returns for the policyholder. Some of the more common types of life insurance are discussed below.

1. Term Life Insurance

Term life insurance provides only pure insurance coverage (i.e., a preset amount of cash if you die while the policy is in force). Since it has no cash value build-up, it is less expensive in the insured's younger years than whole life coverage (which offers cash build-up). As the insured ages, however, the term life premium in annually renewable products becomes significantly more expensive, eventually overtaking the normally level premiums of cash value insurance. It is also possible to buy level premium term policies, which even out the premium obligation over the policy's entire term. By definition, term insurance is protection for a specified term (e.g., 20 years), after which it may automatically expire unless it is a renewable policy.

2. *Cash Value Life Insurance*

Cash value life insurance combines protection and savings. Part of the premium pays for pure life insurance coverage. Part of it accumulates tax-free in the cash value build-up inside the policy, where it is available to the policyholder if it is needed before the policy matures. Cash value policy premiums are usually level throughout the policy's existence.

i.   Whole Life Insurance

A common type of cash value policy is the whole life or level premium policy, sometimes call the life-to-100 policy because it may provide protection to the maximum age of 100, or for the insured's whole life. The cash value component of the whole life policy is possible because the amount of the earlier premiums exceeds the cost of the pure term insurance, where the excess is accumulated in an interest-bearing reserve fund that later offsets the higher cost of protection as the insured ages, thus making the whole life policy a level premium policy. Under a whole life policy, both the premiums and the death benefit are generally fixed.

ii.   Universal Life Insurance

Another type of cash value policy is the universal life policy, which allows the insured to vary the amounts of the premiums, the death benefit and the cash value, thus offering greater flexibility than the whole life policy. The insurance company often reserves the right to change mortality tables and administrative expenses. It is possible to obtain universal life policies with a guaranteed premium that will keep the death benefit in force, until a specified age, regardless of the actual policy performance.

iii.   Joint-Life Insurance

This is a potentially attractive type of cash value life insurance policy for funding buy-sell agreements in some cases. In the context of buy-sell agreements, the joint-life policy pays benefits on the death of the first insured corporate owner (i.e., a "first-to-die policy"), and again on the second death of the second insured corporate owner. The major benefits of this type of insurance are that it (a) insures two or more lives for considerably less expense than individual policies would cost, enabling purchasers to obtain more insurance if needed; (b) allows corporate owners to be insured for different amounts, depending upon the number of shares each owns in the business; and (c) makes insurance possible or more affordable where one corporate owner's poor health may make him or her uninsurable. This type of policy works well with a corporate redemption form of buy-sell agreement, with the corporation owning all of the life insurance.

3. *Split-Dollar Insurance*

Split-dollar is not a type of cash value life insurance, but rather it is a payment arrangement that enables a corporation and stockholder/employee to share or split the cost of the premiums, and share or split the cash value accumulated in the policy. Since the corporation and the stockholder/employee share the cost of the policy, a split-dollar arrangement may be the only option for a small businesses with limited cash flow to purchase life insurance to fund a buy-sell or redemption agreement. The income tax rules governing split dollar arrangements were substantially changed by Treasury Regulations finalized in 2003. The intent of the IRS changes is to tax the economic benefit of the arrangement at higher rates, and also to tax the employee's equity in the policy. The Regulations provide for two types of split dollar "regimes."

i.   Loan Regime

The loan regime generally covers arrangements where the non-owner of the policy pays the premium directly or loans the money to the owner of the policy with the expectation (under a "reasonable person" test) that the amounts paid (or loaned) will be repaid from (or secured by) the policy proceeds. The loan regime is taxed under the regulations governing below market interest loans under section 7872 of the Code.

ii. Economic Benefit Regime

The economic benefit regime applies to endorsement arrangements, or other arrangements that are not split-dollar loans. Under the economic benefit regime, the owner of the policy, which is usually the employer or a trust, is treated as providing a benefit to the non-owner of the policy (often the employee), which is essentially calculated as the value of the life insurance coverage, plus the amount of policy cash value to which the non-owner has access.

4. *Disability Insurance*

A disability buy-sell agreement, funded by disability buy-out insurance, allows the healthy corporate owners to buy the disabled stockholder's interest after a pre-established waiting period, such as two years, during which the extent of the disability can be assessed.

§ 15.06 Estate Freeze Transactions

The assets of the corporate owner will likely appreciate over time. Unless some planning is done, the IRS may eventually take up to 55% of the value of those assets upon the death of the corporate owner. A common estate planning objective, particularly for closely-held business owners, is to pass most or all of that appreciation to younger generation family members. However, disposing of such assets may not be a practical solution. For instance, a transfer of these assets may incur a substantial gift tax, the corporate owner may need the income from the assets, or he or she may not be willing to part with control over the business interest or property. Ideally, the corporate owner would prefer to retain some control over an asset while at the same time having that asset either removed from the corporate owner's estate or having any future appreciation in the asset not taxed as part of his or her estate.

A.   Grantor Retained Annuity Trusts

One popular method of effectively freezing the value of one's estate and then passing the appreciation on to younger generation family members is through the use of a Grantor Retained Annuity Trust ("GRAT"). GRATs are effective vehicles to transfer wealth on a discounted basis while retaining the benefit of the transferred wealth for a period of time. In general, this is accomplished by the grantor contributing assets to a GRAT (such as discounted LLC interests) and retaining the right to receive a specified payout (annuity) from the GRAT for a specific period of time. Once that period ends, the assets remaining in the GRAT pass to the designated beneficiaries. If the grantor dies before the annuity period ends, the full value of the trust assets will be included in his or her taxable estate. The amount of the gift is determined by subtracting the value of the retained interest from the total value of the transfer.

If an individual who owns an asset retains that that asset until death, net income from the asset and the asset itself will be included in the individual's estate. If the same asset is placed in a GRAT and the individual (i.e., grantor) outlives the trust term, the value of the asset remaining in the GRAT at the time of the grantor's death will not be included in the grantor's estate. If the GRAT is successful, the advantages are that asset is removed from the estate at a gift tax value below the current fair market value of the asset (by virtue of the subtraction of the present value of the retained interest) and any appreciation in the asset after the creation of the GRAT will be excluded from the grantor's estate. In 2000, a Tax Court decision made it possible to have **no** taxable gift with a GRAT.[16] However, there has been a recent legislative and executive move to eliminate a zero taxable gift GRAT and to require GRATs have a mandatory minimum term of 10 years.[17] The Tax Relief Act of 2010 did not contain any of these restrictions on GRATs, but should these

---

16.   Walton v. Commissioner, 115 T.C. 41 (2000), *acq.* Notice 2003-72, 2003-44 I.R.B. 964 (IRS NOT Oct 15, 2003).

17.   H.R. 5297: Small Business Lending Fund Tax Act of 2010, which passed the House of Representatives on June 17, 2010; See also the General Explanations of the Administration's Fiscal Year 2010 Revenue Proposals.

restrictions and additional aspects of GRATs eventually take effect, GRATs will likely become less useful as a result of the decreased flexibility.

Again, to determine the amount of the gift, the value of the asset transferred to the GRAT is reduced by the value of the retained annuity stream. The value of the retained annuity stream depends not only upon the value of what was contributed, but also on the annuity amount, the applicable IRS interest rate for the month in which the GRAT is created, the period for which the annuity will be paid, and the grantor's age. If the annuity is identical to the IRS assumed rate under section 7520 for the month of the contribution (that rate is based on the mid-term U.S. Treasury Department bond rate for the month the GRAT begins), the gift is equal to the current value of the transferred asset discounted to reflect the deferral of the gift over the term of years. If the annuity is greater than the IRS assumed rate, the value of the gift will be reduced further.

GRATs are often used in conjunction with LLCs in order to leverage the discounts available through the use of an LLC. Consider the following example.

> *Example:* Assume a senior family member, age 45, owns a block of non-voting stock in his or her business worth $5 million. The first step is to place the stock into an LLC. In return for transferring the interest into the LLC, the senior family member receives a 1% voting interest and a 99% non-voting interest. The voting interest would hold control over the LLC. Next, the senior family member assigns his 99% non-voting interest to a GRAT. Let's assume that after discounting, this non-voting interest would be valued at $3 million [$5 million x (1-0.40)]. The transfer is made in a month when the IRS interest rate under section 7520 is 2.8%.

The GRAT provides that the senior family member is to receive two annual payments of $1,563,314 each (based on an assumed IRS rate of 2.8%). Whatever remains in the GRAT at the end of two years would be distributed to the senior family member's children free of gift or estate tax. A minimal up-front gift is created when the senior family member funds the GRAT, which is charged against his or her applicable exclusion amount ($1 million). If the stock within the LLC does not grow at all, the senior family member will still pass $1,873,372 to his or her children (the two annual payments of $1,563,314 subtracted from $5 million). If the stock appreciates by 10%, the senior family member will shelter $2,767,040; or with 20% appreciation, $3,760,709.

B. Installment Sales

Another estate freeze strategy is for the corporate owner to make a sale of assets that he or she expects will appreciate to a trust that is taxed as a grantor trust for income tax purposes. The basic structure of an installment sale is relatively simple. The grantor selects an asset with an expected return greater than the current applicable federal rate, e.g. his or her business. Next, the grantor sells the asset to a trust for its fair market value. (As has been discussed throughout this chapter, fair market value can be modified through discounting techniques, such as the use of an LLC.) In exchange for the asset, the grantor receives a long-term, interest-only promissory note calling for a balloon payment far in the future – perhaps as long as 20 or 30 years. As a result, only interest is required to be paid during the term of the note with a principal payment equal to the full amount of the note paid at the end of the term. Principal prepayments are permitted at any time, without penalty. The interest rate on the note is the applicable federal rate.[18] The grantor has thus removed from his or her estate an asset that is expected to appreciate in value, and has replaced it with an asset that will not appreciate – the promissory note. All of the capital appreciation of the asset in excess of the interest rate on the note is free of estate tax. The interest on the note is paid back to the seller – providing an income stream for retirement!

The purchaser trust can be for the grantor's family, including spouse and children as desired. The trust should have assets worth at least 10% of the purchase price of the business interest sold, to be safe. This funding can be achieved by a gift from the seller prior to the sale, or the use of an existing, previously funded trust. By having certain administrative provisions in the trust that are set forth in Code section 675, the trust can achieve "grantor trust" status for income tax purposes. When a trust is structured as a grantor trust, the trust's income is taxed to the grantor rather than to the trust or its beneficiaries. A sale of assets by the grantor to a grantor trust is not recognized for income tax purposes. Thus, a sale of an asset to a grantor trust by its grantor is not treated or taxable as a sale for income tax purposes, despite the fact that it would be treated as a completed transfer.[19]

For 2011 and 2012, the federal estate and gift tax changes enacted in Tax Relief Act provide a good opportunity to maximize the benefits of this installment sale technique and to transfer a larger amount to a trust for the benefit of future generations (and in some jurisdictions into perpetuity). For example, in 2011 or 2012 a married couple with no prior taxable gifts could collectively gift $10 million to the grantor trust to provide the 10% "seed" assets prior to the purchase of the business interest. The purchase price or value of the business interest later sold to the trust in exchange for the promissory note could then be $90 million. The assets both gifted and sold to the trust could then appreciate in the trust free of any future transfer taxes assuming the couple also could fully allocate GST Exemption for federal generation skipping transfer taxes to the assets gifted to the trust.

The difference between the interest rate on the promissory note and the actual rate of return on the assets flows to the beneficiaries free from estate and gift tax. For example, if the interest rate is 5% and the rate of return on

---

18. Section 1274(d) of the Code.
19. Section 671-679 of the Code.

the assets is 9%, the trust will make annual payments of 5% of the original sales price to the grantor. All earnings above 5% are retained in the trust for the beneficiaries or used to pay principal on the note.

For gift tax purposes, as long as the sales price of the assets is at least equal to the fair market value of the assets, and as long as the interest rate on the note is at least equal to the applicable federal rate, there is no taxable gift. The IRS treats a sale to a grantor trust as a nonevent for income tax and capital gains purposes.[20] As a result, there is no capital gains tax on appreciated assets sold to the grantor trust, and the trust takes the grantor's basis in the assets. Also, the interest payments on the promissory note are ignored by the grantor for income tax purposes, and the trust takes no deduction for the interest paid. For estate tax purposes, the grantor's estate now only includes the unpaid balance on the promissory note, and the corporate asset sold to the trust is outside the grantor's taxable estate. If the note has not been fully paid at the grantor's death, the IRS may assert a capital gains tax at death, when the trust ceases its grantor trust tax status. Therefore, it is preferable to pay off the promissory note prior to the grantor's death, even if assets in-kind must be used to make payment.

It is important to note that a case involving this technique was challenged by the IRS and then reportedly settled at a 37% discount after being taken to the Tax Court, *Karmazin v. Commissioner*, Tax Court Docket No. 2127-03. The IRS initially asserted in this case that the valuation rules of Chapter 14 of the Code apply to the sale because the notes should be considered equity rather than debt, thus causing the notes to have no value for gift tax purposes. To address the IRS attacks in that case, persons contemplating this type of transaction should consider obtaining personal guarantees from the trust beneficiaries and standby letters of credit from commercial third-party lenders, in addition to having 10% (or more) seed assets in the trust.

Should Congress enact any required minimum term for GRATs, as discussed above, the installment sale technique is likely to gain more favor because of its flexibility, both prior to execution and even after the initial transaction has taken place.

§ 15.07 Sale Of A Business Through A Trust

When a business owner is dealing with ownership of his or her business, he or she generally not too concerned with the income tax consequences upon the sale of the business, much less state income taxes on that sale. However, with proper planning, a significant amount of state income tax savings is possible for business owners in many jurisdictions through the use of trusts.

---

20. Rev. Rul. 85-13, 1985-1 C.B. 184.

Delaware permits the creation of certain trusts that provide significant asset protection during the term of the trust. These asset protection trusts also may allow for significant state income tax savings. Under the applicable Delaware statutes, an individual has the ability to create a trust, whereby the individual may be a beneficiary of the trust and the assets of the trust are not subject to attachment by the individual's future creditors.[21] These Delaware asset protection trusts cannot be formed with the intent to defraud current or future creditors. In order for a person to establish a Delaware trust, the individual may not have any authority to direct distributions from the trust and there must be a Delaware based trustee. Distributions from the trust are made at the discretion of the trustee most often with the assistance of a Distribution Committee.

The trust must be established as a non-grantor trust and should be an incomplete gift for federal gift tax purposes to obtain the desired tax benefits. A non-grantor trust is a trust that will be taxed as a separate entity for income tax purposes. In addition, because the trust is structured to be an incomplete gift for federal gift tax purposes, this allows the transfer of significant assets to the trust without having to use any lifetime gift tax exemption ($1 million) or to pay any gift tax on the transfer to the trust.[22]

Once a trust is established, Delaware law allows a deduction for distributable net income of the trust or for income accumulated, but set aside, for nonresident beneficiaries of the trust.[23] This means that so long as there are no Delaware residents as beneficiaries, the trust will not pay Delaware state income tax. In addition, this trust works only for residents of jurisdictions where the trust is not taxed in that state because there is no resident trustee or there are not enough connections with that state for the state taxing authority to subject the trust to income tax. Prior to utilizing this strategy, a business owner should determine whether his or her state taxing authority is one which will generally not attempt to tax this type of Delaware trust.

Thus, if a business owner outside of Delaware transferred all of his or her stock of the business to a Delaware Trust upon the creation of the business or at some point during the operation of the business and that trust was an incomplete gift and was also considered a non-grantor trust for federal income tax purposes, the income from the stock during the term of the trust would not be subject to income tax in Delaware so long as there were no Delaware beneficiaries of the trust. Operating a business through a Delaware trust may seem like a lot of trouble, but in some instances, the potential benefits would certainly outweigh the burdens. For example, if a business owner lived in a jurisdiction with a state capital gains tax rate of 4% and had a business with a value of $10 million, but a basis in his or her stock of only $2 million, the

---

21.   See 12 Del. Code Section 3570, et. seq.

22.   See PLRs 200148028 and 200612002 (demonstrating that it is possible to establish an irrevocable trust and that the transfer of assets to the trust is an incomplete gift).

23.   30 Del. Code Section 1636.

owner would have significant state income or capital gains tax due if he or she sold all of the stock in the business. However, if the stock were held in a Delaware trust and the trust sold all of the stock, although $8 million would be subject to federal capital gains tax, there would be no state capital gains tax payable by the trust or the beneficiaries (a savings of $320,000).

This strategy has a couple of potential pitfalls which are important to consider. The first was that section 2511(c) of the Code provided that during 2010, any transfer to a trust will be considered a completed gift, unless the trust is considered a grantor trust. Fortunately, section 2511(c) of the Code was repealed retroactively by the Tax Relief Act of 2010, which was enacted on December 17, 2010, thereby eliminating this concern.

The second area of concern is that this strategy has the potential for negative consequences if the proper timing and planning are ignored. Some business owners may transfer the stock in their business to a Delaware Trust and then sell the stock shortly thereafter. While this quick transfer and sale may still avoid state capital gains or income taxes on the sale of the stock in the individual's home state, it is possible that the individual's home state taxing authority would challenge the transaction and try to subject the sale (and the business owner) to state income tax.

§ 15.08 Conclusion

Estate planning for the corporate owner presents a host of problems and opportunities. At the same time, many techniques are available to assist the corporate owner in overcoming these problems. Although the concepts underlying many of these techniques are relatively simple, care must be taken in implementing them in each corporate owner's particular family and tax situation. Setting specific goals and careful planning are keys to successfully transferring wealth, ensuring the continued success of the corporate owner's business and reducing the estate tax burden at death.